STUD...
AND RESPONSE

STUDENT PEER REVIEW AND RESPONSE

A Critical Sourcebook

EDITED BY

Steven J. Corbett
Texas A&M University—Kingsville

Michelle LaFrance
George Mason University

bedford/st.martin's
Macmillan Learning
Boston | New York

For Bedford / St. Martin's

Vice President, Editorial, Macmillan Learning Humanities: Edwin Hill
Senior Program Director for English: Leasa Burton
Program Manager: Karita Frances dos Santos
Executive Marketing Manager: Joy Fisher Williams
Director of Content Development: Jane Knetzger
Assistant Editor: Stephanie Cohen
Content Project Manager: Lidia MacDonald-Carr
Workflow Manager: Lisa McDowell
Production Supervisor: Robert Cherry
Media Project Manager: Melissa Skepko-Masi
Manager of Publishing Services: Andrea Cava
Project Management: DeMasi Design and Publishing Services
Composition: Achorn International, Inc.
Permissions Editor: Kalina Ingham
Senior Art Director: Anna Palchik
Cover Design: William Boardman
Printing and Binding: LSC Communications

Manufactured in the United States of America.

2 1 0 9 8 7
f e d c b a

For information, write: Bedford / St. Martin's, 75 Arlington Street, 8th Floor,
Boston, MA 02116

ISBN 978-1-319-02889-3

Acknowledgments
Text acknowledgments and copyrights appear at the back of the book on pages 425–26, which constitute an extension of the copyright page. Art acknowledgments and copyrights appear on the same page as the art selections they cover.

CONTENTS

Toward Pedagogies of Peer-to-Peer Listening and Trust

Compare the following experiences two writing instructors have had with peer review and response groups:

> From Andrea Lunsford: "On the end-of-term evaluations, I always asked my students what was the best thing about the course—secretly hoping that they would say it was *me*. Fat chance of that. Every single term I asked this question and every single term they responded with three words: 'our peer groups.'"

> From Kevin Davis: "Time after time, I watched students come to class with no draft; draft after draft, I watched students offer unhelpfully general evaluations (such as 'good job') . . . peer review after peer review, I watched students leaving class without a single idea of what to work on or how to go about the work. I grew so frustrated with peer review that, for several years, I discontinued the exercise completely" (211).

These contradictory experiences reflect what we have heard many of our colleagues nationally and locally say about peer response groups in their own classrooms. Though almost universally advocated by writing program administrators (WPAs) and writing across the curriculum and in the disciplines (WAC/WID) leaders, few other pedagogical approaches in writing classes draw such extreme differences of reaction, or elicit such confusion and frustration. Such laments are not new, as demonstrated by the complaints in Thomas Newkirk's piece from 1984 included in this volume (p. 47). Perhaps this explains to some degree a curious discrepancy pointed out by Rich Haswell in his 2005 essay, "NCTE/CCCC's Recent War on Scholarship." While peer response is one of the most ubiquitous pedagogical activities in postsecondary writing classrooms, it remains one of the least studied.

We offer this sourcebook—a collection of foundational, critical, practical, and research-based writing about peer review—to help fill that gap. We want to raise a call for continued practice and study of peer review and response activities originating from the many different subfields of writing studies: composition, rhetoric, WAC/WID, and writing center and peer tutoring theory and practice. This critical sourcebook is intended to provide essential materials for further peer review and response inquiry, practice, and research. In our view, peer response embodies a microcosm of writing studies theory and practice: it incorporates collaborative learning, writing-as-process, writing-to-learn, reader-response, performance, and motivation theories and practices. It asks us to question and map the boundaries of our authority and control as teachers of writing and the designers of writing courses and programs. It raises questions about student diversity and identity, and concerns about technology and digital innovations and constraints. In large part, this is exactly why we have been drawn to study peer pedagogies, coming to understand the promises, perils, and effectiveness of this tool for writing instruction. As the editors of this anthology, we take the position that, simply put, peer response is our best, most promising, and most nuanced pedagogy . . . and it always has been.

To get a sense of how writing instructors think about peer review and response pedagogies, in May of 2010 we sent out a survey to the WPA and WCENTER listservs. Sixty-three respondents took advantage of the open-ended format of the survey. They specified—some at length—a variety of big-picture learning opportunities afforded students during peer response, including more effective realization of community, audience awareness, trust, relationship building, and mutual support. Viewed as a snapshot of thoughts and attitudes about peer response from highly experienced writing instructors (the majority of our respondents had taught for over ten years), those big-picture learning opportunities point to why peer response is utilized so extensively in writing courses across the country.

One respondent, echoing many others, noted that peer response offers students the opportunity to build confidence and a sense of community with other student writers:

> I think that these activities can help students to feel more confident in the classroom. Peer review helps them to develop a vocabulary for talking about writing with others. It can also foster writing partnerships in class—relationships that might not otherwise form if students didn't have such opportunities.

Another respondent, though similarly expressing an overall positive attitude toward peer response, noted how important it is to embrace the difficulties of this complex practice (a caveat offered by only a few other respondents), especially the responsibility of the instructor to prioritize it and *teach* it well:

> All of the opportunities listed above are dependent on whether students are simply directed to do peer review, or are taught how to do it well. The answers I give above presume that "peer review," like any genre, has been defined, modeled, practiced, and given feedback on as part of the class instruction. Without that caveat, the gains may be minimal.

Another interesting finding that stood out in the survey results was the relatively high percentage of respondents who had first learned about peer response in graduate school, either during a practicum or during a workshop or training session on teaching writing. Several others also said that they had first experienced peer review activities as undergraduates or in other graduate school courses. This suggests that those teaching and leading these practicums and workshops are indeed spending valuable time facilitating peer response. Overall, respondents mentioned several things they had learned over the years as they've worked toward successful peer response pedagogies, including

- committing enough time;
- establishing clear goals and objectives so students understand how and why peer review fits into the overall course;
- offering models of effective response strategies;
- building in assessment and accountability measures so students see that teachers value peer review; and
- practicing patience and persistence on the part of all participants.

These responses reflect many of the different strategies and designs discussed in the readings collected in this sourcebook.

It is worth noting that the quest for successful peer review and response pedagogies in rhetoric and writing courses goes back thousands of years. For Quintilian and the Romans, the power of peer interactions was something to be utilized to its fullest potential. James Murphy explains that the Romans used peer critique to systemically instill in (male) students the habits of mind related to effective expression: "What today would be called peer criticism is an integral part of the scheme; in the Roman interactive classroom the student-critic shapes his own critical judgment by assessing publically what he hears and reads" (55). In working toward becoming habitually rhetorical in mind and action, students were encouraged to scrutinize the models of their peers' invention, arrangement, style, memory, and delivery. Instructors encouraged students to compete aggressively with one another as they critiqued peers (see Quintilian I.1.23–25). By habitually practicing the balance of civility with critical rigor, students would exercise strikingly transhistorical habits of mind: curiosity, openness, engagement, creativity persistence, responsibility, flexibility, and metacognition (*Framework for Success in Postsecondary Writing*).

Fast-forward two thousand years to the late 1960s and 1970s, when the foundational tenets of peer review and response were laid by James Moffett, Ken Macrorie, and Donald Murray, who espoused decentering and process approaches, and Peter Elbow, who advocated for "teacherless" classroom experiments as students and teachers negotiated between believing and doubting, listening and talking. These practitioners emphasized the motivational and rhetorical benefits of collaboration and mutual support, downplaying the notion of competition. In the late 1980s, Elbow's collaborations with Pat Belanoff urged writing teachers to coach students on a flexible continuum of response strategies from careful listening/reading toward more full-blown response and critique. Practitioners like Karen Spear and Robert Brooke and colleagues offered a smidgen of theory and a healthy dose of practical advice on how to consider the fine points of utilizing peer response groups in writing classrooms—everything from how many students to include in each group, to some of the roadblocks and pitfalls that can interfere with effective practice. Anne Ruggles Gere complemented these practical and theoretical efforts with her historical work on writing groups in and outside of the academy.

While teacher-scholars were building peer response theories and practices for the classroom—often first-year composition courses—others were exploring peer-to-peer learning across the disciplines, in writing centers and other peer tutoring programs. Although Haswell did not delve into writing center and peer tutoring theory and practice in his review of peer response/review coverage in NCTE/CCCC publications, scholarship from writing center and peer tutoring studies can substantially inform and complement peer critique pedagogies that are ongoing in other sites of writing instruction. The work of Kenneth Bruffee and John Trimbur, for instance, provides (anti)foundational theoretical rationales for the value of peer collaborative learning. Like Elbow, Bruffee (and soon after, writing center practitioners like Muriel Harris and Stephen North) believed there could be substantial, game-changing value inherent in surrendering some control and sharing pedagogical authority with students. Soon the promising bridges between peer review and response and peer tutoring would begin to emerge, including detailed, empirical study of ESL and multicultural students. For example, Marie Nelson's five-year study of developmental, multilingual, and multicultural students, *At the Point of Need*, generated the approach now dubbed the "studio" method (and further discussed in the work of Rhonda Grego and Nancy Thompson), supporting and furthering research on the benefits of collaborative peer interactions with empirical data.

Since these foundational sojourns into peer response, contemporary scholars have continued to ask important pedagogical questions (see, for example, Corbett et al.). People in classroom- and curriculum-based tutoring programs have attempted to build bridges between writing classrooms and writing centers—with developmental students, with linguistically and culturally diverse students, and with students from across the disciplines—with peer response functioning as the crucial connector (see, for example, Corbett). Scholars in our digital age have merged elements of Elbow's "teacherless" classrooms with their own "paperless" technological classrooms and online experiments and innovations (for example, *WriterKEY*; Eli Review; Paulson et al.; Anson; Vieregge et al.; Moxley; Comer and White). Writing centers and other WAC peer tutoring programs have likewise embraced the digital, taking advantage of what web-based pedagogies have to offer. Teacher-scholars in fields outside of writing studies, like education and psychology, have also developed peer sophisticated review and response methods, including the Scaffolded Writing and Rewriting in the Discipline (SWoRD)/Peerceptiv system. Others have married writing in the disciplines with web-based technologies, including Calibrated Peer Review (CPR) for STEM (science, technology, engineering, and math) curriculums.[1] These experiments, along with the use of digital platforms to increase collaborative opportunities and feedback for students, reveal the extent to which most faculty in and out of English recognize the benefits and potentials of peer response activities for developing student writers.

Student Peer Review and Response anthologizes these foundational—as well as forward-thinking—critical works on the use of peer review and response activities in writing classes. As we collected sources to include, we chose readings that would be useful to both newcomers *and* established teachers of writing, as well as those who wish to answer Haswell's call and continue the study of peer response as a significant pedagogy within writing classes. In this collection, we have gathered landmark readings, key empirical studies on students' experience of peer review and response, and advice about designing peer review/response activities with multilingual and diverse students, in disciplinary writing classes, and in digital environments. The sources we've gathered span the theoretical considerations and practical issues related to designing effective peer review and response activities, reflecting the pedagogical grounding—as well as interdisciplinary nature—of composition studies as a field at large. Our hope is that we've provided a useful sourcebook for WPAs, WAC/WID coordinators, writing center directors, and those who coordinate curricular initiatives within writing programs. Instructors who seek to further develop their teaching practices, will also find a number of resources here, as will instructors who want to start using peer response, those who have tried peer response but have had difficulty making it work, and those who want to contribute to the research on peer response.

The readings in this book are divided into six sections. Part One presents foundational theories and lines of inquiry in the field, demonstrating the genesis of conversations on this pedagogical technique. Part Two demonstrates the ways members of the field have taken up or interrogated the assumptions of early proponents of peer review and response activities, critically examining and redeveloping many of the discussion points central to earlier works. Part Three offers practical, ready-to-use pedagogical and logistical suggestions for peer review and response. Part Four concerns the recognition of diverse classroom contexts, including how language, race, gender, ability, and other cultural and personal elements of student life may complicate peer review and response activities. Part Five refocuses the conversation about peer review and response in light of writing across the curriculum and in the disciplines. Finally, Part Six takes up peer review and response in digital environments. All in all, there were many more works we would have liked to include in each section, but could not due to limited space. So, we round out this sourcebook with a list of selected readings and resources for further study.

How we teach (and learn) peer response, including our attitudes toward it, likely goes a long way in determining whether newer writing instructors adopt peer response activities. For students and instructors, at all levels, whose memories of peer response are anything but positive, it becomes important that we proceed in the "unlearning" that might need to happen to overcome lingering ambivalence. Peer response activities can certainly activate and encourage student writers' sense of community, and help students learn to trust more than just the teacher's point of view—but only if instructors can successfully nudge them toward understanding and appreciating the value so many of us see in this collaborative practice. We believe that teachers can realize these goals, but only if we learn to accept our invaluable roles as the conductors of our courses, and the course of our students' learning, while at the same time recognizing and acknowledging the limits of our own pedagogical knowledge, points of view, and abilities. While Lunsford joked about her students not describing *her* as the best thing in their evaluations of the course she taught, we believe they were still offering her a high compliment. For it was in fact Lunsford's conscientious planning, preparation, reflective practice—and trust in her students' abilities as readers and responders—that enabled her students to realize such appreciation for *their* peer response groups. We hope this collection will help teachers everywhere work toward empowering their own students to trust and support each other in similar ways.

NOTES

1. The development and study of Calibrated Peer Review (CPR) in the late 1990s and Scaffolded Writing and Rewriting in the Disciplines (SWoRD) in the mid-2000s explored methods that use web-based and computer-mediated technologies in attempts to balance the quest for enhancing student content-knowledge acquisition with process skills. Developed for chemistry around 1998, CPR has expanded rapidly to hundreds of institutions internationally (see Walvoord et al.; Russell, p. 343). In CPR we are afforded a glimpse into what STEM disciplines value and prioritize in their teaching and learning, including how computer-mediated peer response can help teachers and researchers design more fine-grained, RAD (replicable, aggregate, and data-supported) assessment measures that can lead to improved pedagogies and learning outcomes.

SWoRD/Peerceptiv attempts to synthesize the best of process pedagogies with web-based technologies. The research of developers Kwangsu Cho and Christian Schunn, among others, explores how SWoRD supports both content knowledge and process skills by taking as its model the journal publication process and scaffolding it systematically with the aid of web-based technologies. Further, and in contrast to CPR research, SWoRD researchers draw on some of the same work as writing studies. While reading their theoretical frames, methodologies, and methods we sometimes hear familiar names like Bazerman, Beaufort, Berkenkotter, Ede, Flower and Hayes, and Prior (see, for example, Patchan et al.). Yet, like CPR, and in contrast to most peer response group methods advocated in rhetoric and composition studies, student reviewers are anonymous and they assign grades to each other, privileging isolated numerical scoring and grading over collaborative conversation. Further, Patchan et al. discovered only a moderate (statistically insignificant) difference in the quality of final drafts from students who had received feedback from peers in addition to instructors.

And even though STEM researchers and practitioners are taking some interesting approaches to peer review and response, we have to wonder if the sorts of dialogic, collaborative, and community-building potentials so sought after by the early proponents of peer response from our field are downplayed or downright missing in STEM's more objective assessment quests.

WORKS CITED

Anson, Chris M. "Re: Over-Responders Anonymous." *WPA Listserv*, 24 Apr. 2014, lists.asu.edu /cgi-bin/wa?A1=ind1404&L=WPA-L#130.

Comer, Denise K., and Edward M. White. "Adventuring into MOOC Writing Assessment: Challenges, Results, and Possibilities." *College Composition and Communication*, vol. 67, no. 3, Feb. 2016, pp. 318–59.

Corbett, Steven J. *Beyond Dichotomy: Synergizing Writing Center and Classroom Pedagogies.* The WAC Clearinghouse/Parlor Press, 2015.

Corbett, Steven J., et al., editors. *Peer Pressure, Peer Power: Theory and Practice in Peer Review and Response for the Writing Classroom.* Fountainhead Press, 2014.

Davis, Kevin. "What We Talk about When We Talk about Writing: Initiating Conversations on Writing Quality with Moderated Class Response." Corbett et al., pp. 209–15.

Elbow, Peter. "The Teacherless Writing Class." *Writing without Teachers,* Oxford UP, 1973, pp. 76–121.

Eli Review. *Drawbridge.* http://elireview.com/.

Framework for Success in Postsecondary Writing. Developed jointly by the Council of Writing Program Administrators, the National Council of Teachers of English, and the National Writing Project, 2011, wpacouncil.org/framework.

Haswell, Richard H. "NCTE/CCCC's Recent War of Scholarship." *Written Communication,* vol. 22, no. 2, 2005, pp. 198–223.

Lunsford, Andrea A. "Teacher to Teacher: Tips for New Teachers #7: Effective Peer Groups." *Bedford Bits: Ideas for Teaching Writing,* 16 June 2011, bedfordbits.colostate.edu/index.php/2011/06/16/tips-for-new-teachers-7-effective-peer-groups/.

Moxley, Joe. "Big Data, Learning Analytics, and Social Assessment." *The Journal of Writing Assessment,* vol. 6, no. 1, Aug. 2013, www.journalofwritingassessment.org/article.php?article=68.

Murphy, James J. "The Key Role of Habit in Roman Writing Instruction." *A Short History of Writing Instruction: From Ancient Greece to Modern America,* edited by James J. Murphy, 2nd ed., Hermagoras, 2001, pp. 35–78.

Nelson, Marie Wilson. *At the Point of Need: Teaching Basic and ESL Writers.* Boynton/Cook, 1991.

Patchan, Melissa M., et al. "Writing in Natural Sciences: Understanding the Effects of Different Types of Reviewers on the Writing Process." *Journal of Writing Research,* vol. 2, no. 3, Feb. 2011, pp. 365–93.

Paulson, Eric J., et al. "Peer Review Re-Reviewed: Investigating the Juxtaposition of Composition Students' Eye Movements and Peer-Review Processes." *Research in the Teaching of English,* vol. 41, no. 3, Feb. 2007, pp. 304–35.

Quintilian, Marcus Fabius. *The Institutio Oratoria,* ca. 95. Translated by H. E. Butler, G. P. Putnam's Sons, 1921.

Vieregge, Quentin D., et al. *Agency in the Age of Peer Production.* CCCC/NCTE, 2012.

Walvoord, Mark E., et al. "An Analysis of Calibrated Peer Review (CPR) in a Science Lecture Classroom." *Journal of College Science Teaching,* vol. 37, no. 4, 2008, pp. 66–73.

WriterKEY. Bedford, Freeman, and Worth, www.writerkey.com.

PART ONE

Practical and Theoretical Foundations

Introduction to Part One

The works in Part One lay the groundwork for subsequent pedagogical conversations on the theory, practice, and history of peer review and response. These works, written in the decades that the field of composition was coming to recognize itself as a distinct discipline, speak to concepts now often taken for granted in pedagogical discussions of writing classes—that teaching writing as a process affords students multiple opportunities to come to understand writing and themselves as writers; that collaboration between students (or student and teacher) offers possibilities that the solely teacher-centered classroom might eclipse; that evaluation of student work by the teacher-as-authority may focus students on what the teacher wants over an increasing understanding of writing situations; and that peer group experiences can help students build a number of soft skills such as problem solving, listening, critical reading, and social awareness. As we look back on these foundational works, we realize just how much the pedagogical assumptions included in these texts have worked their way into the field's most basic assumptions about what effective writing instruction entails—demonstrating exactly why we argue that peer review can be considered a microcosm of composition practice itself.

We start things off with a piece from a well-known writing process pioneer, Donald Murray. In this excerpt from "Writing as Process: How Writing Finds Its Own Meaning" (1982), Murray links his process theory of writing to how that theory can be put into practice. Murray begins by emphasizing that the process writing classroom must be a place where experiencing the act of writing is privileged over mastering some sort of content. He goes on to explain that the meaning-making process requires time, space, and—echoing the work of Peter Elbow—the willingness of teachers to let go of some instructional control. Murray moves on to explain how involving students in the response process can build a supportive community of writers who help each other find meaning beyond the dictates of the teacher. Murray then describes the importance of student-teacher conferences and how those meetings feed into the workshop classroom, where students further discuss the details of their writing processes. Murray concludes by emphasizing that writers need thoughtful, patient readers in order to realize their own meanings and processes of meaning-making.

In the second selection, from *Writing Groups: History, Theory, and Implications* (1987), Anne Ruggles Gere hinges her writing pedagogy on successful community-building activities. In this selection, Gere sums up what she's discovered about the history of writing groups inside and outside the academy. She also offers a theoretical understanding of literacy and subsequent implications for classroom work with peer response. As a generative exercise for faculty who teach writing classes and value peer response activities, Gere compares the strengths and weaknesses of writing groups outside and inside academia: What can faculty who place students into peer groups in a classroom setting learn from groups whose members choose to participate and build their own sustainable structures? Gere offers a wide variety of practical considerations gleaned from this comparison, including the choices that practitioners have when trying to build an environment of commitment, confidence, and trust. Gere emphasizes the importance of designing group activities that will nudge student writers toward becoming dialogical members of a literate community.

If the readings in Part One establish the center of our field's long accepted assumptions about the value of and central practices necessary for effective peer response work in writing classes, savvy twenty-first-century readers may also find a naïveté in these foundational texts—a series of sometimes blithe assumptions that the authors in Part Two will begin to unpack, critique, and assail. Even so, as we look back at the recommendations of these foundational authors, it is remarkable to consider how pervasive the ideas espoused in these early works have become in the field of writing studies. The ideal of situating collaboration and peer response as the cornerstones of process pedagogy has worked its way into the most common iterations of composition and appears with some frequency in discussions of WAC/WID (writing in the disciplines) professional development. The next section will model the sorts of reflexive and critical questions necessary for developing a robust pedagogical approach to peer response activities, reminding those interested in peer response activities that our assumptions as teachers always benefit from further critical contestation, reflexive applications, and deeper understandings of our students and their needs, as well as the broader social and institutional contexts that surround and inform them.

1 From *Writing as Process: How Writing Finds Its Own Meaning*

DONALD M. MURRAY

TEACHING THE COMPOSING PROCESS

. . . [My] theory of how a piece of writing finds its own meaning . . . has come out of practice. It is rooted in the experience of making meaning with written language. Theory, however, must return to practice in our field. A writing theory that can not be practiced by teachers, writers, or students and that does not produce increasingly effective drafts of writing must be reconsidered. We also have an obligation to show how the theory can be put into practice. We must show that our students are able to write more effectively and produce pieces of writing that find their own meaning because they understand what happens during the writing act. If we accept the process theory of teaching writing, then we must be able to suggest ways in which our students can experience the writing process.

In teaching the process we have to look not at what students need to know, but what they need to experience. This separates the teaching of writing from the teaching of a course in which the content is produced by authorities—writers of literature, scientists, historians—and interpreted by textbooks and teachers. The writing teacher has no such content. It would be bizarre for the process teacher to deliver a lecture on the process theory of composition in advance of writing—just as bizarre as it would be to deliver a lecture on rhetoric, linguistics, grammar, or any other theoretical concepts before the student writes. Such information would be meaningless to the student. It might even be harmful because the student who hears such information without the perspective of his or her own experience can develop serous misconceptions about the writing process. For example, a student might get the dangerous misconception that writers know the form before they know the content, that students know what they have to say before they say it. I would not write—would not need to write—if I knew what I was going to say before I said it. I must help my students find out through a successful writing experience why that is true.

From *Learning by Teaching: Selected Articles on Writing and Teaching*, Boynton/Cook, 1982, 25–31. Orig. published in *Eight Approaches to Teaching Composition*, NCTE, 1980, pp. 17–31.

In the writing process approach, the teacher and student face the task of making meaning together. The task is ever new, for they share the blank page and an ignorance of purpose and of outcome. They start on a trip of exploration together. They find where they are going as they get there.

This requires of the writing teacher a special kind of courage. The teacher not only has to face blank papers but blank students worried by their blankness, and a blank curriculum which worries the teacher's supervisors. The teacher has to restrain himself or herself from providing a content, taking care not to inhibit the students from finding their own subjects, their own forms, and their own language.

The writing teacher who is writing and, therefore, knows how the stages in the writing process work and how the forces within that process interact, understands the students' natural desire for premature order expressed, in part, by the question, "What do you want?" The teacher must resist the impulse to respond with a prescription. It is better to explain to the students why their writing needs room—time and space—to find its own meaning.

The first day of the writing unit should begin with writing, not talking. The students write and the teacher writes. This beginning is, of course, a symbolic gesture. It demonstrates that the information in the course will come from the student. The students produce the principal text in the writing course.

It is very hard for traditionally trained teachers who are not writing themselves to believe that students can write without instruction from the teacher or without assignment. Teachers often do not have enough faith in their students to feel that the students have anything to say. They also may not realize that much, perhaps most, of the poor writing they see in school is the product of the assignments they give. Most assignments I see guarantee bad writing. In many cases assignments direct students to write on subjects in which they have no interest and on which they have no information. They have to adopt a point of view implicit in the assignments or in the way teachers present them. They have to accept forms and perhaps languages which are not appropriate to their subjects—or their visions of the subjects.

Of course, students like assignments. Why not? They make things easy. The good students know instantly what the teacher wants; the poor students deliver as best they can. And neither group has to make a personal commitment to the writing.

It is important that the writing course which is built on the writing process set that process in action immediately. In fact, this approach might be called the writing/response method. The student writes, then the teacher and the class respond. One device I have used to begin a writing class is to hand out six 3 × 5 cards of different colors. I ask the students to take a card and brainstorm specific details about a person or place, or an event which was important to them. They may also just brainstorm random specifics. After three or four minutes I share my own list with the class. Then I ask them to circle a specific on their own cards which surprised them, or to connect two specifics with an unexpected relationship. I share my surprises with them. Then I tell them to take another card and start with that moment of surprise, or just start freewriting. After three or four minutes I again share my writing with them and ask them to take another card, to continue on, start anew, or switch the point of view. And so we work through the cards. At the end we each share one card, reading it aloud without comment.

I have worked out all sorts of variations of this exercise, and so have teachers to whom I've introduced it. The important thing is that students write upon demand, that they write of what they know, that they are placed under enough pressure so they write what they did not expect to write, that the cards are small enough and switched frequently enough so they have a new chance if one doesn't go well, that the teacher shares his or her writing with them, that they listen to the voices which are coming from the members of *their* writing community, and that they discover that writing is a process of discovery.

Under such conditions I find that writing is produced. Nine hundred and ninety-nine students out of a thousand will write on demand. But if one doesn't write, not to worry. Writing is contagious. It is almost impossible to resist the desire to write in your own voice, of your own concerns, when you are part of a supportive writing community.

SHARING WRITING

Once the writing is produced, it is shared. I have come to believe that this sharing, at least in the beginning, should be done orally. When students read their papers aloud they hear the voices of their classmates without the interference of mechanical problems, misspellings, and poor penmanship. Those problems will have to be dealt with in due time, but first the students—and especially the teacher—should hear the voices which come from the page.

It is equally important, perhaps more important, for the writer to hear his or her own voice. Our voices often tell us a great deal about the subject. The piece of writing speaks with its own voice of its own concerns, direction, meaning. The student writer hears that voice from the piece convey intensity, drive, energy, and more—anger, pleasure, happiness, sadness, caring, frustration, understanding, explaining. The meaning of a piece of writing comes from what it says *and* how it says it.

As the students in the writing class hear a piece of writing, they laugh with the author, grieve with the author, nod in understanding, lean forward to try to learn more. That's how the writing class begins, and that is what carries it forward. The community of writers instinctively understands that each piece of writing is trying to work its way towards a meaning. The community wants to help the writer help the piece of writing find its own meaning.

The experience of sharing writing should be reinforced by the writing conference. Individual conferences are the principal form of instruction in the writing process approach. As we have speculated upon the process by which a piece of writing finds its own meaning, we have seen how important it is to listen to the piece of writing and to pay attention to how that piece of writing is making itself heard. We must, in our conferences, help the student respect the piece of writing, pay attention to what it is trying to say, and experience the process of helping it say it.

We get the student to talk about the paper and to talk about the forces which produced the draft. We do this in conference, and we do it in workshop. I have come to believe that the workshop works best when it begins with a public conference between the writer and the teacher. The teacher gives the student the opportunity to talk about the piece of writing—what the student sees in it, what technical problems the student identifies, what questions the student has for the readers—and encourages the student to talk about the process by which the writing is being produced. The teacher initiates the conference, but soon the class joins in, writers helping writers listen to the evolving writing.

There are few lectures and large group exercises—if any—in the writing class. What is there to say until a draft is heard? Who can predict the proper response to an event which has not taken place? There are, in fact, no classes; there are workshops in which writing is shared. The writers in the workshop study drafts in process to see what meanings are evolving and, thereby, learn to anticipate what may appear on the page as well as read what has appeared.

In my own workshops I publish only the best work. The most effective teaching occurs when the students who have produced that work talk about how they have produced it. This is when I am able to show students what they have learned, and by so doing I constantly learn with them.

> How were you able to get a first draft to work so well?
>
> Well, I don't know. It just seemed to go together.
>
> Well, what did you do before you started to write?
>
> Not much. I didn't make an outline or anything.
>
> Did you think much about the piece of writing you were going to do?
>
> Oh yeah, sure. I think about it all the time, trying out different things, you know, like what you're going to say at the party, or to the girl. Stuff like that, kinda' practicing in your head.

And we're into a discussion of rehearsal as I get this student, and others, to tell about how they do this in their minds and on their pages. I underline, extend, reinforce, and teach what at least some of them have already done so that they know what they've done and may be able to apply it to other writing tasks. Others in the class who have not tried it are encouraged to try it in the future.

This is the way the writing unit unwinds. The attitudes appropriate to rehearsing, drafting, and revising are expressed in conferences and in class by the students and the teacher. The skills of rehearsing, drafting, and revising are refined after they have worked successfully on an evolving draft. Concurrently, the forces of *reading* and *writing*, *collecting* and *connecting* are identified. The students and the teacher share their techniques for developing and controlling these forces, for helping to bring them into effective balance.

The greatest hazard for the teacher is the natural tendency not to respect the forces and instead to supply the student with the teacher's information, to make the teacher's connection, to use the teacher's language, to read what the teacher sees in the text. The teacher must remember, in workshop and in conference, to stand back and give the student room so that the student can give the writing room to find its own meaning. The teacher should not look at the text for the student, not even with the student. The teacher looks at—and listens to—the student watching the text evolve.

The teacher is not coy and does not withhold information that the student needs. But the teacher must practice the patience and restraint of the writer. The writer treats the evolving drafts with respect, trying to help the piece of writing work towards its own meaning. The teacher demonstrates this attitude by treating the student with respect so that the student will respect his or her own evolving writing. By asking helpful questions of the student, the teacher shows the student how to question his or her own drafts: "What did you learn from this piece of writing?" "Where is the piece of writing taking you?" "What do you feel works best in this piece of writing?"

EVALUATION OF WRITING

I am always amused when people feel that a writing course is permissive, that anything goes, that there is no serious evaluation. The fact is there is much more evaluation in the writing course than in the traditional content course. Evaluation in the writing course is not a matter of an occasional test. As the student passes through the stages of the writing process and tries to bring the forces within the process into balance, there is constant evaluation of the writing in process.

This evaluation begins with each word as it is considered and reconsidered in the mind and then as it appears on the paper. The word is reevaluated as the phrase is created and recorded. The phrase is reevaluated as the sentence is created and recorded. The sentence is reevaluated as the paragraph is created and recorded. The paragraph is reevaluated as the page is created and recorded. The page is reevaluated as the entire piece of writing is created and recorded. And then the writer, having once finished the writing and put it away, picks it up and evaluates it again.

In the writing course the writer's evaluation is shared with the teacher or with other writers in the class. The evaluation is evaluated as the writing itself is evaluated. For example:

I don't like the writing at all in this draft. It's gross.

You think it's all gross?

Yeah.

Well, I don't think it's all gross. Some of it may be gross, but what do you think is less gross?

Well, I suppose that description of how to start the snowmobile works pretty well.

Yes, that piece of writing seems to know what it's doing. Why do you think it does?

Well, it seems to be lined up pretty well. I mean, like it goes along, sort of natural.

That's how it seems to me.

Think maybe I should make the rest try to work that way? It's kind of jumbled up now.

Try it if you want.

Each draft, often each part of the draft, is discussed with readers—the teacher-writer and the other student-writers. Eventually the writing is published in a workshop, and a small or large group of readers evaluate it. It is evaluated on many levels. Is there a subject? Does it say anything? Is it worth saying? Is it focused? Is it documented? Is it ordered? Are the parts developed? Is the writing clear? Does it have an appropriate voice? Do the sentences work? Do the paragraphs work? Are the verbs strong? Are the nouns specific? Is the spelling correct? Does the punctuation clarify?

There is, in fact, so much evaluation, so much self-criticism, so much rereading, that the writing teacher has to help relieve the pressure of criticism to make sure that the writer has a bearable amount. The pressure must be there, but it never should be so great that it creates paralysis or destroys self-respect. Effective writing depends on the student's respect for the potential that may appear. The student has to have faith in the evolving draft to be able to see its value. To have faith in the draft means having faith in the self.

The teacher by the very nature of the writing course puts enormous pressure on the student. There are deadlines. The student will write every day. Over my desk hangs the exhortation "nulla dies sine linea," never a day without a line, which is attributed to Pliny and which has hung over Trollope's writing desk and Updike's. I give copies of it to my students, and I practice it myself. There should, in the writing unit, be at least weekly deadlines. There is an unrelenting demand for writing.

Writing means self-exposure. No matter how objective the tone or how detached the subject, the writer is exposed by words on the page. It is natural for students and for writers to fear such exposure. That fear can be relieved best if the writer, the fellow students, and the teacher look together at the piece of writing to see what the piece of writing is saying, and if they listen to the piece of writing with appropriate detachment.

When we write, we confront ourselves, but we also confront our subject. In writing the drafts of this chapter, "How Writing Finds Its Own Meaning," I found meanings I did not expect. I suppose that I was invited to do this chapter because of the definitions and the descriptions of the writing process I have published in the past. I accepted the invitation because I had completed a new description which has since been published elsewhere. But in the months that it has taken me to help this piece of writing find its own meaning I have found new meanings. This is not the chapter I intended to write. The process described here is different from what I have described before. This piece of writing revolted against my intent and taught me what I did not know.

By the time this is published I will, I hope, have moved on. There are those who may be concerned by what they consider inconsistency or disloyalty to my own words. No matter, I have no choice. The pieces of writing I have not yet thought of writing will become different from what I expect them to be when I propose them to myself. My constant is change. My teaching changes from year to year and day to day. I do not teach my students what I have learned in the past. My students teach themselves what we are learning together.

Those of us who teach the writing process are comfortable with the constant change. This sets us apart from many people in the academic world who teach in a traditional or classical mode, believing there are truths which can be learned and passed on from teacher to student, from generation to generation. Their conception has its attractions; it is the one I was taught. But my life as a writer and as a teacher of writing leads me—as similar experience has led others—to a different tradition which some call developmental or truly humanistic. We do not teach our students rules demonstrated by static models; we teach our students to write by allowing them to experience the process of writing. That is a process of discovery, of using written language to find out what we have to say. We believe this process can be adapted by our students to whatever writing tasks face them—the memo, the poem, the textbook, the speech, the consumer complaint, the job application, the story, the essay, the personal letter, the movie script, the accident report, the novel, the scientific paper. There is no way we can tell what our students will need to write in their lives beyond the classroom, but we can give our students a successful experience in the writing process. We can let them discover how writing finds its own meaning.

2 From *Writing Groups: History, Theory, and Implications*

ANNE RUGGLES GERE

PRACTICAL DIRECTIONS

Knowing something of the history and theory of writing groups leads to two sets of implications, one practical and one theoretical. This chapter deals with practical questions, while the next considers theoretical issues.

To discuss practical issues is not, however, to offer a formula for establishing and maintaining effective writing groups. As the history of writing groups in this country illustrates, there is no one "right" way to proceed. Questions of size, procedures, timing, genre, membership, and context have been answered variously by individual groups. Workshops such as those instituted at the University of Iowa and the Breadloaf Writers' Conference share with literary societies and women's clubs a large number of respondents. One advantage of this size, usually twenty-five to thirty people, is that no one individual is reponsible for making a great number of negative comments, and the cumulative effect of repetition can be convincing to the author. Conversely, smaller groups, such as those found in many classrooms and some self-improvement groups, have the advantage of intimacy and a virtual guarantee that all participants will be motivated toward and active in group work.

Some groups elect critics to respond to writers' work while others rely upon spontaneous responses of the whole group. In some groups authors read aloud from written drafts; in others the participants read drafts silently to themselves and then offer either oral or written responses. Sometimes authors are responsible for making notes on comments offered, and in other cases those responding provide written copies of their comments. In school-sponsored writing groups the role of the teacher likewise varies. Some teachers participate equally with students, sharing their own writing and offering their comments along with students; some moderate critique sessions, underlining comments with which they agree and screening out those they think

From "Part III: Implications" in *Writing Groups: History, Theory, and Implications*, Southern Illinois UP, 1987, pp. 99–123.

less appropriate; some leave groups entirely on their own, relying on reports from group moderators about group progress; and still others move from group to group, monitoring behavior, offering suggestions, and modeling effective responses when groups falter.

Use of time likewise varies from one group to another. One group may operate on a strict schedule, allocating a certain number of minutes to each individual in the group and appointing a timekeeper to ensure that all participants receive a hearing. Another may proceed more informally, allowing as much time as an individual author wishes for reading and responding to the work. School-sponsored writing groups usually operate within the constraints of scheduled class time, but sometimes instructors adjust by having classes meet for double sessions or allocating successive days to writing groups to make up for the limitations imposed by a bell ringing after forty-five or fifty minutes. Some groups meet weekly, others monthly, and still others seasonally (such as during the summer months).

Some writing groups concentrate on a single genre, such as poetry or drama, while others include writers who work in a variety of genres. Those who limit group work to a single genre usually maintain that a mixture is distracting, while those who encourage several genres claim that the variety offers participants multiple perspectives. Predictably, group procedures sometimes change with genre. Participants who usually read their work aloud may, for example, distribute copies of poems so everyone can attend to visual effects, line breaks, and other non-aural aspects of poetry. Likewise, groups that usually read one another's work silently may switch to oral reading for dramatic scripts where the sound of the language is more important.

Although groups take a variety of forms they can be categorized into three main types—autonomous, semi-autonomous, and nonautonomous—depending upon the locus and degree of authority. The voluntary constitution of writing groups within literary societies, young men's associations, women's clubs, and in myriad other self-sponsored gatherings identifies them as autonomous. Authority resides within individual members of autonomous groups because they choose to join other writers with whom they are friendly, share common interests, backgrounds, or needs. Autonomous writing groups depend upon members who are willing to give away, temporarily at least, authority over their own writing, indicating that they respect and trust one another enough to surrender their language to one another's critical scrutiny. The sense of empowerment—whether among culturally-deprived students, economically-disadvantaged workers, socially-constrained women, or any individuals who seek more control over their own writing—characteristic of writing groups both past and present results from this simultaneous giving and receiving of authority.

Classroom writing groups are either semi-autonomous or nonautonomous depending upon the instructor's willingness and ability to provide students opportunities to emulate autonomous groups. In nonautonomous groups students never experience the empowerment of using language collaboratively to generate new understandings because the instructor fails to give them the authority to do so. Preparation (or more commonly lack of it), group functioning, assignments or tasks, and evaluation all contrive to prevent members of nonautonomous groups from assuming authority. Instructors have many ways of enabling students to take on a portion of the authority enjoyed by autonomous groups, and when they are successful, classroom groups can become semi-autonomous. This means that individual members experience much of the empowerment characteristic of autonomous groups, but they can never, because of the authority invested in the educational institution and its representative the instructor, become truly autonomous. The following discussion examines autonomous and semi-autonomous writing groups, highlighting the areas where they differ in locus and degree of authority.

For autonomous groups the first issue is finding individual members. Individuals become members of self-sponsored writing groups in a variety of ways, but now, as in the past, most form around similarities of education, class, and goals. College literary societies grew from the efforts of relatively privileged young men seeking a kind of intellectual endeavor not available in the college curriculum, while apprentices who formed self-improvement societies had more practical aims of raising their status in society. Similarly, class markers such as her husband's occupation frequently determined which club a woman might join, but other clubs placed more emphasis on shared goals such as study of specific issues or publication of members' writing. Today's self-sponsored writing groups follow similar patterns of formation, and goals continue to play a large role. Writers whose primary concern is publication, for example, often discourage members who write for their own pleasure because these members may not be "serious" enough. No matter how they happen to join a particular group, individuals in self-sponsored writing groups possess an authority and autonomy unequalled by any school-sponsored group.

One manifestation of this difference appears in the way school-sponsored writing groups are formed. Dividing students into groups is not the first step in establishing classroom writing groups, but when it does occur teachers play a major role in deciding who works with whom. Group composition results from juggling constraints of size (usually four to seven members), heterogeneity (of gender, writing ability, and personality type), and configuration (assigned roles such as recorder or chair). Instructors interested in creating semi-autonomous groups give considerable thought to balancing these factors in a way that passes a measure of authority on to students.

Some teachers minimize their influence by allowing students to determine the membership of their own groups. Others organize students into groups with an eye to diversity in writing ability, gender, and interpersonal skills, and still others have elaborate systems for combining student and teacher preferences. They may, for example, ask students to indicate one or two classmates with whom they would especially like to work and then construct sociograms, placing everyone in a group with at least one preferred individual. Such systems allow students some self-determination without compromising the teacher's concern for diversity in each group.

As all students and all teachers know, authority finally rests with the instructor, but students who have some choice about group membership can move toward a semi-autonomy. A more important contribution to the development of authority among participants in classroom writing groups lies in the preparation for these groups.

Writing groups, both in and out of school, proceed in many right ways, and no single set of guidelines will be effective in all times and circumstances. There are, however, some clear ways for writing groups to go wrong. Most of these fall under the general category of beginning too soon or without sufficient commitment. School-sponsored writing groups require months of preparation, and when I meet teachers who say, "Oh, I tried writing groups and they didn't work," I begin by asking about the preparation.

Establishing trust, developing collaborative skills or discovering those developed outside the classroom, and learning to critique writing constitute the preparation necessary for classroom writing groups. All writers find sharing their work risky because their language is vulnerable to attack by others. Because one's language is such an intricate part of oneself, an attack on language constitutes an attack on the self, and all writers, even those in elementary school, are wary of exposing their language to the criticism of others. Being asked to change one's language means being asked to change oneself, to leave one community and join another, and the fact that this change is the goal of writing groups does not make the process of changing any easier or less threatening. Accordingly, teachers can prepare for writing groups by transforming the class into a community where all members feel secure. This means establishing a climate where put-downs are disallowed, where people are encouraged to express their ideas without fear of recrimination, and where diversity is appreciated, not deprecated.

Teachers can create a supportive classroom community in many ways. They can set an example of respect for others by modeling it in their dealings with all students, and they can use a variety of activities to encourage positive sharing. I have found that asking students to introduce one another or to respond briefly to questions or quotations as part of daily attendance routines quickly establishes the importance and possibility of hearing from everyone in the class (Gere, *Roots* 222–28). Establishing tasks that depend upon group cooperation, requiring frequent reading of student writing to the whole class (either short anonymous observations written when students enter the class and read aloud by the teacher or selections chosen by students from their journals) and including opportunities for role-playing, help solidify a positive classroom climate. Although it is crucial to introduce many community-building activities early in the life of a given class, the need for community building extends beyond the first weeks of the term. Classroom communities, like all other living bodies, need continuing nourishment.

With college and graduate school students, successful writing groups do sometimes function in the absence of supportive classroom communities, but students at this level may have enough confidence in their own abilities to be able to work without a great deal of emotional support. Still, absence of feelings of community and trust in a group exacts a price, one Don Murray describes this way:

> Writing programs usually see workshop as the test by fire, the sort of varsity scrimmage or wargame in which a guy is tested. I am being purposely sexist. Only a few years ago I heard a writer say, "She didn't have the balls to publish in workshop!" That was a point that made me think about my workshop teaching. I heard that quote the same week that a piece of mine was attacked in a workshop of my peers. I knew the lead didn't work; I'd tried all sorts of ways to find a lead that worked, but when a colleague attacked the lead I defended it. (letter)

For Murray the unsupportive emotional climate led to vocal defensiveness, while for other authors it may lead to withdrawal; in any case, the result is the same. Writing groups established without attention to or concern for a prior sense of trust among members risk diminished performances from all participants.

Although necessary, establishing a sense of community does not constitute sufficient preparation for a classroom writing group. Students also need to learn how to work together in groups. Tom Hilgers, who has done extensive research on classroom writing groups, asserts: "The mere creation of collaborative settings for writers is not alone going to generate effective writing. Collaborative skills, like writing skills, must be learned" (12). Learning collaborative skills means, among other things, mastering the social skills needed to work with others in a group and developing the ability to identify and solve problems. Social skills such as stating one's opinion and listening carefully to the contributions of others can be taught prior to establishing writing groups, as instructors encourage class discussion.

If students learn the importance of listening carefully to others before they work in writing groups, they will be more able to function well in such groups. As a preliminary students can develop their listening skills with class dictation exercises. If the instructor reads passages aloud for students to copy, students increase both accuracy and retention of listening (Gere, *Roots* 224). A more difficult and important way of enhancing students' listening skills is for instructors to move away from the traditional recitation style of class discussion where all comments are directed to the instructor (and students make little effort to respond to one another). As Mishler has observed, this type of recitation leads to classroom language where all logical connections remain the teacher's responsibility. If instructors insist that students direct comments to the whole class, respond to one another, and refrain from relying on the teacher to make connections between statements and answer all questions, students' listening skills will improve dramatically. Students will learn to extract meaning from one another's language rather than merely waiting for their opportunity to impress the instructor. In the process they will recognize that their peers give classroom comments careful attention and will become more willing to take risks with their own language.

As students develop listening skills, they become more able to engage in productive problem solving. The ability to identify and solve problems in writing groups takes the specific form of being able to locate and offer constructive suggestions for problems in writing. This means that group members need practice in responding to writing—the kind of practice that teachers can provide by moderating whole-class critique sessions. In such sessions the instructor can highlight useful comments made by students and model others. Implicit in such highlighting will be an acknowledgment of the close relationship between language and feeling, a relationship that contributes to the power inherent in writing groups. In some cases, of course, writing groups remain whole-class activities, but instructor modeling at the outset can make such groups more effective. Another form of modeling involves inviting practiced writing group members to do a "fish bowl" demonstration of their procedures for a class, allowing time for questions from students after the demonstration. Developing listening skills and problem-solving abilities prepares students to participate effectively in writing groups, but the crucial ingredient is commitment.

Teaching commitment to writing groups among students who are required to participate is probably impossible, but commitment can be caught if not taught. Among instructors who tell me their writing groups failed I find a high percentage of diffidence or uncertainty. That is, I find instructors who put students into writing groups because they think it's "good" to do so, not because they know their value firsthand and believe in it. Instructors who introduce writing groups successfully usually are those who have participated in writing groups themselves and know the benefits for their own writing. Part of their success may derive from the fact that such instructors can, by drawing on their own experience, anticipate problems and offer more useful guidance than their inexperienced colleagues. Nevertheless, their commitment to writing groups takes precedence with students, who, like all subjugated groups, read their superiors' feelings expertly.

"Commitment" can be rendered less abstract when put into action. Instructors who claim belief in writing groups give life to that statement by the kind of authority they pass on to students. One of the least effective groups I have observed, for example, worked in a classroom where the teacher asked students to respond to finished pieces of writing. Although they never articulated their complaint, students knew that they didn't have a "real" task; the comments they made would not shape a revision because the writing was completed. Despite her protestations to the contrary, this instructor demonstrated how to make writing groups go wrong. Because this instructor failed to invest their work with the authority of shaping future drafts, students failed to "catch" commitment to the work of the groups.

Another more subtle form of teacher commitment to writing groups centers on the teacher's willingness to take on a new role, not to abdicate responsibility but to assume it differently. One of the critical salvos most frequently aimed at writing groups addresses the issue of teacher responsibility. Critics usually assert that writing groups exist to make teachers' lives easier, pointing to article titles such as "The Efficiency of Student Correction of Compositions" (Tressler), "A Practical Proposition to Take the Drudgery out of the Teaching of Freshman Composition and to Restore to the Teacher His Pristine

Measure in Teaching" (Bernadette), "When the Teacher Stops Teaching" (Putz), or "What Students Can Do To Take the Burden off You" (Hardaway) to sustain their claims. Higley's parody of the writing group meeting in which students carry out a desultory conversation about procedures, making comments such as "What we're supposed to do is say what we think about the writing without taking time to make it up" and "It flowed just right," (682) likewise provides evidence for critics. One group member sits with his head on the desk during the entire session, and after one paper has been discussed, the group decides to take a break. This parody typifies the teacher irresponsibility suggested by some article titles (although it is rarely the substance of these articles) and criticized by those who doubt the value of writing groups. The students portrayed in this parody demonstrate no understanding of or commitment to their task, a sure sign their their instructor has not prepared them sufficiently for writing groups.

Successful classroom writing groups depend upon teachers committed to preparing students with the necessary social and intellectual skills. When this preparation is effective, students become proprietary about their writing groups. In observing school-sponsored groups, I heard a number of students insist that they could not complete their assignments unless the instructor gave them time to work with their groups. Members of self-sponsored groups typically have considerably less overt preparation, but the lack of school-imposed requirements and timetables does not exempt self-sponsored writing groups from all problems. It is more complicated to form a self-sponsored group. Potential participants do not always appear, and writers often roam local conferences looking for others interested in sharing their work. Even when they find one another, members of self-sponsored writing groups wrestle with the issue of commitment. Without the external pressure of school requirements, some individuals find it difficult to attend regular meetings and to prepare writing on agreed-upon schedules. Still, self-sponsored groups need less preparation because a good portion of preparation for classroom writing groups deals, directly or indirectly, with transferring authority from teacher to students, a transfer unnecessary in groups where individual members start from positions of authority.

Yet, as history demonstrates, self-sponsored groups rarely rely entirely upon their own resources. College literary societies leaned upon faculty members; young men's associations evolved into Lyceum groups, partly because the latter provided more structure than individual groups could manage; local chapters of the Chautauqua Literary and Scientific Circle relied upon a prescribed outline to guide their study; and individual women's clubs joined a national federation that provided more resources and structure than could be generated by a single group. In various ways and with differing degrees of success, self-sponsored writing groups of previous generations sought preparation or at least structure from individuals or groups beyond themselves. Individual members' commitment to writing groups grew from the mixtures of need, friendship, and common interests or background that led them to join these groups. In the absence of instructors who can train them in group processes and critical responses, participants devise their own ways of proceeding or they draw upon published resources such as Peter Elbow's *Writing without Teachers*. This usually means that some form of individual or corporate leadership emerges, assuring that all members understand and adhere to agreed-upon procedures.

Commitment is more crucial and easier to assess in self-sponsored groups because, in the absence of school requirements, participants vote with their feet. When participants miss meetings frequently or come unprepared, they are usually signaling a lack of commitment to the group. Some groups, in an effort to insure continuity, will stipulate responsibilities in advance. This was the case with women's clubs, which frequently published programs for the forthcoming year. Other groups try to relieve the burden of continuing responsibility by agreeing to meet for a specified period—such as five months—and then renegotiating for another specified period of time.

Regular attendance does not, of course, provide suffcent support for group survival. Just as is true of classroom groups, commitment takes subtle as well as obvious forms. Bringing "dead" writing, writing on which the author is no longer actively working, can kill a group as quickly as failure to attend. Just as students "know" when an instructor genuinely cares about the success of writing groups, so participants can sense when an author is no longer engaged by a given selection.

Even when preparation and commitment are adequate, no writing group can function effectively without a clear and appropriate task. For groups of mature and experienced writers, directives such as "critique one another's writing" may be adequate, but for most other groups more specific directions are necessary. In school-sponsored writing groups instructors can employ one of several methods for specifying what groups should concentrate on. Instructors can, as Linda Clifton suggests, provide models of the type of writing students are currently working on and ask students to draw on these to develop terminology for defining success in a particular assignment. Students then use these criteria in their writing groups. Alternatively, an instructor can simply review previous relevant lessons before groups assemble so students have a clear idea of what they should look for in one another's writing. Some instructors find it useful to provide students with a list of questions to be asked about a draft: "What is the main point?" "Who is likely to read this?" "Is each point supported adequately?" "Where can the language be made more clear?" Still others follow Harvey Wiener's advice and ask all students to list the two or three questions they need answered about their drafts so they can continue writing. The instructor then collects the questions for everyone to see (56).

To be genuinely effective a writing group's task must also be appropriate to the group's level of functioning. That is, tasks need to be calibrated to what Vygotsky calls the zone of proximal development. In the most general terms, this means giving students assignments they cannot accomplish independently but can, with help from their friends, complete successfully. The specific zone of proximal development for a given group can be identified only by a teacher who works closely with students much as a coach does, watching, encouraging, and suggesting. Such instructors will know how well students can handle features such as "detail" or "transitions," and they will set tasks that push students to move just beyond what they can handle comfortably on their own.

These specifications set an agenda for classroom writing groups, but instructors usually need to go beyond this and detail how the group should proceed. To be effective these details must be very specific, and they should be modeled for students. For example, if students are to read drafts aloud and receive oral comments, they should be told how time is to be divided among group members, the number of times a selection should be read, the form of note taking that will aid effective response, how authors should introduce their writing, and whether authors should receive written comments in addition to oral ones. If each group has a chair or leader, that person's duties should be clarified. Among the functions instructors can assign to chairs are timekeeper, attendance taker, convener, arbitrator, and recorder. If the instructor requires written reports from each chair, the form and content of these reports should be explained.

Others will ask students to fill out rating sheets on which criteria are listed. Sometimes these criteria are specific to a given piece of writing, such as "effective details" and "need more information" for descriptive writing, and sometimes they are generic criteria such as "what I learned from this writing" or "these examples and details clarified or developed the central idea of the essay." Others argue that these sheets become a form of busy work through which students plod mechanically, paying little attention to the writing itself.

In self-sponsored groups the task is both more vague and more specific. The goals—whether self-improvement, freedom from domestic isolation, publication, or a combination of these—that lead a group to form in the first place usually define the task. Groups interested in self-improvement often adopt a course of study that focuses on a specific area (such as "Medieval Art" or "Public Policy in a Nuclear Age") and assign members to write on specific topics. The terms in which such writing is discussed usually concentrate more on content than form, although records of some women's clubs include discussion of writing style. Groups that take publication as their primary goal often give members "assignments" by reporting on the current interests of certain publishers.

Original goals of self-sponsored groups frequently provide a general outline of the task, but, unlike classrooms where instructors provide models and specific guidelines for procedures, accomplishing the given task is often difficult. One set of difficulties comes from defensiveness among participants. Author defensiveness poses a potentially greater problem in self-sponsored groups than it does in school-sponsored ones. With the mediating force of teachers missing, some individuals attach unjustified value to their own writing, defending it furiously against all criticism. The other form of this defensiveness appears in preceding all readings of one's writing with extremely self-deprecating remarks. Certainly this problem is not unique to self-sponsored groups, because students frequently assume the same postures, but without a teacher to intervene, defensive authors can cripple groups. Sometimes groups adopt a light-hearted approach such as the "one apology rule," specifying that authors are allowed to apologize for their work only once during the life of the group, while others impose and enforce prohibitions against author comments.

Disgruntled comments scattered throughout records of literary societies, women's clubs, and other non-school organizations indicate how difficult it is for self-sponsored writing groups to agree upon and adhere to a set of procedures. Michigan's Literary Adelphi sometimes held private critique sessions, presumably to avoid the contentiousness inherent in more public discussions of a work's quality. Minutes of the Seattle Writers' Club contain frequent entries about disagreements among members, difficulties in dealing with a few dominating individuals, and concern that the critic's role had been abrogated by the group. Often the actual recording of a complaint provided sufficient relief, and in other cases groups took action—such as private critique sessions—to alleviate the problem.

When participants are adequately prepared and tasks clear and appropriate, writing groups function best with little interference from outsiders. In school-sponsored groups, teachers may need to attend to logistics such as providing adequate space and designing an effective arrangement of furniture for a number of groups to meet simultaneously, but once groups begin meeting, instructors need do little except monitor groups to see if they are progressing on schedule. Some instructors choose to join one group while others move from group to group, but as Wiener cautions, instructors can undermine the group's authority, and when groups are actually meeting, the best teacher is "the seemingly most idle teacher" (58). The continuing success of self-sponsored writing groups offers further proof that instructors needn't hover over classroom groups.

When writing groups have finished a session, or perhaps a series of sessions, another aspect of their work remains. I refer to evaluation or, as Barnes and Todd call it, *debriefing*. A quick survey of publications on writing groups . . . reveals that most concentrate on claiming the value of or procedures for establishing these groups, but very few discuss evaluation after a group meeting. Yet it is evaluation that transforms the work of writing groups into the kind of learning that enables participants to negotiate their way, as Kenneth Bruffee describes it, into the normal discourse of "knowledgeable peers." By discussing the issues that have arisen in their writing groups, explaining what they have learned, and exploring unresolved issues, participants learn to monitor their own thinking and evaluate their own progress. If instructors lead such discussions skillfully, students can also learn to see relationships among issues as they, for example, recognize similarities among reports from several groups. They can learn to use evidence more convincingly as they offer substantiation for their observations, and they can begin to construct hypotheses as they consider the similarities and differences of what is said. They can, in other words, engage in a variety of cognitive activites that foster learning.

Self-sponsored writing groups may lack structured opportunities for evaluation, but many develop informal substitutes for teacher-directed discussions. My own writing group, for example, has evolved a time for "smoking in the hall" after the evening's readings and responses are finished. During this time participants raise questions, draw conclusions, and talk about what the group is doing at a level of abstraction impossible during the group's "official" working session. Written records of self-sponsored writing groups include little such informal conversation, but the origins of both school- and self-sponsored writing groups suggest the continuing importance attached to evaluative thinking. Literary societies, after all, focused on debate before they turned to writing, and this practice of looking at two sides of an issue created a legacy of critical thinking. Franklin's Junto and the various men's and women's groups that built upon its tradition likewise valued the kind of close examination that fosters intellectual development.

Writing groups, then, do not fit comfortably within any given mold or model—they succeed, or fail, in many ways. But in the most general terms we can assert that they are more likely to succeed when groups are sufficiently prepared and committed, when appropriate tasks are clear and/or agreed upon by all participants, and when debriefing or evaluation is built into the life of the group.

THEORIES OF LITERACY

While practical implications of and for writing groups extend in multiple directions, the theoretical implications take more monolithic form. The single line out of which theoretical implications extend has its roots in the founding purposes of these groups. Whether they began as part of extracurricular groups such as the Female Mutual Improvement Society and the Junto or as part of academic groups such as Zelo and Tabbard; whether initiated in 1771 or in yesterday's classroom; whether populated by adults or school children; whether sponsored by group members or required by teachers—writing groups exist to improve the writing of their members. As such these groups contribute to the development of literacy, and literacy stands at their center. The theoretical implications of writing groups, then, extend into an understanding of literacy—its meaning, purposes, and development.

Discussions of literacy have expanded rapidly in the decades since Jack Goody's 1968 assertion that "surprisingly little attention has been given to the way in which it [literacy] has influenced the social life of mankind" ("Literacy" 1). Goody could substantiate his claim by noting that although humans have been literate for more than 5,000 years, published studies of literacy at the end of the nineteenth century numbered only thirty. Some of this expansion has, no doubt, come in response to the media-inflamed "literacy crisis" of the early 1970s, but the more substantial portion has emerged as scholars in anthropology, political science, economics history, and English studies have reached beyond the traditional boundaries of their respective fields to examine the nature of literacy. Accordingly, the meaning of "literacy" has changed in recent years.

Historically, *literacy* meant ability to read and write, and researchers frequently took signatures on marriage certificates or other legal documents as evidence of literacy (Cippola). More recently, in the United States, for example, literacy has been defined as completion of a specified number of years of formal education or ability to complete set tasks requiring reading and writing. Implicit in all such skill-based definitions of literacy is a technological meaning. To define literacy in terms of skills is to see it as a technology.

Indeed, a number of theorists have made this claim explicitly. Jack Goody, for example, describes literacy as a technology of intellect that, among other things, enables one to "compare side by side utterances that have been made at different times and places" *(Domestication* 11–12). John Oxenham, following Goody's lead, defines literacy as "simply a technology invented for certain practical purposes" (84), and Walter Ong claims that "writing (and especially alphabetic writing) is a technology, calling for the use of tools and other equipment" (81).

Those who assign a technology/skills meaning to literacy assume that the technology of literacy has clear and direct effects on mental functioning. They claim that people who have the ability to read and write can accomplish complex cognitive tasks that are impossible for illiterates. Classical scholar Eric Havelock goes so far as to claim literacy's benefits for the human race. For Havelock, the development of an alphabetic writing system was a pivotal event leading to the spread of literacy in post-Homeric Greece and changing the basic forms of human memory. Walter Ong echoes this view when he claims that "technologies are not mere exterior aids but also interior transformations of consciousness. . . . writing heightens consciousness" (82) and asserts that the printing press gave rise to a new form of intellectual inquiry. Specifically, according to advocates of the literacy as technology theory, literacy enables abstract thought. Greenfield and Bruner assert this relationship, claiming that "writing is practice in the use of linguistic contexts as independent of immediate reference [thereby enabling linguistic manipulation]. . . . Once thought is freed from the concrete situation the way is clear for symbolic manipulation and for Piaget's stage of formal operation in which the real becomes a sub-set of the possible" (175). Goody and Watt, drawing on their work in Africa, claim that "writing establishes a different kind of relationship between the word and its referent, a relationship that is more general and more abstract" and then describe the cognitive transformation that accompanies it *(Literacy* 44). David Olson likewise claims that learning to write changes individuals' cognitive processes.

This chorus of claims for the cognitive benefits of literacy leads, not surprisingly, to exhortations on the importance of spreading literacy. Oxenham, for instance, states that "the skills of literacy are so important to human mental development, the need for 'frontier pushers' so permanent, the possibility of discovering such people in 'deprived' or 'primitive communities' so far from negligible, that the opportunities for literacy should be rationed only for the gravest of reasons" (44). Underlying such exhortation is the assumption that the skill/technology of literacy enhances social and economic advancement, that it will liberate "those who remain fettered in their inescapable poverty and the darkness of ignorance" and help them join the literates "who master nature, share out the world's riches among themselves, and set out for the stars" (Maheu 112). Arguments made by directors of literacy programs throughout the world echo the idea if not the hyperbolic language of this claim.

... Similar assumptions about literacy's capacity to improve minds or at least to enhance one's material circumstances led some individuals to form and/or participate in writing groups. Men whose socioeconomic status excluded them from extensive formal education joined with their peers in an effort to improve their literacy skills. Instructors who shared the conviction that writing groups led participants to produce better prose required their students to respond to one another's writing. Although history provides scanty information on the degree to which these efforts led to material change, the continuing appearance of classroom and self-sponsored groups in which literacy tasks played a central role testifies to the persistence of the technical/ skills definition of literacy. The implications of this connection between a skills/technological definition of literacy and the work of writing groups do not extend very far. Rather, they move in a closed circle: individuals seek writing groups because they wish to improve themselves or their status in life, and the technological/skills meaning attached to literacy confirms the sensibility of their approach and the value of their wish.

The theoretical thinness inherent in this view of literacy results in part from the fact that the technological/skills definition of literacy assigns no cultural content to literacy. It enables a dichotomous view of the world wherein literate people can be clearly distinguished from illiterates. The literates are capable of sophisticated thinking and the illiterates remain forever at a lower level of mental functioning. Like a compass or a yardstick, this "objective" measure of humanity can operate in every time and place to delineate two types of people. Not surprisingly, advocates of the technical model of literacy, of whom Patricia Greenfield is an explicit example, draw on Piaget's category of formal operations to describe the benefits of standing on the literate side of "the great divide" between literates and illiterates. The dichotomous view of literates and illiterates and the unvarying qualities assigned to literacy belie the Cartesian epistemology within which this technical/skills definition operates.

The limitations of the Cartesian-based technology/skills definition of literacy becomes apparent in its inability to address the formation of non-skills-oriented groups or the functioning of *any* autonomous or semi-autonomous writing group. Although they may have been tangentially interested in improving their skills, many of the students who joined literary societies were motivated by a complex set of social, intellectual, and aesthetic concerns that extended beyond mere technique. In the largest sense, they wanted to create a place for themselves in the academic community. Many women's clubs were similarly constituted. Women with no visible need to improve their skills sought to join the larger intellectual comunity in which ideas could be explored and discussed.

Similarly, the functioning of autonomous or semi-autonomous writing groups cannot be explained in technical/skills terms because the technical view of literacy presumes a pre-existing body of knowledge to be assimilated with language serving as the conduit. . . . The collaborative learning of autonomous and semi-autonomous groups can be explained only in terms of a social constructivist view of knowledge that puts language at the center because writing group participants work together to generate much of what they learn. Likewise, . . . the language development of writing groups proceeds along social, not individual, lines. Individuals internalize and transform the language they and their peers have generated, language that operates in what Vygotsky calls their zone of proximal development. Literacy defined as skills of encoding and decoding cannot account for collaborative learning or socially originated language development because autonomous skills can be transported across time and place with no reference to the particular communities in which they function, and collaborative learning and language development operate in specific communities.

In the past decade, an alternative view of literacy has emerged, one much more consonant with the intellectual foundations of writing groups. Supporters of this alternative take exception to the "great divide" theory of the technological/skill definition. They describe it as reductive, arguing that literacy takes a variety of forms and is highly culture-dependent. These revisionist scholars undercut claims for literacy's monolithic qualities and capacity for enhancing intellectual and social development with careful investigation of counter-examples. They point to instances where oral reading skill is not matched by comprehension of what is read (Johanson), where literacy in the absence of formal education does not lead to higher levels of cognition (Scribner and Cole), where the skills of reading and writing function very differently in adjacent communities (Brice Heath), where literacy and textuality can be separated (Stock, Pattison), where literacy does not necessarily yield higher status to its possessors (Cressy, Graff).

This revisionist work in literacy studies assumes that literacy is a complex social phenomenon, that its precise definition varies with social context. Adherents to this "ideology" model, as Street terms it, claim that the nature, development, and use of literacy grows directly out of the immediate social environment. Harvey Graff, one of the earliest of the revisionists, concluded his examination of nineteenth-century literacy by claiming that "the meaning of literacy in mid-nineteenth century urban society can only be understood in context" (292). He went on to generalize his point: "Literacy, finally, can no longer be seen as a universalistic quantity or quality to be possessed however unequally by all in theory. . . . literacy must be accorded a new understanding—in social context. If its social meanings are to be understood and its value best utilized, the 'myth of literacy' must be exploded" (323–24). The myth to which Graff objects relies upon a technological/skill definition of literacy.

In keeping with Graff's assertions, a number of recent studies have examined the nature, development, and use of literacy in terms of the immediate social environment. They take what Brian Street terms an "ideological" view of literacy. Shirley Brice Heath's study of two Piedmont communities gives prominence to how child-rearing, religious practices, and recreational activities contributed to the contrasting manifestations of literacy evident in the adjacent communities of Roadville and Trackton. She notes that language use and instruction in Roadville support "a fixed set of roles and view of the world, and provide a continual test of commitment to existing modes and values of social institutions and relationships" (144) while in Trackton language is for "negotiation and manipulation—both serious and playful" (235). Accordingly, "For Roadville, the written word limits alternatives of expression; in Trackton, it opens alternatives" (235). Arguing against dichotomizing, Heath explains, "in terms of the usual distinctions made between oral and literate tradition, neither community may be simply classified as either 'oral' or 'literate'" (230). In undercutting the oral/literate dichotomy on which the technical/skills definition of literacy depends, Heath demonstrates the need for a more flexible definition, one that can accommodate the varying forms of literacy she has so eloquently chronicled.

Scribner and Cole's study of literacy among the Vai people of Africa shared with Heath's investigation a careful attention to details of development and use of literacy and arrived at similar conclusions about the inadequacy of the "myth of literacy." They found that in the absence of formal education literacy made little difference in intellectual processes and concluded that "there is no evidence in these data to support the construct of a general 'literacy' phenomenon. Although many writers discuss literacy and its social and psychological implications as though literacy entails the same knowledge and skills whenever people read or write, our experimental outcomes support our social analysis in demonstrating that literacies are highly differentiated" (132). Just as Heath calls the oral/literate dichotomy into question, so Scribner and Cole undermine claims of technical/skills literacy for the cognitive benefits of reading and writing. If literacy separated from formal education does not impart demonstrably enhanced capacities for abstract thought, then it cannot be described as the transportable skill that the technical definition implies.

Historical as well as contemporary examinations support the ideological view of literacy. David Cressy, a social historian who studied literacy in Tudor and Stuart England, found wide and unexpected variations among various subgroups in the population. Literacy developed most strongly where it was needed by people and failed to develop where it was not. Cressy observes: "Illiteracy is not a disease, to be eradicated like yellow fever, but rather it is a complex cultural condition linked to expectations and circumstances and rooted in the environment.... Literacy will flourish where those who are offered it are aware of and can experience its benefits" ("Environment" 41). Although he does not address them directly, Cressy could be speaking to literacy advocates such as Oxenham and Maheu who argue that skills of reading and writing should be spread as quickly and broadly as possible. In demonstrating that cultural contexts shape the needs and uses of literacy,

Cressy shows the inherent fallacy of assuming that everyone needs literacy to the same degree.

Recent literacy studies not only reveal the weaknesses of the technical/ skills definition, they also yield new, broader definitions of literacy. Brian Stock, drawing on his examination of literacy in the eleventh and twelfth centuries, claims: "Literacy is not textuality. One can be literate without the overt use of texts, and one can use texts extensively without evidencing genuine literacy" (7). For Stock, genuine literacy refers to culturally defined norms of learning, and in the medieval period these were frequently oral. Robert Pattison makes a related point about literacy in contemporary society by defining it as "consciousness of the questions posed by language coupled with mastery of those skills by which a culture at any given moment in its history manifests this consciousness" (5). According to Pattison, this consciousness need not involve skills of reading and writing, and he predicts that electronic media will propagate the "new literacy" of our society (205). The meaning of literacy thus extends from encoding and decoding written symbols to understanding meaning in a specific social context.

Studies operating under the ideological definition assume that literacy means joining a specific community through understanding the issues it considers important and developing the capacity to participate in conversations about those issues. As used here, the term *conversation* refers to Kenneth Bruffee's use of the word, the "conversation of mankind" that enables reflective thought and results from social engagement in intellectual pursuits. Mastery of skills such as reading and writing may be essential to joining a specific literate community, but while necessary, these skills are not sufficient because ability to encode and decode does not of itself guarantee anyone admission to a literate community. Some composition instructors who have tried to join a community of, say, physicists, know too well how inadequate reading and writing skills can be. Furthermore, as Elizabeth Eisenstein has noted, not all who master the written word become members of a book-reading community, a community in which members read to learn once they have learned to read. In other words, literacy defined in technological/skill terms does not suffice for membership in literate communities.

Writing groups, seen in terms of this broader definition that links literacy and community, take on large implications. If becoming literate means joining a community, and if literacy varies from one community to another, then complaints about "illiteracy" speak to the fact that individuals have not absorbed sufficiently the mores of a given community, whether that community be a college class or the more amorphous "American culture." This problem, one facing both educators and the larger society, cannot be addressed by moving "back to the basics" and placing a "greater emphasis . . . on reading, writing and arithmetic" (Fadiman and Howard 123). But it is a problem with particular urgency for English studies because, as E. D. Hirsch has noted, English has a unique nationalizing function in American eduation ("Formalism" 351). If citizens are to become members of intellectual and social communities beyond those into which they are born, they are likely to do so in English classes. Defining literacy as membership in a given community means identifying one of literacy's central purposes as prescribing the terms by which individuals enter certain communities. Accordingly, composition instructors, in particular, face the task of initiating students into communities of educated people. Indeed, Patricia Bizzell has argued that composition classes should introduce students into academic discourse communities and that "to neglect the context of writing and knowledge is to risk committing a new version of the social injustice attributable to the old composition course" (205). Bizzell refers to the social injustice of excluding some individuals from the literate community, usually an academic one, to which they seek entry.

Writing groups offer a means for individuals, both in and outside of school, to enter literate communities. The collaboration and language development inherent in writing groups insure that participants will begin to develop the cognitive abilities essential to literacy in the broad sense. In addition, evidence from studies of early literacy demonstrates that the processes by which children initially become literate have much in common with what occurs in writing groups.

Gumperz and Dyson, in their respective examinations of emergent literacy in young children, find that youngsters succeed in becoming literate to the extent that they learn to use language in new ways. Children in the early years of elementary school find occasions for broadening their repertoires of language use during the interaction of "sharing time." As they narrate events from their lives, children learn to develop a coherent oral text, to consider the perspectives of others, and to adjust their language accordingly. Similarly, the collaboration of writing groups offers participants of more advanced years opportunities to observe and practice new forms of language that they can internalize as part of their own language development.

Joining a community of any sort depends upon affective qualities as well as cognitive ones, and literate communities are no exception. Attitude plays a large part in individuals' ability and willingness to become literate or to participate in literate communities. Persons who have negative feelings about reading and writing are much less likely to participate in literate communities than individuals who feel positively disposed toward these activities. Stereotypical responses of "I'd better watch my language" or "I never did like to write" that greet English teachers in social situations indicate the degree to which negative attitudes toward literacy infect the general population, and these negative attitudes can lead individuals to exclude themselves from communities where literacy plays a significant role.

Powerful evidence of these negative attitudes takes the form of aliteracy. Aliterates do not lack technical skills, but because they have no sense of belonging to the literate community, they withdraw. Like Bartleby, they "prefer not to" read and write. Statistics on newspaper circulation provide one indication of this phenomenon. From 1970 to 1981 daily circulation of newspapers dropped 7 percent, the number of books published has dropped 5,000 over the last several years, and teenagers do little reading for pleasure, preferring to spend time on movies and television (Thimmesch 3–4, 29, 37). Causes of aliteracy are difficult to define precisely, but at a recent symposium representatives of television, newspapers, magazines, education, and publishing companies speculated that the causes include teaching, which robs students of "some of the enjoyment in reading" (Thimmesch 4). Failure of community underlies this statement, for it is in community that individuals learn to enjoy reading and writing.

The losses incurred by aliteracy include "critical thinking skills, predicting skills and argumentation skills" and exercise of the voting franchise. Ultimately, aliteracy may lead to a two-class system of an educated elite and an aliterate majority (Thimmesch 18, 24). In such a situation, "if the gap between the educated minority and the undereducated mass becomes too great, the opportunities for political manipulation will grow" and the democratic system of government will be threatened (Thimmesch 39).

In many ways these claims echo Thomas Jefferson's famous statement about newspapers in a democracy: "Were it left to me to decide whether we should have a government without a newspaper, or newspapers without a government, I should not hesitate a moment to prefer the latter. But I should mean that every man should receive these papers and be capable of reading them." If we assume "receive" to include motivation in its meaning, then Jefferson's juxtaposition of "receive" and "be capable of reading" implies that a combination of skill and attitude is essential to membership in a literate community, and that reinforces the Thimmesch statement about the importance of literacy to democracy.

Becoming literate enough to be willing to participate in a democracy means becoming part of a community, and instructors need ways to help students into the literate community. Writing groups offer one way. Founders of college literary societies, of young men's associations, of women's clubs, and of other self-sponsored groups all understood, implicitly or explicitly, that literacy is a social activity and that the best way to become more literate was to join with others. Instructors who have established classroom writing groups likewise operated on the assumption that literacy thrives in a community. To be sure, the value of writing groups varies with the effectiveness of their functioning, and only those groups with adequate preparation, commitment, and clarity of task can ease students into a literate community. When writing groups work well, however, they enhance students' chances of joining the literate community of which that group is a part.

Historical origins point to the connection between writing groups and literate communities. As this book has shown, students and non-students initiated writing groups because they "knew" that literacy belongs to a community. One of the attributes most frequently credited to writing groups is a positive attitude. Variously expressed as motivation toward writing, a warmer classroom climate, and enthusiasm for revision, this positive attitude can counter the negativism that leads to aliteracy. Educational movements and specific historical events have come and gone, but the pervasive motivation toward creating communities of literacy has endured and prevailed. Differences of age, circumstance, and historical period disappear before this common motivation.

Finally, writing groups...focus on the social dimension of writing, reminding participants that literacy does not function in isolation. In writing groups, people can become part of a community that takes aesthetic pleasure in a fine sentence, distinguishes between a convincing argument and one that fails to convince, and delights in clear and effective presentation of an idea. The product of writing groups, the polished prose, has importance, but even more significant is the process of the group, the means by which individuals experience and eventually become part of a literate community.

WORKS CITED

Barnes, Douglas, and Frankie Todd. *Communication and Learning in Small Groups.* London: Routledge, 1977.

Bernadette, Sr. Miriam. "Evaluation of Writing: A Three-Part Program." *English Journal* 54 (1965): 23–27.

Bizzell, Patricia. "College Composition: Initiation into the Academic Discourse Community." *Curriculum Inquiry* 12 (1982): 191–207.

Brice Heath, Shirley. *Ways with Words.* Cambridge: Cambridge UP, 1983.

Bruffee, Kenneth. "The Way Out: A Critical Survey of Innovations in College Teaching with Special Reference to the December, 1971 Issue of *College English.*" *College English* 33 (1972): 457–68.

———. "The Brooklyn Plan: Attaining Intellectual Growth through Peer-Group Tutoring." *Liberal Education* 64 (1978): 447–68.

———. "Collaborative Learning: Some Practical Models." *College English* 34 (1973): 579–86.

———. *Short Course in Writing.* 1980. Boston: Little, 1985.

———. "Collaborative Learning and the 'Conversation of Mankind.'" *College English* 46 (1984): 635–52.

Cippola, Carlo. *Literacy and Development in the West.* London: Pelican, 1969.

Clifton, Linda. "What If the Kids Did It?" *Washington English Journal* 7 (Winter 1985): 12–16.

Cressy, David. *Literacy and the Social Order: Reading and Writing in Tudor and Stuart England.* Cambridge: Cambridge UP, 1980.

———. "The Environment for Literacy: Accomplishment and Context in Seventeenth-Century England and New England." *Literacy in Historical Perspective.* Ed. Daniel Resnick. Washington: Library of Congress, 1983. 23–42.

Dyson, Anne. "Learning to Write/Learning to Do School: Emergent Writers, Interpretations of School Literacy Tasks." *Research in the Teaching of English* 19 (1984): 233–64.

———. "Second Graders Sharing Writing: The Multiple Social Realities of a Literacy Event." *Written Communication* 2 (1985): 189–215.

Eisenstein, Elizabeth. *The Printing Press as an Agent of Change.* New York: Cambridge UP, 1979.

Elbow, Peter. *Writing without Teachers.* New York: Oxford, 1973.

Fadiman, Clifton, and James Howard. *Empty Pages: A Search for Writing Competence in School and Society.* Belmont, CA: Fearon, 1979.

Gere, Anne Ruggles, ed. *Roots in the Sawdust: Writing to Learn across the Disciplines.* Urbana: NCTE, 1985.

Goody, Jack, ed. *Literacy in Traditional Societies.* New York: Cambridge UP, 1968.

Graff, Harvey J. *The Literacy Myth: Literacy and Social Structure in the Nineteenth-Century City.* New York: Academic, 1979.

Greenfield, Patricia, and Jerome Bruner. "Culture and Cognitive Growth." *Handbook of Socialization: Theory and Research.* Ed. David Goslin. New York: Rand, 1969.

Hardaway, Francine. "What Students Can Do to Take the Burden off You." *College English* 36 (1974): 577–80.

Havelock, Eric. *Preface to Plato.* Cambridge: Harvard UP, 1963.

Higley, Jerry. "The New Comp." *College English* 37 (1976): 682–83.

Hilgers, Thomas. "Toward a Taxonomy of Beginning Writers' Evaluative Statements on Written Compositions." *Written Communication* 1 (1984): 365–84.

———. "On Learning the Skills of Collaborative Writing." CCC Convention. New Orleans, April 1986.

Hirsch, E. D. "English and the Perils of Formalism." *American Scholar* 53 (1984): 369–79.

Johansson, Egil. "The History of Literacy in Sweden." *Literacy and Social Development in the West: A Reader*. Ed. Harvey Graff. Cambridge: Cambridge UP, 1981. 151–82.

Maheu, R. World Congress of Ministers of Education on the Eradication of Illiteracy. Speech and Messages, UNESCO. Teheran, 1966. Quoted in *Modes of Thought*. Ed. Robin Horton and Ruth Finnegan. London: Faber, 1973.

Mishler, Elliot. "Implications of Teacher Strategies for Language and Cognition: Observations in First Grade Classrooms." *Functions of Language in the Classroom*. Ed. Courtney Cazden, Vera John, and Dell Hymes. New York: Teachers College Press, 1972. 267–98.

Murray, Donald. *A Writer Teaches Writing*. Boston: Houghton Mifflin, 1968.

———. "Finding Your Own Voice: Teaching Composition in an Age of Dissent." *College Composition and Communication* 20 (1969): 118–23.

———. "Internal Revision: A Process of Discovery." *Research on Composing*. Ed. Charles Cooper and Lee Odell. Urbana: NCTE, 1978.

———. Letter to the author. 26 September 1984.

———. *A Writer Teaches Writing*. 2nd ed. Boston: Houghton, 1985.

Olson, David. "From Utterance to Text: The Bias of Language in Speech and Writing." *Harvard Educational Review* 47 (1977): 257–81.

Ong, Walter. *Ramus, Method, and the Decay of Dialogue*. Cambridge: Harvard UP, 1958.

Oxenham, John. *Literacy: Writing, Reading and Social Organisation*. London: Routledge, 1980.

Pattison, Robert. *On Literacy*. New York: Oxford UP, 1982.

Piaget, Jean. *The Construction of Reality in the Child*. New York: Basic, 1954.

———. *Language and Thought of a Child*. New York: Basic, 1954.

Putz, Joan. "When the Teacher Stops Teaching: An Experiment with Freshman English." *College English* 32 (1970): 50–57.

Scribner, Sylvia, and Michael Cole. *The Psychology of Literacy*. Cambridge: Harvard UP, 1981.

Stock, Brian. *The Implications of Literacy. Written Language and Models of Interpretation in the Eleventh and Twelfth Centuries*. Princeton: Princeton UP, 1983.

Street, Brian. *Literacy in Theory and Practice*. Cambridge: Cambridge UP, 1984.

Thimmesch, Nick. *Aliteracy: People Who Can Read But Won't*. Washington D.C.: American Enterprise Institute for Public Policy Research, 1984.

Tressler, Jacob. "The Efficiency of Student Correction of Compositions." *English Journal* 1 (1912): 405–11.

Vygotsky, Lev. *Thought and Language*. Trans. Eugenia Hanfmann and Gertrude Vakar. Cambridge: MIT, 1962.

———. *Mind in Society: The Development of Higher Psychological Processes*. Ed. Michael Cole et al. Cambridge: Harvard UP, 1978.

Watt, Homer A. "The Philosophy of Real Composition." *English Journal* 7 (1918): 153–62.

Wiener, Harvey. "Collaborative Learning in the Classroom: A Guide to Evaluation." *College English* 48 (1986): 52–61.

PART TWO

Shaking the Foundations: Questioning and Revaluing Assumptions

Introduction to Part Two

This section offers works that speak directly to—and question—the foundational texts of Part One. We include here essays, from a span of three decades, that offer a number of important challenges to assumptions active in discussions and descriptions of peer response pedagogies for students and teachers. Authors included here raise questions about the pitfalls of peer response, dig more deeply into what makes for truly effective peer response designs, and offer a sense of the student experience of and sensibilities around peer activities in writing classes. It is worth noting that the scholars in this section began to employ case studies, alternative theories, and methods to better understand what happens in peer groups, as well as to expand the practice of peer review and response in compelling ways. The works collected here provide a valuable starting point for the research-minded in our field, offering a strong sense of notable research questions and models that have been employed in uncovering stronger empirical and qualitative understandings of peer response in action.

In the first selection, "Direction and Misdirection in Peer Response" (1984), Thomas Newkirk questions the "attacks" made on teachers' evaluative authority by the likes of James Moffett and Peter Elbow. Newkirk offers one of the first empirical studies of college peer review and response groups in his attempt to find out if students provide feedback in line with the goals of the course, an attempt that would motivate and inform subsequent inquiries. Newkirk found that students in his study used widely different criteria and stances in reviewing and responding to their peers' work. Based on his findings, Newkirk suggests that students need to be treated like "apprentices," and teachers need to view the practice of peer response as a reciprocal pedagogy between all participants.

In our second selection, "Peer Response Groups in the Writing Classroom: Theoretic Foundations and New Directions" (1988), Anne DiPardo and Sarah Warshauer Freedman continue Newkirk's refrain, lamenting the lack of empirical study of peer response groups (a concern that continues well past the turn of the millennium). In their ambitious study, the authors offer a comprehensive review of the literature on collaborative learning and peer response groups up to that time. Informed by Vygotsky's theories of social interaction and language development, the authors build a conceptual frame for future research investigations—one of the first calls in the field for a stronger understanding of how composition classrooms prepare students to transfer what they know about writing between different contexts. The implications and suggestions DiPardo and Freedman offer pivot on the ways instructors and students may realize Newkirk's pedagogical "reciprocity"—a process of productively sharing instructional authority. The authors advocate a more flexibly-conceived classroom environment wherein students have abundant choices in how, when, and with whom they give and receive productive feedback in their meaning-making and learning processes.

In our third selection, "Habits of Mind: Historical Configurations of Textual Ownership in Peer Writing Groups" (1998), Candace Spigelman interweaves concepts related to the history of authorship and intellectual property with case studies of four diverse students in a writing group. Spigelman makes a compelling argument for the ways students conflictingly view writing as both their "own" intellectual property, while at the same time understanding that it can also become appropriable "communal" property during the acts of peer review and response. Spigelman argues that there is great pedagogical value in helping students come to terms with moving beyond the particular "habits of mind" they bring to peer groups, and in realizing the potentially productive dialectical tension between viewing their writing as both private *and* communal.

Lynne Belcher, in our fourth selection, "Peer Review and Response: A Failure of the Process Paradigm as Viewed from the Trenches" (2000), briefly reports on a survey of thirty writing instructors from the WCENTER and ECOMPL listservs conducted in the year 2000. Although Belcher's review finds that most respondents did not view peer review as particularly useful for students in learning to write or as time-saving for teachers in providing feedback, she reports that almost all respondents recommended that new instructors utilize peer response in their instruction. The instructors surveyed seemed to view peer response as more integral to fostering critical reading, rather than writing, skills.

Complementing and complicating the previous essays and our own survey results, our fifth and sixth selections likewise draw on surveys of students, instructors, and/or program leaders in their investigations of the pros and cons of peer response practice. In "Peer Review from the Students' Perspective: Invaluable or Invalid?" (2007), Charlotte Brammer and Mary Rees surveyed 328 students (a 25 percent response rate) in first-year and upper-level writing intensive courses at a private university. Their findings reveal that 92.7 percent of students they surveyed across the disciplines found some value in participating in peer response activities. Moreover, when such activities were part of every writing assignment, students were much more likely to report viewing peer response as "usually" or "always" helpful. Students who reported more preparation in terms of procedural methods valued peer response more, and students who experienced more explicit and multimethod instruction felt more confident and perceived more value in performing peer response.

Next, Pamela Bedore and Brian O'Sullivan report on a study of peer response in first-year composition at a research university in "Addressing Instructor Ambivalence about Peer Review and Self-Assessment" (2011). They surveyed students in two courses, and conducted in-depth focus groups and interviews with the program director, three instructor training coordinators (ITCs), and five graduate instructors. Findings from this study are quite varied and include that (1) student writers (and program leaders) often view peer review and response activities more positively than instructors; (2) the most successful peer response efforts are the result of the inclusion of this pedagogical technique from the beginning to the end of a course; (3) students often had a tough time distinguishing (and instructors had a tough time explaining) the differences in goals for peer review activities, forms of self-assessment, and instructor feedback; and (4) instructors are ambivalent about the trade-offs of including peer response pedagogies, such as the balance between learning opportunities for students and perceptions of teacher authority.

These readings offer a historical snapshot of the work that has been undertaken to expand our initial understandings of peer response. Far from comprehensive, however, the works included here also reveal the degree to which peer response remains an under-studied pedagogical approach within the conversation about effective writing instruction. Many questions remain for researchers interested in the social nature of writing development—how group dynamics may impact or impel learning experiences around writing and how peer groups may or may not be a site to further understand writing transfer. We hope these readings will inspire current and new generations of researchers to renew exploration of the benefits and limitations of peer review and response activities.

3 *Direction and Misdirection in Peer Response*

THOMAS NEWKIRK

The late sixties and early seventies saw a concerted attack on the teacher-as-audience. James Moffett claimed that the teacher's authority as evaluator disrupted any natural relationship that a writer might have with an audience.[1] Peter Elbow argued for a "teacherless writing class" where responses came solely from peers.[2] In response to these and other attacks, many freshman English textbooks began to identify the audience for writing as someone other than the teacher. Some urged students to consider their peers to be the primary audience; others advised students to define an appropriate audience (peers being one possibility) and to write for that audience. The writing would then be judged by its effectiveness and appropriateness for the intended audience.[3]

Despite the heavy emphasis on peer evaluation, there has been no systematic investigation of the responses of the peer audience. If students are asked to write for their peers, one must assume that the evaluation criteria used by these peers are consistent with the goals of the writing course. But is this the case? If students approach peers' writing with values, interests, and emphases different from those of writing instructors, the status of the peer response becomes problematical.

In order to examine possible differences between instructor and peer evaluations, I conducted a study which posed three questions:

(1) Do instructors in Freshman English give four selected papers evaluations that differ significantly from evaluations given by students in Freshman English?

(2) Are instructors in Freshman English able to predict the differences between their evaluations and the students' evaluations?

(3) What are the reasons for the different evaluations?

For this study I selected one group of ten instructors in Freshman English at the University of New Hampshire and another group of ten students currently taking the course. The ten students were selected from a group of

From *College Composition and Communication*, vol. 35, no. 3, 1984, pp. 301–11.

twenty student volunteers. In order to ensure a range of writing abilities in this group, I asked the instructors of these twenty students to rate them in the top, middle, or bottom third of their class based on the four or five papers they had seen to date. From the twenty, I then selected three students rated in the top third, four rated in the middle third, and three rated in the bottom third.

I met with each of the twenty subjects individually for about one and a half hours. Subjects were asked to read four papers and were given as much time as they needed to read, reread, and review. After each paper was completed, I interviewed the student to explore his or her evaluation. This interview was taped and later transcribed. After all of the papers were read, each subject made two ratings:

(1) They gave each paper a general impression rating of 1–10.

(2) They ranked each paper 1–4.

In addition, instructors were asked to predict the students' rankings of the papers. Finally, subjects were asked to explain the reasons for their rankings.

The four papers chosen for evaluation were all written by students in introductory writing courses at the University of New Hampshire. All four are essays in which the writer uses personal experience to support generalizations. The spelling and punctuation of all the papers were corrected so that errors of this type would not figure into the evaluations.

To give a sense of the task for each subject, I will present excerpts and brief summaries of each paper.

a. "Mailaholic." In this paper the writer attempts to show her addiction to receiving mail. Near the beginning of the paper, she writes

> I am a mailaholic.
> I am addicted to letters, receiving, sending, reading, writing, and addressing them. I revel in stationery stores; picking and choosing the "right" paper for me. Should I get the Muppets, Snoopy, or something sophisticated with flowers on it?
> Stationery is nothing without stamps. Flag stamps, wild animal stamps, stamps with morals, purple stamps with B's on them. One-cent stamps, thirteen, fifteen, and now eighteen-cent stamps. Post offices drive me wild!

b. "Friendships." This paper is built on an extended metaphor comparing the author's friends to the various positions on a baseball team. She begins the comparison with her own position:

> I am on the mound. I am a pitcher. No one plays the game unless I throw the ball. Everything is determined by how I pitch the ball. The catcher would be my best friend, giving me advice, keeping my spirit up and my concentration on the game. If I threw a wild pitch, she would sacrifice her body to save the ball. She would dig bad pitches out of the dirt and throw the ball back to me so I can get back on the mound and

pitch again. When I am doing poorly she would call "time out" and walk to the mound to build up my confidence and when I strike a batter out, we rejoice together.

c. "Problems of Eminent Domain." This paper attempts to show the injustice of the law of eminent domain as it was used to purchase part of a farm owned by the writer's parents. Midway through the paper, she describes her parents' financial status:

> At the present time, my parents' financial status is questionable. The amount they received this summer for the land is $56,000. This payment was made for 64 acres of some of the most valuable land in New York State. The amazing fact that my parents received the same amount of money that a couple can earn in three years, for a section of land that took my parents a lifetime of work to obtain, reveals that something must be unfair. The state offered my parents $56,000 for putting them out of business. To pay a couple $56,000 for putting out of business a 36 dairy cow operation is outrageous. The amount wouldn't even be able to purchase a hot dog business from a local vendor.

d. "Grossmans . . . Love It or Leave It." This paper describes the writer's disillusionment with this summer employer and his sympathy for workers who don't consider alternative employment. In the paragraph below, he describes one of his co-workers:

> I had heard stories about a salesman named Truman before I met him. When I started to work, Truman happened to be on vacation. If you worked full-time for a year you were entitled to a two-week vacation. Truman had worked for Grossman's for ten years. "Great to be back," he said as he came through the door. I remember how strange it sounded at the time; I guess it sounded funny because he really meant it. Truman, who never bothered to take his cigarette out of his mouth when he was talking, is the type of person you have many conversations with but you have difficulty remembering what any one of them is about; but you can always remember what brand of cigarette he smokes.[4]

The results of the ratings and ranking are shown in Tables 1, 2, and 3. Table 1 compares the holistic (1–10) ratings given by the two groups. Table 2 compares the rankings (1–4) given by both groups, and Table 3 compares teachers' predictions of student rankings with the actual rankings. From these data, two conclusions seem justified:[5]

(1) Students and instructors differed in their evaluations of "Grossmans . . . Love It or Leave It" and "Friendships."

(2) Instructors were able to predict correctly some differences in the ranking of "Grossmans . . . Love It or Leave It" and "Friendships." But for "Friendships" particularly, they were unable to anticipate the magnitude of the difference.

The transcripts suggest three major reasons for the differences in the evaluations.

Table 1   Average Point Rating (10 = high, 0 = low)

	Mailaholic	Friendships	Eminent Domain	Grossmans
Students (N = 10)	6.5	6.7	7.0	6.6
Teachers (N = 10)	6.0	3.9	6.5	7.3

Table 2   Average Ranking (1 = high, 4 = low)

	Mailaholic	Friendships	Eminent Domain	Grossmans
Students	2.5	2.7	2.3	2.7
Teachers	2.3	3.9	2.2	1.6

Table 3   Accuracy of Predictions (1 = high, 4 = low)

	Mailaholic	Friendships	Eminent Domain	Grossmans
Students' Rank	2.5	2.7	2.3	2.7
Teachers' Prediction of Student Rank	2.1	3.6	2.3	2.1

The Role of Identification of Peer with Writer

In three of the four papers, the writers are dealing with experiences common to the experiences of students reading the papers. For that reason, many students claimed they could "relate to" the paper. The sheer frequency of statements of this type suggest that this willingness to identify with the author is a powerful determiner of student response. Some examples:

Response to Mailaholic

I thought it was a good paper. It was interesting to read. I feel the same way she does about mail, like when she says she feels depressed when she doesn't get mail in her mailbox, and somebody else had like 10 letters in their mailbox, it kind of makes you unhappy.

Response to Friendships

I could understand her analogy. When she started talking about her mother being the umpire and how her beer drinking friends her mother would always say are illegal, I could see a mother doing that because that's what my mother always does.

Response to Eminent Domain

Having lived in New England I've heard of people having their land taken. In fact, I knew a family who had their land taken for a highway to be put in and it's especially bitter after you've worked the farm for so many years.

Response to Grossmans

> I worked at a company and there were people there that worked there full-time, and I just look at them and laugh like he (the writer) did and just say "Are you going to do this for the rest of your lives?" Don't they want to get out of that rut? Then they'll say, "I'm making a lot of money now," or "I have this and I bought a new car with this." He doesn't know about the interest and stuff, but at least he has a car.

One student defined the general principle upon which these responses are built as follows:

> I suppose when a reader reads a paper, it's a lot easier if the person can relate to it, has some background and says, "I can relate to this because it seems the same kind of thing happened to me." And it's a lot easier if the reader knows something about what the writer is talking about.

This kind of personal identification, however, was virtually absent in the teacher protocols.

This discrepancy could account for some of the disagreement in the evaluation of "Friendships." For instructors the extended metaphor was unsuccessful; one even claimed that the paper would make for a good Abbott and Costello comedy routine. But the general criticism was that the metaphor ends up keeping the writer from exploring friendships. A typical response:

> . . . it's a fairly simple paper. The author takes one metaphor and extends it for three pages. It doesn't work well because the author stayed too long in the realm of images. It doesn't really say very much about friendships.

A number of students agreed with this assessment, but many found the analogy far more informative than the instructors did.

Contrast this instructor's evaluation with that of a student who chose "Friendships" to be the best of the four papers.

> I really liked the idea because you can really tell that they're complex relationships she has with each friend. You can tell that she has different relationships with every friend she has. And she wants to convey that to us and I think this idea (the baseball metaphor) gets that point across in the paper, that she has a really complex relationship with her friends.

What to most instructors was "simple" is to this and several other students "really complex." A possible reason for this discrepancy is that the instructors expect elaboration to be done by the writer; for example, they claimed the connection between the spectators and the pitcher in the metaphor needed to be specifically drawn out. Students are more willing to do some of this elaboration *as readers.* If readers have had a similar experience, they are ready to use that background to extend what has been written. Because they "read in" details, they see a complexity that the teacher does not. Because the very limited comparison of mother to baseball umpire reminds them of their own mothers' rule-making authority, those few sentences are invested with a richness not granted to them by instructors. This contrasting willingness to "read in" elaboration is one of the distinguishing differences in the strategies of the two groups.

On two occasions students commented on this difference. One student noted that "Mailaholic" has "the tone of an English paper." Curious, I asked what he meant by that:

> It's more declaratory than inspired. It's very much plotted; it's not pulling along by its own weight. When you write a magazine or newspaper article what you put and how much you put is controlled by whether or not you're going to be exciting or interesting. *Whereas in an English paper you know you can develop as far as you want, as long as you do it well. I think she's taken a little advantage of the reader.* She'll ask a question at the beginning of the paper and then elaborate on it. Make a blanket statement, elaborate on it. (emphasis added)

Another student when asked to predict which paper teachers would select as the best, chose "Mailaholic":

> *She's taking something that seems menial to people and she's making it a big deal. And I think they like to see stuff like that.* I think they like to see students write about something like a tree and make it flowery, make it come alive. So I think they would like [Mailaholic] because it's no big deal to get mail and she made it sound like it was really something. *She talks about different characteristics and stuff.* (emphasis added)

Both students seem to suggest that elaboration pays off when writing an "English paper" but for themselves and for real world writing, it can be a bad habit.

THE ROLE OF ORIGINALITY

One reason for the relative popularity of "Friendships" was the fact that the writer tried a method of exposition that students found original. Note the similarity in the following three responses, written by three different students:

> I thought it (Friendships) was very creative and imaginative and I think it was well put together. And the writer wasn't just telling a story. I think that teachers would feel the same way about that; they like to see a creative mind instead of just reading about certain events.

> I never thought of friendships like this. I wrote a friendship paper for English and I never thought of it. I thought it was really neat in a way. I would have never thought of my friends as a baseball team like this is doing. . . . It's like a different way of writing a paper on friendships. I've never seen one done this way.

> I like the Friendships one because I liked the way she applied the baseball diamond comparison. I would have never thought of that. . . . I think

teachers [would prefer "Friendships"] because they'll like the unique approach to the friendships whereas "Grossmans" [the first choice of this student] was just a straightforward kind of paper.

A similar scale of values underlies all of these responses. All three students compare the approaches taken in "Friendships" to another possible approach to the topic. In the first, the students claim that the writer "wasn't just telling a story"; one suspects that the second writer, in comparing her own paper on friendships to this paper, realized that she had taken a more conventional approach (written a "story"?), and she was humbled by the comparison to this new approach; and in the third the student predicts that teachers will prefer an original to a "straightforward kind of paper." All of these responses suggest that there is a genre of English paper which they call a "story" that they feel comfortable with. A "story" is not necessarily a narrative, but is more a presentation of facts and experiences in which the shaping hand of the writer is not explicitly evident. In "Friendships" the shaping hand is clearly evident; the metaphor precludes a "straightforward" presentation of facts or experiences. Even one student who found problems with the metaphor predicted the "attempted use of the [comparison] would probably impress teachers."

They were wrong. While instructors occasionally acknowledged the originality of the approach, their major complaint was that the metaphor ended up limiting the student:

> . . . . it seems that the author while writing this paper had that metaphor and thought, "Gee, this is really neat" and just filled it out completely. I haven't found out much about this person's friendships. The metaphor is so all-encompassing that it sort of sucks up the whole idea.

This discrepancy in responses may be due to different reading backgrounds in the respondents. Students reading "Friendships" probably have had few previous reading encounters that dealt with extended metaphors. Consequently, they are not familiar with the conventional criteria for the use of extended metaphors, specifically with the usual requirement that they must be used to clarify the subject. Instructors who, as graduate students in English, are immediately familiar with the use of figures of speech, could easily see that this student's use of the figure violated a basic convention for its use. One still might question, however, whether the student should have been given more credit for "the attempted use" and whether a uniformly critical reaction might convince a student to return to writing "stories."

THE ROLE OF STANCE

The question of stance goes beyond differences in specific criteria used by the two groups; it deals more with the role the reader takes in reading a student paper. The issue of stance can be illustrated by the example of a teaching assistant in a writing course. On the first day of class he informed his students that since he would be the audience for their papers, he would put on the board a list of subjects that he was interested in and encourage students to write on them. The director of the Freshman English program was horrified to hear of this; he felt that it was highly inappropriate to force students to write to the instructor's *individual* interests.

But the instructor was doing nothing more than any reader does; we generally choose to read in areas of interest and avoid styles of writing or subjects that do not appeal to us. We indulge our idiosyncracies—and call it "taste." This private stance is counterproductive in the classroom, though, because the instructor must acknowledge a wider range of interests and stylistic possibilities. In a sense, the instructor represents the standards and range of interests of an evaluative community. Take as an example a paper I received a couple of years ago, "Why Cheerleading Is a Sport." Now, as a jaded product of the late 60's, I would not choose to read this piece unless the approach was satirical (which it definitely was not). As an instructor, though, I took it seriously and worked with the writer to develop arguments that might persuade an intelligent reader unafflicted with my biases. I suspect that much of the criticism of the "teacher-as-audience" is actually criticism of teachers who allow their idiosyncracies to become the source of evaluation.

Not only is the instructor's range of interest wider, but the focus is different. To evaluate writing the instructor must direct considerable attention to ways in which the text meets or fails to meet criteria implicit in the genre in which the student is writing, for at some point the teacher must give a critical response. In order to give a response, an instructor must view the text as opaque; it is a tangible, seeable representation of a set of decisions made by the writer.

The student responses suggest that students have only partially been able to adopt this stance; many still read like private readers. In some cases this was evident when students said they could "relate to the paper"; in others it appeared when they claimed that they liked a paper because they liked the topic. But in some cases the students' responses suggested that they were reading to learn, to be persuaded, to be amused. They were granting the text transparency. They were not looking at the window but the view the window allows them. For example, one student reacted as follows to the description of Truman in Grossmans:

> It was especially effective for me when he started talking about Truman in the three-room apartment with his wife and five kids. I can't even think about that. It just makes you think that these people are so much poorer than most people I know.

An instructor commenting on this section of the paper would more likely have referred to the writer's effective characterization of Truman or to the effective choice of details that describe the situation. But this student talks, not about the strategy of the writer, but about the reality being described, not the window but the view.

IMPLICATIONS

The results of this study are consistent with those of an earlier study I con-ducted[6] and suggest strongly that students and instructors in Freshman English at the University of New Hampshire frequently use different criteria and stances in judging student work. For this reason, the two groups might profitably be viewed as distinct evaluative communities. This position has powerful implications for instruction.

The study raises serious questions about the advice given to students encouraging them to "write for their peers." Such advice embodies two criti-cal assumptions: that the teacher is fully aware of the criteria that the peer audience applies to students' writing, and that those criteria are consistent with the aims of an introductory writing course at the college level. In the case of "Friendships," instructors were unable to anticipate its appeal to students, and one might argue that even if they had been able to anticipate its appeal, they would have been reluctant to accept the students' judgment. They would have been reluctant to reward a paper that fell so short of their expectations about explicitness and about the use of the extended metaphor.

If teachers have this difficulty in anticipating—and accepting—the stan-dards of the student audience which the teachers meet regularly, how much more difficult is it for the teacher to anticipate responses of less familiar audi-ences. If students are encouraged to write for any audience with the assurance that the paper will be assessed on its effectiveness with the intended audience, one must assume that the instructor possesses a virtually complete knowledge of how various audiences respond to prose. I suggest that few teachers have this complete knowledge; we fall back on using the criteria of the community to which we belong.

The danger, then, is to say one thing and do another: to claim to take one position (assessing writing on its probable effect with any intended audience) and to actually take another (assessing on the basis of the norms of the aca-demic community). This discrepancy will only heighten the cynicism that many students have about evaluation.

This study also suggests the limitations of peer groups for providing a fully adequate response to a student paper. My own experience working with beginning teaching assistants suggests that many begin with unrealistic expecta-tions about the peer audience; when peers respond in a way that "misdirects," the instructor is caught in a dilemma—either to allow the "misdirection" to occur or to enter a dissenting opinion and thereby seem to veto a class deci-sion. Even when the instructor has been careful to go over criteria with the stu-dents, he or she will often find these criteria applied with different results by students and teacher. The teacher's "detail" may differ from the student's "detail."

Nothing I have said should be construed as arguing for the elimination of the peer workshop; students need practice applying the criteria that they are now learning. But rather than being viewed as the "natural" audience for fellow-students' writing, they might more profitably be viewed as apprentices, attempting to learn and apply criteria appropriate to an academic audience. It follows that the teacher's role in the workshop should not be passive. If students are to enter into the evaluative community of the instructor, they need to see the norms of their new community applied to student work. To use Frank Smith's term, they need access to demonstrations; terms like "detail," "transitions," "order," have meaning only as they are applied; the instructor needs to make his or her application of these criteria as accessible as possible.

This study also raises questions about the shorthand comments that teachers frequently use to mark papers. Many of these comments are informative only if one can assume a common critical vocabulary. For example, James McCrimmon in his much-used text *Writing with a Purpose* suggests the use of abbreviations like "det" for "detail inadequate."[7] But the use of this correction symbol will be successful only if instructor and student agree on what constitutes a detail and on what constitutes adequacy. The results of this study suggest that students are more willing to identify with a text and "read in" details that the writer has not included; their view of adequacy may differ from that of their instructors, who expect greater explicitness.

As the student masters the norms of this academic community, comments like "detail inadequate" can take on meaning. It is not uncommon for an abbreviated comment to be fully informative to an experienced student. But for the student about to enter a new community, "det" is not enough.

The instructor stands as the representative of a larger community and has the responsibility of making the norms of that community clear and plausible—even appealing. Correction symbols, checklists, grades, rating scales, or even peer workshops do not offer beginning students a full enough picture of how these norms work. Most presume that the major work of teaching has been done, that teacher and student are working on the same wavelength—when in many, if not most, cases they are not. These norms will be made clearer if we as teachers expose what goes on when we read—if we illustrate, if we demonstrate how they work.

In addition to the need for clarity and fullness of response, the study suggests, I hope, the value of paying serious attention to students' own comments about writing. When I began collecting student responses, I tended to view those that differed from my own as "misreadings." Like one of Plato's advantaged souls, I assumed that I soared higher and had a clearer view of The Good than my lower-altitude students. My job was to help them ascend. But as I reread the student comments, I began to see their plausibility, their coherence. They no longer appeared erratic; rather they seemed to arise from reasonable assumptions about writing. I was no longer confronted with misreadings, but with different, equally logical readings.

As a result I try to listen longer and better when a student explains a judgment, always assuming it makes sense. Previously I would have rushed in, eager to change what I had not tried to understand.

NOTES

1. James Moffett, *Teaching the Universe of Discourse* (Boston: Houghton-Mifflin, 1968), p. 193.
2. Peter Elbow, *Writing without Teachers* (New York: Oxford University Press, 1973).

3. See, for example, Sylvan Barnet and Marcia Stubbs, *Practical Guide to Writing*, Fourth Edition (Boston: Little, Brown and Company, 1983), and Maxine Hairston, *A Contemporary Rhetoric*, Second Edition (Boston: Houghton Mifflin, 1978).

4. Full copies of the papers used in this study are available upon request. Write to Thomas Newkirk, English Department, University of New Hampshire, Durham, NH 08324.

5. A subsequent study with a larger sample, 72 students and 20 teachers, found the same discrepancy for "Friendships" and an even greater discrepancy for "Grossmans."

6. Thomas Newkirk, "How Students Read Student Papers: An Exploratory Study," to be published in the new journal, *Written Communication.*

7. James McCrimmon, *Writing with a Purpose*, Seventh Edition (Boston: Houghton Mifflin, 1980), inside cover.

4

Peer Response Groups in the Writing Classroom: Theoretic Foundations and New Directions

ANNE DiPARDO AND
SARAH WARSHAUER FREEDMAN

T he past 20 years have been for writing teachers a time of intense fermentation, reflection, and innovation. The reasons are many, resting partly in social and demographic change and partly in a professional paradigm shift generated by research into how writers write (Hairston, 1982). Practice has suggested research and research has suggested practice, but not always has there been a perfect synergy between the two. Peer response groups, warmly advocated by a number of theorists and teachers (Beaven, 1977; Bruffee, 1978; Elbow, 1973; T. Hawkins, 1976; Healy, 1980; Macrorie, 1979; Moffett, 1968; see Gere, 1987, for a complete catalog of the work on peer response groups), present an interesting case in point. Although practitioner endorsements commonly share the assumption that the writing process is somehow supported by having students gather together for the purposes of providing one another with feedback on writing, response groups have been seldom studied to illuminate just what processes are thereby supported, or how. Thus, although writing groups have assumed an important place in educational practice, teachers are left to reflect upon them mostly in light of their own experiences or those of colleagues. Freedman's (1987b) national survey of 560 successful teachers of writing points out that practitioners are deeply divided as to the efficacy of the small-group approach. The conflicts felt by practitioners are paralleled in the small body of research so far conducted on response groups, which has produced strongly disparate findings about their success (e.g., see Berkenkotter, 1984, and Newkirk, p. 47 in this volume, for negative findings about groups as compared with Gere & Abbott, 1985, Gere & Stevens, 1985, and Nystrand, 1986, for positive findings).

Further complicating discussions of groups in the writing class is the fact that besides their most common function of responding to writing, groups may serve other functions as well. In a study of two ninth-grade writing classrooms, Freedman (1987a) found groups used in four distinct ways: for responding to writing, thinking collaboratively, writing collaboratively, and editing

From *Review of Educational Research*, vol. 58, no. 2, June 1988, pp. 119–49.

student writing. Most of the literature about groups in the writing class is concerned with groups that function mainly to provide students with opportunities for responding to one another's writing, including opportunities for editing.

Some who discuss response groups assume that they function for thinking and writing collaboratively (e.g., Bruffee, 1973, 1978, 1984, 1985; Gebhardt, 1980; Gere, 1987). As Gere notes,

> Writing groups are generally catalogued under the heading "collaborative learning," a form of learning that includes a variety of learner-centered activities ranging from convening small groups to solve problems in a math class to organizing book groups that meet to discuss texts selected by members. (p. 55)

In Freedman's (1987a) study of groups in two ninth-grade classrooms, however, collaborative groups are more narrowly defined. The groups that function most collaboratively are not those attending to the writing of a particular individual but, rather, those that involve working together to solve a single problem or coauthor a single text. Freedman concludes that groups function collaboratively only if the members work together on a group-owned product. She still recognizes, however, the possibility of collaborative events that may occur within the ongoing activities of response groups. Even with this more restricted definition of collaboration, some of the research on collaborative learning in general may thus serve to illuminate aspects of the teaching-learning process particular to writing response groups; but because response groups are intrinsically less collaborative than groups working together toward a single, cooperatively owned product, existing research on collaborative learning cannot fully explain response group dynamics.

Some research has examined the potential of collaborative student writing, usually with the use of microcomputers (Daiute & Dalton, in press; Dickinson, 1986; J. Hawkins, Sheingold, Gearhart, & Berger, 1982; Levin, Reil, Rowe, & Boruta, 1985; Reil, 1985). Other research argues the merits of groups organized for thinking collaboratively about problems related to writing (Hillocks, 1981, 1984, 1986). Although collaborative writing and thinking groups hold interesting potential, they present distinctly different sorts of learning-teaching occasions than do response groups in which the group members work in turn with different individuals on their individually owned products. These other kinds of collaborative groups used in writing instruction warrant further investigation, but because the questions they provoke and the approaches for examining them are of a wholly different order, we will limit our discussion to the more commonly practiced and studied writing response group. We will discuss notions of collaboration only as they relate to the activities of the response group.

The existing confusion about response groups suggests a need not only for more research, but also for a conceptual framework to contain and inform such inquiry. The purpose of this review will be to lay a theoretic foundation for research on response groups in order to suggest questions that further studies might explore—such questions, for instance, as how response groups fit into the larger social and instructional context of the writing class, what factors internal to response groups influence how peer group learning can take place, and how students give and receive response to and from one another.

Not specific to the writing classroom, several frameworks have been proposed for classifying studies of groups in classrooms (e.g., Peterson, Wilkinson, Spinelli, & Swing, 1984; Webb, 1982). In reviewing research on connections between group processes and student learning, Webb shows that some studies relate features of the learning situation—such as ability grouping and ethnic composition in groups—to interactional patterns in the groups. She then shows that other studies relate interactional patterns—such as giving help, receiving help, and on- or off-task behavior—to individual achievement measures. Webb's framework relates the two sets of studies by tracing a path from factors that influence group process, to group processes, and then to evidence that learning has taken place. By drawing these connections, she argues for a process-product paradigm. Her approach is aligned with earlier reviews of the relative merits of different cooperative group methods (Sharan, 1980) and of the use of groups in cooperative learning (Slavin, 1980).

In introducing their collection of research on small groups (Peterson, Wilkinson, & Hallinan, 1984), Peterson and Wilkinson (1984) describe three dominant research paradigms for studying groups: the sociological, the sociolinguistic, and the process-product. The sociological paradigm is concerned with issues that affect how students are placed in groups and then the consequences of their placement (e.g., ability and ethnic groupings). The sociolinguistic paradigm describes the communicative (verbal and nonverbal) interactions among students within groups and has been used mostly to study reading groups in elementary classrooms. The process-product paradigm attempts to correlate measurable group processes with measurable outcomes. Peterson and Wilkinson argue for an integration of these perspectives and in a chapter in their volume demonstrate a combining of the process-product and sociolinguistic approaches in a study of elementary mathematics teaching (Peterson, Wilkinson, Spinelli, & Swing, 1984).

Because of the special properties of response groups used during writing instruction, these general frameworks, which are not built specifically to address issues particular to the teaching and learning of writing, must be tailored to account for the special properties of response groups in writing classrooms. The process-product model alone is insufficient. In the case of writing, this model is not easy to apply because progress in writing is difficult to measure and often occurs over extended periods of time. Even when no one-to-one relationship can be found between talk in groups and improvement on an individual piece of writing, learning might still be occurring in groups. Alternatively, even if a writer makes measurable improvement on a piece of writing that can be connected to talk in a group session, the writer may not have learned a concept that he or she can apply to a new writing situation. Little is known about what is involved in transferring writing skills from one task to the next. Only a sociolinguistic model leads to increased understandings of the internal dynamics of the groups and the kinds of interactions that can lead to language learning. As Peterson and Wilkinson suggest, it seems important to start with a sociolinguistic understanding of group processes and to begin to build toward product measures that are meaningful.

In order to build a conceptual framework for informing research on the use of groups in writing instruction, we will begin with theories of the teaching and learning of writing and issues specific to writing groups. More general theory on group learning will be considered in reference to issues specific to the teaching and learning of writing.

Because response groups are not a novel innovation but already an integral part of many writing classrooms, we begin by tracing their emergence in the classroom, examining the reasons commonly given for their use, and exploring issues of power and classroom control associated with the use of these groups. In the first section, we concentrate both on issues raised in the substantial pedagogical literature on groups and on issues raised in the research literature, considering the work of teachers and theorists as well as empirical studies. Our aim in this section is not to provide a critical review but instead to explicate themes of theoretic importance: the relationship of peer response groups to the process approach to teaching writing, the role of peer-based learning in the classroom, and issues concerning interactional patterns in groups as opposed to dyads.

In the second major section, we examine how Vygotsky's theory of development, which emphasizes the importance of social interaction to language learning, suggests ways that groups might support students' acquisition of written language. Vygotsky's theories suggest a close relationship between talk and writing and the importance of a research framework that leads to understanding how social interactions, in this case in the form of peer talk, can contribute to writing development.

In the third section, we provide a critical review of the small body of research on peer response groups in writing instruction. This section is organized around two key issues that emerge from the synthesis of theoretical and practical concerns: (a) the degree of teacher control over the groups and the effects of control structures, and (b) the kinds of social interactions within groups, with attention to how those interactions relate to the larger instructional context and to teaching and learning in the groups. Finally, we point to alternative conceptions of peer talk about writing and directions for future research.

Our intention is not to provide an exhaustive critical review of the literature on small-group learning, but to examine that work which contributes to a theoretic frame for organizing issues important to pedagogy and research on response groups in the writing classroom.

HOW WRITING GROUPS FUNCTION IN THE CLASSROOM: ISSUES FROM PRACTICE

Groups and the Process Approach

Myers (1986) and Gere (1987) remind current practitioners that the small-group approach to writing instruction is not so new as most suppose. Gere, in her extensive history of the use of and research on writing groups, shows that "writing groups have existed as long as writers have shared their work with peers and received commentary on it" (p. 9). She traces the history of groups in the United States back to the early days of the colonies when they were part of literary societies, documenting their use in classrooms as early as the last part of the 19th century.

Both Myers and Gere point to Sterling Andrus Leonard's Dewey-inspired textbook, *English Composition as a Social Problem* (1917), for an enthusiastic discussion of many of the same group techniques generally thought of as "new" today: Elementary-age students are to meet in groups to respond to each other's papers; they are encouraged by their teacher to invent any necessary terminology and, above all, to avoid harsh, nitpicky criticism. Embracing Dewey's vision of the school as miniature community, Leonard seeks to create harmonious, cooperative relations among students as they pursue together shared educational goals, mirroring in the process the image of an ideally functioning society. As Myers points out, Leonard's philosophy is echoed in recent works by advocates of the small-group approach, including Elbow (*Writing With Power,* 1981) and Bruffee (*A Short Course in Writing,* 1985), both of whom encourage positive, supportive interactions among writing group members, and emphasize the salutary effects of requiring small groups to push toward collective "consensus."

The philosophic underpinnings motivating the use of groups in the early part of this century and today are similar, but much has changed since Leonard's time that affects how we view groups in the writing classroom. English instructors may still be scrambling, as they were in Leonard's day, to establish their own professional status (Myers, 1986, p. 158), but the challenge presented by our rapidly expanding knowledge of how writing is best taught and learned changes the tone of the struggle. From Kuhn's *The Structure of Scientific Revolutions* (1963), Hairston (1982) borrows the term "paradigm shift" to describe the change generated by the profession's new knowledge of writing and writers. According to Kuhn, disciplines are governed by conceptual models which, when threatened by emerging anomalies, are gradually forced to give way to reformed or even wholly different paradigms. Such is the case, argues Hairston, with writing instruction, as the traditional product-centered model is questioned in light of recent work by linguists, cognitive psychologists, anthropologists, and composition theorists. Hairston goes on to list key features of the new paradigm: It focuses on writing as a process, with instruction aimed at intervening in that process; it teaches strategies for invention and discovery; it emphasizes rhetorical principles of audience, purpose, and occasion, with evaluation based on how well a given piece meets its audience's needs; it treats the activities of prewriting, writing, and revision as intertwining, recursive processes; and it is holistic, involving nonrational, intuitive faculties as well as reason (p. 86).

A moment's consideration of Hairston's list begins to suggest some reasons for the appeal of the small-group approach: Groups present an arena for intervening in the individual's writing process, for working collectively to discover ideas, for underscoring the writer's sense of audience, for interacting with supportive others at various points in the composing process, and even, perhaps, for developing the writer's intuition. Emig (1979), who has written a similar description of the new paradigm, underscores the important role social exchange can play in the writing process. Seen formerly as "a silent and solitary activity" with "no community or collaboration," writing is now acknowledged as a process "enhanced by working in, and with, a group of other writers, perhaps especially a teacher, who gives vital response including advice" (pp. 140–141). At this point, Emig makes a special case for peer groups that have the particular function of responding to group members' writing.

The role small groups can play in expanding the audience for student writers is further emphasized by rhetorical theory and research findings that show the importance of writers' concepts of audience. Flower (1979), in a study of more and less successful college-age writers, finds that successful writers pay more attention to audience needs than do less successful writers. Flower's findings are based on what writers say when asked to think aloud as they write in testlike conditions. Although it is not known whether the same results would be found with younger writers, or writers writing in more natural conditions, and although thinking aloud may alter the nature of the writing process itself, one can still conclude that more successful writers, under certain conditions, are more conscious of audience than their less successful counterparts. Peer groups provide one way to make audience needs concrete and to help writers who otherwise might not focus on those needs to do so.

Britton, Burgess, Martin, McLeod, and Rosen (1975), studying the writing process with very different research techniques, reach similar conclusions. Britton and his colleagues collected 2,122 writing samples from 500 secondary students, produced under natural conditions in British school settings. The researchers then independently coded the writing samples to indicate the audience that the students had in mind as they wrote. They found the "teacher-examiner" to be the audience for 40% of the writing produced by first-year (U.S. sixth-grade) students, increasing to 60% of the audience for seventh-year (U.S. twelfth-grade) students. Britton and his colleagues conclude by urging schools to broaden the audience for student writing so that the audience demands in school more closely match the varied writing demands in the world outside school. Peer groups could certainly play an important role in helping promote such a goal.

Besides broadening and emphasizing the audience for writing, groups have also been seen as a way to support the shift from a product to a process emphasis in writing instruction. Recent research on the writing process argues the importance of allowing students time to go through an elaborated writing process in which they have opportunities to think about their topics as well as to revise their work to meet the needs of their readers (Flower, 1979). Peer groups can play a number of roles in that expanded process. More specifically, Freedman (1987b) finds through her national surveys of successful teachers that these teachers provide for response to students' ideas and their writing throughout the writing process, not just at the time the students hand in their final versions. Peer groups can assist teachers, who are generally overworked, in providing such ongoing response to student writing.

From Process to Peer-Based Interactions: Issues of Power

As one considers how small groups support the larger goals of writing instruction, perhaps even deeper and more significant than their potential in supporting the writing process are new understandings of the role social interaction plays in the teaching and acquisition of written language. Vygotsky (1978, 1986), whose developmental theory assigns a pivotal role to social interaction, has prompted composition theorists and researchers to begin examining how working together promotes students' progress. Vygotsky's attention to social processes has helped produce a conceptual climate wherein peer-based learning of all kinds has acquired a provocative new role.

One vocal proponent of writing groups (Bruffee, 1984) points to Vygotskian theory as a conceptual foundation for the approach, but, as we will see, this is one of many sketchily developed points in the pedagogic literature on groups which warrants further discussion. Our next major section will return to the question of how Vygotskian theory might be applied to groups and what such a framework suggests to both research and practice, but for now we will pursue the issues of power and control raised by the use of truly student-centered response groups.

Bruffee (1984, p. 6), a leading proponent of writing response groups, argues for the benefits of peers working together to foster a kind of peer-based learning that takes power away from the teacher and puts it in the hands of the students. He cites both Kuhn (1963) and Rorty (1979) in arguing that knowledge is not a static given but is "socially justified," evolving as communities of "knowledgeable peers" interact, thus shaping, extending, and reinforcing one another's ideas. It is this sort of self-governed dynamic that we must allow our students, Bruffee (1978) argues, if they are to discover the "social and emotional foundation upon which intellectual work rests" (p. 462). As an example of learning based in a community of "knowledgeable peers," Bruffee cites M. L. J. Abercrombie's *The Anatomy of Judgement* (1960), a study that documents how peer influence works through a process of group discussion to develop the diagnostic judgment of medical students at the University of London. Bruffee has argued (1973) that, although such peer-based learning is indeed the norm in the professions and in business, it has traditionally been absent from the classroom—a gap that becomes even more noteworthy considering the potent influence of peer dynamics throughout one's school years. Without examining in any depth the nature of group tasks or interactions, Bruffee tends to assume that all such peer-based work is collaborative.

A number of researchers, using different research paradigms and working with students of different ages, have shown the strength of peer influence on learning. Labov (1982), for instance, has studied the importance of peer networks in shaping the language and value systems of inner-city adolescents. Corsaro (1985), working with a nursery school class, and Dyson (1987, 1988), working with a combined first/second-grade class, have conducted observational case studies of interactions among peers in school, suggesting the increasingly important role of peer friendship as an influence on learning.

Also drawing upon data gathered through naturalistic observation, Cooper, Marquis, and Ayers-Lopez (1982) have studied spontaneous speech among kindergarten and second-grade children, documenting instructional episodes initiated with varying degrees of directness by peer learners. All instructional episodes are then categorized as concerned with either "instructional issues" (such as procedures for assignments), or "substantive issues" directly involving the subject matter under study. Finding 79% of the learner-initiated episodes to be concerned with substantive issues, Cooper et al. conclude "that children are viewed by their peers as having information that is of central import in classroom learning" (p. 189).

In a more controlled sociolinguistic study, Steinberg and Cazden (1979) have observed seven emotionally disturbed 11- and 12-year-old children enacting "instructional chains" wherein one student, after receiving appropriate training, assumed the task of tutoring the others on a given lesson. Steinberg and Cazden's analysis, focusing on linguistic changes which signal a negotiation between peer and teacher roles, reveals how these students succeeded in juggling the dual demands of managing social relationships and communicating new information. These student-tutors are seen building upon their status as peers to create an effective teaching-learning environment, dealing with disruptive peers, for instance, in an effective but nonthreatening manner that eluded their regular classroom teacher.

In a study comparing fourth graders' performance on combinatory logic tasks in a laboratory setting versus a more loosely structured group activity, Newman, Griffin, and Cole (1984) discover another way in which peer interaction supports learning: by giving students an opportunity to formulate their own goals for a task rather than simply accepting goals enforced by a teacher or researcher. When given one-on-one instruction in the laboratory setting, many students fail to fully comprehend the assigned task; but when the same students are allowed to explore together a similar task—this time within the context of a higher level problem—they eventually "discover the task on their own" (p. 188), resulting in superior achievement. Although it is not clear whether peer-based learning or the context of a higher level problem (or both) is responsible for these superior gains, Newman, Griffin, and Cole conclude that the "hierarchical division of labor" (p. 188) present in the laboratory setting—as it is in the traditional classroom—obscures the learner's sense of the larger purpose and meaning of a task by removing higher level goals from his or her control. More research is needed, they suggest, to compare how the tasks are made to happen in a laboratory setting versus how they can be "made to happen in everyday situations where there is no teacher" (p. 189), but where peers may present a possible source of help for one another.

Other researchers and theorists suggest that the comfort level of peer interactions can support cognitive growth. For instance, Michaels and Foster (1985), in a study of a first-grade class's "sharing time," show how peer teaching can enhance language learning even among very young children as they play to an audience of "sympathetic but discriminating" classmates (p. 157). Social skills theorist Argyle (1976) argues that because peers share similar cognitive constructs, they can communicate more readily with one another than they can with a teacher—that although they may not know as much as their instructor, peers hold special potential to build one another's confidence, social skills, and motivation.

Although research has thus suggested various ways in which peers working together can uniquely support or complement the instructional goals of school, there is some evidence that teachers feel threatened by the sheer force of peer influence and its potential to undermine the organizational norms of school (Sieber, 1979). When advocates of writing groups point enthusiastically to the power of peer dynamics (see, for instance, Bruffee, 1978, p. 449), they often do so without reviewing the body of research which suggests ways in which this power may be productively channeled toward instructional ends. Teachers are thus left to wonder if the student-centered approach is truly practical, given the realities of classroom management and need for discipline.

Some teachers have responded to this dilemma by coming up with new ways to involve students without completely unleashing the power of peer dynamics. Graner (1987), for instance, laments the fact that "allowing students to operate in peer groups requires teachers to give up a large measure of classroom control," making it "virtually impossible for the teacher to guarantee that these discussions do not become small talk or social chit-chat" (p. 41). He proposes as an alternative what he calls the "Revision Workshop," a whole-class lesson in which stronger and weaker specimens of student writing are compared and revision strategies discussed, with students then given an opportunity for individual, silent work on their own revisions. In emphasizing that the approach "does not require that teachers surrender any classroom control" (p. 43), Graner intends to reassure teachers that they can include the benefits of peer response in their classrooms while maintaining sole authority over its form and substance. But by denying peers the opportunity to interact as peers, constraining their feedback within the guidelines of teacher-led discussion, Graner eliminates not only the instructor's surrender of power but also the students' chance to receive feedback that truly diverges from that of a "teacher-examiner" (Britton et al., 1975). Such approaches as Graner's, while intending to solve the immediate logistical and political problems inherent in instituting a small-group approach, commonly reflect significant misunderstanding concerning the role of social interaction in the acquisition of written language.

Even instructors moving more boldly toward the use of response groups often search for ways to limit their autonomy. Indeed, how groups are framed serves as a powerful indicator of an individual instructor's theory of what it means to "teach the writing process" (Freedman, 1987b) and to interact in support of that process. Some teachers, following the tradition of Elbow (1973) or Macrorie (1979), offer only a bare minimum of guidance to groups, leaving students to devise strategies for responding to one another's writing that are largely intuitive and highly individual. Others, while interested in the potential of peer response, feel uneasy about surrendering so much classroom control to their students and continue to look for ways to guide and shape the group process. A common means of preserving some degree of teacher-centered control is the use of such procedural heuristics as lists of questions and reminders ("editing sheets") to channel response (see, for instance, Lamberg, 1980). There is evidence, however, that as much can be lost as gained by such strategies. In her study of peer groups in two ninth-grade classrooms, Freedman (1987a) finds that use of editing sheets correlates with a marked reduction of student-to-student talk. Such devices lessen the extent to which small groups are truly peer-run collectives and, in the most extreme case, move toward a mere parceling of tasks traditionally completed by an instructor, with students attending so closely to teacher-mandated concerns that groups no longer serve the function of providing a wider, more varied audience for student writing.

A teacher's use of peer groups may thus reflect a profound conceptual shift, or amount to little more than pursuing a traditional teacher-centered agenda within a parceled class. This is not to say that a teacher must turn over complete control to groups in order for them to be productive. Given the power of peer dynamics to either subvert or support educational goals, teachers' desires to monitor group activities seem reasonable indeed. The real issue is how to devise ways in which teachers and students might productively share power, but on this point the literature has been largely silent. Although a small portion of the research on group learning looks at spontaneous instructional events wherein roles shift and democratic peer teaching occurs (e.g., Cooper, Marquis, & Ayers-Lopez, 1982; Freedman, 1987a; Freedman & Bennett, 1987), far more common is study of highly structured peer engagements wherein students are trained to assume the role of teacher (e.g., Mehan, 1979; Palincsar & Brown, 1984; Steinberg & Cazden, 1979). Similarly, practitioner endorsements of response groups have failed to address in any in-depth manner the problem of how to encourage feedback that is spontaneous and natural rather than mere mimicry of a teacher. Because response groups function within a larger instructional context, it is important to attend to ways in which the classroom as a whole can encourage or discourage peer talk during writing. From this wider vantage point, the issue of teacher-versus-student power may be envisioned anew: Peers' being empowered to interact with one another need not be seen as subtracting from the teacher's power to design, monitor, and participate in the learning environment.

Groups Versus Dyads

In examining how students learn from a peer acting as a teacher, many studies of student groups fail to chart precisely the distinctions and similarities between dyadic interactions in which a teacher or more proficient peer provides tutoring. Similarly, in the literature on writing instruction peer tutoring in dyads and group work are often mentioned together as possible alternatives to more traditional instruction, often with no substantive discussion of how much one-to-one and small-group arrangements differ in form and purpose. Sometimes training students in individual peer tutoring is seen as basically the same thing as training them to work together in groups. Bruffee (1978), for instance, refers to the essential similarity between one-on-one peer tutoring "and its classroom counterpart, the organized, progressive, collaborative peer criticism" (p. 451). Brannon and Knoblauch (1984) move toward a sharper distinction, suggesting that whereas students receiving response from groups of classmates benefit from widely ranging feedback on their writing, individual tutoring encourages more searching self-analysis of the writer's ideas and strategies (p. 45). Spear (1984) takes the argument one step further, proposing that subjection to multiple points of view in group sessions enables the writer to "anticipate other points of view and to reflect with detachment upon the value of one's ideas" (p. 74). In a review of research into peer group work around a variety of (nonwriting) tasks, Damon (1984) has noted that one-on-one tutoring seems most suitable to those situations "where there is a need for supplementary bolstering of adult instruction," whereas student groups are better suited to acquiring "basic reasoning skills" (Damon, p. 338, cites Sharan, 1984, and Slavin, 1980, on these points). Indeed, peer tutoring sets up the role of tutor and tutee, matching more closely a hierarchical teacher-student relationship than a more coequal student-student relationship.

Such general comparisons lead to the conclusion that there are major differences between one-on-one and small-group collaboration in writing instruction. While collaboration may occur in dyadic tutoring exchanges, one would suspect that peer-run collaboratives might be characterized by more complicated interdynamics. No research to date has compared interactions in dyadic tutoring with those of writing groups, and in the theoretic and pedagogic literature on the subject, the boundary between these two commonly proposed forms of collaborative learning continues to be blurred. Dyads do, however, present a useful lens through which to view the role of social interaction in the teaching-learning process; indeed, investigations of dyadic interaction have played a significant role in the development of language learning theory.

Summary

Peer response groups may not be a wholly novel innovation, but in the context of today's conceptual climate they present practitioners with newly defined opportunities and dilemmas. On the one hand, teachers embracing a process approach to writing instruction are drawn to the idea of having peers provide ongoing response to one another on multiple drafts of their work. Not only does peer response free overworked teachers from the task of providing such detailed feedback personally, but it also emphasizes and broadens the student writer's sense of audience and the role of talk during writing. On the other hand, teachers are concerned about the surrender of classroom power peer groups generally entail. Ironically, in attempting to build a teacher-mandated agenda into the structure of response groups, instructors may erode rather than enhance their potential by encouraging students to role-play the teacher instead of interacting as peers. Given the paucity of research focused specifically on response groups, teachers are often unsure as to how the power of peer dynamics might be productively channeled toward enriching the learning environment for student writers.

How Vygotsky's Developmental Theory Supports Group Work

Vygotsky's theories, which emphasize that learning is a result of social interaction, provide a framework that can usefully inform studies of learning in response groups in the writing classroom. Although his theories were developed through studies of dyadic interaction, it is possible to extend them to examine small groups (e.g., Damon, 1984; Forman & Cazden, 1985; Freedman, 1987a).

Vygotsky (1978) says that all "good learning is that which is in advance of development" (p. 89) and involves the acquisition of cognitive skills just beyond the student's independent grasp. Such learning, Vygotsky argues, is accomplished through social activity in what he calls the student's "zone of proximal development." He defines the zone as "the distance between the actual developmental level as determined by independent problem solving and the level of potential development as determined through problem solving under adult guidance or in collaboration with more capable peers" (p. 86). In this zone, continues Vygotsky, lie those functions "not yet matured" but "in the process of maturation," functions that can be termed the "buds" or "flowers" rather than the " 'fruits' of development" (p. 86). Once an aspect of development comes to fruition, the child (or, indeed, the adult) is able to proceed independently. Thus, the "actual developmental zone," which can be gauged through traditional assessment procedures, gives information about development but not about potential, because "the actual developmental level characterizes mental development retrospectively, while the zone of proximal development characterizes mental development prospectively" (p. 87). Thus two students may display a similar degree of completed mental development, but their "developmental dynamics" may be quite different, allowing one to go much further than the other when both are given equal help (p. 87).

Bruner (1978) has coined the term "scaffolding" to describe the instructional strategies of the expert or "more capable peer" interacting with learners in their respective zones of proximal development. Cazden (1979, p. 11) adds a useful caution: Although the metaphor is helpful to a point, Vygotsky's theory calls for a special sort of assistance for the learner, which, rather than being completely discarded as a scaffold is, is "replaced by a new structure for a more elaborate construction" as the developing student moves forward through the zone of proximal development, building on completed learning ("development") to pursue more complex, sophisticated tasks. Thus, although the image of a scaffold effectively captures the idea that, in Bruner's words, "the tutor or aiding peer serves the learner as a vicarious form of consciousness until such a time as the learner is able to master his own action through his own consciousness and control" (1985, p. 24), it is important to remember that Vygotsky envisioned a more dynamically interpersonal, flexible phenomenon than this term connotes.

In applying the concept of scaffolding to group interactions in the writing class, it is also important to consider the range of abilities of students attempting to enhance one another's learning. That is, although Vygotsky specified that a "more capable peer" can offer suitable supports to the learner progressing through the zone of proximal development, when students are randomly placed in groups (as is most often the case in writing classes), it is conceivable that generally weaker writers may end up offering support or advice to generally more able writers. Given the multifaceted nature of writing, it is altogether feasible that any particular student may be more astute than another in addressing a given feature of a finished text or, indeed, any feature of the process leading to the production of that text.

But although students of varying abilities may be able to offer one another helpful pointers throughout the composing process, Vygotsky's emphasis on the social nature of learning suggests that learning to write is much more than simply absorbing bits of knowledge or mastering discrete skills. Wertsch (1979a) argues that Vygotsky was more interested in "communicative social interaction" than "language systems or narrowly defined verbal phenomena," comparing this emphasis on language as social act to Wittgenstein's "language-games," wherein "understanding an expression depends on understanding the flow of activity in which the interlocutors are engaged" (p. 5). Wertsch notes that Vygotsky's title *Thought and Language* might have been more accurately translated as *Speech and Language* to better reflect his preoccupation with the "social activity of speech," as opposed to the "structure of language systems" (p. 4).

In the United Kingdom (Barnes, Britton, & Rosen, 1969; Barnes & Todd, 1977, 1981) and increasingly in the United States (Cazden, 1986), researchers have turned their attention to ways in which students' conversations bring together cognitive and social aspects of language learning. Meaning is thus reenvisioned not as static given handed down by a knowledgeable instructor, but as the ever-evolving product of social interaction.

Acceptance of the Vygotskian premise that the genesis of reasoning for oneself through "inner speech" lies in social speech prompts one to embrace the importance of talk in the classroom, and, more specifically, to advocate building an environment rich in peer talk. As Cazden (1986) points out, peer interaction not only provides an abundant source of conversation, but it also allows students to try out a range of roles they would otherwise be denied in the "asymmetrical" power structure of traditional student-teacher participant structures. Among themselves, Cazden argues, peers both receive and give advice, both ask and answer questions, assume the role of both novice and expert. In examining the importance of verbalizing during learning, Durling and Schick (1976) find that vocalizing to a peer is more effective than vocalizing to an experimenter, thus providing empirical evidence of the importance of learners viewing themselves as teachers, not just as students. Freedman and Bennett (1987) have documented how groups in two ninth-grade writing classrooms afford students the opportunity to adopt different roles from those they play in whole-class interactions: A habitual follower may suddenly emerge a leader, for instance, or vice versa.

Beyond freeing students from writing to a lone audience of "teacher-examiner" (Britton et al., 1975), peer group talk about the activity of writing is thus aligned with the Vygotskian premise that writing is a deeply social act—an act that encompasses far more than the goals and conceptions of any individual instructor. The kinds of supports students can offer one another can thereby be seen as extending beyond assistance in mastering teacher-mandated goals to the rich range of communicative function that full language mastery entails.

The Social Context of Schools and Vygotsky's Theories: Tensions and Possibilities

Although Vygotsky's theories of development seem useful to understanding the teaching and learning of writing, there are as yet many gaps in our understanding of how his theories can be applied to actual teaching-learning situations. What, for instance, are the chances of this type of calibrated interaction taking hold among peers, particularly groups of peers, interacting around specimens of their writing? Greenfield (1984) has pointed out the particular difficulty of constructing and calibrating social interactions suitable to assist learners with complex tasks such as language learning. Although the cognitive challenge implied in groups working on writing has not been formally assessed, one might surmise that it constitutes a considerable social and cognitive burden.

Research indicates certain built-in impediments to teacher-structured response groups in writing classrooms. For example, Freedman (1987a, 1987b) discusses the essentially hierarchical structure of most classrooms where the premium is placed on competition and individual achievement. Theorists offer some clues, however, to what peer collaboration might look like under optimal conditions, although the picture remains rather sketchy—especially where school-based literacy tasks are concerned. Some of the existing examinations of the Vygotskian model in action do involve linguistic tasks, revealing how mothers construct language-learning supports for young children (e.g., Ninio & Bruner, 1977; Rogoff & Gardner, 1984) or how native speakers support nonnative speakers (Wong-Fillmore, 1976). Although such studies provide useful illustrations, they offer no information about the cognitive and social capacities needed to interact supportively in classroom settings, nor do they address problems encountered by students (at any level) attempting to replicate early language learning in the home.

Indeed, a number of researchers indicate that social interactions that support learning—whether between teacher and student or among peers—are far less likely to occur in school-based learning. Cazden (1979), for instance, suggests that a dramatic shift will occur in children's interactional patterns as they leave the home environment and enter the classroom and that the mismatch between home and school creates interactional difficulties for children from nonmainstream communities when they enter school. Heath (1983) follows working-class and middle-class children from their home environments into the classroom and describes the nature and consequences of differing interactional demands. She finds that the black and white working-class children whom she studied come to school with well-established narrative patterns that are different from one another, and that both are unlike those that dominate the classroom. Their learning is made difficult because the interactional environment in the classroom does not build from or understand the patterns these children learn at home. Heath shows that if teachers are sensitive to the needs of different learners and adjust classroom interactions to better account for what different learners do and do not know, students from varied backgrounds can have success in schools. The Kamehameha Early Education Program in Hawaii has come to similar conclusions in work with native Hawaiian students (Au, 1980; Au & Jordon, 1981; Au & Kawakami, 1984; Au & Mason, 1983; Calfee et al., 1981).

In their study of "reciprocal teaching," Palincsar and Brown (1984) suggest ways of getting students to assume the points of view of teachers and to take control of their learning. Teachers, working in the zone of proximal development, gradually hand over control of the task to seventh-grade students who are experiencing difficulty with reading comprehension. Given a wealth of structured, explicit instructions and extensive modeling of the prescribed strategies by an expert, the students are able to succeed in learning to pose teacher-type questions about texts with "sizeable gains on criterion tests of comprehension, reliable maintenance over time, generalization to classroom comprehension tests, transfer to novel tasks that tapped the trained skills of summarizing, questioning, and clarifying, and improvement in standardized comprehension scores" (p. 117). Because they focus fairly narrowly on mastery of isolated skills and have students closely imitate a teacher's behavior, Palincsar and Brown's seventh graders stop short of the range of problems typically tackled in writing groups; but the study is nonetheless a valuable exploration of how Vygotskian theory might begin to be translated into the practice of peer talk as teachers think about how to help peers work productively together.

Although student-centered learning may seem novel within the classroom, even the casual observer is aware that children outside school engage regularly in group problem solving, notably without instruction or monitoring from a teacher. Newman, Griffin, and Cole (1984) show how cognitive tasks carried out individually in the classroom are often divided and approached cooperatively in after-school clubs (p. 137), a reflection of the fact that the collaborative mode—first mastered in the child's earliest, home-based learning experiences—remains the norm outside of school. Newman et al. argue that young children experience a kind of culture shock as they move from the cooperative environment of the home into the classroom, where the premium is on individual problem solving and where cooperation among peers is called cheating (p. 137).

Forman and Cazden (1985) have noted that one problem with channeling this capacity for collaborative work toward the goals of schools is that too little is known about how peers interact. So strong is our Western, industrial-society bias toward individual achievement, they argue, that neither psychologists nor educators have looked at how students "work together to produce something that neither could have produced alone" (p. 329). To compare the types of strategies that emerge when students work together or individually on a problem, Forman conducted a study in which four pairs of 9-year-olds worked together on chemical reaction problems involving combinatory logic while a control group worked individually. On an initial posttest, dyads demonstrated striking gains over the singletons. Perhaps even more interesting are the insights into students' problem-solving patterns yielded by the study. Styles of collaboration, for instance, are of varying depths, ranging from "parallel," where students share materials and comments but fail to otherwise monitor one another's work, to "associative," where some information is exchanged about various combinations selected without any further coordination of the students' roles, to "cooperative," where students constantly monitor each other's tasks, carefully coordinating roles (p. 338). Particularly in this "cooperative" mode, students tend to argue about conflicting solutions en route to a shared one, thus fulfilling the hypothesis of Piagetian theorist Perret-Clermont (1980) that cognitive conflict serves as a "mediator between peer interaction and cognitive reorganization" (Forman & Cazden, p. 339).

But where Piaget looked for cognitive conflict to promote growth-inducing disequilibrium, Forman and Cazden (1985) argue that "he was not interested in describing or explaining social processes as a whole" (p. 340). They turn to Vygotsky for his insights into the interactional transformation of interpsychic into intrapsychic regulation that can occur among peers. Vygotsky's theories lead them to conclude that this transformation is achieved when peers assume "separate but complementary social roles" (p. 341), one student observing, guiding, and correcting while the other performs the task. Thus, the students are able to accomplish together what neither can do alone, much as if they have been tutored by a "more capable" peer. Peer dyads can allow for many of the same learning opportunities as tutoring offers, conclude Forman and Cazden, by providing an "impetus for self-reflection encouraged by a visible audience," the "need to respond to peer questions and challenges," and by requiring the student to "give verbal instructions to peers" (p. 344) — that is, to take on the cognitive challenge of role-playing the expert. Although they acknowledge that "a Piagetian perspective on the role of social factors in development can be useful in understanding situations where overt indices of cognitive conflict are present" (p. 343), Forman and Cazden suggest that "if one wants to understand the cognitive consequences of other social interactional contexts, Vygotsky's ideas may be more helpful" (p. 343).

Throughout this section, the focus has been on collaborative activity that involves students' working together to solve a group-owned problem. The very nature of the activity of individual writing and how writing gets accomplished needs further examination. Dyson (1987, 1988) has begun to explore the role of the peer collective in the composing process of the individual, showing how informal group talk can be promoted in the elementary classroom in ways that allow students time for productive collaboration as they produce individual pieces.

Piaget Versus Vygotsky

Gere (1987) discusses the consequences of Vygotskian as opposed to Piagetian theory for the study of response groups. She claims:

> In Piagetian terms, writing groups provide a means to the end of individual performance in writing, but they are finally peripheral because the essence of writing lies in the individual effort of opening the mind's locked lid. Vygotsky's insistence on the dialectic between the individual and society, however, puts peer response at the center of writing because it makes language integral to thinking and knowing. (pp. 83–84)

By contrast, Damon (1984) argues that although the Piagetian and Vygotskian models of peer instructional interaction may at first appear oppositional, they can in fact be seen as mutually complementary. In the Piagetian view, he notes, peers provide a compelling source of cognitive conflict—especially because peers speak on a similar level, usually with a directness that seems comparatively nonthreatening. (Buckholdt & Wodarski, 1978, have similarly suggested that students learn more readily in interactive groups because peers can easily understand one another's language.) Because peer feedback is taken seriously, peer disagreements readily produce both social and cognitive conflict, which pressures peers to become aware of views other than their own, to reassess the validity of their own points of view, and to learn to justify their opinions and communicate them to others (see Johnson & Johnson, 1979, for an empirical study demonstrating the importance of interpersonally induced conceptual conflict in group learning). In contrast to Vygotskian theory, the Piagetian framework, as illustrated currently in the Geneva school by researchers such as Doise and Mugny (1981), emphasizes peer interaction as a trigger for change in that cognitive dissonance may set the learning process in motion; growth is seen as the product of restructuring the child's internal reasoning processes. Damon notes that, on the other hand, a Vygotskian view of peer interaction stresses the gradual internalization of intellectual processes (such as verification, spontaneous generation, and criticism) that are activated as peers communicate with one another. Vygotskian theory thus promotes the view that "peer feedback not only initiates change" but also "shapes the nature of change itself" (Damon, p. 333).

Although we agree with Damon that the Piagetian and Vygotskian frameworks for viewing group learning are not in all instances incompatible, we hold that they present distinctly different views of the teaching-learning process. On the one hand, Piaget (1970) asserts that social interaction plays a role in promoting learning, but that it is necessarily secondary to development: "The very fact that the stages follow the same sequential order in *any* environment," he writes, "is enough to show that the social environment cannot account for everything" (p. 721). Vygotsky (1978), on the other hand, assigns a much more profound significance to the "social environment" that Piaget downplays: "Learning awakens a variety of internal developmental processes," he writes, "that are able to operate only when the child is interacting with people in his environment and in cooperation with his peers" (p. 90). In Piaget's view, development leads learning; in Vygotsky's view, learning leads development, and does so through the mechanism of social interaction. Despite Piaget's impressive contributions to cognitive theory, Vygotsky speaks more directly to the issue of how social interaction facilitates learning, and assigns it a central role indeed.

The contrast between Piagetian and Vygotskian theory is further highlighted in their differing definitions of what each terms "egocentric" speech and what Vygotsky's followers term "private" speech (Wertsch, 1979b). In Piaget's use of the term, "egocentric" speech indicates a child's inability to consider the needs of others. It precedes social speech, which is "de-centered," and allows the speaker to account for an audience. Egocentric speech is indicative of learners still adrift in their own narrow, presumably unchallenged views. At most, group interaction might provide an antidote to such egocentrism by promoting cognitive conflict that the learner then works out alone, ultimately restoring equilibrium.

Vygotsky (1978), on the other hand, sees children's private speech as "the transitional form between external and internal speech" (p. 27). All speech is social; therefore, private speech is "embedded in communicative speech" and functionally is a precursor of and "the basis of inner speech" (p. 27). Thus, whereas Piaget argues (1959) that these egocentric utterances constitute a self-directed "soliloquy" (p. 256), which disappears as the child becomes socialized, Vygotsky (1986) hypothesizes that "egocentric speech is actually an intermediate stage leading to inner speech" (p. 32). Vygotsky argues that this private speech, rather than simply dying out, " 'goes undergound' " (p. 33) as it is transformed into "inner speech," that is the raw material for independent reasoning.

In discussing Vygotsky's view of private speech, Wertsch and Stone (1985) note an intriguing anomaly that has some bearing on talk in writing groups: Before children fully appreciate that private speech can serve a "self-regulative" function as collaboration yields to autonomy, learners may continue producing such speech in "potentially communicative settings" for a time (p. 172). Such talking to oneself in the presence of others, far from reflecting Piagetian egocentrism, is seen as indicative of cognition's social roots. Although Vygotsky developed this aspect of this theory in response to his observations of young children, an important part of the work of writing groups emerges as a striking parallel. A teacher studied by Freedman (1987a) articulates the often-heard concern: "I want kids to *HEAR* their own writing," she asserts. "Other kids' suggestions can be an added benefit, but I really want them to hear their own work, critically" (p. 12). Such activities as listening metacognitively to one's own work or "thinking aloud" in the presence of others—activities more accurately described as "self-monitoring" rather than communicative—can be linked theoretically to Vygotsky's view of the child's private speech. In her study of response groups, Freedman found that this kind of self-monitoring occurred regularly as ninth grade students read their writing aloud to others.

An additional tension between Vygotskian and Piagetian theories arises from Piaget's emphasis on cognitive conflict versus Vygotsky's emphasis upon cooperation. Although it seems rather obvious that both might be of benefit, pedagogic literature advocating the use of writing groups continues to stress the supposed importance not only of cooperating but of reaching consensus. In a recent *College English* article, Wiener (1986) echoes this argument, suggesting that where group members fail to achieve consensus, collaboration gives way to a mere delegating of traditional tasks (p. 55). Citing Bruffee's (1985, p. 45) prescription that tasks lead to "an answer or solution that can represent as nearly as possible the collective judgement and labor of the groups as a whole," Wiener stresses that a push toward ultimate agreement should be clearly implicit in all assigned tasks. According to Wiener, although the teacher should keep a distance from the students' collaborative workings, as the class meets once again as a whole, the teacher's job becomes one of helping students synthesize apparent contradictions among the conclusions reached by various groups (p. 58). Meanwhile, Myers (1986), one of the few theorists to challenge this emphasis upon consensus, argues that many of the popular appeals for collaborative learning—whether spearheaded by Leonard in the last century or Elbow and Bruffee in this one—encourage conformity to the status quo by stifling ideological differences. "Bodies of knowledge cannot be resolved into a consensus," he writes, "without one side losing something" (p. 167).

Vygotsky does not claim that the process of reaching consensus is a necessary feature of group cooperation. Indeed, it remains to be seen whether such consensus may be construed as an index of group cooperation. Disagreement among group members, whether resolved or unresolved, marks an instance where Piagetian theory complements Vygotskian theory without necessarily contradicting it. When student writers disagree, they are not only encouraged to reconsider and deepen their positions, but are confronted with a larger dilemma: that readers (even readers who are also writing instructors) hold differing positions of what constitutes quality writing, that a text embraced enthusiastically by one may be rejected by another. One commonly stated rationale for implementing writing groups is that students need to develop a sense of audience, and some disagreement is of course a hallmark of almost any audience numbering more than one. As students model for one another the disparate response that mirrors feedback in the world outside the English class, they provide a socially based learning support that is aligned with Piaget's notion of cognitive dissonance but not at all in opposition to a Vygotskian framework. Indeed, such a "microaudience," in challenging students to negotiate between receptivity and adherence to authorial intention (see Berkenkotter, 1984), could indeed function as an interactive support. Urging students to reach premature or inappropriate agreement may short-circuit this process, imposing unnatural constraints on the human penchant for argument. It is

through "collective argument," Vygotsky (1981) notes, that "the higher functions of child thought at first appear" (see Genishi & DiPaolo, 1982, for a sociolinguistic examination of the role of argument in preschool education); and
there is ample reason to believe that argument, whether resolved or not, continues to play an important role in a writer's growth. In a recent study of
fourth and fifth graders writing collaboratively on microcomputers, Daiute
and Dalton (in press) find that both resolved and unresolved conflicts correlate with individual gains in writing ability as the students learn together to
play and experiment with language.

Though consensus may play a relatively more important role where one
text (as in collaborative writing) or one solution (as in joint problem solving)
is the goal, the importance of pushing toward agreement may still be over-
stressed. Certainly, where the context is the more common paper response
group, this mistaken emphasis on consensus brings into focus a larger confusion regarding how student collaboration is to function.

RESEARCH ON PEER RESPONSE GROUPS

Introduction

Given their relatively recent surge in popularity, response groups have as yet
been the subject of only a small body of empirical literature, some of which is
constricted by a rather narrow frame of vision. Because issues of classroom
power figure so prominently in the use of response groups, it is particularly
important that researchers consider the relative degrees of teacher versus student
control which characterize specific instances of group work. Further, because
Vygotskian theory suggests a close correspondence between the nature of interaction and learning occurring in groups, there is a need for careful analysis of
the internal social dynamics of groups. Both issues are directly tied to the
agenda and style of the classroom as a whole, further underscoring the efficacy of examining groups within a larger instructional milieu.

Of the many ways writing teachers set up response groups, each structure may influence how members of a group will interact and what kind of
feedback will be offered; correspondingly, how groups are framed will influence the findings from research. For instance, strategies designed to retain a
degree of teacher control will impact importantly on group dynamics, thereby
suggesting a number of considerations: Is student attention channeled toward
certain features of the texts by specific, teacher-generated guidelines, or do
students look more generally for features that bother or impress them as individuals? Are students directed to address the various components of evaluation in a particular order, and with a particular emphasis? Are they to
look only at the ideas and issues presented, or attend at some point to more
mechanical concerns such as syntax, style, spelling, and punctuation?

In terms of internal dynamics, it is important to look at the relationship
between various teacher-imposed control structures and the social interaction
in groups. For instance, if groups are given directives, is the broader social

context of the classroom one that ensures that these teacher directives will be followed? What is the effect of directives that are followed on social interaction? For example, is student feedback to be presented orally, in writing, or both? How much interaction is there around different topics? What about passive group members? Should everyone, as Perl and Wilson (1986) suggest, be required to give at least some feedback on each paper? What if no one can think of anything to say?

Our consideration of how Vygotskian theory might inform the pedagogic controversy surrounding writing response groups directs particular attention to these issues of teacher versus student control and the nature of social interaction in groups. Therefore, the following discussion of research on response groups will examine each study in terms of how it considers aspects of classroom organization that affect the nature of the interaction within groups and in terms of how it considers issues internal to the workings of the groups themselves.

Review of Research

Gere and Stevens (1985) and Gere and Abbott (1985) compare writing group language across fifth-, eighth-, and eleventh-grade levels. Although they do not study the context for the groups or issues of control, they do say that the groups they studied follow the same format, modeled on Elbow's "teacherless" writing class. The teachers in the study learned the technique when they participated in Writing Project workshops. In the groups, drafts are to be read aloud twice, with group members listening the first time, taking notes the second time (no one besides the writer has access to a written version of the essay), and then offering oral response.

The focus of the Gere and Stevens and Gere and Abbott studies is on the internal workings of the groups. They record naturally occurring group sessions on audiotape and later transcribe them. Each "idea unit" of talk (Chafe, 1980) is then coded to indicate whether it "informs," "directs," or "elicits," and to indicate whether it reflects a focus on the group itself or the paper under discussion. Gere and Stevens find that the most commonly occurring idea unit "informs" group participants about the content of the writing being discussed. The study offers reassuring evidence to teachers that response groups receiving fairly minimal guidance are capable of staying on task. Beyond that, Gere and Stevens argue that student talk tends to be far more specific to a particular text than are teachers' written comments. Since they did not study teachers' comments, the basis for the comparison remains unclear. They claim, though, that teacher comments "may be said to attempt to form student writing by conforming it, that is, by trying to realize its potential similarity to a paradigm text by asking the writer to conform to certain abstract characteristics of 'good' writing" (1985, p. 101). Students' comments, on the other hand, are found to be attentive to the writer's intended meaning, "a meaning which is often compounded of a variety of questions, comments, and criticisms of quite different 'interpreters' who may each find a different 'meaning'" (p. 103). Gere and

Stevens conclude that student response is thus not only more specific, but richer and more varied than teacher feedback alone.

Gere and Abbott (1985) find further that grade level affects the topics students discuss in groups, with younger students attending more to content and with older students attending more to form. Further, discussions of narrative as opposed to expository texts influenced the topic of discussion, with narratives evoking more discussion of content and with exposition evoking more phatic comments. They also found that older students talking about expository texts spend less time "informing" group members about the content of the writing.

In neither Gere study does the coding system allow the researchers to examine the nature of the interaction among the students, because the talk of each speaker is coded as a unit of meaning, not as it functions as part of an interactional sequence of meaning-making.

Nystrand (1986) and Nystrand and Brandt (in press) studied 250 students participating in 13 college-level classrooms, some centering solely around group work and completely student-centered and others teacher-centered and not using writing response groups. Although these studies do not explicitly address issues of control, they do discuss both the context and interactional dynamics of the response groups examined. Nystrand's (1986) approach follows a process-product model, in which he compares the relative success of the different classroom structures by measuring student improvement across the semester. He finds that students who work in groups evidence greater gains in their writing of personal essays than those who do not and that those who work in groups come to conceptualize revision as reconceptualization, whereas those who do not conceptualize it as editing. Nystrand also offers an interesting analysis of essential differences in how different types of groups deal with problems, adding a detailed analysis of the internal group dynamics for five of the groups across the semester. Some groups, for instance, seem to consider their task complete once they summarily label a general problem, failing to examine the trouble source in any great detail. Other groups talk at length about ideas—a potentially useful strategy if the writer needs help finding a focus, but which more often leads students off the subject. He associates group success with whether students all have photocopies of the writing under discussion. He finds that when group members both listen to a paper being read aloud and follow along on a copy of the written text, they are more likely to attend to higher order considerations (such as structure and presentation of the paper's central argument), whereas merely listening results in more attention to lower order problems (such as word choice). He finds that successful groups focus discussion on issues of genre, topic, and comment. Nystrand asserts that the best groups are characterized by "extensive collaborative problem solving," where the group joins together in addressing one rhetorical problem after another in a concrete and cooperative manner, thus creating an environment—not unlike that of initial language acquisition—in which the learner continuously tests hypotheses about the possibilities of a written text. Nystrand argues that such groups serve an important function in helping students "anticipate potential trouble sources *as they write* [emphasis in the original]" and "develop a sensitivity to the possibilities of text, which effectively enables them to monitor their composing processes" (pp. 210–11).

In an extension of this work, Nystrand and Brandt (in press) connect talk in groups to student revisions. They collected drafts and revisions from students in both types of classes, asking the students to also describe what they would like to revise after they wrote their first draft. After they had completed their revisions, the students were asked "to assess both the strengths and weaknesses of their revisions" (p. 7). Trained raters found that students who worked together in groups produced "higher quality" revisions and were more aware of their needs and accomplishments than those who received only teacher feedback. In addition, the overall quality of the revised piece of writing was judged better for students who were in classes in which they worked in groups. Nystrand and Brandt also expand the analysis of the five students whose groups were videotaped and connect the group talk to the students' subsequent revisions. They conceptualize the "conversations and revisions in terms of 'entry points'" (p. 12). In other words, they ask, "At what level of text did the peer group 'enter' a draft under consideration and, likewise, at what level of text did the writer 're-enter' the text during revision?" (p. 12). The analysis of the talk in terms of genre, topic, and comment is expanded to the revisions. They found that they could predict the revision based on the talk, with the extent of the discussion predicting the extent of the revision and with talk on one level of text tending to implicate changes at other levels. They also found that the most common entry point was genre.

Unlike Gere's analysis, Nystrand's allows an examination of the interactive nature of talk in the groups. Nystrand is also clear that the groups occur in a student-centered context. He describes the context as follows:

> Students . . . meet regularly in groups of four or five, and the same groups meet three times a week over the course of the term for the purpose of sharing and critiquing each other's writing. The instructor assigned few if any topics and gives students no checklists to use in monitoring their discussion. Rather, students keep journals and prepare pieces of exposition from these notebooks for presentation to classmates at every class meeting. Students are required to prepare a new paper or a substantial revision for each class. They are instructed to consider the extent to which the author achieves his or her purpose; they are to avoid checking spelling, punctuation, and usage; and they are required to provide each member of their group with a photocopy of their work. Periodically the instructor collects the best papers from each student for evaluation, but she does relatively little direct instruction, and intervention in these groups is minimal. (1986, p. 180)

Other smaller scale, naturalistic studies of college-level peer response groups contradict Nystrand's thesis. Limited not only in size but in their failure to consider the context and internal dynamics of writing groups, these studies nonetheless raise some provocative cautions that warrant further exploration. Newkirk (1984, p. 47 in this volume), for instance, questions how well peer feedback supports the goals set by a writing teacher. In his study, 10 students at the University of New Hampshire were evaluated by 10 teachers and peers on four different writing tasks. Striking differences emerged between teacher and student feedback, and, in contrast to Nystrand's findings, Newkirk finds student responses lacking in a number of ways. First, his analysis reveals that strong peer identification among the students makes them more willing than their teachers to fill in missing elaboration as they read, thus rendering them more tolerant of what the teachers consider thin or undeveloped prose. Second, the students tend to reward a rather clumsy attempt at extended metaphor in one paper on the assumption that it is the sort of thing their teachers would like. Finally, Newkirk points out key differences in reader stance—the teachers were more often willing to put aside personal opinion and help students express their own ideas, whereas the student respondents tended more fully to indulge their own opinions and idiosyncrasies, sometimes simply rejecting an idea rather than helping a writer better express it. Based on his findings, Newkirk concludes that in asking students to write for their peers, teachers may not be giving them the best preparation for school writing. He acknowledges a dilemma: On the one hand, if students are told to consider audience but then allowed to write only to the academic community, cynicism may be fostered; on the other hand, if peer feedback is "vetoed" in teacher evaluations, the value of student collaboration may be lost. Newkirk argues that the answer lies in careful demonstration of response strategies before peer sessions take place, and in helping students realize that they are in the role of apprentices, not experts. Although teachers should listen carefully to student responses and not assume misreading, Newkirk maintains that they should also be aware that student response can diverge from teacher intent in unpredictable and what some would consider unsatisfactory ways.

Indeed, where group work is seen as a parceling of tasks normally completed by the teacher, any digressions from a given instructor's response norms might be seen as a major flaw; but where groups are conceived as having a more fully collaborative life of their own, providing an extended social context in which to give and receive feedback, failure to match a teacher's response mode perfectly does not present such a consuming concern. Also, the kind of peer response that grows over time in the setting Nystrand describes is likely to be qualitatively different from the kind of response an individual student gives when suddenly presented with a piece of writing. It becomes difficult to interpret Newkirk's findings in relationship to the context of the peer response group.

In another study of college-level response groups, Berkenkotter (1984) examines the sometimes confusing task student writers face in reconciling their own imperatives with the suggestions of others. In case studies of three students in her freshman composition course, Berkenkotter finds that each responds differently to reader feedback, depending on the individual writer's "personality, level of maturity, and ability to handle writing problems" (p. 313). She collected think-aloud protocols from the students as they were composing and revising as well as tape recordings as they worked in groups and met one-on-one with her. She does not analyze the talk in the groups, nor does she attempt to connect the student writing in any systematic way to the work in the groups. In her descriptions of the students, she relates that one abrasively resisted others' suggestions; another maintained inner-directed control of her text despite confusing suggestions by her group; a third was so responsive to the sometimes hypercritical feedback of her group that she lost sight of her real purpose for writing, regaining it only as she began to take a more adversarial stance toward her group. Stressing that we do not yet know much about the process by which students gain authority over their texts, Berkenkotter urges caution in classroom use of peer response groups, where the interplay of "subtle emotional and intellectual factors" can leave some students feeling more confused than enlightened (p. 318). Because Berkenkotter provides no information about how the peer groups functioned in relationship to the rest of the instructional context, it is unclear whether they were teacher or student controlled. Berkenkotter also provides no detailed analysis of the inner workings of the groups.

In an ethnographic study of two ninth-grade writing classes, Freedman (1987b) looks at how peer groups function within learning environments informed by diverging instructional theories. In addition to providing the context for the groups, she presents a detailed analysis of the talk in the groups (Freedman, 1987a; Freedman & Bennett, 1987). In one classroom, the teacher depended on peer response as central to her teaching; from no other source in the classroom context could students get substantive help during the writing process. Overall, the teacher did not relinquish control of the groups; she gave them specific directions and had group members complete sheets she prepared for assessing one another's work. An analysis of the patterns of the talk in the groups shows that the students were oriented to the teacher and the teacher's tasks rather than to one another's writing. They were as concerned with completing the sheets in a way that would please the teacher as they were with interacting with one another. They refused to offer evaluative commentary. In the end, rather than serving as a comfortable setting where students could collaborate, these groups functioned more as a time for individual writers to complete teacher-given tasks. On a more positive note, however, the students read their work aloud and at that point they showed evidence that they reflected on their writing and anticipated what their peers were thinking. In this sense, they were becoming aware of the needs of the reader.

The other teacher in Freedman's study did not rely on peer response during the writing process. Although this teacher used groups frequently, he set them up mostly as forums where students could work collaboratively to solve a specific problem he posed to the group—such as finding support for a character's traits in a piece of literature. When this teacher did set up response groups, students spent much time off task. The students in his class had frequent one-to-one conferences with their teacher about their writing.

In both classrooms there was plentiful social interaction during writing. It is important to remember that the peer group is not the only arena for such interaction. Freedman (1987a) and Freedman and Bennett (1987) make no attempt to connect the student writing to talk in the groups; however, in two case studies, one from each classroom, Freedman (1987b) does show how students' writing grows in relation to the entire stream of social interaction in the instructional environment.

Along with Freedman and Bennett (1987), Hillocks (1981, 1984, 1986) emphasizes that groups in writing classes serve widely varying functions. He categorizes instructional approaches that rely on small groups as either "natural process" or "environmental" and argues that the two use small groups toward different ends. Hillocks places in the natural process mode those classes where students are given little or no direct instruction in the qualities of good writing; students in such classes may meet often in response groups, but they are given broad instructions and asked ultimately to come up with their own criteria for commenting. Nystrand's student-centered approach would likely fall here. Classes in the environmental mode, though also featuring high levels of peer interaction, structure small-group discussions toward solving well-defined problems relevant to particular features of the writing process. According to Hillocks, a typical environmental activity might consist of a teacher's first leading "a brief discussion of student writing, helping students apply a set of criteria to it," then asking students to "apply the same criteria to other pieces of writing, not only judging the piece but generating ideas in response to several questions about it in order to improve it" (1984, p. 144). Although students learn identifiable writing skills in environmental mode classrooms, the lesson comes through interactive problem solving—not through listening to presentational-style lectures. A classroom in Hillocks's "individualized" mode and in his "presentational" mode, with its emphasis on teacher-led discussion and lecture, would be unlikely to include small groups at all. Hillocks finds, through a meta-analysis of 29 experimental studies, that of the four modes the environmental is the most productive (1984, p. 147)—a finding that raises certain concerns about the wide use of natural-process-style response groups, where students are turned loose upon the rather far-reaching, often ill-defined task of commenting on one another's work. Hillocks's results, however, are difficult to interpret. He reports a lack of homogeneity among the different natural process studies in his meta-analysis ($H = 23.15$ as opposed to $H = 12.83$ for environmental classrooms) (1984, pp. 196–97). As Witte (1987) points out, the meta-analysis is based on measurable improvement on a scale of writing quality, but the nature of the scale may differ across studies (p. 206). Furthermore, Hillocks's inferences about the mode of instruction actually used in the studies are questionable. As Larson (1987) asks, "How accurately can one suggest that the teaching one sees fits approximately (let alone tightly) into one of the four categories?" (p. 209). According to the theoretical frame we have put forth, the instructional mode would not be the key variable; rather, the degree and type of social interaction would. Hillocks provides no information about the extent to which the instructional mode correlates with particular kinds of social interactions.

Certainly, Hillocks's findings in favor of a more structured approach are contradicted by Nystrand's research. Nystrand demonstrates that student-centered group teaching at the college level can be highly effective. Newkirk and Berkenkotter, meanwhile, demonstrate that at this level peer influence can as easily subvert as support educational goals, a conclusion supported by numerous anthropological studies of schooling (for an overview and discussion of these, see Sieber, 1979). The problem of how to channel the power of peer influence effectively thus emerges, and herein lies a central issue: Although "collective forms of pupil behavior" have been seen as "intrusive elements in the school, obstructive to the accomplishment of its formal goals" (Sieber, p. 208), collaborative learning advocates urge teachers to relinquish a large chunk of their power to independently functioning peer groups. Some teachers attempt to qualify this surrender by prescribing tightly knit, carefully detailed guidelines to groups (for instance, asking response groups to answer a series of questions about each paper rather than simply discussing whatever seems most important to them as in the Freedman study). The issue of teacher versus student control is complicated further by the traditional grading system. As Gere and Abbott (1985) and Freedman (1987a) point out, asking secondary and elementary students to provide independent response to each other's papers does not necessarily reduce the importance they attach to the grades they will eventually receive from a teacher. The Nystrand studies offer the only clear evidence of what happens when the teacher truly surrenders control to the students, and it is important to remember that his study is at the college level. By contrast, Hillocks (1981, 1984, 1986), in advocating the use of groups within an "environmental mode" classroom, argues for teacher control of a particular type.

A number of questions remain unanswered about the nature of collaborative learning in general and peer response in particular. More studies are needed of the actual functioning of peer talk within writing classrooms, with full descriptions of the classrooms themselves and how classroom structures relate to peer structures. In particular, such studies need to consider the larger instructional context as well as the internal dynamics of groups themselves. Because groups are so enmeshed in the larger world of the classroom—its power dynamics and social structure, its patterns of communication, its overarching instructional agenda—they must ultimately be studied within that context as they both help shape it and are in turn shaped by it. Important questions include the following:

- How does peer talk about writing function in the writing classroom?
- How does peer talk fit the rest of the instructional agenda?
- When talking together, how do students give and receive response and support?

Answers to such questions could begin to show (a) the influence on group function from the larger instructional context that is created by a teacher's philosophy of teaching writing, (b) actual patterns of students' communicative interactions during group sessions, (c) ways that social dynamics within peer groups influence the ways that students approach academic tasks in groups, and (d) ways that students solve intellectual problems.

CONCLUSION

Whereas some practitioners continue to endorse response groups as an ideal means of broadening and emphasizing students' sense of audience throughout the composing process, others are expressing misgivings about their efficacy and, more specifically, the dispersal of centralized power they generally entail. Meanwhile, theories of development present some compelling arguments for how peer talk might support the writing process, with the Vygotskian perspective in particular suggesting the benefits of a more richly interactive classroom environment than that provided by the traditional, teacher-dominated norm. To bring together the experience of practitioners and the vision of theory, research is needed that not only provides more information about what goes on in various types of peer interactions but also fosters conceptually grounded understandings of how peer dynamics can support the larger goals of writing instruction.

In thinking about peer talk in support of writing development, we need first to delineate the larger rationale for engaging peers in the process of giving and receiving feedback. The Vygotskian view of writing as a deeply social, necessarily flexible act can not only inform empirical explorations of peer response to writing but can also help practitioners productively reframe their concerns about the role of peer dynamics in the teaching-learning process. Where use of peer response is not accompanied by a philosophic shift that suggests the benefits of peers' working and talking together in a manner that is at once academically serious and supported by the peer structure, writing instructors will always feel frustrated at the failure of peers to perfectly mirror the substance and style of teacher feedback. Learning to write is, of course, more than learning to write for a teacher, demanding as it does an ever-shifting, complex negotiation between writers and their particular audiences. Ironically, although this realization has prompted practitioners to introduce response groups into their classrooms, the tendency has been to undermine their potential by channeling peer dynamics toward teacher-mandated guidelines, thereby subtracting from the process the crucial element of student empowerment and denying group members authority to become decision-making writers and readers.

Ultimately, the success of peer response to writing lies in issues broader and deeper than the simple retention or surrender of teacher power. Indeed, a Vygotskian vision of individual development suggests a cooperative environment wherein power is productively shared—a classroom that could more properly be called a resource room, its teacher more properly a knowledgeable coach, its students more properly one another's colleagues. Learning in such an environment becomes less a matter of following teachers' directives and more a matter of teachers and students mutually engaged in talking and reading and writing, in giving and receiving feedback across varied audiences and at varied points in the writing process.

Because the classroom filled with student talk represents a marked departure from what has long been the American norm, it requires a revolution not only in the teacher's concept of language learning, but also in the home and school communities that shape students' ideas concerning what it means to be in school. The current interest in group learning notwithstanding, traditional attitudes hold powerful sway, inappropriate expectations constricting our sense of what is possible and most productive. A case in point is Emig's (1979) story of an evaluating administrator who postponed his visit to a classroom where students were talking in small groups, explaining to the teacher that he would return when she was "teaching"—teaching, that is, in the sense of lecturing and tightly controlling, strategies still most expected and therefore accepted, but of limited usefulness.

Peer response groups represent a step toward allowing student talk its due role in fostering the writing process, but, given the philosophical assumptions that still permeate most classrooms, such groups are but a small movement in this promising, still largely unrealized direction. Tensions abound between what groups are purported to offer and how practitioners frame them; too often, what is termed "peer interaction" amounts to little more than teacher-initiated, teacher-controlled episodes in which students follow explicit directives and take turns role-playing their instructor. At best, such interaction is a kind of conspiracy geared less toward communicating peer-to-peer than pleasing a teacher and thereby achieving satisfactory grades. Thus, in many classrooms where response groups are present, the gathering of chairs into small circles leaves the traditional conceptual landscape essentially untouched.

An occasional peer response episode does little to create a larger environment offering ongoing social supports for writers. As long as students are directed to share their work at a day and time arbitrarily deemed appropriate by a teacher, much of the recursive, organic nature of the writing process is obscured. Indeed, the isolated opportunities for peer talk that response groups offer may not always provide the most timely or effective support for developing writers. What if a student would rather read a given piece to a teacher? What if a student prefers to work alone? What if a student isn't ready to share a specimen of writing on the appointed day? What if response is needed earlier, as ideas are just beginning to form, as the first tentative words emerge?

Ideally, peer talk about writing should occur in an environment that is flexible and attentive to the role of individual differences and that fosters communication about issues of genuine significance to students—a workplace organized and guided by a teacher, but offering the writer opportunities to solicit feedback from peers as well as from the teacher in support of one's evolving, individual needs.

In a collaborative classroom, teaching springs free of its traditional connotations, shedding the urge to dominate in favor of a less intrusive monitoring and shaping. If peer interactions in support of the academic work of writing are to take root and flourish, they must be grounded in a theoretic foundation that embraces this distinctive vision of the teaching-learning process, which allows instructor and students to take their respective places as members of a diversified community of learners—dynamically interactive and, like the business of becoming a writer, forever in process.

The project presented or reported herein was performed pursuant to a grant from the Office of Educational Research and Improvement/Department of Education (OERI/ED), Center for the Study of Writing. However, the opinions expressed herein do not necessarily reflect the position or policy of the OERI/ED, and no official endorsement by the OERI/ED should be inferred. The authors would like to thank Vera John-Steiner and the anonymous reviewers who contributed substantially to the final version of this manuscript.

REFERENCES

Abercrombie, M. L. J. (1960). *The anatomy of judgement: An investigation into the processes of perception and reasoning.* New York: Basic Books.

Argyle, M. (1976). Social skills theory. In V. L. Allen (Ed.), *Children as teachers: Theory and research on tutoring* (pp. 57–73). New York: Academic Press.

Au, K. (1980). Participation structures in a reading lesson with Hawaiian children: Analysis of a culturally appropriate instructional event. *Anthropology and Education Quarterly, 11,* 91–115.

Au, K., & Jordon, C. (1981). Teaching reading to Hawaiian children: Finding a culturally appropriate solution. In H. Treuba, G. Guthrie, & K. Au (Eds.), *Culture and the bilingual classroom: Studies in classroom ethnography* (pp. 139–152). Rowley, MA: Newbury House.

Au, K., & Kawakami, A. (1984). Vygotskian perspectives on discussion processes in small-group reading lessons. In P. Peterson, L. C. Wilkinson, & M. Hallinan (Eds.), *The social context of instruction: Group organization and group processes* (pp. 209–225). Orlando, FL: Academic Press.

Au, K., & Mason, J. (1983). Cultural congruence in classroom participation structures: Achieving a balance of rights. *Discourse Processes, 6,* 145–167.

Barnes, D., Britton, J., & Rosen, H. (1969). *Language, the learner, and the school.* Harmondsworth, England: Penguin.

Barnes, D., & Todd, F. (1977). *Communication and learning in small groups.* London and Boston: Routledge & Kegan Paul.

Barnes, D., & Todd, F. (1981). Talk in small learning groups: Analysis of strategies. In C. Adelman (Ed.), *Uttering, muttering: Collecting, using and reporting talk for social and educational research* (pp. 69–77). London: Grant McIntyre.

Beaven, M. (1977). Individualized goal setting, self-evaluation, and peer evaluation. In C. Cooper & L. Odell (Eds.), *Evaluating writing: Describing, measuring, judging* (pp. 135–156). Urbana, IL: National Council of Teachers of English.

Berkenkotter, C. (1984). Student writers and their sense of authority over texts. *College Composition and Communication, 35*(3), 312–319.

Brannon, L., & Knoblauch, C. H. (1984). A philosophical perspective on writing centers and the teaching of writing. In G. Olson (Ed.), *Writing centers: Theory and administration* (pp. 36–47). Urbana, IL: National Council of Teachers of English.

Britton, J., Burgess, A., Martin, N., McLeod, A., & Rosen, H. (1975). *The development of writing abilities (11–18).* London: Macmillan Education.

Bruffee, K. (1973). Collaborative learning: Some practical models. *College English, 34,* 579–586.

Bruffee, K. (1978). The Brooklyn plan: Attaining intellectual growth through peer-group tutoring. *Liberal Education, 64,* 447–468.

Bruffee, K. (1984). Peer tutoring and the "conversation of mankind." *College English, 46,* 635–652.

Bruffee, K. (1985). *A short course in writing* (3rd ed.). Boston: Little, Brown.

Bruner, J. (1978). The role of dialogue in language acquisition. In A. Sinclair (Ed.), *The child's conception of language* (pp. 241–256). New York: Springer-Verlag.

Bruner, J. (1985). Vygotsky: A historical and conceptual perspective. In J. Wertsch (Ed.), *Culture, communication, and cognition* (pp. 21–34). Cambridge, England: Cambridge University Press.

Buckholdt, D., & Wodarski, J. (1978). The effects of different reinforcement systems on cooperative behaviors exhibited by children in classroom contexts. *Journal of Research and Development in Education, 12,* 50–68.

Calfee, R., Cazden, C., Duran, R., Griffin, M., Martus, M., & Willis, H. (1981). *Designing reading instruction for cultural minorities: The case of the Kamehameha Early Education Program.* New York: Ford Foundation, Division of Education and Research.

Cazden, C. (1979). Peekaboo as an instructional model: Discourse development at home and at school. *Papers and Reports on Child Language Development, 17,* 1–19.

Cazden, C. (1986). Classroom discourse. In M. C. Wittrock (Ed.), *Handbook of research on teaching* (3rd ed., pp. 432–463). New York: Macmillan.

Chafe, W. (Ed.). (1980). *The pear stories: Cultural, cognitive, and linguistic aspects of narrative production.* Norwood, NJ: Ablex.

Cooper, C. R., Marquis, A., & Ayers-Lopez, S. (1982). Peer learning in the classroom: Tracing developmental patterns and consequences of children's spontaneous interactions. In L. C. Wilkinson (Ed.), *Communicating in the classroom* (69–89). New York: Academic Press.

Corsaro, W. A. (1985). *Peer friendship in the nursery school.* Norwood, NJ: Ablex.

Daiute, C., & Dalton, B. (in press). "Let's brighten up a bit": Collaboration and cognition in writing. In B. Rafoth and D. Rubin (Eds.), *The social construction of written communication.* Norwood, NJ: Ablex.

Damon, W. (1984). Peer education: The untapped potential. *Journal of Applied Psychology, 5,* 331–343.

Dickinson, D. (1986). Cooperation, collaboration, and a computer: Integrating a computer into a first-second grade writing program. *Research in the Teaching of English, 20,* 357–378.

Doise, W., & Mugny, G. (1981). *Le développement social de l'intelligence.* Paris: Interéditions.

Durling, R., & Schick, C. (1976). Concept attainment by pairs and individuals as a function of vocalization. *Journal of Educational Psychology, 68,* 83–91.

Dyson, A. H. (1987). Unintentional helping in the primary grades: Writing in the children's world (Tech. Rep. No. 2). Berkeley, CA: Center for the Study of Writing. Also to appear in B. A. Rafoth & D. L. Rubin (Eds.), *The social construction of written communication.* Norwood, NJ: Ablex.

Dyson, A. H. (1988). Drawing, talking, and writing: Rethinking writing development (Occasional Paper No. 3). Berkeley, CA: Center for the Study of Writing.

Elbow, P. (1973). *Writing without teachers.* London: Oxford University Press.

Elbow, P. (1981). *Writing with power.* London: Oxford University Press.

Emig, J. (1979). Non-magical thinking: Presenting writing developmentally in schools. In C. Frederiksen & J. Dominic (Eds.), *Writing: The nature, development and teaching of written communication* (Vol. 2, pp. 21–30). Hillsdale, NJ: Erlbaum.

Flower, L. (1979). Writer-based prose: A cognitive basis for problems in writing. *College English, 41,* 19–37.

Forman, E., & Cazden, C. (1985). Exploring Vygotskian perspectives in education: The cognitive value of peer interaction. In J. Wertsch (Ed.), *Culture, communication, and cognition: Vygotskian perspectives* (pp. 323–347). Cambridge, England: Cambridge University Press.

Freedman, S. W. (1987a). *Peer response in two ninth-grade classrooms.* (Tech. Rep. No. 12). Berkeley, CA: Center for the Study of Writing.

Freedman, S. W. (1987b). *Response to student writing* (Research Report No. 23). Urbana, IL: National Council of Teachers of English.

Freedman, S. W., & Bennett, J. (1987). *Peer groups at work in two writing classrooms* (Grant No. OERI-G-008690004). Washington, DC: Office of Educational Research and Improvement.

Gebhardt, R. (1980). Teamwork and feedback: Broadening the base of collaborative writing. *College English, 42,* 69–74.

Genishi, C., & DiPaolo, M. (1982). Learning through argument in a preschool. In L. C. Wilkinson (Ed.), *Communicating in the classroom* (pp. 49–68). New York: Academic Press.

Gere, A. R. (1987). *Writing groups: History, theory and implications.* Carbondale: Southern Illinois University Press.

Gere, A. R., & Abbot, R. D. (1985). Talking about writing: The language of writing groups. *Research in the Teaching of English, 19,* 362–379.

Gere, A. R., & Stevens, R. (1985). The language of writing groups: How oral response shapes revision. In S. W. Freedman (Ed.), *The acquisition of written language: Response and revision* (pp. 85–105). Norwood, NJ: Ablex.

Graner, M. (1987). Revision workshops: An alternative to peer editing groups. *English Journal, 76*(3), 40–45.

Greenfield, P. M. (1984). A theory of the teacher in the learning activities of everyday life. In B. Rogoff & J. Lave (Eds.), *Everyday cognition: Its development in social context* (pp. 117–138). Cambridge, MA: Harvard University Press.

Hairston, M. (1982). The winds of change: Thomas Kuhn and the revolution in the teaching of writing. *College Composition and Communication, 33*(1), 76–88.

Hawkins, J., Sheingold, K., Gearhart, M., & Berger, C. (1982). Microcomputers in schools: Impact on the social life of elementary classrooms. *Journal of Applied Developmental Psychology, 3,* 361–373.

Hawkins, T. (1976). *Group inquiry techniques for teaching writing.* Urbana, IL: NCTE/ERIC.

Healy, M. K. (1980). *Using student writing response groups in the classroom.* Berkeley, CA: Bay Area Writing Project.

Heath, S. B. (1983). *Ways with words: Language, life, and work in communities and classrooms.* Cambridge, England: Cambridge University Press.

Hillocks, G., Jr. (1981). The response of college freshmen to 3 modes of instruction. *American Journal of Education, 89,* 373–395.

Hillocks, G., Jr. (1984). What works in teaching composition: A meta-analysis of experimental treatment studies. *American Journal of Education, 93,* 107–132.

Hillocks, G., Jr. (1986). *Research on written composition: New directions for teaching.* Urbana, IL: ERIC Clearinghouse on Reading and Communication Skills.

Johnson, D., & Johnson, R. (1979). Conflict in the classroom: Controversy and learning. *Review of Educational Research, 49,* 51–70.

Kuhn, T. (1963). *The structure of scientific revolutions.* Chicago: University of Chicago Press.

Labov, W. (1982). Competing value systems in inner-city schools. In P. Gilmore & A. A. Glatthorn (Eds.), *Children in and out of school* (pp. 148–171). Washington, DC: Center for Applied Linguistics.

Lamberg, W. (1980). Self-provided and peer-provided feedback. *College Composition and Communication, 31,* 63–69.

Larson, R. (1987). Review of *Research on written composition: New directions for teaching. College Composition and Communication, 38*(2), 207–211.

Leonard, S. A. (1917). *English composition as a social problem.* Boston: Houghton.

Levin, J., Reil, M., Rowe, R., & Boruta, M. (1985). Muktuk meets Jacuzzi: Computer networks and elementary school writers. In S. W. Freedman (Ed.), *The acquisition of written language: Response and revision* (pp. 160–171). Norwood, NJ: Ablex.

Macrorie, K. (1979). *Telling writing.* New York: Hayden.

Mehan, H. (1979). "What time is it, Denise?": Asking known information questions in classroom discourse. *Theory Into Practice, 28*(4), 285–294.

Michaels, S., & Foster, M. (1985). Peer-peer learning: Evidence from a student-run sharing time. In A. Jaggar & M. T. Smith-Burke (Eds.), *Observing the language learner* (pp. 143–158). Urbana, IL: NCTE/IRA.

Moffett, J. (1968). *Teaching the universe of discourse.* Boston: Houghton Mifflin.

Myers, G. (1986). Reality, consensus, and reform in the rhetoric of composition teaching. *College English, 48,* 154–171.

Newkirk, T. (1984). How students read student papers: An exploratory study. *Written Communication, 1*(3), 283–305.

Newman, D., Griffin, P., & Cole, M. (1984). Social constraints in laboratory and classroom. In B. Rogoff & J. Lave (Eds.), *Everyday cognition: Its development in social context* (pp. 172–193). Cambridge, MA: Harvard University Press.

Ninio, A., & Bruner, J. (1977). The achievement and antecedents of labeling. *Journal of Child Language, 5,* 1–15.

Nystrand, M. (1986). Learning to write by talking about writing: A summary of research on intensive peer review in expository writing instruction at the University of Wisconsin-Madison. In M. Nystrand (Ed.), *The structure of written communication* (pp. 179–211). Orlando, FL: Academic Press.

Nystrand, M., & Brandt, D. (in press). Response to writing as a context for learning to write. In C. Anson (Ed.), *The discourse of commentary* [working title]. Urbana, IL: National Council of Teachers of English.

Palincsar, A. S., & Brown, A. L. (1984). Reciprocal teaching of comprehension-fostering and monitoring activities. *Cognition and Instruction, 1*(2), 117–175.

Perl, S., & Wilson, N. (1986). *Through teachers' eyes: Portraits of writing teachers at work.* Exeter, NH: Heinemann.

Perret-Clermont, A. N. (1980). *Social interaction and cognitive development in children.* New York: Academic Press.

Peterson, P., & Wilkinson, L. C. (1984). Instructional groups in the classroom: Organization and processes. In P. Peterson, L. C. Wilkinson, & M. Hallinan (Eds.), *The social context of instruction: Group organization and group processes* (pp. 3–12). Orlando, FL: Academic Press.

Peterson, P., Wilkinson, L. C., & Hallinan, M. (Eds.). (1984). *The social context of instruction: Group organization and group processes.* Orlando, FL: Academic Press.

Peterson, P., Wilkinson, L. C., Spinelli, F., & Swing, S. (1984). Merging the process-product and the sociolinguistic paradigms: Research on small-group processes. In P. Peterson, L. C. Wilkinson, &

M. Hallinan (Eds.), *The social context of instruction: Group organization and group processes* (pp. 125–152). Orlando, FL: Academic Press.

Piaget, J. (1959). *The language and thought of the child* (3rd ed., M. Gabain, Trans.). London: Routledge and Kegan Paul.

Piaget, J. (1970). Piaget's theory. In P. H. Mussen (Ed.), *Carmichael's manual of child psychology* (3rd ed., Vol. 1, pp. 703–732). New York: Wiley.

Reil, M. (1985). The Computer Chronicles Newswire: A functional learning environment for acquiring literacy skills. *Journal of Educational Computing Research, 1*(3), 317–337.

Rogoff, B., & Gardner, W. (1984). Adult guidance of cognitive development. In B. Rogoff & J. Lave (Eds.), *Everyday cognition: Its development in social context* (pp. 95–116). Cambridge, MA: Harvard University Press.

Rorty, R. (1979). *Philosophy and the mirror of nature.* Princeton, NJ: Princeton University Press.

Sharan, S. (1980). Cooperative learning in small groups: Recent methods and effects on achievement, attitudes and ethnic relations. *Review of Educational Research, 50,* 241–271.

Sharan, S. (1984). *Cooperative learning.* Hillsdale, NJ: Erlbaum.

Sieber, T. (1979). Classmates as workmates: Informal peer activity in the elementary school. *Anthropology and Education Quarterly, 10*(4), 207–235.

Slavin, R. E. (1980). Cooperative learning. *Review of Educational Research, 50,* 315–342.

Spear, K. (1984). Promoting cognitive development in the writing center. In G. Olson (Ed.), *Writing centers: Theory and administration* (pp. 62–76). Urbana IL: National Council of Teachers of English.

Steinberg, Z., & Cazden, C. (1979). Children as teachers of peers and ourselves. *Theory Into Practice, 18*(4), 258–266.

Vygotsky, L. S. (1978). *Mind in society.* Cambridge, MA: Harvard University Press.

Vygotsky, L. S. (1981). The genesis of higher mental functions. In J. V. Wertsch (Ed.), *The concept of activity in Soviet psychology* (pp. 144–188). Armonk, NY: Sharpe.

Vygotsky, L. S. (1986). *Thought and language* (Alex Kozulin, Trans.). Cambridge, MA: MIT Press.

Webb, N. (1982). Student interaction and learning in small groups. *Review of Educational Research, 52,* 421–445.

Wertsch, J. (1979a). From social interaction to higher psychological processes: A clarification and application of Vygotsky's theory. *Human Development, 22,* 1–22.

Wertsch, J. (1979b). The regulation of human action and the given-new organization of private speech. In G. Zivin (Ed.), *The development of self-regulation through private speech* (pp. 79–98). New York: Wiley.

Wertsch, J., & Stone, C. (1985). The concept of internalization in Vygotsky's account of the genesis of higher mental functions. In J. Wertsch (Ed.), *Culture, communication, and cognition* (pp. 162–179). Cambridge, England: Cambridge University Press.

Wiener, H. S. (1986). Collaborative learning in the classroom: A guide to evaluation. *College English, 48,* 52–61.

Witte, S. (1987). Review of *Research on written composition: New directions for teaching. College Composition and Communication, 38*(2), 207–211.

Wong-Fillmore, L. (1976). *The second time around: Cognitive and social strategies in second language learning.* Unpublished doctoral dissertation, Stanford University, Stanford, CA.

5

Habits of Mind: Historical Configurations of Textual Ownership in Peer Writing Groups

CANDACE SPIGELMAN

Recently I came across the following entry in one of my student's journals: "I like the writing groups, but I don't use the advice because then the paper would not be *my own*. I feel that my writing is *my writing* and should not be based upon what advice is given by others" (emphasis added). Barbara was one of the best students in my basic writing class that semester. In her essays, she raised intelligent questions, and she took a great deal of pride in her writing and in her grades. During peer groups, both small groups and one-on-one, she actively participated, providing serious readings of her peers' texts as well as thoughtful commentary. So her comments came as a surprise to me. If she valued peer comments and if she gave them herself, why would she not want to use peer feedback to improve her own writing? Where do students get their understanding of what it means to "own" one's text? How do these beliefs shape their practices in writing groups?

In this paper I want to argue that students' attitudes about authorship and intellectual property rights are, among other things, evidence of certain cultural "habits of mind," habits which are shaped throughout their lifetimes and which they bring to their interpretations of the writing group experience. To understand these habits, I first look at Western historical influences that have contributed to current concepts of textual ownership. Writing groups, I believe, mirror the tensions between the public and the private, the individual and the communal, that occur in every sphere when the question of intellectual property arises. By examining historically the complex, deeply enmeshed relationship between the reading (and writing) public and the writer for control of the text, I show that the tensions that arise from this relationship emerge across cultural periods. However, at different times, in response to specific economic and social conditions, either an individual or a communal perspective will seem to dominate.

I begin with an historical overview of perceptions of literary products as public and/or private property and then explore conflicts in legal notions of textual ownership relating to the "fiction" of private labor in the debate over

From *College Composition and Communication*, vol. 49, no. 2, 1998, pp. 234–55.

copyright and the "problem" of the idea/expression dichotomy in American Constitutional law. Much of my discussion focuses on values and practices of students in one writing group in a first-year composition class at a branch campus of Penn State University. This material comes from a larger, more comprehensive case study describing four student writers as they attempted to negotiate the public and private demands of textual production during their peer group meeting.[1]

In this essay, I interweave themes relating to the history of authorship and intellectual property with observations and quotations from student writers in an effort to mark the resonance between the tensions implicit in Western cultural values relating to textual ownership and the beliefs and behaviors of the writing group members. At the same time, the students' responses to their writing group situation provide a helpful lens through which to review the historical development of intellectual property as well as to think about its implications for writing group pedagogy.

COMPETING WORLD VIEWS OF TEXTUAL OWNERSHIP

We tend to think of the long "pre-modern" era as a time when ideas and even texts themselves were generally not represented by a single author's name, when literary plots and intellectual arguments circulated in the public domain. From the Classical period through the Middle Ages and into the Renaissance, the author, when identified at all, was recognized as only one of many who took part in the production and circulation of a composition (Woodmansee, "On the Author Effect" 15).[2] But amidst this active public circulation of ideas, writers nevertheless seem to have possessed a particular notion of textual ownership, understood even then as an investment in or "claim" to one's writing as an object of pride and personal achievement. Ancient Greek and Roman critics insisted that writers openly acknowledge their sources, and those who imitated without crediting their models were denounced (White 3–19).[3] Furthermore, in late medieval England and on into the 16th century, the circulation of literary material among colleagues was balanced by a justifiable anxiety that a fellow writer would copy one's work and claim it as his or her own (Shaw 327). And as early as 1590, English writers sought to preserve their manuscripts in their original form by having them printed before selling them, since subsequent owners could introduce modifications (Feather 471). At a time when it was not easy to think of ideas as having a solid, commodifiable form or to imagine them as private and personal possessions, writers were investing in and protecting their works *as if they were* products of autonomous achievement.

If indeed writers have always felt a powerful sense of ownership about their work, then perhaps the "communal" pre-modern literary climate was more complex than we generally suppose. For what we find in this earlier time, before widespread literacy and printing gave authors a viable means of earning a living, is a definition of "ownership" that permits both the public and the author to claim the written text, albeit in different and uneven ways: the primary writer may incorporate ideas from the community, from other writers, and once the text is circulated, readers may likewise adapt it to their purposes; at the same time, the writer exerts a countervailing pressure to possess the text and to retain ultimate control over it.

In contrast to the communal notion of authorship that dominates our image of the literary climate in the pre-print period, after Gutenberg it is the image of the individual, first as "author-producer" and, later, as "authorial-genius," that ultimately achieves center stage.[4] But it is important to recognize that such "modern" developments as print technology, widespread literacy, and capitalist economics do not reduce the tension between the public and the private. Rather, they change the way that writers and textual ownership are perceived. With the early modern period, the products of intellectual labor became commodities that an "owner" might exchange for social and material goods. It would be quite some time, however, before the owner and the author were collapsed into one: for much of the long history of "authorship," few writers could hope to make a living as "professional authors." Generally, writers quickly sold their manuscripts for a one-time payment, and profits were realized by those who could reproduce and circulate them swiftly and cheaply (Lunsford and Ede, *Singular* 80–81).

However, in the Anglo-American tradition, the lengthy process of commodifying intellectual property eventually gave the writer the status of autonomous and private "creator," or "author."[5] From the Romantic poets onward, authors have been esteemed for their separation from rather than collaboration with others—although during the Romantic period itself, the notion of the autonomous author-genius was not reflective of actual writing practices, which continued (and continue) to be corporate and collaborative.[6] Nevertheless, the myth of private authorship retains a cherished hold on our popular literary world view.

Yet, recent developments in electronic technology such as the Internet, with its public bulletin boards, email, hypertext, and other forms of reader/writer interaction have the potential to once again blend the lines between public and private intellectual property. In college labs, networked systems enable students to engage in ongoing conversations with their classmates and instructors. In addition, software packages that provide for interactive conferencing allow students to actively collaborate in—that is, help to write—each other's papers. At the same time, while web sites make information easily accessible, there is growing debate about whether and how technological networks should be owned and controlled.[7] Postmodern technology will perhaps change our world view once again, but this newer communal view of textual ownership must necessarily reflect our ways of thinking about authors and texts for the last 300 years.

NEGOTIATING COMPETING WORLD VIEWS IN WRITING GROUPS

With its emphasis on the communal aspects of textual ownership, writing group theory reflects an urge to reproduce the public side of pre-print literary production, free of the cumbersome pull of the author's desire. At the same time, student writers and readers, who are immersed in a world view colored by a significantly evolved history of commercial and literary practices, will obviously bring these notions of authorship and ownership to the group process as well. Certainly such tensions were at work shaping the world views of the four students whom I observed, who appeared to be perpetually trying to balance and accommodate a number of contradictory perspectives.

Prior to the study, the student participants—Andrew, Lori, Julie, and Edward—had worked in several different writing groups and had also served as reader-responders in one-on-one peer exchange. Lori, Julie, and Edward were white, traditional-aged, first-year students. Edward had been born in Russia but spoke English fluently. The three first-year students had all taken a basic writing course during the previous semester. Andrew, an African-American student, was a twenty-two-year-old junior who had transferred to the campus to pursue a baccalaureate degree after three years at another university.

From their interview comments and by their actions on the videotape of the group meeting, it was clear that Andrew, Lori, Julie, and to some degree Edward came to the writing group *expecting* to share and pool ideas. Their definitions of effective peer groups anticipated a conception of peer texts as public, exchangeable documents, and their list of criteria underscored their expectations that group members would provide comprehensive, helpful advice. According to this view, peers must, first of all, listen to the content of each other's papers. Andrew explained that group members must be "honest, and you can't be afraid to hurt somebody's feelings because, in the long run, you're trying to help them get a better grade." Lori pointed out that an effective peer reader "notices" and having read a peer's paper, "knows what kind of point you're trying to make." When group members don't understand a writer's point, Lori said, they must raise questions about it.

The participants also believed that peers must work together to generate useful ideas for individual essays. Julie defined an effective group as one in which "people listen to your paper and actually give you . . . suggestions. Like when you're reading, they'll point out something and say, 'How 'bout you say this instead.'" At the same time, Lori wanted the peer group to help the writer to conform to the demands of the assignment itself as well as to the demands of standard written English: "Once you read your paper [aloud], them giving you suggestions and telling you, like, where you need to fix things, like, where you have errors and where you need to be fixed." Writers, as Lori saw it, should naturally accept "contributions" from the group as these suggestions benefit the individual's paper. According to these students, then, writing groups demonstrate the value of group invention by providing avenues for the writer's thinking and writing, and they expected textual exchange and appropriation to be integral to writing group dynamics.

At the same time, the students appreciated their own creative efforts. That is, at least within this particular peer group context, they recognized themselves as "authors" who brought their own personal insights to their work, and who ultimately would be graded for their individual efforts.[8] In his interview, as Andrew explained his writing process, he characterized himself as an "author":

> I try to [think] a whole lot about what I'm saying. . . . I try to talk my paper, like when a reader reads it, it's like I'm talking to them. . . . So I try to keep it, like a constant, like a nice little rhythm going. I usually only use words that I usually speak . . . I usually try to not use too many big words . . . [and I] always, always get into character.

By writing, Andrew established authority over his text. As he saw it, his choices of what to include and what to omit were based on his intentions and his knowledge of what would be effective in a particular case. Likewise, Edward emphasized his role as autonomous decision-maker following a peer group session. In order to decide which suggestions to include and which to ignore, Edward explained, "I'll read the paper over again, and then I'll take the suggestions and work with them. I'll write another paragraph, and I'll see if it goes." As a writer, Edward decided about his essay's content: "If it works, I'll use it; if it doesn't, I will not use it."

Edward's and Andrew's strong sense of textual authority contrasted with the more tentative perspectives of Julie and Lori. In response to the question, "Do you have a sense of your paper being taken over if the teacher or tutor or someone else asks you to make . . . changes?" Julie asserted, "No, because usually when I write a paper out, when I start off writing a paper, I'm not too sure. Like I know that there is something missing in my paper or, you know what I mean, it's not perfect. . . . I'm usually going into it with a little bit of difficulty, and I always need that suggestion."

Lori's response suggested more confidence in herself as a writer who could both consider and evaluate her peers' suggestions. For example, she said that she appreciated when the members of the writing group helped to provide "other suggestions I didn't think of on my own, . . . and they'll have a different view or they'll think in a different way and that's good to add into your paper." When Lori "added in" her peers' analysis of a reading, she weighed their arguments against her own and determined their value and relevance to her essay. However, as we noted above, Lori valued group feedback for indicating "where you need to fix things, like where you have errors and where you need to be fixed." Such metaphors suggest that Lori envisioned her writing (and perhaps herself) as somewhat damaged and in need of repair.

In this peer group, the students made a valiant effort to place their texts in the public domain, to appropriate and to be appropriated, at the same time that they retained their roles as autonomous writers who would submit their essays as individual projects and who would be evaluated accordingly. Operating within a dialectical situation, Julie, Lori, Andrew, and Edward attempted to straddle and accommodate competing world views by constructing two worlds simultaneously: in one, they were collaborators, shared owners in the production of their peers' drafts; in the other, they were solitary "authors," soliciting feedback from helpful peers. More than they realized, these writing group members were re-enacting the tensions that emerge in the gap between the public and private world views of every literary era. They dramatize that these conflicts are never fully reconciled: the outcome is always dialectical and the question of ownership continually unresolved. This dialectic will become increasingly visible in the peer group portions relating to intellectual labor and academic integrity that follow.

THE LEGAL DISCOURSE OF PRIVATE INTELLECTUAL LABOR

The modern notion of the author as a singular individual who holds both a personal and a financial investment in his or her work was influenced to some degree by various legal arguments surrounding copyright, in the discourse of the author's labor. Although these arguments provide an interpretive framework for understanding students' notions of textual ownership, I want to stress from the start that, aside from some general sense that each published book has a copyright, few students bring to the composition classroom any familiarity with the history of copyright legislation. However, they do harbor certain assumptions regarding the relationship between the writer's intellectual activities and his or her text as property, a notion that has roots in the legal discourse of the debate over copyright.

As it was argued in 18th-century England, this debate between London and provincial booksellers was primarily a suit to control the rights to reproduce and distribute literary property.[9] Within the discourse of the copyright arguments, there was no question of the author's ownership of his pen and ink manuscript or right to sell that manuscript for a pre-determined fee (Rose 54–5). (In this section, I deliberately use the male pronoun to reflect the perspective of the period in which these debates were waged.) But the copyright issue turned on a different conception of ownership entirely: the concept of ideas as intellectual property. And while the copyright question was economic in principle, it contributed to the literary notion of authorship that we sustain today. Briefly, a series of legal cases tested the validity and limits of what is considered the first copyright act, the 1709 Statute of Anne. This statute dramatically restricted the power of the London booksellers, who had held, in effect, a perpetual monopoly on valuable books. As a result, when their copyrights began to run out, they sought to overturn the restrictions of the Statute of Anne on a case-by-case basis. In bringing suit, the tactic used by both the London booksellers and their opponents, booksellers in the provinces who wanted access to profitable works, was to invoke the rights of authors.[10]

Of particular interest are the legal arguments the London booksellers derived from Locke's *Two Treatises of Government*.[11] According to Locke, a person's body is naturally his own property, as are the things his body produces through labor. The London booksellers argued their case by focusing on the fundamental right of the author to own intellectual property just as a landowner owned the products of his harvest.[12] In the process, they solidified the view of the author's work as his personal possession by virtue of his intellectual labor. At the same time, the concept of the text was altered: now not only the pen and ink manuscript, but also its ideas, and eventually its style, attained exchange value and became linked inextricably with the rightful property of the author.

Arguments for the author as proprietor contributed to a view of writing as solitary intellectual work, but as I have tried to show, it changed nothing about the actual production of written texts, which have always, directly or indirectly, borne the influence of other texts and other "writers." In fact, as we will see below, the ways in which one text influences another continues to be the crucial "flip side" of copyright discussion, invoking as it does the critical necessity of public access to "protected" works for generating new ideas and new texts. Equally significant, copyright arguments have always unproblematically assumed a one-to-one correspondence between the single author and his or her work, as Ede and Lunsford have so clearly illustrated in *Singular Texts/Plural Authors*. It is ironic, but telling, that Wordsworth, whose own work was so greatly influenced by his collaboration with Coleridge, actively lobbied for the extension of copyright laws on the grounds that the author genius is entitled to financial security as he labors to produce original works for posterity (Woodmansee and Jaszi, "Law" 770–71).

The writing group events described below dramatize the inescapability of collaborative influence. At the same time, they alert us to the "dream" of writing as private, autonomous labor in which the discourse of the early copyright arguments was grounded, and which remains inscribed in the values of developing student writers. Like copyright lawyers, the writing group participants invested textual ownership in the notion of labor. But because they had to confront the fact that in practice intellectual labor may be both shared and private, when they attempted to measure textual ownership by the level of labor invested in the production of a particular text, they ended up telling competing "stories" of their composing processes. At times, they invoked a discourse of shared labor to talk about their contributions to the making of meaning in their peer's essays. At other moments, their discursive constructions undermined notions of multiple-authorship and refocused on the individually authored and individually owned text.

THE DISCOURSE OF INTELLECTUAL LABOR IN PEER WRITING GROUPS

The historical construct of the author as private laborer/owner must inevitably conflict with the public concept of labor implicit in writing group theory, which calls upon students to create their own essays in an atmosphere of oral and written exchange. In this study, the writing group operated within a multilayered, intertextual context: as part of their essay assignment, the students were required to reflect on their assigned readings; they also had recourse to both small-group and whole-class discussion of these readings, and in the case of Julie and Lori, the benefit of each other's initial drafts on the same topic.[13]

Yet, when asked to explain their beliefs about textual ownership, the students repeatedly invoked the Lockean concept of private intellectual labor. Edward, for example, said that he felt a strong "sense of ownership" about his essay, "My Language," because he had "done all of the work for it. It was completely mine, thought by me and written by me." Andrew stressed the time

and effort involved in composing his papers and the sense of personal investment he felt when a draft was finished. He "owned" his essay, he explained,
by virtue of the labor involved in its production:

> Of course [I own it]. That goes without saying . . . Just for the simple fact
> that the time and effort that you put in the paper, you know . . . Anything
> you put your name on you should be proud of. So I mean, [after] all the
> hours that you take the time to write it, you want to think it's yours.

Yet these expressions of private property were noticeably absent when
the students described their active participation in the group, where their
equally-shared labor led to their expression of shared authorship of the working drafts. Here, group members were involved in discussion of a minor issue
of grammar in Edward's introductory paragraph. Edward had written "Did
you ever have a feeling in your stomach that wasn't right? When everything
just feels all different and you felt lost." The group collectively attempted to
revise the "offending" sentences for greater coherence and style.

> JULIE: For the first, "Did you ever have a feeling in your stomach that just
> wasn't right," then you don't have to put "when." You can just put "every-
> thing feels all different."
>
> EDWARD: After what? "Did you ever have that feeling in your stomach"?
> What should I do?
>
> JULIE: You just write . . . "Everything just feels," or something. It sounds like
> you're asking another question.
>
> EDWARD: "Feels different"?
>
> JULIE: Everything feels different to you.
>
> ANDREW: I think that is another question. I think you should keep the "when."
> He should put a question mark at the end of the sentence.

This discussion continued for several minutes as various group members
attempted to reword or rewrite the sentence. In the interviews, when the students described this writing group event, they repeatedly emphasized their
shared responsibility in the evolution of the text. Notice the dominance of the
pronoun "we" to express collective agency in Lori's follow-up session.

> See, *we* couldn't get the first two sentences right because there was two
> questions in a row, and *we* were trying to figure that out. It took so long
> to figure out what *we wanted*. Like if *we wanted* two questions or we
> wanted to make it one question. That's what we were trying to figure
> out. . . . We weren't sure if *we should put* a question mark. . . . Two separate
> questions *we ended up with*, I think, like, the way we had it. *We* couldn't
> figure out anything. (emphasis added)

Likewise, Julie explained, "*We* just tried to change it [Edward's wording],
but *we* kept it. I tried to change it. . . ." Later she added, "But then he didn't have
a question mark there, so *we made it* a question." In retelling the story, both students described Edward's paper as the group's possession. The group was in

charge of "get[ting] the first two sentences right." The concern was with what the group "wanted" (one question or two). Throughout the transaction, there was no mention of a single author; in fact, the students made no reference to Edward as author or authority over the sentences they are working with.

Significantly, expressions of collective labor and, therefore, collective authorship were not limited to editorial activities. One of the most productive efforts in the writing group session occurred as the students were helping Andrew develop paragraphs of support for his essay on multicultural societies. In the last paragraph of his rough draft, Andrew had written about his departure from an insulated African-American neighborhood for the multiethnic experience of college: "It was not until my freshman year at Drexel University that I was exposed to other nationalities, for Drexel University's enrollment was 7% minority." The students empathized with Andrew's experience and framed a series of questions to elicit his elaboration of detail. These questions began with Lori's asking, "After this part, 'I was exposed to nationalities,' like, how did that make you feel? Did you like that? How did you like being involved with other people?" Following Lori's lead, Julie and Edward enthusiastically formulated their own questions for Andrew to consider:

> JULIE: What was it . . . ? Yeah.
>
> ANDREW: It was a good thing, you know. It was different. You realize . . . growing up with only one type of people . . .
>
> EDWARD: Well, tell.
>
> JULIE [*writing*]: How were your feelings? What was different? How were you treated?
>
> [*Andrew writes*]
>
> EDWARD: And how did you treat others?
>
> JULIE [*writing*]: How did you treat others?
>
> LORI: Did you like the way you felt?

When the students were asked to explain this section of the videotape, both Lori and Julie described it as a shared activity. Lori said, "We told him to put an example in. He said, like, he went to a college where he was, like, the only black person, and we told him, like, 'How did that make him feel? Put an example of, like, what it made you feel and stuff.'" Julie also saw the effort as quite collective: "We're saying to use examples, like, how did he feel when he went to a different college? What was different? How was he treated? How did he treat others? Like, because he went to a predominantly black high school."

Finally, the videotape of both these sequences revealed a remarkable amount of writing by all the members of the group, not just the writer whose essay was at that moment before the group. In Edward's section, peer group members both spoke and wrote alternative sentence clusters in an attempt to rephrase the sentence under consideration. Likewise, Julie wrote out the list of questions that the group members had raised about Andrew's experience.

At the end of the session, they offered these written suggestions to the appropriate writer for future consideration. In this way, besides the work of generating sentences and ideas, peers shared in the actual physical labor of writing the revised draft.

The group members' assertions contrasted strikingly with the primary writer's description of the same events. In every case, the primary writer's discourse mirrored early copyright arguments: private ownership by reason of private labor. For example, Edward tried to minimize the group's investment in rewriting his sentences. The writing group, he explained, was "just helping me to decide, . . . [h]elping me make it stronger. Like this was just an idea. It wasn't anything. They're helping me make the sentence more meaningful." In Edward's telling, the writer retained ownership of the text. *Me* was distinguished from *they* as a separation that reinforced the ownership/assistance role. According to Edward, there were two "sides" to this discussion and it was the writer who finally chose which position to accept: "Like, they were deciding. Andrew wanted it to stay the same. Julie wanted to change it, so I was trying to [inaudible] an idea. I was sticking mostly with Andrew *since I wrote it that way.*"

Finally, as part of their assignment, the students were required to refer to one of their required readings. Although his peers had actively assisted Edward, by finding and explaining the appropriate reference, Edward downplayed the group's contribution: "I did not have me compared to . . . Rodriguez, which was the whole basis of it. I couldn't know how to do it, so Julie was just telling me, you know, how I can go about comparing myself, and then she offered me her group essay or quiz about the topic of Rodriguez that was there." Edward pointedly emphasized his own invention: "So I read that [the quiz document] real quick and got an idea that came out to be this [paragraph]. . . . I just made notes on my own paper and my draft, right here, and I just elaborated it right here [in the final draft]." In telling the story this way, he limited his peers' influence to the immediate present of the group meeting while the final draft resulted largely from his own efforts.

Likewise, in discussing changes to his paper, Andrew emphasized his status as the essay's author.

> ANDREW: Oh, before I started reading my paper, I told them I came into, like, a writer's block and I started the paragraph, but I didn't know if that was a good direction to go with or to. So when I asked for suggestions and they said, "Yeah, that's a good direction to go in. You want to include all these things in your story, or your personal narrative part, for the reader, just so they can understand.". . .
>
> CS: . . . Do you feel more comfortable with the paper now that you added those things in? . . . Do you feel closer to where you wanted to go initially?
>
> ANDREW: Yeah, I was hesitant. See they just helped me along my road.

Like a solitary traveler, Andrew asked for directions; his peers gave him assistance and advice, but they "just" helped out, confirming that his path was the right one.

Julie and Lori, too, underplayed the group's role in the production of their revised drafts, characterizing their peers as assistants, not co-writers. At her interview, Julie acknowledged unproblematically the intertextual dynamics that led to her revision. "Lori and I had the same topic," she explained, "so listening to her helped me, you know, jot down some ideas and put my paper in a better perspective." But when I suggested that she might have "used Lori's ideas," she became defensive, saying, "I *just* read over—just looking at her paper, you know, helped me realize [where] I was going. . . ." In light of the fact that Julie had made fundamental changes in her essay's central argument in response to her group's advice, her reactions were particularly telling.

The student writers appeared to be wary of what they saw as possible traps set by me, an authority figure (interviewer/instructor/representative of the university) who might secretly think they had done something wrong. Their deeply entrenched belief that private labor was the institutional test of authorship could be mitigated by assuring me that their peers were "just helping." But beyond this, the phrase "just helping" tended to secure for the writer primary ownership of the text by emphasizing his or her major contribution to the task of composition. At the same time, however, its invocation illuminates the tension between such perceptions and the students' actual behavior in their peer group, where the relationship between public and private labor was far more enmeshed.

THE IDEA/EXPRESSION DICHOTOMY IN LAW AND WRITING GROUPS

The discourse of the copyright debate, which stabilized the commonplace relationship between intellectual labor and private ownership, simultaneously invoked the name of the author to argue that the text was a public object and that restricting the legal terms of proprietorship would encourage the dissemination of cultural and learning. Although it was actually only a ploy to undermine the monopoly of the London Booksellers, the document that was to become the Statute of Anne was entitled "An Act for the Encouragement of Learning, by Vesting the Copies of Printed Books in the Authors or Purchasers of such Copies, during the Times therein mentioned." By suggesting that writers owned their texts for a limited duration, supporters of copyright attempted to elevate writers to the status of property owners, but at the same time, their arguments actually divested the text of its status as private property.[14] Within the original copyright debates were the twin concepts that form the base of American copyright legislation: that the author, as first creator, has a basic right to profit from and to protect his property; at the same time, that the public (which includes future writers) has a right to benefit from the dissemination of ideas in order to further learning and creative production.[15] In this way, the public derives the cultural benefit of the author's labor while the writer sustains sufficient financial security to make textual production worthwhile. At the same time, the legal authorization of "fair use," giving individuals limited access to documents that are protected by copyright, helps to promote the dissemination of ideas into the public sphere without penalizing the livelihood of writers, on the one hand, or scholars and future artists, on the other.

In order to accomplish this feat, American law sustains a rather complicated concept of what may justly fall within the domain of copyright protection. The so-called "idea/expression dichotomy" asserts that ideas are considered to be within the public domain while their expression may be protected as private property.[16] Splitting ideas from their expression, content from form, is a perplexing operation, and, in the real world of readers and writers, perhaps impossible, yet this distinction continues to operate in legal arguments. For the writing group participants, constructions of honest appropriation, as opposed to dishonest theft, often rested on their perceived ability to separate their words and the words of others from a particular formulation determined as "the writer's ideas." What is interesting about their approach is that it more closely resembles the legal distinctions in the idea/expression dichotomy of copyright law than it does contemporary academic rules for avoiding plagiarism, and yet it was understood by students in reference to the latter. That is, three of the students in the writing group employed the principles of copyright law (or the inverse of that law) in order to remain within the boundaries of what they understood as ethical academic scholarship.

In separating form from content or expression from ideas, copyright law differs from our common conception of literary borrowing or stealing, in which the unacknowledged appropriation of either ideas or words is deemed unacceptable. Plagiarism can and often does occur when the literary item is not copyrighted, and, in fact, the citation procedures that ensure academic honesty tend to be more rigid than those that apply to copyright legislation. In copyright, words alone are protected from appropriation without acknowledgment, but to avoid plagiarism both an author's "ideas" and his or her "wording" must be credited. In writing groups, students frequently reformulate each other's sentences, suggest additional arguments, and provide embellishments for an essay's development. To some degree, the transience of speech makes for a more flexible style of exchange. Because readers are present for oral interpretation and response, their suggestions to writers may be received as verbal offerings (gifts) or viewed as part of a communal pool of ideas. In either case, the rhetorical situation of the writing group may place readers' comments and even peers' essays outside the rigid parameters of traditional scholarly behavior. In these situations, theoretically, there should be no need for a distinction between form and content. Nevertheless, as I will illustrate, when students revise their papers, they frequently do distinguish between the use of ideas and expressions, based on their own varied interpretations of the "legal" and "ethical" requirements for what they take to be honest scholarship.

As Andrew saw it, writers demonstrate their integrity as they reshape ideas into their own words. It is the words themselves that make the artist, that demonstrate the work that has been done. Andrew felt that using another student's words "would make me feel like I didn't put the work or effort in myself." "When you take somebody else's [words]," he says, ". . . that shows no thought on your behalf." In addition, since a writer's or peer's words are his own possession, using them is a kind of theft. "You can use the idea to make it relate to your paper. But his words are his words. I mean that's—, might as well just cut and paste." Since ideas are appropriable but words are not, Andrew said, he must actively work with his peers' ideas to recast them in his own particular language.

Lori, too, distinguished between the ownership of ideas and words, and, like Andrew, used this as a determining criteria for ethical scholarly behavior. Lori explained that it was important to "put your own words down . . . because it's just your paper." Although Lori said that she found peer group activity very useful, her method of applying peer group suggestions was consistent with her belief that "it's your paper and you should have your own words":

> Well, I usually write them [peers' suggestions] down at the end of the paper, like, right when they say them so I won't forget. And then I'll try and fit them in where they will go when I revise the paper in the computer. When they tell me something, I'll write it down—just like a note, just so I know, and then I'll go home and, like, write it out more in, like, sentence form and then try and fit it in where it will fit.

Lori stressed that she "just make[s] a note" to simply jog her memory. Then she wrote it out in her own words "in sentence form." In other words, an idea became hers when she collapsed it as a note and then resurrected it in sentence form. It was now *her* idea in *her* sentence. In this process of reduction, she neutralized the suggestion to a non-possessable phenomenon (the idea), while the process of the addition of her own words made the written product hers alone.

Both Lori's and Andrew's investment in word choice sustained the legal notion that the author's "expression" is protected by law although its "idea" remains part of the common sphere. For Edward, on the other hand, the principle of the idea/expression dichotomy was reversed. Edward's responses in the following segment are illustrative of his position that original, independent ideas circumscribe the writer's domain, but the words he or she chooses are susceptible to any number of external alterations. I asked Edward about the sentence he had written to begin his fourth paragraph, "I can use Russian in situations where I wouldn't be comfortable using English." This sentence, which the writing group wanted clarified, appeared in his rough draft in his tutor's handwriting. Edward explained: "So my tutor suggested that in a sort of similar sayings: . . . sometimes I can use Russian . . . basically the same thing I said only worded it, . . . she worded it more effectively."

CS: . . . So these are really pretty much her words.

EDWARD: Her words, yes.

CS: Okay. Why is it okay to put her words here when we say that you can't use the words of others?

> EDWARD: Because her words came from my idea. . . . She didn't just say, "Why don't you say for your story, 'Sometimes I use Russian.'" She read my topic sentence and her being a professional, she can turn that into a better sentence.

Edward perceived a dramatic difference between the appropriation of others' words, in the form of reconfigured syntax, vocabulary, or grammar, and the appropriation of their ideas. The writer generates ideas (concepts, themes, arguments, relevant examples) while others—tutors, peers, and teachers—function in an editorial capacity, helping the writer achieve his or her original intention. As a non-native speaker of English, Edward's view that "fair use" included the adoption of others' words was certainly related to his own need to translate his ideas into a second language.[17]

Unlike her peers, who applied the copyright distinction between words and ideas, Julie invoked the ethics of academic scholarship by asserting that both ideas and words were off limits for direct appropriation. If peer group members suggested words or ideas for her paper, Julie said, she would "try to change it around and put it in my own words." According to Julie, in writing groups, students should benefit from the discussion of broad concepts, but they should not "steal" each other's ideas for papers. As an example of this process, Julie explained that in order to revise her essay, she used the talk and writing of her peer group to help her decide what she thought about the issue at hand. Their contributions, she asserted, made the topic more relevant and meaningful to her and gave her a perspective. As a result, she was able to "personalize" the topic and then to write about it.

Significantly, Andrew, Lori, and Edward invoked, in various forms, the distinctions between ideas and their expression so crucial to the arguments over authorship and textual ownership in the copyright debates of the 18th century and represented in American copyright law, at least until quite recently. For notwithstanding its economic motivations, intellectual property legislation seems, on the one hand, to have anticipated postmodern aesthetics, at least in its early recognition of importance of intertextuality and "influence" in artistic production. But, on the other hand, as Peter Jaszi points out, contemporary copyright law is also moving in the opposite direction: limiting public access to and use of both published and unpublished documents, extending the years a work is protected by copyright, and appealing to "moral rights" interpretations.[18] Once again, legal discourse is invoking the author-construct in the name of the author-genius. Yet, as Andrea Lunsford and Susan West make clear, recent judgments and proposed legislation designed to "protect" ostensible creators actually serve to inhibit public access and at the same time to protect the commercial (and the ideological) interests of large corporations and other third parties, who hold the rights to much of the intellectual property that is produced today (389–90). Owing to these recent changes, Lunsford and West underscore our discipline's need to be concerned with the debate surrounding the "ownership" of language and its implications for the public dissemination of information and ideas. Such findings, they stress, have significant implications for teachers of composition who work in an environment in which many of the questions of public and private converge.

CONCLUSION: THE DIALECTICS OF OWNERSHIP

Obviously, most first-year writing students do not develop their attitudes toward textual ownership out of a knowledge of legal issues or historical controversies concerning ownership and copyright. However, the positions so clearly framed in this debate and the subsequent legal decisions that emerged from it reflect a general discourse of ownership that has endured over centuries. Student writers do, indeed, think of themselves as textual "owners" (at least to the extent that they can think of themselves this way, given the competing urgencies of teacher evaluation and appropriation) because they "know" that writers "own" their texts. They may feel the urgency to hide or hoard their words, their thoughts, their ideas, in part because they fear fellow students will "steal" them, or because, in conceiving of their compositions as individually wrought objects, they have "forgotten" the role others may play in textual production. So complicit is popular sentiment with legal discourse that the "author's rights" argument seems almost commonplace and totally consistent with the attitudes of some of the students I interviewed for my research. Several confided that they planned their absences for peer review days so that their peers could not "steal" their ideas. One student was so fearful of intellectual theft that she would not discard her rough drafts in the trash receptacle in the public computer lab. Of course, students may also hide their compositions from their peers because they feel embarrassed or inadequate, and these issues too may have something to do with notions of textual ownership.

But another part of what I would call the continuing discourse of textual ownership involves its public side. As Lori, Andrew, Edward, and Julie demonstrated, students *do* share in writing groups as often as they do not. They read their essays aloud, and often they appropriate sections of each other's texts and refigure them in their own papers. This willingness to collaborate also comes out of an enduring, albeit unstable, conception of the product of the writer's labor as at once his or her own and, at the same time, under particular circumstances, appropriable by others. As this brief historical overview suggests, the phenomenon of textual ownership is always irredeemably dialectical. Nowhere is this clearer than in productive peer groups where students grapple with the various tensions that comprise the writing group context.

Teachers of composition who use peer groups might productively tap these tensions by organizing their first-year writing classes around the topics of intellectual property and textual ownership. Using their own essays as well as published texts, students might be encouraged to question the various historical, cultural, and institutional ways in which knowledge, understood as private and public intellectual property, has been defined and located. Questions might be raised about whether a text can be at once both private *and* communal property: whether it is possible for a student to retain a tentative hold on the text he or she has written and also effectively collaborate, under what conditions this might occur, and why we might want it to take place. Students might also articulate and investigate many of their own preconceived notions relating to conventions for attribution and scholarly appropriation. Such discussion would clarify these issues, helping students to see where their interpretations of academic conventions differ from the actual requirements of scholars using sources to investigate a field.[19] Students might consider their responsibility to peer ideas and, at the same time, consider situations in which the general discourse of a community renders acknowledgment unnecessary.[20] All in all, by investigating issues of intellectual property, students can be helped to develop more nuanced and productive theories of ownership than those unexamined theories or "habits of mind" that they bring to the writing group classroom.

NOTES

1. This series of case studies completed a year-long investigation of intellectual property issues involving observations of writing groups in three composition classes, surveys of 40 students, and 17 pilot-study interviews. During one semester, Edward, Andrew, Lori, and Julie, the case study subjects, allowed me to "follow" them through their writing classes. In addition to tapping their peer group meeting, each student participated in several individual interviews and provided me with copies of all their assigned papers as well as rough and final drafts, class notes, and meeting notes relating to the essays that were discussed in their peer group session.

2. In borrowing the topics and arguments developed by his predecessors and peers, Seneca can argue in *Letters* that he is "not pilfering them, as if they belonged to someone else . . . for they are common property." He adds further that "the best ideas are common property" and "whatever is well said by anyone is mine" (qtd. in White 7). Boccaccio, Chaucer, and Shakespeare did not acknowledge the sources of their productions, and we can assume that the audiences' familiarity with a work's plot and characters was central to their appreciation of it. Likewise, published writers, including Ben Jonson, routinely appropriated from their peers (Miller 86–87).

3. In *The Natural History*, Pliny the Elder states that the literary pirate has "the mark of a perverted mind . . . to prefer being caught in a theft to returning [that is, by acknowledgment] what we have borrowed" (qtd. In White 16).

4. Walter J. Ong argues that printing "encouraged human beings to think of their own interior consciousness and unconscious resources as more and more thing-like . . . to sense that its [their minds'] possessions were held in some sort of inert mental space" (120; see also Ross; Eisenstein).

5. In "The Genius and the Copyright: Economic and Legal Conditions of the Emergence of the 'Author,'" Martha Woodmansee traces the emergence of the concept of the author-genius to a reconfiguration of the concept of authorship by 18th-century German writers seeking legal protection for their intellectual labor. In England, on the other hand, the concept evolved instrumentally from the commercial interests of publishers, rather than writers (Rose; Jaszi "Toward a Theory"). Eventually, however, the "author" as originary genius and proprietor elided to produce what Woodmansee describes as "our modern fiction of the author as the sole creator [and owner] of unique, original works" ("Author Effect" 25; also see Kaplan).

6. According to Woodmansee, Samuel Johnson's major and lesser-known writings involved elements of the collective and collaborative, from appropriating parts of published articles to ghost writing sermons for colleagues ("Author Effect"). During and after the Romantic period, writers, including Coleridge and Wordsworth and Eliot and Pound, continued to share, borrow, and steal each other's work. In other situations, known writers, such as Keats and Dreiser, collaborated with less well-known "significant others" to produce texts for which they received sole credit. Finally, Coleridge apparently translated the writings of German philosophers and published the passages as his own "original" works. For a thorough account of the collaborative activities of novelists and playwrights, see Jack Stillinger's *Multiple Authorship and the Myth of Solitary Genius*. Thomas Mallon's *Stolen Words* provides examples of literary theft as well as "silent collaborations" among authors and scholars.

7. Martha Woodmansee and Peter Jaszi describe the legal-commercial complexities of electronic data technology in this way: "In short, a battle is shaping over the future of the Internet and its successors. On one side are those who see its potential as a threat to traditional notions of individual proprietorship in information and who perceive vigorous extension of traditional copyright principles to the new information environment as the solution. On the other side are those who believe that the network environment could become a new cultural 'commons' if its development is not stifled by premature or excessive legal controls" ("Law" 779–80). In September 1995, the National Information Infrastructure Task Force's Working Group on Intellectual Property Rights delivered their report (termed the "White Paper"), and subsequently, the NII Copyright Protection Act of 1995 was introduced in Congress. The report suggests that copyright violation could be broadly applied to browsing and/or using on-screen documents and suggests extreme limits on "fair use." For a detailed description of these developments, including impressive intervention by the Digital Future Coalition (with representation from NCTE, CCC, and MLA), see Andrea Lunsford and Susan West. The Association of Research Libraries in conjunction with The Coalition for Networked Information reports progress on congressional activities at http://arl.cni.org/info /frn/copy/frncopy. html. In December 1996 and again in March 1997, members of the World Intellectual Property Organization (WIPO), which includes the United States, met at a diplomatic conference in Geneva to consider proposals for updating copyright laws relating to electronic technology. A meeting addressing intellectual property in databases is scheduled for September 1997. In the meantime, the WIPO, in cooperation with the Ministry of Education and Culture in Spain, will hold an International Forum on The Exercise and Management of Copyright and Neighboring Rights in the Face of the Challenges of Digital Technology in mid-May. The DFC may be contacted at dfc@alawash.org and at http://www.ari.net/dfc.

8. Andrea Lunsford and Lisa Ede argue that despite the efforts of some teachers to engender a collaborative approach, "day-to-day writing instruction in American colleges and universities still reflects traditional assumptions about the nature of the self (autonomous), the concept of authorship (as ownership of singly-held property rights) and the classroom environment (hierarchical, teacher centered)" ("Collaborative Authorship" 425). However, care must be taken not to press too far in the opposite direction. Writing classes have long been sites of textual appropriation rather than textual investment, owing to the power relations of classrooms and institutions, and it was, ironically, in response to concerns about such appropriation that attentive writing teachers began to encourage their students to assert their authority and ownership of textual meaning. Classroom writing groups are, in fact, a way to help students gain textual authority by identifying themselves and each other as writers.

9. Mark Rose's "The Author as Proprietor: *Donaldson v. Becket* and the Genealogy of Modern Authorship" provides the background material for my discussion of the evolution of the discourses of private and public ownership as these emerged in the legal debate over copyright.

10. Rose credits Lyman Ray Patterson for his observation that the emphasis on the author in reference to the Statute of Anne was clearly a strategy to undermine the London booksellers' monopoly. According to Patterson, "the monopolies at which the statute aimed were too long established to be attacked without some basis for change. The most natural and logical basis for the changes was the author" (147; qtd. in Rose 57; see also Kaplan; Jaszi, "Author Effect").

11. The insistence on the author's right to own the fruits of his labor, a central argument in the discourse of copyright, is based on Locke's assertion that "Though the Earth, and all inferior Creatures be common to all Men, yet every Man has a *Property* in his own *Person*. This no Body has any Right to but himself. The *Labour* of his Body, and the *Work* of his hands, we may say, are properly his. Whatsoever then he removes out of the State that Nature hath provided, and left it in, he hath mixed his *Labour* with, and joyned to it something that is his own, and thereby makes it his property" (17, emphasis added).

12. For example, in 1774, in his *Observations on Literary Property*, William Enfield writes "In this various world, different men are born to different fortunes: one inherits a portion of land; he cultivates it with care, it produces him corn and fruits and wool: another possesses a fruitful mind, teeming with ideas of every kind; he bestows his labour in cultivating *that*; the produce is reason, sentiment, philosophy" (qtd. in Rose 65).

13. The writing assignments were based on readings in the course text, Ford and Watters' *Coming from Home: Readings for Writers*, Toni Morrison's "A Slow Walk of Trees," Richard Rodriguez's "Public and Private Language," and Simon J. Ortiz's "The Language We Know." In small and large group discussion, the students responded to the question "Do the attitudes of parents and family generally prescribe the political and social values of the children? Under what circumstances might alternatives or conflicts arise?" This question related to Toni Morrison's essay, which described the influence of Morrison's family members on her notions of racial tolerance and

intolerance. Both Lori and Julie addressed these issues in their essays. In response to Rodriguez's essay, students weighed the advantages and disadvantages of cultural assimilation and multiculturalism. This became the topic for Andrew's paper. Simon Ortiz's essay examined the impact of an individual's primary spoken language on his or her cultural and personal identity. Edward's essay was influenced by Ortiz's discussion.

14. In the 1747 case of *Donaldson v. Becket*, the cultural significance of the text and its rightful place in the public domain were underscored by Lord Camden's argument that ideas could not be considered property, for to do so would be to hold learning hostage to an elite group "who will set what Price upon it their Avarice chuses to demand, 'till the Public becomes as much their Slaves, as their own Hackney Compilers are" (qtd. in Rose 68).

15. Article I, Section 8, of the *United States Constitution* states that Congress shall have the power to "promote the Progress of Science and the useful Arts, by securing for limited Times to Authors and Inventors the exclusive Right to their respective Writings and Discoveries." Stressing the conflict of aims implicit in copyright doctrine, Peter Jaszi asserts that its structure may be understood as "a function of the impossibility of serving one of the described objectives without disserving the other. Many particular doctrinal constructs thus are simply attempts to mediate the basic contradiction between public benefit and private reward. Their instability is guaranteed because the two goals are irreconcilable" ("Toward a Theory" 464).

16. This position was articulated by Justice Erie in *Jeffreys v. Boosey*, 4 H.L. 815, 867 and was first applied in the United States in 1898 in the case of *Holmes v. Hurst*: "The right thus secured by the copyright act is not a right to the use of certain words, because they are the common property of the human race, and are as little susceptible of private appropriating as air or sunlight; nor is it a right to ideas alone, since in the absence of means of communicating them they are of value to no one but the author. But the right is to that arrangement of words which the author has selected to express his ideas . . ." (qtd. in Lindey 281).

17. Edward's perceptions are congruent with the United States Supreme Court's 1853 ruling that a German translation of Harriet Beecher Stowe's *Uncle Tom's Cabin* was not an infringement of copyright. In *Stowe v. Thomas*, it ruled that protection applied to exact copies of the work, or in Stowe's case, the English version alone. Edward, however, would disagree with the position that "an author's exclusive property in a literary composition" did not extend to his or her "conceptions and inventions" (207).

18. Peter Jaszi cites a number of recent decisions in favor of the financial well-being of the "original author" rather than the perpetuation of culture through contact and derivation from previous works as well as cases where the court has refused to engage issues relating to authorial collaboration and other corporate modes of production ("Toward"; "Author Effect"; Jaszi and Woodmansee "Law"). Furthermore, Congress seems intent on lengthening the term of copyright protection: in the Copyright Act of 1976 the term was extended to the life of the author plus 50 years; on February 5, 1997, H.R. 604, the Copyright Term Extension Act, was introduced proposing an addition of 20 years to the existing term of copyright protection for both new and currently protected works. Much of the impetus for new legislation is associated with the United States' adoption in 1988 of the principles of the Berne Convention. According to Patricia Brennan, "the major changes for the U.S. copyright system as a result of Berne were: greater protection for proprietors, new copyright relations with 24 additional countries, and elimination of the requirement of a copyright notice on copyrighted work" (2). The constituents of the Berne Convention arrived at their concept of the "author" and the "work" by way of a different set of theories and practices than did the United States and England. Their legislation has always been interpreted from a "moral rights" perspective, which gives the writer control over his or her text's circumstances of dissemination, circulation, and presentation. Moral rights doctrine rests on the principle that the author and the creation are one and the same (Jaszi, "Toward" 497). According to Jaszi, following Benjamin Kaplan, the recent narrowing of U.S. copyright in favor of the "author" is "the legislative expression of unreconstructed faith in the gospel of Romantic 'authorship'" ("Toward" 500).

19. In her article "Plagiarisms, Authorships, and the Academic Death Penalty," Rebecca Moore Howard argues that many of the "errors" students make in handling academic citation conventions are indicative of their efforts to approximate academic discourse and, as such, should be tapped as pedagogic strategies. Further, she contends that contemporary theory and writing practices indicate a need for revised definitions of plagiarism and revised policies for dealing with student infractions.

20. In *Readings in the Arts and Sciences*, Elaine Maimon suggests that students might be taught to write acknowledgments or prefatory notes to indicate peer assistance in the composition of their essays (387).

WORKS CITED

Brennan, Patricia. "Timeline: A History of Copyright in the U.S." Association of Research Libraries. Available online: arl.cni.org/info/frn/copy/timeline.

Eisenstein, Elizabeth L. *The Printing Press as an Agent of Change*. Cambridge: Cambridge UP, 1980.

Feather, John. "From Rights in Copies to Copyright: The Recognition of Authors' Rights in English Law and Practice in the Sixteenth and Seventeenth Centuries." *Cardozo Arts and Entertainment* 10 (1992): 455–73.

Ford, Marjorie, Jon Ford, and Ann Watters, eds. *Coming from Rome: Readings for Writers*. New York: McGraw, 1993.

Howard, Rebecca Moore. "Plagiarisms, Authorships, and the Academic Death Penalty." *College English* 57 (1995): 788–806.

Kaplan, Benjamin. *An Unhurried View of Copyright*. New York: Columbia UP, 1967.

Jaszi, Peter. "On the Author Effect: Contemporary Copyright and Collective Creativity." Woodmansee and Jaszi, eds. *Construction* 29–56.

———. "Toward a Theory of Copyright: The Metamorphoses of 'Authorship.'" *Duke Law Journal* (1991): 455–502.

Lindey, Alexander. *Plagiarism and Originality*. New York: Harper, 1952.

Locke, John. *The Second Treatise of Government*. Ed. Thomas P. Peardon. New York: Liberal Arts P, 1952.

Lunsford, Andrea A., and Lisa Ede. "Collaborative Authorship and the Teaching of Writing." Woodmansee and Jaszi, *Construction* 417–38.

———. *Singular Texts/Plural Authors: Perspectives on Collaborative Writing*. Carbondale: Southern Illinois UP, 1990.

Lunsford, Andrea A., and Susan West. "Intellectual Property and Composition Studies." *CCC* 47 (1996): 383–411.

Maimon, Elaine P., Gerald L. Belcher, Gail W. Hearn, Barbara F. Nodine, and Finbarr W. O'Connor. *Readings in the Arts and Sciences*. Boston: Little, Brown, 1984.

Mallon, Thomas. *Stolen Words: Forays into the Origins and Ravages of Plagiarism*. New York: Ticknor, 1989.

Miller, Susan. *Rescuing the Subject: A Critical Introduction to Rhetoric and the Writer*. Carbondale: Southern Illinois UP, 1989.

Ong, Walter J. *Orality and Literacy: The Technologizing of the World*. London: Methuen, 1982.

Rose, Mark. "The Author as Proprietor: *Donaldson v. Becket* and the Genealogy of Modern Authorship." *Representations* 23 (1988): 51–85.

Ross, Marlon B. "Authority and Authenticity: Scribbling Authors and the Genius of Print in Eighteenth-Century England." *Cardozo Arts and Entertainment Law Journal* 10 (1992): 495–521.

Shaw, Peter. "Plagiary." *The American Scholar* (1982): 325–37.

Stillinger, Jack. *Multiple Authorship and the Myth of Solitary Genius*. New York: Oxford UP, 1991.

Stowe v. Thomas. Federal Cases 23 (1853):201–08.

United States Constitution, Art I, Clause 8, Section 8.

White, Harold Ogden. *Plagiarism and Imitation During the English Renaissance: A Study in Critical Distinctions*. Cambridge: Harvard UP, 1935.

Woodmansee, Martha. "The Genius and the Copyright: Economic and Legal Conditions of the Emergence of the 'Author.'" *Eighteenth Century Studies* 17 (1984): 425–48.

———. "On the Author Effect: Recovering Collectivity." Woodmansee and Jaszi, *Construction* 15–28.

Woodmansee, Martha, and Peter Jaszi. "The Law of Texts: Copyright in the Academy." *College English* 57 (1995): 769–87.

Woodmansee, Martha, and Peter Jaszi, eds. *The Construction of Authorship: Textual Appropriation in Law and Literature*. Durham: Duke UP, 1994.

6

Peer Review and Response: A Failure of the Process Paradigm as Viewed from the Trenches

LYNNE BELCHER

In 1972 when Donald Murray argued that writing should be taught as a process not a product, he foresaw many implications for teaching the process rather than the product. The first implication Murray lists in his essay "Teach Writing as a Process Not Product" is "The text of the writing course is the student's own writing. Students examine their own evolving writing and that of their classmates, so that they study writing while it is still a matter of choice, word by word" (91). Ten years later, Maxine Hairston argued for a paradigm shift in the teaching of writing in her "The Winds of Change: Thomas Kuhn and the Revolution in the Teaching of Writing." She argued that the new paradigm should focus on the writing process, a process that involves the intervention of readers in students' writing during that process. She also argued that students benefit "far more from small group meetings with each other than from the exhausting one-to-one conferences that the teachers hold" (17).

Clearly, the process method of teaching writing involves reader intervention by students in the writing of their classmates. But how successful has that intervention been in the writing that students produce? Since this part of the paradigm is so important to teaching writing as a process, we need to have some idea as to how well it has worked.

A careful examination of what instructors see happening as student readers intervene in the writing process of their classmates will show how this part of the process paradigm has failed. Students, for the most part, have not, as Murray argued, examined "their own evolving writing and that of their classmates . . . word by word." Nor has small group work been a greater benefit to student writers than the "exhausting one-to-one conferences" between teacher and student writer, as Hairston argued. What seems to be an essential part of the process paradigm has been a failure in that it has not worked in the way many had hoped.

Much has been written about the work of peer response groups in the past, building on the work of Elbow and Bruffee, but much of that research

From *Reforming College Composition: Writing the Wrongs*, edited by Ray Wallace et al., Greenwood Press, 2000, pp. 99–111.

has focused on what small numbers of students do when they respond to the writing of their classmates. The research generally can be classified into three categories: historical perspectives of peer review and peer response groups, descriptions of what peers do when they respond to the writing of their classmates, and suggestions for improving peer responses. Ann Ruggles Gere's book on peer groups written in 1987 includes both a historical perspective and an exhaustive bibliography. Muriel Harris includes a brief history in her comparison of writing center tutorials with peer response groups. Harris points out that "peer response, having been the subject of numerous studies, has a track record of conflicting results" (377).

Much of the research concluding with claims of the effectiveness or ineffectiveness of peer response begins with descriptions of what peers do when they respond to the writing of their classmates. Thomas Newkirk (p. 47 in this volume), Anne Ruggles Gere and Robert D. Abbott, Nancy Grimm, Nina Ziv, and Diana George among others have studied what peer reviewers actually do. Most of them conclude that more research needs to be done. Ronnie Carter concludes that though females outperform males as peer reviewers, "this study points out the lack of demonstrable *short-term* gains in peer evaluation by itself" (13). Carter also concludes that more research needs to be done (15).

Some researchers have tried to help make peer response more effective by looking at what instructors can do to better prepare their students to be good critical readers and responders. Mara Holt suggests a method for helping instructors understand "the kinds of peer criticism that students can fruitfully engage in" (391). Karen Spear in her book *Sharing Writing: Peer Response Groups in English Classes* explains not only what peer writing groups do but also how they can be used more effectively in composition classes. More recently, Candace Spigelman looks at the tension students feel about the ownership of texts in peer writing groups and how that tension can be used productively (p. 91).

None of the research really examines what instructors who actually teach multiple sections of writing classes every semester think about the quality of peer responses and whether or not the use of peer response groups actually frees instructors from one-to-one conferencing. To that end, I surveyed writing instructors on two e-mail lists concerned with writing and writing instruction: WCENTER@ttacs6.ttu.edu and ECOMPL@listserv.nodak.edu. The survey reads as follows:

Name:
Semester class load:
Number of writing courses per semester:
Enrollment limits in first year composition:

1. Do you use peer review as part of your instruction in the writing process?
   Yes   No   If you don't, why not?

2. What kind of information do you ask peer reviewers to consider?
   Global revision   Paragraph and sentence level revision   Editing

3. How would you describe the quality of the peer comments?
   Excellent   Good   Fair   Poor

4. Do you grade peer reviewers on their comments?
   Yes   No   If you answered yes, why?   If you answered no, why not?

5. Do you think using peer reviewers makes your job easier or harder?
   Easier   Harder   No difference

6. Do you think using peer reviewers saves you time?
   Yes   No   If yes, how does it save you time?   If not, why not?

7. Which do you think is more effective in helping students revise their work?
   Small groups of peer reviewers working together
   One-to-one conference between teacher and student

8. Would you recommend that a new writing instructor make use of peer review as a part of writing instruction?
   Yes   No   Why or why not?   Other comments?

Survey Findings

Kinds of and Locations for Colleges/Universities

Though I did not ask for information about the size and the mission of the schools where the respondents teach, those who answered the survey either included college/university web site addresses or used institutional addresses in their survey responses. I was able to visit the web sites of the schools for all but one respondent who had a commercial e-mail address. Ten of those thirty respondents (33 percent—totals will not always equal 100 percent since those numbers have been rounded off) teach at regional universities where undergraduate education is the primary focus, though most of these schools have some graduate programs. Two (7 percent) of those respondents teach at liberal arts colleges where the focus is on undergraduate education. Four of those respondents (13 percent) teach at liberal arts colleges with religious affiliations and a focus on undergraduate education. One respondent (3 percent) teaches at a larger Catholic university. Six of those respondents (20 percent) teach at community colleges, and five respondents (17 percent) teach at large, land-grant universities, though two of those respondents identified themselves as TA's, two were identified as part-timers, and one was identified as a lecturer. One respondent (3 percent) teaches at a professional/technical university, and one respondent (3 percent) teaches advanced placement writing classes at a high school.

Respondents teach in a variety of places; eighteen states and Australia are represented in the survey. Pennsylvania is most represented with four respondents while Texas and Kansas have three each. New York, Georgia, Wisconsin, and North Carolina are each represented by two respondents. Wyoming,

Indiana, North Dakota, Illinois, Nebraska, Massachusetts, Utah, Virginia, Iowa, Connecticut, Georgia, and Colorado are each represented by one respondent.

What I was looking for with the surveys is instructors' attitudes about using peer response work in the classroom. I wanted to see what it is teachers think they are accomplishing when they use peer review. I was also interested in what instructors think of the quality of the comments their students make about other students' writing. I wondered if teachers think using peer review allows students to understand writing word by word and if making use of peer reviewers frees instructors from the demanding work of one-to-one conferences.

Semester Course Loads

Respondents reported that semester course loads range from five classes to one class, though many who teach smaller loads are either running writing centers/labs or are graduate students. In cases where respondents reported two different loads (e.g., three classes for fall, two for spring), the greater number was recorded since those respondents teach the greater number of classes at least one semester of each year. The responses to the question on semester class load are as follows:

5 classes per semester—two   (6 percent)
4 classes per semester—nine   (29 percent)
3 classes per semester—eight   (26 percent)
2 classes per semester—eight   (26 percent)
1 class per semester—four   (13 percent)

Respondents teach an average of 2.9 classes per semester. Eight of the respondents who say they teach either one or two courses a semester explain that they also work in or direct a writing center. Two other respondents identified themselves as graduate students.

Writing Course Load per Semester

Respondents also indicated the number of writing classes they teach each semester:

5 writing courses per semester—two   (6 percent)
4 writing courses per semester—three   (10 percent)
3 writing courses per semester—five   (16 percent)
2 writing courses per semester—sixteen   (52 percent)
1 writing course per semester—four   (13 percent)

Respondents teach an average of 2.35 writing classes per semester.

Enrollment Limits in First Year Writing Courses

Enrollments in first year composition courses range from 16 to 30 students, though five respondents say that the enrollment limits are regularly exceeded. These are the enrollment limits indicated by respondents:

30 student limit—one ("routinely raised")	(3 percent)
28 student limit—one	(3 percent)
27 student limit—one	(3 percent)
25 student limit—twelve	(39 percent)
24 student limit—one	(3 percent)
23 student limit—one	(3 percent)
22 student limit—five	(16 percent)
20 student limit—seven	(23 percent)
16 student limit—one ("sort of" limit)	(3 percent)

Class size average is 22.5 students for respondents.

Peer Review as Part of Instruction in the Writing Process

All thirty-one respondents said they use or have used peer review as part of instruction in the writing process. One respondent claimed to be "currently rethinking" using peer review. This respondent said, "I have tried a variety of ways to peer edit. Very few of them [peer reviewer comments] have had positive results; most of the time peer [reviewer] comments are too vague, [peer reviewers] comment on things that are a matter of personal style, or [peer reviewers] are just plain wrong." Another respondent said, "I have used it [peer review] quite a bit in the past. I'm taking a couple of semesters to try teaching without it right now." Though all the respondents have used peer review, not all of them are satisfied with the results.

Kinds of Information Solicited from Peer Reviewers

Most respondents (thirty) said they ask peer reviewers to consider global revision in their responses to their classmates' papers. Almost as many respondents (twenty-one) solicit paragraph and sentence-level revision comments. Almost half of the respondents (fourteen) said that they have peer reviewers make editing comments about their classmates' papers. One respondent said that students are required to write "two-page critiques referencing audience, purpose, content, and style." Only one respondent asks students to review "mainly sentence level and editing."

The Quality of Peer Comments

The respondents were asked to comment on the quality of the peer review responses, identifying those comments as excellent, good, fair, or poor. Some respondents said the comments cover a wide range of quality while others said that the quality of the comments improves over the course of the semester. Here is how the respondents categorized the quality of peer reviewers' comments:

Excellent — two

Good — fifteen

Fair — twelve

Poor — seven

(The total is higher than thirty-one because some respondents identified several categories.)

Three respondents said the quality of peer comments improves over the semester. Nine respondents said there is a wide range in the quality of the comments by peer reviewers. One respondent said the quality of peer review comments is "fair to poor, usually. I also think they don't take it too seriously . . . I really wish I could figure out how to induce them to take it more seriously. (One time I tried anonymous peer reviews to see if people would be more candid. Not really — although one usually quiet, diplomatic student wrote a scathing peer review.)"

One respondent voiced the frustrations that many composition instructors must sometimes feel about peer review comments: "I've never been completely satisfied with the way it's gone, and students have consistently indicated on course evaluations that they are frustrated with it. I've tried modeling the process on sample papers. I've tried giving them detailed guidelines for comments. I've tried providing minimal guidance; I've tried putting students in peer revision groups that they stay with all semester. I've tried moving them to new partners every time. The main problem has been lack of thoughtful and useful commentary and/or commentary that directly contradicts my advice to the student. For this reason, students have seen it as a waste of time if not downright counterproductive."

One respondent said that the quality of peer comments is "excellent to poor; some students don't offer any constructive feedback at all; others are excellent at responding — it's too hard to give an overall judgment except to say that I find it valuable enough to continue." For many of the respondents, it seems that in spite of (or because of) the quality of the comments, they will continue to use peer responses to drafts of papers in their classes.

Grading Peer Reviewers on Their Comments

Respondents were asked if they grade the peer reviewers on their comments. Twelve (39 percent) said they do, while eighteen (58 percent) said they do not. Four respondents said they include peer comments as a grade for participation. Seven said they periodically review peer comments. Many respondents commented about the value of grading or not grading peer review comments. One respondent said that the review comments aren't graded, "but I make them sign off on their comments and I review the peer review sheets to identify weaknesses in their process and then focus on those areas more for the next review. A peer review is just as much a learning process for the reader as it is for the writer. This is practice to help them understand how to find mistakes in their work and how to offer critiques of others' work in a manner that is helpful." Other respondents expressed the idea that peer review comments are as much a learning experience for the reader as for the writer.

Several respondents said they do grade the peer review comments as a way to get students to take responding to drafts seriously. One respondent who grades the peer review comments said that "Sad to say, if students know they are accountable, most seem to take the activity more seriously." Another said, "I have found that students spend more time and give better comments when they know they are being held accountable."

Several respondents said they do not grade review comments because of a lack of time: "I think maybe I should [grade the review comments] because that might make students take it seriously," but this respondent also said that the comments are not graded because the respondent is already "too busy." Another respondent replied "no" to the question about grading peer review comments because "I already have too much work with forty-four students." Others said they do not grade the comments but for different reasons: "I am more interested in the social aspect of writing for real readers. Also, I give grades only on midterm and final portfolios, based on writing quality, amount of work (i.e., how much revising, what depth of revising), and participation. Any individual set of peer comments is only a small part of the overall picture. I do ask for peer evaluation of midterm and final portfolios, and I comment on those one- to one-and-a-half-page evaluations as part of the feedback which the portfolio author receives." Another respondent said that "I think that would inhibit the comfort level of the groups. I don't want it to be competitive. Also the logistics would be a problem. I can't sit in on all the groups at the same time." Though not all respondents grade the comments of the reviewers, they do seem to spend time looking at the kinds of comments reviewers are making in order to help reviewers become better critical readers.

Peer Reviewers Make Instructor's Job Harder and Easier

Respondents were asked if using peer reviewers makes their job in the classroom easier or harder. Many respondents did not like the choices for answers and so came up with other answers. Ten respondents (32 percent) did say that the use of peer reviewers makes their jobs easier. Five (16 percent) said it makes their jobs harder. Nine (30 percent) said using peer reviewers makes no difference in their workload. Two (6 percent) said it makes their jobs both easier and harder while three (10 percent) said it makes their jobs neither easier nor harder. One respondent (3 percent) said it makes the job more interesting while another (3 percent) said it makes the job different. Many respondents had more to say. One respondent believes using peer reviewers makes the job harder "because I spend a great deal of time trying to teach them the fundamentals of peer review and then I spend time constructing a variety of different peer reviews. It also takes time to evaluate the success of each peer review session." Another respondent said that using peer reviewers makes the job "harder, I think. . . . I'm always tinkering with the process to try to make it work better. I love the idea in theory—and have found it useful in grad courses—but I think it needs to be done differently." Another respondent said that using peer reviewers makes the job harder, "but that's not a bad thing." One respondent who believes using peer reviewers makes the job harder said that, "ideally, it should make it easier. If students are responding as engaged and intelligent readers they should provide backup for my comments and provide insights of their own that I might have missed. However, this has rarely been the case. Instead, I've had to do a lot of extra work preparing guidelines, checking that they did it, etc. That's why I've decided to give it a break for a few semesters. Maybe I'll get some fresh ideas, a new perspective, and try it again."

Respondents who reported that using peer reviewers makes their jobs easier had a variety of reasons for answering as they did. One respondent said, "I'd say that classes involving a lot of workshopping are easier for me—because that's what I know. It has little to do with the time I spend reading papers, however. It has more to do with how class time is spent, and how much I have to allocate in preparing for it. I also sleep better at night knowing that my comments aren't the only comments they are depending on." One respondent said that using peer reviewers makes the job "easier; one less day that I have to lecture, which is often a waste of time anyway." Another said that using peer reviewers makes the job neither easier nor harder: "If I didn't use them I would read every draft, but since I do use them I spend a lot of time modeling and teaching students how to respond to one another's writing." One respondent reflected the views of many in saying, "It helps students to see a variety of opinions (hopefully), but it also gives me more work to do in checking over the responses to grade them."

Peer Reviewers Do Not Save Time for Instructors

Respondents were also asked if using peer reviewers saves time for instructors. While eleven respondents (35 percent) said that using peer reviewers saves them time, seventeen (55 percent) said it does not. Two (6 percent) weren't sure, and one respondent (3 percent) said that saving time isn't a priority. One of those "yes" votes was a probably: "Probably yes, because it teaches critical thinking skills as it has students review their own writing and their knowledge of writing." Another said the time it takes to make use of peer reviewers is "time better spent. . . . Because I don't have to personally respond to every paper, I get better writing from students when I do see it, and I'm teaching them not to be dependent on me for feedback. It doesn't save time compared to a pure lecture, though, because I have to make up peer review sheets and guidelines, facilitate those groups and actively engage students in the process of peer review." One respondent said that "the students quickly begin making comments about problems I used to have to tell them about." Another said that "the peer review substitutes for a conference with me. The papers don't end up as good, but they learn more about working in such groups." Another respondent said, "I don't use it as a substitute for my own work."

Most of those who said that using peer reviewers does not save them time noted that it actually takes more time: "I need to spend a great deal of time setting them up to be good reviewers—that usually takes at least half the semester. Then I work on checklists and comment sheets for each assignment. That takes time. Then I go over the peer comments with my students in conference. . . . Just conducting class and conferences would be less time consuming, but I want my students to learn how to be good writing partners later, so I think the time is worth it." Another echoes that concern: "It is another means to giving feedback on work in progress, and thus can relieve me of some of that load, but students need to learn how to review others' work, and that must be built into class time and practiced." Many of those who said using peer reviewers does not save them time explained that they respond to drafts of papers as well as have peer reviewers respond to them.

Some respondents pointed out that peer review is probably a greater benefit to the reader than to the writer: "The main benefit I see is to the reader, not the writer. The comments they made toward the beginning of the semester were mostly about surface error, even though they had strict instructions to discuss only content issues—I think that is because they didn't really understand what I meant or how to do it. . . . Because I think the helpfulness of their comments is limited until they get some experience, I also read and comment on all their drafts, and meet with them individually. . . . If you start out teaching kids who are more comfortable with writing, then maybe peer editing as a source of information for the writer is more realistic. For me, it is still extremely useful—just more so for the reader." Another respondent expressed a common opinion: "peer review (as you know) doesn't just happen, but like everything has to be taught, modeled, what-have-you." One respondent found that question about saving time "absurd." This respondent said that after many years of teaching, "saving time has not been a priority in my teaching."

Teacher Conferences Are More Effective Than Peer Reviewers

Almost half of the respondents (fourteen—45 percent) believe that one-to-one conferences between teacher and student are a more effective intervention method than peers working together. Three respondents (10 percent) believe peer groups are more effective than student/teacher conferences. Two respondents (6 percent) said a mixture is effective while four (13 percent) said each is equally effective. Four respondents (13 percent) said teacher conferences have a different purpose than peer reviews, and two respondents (6 percent) said each has its strengths and weaknesses. Two respondents (6 percent) said that teacher/student conferences are more effective for the short term but that peer review work has a long-term effect. One respondent said "students learn more from each other than from the teacher and that knowledge is more deeply structured or implanted when students are able to work together to internalize it. Ultimately, students just learn more from collaborative groups than from a teacher trying to impart knowledge." Another respondent supporting the effectiveness of peer review work summed up that opinion by saying, "Students learn more by giving advice than by getting it."

Those who responded that teacher/student conferences are more effective than peer review work seem confident of their opinions about this issue, saying "no question about it" and "definitely one-to-one conferences between teacher and student." One respondent said that "students often ignore peer comments, and many students just can't figure out how to give useful suggestions." Another respondent said, "I am a great fan of one-on-one conferences, and this year have finally managed to bring each in under twenty-five minutes." Another said, "Although peer reviewers are quite useful as a way of giving the student an audience, I think the one-to-one conference between teacher and student is hard to beat. I find I can verbalize suggestions for writing improvement better than the students can." One respondent explained that although a one-to-one conference between teacher and student is a better method, "I can't use it with my teaching load. Too bad."

The fourteen respondents who have mixed opinions about which method of intervention is more effective have a variety of reasons for their mixed opinions. One respondent uses "a mixture of small groups and occasional larger ones. The first for active participation, the second for seeing more how other people comment, and seeing the wide range of things that can be said about student work. One-on-one conferencing can be very effective, but I think only if the students want to—I'm hesitant to assign whole classes to come and see me individually." Another respondent said, "They have different uses. I use small groups to comment on things like coherence and the quality of evidence—that is effective because it lets students develop a 'metalanguage' for analyzing writing. But if student reviewers are less able to say why a text appears disjointed, etc. or how it could be improved, then a teacher-student conference is important." Another respondent said, "Both are effective; for the short-term goal of getting a good grade on the paper at hand, the one-to-one works better, but perhaps for long-term, general growth as a writer, the peer conference is better because writers can see how real people react to confusing, unclear writing, and that makes a strong impression and provides motivation to write more clearly." One respondent who said that both methods are effective added, "But small groups without teacher guidance at the individual level is, I'm afraid, a cop-out. Peers simply do not know what we (presumably) know about the writing process."

New Instructors Should Use Peer Review

Thirty (97 percent) of the thirty-one respondents would recommend that a new writing instructor make use of peer review as part of writing instruction. Some respondents were quite emphatic in their recommendations while others gave more qualified answers. One respondent said, "Beyond the obvious goal of helping each other improve their writing, I think the peer groups have other benefits that are more intangible. Having a real audience fosters the sense of writing as genuine communication as nothing else can. I encourage them to discuss the concepts and learn from each other about all kinds of ideas. They get ideas for their own future writing. They find out that not everyone else is a fabulous writer—that they have similar frustrations with writing. They also are exposed to those students who take the same assignment they had and develop something really insightful and eloquent. Students actually become part of that community of writers we read about." One respondent who has had negative experiences with using peer reviewers said, "Despite my bad experiences with it, I know there are others who've found it very useful. I certainly think new teachers should try it out in a couple of different formats. They may find it very helpful and interesting." One respondent pointed out that "Peers listen to peers—you and I do it, too—but new writing instructors need to learn how to teach peer review—it doesn't just happen." Another respondent believes new instructors should use peer review "Just to begin the practice of de-centering the classroom from the beginning— it's a difficult transition to make." One respondent said that "whether I recommend this or not depends upon the teacher's personality. Peer reading may or may not suit what the teacher wants to do. Although I use peer reading in both comp. classes, many teachers find the second semester of peer reading a waste of time."

CONCLUSION

The original motivation for this survey was my own frustrations with what I saw as the failure of peer review to do what I hoped it would do: free me from the exhausting work of either reading drafts of students' papers or having individual conferences with students, something that is difficult to do while teaching four classes, two of which are writing classes. Since reader intervention is such an integral part of the process paradigm, I have always worried about the problem of giving feedback to all students. Making use of peer responders has not solved this problem for me. Other composition instructors seem to be more optimistic about this practice, though many do not see peer review as a way for writers to learn about writing or as a time-saver for instructors. They see peer review as a way for students to learn how to read critically. The dedication to teaching of the respondents to this survey and their willingness to work long and hard at what they do are impressive. I am amazed at the time and energy this hard-working group of professionals must put into their teaching.

When I was in graduate school in the early 1980s, one of my professors said that teaching writing as a process is much easier than teaching it as a product. I have always wondered how that could be possible given the demands of teaching writing as a process with multiple drafts and constant feedback. I now understand that my professor could say that because most of the people teaching in graduate programs do not teach first-year composition or only teach an occasional honor's section. According to the October 1998

PMLA, 96 percent of all writing classes in Ph.D.-granting English departments are taught by graduate students, part-timers, or full-time non-tenure-track faculty members (1157). Also, according to *PMLA*, "between one-half and two-thirds of the total number of professorial-rank appointments are located outside doctorate-granting research institutions" (1166).

Many of us end up teaching three to five classes a semester with half of those classes being writing classes. Not only do we have to teach our students how to write, we have to teach them how to read. What most of us do as composition instructors is complicated, demanding, and time-consuming. Yet in higher education, our work is marginalized at best. Those who teach us may do most of the research and may be among the most recognized in the profession, but they seldom do the work of a composition teacher, and they certainly cannot understand the time that is involved in teaching writing as a process. We do not need another paradigm shift in the teaching of composition; we need a revolution.

WORKS CITED

Bruffee, Kenneth A. *A Short Course in Writing Practical Rhetoric for Teaching Composition through Collaborative Learning.* 3 ed. Boston: Little, Brown, 1985.

Carter, Ronnie. *By Itself Peer Group Revision Has No Power.* ERIC, 1982. ED 226 350.

Elbow, Peter. *Writing without Teachers.* New York: Oxford UP, 1973.

George, Diana. "Working with Peer Groups in the Composition Classroom." *College Composition and Communication* 35.3 (1984): 320–26.

Gere, Anne Ruggles. *Writing Groups: History, Theory, and Implications.* Carbondale: Southern Illinois UP, 1987.

Gere, Anne Ruggles, and Robert D. Abbott. "Talking About Writing: The Language of Writing Groups." *Research in the Teaching of English* 19.4 (1985): 362–85.

Grimm, Nancy. "Improving Students' Responses to their Peers' Essays." *College Composition and Communication* 37.1 (1986): 91–94.

Hairston, Maxine. "The Winds of Change: Thomas Kuhn and the Revolution in the Teaching of Writing." *College Composition and Communication* 33.1 (1982): 76–88. Rpt. in *Rhetoric and Composition: A Sourcebook for Teachers and Writers.* Ed. Richard L. Graves. Upper Montclair: Boynton/Cook Publishers, 1984. 14–26.

Harris, Muriel. "Collaboration Is Not Collaboration Is Not Collaboration: Writing Center Tutorials vs. Peer Response Groups." *College Composition and Communication* 43.3 (1992): 369–83.

Holt, Mara. "The Value of Written Peer Criticism." *College Composition and Communication* 43.3 (1992): 384–92.

Murray, Donald. "Teach Writing as a Process Not Product." *The Leaflet.* New England Association of Teachers of English, November 1972, 11–14. Rpt. in *Rhetoric and Composition: A Sourcebook for Teachers and Writers.* Ed. Richard L. Graves. Upper Montclair: Boynton/Cook Publishers, 1984. 89–92.

Publications of the Modern Language Association of America. Final Report of the MLA Committee on Professional Employment. New York: *PMLA* 113.5 (October 1998): 1154–77.

Spear, Karen. *Sharing Writing: Peer Response Groups in English Classes.* Portsmouth: Boynton/Cook Publishers, 1988.

Ziv, Nina. *Peer Groups in the Composition Classroom: A Case Study.* ERIC, 1983. ED 229 799.

7

Peer Review from the Students' Perspective: Invaluable or Invalid?

CHARLOTTE BRAMMER AND MARY REES

Peer review is well established as an important theoretical component of the writing process. Early practitioners of process writing such as Peter Elbow, Kenneth Bruffee, Donald Murray, and Anne Ruggles Gere studied, discussed, published, and lived collaborative learning at a time when the "chalk and talk" lecture routine was standard throughout higher education. Thanks to their vision, the process of having students critique each other's papers has become commonplace in the composition classroom and in English composition textbooks. According to one survey, experienced instructors believe that all new teachers of composition should use peer review to at least some extent (Belcher, p. 110 in this volume). Although the emphasis on decentralizing the role of teacher once made peer review a cutting edge, progressive activity, it is now as entrenched as the old routine of lecture, write, and correct. Yet we frequently hear students complain bitterly that peer review is a waste of time or blame their peers for not "catching all the mistakes." We also hear colleagues grumble that students' papers are poor in quality and that students do not stay on task during the peer review process. While such behaviors and responses do not support the theory, they are a reality in many educational settings.

Only a few instances of empirical research examine what the students themselves think of their participation in peer review. Perhaps because peer response is practically instinctive to those of us who teach writing, few have felt the need to study the student perspective. Instead, studies have focused on the quality of peer comments, their effect on the revision process, and the best methods for conducting peer review. A few studies have indeed examined student attitudes (see Asraf; Murau; McGroarty and Zhu), but within the last decade, in particular, these studies have focused on second-language (L2) writers. Such focus provides valuable insight for both first-language (L1) and L2 teachers, but an examination of specifically L1 environments provides a useful comparison to L2 studies.[1] This lack of knowledge of student perception of the peer review process coupled with a concern about the difficulties

From *Composition Studies*, vol. 35, no. 2, Fall 2007, pp. 71–85.

inherent in group work motivated this study. In the remainder of this article, we report the results of faculty and student surveys from one university as a way of revisiting peer review and its value to the writing process.

A REVIEW OF PEER REVIEW RESEARCH

Despite some continuing romantic emphasis on the solitary author, most composition scholars have established quite firmly that the composing process is social, and peer review is an integral part of that process. According to Bruffee, learning to write is not only a matter of knowing the elements of composition, but also involves the student's acculturation into the collegiate, educated world—a process vital to the student's ability to succeed (*Collaborative* 9). Arguing from a historical perspective, Gere asserts that, among other things, writing groups can help students overcome the alienation that occurs when writers create work that does not have an audience. Those who write solely "for the teacher" will find it difficult to predict their audience needs, which will increase their sense of isolation (10). Viewing writing as a social-interactive phenomenon, Martin Nystrand posits that "meaning is a social construct negotiated by writer and reader through the medium of text" (78). Robert Brooke notes the importance of peer audiences when he defines the goals of writing groups as helping each student to "understand the ways in which writing can be useful in many areas of one's life, as well as to have experiences which adapt writing to any of those uses" (9).

Many teachers, however, find that establishing a productive community of collaborative writers is anything but easy. As one faculty member notes, "It doesn't save time" (qtd. in Belcher p. 117). The sheer number of essays devoted to explaining *how* to conduct peer reviews attests to its complexity and required commitment. Although group work has found widespread acceptance, even Bruffee admits that "institutionalized educational collaboration in whatever form . . . is never unproblematical" ("Collaborative" 14). Hephzibah Roskelly asserts that collaborative groups in writing classrooms experience a conflict in aims: socializing, working toward "being let into the 'academic club,'" and criticizing, "transforming structures by asserting the value of those without membership" (124). John Trimbur, himself an advocate of process writing, urges us to remember that we cannot eliminate power structures from writing groups, and therefore theories of collaboration must grapple with the fact that writing groups have the potential to reinforce conformity rather than negotiate new meaning.

Just as the theoretical perspectives acknowledge the complexity of peer review, practitioner advice is likewise varied. For example, Fiona Paton provides a list of peer review guidelines that includes critiquing a model paper and creating a new peer review checklist for each rhetorical task (294). Working from a different pedagogical stance, Jetta Hansen and Jun Liu suggest scaffolding the peer review process by modeling a paper through three steps: critical reading, suggesting revisions, and revising (35). Lisa Cahill extends this scaffolding by emphasizing collaboration at every step of the writing process, including involving students in creating peer review sheets. Susan Miller recommends involving the teacher directly in the process by having conferences with groups of four students at a time. In fact, there are probably as many different ways to conduct peer review as there are instructors to conduct it; the question then becomes, what elements of peer review must gain pedagogical priority?

To answer this question, in part, we turn to the scholarship of L2 peer review. Studies that measure students' attitudes toward peer review are more frequent in L2 than L1 environments, but findings sometimes are based on mixed groups or are otherwise applicable to the L1 experience. For example, Andrea Murau found that both L1 and L2 students had mixed feelings about peer review, and several of those surveyed (up to 20%) would not participate in peer review if it were not required—even though they found it helpful. This survey also found that L2 students experienced a high degree of anxiety during the peer review process while L1 students felt more comfortable (73). In addition, Ratnawati Asraf's study of L2 first-year writers indicates that students see the value of peer review, but often give poor advice to their peers; thus, Asraf concludes that peer review may be most useful to writers who are proficient in the language (unless less proficient writers are given constant teacher oversight). Conversely, in their survey of L2 writers, Olga Villamil and María C. M. de Guerrero found that "[m]ost changes were incorporated" and were "95% correct" or in line with the professors' comments. Mark Simkin and Nari K. Ramarapu also discovered that computer science students trust peers to the extent that the majority of them are comfortable with the practice of peer rating, in which other students grade their term papers (256).

Such conflicting results lead us to question the effectiveness of peer review and student perceptions of it. To that end, we designed this study to measure whether and how peer review is used and valued in writing classrooms. We began with several key questions:

1. Does the frequency of peer review relate to perceived value of peer review for students and writing faculty?

2. Does the perceived value of peer review relate to the use of required and/or optional peer review?

3. Does student self-confidence in peer review relate to perceived value of peer review?

4. Does student self-confidence in peer review relate to perceived instruction in peer review?

5. Does perceived value of peer review relate to instruction in peer review, for both students and writing faculty?

Methods

This study was conducted at a private master's-level comprehensive university in the southeastern United States. The university core curriculum includes a first-year course sequence, Communication Arts I and II, which emphasizes both writing and speech (unlike more traditional first-year writing courses). Students are also required to take two upper-level writing-intensive courses; most students complete this requirement through courses in their major. These discipline-specific writing-intensive courses are regularly reviewed as part of the university's writing across the curriculum program. Peer review is encouraged at all levels of writing-intensive courses. Data was gathered during the spring semester to ensure that most students had completed at least one writing course at the university. We conducted the study near the end of the semester when most courses require lengthy paper assignments; we felt the timing would ensure that students had a rich writing experience that would be fresh in their minds.

This particular university provides an appropriate location for this study, at least in part because of its homogenous population, which supports greater confidence in the study results.[2] The university is certainly working to increase campus diversity, but the profile is typical of many private institutions: largely white, middle-class, suburban, with selective enrollment.[3] Approximately 65% of incoming students are female; 35%, male. We asked 72 faculty members who teach either the first-year Communication Arts courses or upper-level writing-intensive courses to participate in the study; of the 22 faculty respondents (30.5% response rate) who completed the survey, 19 self-identified as white and three abstained from providing any demographic data. Nine respondents were male; 10 were female. The faculty respondents represent 11 disciplines, although eight claimed English or "core" as their disciplines. We asked the writing faculty who agreed to participate in the study to survey their students.[4]

Judging from average enrollments in the first-year and upper-level writing-intensive courses, we estimate that 1,296 students were asked to take the survey. We received responses from 328 students (25% response rate). The number of faculty and student survey responses is in keeping with our average 1:15 faculty-to-student ratio in our writing courses. Thus, while the overall response rate is low, the per class response rate is strong (approximately 82%). Of the 328 student respondents, 208 (63%) were female; 103 (31%) were male. Seventeen respondents did not provide demographic data. This female-to-male ratio is consistent with the university's student body. Also in keeping with the university's overall demographic, 276 (84%) student respondents self-identified as white. The university has a small group of minority students, and this limited diversity is reflected in the study: 3.4% self-identify as African American, 1.8% as other, less than 1% as either Asian or Latina. Approximately 9% chose not to indicate ethnicity. That said, the students represent a fairly even spread across 30 majors and concentrations, with only 12.8% undeclared. Business was the largest declared concentration, with 40 (12.2%).[5]

RESULTS

The aggregate averages from the course evaluation results (see Table 1) suggest that peer review is used in most of the university's first-year writing classrooms, but most students find peer review "not very helpful." The numbers improve

TABLE 1 Questions from First-Year Course Evaluations (n=27 sections)

Question & Response	Aggregate Average	Section Average
How often was peer review used in your class? 1. Always; 2. Usually; 3. Occasionally; 4. Seldom; 5. Never	2.39	1.85
How helpful was peer review in revising your paper? 1. Very helpful; 2. Somewhat helpful; 3. Not very helpful; 4. Not helpful; 5. A waste of time	3.06	2.37

when averages for individual class sections are combined. The section averages indicate that peer review is used "usually" to "always" in the first-year writing courses and that students find them "somewhat helpful."

According to the frequency counts and percentages in the faculty survey (see Table 2), most faculty (73%) claim to use peer review in their classrooms either "usually" or "always." This result is consistent with their view that peer review is a valuable part of the writing process (mean=3.77 on a 5-point scale) and their belief that peer review improves student writing (mean=3.45 on a 5-point scale). Similarly, most faculty require students to complete some form of peer review (72.7% require in-class peer review; 36.4% require out-of-class) and spend at least some class time preparing students to review each others' papers. This preparation seems to take the form of lecturing (50%), demonstrating "good peer reviews" through paper sharing (36.4%), and providing students with handouts (40.9%). Faculty consensus seems to break down over how often to assess peer review; however, there is a significant correlation between how much faculty value peer review as part of the writing process and how frequently they choose to assess it (Pearson's r =.001).

Approximately two-thirds of student respondents reported that they [1] used peer review for more than half of their major writing assignments and [2] found peer review either "occasionally" or "usually" helpful in revising their papers (see Table 3). This finding held across academic rank and discipline. For most students (some 80%), peer review was required. Importantly, most students prefer some form of peer review: only 7.3% preferred not to participate in peer review [χ^2 (4, n=328) =20.988, p=.000]. Student preferences for type of peer review vary, with "required peer review" and "friend or family member" receiving the most responses. Only one-third of the student respondents see value in in-class peer review, which is how peer review is generally practiced in this university's first-year composition classes, and only 16% want to seek assistance from the university's resource center.[6] Most students are at least somewhat confident in their ability to review peers' papers and are taught to conduct peer review by handouts and lectures. (There were no significant differences between responses from males and females.)

TABLE 2   Faculty Survey Results

Question	Response
How often do you use peer review in your courses?	1. Never (0); 2. Seldom (4 / 18.2%); 3. Occasionally (2 / 9.1%); 4. Usually (7 / 31.8%); 5. Always (9 / 40.9%)
Peer review is a valuable part of the writing process.	1. Disagree to 5. Agree (range=2-5; mean=3.77; SD=.922)
Peer review improves the quality of student writing.	1. Disagree to 5. Agree (range=2-5; mean=3.45; SD=.800)
What types of peer review do you use? (select all that apply)	1. Required in-class peer review (16 / 72.7%); 2. Required out-of-class peer review (8 / 36.4%); 3. Encouraged students to ask friends to review papers (6 / 27.3%); 4. Encouraged students to visit Communication Resource Center (13 / 59.1%); 5. Other (5/ 22.7%)
Do you assess peer review?	1. Never (1 / 4.5%); 2. Seldom (5 / 22.7%); 3. Occasionally (6 / 27.3%); 4. Usually (6 / 27.3%); 5. Always (4 / 18.2%)
How much time to you spend preparing students for peer review?	1. None (1 / 4.5%); 2. Less than half a class (17 / 77.3%); 3. More than half a class (4 /18.2%)
How do you teach peer review? (select all that apply)	1. I give no formal instruction in peer reviewing (3 / 13.6%); 2. I give students a handout on how to peer review (9 / 40.9%); 3. I lecture on how to peer review (11 / 50%); 4. I use role play to demonstrate how to peer review (3 / 13.6%); 5. I share a paper and demonstrate good peer review (8 / 36.4%); 6. Other (5 / 22.7%)

The results indicate that frequency of peer review as part of producing major writing assignments relates positively to perceived value of peer review for students [χ^2 (18, n=328) =142.290, p=.000]. In other words, when students participated in peer review for most or all of their major writing assignments, they were more likely to consider peer review as "usually" to "always" helpful. Similarly, perceived value of peer review for students correlates positively with required in-class peer review [χ^2 (5, n=328) =20.156, p=.001]. Requiring students to complete in-class peer reviews seems to encourage them to view peer review as more important or more helpful. While seemingly at odds with students' dislike of in-class peer review, this correlation is consistent with the finding that students who reported more preparation, in terms of methods—in how to peer review—also valued peer review more [χ^2 (4, n=312) =10.361,

TABLE 3   Student Survey Results

Question	Response
How often do you use peer review as a part of producing major writing assignments in your course?	1. Never (42 / 12.8%); 2. With less than half of the major writing assignments (81 / 24.7%); 3. With more than half of the major writing assignments (68 / 20.7%); 4. With all major writing assignments (137 / 41.8%)
If peer review is used in class, how helpful is peer review in revising your paper?	1. Not helpful at all (15 / 4.6%); 2. Seldom helpful (59 / 18%); 3. Occasionally helpful (102 / 31.1%); 4. Usually helpful (107 / 32.6%); 5. Always helpful (35 /10.7%). *Note that n=10 (3%) did not respond to this question*
What type(s) of peer review do you use? (select all that apply)	1. I participate in required in-class peer review (264 / 80.5%); 2. I participate in required out-of-class peer review (98 / 29.9%); 3. I ask classmates to peer review even when it is not required (67 / 20.4%); 4. I ask a friend or family member to review my papers (159 / 48.5%); 5. I go to the Communication Resource Center for peer review (69 / 21%); 6. Other (8 / 2.4%)
Which type of peer review do you prefer?	1. Required in-class peer review (111 / 33.8%); 2. Required out-of-class peer review (33 / 10.1%); 3. To ask classmates to peer review even when it is not required (37 / 11.3%); 4. To ask a friend or family member to review my papers (122 / 37.2%); 5. To go to the Communication Resource Center for peer review (54 / 16.5%); 6. (Other) (13 / 4%); 7. Not to have my papers peer reviewed (24 / 7.3%)
I am confident of my ability to review a peer's paper.	1. Never (10 / 3%); 2. Seldom (89 / 27.1%); 3. Occasionally (66 / 20.1%); 4. Usually (165 / 50.3%); 5. Always (64 / 19.5%)
How have you been prepared to review a peer's paper? (select all that apply)	1. I have had no formal instruction in peer reviewing (90 / 27.4%); 2. I was given a handout on how to peer review (137 / 41.8%); 3. I listened to a lecture on how to peer review (107 / 32.6%); 4. I watched / participated in role play of peer review (44 / 13.4%); 5. I was given a paper that demonstrated good peer review (71 / 21.6%); 6. Other (34 / 10.4%)
Other thoughts or comments.	160 / 48.8% responded

$p=.035$]. Specifically, students who were prepared to carry out peer review through two or more teaching methods (e.g., handout, lecture, and paper demonstration) were more likely to find peer review helpful.

These positive impressions of peer review seem to be enhanced by student self-confidence in their ability to peer review. Students who are more confident in their ability to review peers' papers also value peer review as an important part of the writing process [χ^2 (4, n=318) =15.443, $p=.004$]. Not surprisingly, students who receive more instruction in how to peer review are more confident in their ability to review others' papers. Students who reported that instructors used two or more methods in teaching the process of peer review also reported more confidence in their ability to peer review [χ^2 (4, n= 322) =15.575, $p=.004$]. Attempts to correlate specific pedagogical methods for peer review with student confidence were unsuccessful with this sample size.

The final question on the student survey was *What other thoughts or comments do you have about peer review?* Of the 328 students who completed the surveys, 160 (49%) chose to respond. Of these 160 comments, 92 (57.5%) expressed positive impressions about peer review, and 66 (41.3%) were negative. Comments such as *Very helpful in getting input other than my own!* were coded as positive, while comments such as *Peers never seemed to be willing to be open and give honest feedback* were coded as negative. Two comments could not be coded as positive or negative: (1) *There was a big emphasis on it freshmen year but I haven't done it since then* and (2) *I would have liked to have gotten more instruction on how to peer review. That way I would be more confident in my peer reviewing skills and the skills that other students in the class had.* While the second comment could be construed as leaning toward positive, we decided that it did not fit the spirit of the other comments we had coded as positive.

In addition to coding the free-response comments as positive or negative, we also coded for topics that emerged from the data, specifically (1) busy-work, notions that peer review was a waste of time or simply "free days"; (2) reviewer dependent, the idea that the value of peer review is directly related to the quality of the reviewer; (3) proofreading/editing, the idea that peer reviewing is synonymous with checking for errors; and (4) other, comments that did not fit within the other three categories. Of the 160 responses to the last question on the student survey, we coded 60 for topic; 100 responses simply expressed positive or negative opinions of peer review (e.g., *Peer review is great!*). Of those 60 comments, 31 (52%) remarked about the value of the reviewer, and 28 (47%) focused on proofreading or editing. Eight comments referred to peer reviewing as busywork. All but two comments fit one of the three categories; five comments included references to both the value of the reviewer and proofreading.

CONCLUSIONS

This study suggests that we have much work to do in helping students understand what peer review is (collaborative learning), and, more pointedly, what it isn't (proofreading). An extensive L2 study by Villamil and de Guerrero finds that, of changes suggested in peer review that were incorporated, "grammar was the most revised aspect whereas organization was the least attended to" (508). These findings of Villamel and de Guerrero are corroborated by research conducted by Asraf Ratnawati, who found that L2 students were extremely concerned about grammatical errors even though the assignment in question was not to be graded (76). Although the respondents to our survey were not L2 learners, they also had a clear expectation that peer review should help them catch proofreading errors. Likewise, Murau's study of both native and non-native speakers finds that both student groups appreciate peer review because it can help with, in their words, "minor mistakes" in "grammar, vocabulary" (74). This student concept of peer review is so common that Fiona Paton advises instructors to "be aware, however, that most first-year students will approach peer review as a proofreading exercise and will tend to remain on the level of correcting spelling and punctuation" (292). This misunderstanding of the theoretical goals of collaborative learning is surprising in light of the fact that collaboration in the writing classroom has been common for at least twenty years.

Student surveys in our study revealed a similar concern related to the perceived ability of the peer reviewer and his/her investment in providing quality feedback. While this study was not designed to investigate this aspect of peer review, many students indicated that they did not trust their peers to review their papers, stating that *I've never understood how having all students, including those who make C's & D's on papers, is beneficial. If they can't write a good paper, why do I want them to correct mine?* (Student survey #308). Of the 52% of the free-response comments that focused on the quality of the reviewer, most expressed concerns about classmates' dedication and ability to peer review. For example, one student responded, *I don't trust my peers to review my paper. I don't think they can do it competently, just like I don't think I can give a good peer review b/c I am a horrible writer* (Student survey #272).

Even at a university with limited diversity, students enter the writing classroom with varying writing experiences and skills. Some may have written extensively in high school and developed fairly robust composing processes, including peer review skills, while others may have written only sparingly. Some students are confident in their writing abilities while others would rather give a speech or jump from the proverbial airplane than write a paper. If the developed writer laments the lack of "qualified peers" available for review, he or she may be correct on some levels: the excellent student writer may not have a true peer if that student defines a peer as someone of equal skills. Again, we suspect that students do not understand the purpose of peer review and its value in a developed writing process.

The literature on both L1 and L2 studies shows that this attitude of distrust toward the peer reviewer is not uncommon. In a 1992 study, Kate Mangelsdorf finds that 77% of L2 students surveyed who did not like peer review were afraid that their peers would not provide valid advice (qtd. in Murau 2). A similar study, in 1997, finds much the same results: one surveyed L2 writer states, "Peer revision is a positive side to writing, but your peers do not always give you valuable feedback. Often my writing has changed for the worse when I receive comments from my peers" (qtd. in McGroarty and Zhu 31). In *Collaborative Learning: Higher Education, Interdependence, and the Authority of Knowledge*, Bruffee refers to a long example provided by David L. Rubin discussing "Zelda" and her difficult experience learning to trust her peer reviewers, an experience he finds representative of many writers. Perhaps because of this distrust, most students in our survey prefer to choose a friend or family member whom they know and in whom they have confidence, a preference which is indicated in Murau's study as well. Murau notes that "the trust of a good friend also seemed to be a factor when choosing a reviewer for LI and L2 writers" (75). To the student, it seems only logical that for a peer to be helpful he or she must be at least as skilled as the writer.

Helping students to accept that collaboration rather than correction is the goal of the writing group is essential to the successful peer review session.[7] The conclusion that McGroarty and Zhu reach is one that many instructors (Hansen and Liu; Cahill; Paton; etc.) have reached through practice: thorough preparation for peer review is vital to its success. Possibly, such preparation will offset the sense many students have that peers are not helpful, both by teaching students how to be effective reviewers and by teaching student writers what kind of help to look for (and appreciate) from peer reviewers. Our study suggests that providing handouts and lecturing are insufficient methods for demonstrating the collaborative value of peer review. The results of this survey indicate that professors must invest a great deal of class time to ensure a productive peer review, a finding in keeping with current literature on the subject. For example, Paul Rollinson suggests that "pre-training" for peer review focus on three areas: (1) raising awareness, (2) productive group interaction, and (3) productive response and revision. Like many others, he also recommends teacher feedback after peer review. Altogether, these perspectives suggest that the teacher spend substantial time focusing on the activity.

Although we agree with Paton that "[p]roductive peer review requires a typed and completed draft representing the student's best effort to that point" (293), more emphasis on peer review as a global activity may be in order. Students should not seek only to "correct" errors but should see peer review as a brainstorming process as well as an editing process. Perhaps we should revise and re-create our notion of peer review as an ongoing part of the process, a part that begins with brainstorming and is revisited at various reiterative stages throughout the composing process.

Such a re-visioning would require instructors to rethink the way they currently conduct peer reviews. For example, the results of this study support the importance of building rapport among classmates if our goal is to encourage productive peer review. Students need to create a sense of shared community in order to develop dialogues of trust and to build confidence in their classroom peers. Handouts and lectures cannot accomplish this task. Lisa Cahill argues that peer review needs to be "more than a series of questions that function in the textual vein" (304). Similarly, Gayle Nelson and John Murphy reinforce such collaborative learning theory, finding that the number of peer reviewer suggestions implemented in students' final essays depended on the communication environment of the reviewers/writers (cooperative or defensive) (140). This indicates that instructors need to continue to build collaborative groups that encourage rapport, moving away from lists of peer review questions that lead to a lot of writing, but little interaction.

Students seem to take their cues from instructors. If we stress the importance of peer review, our students are more likely to do so, but if we just go through the motions, perhaps passing out recycled handouts, our students will pick up on our lack of dedication and act accordingly. The results from our study suggest that when students perceive purpose for the peer review (as opposed to an activity to take up class time, aka "busywork") and faculty commitment to peer review (evidenced through regular practice, devotion of class time to preparing students to conduct peer review and actually doing peer review), they are more likely to feel confident about being able to review their classmates' papers and seem to value the peer review process. And if we value peer review as a critical component of a fully elaborated writing process and accept the social interactive perspective of writing, then we must take the necessary steps to allow students to learn to trust their classmates as "true peers."

NOTES

1. Other researchers have noted that L1 and L2 students have different composing processes, language use, cultural perspectives, and motivation (see Silva, 1993; Atkinson and Ramanathan, 1995; Nero, 1997). We cannot assume that research on L2 learners always applies directly to L1 learners; however, we must acknowledge that similarities exist. As writing instructors, we must continue to search for ways in which L2 studies can inform L1 and vice versa.

2. According to Maxwell, "A small sample that has been systematically selected for typicality and relative homogeneity provides far more confidence that the conclusions adequately represent the average members of the population than does a sample of the same size that incorporates substantial random or accidental variation" (71).

3. ACT composite middle 50% range for entering freshmen is 23–28.

4. We do not know for certain whether all 22 faculty who completed the survey also had students complete the surveys, but most bundles of student surveys were accompanied by one faculty survey.

5. *Data Collection Procedures:* Faculty who taught as part of the first-year Communication Arts program or upper-level, writing-intensive courses were invited to participate via email. Faculty who elected to participate had the option of using electronic or paper surveys. We asked faculty to complete the faculty survey and to have their students complete (paper) student surveys. We worked to triangulate this study, working with both quantitative and qualitative data. First, we included two questions on all course evaluations for 27 first-year Communication Arts courses. These evaluations were completed in campus computer labs during class time as part of the regular course evaluation process. Student enrollment for these courses was 502; of those, 398 students completed evaluations (79.28% response rate). The evaluations were anonymous, and to ensure faculty and student privacy, only aggregate responses to the questions were provided. Second, we created one survey for writing faculty and another survey for students in writing-intensive courses. The surveys consisted of seven questions, including Likert-type evaluative questions as well as specific response and open-ended questions for gathering qualitative data.

Data Analysis Procedures: Much of the data was analyzed using frequency counts and percentages. Where appropriate, primarily with student surveys, SPSS® software was used to calculate correlations and statistical significance. Likert-type and multiple choice responses were assigned specific numerical values as nominal variables for computational purposes. Free-response or open-ended questions (e.g., responses where we asked respondents to explain "other") were assessed qualitatively, meaning we allowed categories to sift out from the data rather than imposing preconceived categories. After carefully reviewing and discussing the free responses, we coded free responses to question #7 on the student survey in two ways: (1) as either positive or negative toward peer review and (2) topically (whether the comment focused on the reviewer, etc.). Other free responses were not coded at this time. After agreeing on appropriate categories and defining those categories, both researchers coded the data separately (92% agreement rating) and reached consensus through discussion on disputed codes. We worked to use this study as a preliminary exploration into the numbers of peer review.

6. Frankly, we were somewhat dismayed at finding that so few of our own students appreciated the university's Communication Resource Center (CRC—our writing/speaking center). Tutors in the CRC are undergraduates who were recommended, usually by their first-year Communication Arts' instructor, to the center's director. Not surprisingly, such recommendations are based on students' excellence in writing and speaking assignments during that first-year course. While we believe our tutors offer strong support to fellow students and work collaboratively with fellow students on writing and speaking assignments, we are aware that, as Trimbur points out, undergraduate tutors must learn "to negotiate the conflicting claims on [their] social allegiances" ("Peer Tutoring" 121). This is no small task.

7. In the study by McGroarty and Zhu, the student who showed dissatisfaction with peer review was one of a control group of students who received limited training in peer review techniques. The authors then examined the control group's perception of the peer review process, the validity of group members' comments on the papers of others, and their teacher's "feel" for how effective peer review was. Results show that the control group had a generally negative experience in all aspects examined. These student comments seem quite similar to those of our own students. McGroarty and Zhu's study, however, is most valuable for examining what happens when peer review is taught early on as a skill: students in the experimental group that received extensive instruction in peer review had a far more positive experience.

WORKS CITED

Asraf, Ratnawati. "Teacher Comments in Teaching Writing: A Critique of Peer Review." *The Gombak Review* 4.1 (1999): 64–82.

Atkinson, Dwight, and Ramanathan, Vai. "Cultures of Writing: An Ethnographic Comparison of L1 and L2 University Writing/Language Programs." *TESOL Quarterly* 29.3 (1995): 539–68.

Brooke, Robert, Ruth Mirtz, and Rick Evans. *Small Groups in Writing Workshops: Invitations to a Writer's Life.* Urbana: NCTE, 1994.

Bruffee, Kenneth. "Collaborative Learning and the 'Conversation of Mankind.'" *College English* 46.7 (1984): 635–52. Rpt. in Villanueva 393–414.

———. *Collaborative Learning: Higher Education, Interdependence, and the Authority of Knowledge.* 2nd ed. Baltimore: Johns Hopkins UP, 1999.

Cahill, Lisa. "Reflecting on Peer Review Practices." Roen et al. 301–06.

Ede, Lisa, and Andrea Lunsford. "The Pedagogy of Collaboration." *Singular Texts, Plural Authors: Perspectives on Collaborative Writing.* Carbondale: Southern Illinois UP, 1990. Rpt. in *The Allyn and Bacon Sourcebook for College Writing Teachers.* Ed. James C. McDonald. Needham Heights: Allyn and Bacon, 1996. 53–71.

Gere, Anne Ruggles. *Writing Groups: History, Theory, and Implications.* Carbondale: Southern Illinois UP, 1987.

Hansen, Jetta G., and Jun Liu. "Guiding Principles for Effective Peer Response." *ELT Journal* 59.1 (2005): 31–38.

Maxwell, Joseph A. *Qualitative Research Design: An Interactive Approach.* Applied Social Research Methods Series 41. Thousand Oaks: Sage, 1996.

Miller, Susan K. "Using Group Conferences to Respond to Essays in Progress." Roen et al. 307–18.

McGroarty, Mary E., and Wei Zhu. "Triangulation in Classroom Research: A Study of Peer Revision." *Language Learning* 47.1 (1997): 1–43.

Murau, Andrea M. "Shared Writing: Students' Perceptions and Attitudes of Peer Review." *Working Papers in Educational Linguistics* 9.2 (1993): 71–79.

Nelson, Gayle L., and John M. Murphy. "Peer Response Groups: Do L2 Writers Use Peer Comments in their Drafts." *TESOL Quarterly* 27.1 (1993): 135–41.

Nero, S. J. "English is My Native Language . . . or So I Believe." *TESOL Quarterly* 31.3 (1997): 585–92.

Nystrand, Martin. "A Social-Interactive Model of Writing." *Written Communication* 6.1 (1989): 66–85.

Paton, Fiona. "Approaches to Productive Peer Review." Roen et al. 290–300.

Roen, Duane, Veronica Pantoja, Lauren Yena, Susan K. Miller, and Eric Waggoner, eds. *Strategies for Teaching First-Year Composition.* Urbana: NCTE, 2002.

Rollinson, Paul. "Using Peer Feedback in the ESL Writing Class." *ELT Journal* 59.1 (2005): 23–29.

Roskelly, Hephzibah. "The Risky Business of Group Work." *The Writing Teacher's Sourcebook*. 4th ed. Ed. Edward P. J. Corbett, Nancy Myers, and Gary Tate. New York: Oxford UP, 2000. 123–28.

Silva, T. "Toward an Understanding of the Distinct Nature of L2 Writing: The ESL Research and Its Implications." *TESOL Quarterly* 27.4 (1993): 657–77.

Simkin, Mark G., and Nari K. Ramarapu. "Student Perceptions of the Peer Review Process in Student Writing Projects." *Journal of Technical Writing and Communication* 27 (1997): 249–63.

Trimbur, John. "Consensus and Difference in Collaborative Learning." *College English* 51.6 (1989): 602–16. Rpt. in Villanueva 439–56.

———. "Peer Tutoring: A Contradiction in Terms?" *The Writing Center Journal* 7.2 (1987): 21–27. Rpt. in *The Harcourt Brace Guide to Peer Tutoring*. Ed. Toni-Lee Capossela. New York: Harcourt, Brace, Jovanovich, 1998. 117–23.

Villamil, Olga S., and María C. M. de Guerrero. "Assessing the Impact of Peer Revision on L2 Writing." *Applied Linguistics* 19 (1998): 491–514.

Villanueva, Victor, Jr., ed. *Cross-Talk in Comp Theory: A Reader*. Urbana: NCTE, 1997.

8

Addressing Instructor Ambivalence about Peer Review and Self-Assessment

PAMELA BEDORE AND BRIAN O'SULLIVAN

I think we all struggle. This is something we talk about around the water cooler or the coffee machine at the Writing Center. Which is, how do we teach peer review? How do we model it? How do we teach it? Not just, why it's useful, but how to actually do it. I mean, we've had so much trouble finding an effective way to teach it.

(GRADUATE-STUDENT WRITING INSTRUCTOR)

INTRODUCTION

"Around the water cooler or the coffee machine," much of the talk about peer review and self-assessment at our writing program seemed tinged, if not saturated, with frustration. We heard about the peer who could only say "great job!," the student who felt "dissed" by fellow students, and the writer who self-castigated instead of self-critiquing. These disaffected figures seemed to be to a new generation what the bespectacled, red-pen-wielding instructor and enforcer of grammatical correctness was to the compositionists of the sixties and seventies. As junior writing program administrators at a research-extensive university, and members (more or less) of our instructors' generation, we sympathized with them—but we also wondered why there seemed to be such a disparity between their view and that of the composition and rhetoric literature and lore that informed our program.

Like many first-year writing programs, ours had a deep commitment to peer review and self-assessment. We followed in the tradition of the University of Minnesota Writing Workshops, where heavy stress was placed on modeling the professional peer review process. We also followed the same collaborative principles in assessing our program as a whole that we followed in assessing and developing student writing, so we sought feedback from the undergraduate students in the first-year writing class as well as the graduate-student instructors teaching the class. Our preliminary studies—broadly distributed surveys—suggested that instructor concerns about peer review and self-assessment might run deeper than doubts harbored by students. We thus dug

From *WPA: Writing Program Administration*, vol. 34, no. 2, Spring 2011, pp. 11–36.

more deeply into instructor attitudes on teaching collaborative assessment by conducting focus groups of instructors and interviews of the program director and the Instructor Training Coordinators (ITCs) responsible for their pedagogical training.

This paper employs our findings about instructor attitudes towards collaborative assessment to argue that WPAs must more actively engage instructors of first-year writing in honestly expressing and addressing their own attitudes towards peer review and self-assessment. Our instructors and ITCs show an active and thoughtful ambivalence that results in part from an underestimation of the degree to which students and/or other instructors value collaborative assessment as a goal, and in part from legitimate concerns about the viability of these teaching practices. Finally, we provide discussion of nine themes that can be productively deployed in faculty development to discuss instructor ambivalence about collaborative assessment.

This article is not about whether first-year writing programs should or should not utilize peer review and self-assessment. We assume that the learning goals of most such programs include the abilities to critique one's own writing productively as well as that of others. Whether we teach critique of others' writing through an activity called "peer review" or through "collaborative writing," "writing groups," "workshops," or other methods, we ask students to review each other's work, and whether we call critiquing one's own writing "self-assessment," "reflective writing," an exercise in "self-efficacy," or simply an aspect of revision, we surely want students to do it. The authors, and in general their participants, do not doubt the necessity of these goals or activities. But we do believe that instructors' doubts about peer review as it is actually practiced in many classrooms are serious and worthy of careful consideration and dialogue.

Engaging these doubts must begin by teasing apart and defining peer review and self-assessment. In the program in which both of us worked, peer review and self-assessment, along with instructor feedback, were closely linked in what we came to think of as "collaborative assessment." We liked—and still like—this collaborative assessment model and the ways in which it embodied give and take between writers and readers. Yet our results suggest that instructors' concerns sometimes result from a hazy view of the distinctions between the responsibilities of a peer reviewer and those of a self-critical writer. Seemingly opposite but deeply similar problems of definition may face programs that teach peer review and self-assessment separately and do not link them to instructor feedback; students in such programs may not learn to define the roles of writer and different kinds of readers in relation to each other.

LITERATURE REVIEW

Collaborative assessment is based on the principle that dialogue produces better understanding and evaluation than a single perspective. Much of the literature on peer review and self-assessment values these practices for their potential to remove the instructor from the position of sole authority on student writing, an element our instructors warmly embraced in discussing their teaching philosophies. Since the 1960's, peer review and self-assessment have been major elements in efforts to foster "writing without teachers" (Elbow), to displace "teacher talk" and the morbidly ossified academic discourse dubbed "Engfish" (Moffett), and to introduce students to the "conversation of mankind" (Bruffee). Increasingly, theorists have argued for giving students a more substantial, consequential voice in writing assessment (see, for example, White, Huot, and Inoue).

On the other hand, peer response has been critiqued by those who value maintaining the instructor's centrality. "A teacher's definition of 'better writers,'" as Brooke, Mirtz, and Evans note, determines the relative importance of student and instructor feedback in meeting course goals. David Bartholomae, they observe, argues against peer response because he believes the function of composition is to make writers "better" by leading them towards greater mastery of the conventions of academic communities, and peers who are equally deficient in knowledge of these conventions cannot lead each other towards such a goal. For Brooke, Mirtz, and Evans, on the other hand, "to be better writers means . . . to understand the ways in which writing can be useful in many areas of one's life, as well as to have experiences which adapt writing to any of those uses" (9). For these goals, small groups and peer response seem indispensable; they act as "invitations to a writer's life," allowing students to experience authentic communication with readers (12).

Constructions of students' individuality have concerned some scholars examining aspects of collaborative assessment. For instance, Candace Spigelman (p. 91 in this volume) studies student responses to show how peer review in writing groups uncomfortably conflicts with the ideology of individual ownership, even though it is ultimately productive in challenging students to recognize the social dimension of writing. Similarly, Susan Latta and Janice Lauer ask whether the "selves" under review in formal self-assessment exercises may find themselves subjected to scrutiny that limits their expressive freedom and heightens their writing apprehension. Additionally, Peggy O'Neill argues that self-assessment, when required but not dialogically engaged by peers and the instructor, degenerates into what Michel Foucault would describe as "ritualistic discourse"—a rote confession, invoked as part of a regimen of evaluation, classification and discipline—not as an organic part of revision and learning. Consequently, O'Neill agrees with Glenda Conway that "required reflection is ethical only if it exists as an ongoing component of a course and if the teacher of that course openly discusses his or her reactions to reflections with students" (Conway 92). All these compositionists are concerned with the subjectivity of the student; none fully addresses the question of whether collaborative assessment undermines or conceals a teacher's authority—a very real question for many of the graduate-student instructors with whom we worked.

These concerns also resonate in Jane Bowerman Smith and Kathleen Blake Yancey's collection of essays, which attends to self-assessment on the part of both students and instructors. Thomas Hilgers, Edna Hussey, and Monica Stitt-Bergh note that "teachers embrace the theoretical promise of self-assessment, although few devote much time to its practice" (9), marking a need to return attention to the now decentered instructor. While Hilgers et al., along with several other authors in the collection, focus on students' assessments of their own writing, others focus on instructors' self-assessment of pedagogy. Sandra Mano, for example, recounts the story of her own need for self-assessment in the process of engaging with, and ultimately transforming, a culture of teaching assistants around pedagogical practices. Mano reports difficulty in compelling new graduate-student composition instructors to adopt a process-based collaborative pedagogy, including peer review; new instructors questioned her authority and expertise and clung to their own prejudices about how to teach. Mano's own self-assessment alters her approach to teaching the pedagogy of collaborative assessment when she realizes that student concerns about collaborative assessment must be met with a willingness to "share power with the graduate students" (164).

We agree with Mano that self-assessment is a critical element of pedagogical transformation, and in our study we invited instructors as well as students to collaborate in the program's self-assessment. Any study that draws on voices of students, instructors, and administrators to assess an aspect of a writing program will inevitably be a study *in* collaborative assessment; by making it also a study *of* collaborative assessment in the classroom, we thematize the problem of collaboration rather than allowing it to be marginalized.

Our attention to instructor attitudes about collaborative assessment extends recent work in the field. In their study on attitudes towards peer review, for example, Charlotte Brammer and Mary Rees administered companion surveys asking faculty about their use of peer review in the classroom, and asking students about its effectiveness and their voluntary use of the practice outside the classroom. Although they report briefly on faculty responses, most of Brammer and Rees's analysis focuses on student attitudes as they make recommendations for ways in which faculty can provide more effective contexts for successful peer review. They acknowledge the importance of instructor attitudes, to be sure: "Students seem to take their cues from instructors. If we stress the importance of peer review, our students are more likely to do so, but if we just go through the motions, perhaps passing out recycled handouts, our students will pick up on our lack of dedication and act accordingly" (p. 132). Their productive analysis of student attitudes sets the stage for an equally productive analysis of instructor attitudes. How can we explain the phenomenon of instructors just going through the motions? Why might instructors lack dedication to peer review? In Lynne Belcher's informal survey of 31 writing instructors regarding their practices and experiences with peer review, she provides more questions than she answers. Belcher finds that although 30 of her 31 respondents recommend peer review as a teaching strategy for new instructors, their responses to individual questions about specific aspects of teaching peer review were far less positive.

METHODS

We conducted our study at a research-extensive university in which the first-year writing course was the only required course for all undergraduates. The course was supervised by a free-standing writing program and taught almost exclusively by graduate students, most from English and some from other departments. Instructors designed individual course topics and syllabi within broad program requirements that included instructor feedback in dialogue with peer review and self-assessment. Collaborative assessment was incorporated into all components of training, including the five-credit writing pedagogy course in the summer before instructors began teaching, the two-credit pedagogy workshop (in the form of small mentoring groups) in their first year of teaching, and several brown-bag pedagogy meetings open to all instructors. Instructors were free to choose from among existing models of peer review and self-assessment or to design their own.

In a survey, students rated self-assessment 2nd and peer review 14th out of fifteen writing skills targeted by the first-year writing course. . . . In terms of the value of the skills to their future writing, students ranked self-assessment 5th and peer review 15th. Since the program philosophy explicitly linked peer review and self-assessment, we found the disjunct in how students saw the two skills surprising, especially when we considered that the program had been emphasizing peer review longer than self-assessment. We had an anecdotal sense that not all instructors felt comfortable teaching these elements of writing, so we designed a companion survey that asked instructors to rank their ability to teach the fifteen skills and their perception of the value of these skills in students' future writing. . . . In ranking their own ability to teach the fifteen target skills, instructors ranked self-assessment 14th and peer review 15th. In terms of the value of the skills to students' future writing, instructors ranked self-assessment 9th and peer review 15th. In trying to understand why peer review was ranked so low across constituencies while self-assessment was ranked rather high by students but very low by instructors, we turned to student focus groups, where we heard relatively positive feedback about both peer review and self-assessment. We recognize, of course, that student responses may lack reliability, especially when students are speaking in person with a focus group leader who may be perceived as an authority figure. Nonetheless, it seems telling that in both student focus groups, students included peer review in response to the opening question, "What was most helpful about your writing class?" It seemed that students viewed self-assessment and, to a degree, peer review more positively than their instructors did, and we wanted to understand why.

We used selected quotations from student focus groups in designing focus group questions for instructors. The resulting questions were designed to elicit more detailed responses about collaborative assessment. . . . These focus groups were moderated by psychology graduate students with focus group experience who were not writing instructors but who worked at the

Writing Center (as did some of the focus group participants). We also conducted interviews of the faculty member who directed the Writing Program
and three Instructor Training Coordinators (ITCs) who had been advanced
graduate students when they served in that role, although one was a professor at another institution by the time we interviewed her. . . . All study instruments had IRB approval, and participant names have been changed to preserve anonymity.

This paper provides a qualitative analysis of the focus groups and interviews, discussing the attitudes of a small number of people (nine participants
in total: five instructors, three ITCs, and one program director). We chose this
approach over broader assessment tools like surveys because, like Eubanks
and Abbott, we believe that focus groups allow us to "bridge the gap between
potentially superficial quantitative methods and potentially subjective naturalistic methods" (33). Our results, based on intensive study of the comments
of this small group of instructors and administrators, are deeper than they are
wide, but from our perspectives as WPAs now working at different institutions, we are confident that the ambivalence reflected by this small group of
participants at a single institution is hardly unique. After all, this institution
has a deep commitment to collaborative assessment; this study itself results
from that commitment. Doubts reflected within this program might be even
more pronounced in other institutional contexts.

We did three separate strands of analysis to better understand our data.
In our quantitative coding, we used the utterance as the basic unit. For the
focus groups, all utterances were under 140 words, since participants interrupted each other often. For the interviews, we occasionally broke up the lon-
gest monologues (several were over three hundred words) into two or three
utterances based on their content in order to count them more accurately. To
determine significant utterances, we counted as trivial any utterance asking
for clarification such as "could you repeat the question?" and any utterance
that didn't specifically address elements of collaborative assessment, such as
"I used to be a grant writer." In the focus groups, we also removed utterances
that marked only agreement, i.e., comments whose entirety was "yes," "right,"
"I agree," etc. We found our focus group members to be highly supportive of
each other's statements, with 20% of all utterances and 32% of non-trivial
utterances marking simple agreement. Although the program director and the
graduate-student ITCs were asked the same interview questions, we report
on them separately since their responses tell quite different stories, perhaps
unsurprisingly given their different institutional positions. We analyzed a
total of 743 codeable utterances, 379 from instructors, 311 from ITCs, and 53
from the program director.

In processing the transcripts, the two investigators separately coded all
utterances and then met to adjust to a single set of codes. This activity simultaneously allowed us to develop a useful set of robust quantitative data and to
more deeply interrogate each of the utterances that had been made; in short,
this tedious process made us extremely familiar with our transcripts. We report

here on three sets of codes: a relatively simple identification of positive/negative attitudes in our participants, a count of adjectives referring to the attitudes of others, and a more nuanced identification of recurring themes. We coded utterances as "positive" or "negative" when they expressed commitment or skepticism, respectively, about either the process or the results of peer review, self-assessment, or instructor feedback that responded to peer review and self-assessment. Thus, we coded as negative utterances such as "I find that students don't really engage with self-assessment" or "peer review always makes me feel bad." We coded statements neutral when they described collaborative assessment practices without value judgments or evaluation; for example, "I put my students in pairs for peer review," or "In my class, peer review is worth 5% of your grade." We coded as mixed those utterances that included both positive and negative attitudes towards collaborative assessment, such as "I think peer review is helpful to students, but it's very hard to teach."

In coding for respondents' own attitudes about peer review and self-assessment, we found that we had to separate their characterizations of the attitudes of others carefully. We found these characterizations interesting in their own right, so we coded for perceptions of undergraduate student attitudes on the part of instructors and ITCs, and of instructor attitudes on the part of ITCs and the program director. As an index of these attitudes, we compiled a list of the adjectives used to describe them. Finally, we identified recurring themes underlying our participants' discussions of peer review and self-assessment, and we coded for mentions of those themes.

RESULTS AND DISCUSSION

Our main finding is a deeply rooted ambivalence about collaborative assessment in graduate-student instructors and administrators, in contrast to a much more serene commitment to this practice in the full-time faculty member directing the program. While we recognize the limitations of comparing the views of a single person to those of a small group, the director's views are representative of the predilection in favor of collaborative assessment common to many WPAs, as shown in our literature review. The contrast between the program director and the graduate-student ITCs and instructors can be seen quite starkly in Table 1.

Note the significant difference between the director and the graduate students, especially in the fact that over half the program director's comments are based in positive attitudes towards collaborative assessment, while only about one quarter of utterances made by graduate students are positive. There are also differences between the graduate students who serve as administrators in the program and those whose duties are only instruction; most notably, almost 30% of instructor utterances about collaborative assessment reflect negative attitudes, nearly double the percentage of those made by the ITCs charged with teaching them. Note too that over one third of comments by graduate students—instructors and ITCs alike—reflect mixed attitudes. In

TABLE 1   Positive/Negative Attitudes towards Collaborative Assessment by Group

	Positive	Negative	Mixed	Neutral
Program Director (1 participant, 53 utterances)	54.7% (29)	3.8% (2)	22.6% (12)	18.9% (10)
ITCs (3 participants, 311 utterances)	29.3% (91)	15.1% (47)	38.9% (121)	16.7% (52)
Instructors (5 participants, 379 utterances)	24.5% (93)	28.5% (108)	34.8% (132)	12.1% (46)

many cases, the mixed label refers to a participant articulating a benefit of a practice in the same breath as an anxiety about teaching it. For example, in describing as effective her practice of modeling reader comments for her students, Ann immediately added, "I mean, assuming that I do it properly or well."

Separating our data by participant yielded one insight: the one male instructor in our sample had an attitude profile far closer to that of the program director than to his peers (his 25 utterances were 44.0% positive, 16.0% negative, 32.0% mixed and 8.0% neutral). Obviously, we cannot generalize based on such a small sample size, but the impact of gender on (graduate-student or other) instructor attitudes may be ripe for future research.

Further separating our data by element of collaborative assessment discussed (peer review, self-assessment, or both) showed similar attitudes towards each element. However, instructors were more likely to speak of peer review and self-assessment separately, with only 13.1% of their utterances addressing the two practices working in concert, while those responsible for their training more often linked the practices (28.9% of ITC utterances and 34.0% of program director utterances). This suggests that the theoretical links between peer review and self-assessment may not always translate fluidly into classroom practice.

In attempting to better understand the ambivalence of our participants, we counted the number of times they characterized the attitudes of others. Our transcripts revealed characterizations of student attitudes that resonated with conversations we've had with each other and with faculty at this and other institutions. We found 107 instances in which graduate students characterized undergraduate student attitudes, with 70 of these characterizations falling under negative valences, 33 under positive, and 4 under neutral. The most repeated terms are: hated (9 mentions), comfortable (6), resistant (6), disliked (5), critical (4), frustrated (4), not mean (4), and trusting (3).

These characterizations tell an interesting and somewhat contrapuntal story. The majority of terms were mentioned only once or twice, and so we grouped the terms based on their contexts in three categories: general attitudes towards collaborative assessment; dispositions towards collaborative assessment; and attitudes about the outcomes of collaborative assessment. Broadstrokes characterizations of students' general attitudes towards collaborative assessment are quite negative, with students described as "hating" or "disliking" collaborative assessment a total of 14 times, while they were described as "loving," "liking," or "enjoying" it only 4 times.

In terms of student disposition towards collaborative assessment, we find a less significant gap between negative and positive characterizations, although the negative terms chosen seem more charged than the positive ones. The 31 negative characterizations can be broken into three main categories: 11 mentions of aggression (which includes antagonistic, competitive, critical, harsh, mean, and uncivil); 10 of resistance (inattentive, lost, reluctant, resistant, and uninvested); and 10 of fear (anxious, dreading, fearful, hesitant, insecure, intimidated, nervous, and touchy). The 25 positive characterizations can be broken into four main categories: 12 of comfort (comfortable, not in danger, safe, and trusting); 9 of civility (civil, honest, nice, nonjudgmental, and not mean); 3 of willingness (cooperative, game, and open-minded); and 1 of happiness ("students are happy to do peer reviews").

While instructors showed an active ambivalence about the value of collaborative assessment in the face of its difficulty, their perceptions of how students saw the outcomes of peer review and self-assessment were quite negative. Here we get 18 negative characterizations and only 5 positive ones. The negative descriptors can be divided into categories of injury (chastised, demoralized, devastated, exposed, horrified, hurt, sick, traumatized) and fatigue (annoyed, frustrated, hassled, overwhelmed, and "self-assessed-out"). While these negative adjectives tend towards the dramatic, those we categorized as positive represent an emotive range: excited, enlightened, appreciative, not offended, and surprised (that it worked).

The tendency of instructors to see student attitudes as largely negative may well be underestimating student buy-in of collaborative assessment. At this institution, after all, student surveys ranked self-assessment quite highly in terms of effectiveness of instruction and future usefulness, and despite lower survey rankings, peer review came up spontaneously as one of the most effective writing tools in student focus groups.

Similarly, those responsible for training writing instructors may also be underestimating instructor buy-in of collaborative assessment or interpreting ambivalence as resistance. We hope that this article, like Belcher's informal survey of instructors on peer review, will be useful to WPAs in understanding the complexity of attitudes instructors may be bringing to teaching collaborative assessment. The WPAs in our study characterized instructor attitudes more negatively than did the instructors they were working with. Their characterizations of instructor attitudes included 26 mentions of negative attitudes, 9 of positive attitudes, and 3 of neutral attitudes. The most common negative attitudes were resistant (9 mentions), overwhelmed (4), and skeptical (3). Negative attitudes were discussed in fairly strong language, including

TABLE 2   Mention of Themes, Ranked[1]

	Director (1 participant, 53 utterances)	ITCs (3 participants, 311 utterances)	Instructors (5 participants, 379 utterances)	Total (743 utterances)	Rank
Difficult to teach	8	83	105	196 (26.4%)	1
Audience (CA helping students think about audience)	12	40	55	107 (14.4%)	2
Democratic classroom (CA distributing power)	4	38	65	107 (14.4%)	3
Transfer of skills to future writing contexts	3	23	39	65 (8.7%)	4
Superficiality of comments	0	24	36	60 (8.1%)	5
Instructor negative experience	1	9	37	47 (6.3%)	6
Instructor positive experience	0	7	33	40 (5.4%)	7
Grade	1	17	15	33 (4.4%)	8
Instructor invisibility	2	14	13	29 (3.9%)	9
Deception (Instructor deceiving students)	0	5	11	16 (2.1%)	10

anxious, fearful, struggling, frustrated, and hating. Only two of the positive attitudes were mentioned more than once: embracing and converted. Other positive attitudes were described in fairly weak language: accepting, good-hearted, hard-working, inspired, and surprised that it worked.

Faced with what they saw as resistant and skeptical cadres of new instructors, the director and ITCs were focused more on the problem of persuading these instructors of the benefits of proven pedagogical methods than on collaboratively reevaluating these methods. The positive characterizations suggest something about the trainers' goals; they wanted new instructors to good-naturedly accept the prescribed methods, and to be so pleased with the results that they would even "convert." Gretchen recalls her own "conversion experience" when she first taught in the program: "You know, I'd never worked with this model, and it took me a while. I was skeptical . . . I tried a couple of times, failed a couple of times. Eventually, one day it was a success, and I said, wow, this is great, this could work, and I was converted at the point." This missionary language was used lightly, not to elevate the ITC above the new instructors, but to identify with them. Helen, the incumbent ITC, recalled an exercise in which these concerns were addressed head-on in training. She and the director asked new instructor trainees to reflect on their best and worst experiences of receiving feedback on their writing. She shared her own most prominent memory of writing feedback, in which a faculty member had told her that, by summarizing too much and not critiquing enough, she was reducing herself to the state of a "mechanical tour guide." Recalling this sensitized her to students' anxieties about receiving each other's feedback—and to instructors' anxieties about requiring such feedback. By having instructors discuss their own experiences, she hoped to help them understand and perhaps transcend the personal origins of their own ambivalence about using collaborative assessment in their classrooms. At the same time, listening to the instructors' stories might inform the program's continuing efforts to reassess and readjust its approach to collaborative assessment.

The instructors' ambivalences are located, we found, in nine key issues, and we provide discussion and analysis of these themes so WPAs can use them as points of departure for discussions with instructors. While three themes were predominantly discussed as negative (difficult, superficial, deception) and three were almost always positive valenced (audience, democracy, transfer), the others were more complexly characterized. Table 2, which shows the number of times each group mentions a specific theme, reveals the depth of ambivalence our participants experienced in thinking about collaborative assessment.

THEME 1: THE DIFFICULTY OF TEACHING COLLABORATIVE ASSESSMENT

As the most prevalent theme in our study, mentioned in over one quarter of all utterances, the difficulty of assessing writing—whether one's own or a peer's—must be central to conversations about teaching collaborative assessment. As revealed by the literature and by studies such as Belcher's, collaborative assessment has many benefits. And yet, it is also very hard to teach, and instructors should be aware of that and should be encouraged to discuss the challenges it poses in the classroom without feeling that they have failed. Our participants identified several specific sites of challenge: the difficulty for students to take on another person's perspective, the overwhelming nature of the material generated by collaborative assessment, its interconnectedness with other portions of the course, and ambiguity about the instructor's role.

In one of the focus groups, Carla articulated a difficulty students often face when receiving peer feedback: "And you have to put yourself now in that person's [the peer's] perspective, kind of outside, and try to understand what they don't understand." Ann agreed, noting that students sometimes find it harder to respond to a good peer review than to produce one: finding a problem is the easy part, but then the writer must ask, "'how do I revise, if I just found out that my paragraphs just don't make sense, how do I actually make it operational?'" The challenge of getting students to respond effectively to feedback is often equally present when students receive instructor feedback, and having students consider multiple readers—the instructor, the peer, and the self, at minimum—we hope prompts student writers to develop broader perspectives on the quality and presentation of their own arguments.

These multiple perspectives were, as ITC Fiona said, both "great" and "overwhelming"; they complicated the writing process even as they enriched it. The only way to resolve the complexities introduced by one round of self-assessment or peer review seemed to be another round of self-assessment and peer review, ad infinitum. "But," Ann said, "I'm not advocating a third synthesis of each paper. And the second peer review. And having peers read everything." To which Carla responded, "But ideally, that's what needs to happen." Ann and Danielle agreed; to teach collaborative assessment well seemed to require teaching it forever.

And it also seemed to require teaching peer review and self-assessment constantly and integrating it into every part of a course. As Carla said, peer review involves "all of those things that have to do with what we think of as reasoning and writing." To which Ann replied, "Gosh, and we throw it in in, like, week two or three." The conversation went on to consider whether peer review should be taught only later in the semester, with instructors coming to the consensus that although peer review may call upon more skills than students have early in the semester, it is also essential in helping them build those skills.

Despite this commitment to collaborative assessment, though, instructors sometimes faced anxiety in defining their own role, as Fiona articulated: "is it [the instructor's role] just to facilitate the comments that come from the writer him or herself and the peer reviewer, or actually serve as an arbiter of who's right and who's wrong?" This challenge is one of the instructor not only defining her own role, but also maintaining a careful balance where student input on their own or each other's writing is respected but also "corrected" as such corrections help students improve writing.

THEME 2: ATTENTION TO AUDIENCE

The most frequently mentioned positive characterization of collaborative assessment, unsurprisingly, celebrated its ability to help students engage with audiences, real and imagined, in their writing. In thinking about audience, one instructor cited Linda Flower's work on moving from writer-based to reader-based prose, a philosophy consonant with that of the program director, who recommended an approach where reader-based prose could be achieved through peer review, self-assessment, and instructor feedback all working together to create a complex sense of audience for students. Multiple perspectives, the program director said, "help them see that there are different minds out there, and get to the heart of an important communication principle, which is that each mind is unique, and that our goal as a writer is to do our best to communicate as clearly as possible our text to whatever intended audience we might have."

THEME 3: DEMOCRATIC CLASSROOM

Our participants were attracted to using collaborative assessment to build a democratic classroom, but also saw in it some inherent tensions. For example, in explaining the potential of collaborative assessment to empower students in the classroom, Carla referred to a teaching philosophy she had recently composed: ". . . writing about how my students always had more interesting things to say than I do, in every class period, and how I think that's the goal of this kind of community that you create, with a student-centered work, that you [the instructor] would start to become less and less the voice, and how there are all these other voices that are equally valid." A confident instructor might be comfortable with admitting that students provide feedback superior to the instructor's, but this position might be difficult for a newer instructor whose authority still feels tenuous. And creating the kind of community Carla espouses, which means deconstructing the hierarchy students expect, is what she sees as "the hardest part of teaching peer review." Danielle agreed with Carla's assessment of both the difficulty and importance of getting students beyond a hierarchical model of writing in which only the instructor's assessment is valued, characterizing the process of getting students "dependent on their own instincts in terms of giving and receiving feedback" as "weaning" students from the instructor. Through this move, students who have completed the class "can still be reflective about their own writing, which is what peer review is supposed to help them do." Although this connection of the student-centered, democratic classroom to the transfer of writing skills into future contexts is clearly discussed as an ideal of collaborative assessment, some anxieties over this approach lingered with instructors, as seen when they mentioned instructor effacement and invisibility.

THEME 4: TRANSFER OF SKILLS

Collaborative assessment's transferability as a skill that would be useful in other contexts and future writing was mentioned in almost 10% of all utterances, not only as an ideal, but through a variety of examples that might be helpful to other WPAs in training instructors. Helen, one of the ITCs, recounted a successful experience in which a former student from her first-year writing class had asked for feedback on a personal statement for medical school: "And he, at a certain point, without any comment from me, he had sent me his first draft, and he gave me a self-assessment. I was like, 'it works, I did it, oh my gosh!'" Danielle, an instructor, reported that requiring formal self-assessment from her students had transferred into her own writing practice, explaining that she now writes a little self-assessment statement to her advisor every time she submits portions of her dissertation for feedback.

The potential of self-assessment to transfer to contexts outside the classroom was more often mentioned than that of peer review, and two participants specifically mentioned that students were less likely to participate in peer review after the class was over. This view is at odds with the finding in both Brammer and Rees and in our student focus groups that students report that they do participate in voluntary out-of-classroom peer review.

THEME 5: SUPERFICIALITY OF COMMENTS

The concern that students make only superficial comments on peer reviews and self-assessments came up so often we separated it from the broader issue of the difficulty of teaching collaborative assessment, although the two are clearly related. Carla and Danielle particularly worried about the stronger students in their classes, using their own experiences as strong undergraduate writers who were frustrated by superficial peer feedback in explaining that "the better writers don't necessarily get the depth and width they need. They know they'll get it from you, which is why they wait for it" (Danielle). Our participants connected the concern of superficial comments to the larger skill of critical reading, noting that responding to writing requires students to read critically, and might even help them develop that skill.

It seems to us that faculty development workshops with concrete examples of questions that lead students to engage more deeply with the writing they are reviewing—whether their own, a peer's, or a published author's—would be useful in providing instructors tools to combat the challenge of superficial comments. We also wondered if writers were expecting too much direction from their peers. Perhaps instructors were not fully distinguishing the goals of peer review from the goals of instructor feedback and self-assessment. Perhaps the "depth and width" students hoped for from their peers included specific edits that would solve their problems, whereas simply pointing out certain problems might have been a more reasonable expectation.

THEME 6: THE GRADE

Although we did not ask about grades directly, they were mentioned 32 times by our participants, in a variety of keys. Our participants worried that the importance of the grade had the potential to undermine the value students placed on collaborative assessment, since students would pay more attention to instructor feedback than to their own or their peers' critiques. This problem can be mitigated, some instructors suggested, by grading the collaborative assessments themselves. Although all agreed that such grades should be worth a relatively small percentage of the class grade, discussions about how deeply integrated assessment strategies are with writing development led some instructors who had not previously graded peer reviews and self-assessments—or who had graded them under the rubric of participation—to consider putting a higher numerical value on these activities.

THEME 7: INSTRUCTOR EFFACEMENT

The idea that collaborative assessment allowed an instructor to be "as invisible as possible" (Danielle) in her own classroom came up almost thirty times, and these references were not easily categorized as positive or negative. Members of one focus group expressed agreement at Danielle's approach on peer review days of effacing herself in favor of creating "a day that's just about them and their writing." Much later in the same focus group, Ann imagined peer review and self-assessment working in an idealized way and asked: "So I mean, who needs an instructor at this point?" For these graduate-student instructors, relatively new to teaching, effacing themselves seemed at once philosophically resonant and perhaps all too easy. After all, they were approaching teaching from near the bottom of the academic hierarchy, and they may not have felt they had much power and authority which they could share with students.

THEME 8: INSTRUCTOR DECEPTION

In 2% of utterances, instructors and ITCs admitted that they fear they are deceiving students; this percentage is small, to be sure, but even sixteen mentions of such a delicate matter seem worth exploring. In explaining the principle that all readers are valid in a model of teaching writing that embraces peer review and self-assessment alongside instructor feedback, Gretchen expressed a concern about the potential clash between principles and realities: "I admit that I'm deceiving them. I say, I'm just your reader, but I'm in essence ultimately giving them a grade, so I know that this is difficult to balance." A similar concern came up in one of the focus groups when instructors discussed the ways in which they used student self-assessments as "almost like evaluations all year long." Danielle said "I have to say, it's almost a little selfish as I think about it. But the self-assessments I've had them do so far, I think, are more useful for me necessarily than they are for them . . . I don't know what they're getting out of it!" It may seem clear to administrators that students actually "get a lot out of it" when instructors closely monitor their progress and respond accordingly. However, to Danielle, this benefit seemed indirect, and thus, requiring self-assessments does not seem truly student-centered; as a result, she admitted, she doesn't always require this practice despite the program mandate to do so. Instructor concerns about "deception" and "selfishness" suggest that their resistance does not merely come from an unwillingness to engage in difficult practices; it grows out of a well-reasoned and considered concern about the trade-offs inherent in creating a collaborative classroom.

THEME 9: INSTRUCTOR EXPERIENCES WITH COLLABORATIVE ASSESSMENT

Our graduate-student instructors knew the collaborative classroom from both sides, and they often referred to their own experiences as students. Participants mentioned positive experiences, especially in considering recent experiences of tough but supportive dissertation groups and the use of self-assessment to communicate more effectively with advisors. In thinking about their undergraduate experiences, though, they focused largely on the negative, and they used quite strong language in doing so. Ann, for example, characterized her undergraduate experiences as "demoralizing" and "traumatic." Carla, in agreement, described undergraduate writing classes in which peer feedback was "either completely useless or incredibly hurtful," saying that she was left feeling that "I'm never going to let anyone see my work ever again as long as I live." Even now, as she neared the end of her doctoral program, Carla said: "I'm just absolutely deathly afraid of anyone reading my work," adding, "except my adviser." For Carla, processing these personal experiences was important as a teacher, since these allowed her to monitor her student reactions. As she said, "I don't want my students to be leaving my class and think they never want anybody seeing their work again. That's absolutely the worst possible scenario."

Our participants also described negative experiences with self-assessment. Ann said she doesn't do self-assessment as a graduate student, "unless you consider harsh, brutal self-criticism to be self-assessment." Her colleagues did. For Danielle, who was an undergraduate education major, formal self-assessment was a common assignment, and her recollection of the experience was blunt: "I hated writing them as a student, so as a professor, I feel that it's just mean." This observation led to a discussion of resistance summarized by Carla: "Yet even if you try to sell it [self-assessment], it comes through—all the resistance, it comes through."

The resistance to peer review and self-assessment instructors recalled from their undergraduate days was based in different challenges. They tended to see self-assessment as tedious or boring, but characterized peer review as carrying the potential of harm and even "violation" (Ann). Although the two practices have deep philosophical links, such different reactions emphasize the need to also provide instructors with tools to discuss them separately. Our participants' often negative undergraduate reactions to collaborative assessment were mitigated by more positive experiences as graduate students and by seeing both peer review and self-assessment work in the classes they were teaching. It seems likely that discussing such reactions with other instructors—and perhaps even with first-year writing students—would be beneficial in helping instructors move collaborative assessment into their comfort zone.

CONCLUSION

In analyzing our instructor focus groups, we find that instructors, through their own collaborative self-assessment, can productively revise their attitudes towards collaborative self-assessment by recognizing how those attitudes are rooted in their own experiences and prejudgments. We also find that instructors' complex reactions to collaborative assessment—a continuing tension between embracing and resisting the approach—are founded in thoughtful and principled self-assessment and peer review which should be heard out by administrators.

And the communication must be two-way. It is important that WPAs, where possible, share local assessments with their instructors. On a more general level, articles about the theory and practice of collaborative assessment in pedagogy classes might be productively accompanied by studies of student attitudes. For example, Brammer and Rees' study suggests that student attitudes tend toward the mixed rather than the negative. They find, after all, that despite complaints, only 7.3% of their student participants "preferred not to participate in peer review" (p. 126). This correlates with our more anecdotal findings through student focus groups, where they characterized collaborative assessment practices in a number of ways, ranging from "boring" to "very helpful," and where they reported often engaging in informal peer review by asking friends and roommates for feedback on papers.

Rather than pure dislike, we found in instructors true ambivalence: not a lukewarm acceptance or an indifference to these practices, but strong attraction coexisting with strong aversion. On one hand, instructors were drawn to collaborative assessment because it provided a productive context for students to address issues of audience, it promised to shift from them the burden of evaluative power and create a less hierarchical classroom, and they believed it to be a transferable skill that would help students in future writing. On the other hand, they doubted collaborative assessment because it was inherently difficult to teach, it threatened to erode their necessary authority in the classroom, and it concealed their real power rather than honestly distributing some of it throughout the classroom. Instructor attitudes were also heavily inflected by memories of their own often negative experiences with collaborative assessment as undergraduates. Overall, their ambivalence about peer review and self-assessment reflected a sober and realistic view of the risks of collaborative assessment from their perspective at the margins of academia.

For example, despite the program's solid philosophical basis for integrating peer review and self-assessment, perhaps instructors are prudential in separating these practices as they reflect on their teaching experiences; perhaps they have found that the two practices pose different problems, and WPAs should provide instructor training that allows for conceptually distinguishing them instead of (or in addition to) collapsing them. In order to model rhetorical understandings of writing as communication from writer to reader, programs and instructors should provisionally define the roles of writer and reader. Peer reviewers, as readers, can be told that they are not responsible for "fixing" or reconceptualizing the paper, but for telling other writers what they find clear and persuasive and what they do not; the self-assessors, as writers, can be told that they remain "in charge" of the paper and are not responsible for addressing every whim of every reader.

We say "can be told" because models of the reader-writer relationship are many and various; therefore, writing programs should neither rigidly define peer review and self-assessment for everyone, nor allow these terms to remain undefined or hazily defined within each classroom. Writing programs should recognize that instructors—and particularly graduate-student instructors, who may still be negotiating with their committees over ownership of their own writing—may have their own anxieties and misgivings about sharing their own work or explicitly evaluating it for themselves, and may therefore have difficulty asking students to share or self-evaluate without carefully delimiting those activities to create protective boundaries. And other instructors may passionately believe in intense, almost unbounded collaboration between readers and writers. Therefore, we recommend that programs ask instructors to define and delimit the responsibilities of peer reviewers and self-assessors collaboratively within broad parameters informed by the literature (and perhaps using exercises similar to the focus group conversations we used in our study) and that programs also help instructors more specifically define those responsibilities for their own individual pedagogies and courses.

We argue that instructors concerned about possible negative reactions from students should reconsider whether these concerns stem from their own ambivalence about peer review and self-assessment, and that those training new instructors should actively engage with such ambivalence, recognizing its validity without abandoning commitment to the ideals of collaborative assessment. While our graduate-student instructors were ambivalent about teaching collaborative assessment in first-year writing courses, they showed confidence in the value of the conversation they were having, which was essentially a form of collaborative assessment of their own pedagogical practices. For us, the focus groups demonstrated the need for instructors to work together collaboratively and supportively to examine their own experiences and attitudes as writers—particularly in terms of collaborative assessment—and the ways in which these shape their emerging identities as instructors.

NOTE

1. Some utterances were counted under multiple themes, while others mentioned none of these themes. The percentages are calculated by the number of utterances mentioning the theme over the total number of utterances (743).

WORKS CITED

Bedore, Pamela, and Deborah Rossen-Knill. "Informed Self-Placement: Is a Choice Offered a Choice Received?" *WPA: Writing Program Administration* 27.4 (2004): 55–78. Print.

Brooke, Robert, Ruth Mirtz, and Rick Evans. *Small Groups in Writing Workshops: Invitations to a Writer's Life.* Urbana: NCTE, 1994. Print.

Bruffee, Kenneth A. "Collaborative Learning and the 'Conversation of Mankind.'" *College English* 46.7 (1984): 635–52. Print.

Conway, Glenda. "Portfolio Cover Letters, Students' Self-Presentation, and Teachers' Ethics." *New Directions in Portfolio Assessment: Reflective Practice, Critical Theory, and Large-Scale Scoring.* Ed. Laurel Black, Don Daiker, Jeffrey Sommers, and Gail Stygall. Portsmouth, NH: Boynton/Cook, 1994. 83–92. Print.

Elbow, Peter. *Writing Without Teachers.* Oxford: Oxford UP, 1973. Print.

Eubanks, Philip, and Christine Abbott. "Using Focus Groups to Supplement the Assessment of Technical Communication Texts, Programs, and Courses." *Technical Communication Quarterly* 12.1 (2003): 25–45. Print.

Flower, Linda. "Writer-Based Prose: A Cognitive Basis for Problems in Writing." *College English* 41.1 (1979): 19–37. Print.

Hilgers, Thomas L., Edna L. Hussey, and Monica Stitt-Bergh. "The Case for Prompted Self-Assessment in the Writing Classroom." Smith and Yancey 1–24.

Huot, Brian. "Toward a New Discourse of Assessment for the College Writing Classroom." *College English* 65.2 (2002): 163–80. Print.

Inoue, Asao B. "Community-Based Assessment Pedagogy." *Assessing Writing* 9.1 (2004): 208–33. Print.

Latta, Susan, and Janice Lauer. "Some Issues and Concerns from Postmodern and Feminist Perspectives." Smith and Yancey 25–34.

Mano, Sandra. "Negotiating TA Culture." Smith and Yancey 157–68.

Moffett, James. *Teaching the Universe of Discourse.* Boston: Houghton Mifflin, 1968. Print.

O'Neill, Peggy. "Reflection and Self-Assessment: Resisting Ritualistic Discourse." *The Writing Instructor* 2.1 (2002): n. pag. Web. 30 June 2010.

Smith, Jane Bowerman, and Kathleen Blake Yancey, Eds. *Self-Assessment and Development in Writing: A Collaborative Inquiry.* Cresskill: Hampton P, 2000. Print.

Spigelman, Candace. "Habits of Mind: Historical Configurations of Textual Ownership in Peer Writing Groups. *CCC* 49.2 (1998): 234–55. Print.

White, Ed. "The opening of the Modern Era of Writing Assessment: A Narrative. *College English* 63.3 (2001): 306–20. Print.

PART THREE

Theory into Practice

Introduction to Part Three

The essays collected in this section offer the practical insights and experience of teacher-scholars, who weigh the opportunities and challenges of peer review and response as they offer well-informed, ready-to-apply suggestions and insights on successful practice. Those interested in how experienced writing instructors design and support peer response activities in their own classes will find the strategies here useful in developing their own goals and course designs. Readings in Part Three particularly focus on the contexts of first-year writing courses and the needs of students who are new to the contexts of writing for college. While the authors each treat the nuts and bolts of collaborative work in peer groups, they also reveal a deep concern for pedagogies of sharing and listening.

Our first selection, excerpted from Peter Elbow and Pat Belanoff's third edition of *Sharing and Responding*, is a must-read for anyone seriously interested in better peer review and response practice. Originally published in 1989, sixteen years after Elbow's *Writing without Teachers*, this concise, easy-to-navigate book fleshes out many of Elbow's foundational tenets and treats peer sharing and responding in quite practical terms. In illustrating why student writers need an audience of readers willing to listen first and advise later, Elbow and Belanoff illustrate a continuum of practice from simple sharing and reading (listening) to more full-blown criterion-based feedback and critique (responding). Along the way, the authors touch on such well-known Elbowisms as "summary and sayback," "movies of the reader's mind," and "believing and doubting." Elbow and Belanoff ultimately provide suggestions for smart, systematic ways that teachers of writing can help student writers develop the requisite trust and patience in learning to respond to one another's work.

In a chapter from a collection he edited with Ruth Mirtz and Rick Evans (*Small Groups in Writing Workshops* [1994]), Robert Brooke takes up where Elbow and Belanoff left off. In the book's first chapter, readers get a much more intimate sense of what the peer response experiences were like for the authors and their students. Influenced by the work of Bruffee, Elbow, Gere, Linda Flower and John Hayes, and Ann Berthoff, Brooke attempts to illustrate how students learn the rules of written language in ways similar to how children learn oral language—through intensive interaction with both oral and written conversations with their peers and teachers. While ultimately arguing for the benefits of peer writing groups, Brooke also describes potential drawbacks (such as students negotiating sensitive private/public writing issues with others or reconciling their experiences with writing teachers who do not value peer-to-peer collaborative learning, or negotiating diversity among peers). Like Elbow and Bruffee, the author argues that the more we work against the grain of our culture's view of the prevailing role of the teacher as controller of classroom discourse and behavior, the more we might develop the potential for multivoiced, shared pedagogical authority. Illustrating this belief with fine-grained reporting from students, Brooke offers readers detailed ways to design and implement all phases of peer response activities.

Our third and fourth selections hail from a section of the collection *Strategies for Teaching First-Year Composition* (2002) that was dedicated to peer response activities. Susan K. Miller's "Using Group Conferences to Respond to Essays in Progress," similar to Spigelman's essay included in Part Two, seeks to combine the best of peer response activities detailed by Brooke, Mirtz, and Evans with the types of teacher-student conferences described by Muriel Harris in *Teaching One-to-One*. Miller discusses the value of having students listen and respond to one another's works in progress while the teacher takes an active role with the group. Her essay offers an example of student response and a discussion of how that peer feedback affected subsequent drafts of a student's work in fruitful ways. Of note to those interested in researching peer response activities: Miller's innovative method has become a foundation of peer response research.

In the fourth selection, "Reflection on Peer-Review Practices," Lisa Cahill revises typical notions of what it means to foster an environment of authentic peer-to-peer listening and responding. Like Karen Spear's work fourteen years earlier, Cahill realizes that having students fill out long, detailed Q&A worksheets might not be the most helpful method of performing peer response. She narrates her own movement from a rigidly formal method to a much more fluid, flexible practice that encouraged students to engage in the communal, trust-building processes of listening and talking about each other's writing. Cahill describes how she came to realize that allowing students much more freedom and responsibility to manage their own groups, generate their own questions, and negotiate their own differences would instantiate more valuable, long-term communicative and composing aptitudes.

The authors collected here in Part Three each affirm that pedagogies of sharing and responding are central to the core learning that writing classes make available to students. While these pedagogical centers may seem simplistic or reductive in an age dominated by concerns for writing transfer, the authors in this section remind us that when we ask students to read and respond to the work of their peers we are providing a unique opportunity for different forms of student-driven learning to emerge. These readings also remind us that strong course design—of any sort—begins with instructors' reflexive understanding of their own goals for student writers. Creating appropriate spaces for student reflection and engagement may take some experimentation and attention from writing instructors. The authors collected in this section all suggest that time spent thinking through peer response activities is time well invested.

9

From Sharing and Responding

PETER ELBOW AND PAT BELANOFF

SUGGESTIONS FOR USING "SHARING AND RESPONDING"

There are more techniques here than you can use on any one occasion. But we want you to try them all out in order to learn the wide range of options you have for feedback. Then you will be in a position to ask for the kind of feedback that is right for you, depending on your preferences or temperament, the kind of piece you're working on, and the stage it's at. Many people don't like getting feedback on their writing because they feel that they are "on the chopping block." They don't realize how many options they could ask for, and so they end up helplessly putting themselves in the hands of readers. "Sharing and Responding" will help you take charge of the process of getting responses.

We also urge you to try out these techniques in order. They go from quicker to more time-consuming, from easier to harder, and from safer to riskier. This progression builds a feedback situation of support and trust. Don't assume, though, that the later kinds of responding are better: Some of the earliest ones remain the most useful despite being quick and easy.

OUR UNDERLYING PREMISES AND CONVICTIONS

We find that most students are reluctant to judge or evaluate each other's writing and give advice about how to improve it. We think they are right. Evaluation and advice are not what writers need most. What writers need (and fortunately it's what all readers are best at) is an *audience*: a thoughtful, interested audience rather than evaluators or editors or advice-givers. In the long run, you will learn the most about writing from feeling the *presence of interested readers*—like feeling the weight of a fish at the end of the line. You can't trust evaluations or advice. Even experts on writing usually disagree with each other. And even when they agree about what is weak, they often disagree about how to fix it.

From "Cover Letter" and "Summary of Kinds of Responses" in *Sharing and Responding*. 3rd ed., Random House, 2000, pp. 3–16.

Therefore we urge you to follow a crucial principle for feedback: Don't let anyone give you evaluation or advice unless they also give you the perceptions and reactions it is based on, that is, unless they describe *what they see* and *how they are reacting*. For example, if a reader says, "The organization is confusing in your piece," make sure she goes back and describes the sequence of parts in your piece as she sees them, and/or the sequence of her reactions as she was reading: When did she first start feeling confused, and what kind of confusion was it? What was going on in her mind and feelings at different points?

Many students have never written except in school, never given their writing to anyone but a teacher, and always gotten some kind of evaluative response. But it's hard for writers to prosper unless they give their work to a variety of readers, not just teachers, and get a variety of responses: no response, nonevaluative responses, evaluative responses. The suggestions here will give you the variety of audience relationships you need to develop a more productive sense of audience.

You will improve your writing much faster if you let us and your teacher help you build a community in your classroom: a place where people hear clearly even what is mumbled, understand what is badly written, and look for the validity even in what they disagree with. Eventually you will learn to write to the enemy—to write surrounded by sharks. But you will learn that necessary skill better if, for a while, you practice writing to allies and listening to friends.

TWO PARADOXES OF RESPONDING

First paradox: the reader is always right; yet the writer is always right. That is, readers get to decide what's true about their reactions—about what they see or think or feel. It's senseless to quarrel with readers about their experience of what's happening to them (though you can ask them to explain their experience more fully).

Nevertheless, you as the writer get to decide what to do about any of this feedback from readers, what changes to make, if any. You don't have to follow their advice. Just listen openly and swallow it all. You can do that better if you realize that you get to take your time and make up your own mind.

Second paradox: the writer must be in charge; yet the writer must sit quietly and do nothing. As writer, you must be in control. It's your writing. Don't be passive or helpless. You get to decide what kind of feedback, if any, you need. Are you trying to improve this particular piece? Or perhaps you don't care so much about working on this piece any more but just want feedback on it to learn about your writing in general. Or perhaps you don't want to work on anything but just enjoy sharing this piece and hearing what others have to say. Don't let readers make these decisions for you. Ask for what you want and don't be afraid to stop them if they give you the wrong thing. For example, sometimes it's important to insist, "I'm still very tender about this piece. I just want to hear what it sounds like for now and not get any feedback."

Nevertheless you mostly have to sit back and just listen. If you are talking a lot, you are probably blocking good feedback. For example, don't argue if they misunderstand what you wrote. Their misunderstanding is valuable, and you need to understand it in order to see how your words function. If they want to give you feedback you didn't ask for—or not give you what you ask for—they may have good reasons. If you aren't getting honest, serious, or caring feedback, don't blame your readers. You may not have convinced them that you really want it.

HOW WE WROTE "SHARING AND RESPONDING"

In our first drafts of the *Community of Writers* book, we put all our sharing and responding suggestions in the workshops themselves. But then we ran into a dilemma. We realized that we wanted to give students and teachers lots of choice of which workshops to use and what order to use them in. Yet we didn't want to give that much choice about which feedback techniques to use and which order to use them in. For it's crucial to us that you go through a progression that gives the best learning and builds the most trust. Because of this dilemma, we hit on the plan of having a separate "Sharing and Responding" guide (though we have also kept a few suggestions in each workshop).

Also, this part in the first edition of our textbook was too complicated: too many kinds of response were arranged in groupings which were too complex. We realize now that as we worked out this book for the first time, we built too much of our background thinking into the structure itself. Writers often speak of the principle of "scaffolding": structures put up in order to help construct the building in the first place—but which can be taken down after the building is done. We had too much scaffolding in the first edition. You'll find the same thing sometimes happens to you. You'll write something and it comes out complicated; but once you've got it written, you finally understand it better and you can then revise to make it simpler.

And, now for this third edition, we have changed the sample essays. Some of our students and reviewers told us it would be helpful to have essays on topics more relevant to today's world and the kinds of problems they might meet up with in their own lives. We think the two essays we selected confront such problems. We hope you agree. But whether you do or don't, we'd like to have responses from you since, like you, we can profit from readers' responses. . . .

Summary of Kinds of Responses

Here is an overview of 11 different and valuable ways of responding to writing and a few thoughts about when each kind is valuable. . . . After you have tried them out, you can glance back over this list when you want to decide which kind of feedback to request.

1. SHARING: NO RESPONSE

Read your piece aloud to listeners and ask: "Would you please just listen and enjoy?" You can also give them your text to read silently, though you don't usually learn as much this way. Simple sharing is also a way to listen better to your own responses to your own piece, without having to think about how others respond. You learn an enormous amount from hearing yourself read your own words or from reading them over when you know that someone else is also reading them.

No response is valuable in many situations—when you don't have much time, at very early stages when you want to try something out or feel very tentative, or when you are completely finished and don't plan to make any changes at all—as a form of simple communication or celebration. Sharing gives you an unpressured setting for getting comfortable reading your words out loud and listening to the writing of others.

2. POINTING AND CENTER OF GRAVITY

Pointing: "Which words or phrases or passages somehow strike you? stick in mind? get through?" Center of gravity: "Which sections somehow seem important or resonant or generative?" You are not asking necessarily for the main points but for sections or passages that seem to resonate or linger in mind. Sometimes a seemingly minor detail or example—even an aside or a digression—can be a center of gravity.

These quick, easy, interesting forms of response are good for timid or inexperienced responders, or for early drafts. They help you establish a sense of contact with readers. Center of gravity response is particularly interesting for showing you rich and interesting parts of your piece that you might have neglected, but which might be worth exploring and developing. Center of gravity can help you see your piece in a different light and suggest ways to make major revisions.

3. SUMMARY AND SAYBACK

Summary: "Please summarize what you have heard. Tell me what you hear as the main thing and the almost-main things." (Variations: "Give me a phrase as title and a one-word title—first using my words and then using your words.") Sayback: "Please say back to me in your own words what you hear me getting at in my piece, but say it in a somewhat questioning or tentative way—as an invitation for me to reply with my own restatement of what you've said."

These are both useful at any stage in the writing process to see whether readers "got" the points you are trying to "give." But sayback is particularly useful at early stages when you are still groping and haven't yet been able to find what you really want to say. You can read a collection of exploratory passages for sayback response. When readers say back to you what they hear—and invite you to reply—it often leads you to find exactly the words or thoughts or emphasis you were looking for.

4. What Is Almost Said? What Do You Want to Hear More About?

Just ask readers those very questions.

This kind of response is particularly useful when you need to *develop* or enrich your piece—when you sense there is more here but you haven't been able to get your finger on it yet. This kind of question gives you concrete substantive help because it leads your readers to give you some of *their ideas* to add to yours. Remember this, too: What you imply but don't say in your writing is often very loud to readers but unheard by you and has an enormous effect on how they respond.

Extreme variation: "Make a guess about what was on my mind that I didn't write about."

5. Reply

Simply ask, "What are *your* thoughts about my topic? Now that you've heard what I've had to say, what do *you* have to say?"

This kind of response is useful at any point, but it is particularly useful at early stages when you haven't worked out your thinking. Indeed, you can ask for this kind of response even before you've written a draft; perhaps you jotted down some notes. You can say, "I'm thinking about saying X, Y, and Z. How would you reply? What are your thoughts about this topic?" This is actually the most natural and common response to any human discourse. You are inviting a small discussion of the topic.

6. Voice

(a) "How much voice do you hear in my writing? Is my language alive and human? Or is it dead, bureaucratic, unsayable?" (b) "What kind of voice(s) do you hear in my writing? Timid? Confident? Sarcastic? Pleading?" Or "What kind of person does my writing sound like? What side(s) of me come through in my writing?" Most of all, "Do you trust the voice or person you hear in my writing?"

This kind of feedback can be useful at any stage. When people describe the voice they hear in writing, they often get right to the heart of subtle but important matters of language and approach. They don't have to be able to talk in technical terms ("You seem to use lots of passive verbs and nominalized phrases"); they can say, "You sound kind of bureaucratic and pompous and I wonder if you actually believe what you are saying."

7. Movies of the Reader's Mind

Ask readers to tell you honestly and in detail what is going on in their minds as they read your words. There are three powerful ways to help readers give you this kind of response: (a) Interrupt their reading a few times and find out what's happening at that moment. (b) Get them to tell you their reactions in the form of a *story* that takes place in time. (c) If they make "it-statements" ("It was confusing"), make them translate these into "I-statements" ("I felt confused starting here about . . .").

Movies of the reader's mind make the most sense when you have a fairly developed draft and you want to know how it works on readers, rather than when you're still trying to develop your ideas. Movies are the richest and most valuable form of response, but they require that you feel some confidence in yourself and support from your reader, because when readers tell you honestly what is happening while they are reading your piece, they may tell you they don't like it or even get mad at it.

8. METAPHORICAL DESCRIPTIONS

Ask readers to describe your writing in terms of clothing (e.g., jeans, tuxedo, lycra running suit), weather (e.g., foggy, stormy, sunny, humid), animals, colors, shapes.

This kind of response is helpful at any point. It gives you a new view, a new lens; it's particularly helpful when you feel stale on a piece, perhaps because you have worked so long on it. Sometimes young or inexperienced readers are good at giving you this kind of response when they are unskilled at other kinds.

9. BELIEVING AND DOUBTING

Believing: "Try to believe everything I have written, even if you disagree or find it crazy. At least *pretend* to believe it. Be my friend and ally and give me more evidence, arguments, and ideas to help me make my case better." Doubting: "Try to doubt everything I have written, even if you love it. Take on the role of enemy and find all the arguments that can be made against me. Pretend to be someone who hates my writing. What would he or she notice?"

These forms of feedback obviously lend themselves to persuasive essays or arguments, though the believing game can help you flesh out and enrich the world of a story or poem. Believing is good when you are struggling and want help. It's a way to get readers to give you new ideas and arguments and to improve your piece in all sorts of ways. Doubting is good after you've gotten a piece as strong as you can get it and you want to send it out or hand it in—but first find out how hostile readers will fight you.

10. SKELETON FEEDBACK AND DESCRIPTIVE OUTLINE

Skeleton feedback: "Please lay out the reasoning you see in my paper: my main point, my subpoints, my supporting evidence, and my assumptions about my topic and about my audience." Descriptive outline: "Please write *says* and *does* sentences for my whole paper and then for each paragraph or section." A *says* sentence summarizes the meaning or message, and a *does* sentence describes the function.

These are the most useful for essays. They are feasible only if the reader has the text in hand and can take a good deal of time and care—and perhaps write out responses. Because they give you the most distance and perspective on what you have written, they are uniquely useful for giving feedback to yourself. Both kinds of feedback help you on late drafts when you want to test out your reasoning and organization. But skeleton feedback is also useful on early drafts when you are still trying to figure out what to say or emphasize and how to organize your thoughts.

11. CRITERION-BASED FEEDBACK

Ask readers to give you their thoughts about specific criteria that you are wondering about or struggling with: "Does this sound too technical?" "Is this section too long?" "Do my jokes work for you?" "Do you feel I've addressed the objections of people who disagree?" And of course, "Please find mistakes in spelling and grammar and typing." You can also ask readers to address what they think are the important criteria for your piece. You can ask too about traditional criteria for essays: focus on the assignment or task, content (ideas, reasoning, support, originality), organization, clarity of language, and voice.

You ask for criterion-based feedback when you have questions about specific aspects of your piece. You can also ask for it when you need a quick overview of strengths and weaknesses. This kind of feedback depends on skilled and experienced readers. (But even with them you should still take it with a grain of salt, for if someone says your piece is boring, other readers might well disagree. Movies of the reader's mind are more trustworthy because they give you a better picture of the personal reactions *behind* these judgments.)

Procedures for Giving and Receiving Responses

We've briefly summarized your choices among *kinds of response*. Now we want to emphasize that you also have important choices among *procedures for getting responses*. It's important to test these out, too—to see which ones are the most helpful for you in different situations.

EARLY OR LATE DRAFTS?

Responses are helpful on both early and late drafts; indeed, it's a big help to discuss your thinking even before you have written at all. (For very early drafts, these response modes are particularly helpful: pointing, center of gravity, summary, sayback, almost said, and reply.) At the other extreme, it can be helpful and interesting to get feedback even on *final drafts* that you don't plan to revise any more: You will learn about your writing and about how readers read. When poets and fiction writers give readings, the goal is pleasure and celebration, not feedback. (Keep your eye out for notices of readings by poets and writers in local schools, libraries, and bookstores. They can be fun to attend.)

Pairs or Groups?

On the one hand, the more readers the better. Readers are different, and reading is a subjective act so you don't know much if you only know how one reader reacts. On the other hand, more readers take more time and you can learn a lot from one reader if she is a good one—if she can really tell you in detail about what she sees and what goes on in her head as she reads your words. Also, it's easier to build an honest relationship of trust and support between just two people. (If you know you are working on something important and will want to get feedback at various stages, you can use your trusted readers one or two at a time.)

You can have it both ways too—getting the multiple perspectives of groups and the trust and support of pairs—by first getting brief feedback from a group and then dividing into pairs for fuller responses (or vice versa).

New Faces or the Same Old Faces?

If you change readers, you get variety and new perspectives. But good sharing and responding depend on a climate of safety and trust. Certain things can't occur until reader and writer have built up trust, and that takes longer than you might think. Most writers find one or two trusted readers or editors, and rely on them over and over.

Share Out Loud or Give Readers Copies on Paper?

The process of reading out loud brings important learning: You can feel strengths and weaknesses physically—in your mouth as you pronounce your words and in your ear as you hear them. And you can tell about the effects of your words by watching your listeners. Reading out loud is more alive. But if your piece is very long or time is short, you will need to give paper copies. Paper texts give readers more time to read closely and reflect on your writing, especially if the material is technical. Remember, however, that if listeners can't follow your piece as you read it out loud, it is probably not clear enough.

Perhaps the most efficient way to get the most feedback in the shortest time is to circulate paper copies around a group; at every moment, everyone is reading someone's paper and writing feedback. (You have the choice of whether to let readers see how previous readers responded.) But efficiency is not everything; this method is not very sociable. You can also combine the two modalities by reading your paper out loud but giving listeners a copy to follow. (Computers and photocopy machines make it easier to create multiple copies.)

Writers have always used the mail to share writing with readers and get responses, but electronic mail and fax machines have encouraged many more people to "meet" across hundreds and thousands of miles. Some people use these media not just for transmitting pieces of writing and responses but even for "real time" conversation about the writing.

ABOUT READING OUT LOUD

You need to read your piece twice. Otherwise listeners can't hear it well enough to give helpful responses. But if you don't want to read it twice in a row (which can feel embarrassing), there is a good solution. Have each person read once for no response; then have each person read again for response. Listeners need a bit of silence after each reading to collect their thoughts and jot down a few notes; this way no one will be too influenced later by hearing the responses of others.

Also, it can be interesting and useful to have the second reading given by someone other than the writer. This way listeners get to hear two different "versions" of the words. When someone reads a piece of writing out loud, that in itself constitutes feedback: it reveals a great deal about what the reader sees as the meaning, emphasis, implications, and voice or tone of the piece. Some critics and writers say that a set of words is not "realized" or "complete" until read out loud — that words on the page are like a play script or musical notes on a page, mere ingredients for the creation of the real thing, which is a performance.

Some writers get others to give both readings, but we think that's sad because you learn so much from reading your own words. If you feel very shy or even afraid to read your writing, that means it's even more important to do so.

RESPONDING OUT LOUD OR ON PAPER?

Both modes are valuable. Spoken responses are easier to give, more casual and social. And it's interesting for responders to hear the responses of the others. Written responses can be more careful and considered, and the writer gets to take them home and ponder them while revising.

There's an easy way to combine written and spoken responding. First, all group members give copies of their paper to everyone else. Then members go home and read all the papers and take a few notes about their responses to each one. But each member has responsibility for giving a careful written response to only one paper. When the group meets for sharing responses, the person who wrote out feedback starts by reading what he wrote (and hands his written feedback to the writer), but then the others chime in and add responses on the basis of their reading and notes. This method is particularly useful if there isn't much time for group work or if the pieces of writing are somewhat long.

HOW MUCH RESPONSE TO GET?

At one extreme, you'll benefit from no response at all—that is, from private writing where you get to ignore readers for a while, and from mere sharing where you get to connect with readers and feel their presence but not have to listen to their responses.

At the other extreme, it's crucial sometimes to take the time for extended and careful response—perhaps in writing—from at least one or two readers. We urge you to create some occasions where you ask a reader or two to take your paper home and write out at least two or three pages that provide (a) a description of what they see (skeleton or descriptive outline, description of voice, and so forth); (b) a description of how they reacted (movies of their minds—what the words *do* to them); (c) what they see as strengths and weaknesses of your paper and suggestions for improving it. If your teacher asks for this extensive approach to feedback, she will probably ask you to write out your reactions to those responses, in particular whether you think their evaluation and advice make sense or not and why.

A middle course is to get two to four minutes of response from each reader. This won't give you the complete story of the readers' perceptions or reactions, but it will give you the most powerful thing of all: the leverage you need to imagine what your piece of writing looks like through someone else's eyes. Sometimes just one tiny remark is all you need to help you suddenly stop seeing your words *only* from your own point of view and start experiencing how differently they sound to someone else.

WAYS TO HELP RESPONSE PAIRS OR GROUPS WORK BETTER

When it comes to people working together on difficult activities (and nothing is more "difficult" than showing your own writing), there are no magic right methods. But there are some helpful rules of thumb.

First, remember that even though you may feel naked or vulnerable in sharing your writing, especially if it is an early draft, readers will be just as naked and vulnerable if they give you good feedback. To give accurate movies of the mind is a generous gift: honest readers are willing to be guinea pigs and let you see inside their heads. And this kind of honesty goes against many habits and customs of student life. Classmates won't give you this gift unless you treat them with great respect *and* are very assertive about insisting that you really want good feedback. (As teachers, we used to shake our fingers at students who weren't giving much feedback and try to cajole them into being "more responsible responders." But that never seemed to help. We discovered we could get better results by turning back to the *writer* and saying: "Are *you* willing to put up with not getting feedback? *We* can't make them do it. Only you can.")

Try to avoid arguments between responders or between writer and responder. Arguments waste time, and they make responders less willing to be honest. But most of all, you usually benefit from having different and unreconciled points of view about your text. Don't look for a "right answer" but for how your writing looks through different sets of eyes. And when readers disagree, that brings home the central principle here: *You* get to make up your own mind about how to interpret the feedback, how seriously to take it, and what changes to make, if any.

When working in groups, always make sure someone agrees to watch the time so that people at the end don't get cheated.

Spend some time talking about how the feedback process is working. Try taking a few moments now and then to write out informal answers to these questions.

- What works best in your group?
- What is not working well?
- Do you wish members were more critical of your work? less critical?
- Which has been the most helpful to you, oral or written responses?
- Does your group work best with detailed instructions? with little guidance?
- Is there someone who always seems to take charge? or who doesn't participate much? How do you feel about this?

You can share these responses yourselves and identify problems and discuss ways to make things work better. You can make these comments anonymous if you wish by giving them to another group to read to you. Your teacher may ask for these responses and use them as a basis for full-class discussion.

FINAL NOTE

Does this seem too complicated? All these kinds of responses and ways of giving them? There is, in fact, a lot to learn if you want to get useful responses and give them. But *after* you and your friends have tried out all these techniques and built up a relationship of trust, you can make the whole feedback process become simple. You don't have to decide on any particular kind of feedback to ask for; you can just say, "Tell me about your responses" or "Just write me a letter." You can trust them to give you what is most valuable. But if you leave it wide open this way *before* readers have practiced all these responding techniques, you often get nothing—or even get something hurtful or harmful. It won't take you too long to try out the 11 kinds of feedback, especially since you can sometimes use more than one in one session.

10 Invitations to a Writer's Life: Guidelines for Designing Small-Group Writing Classes

ROBERT BROOKE

It's 8:32 a.m., mid-February, and I'm fumbling with keys at my office door, trying not to spill the large toasted coconut coffee I've carried over from the Union. Arnold (twenty years old, John Lennon glasses, the first week of what will be a beard beginning to grow in) is already waiting outside my door.

"I wanted to show you the pen I bought," he says once we get inside my office. "I was reading Natalie Goldberg [*Writing Down the Bones*] last night, where she says you need to consider the kind of tools you use, you know, what kind of pen and notebook makes you feel like writing, so I went down to Nebraska Bookstore and bought three different fountain pens. Neat, huh?"

He hands me a bright green cartridge pen with a gold clasp, and he beams.

"I tried all last week to write two hours a night after my roommate went to bed, but it isn't working," Arnold continues. "He keeps having his girlfriend over, and they stay up really late watching TV. So, instead, I think I'll try writing whenever I can between classes and at work. How do you fit your writing time in? You always seem so busy."

–Excerpt from Robert Brooke's teaching journal

I remember that very first workshop, which you led to get us started, got me off on the idea of how others influence our lives. I started out with just thoughts that went in no particular direction, and that eventually became a short little piece, only about half a page, but I explored the idea a little more, and was later able to use that as a start for a poem. It's weird how that took so long to take off. I kept telling myself I would start the poem, I would look at the short piece I had written, and felt absolutely nothing. But I knew I had to put this in a poem. One night I just sat down and wrote it, and somehow the thoughts found their way out, more clearly and concisely than I remember them filtering through my head. I remember looking down at the page and thinking that was what I needed to say, there

From *Small Groups in Writing Workshops: Invitations to a Writer's Life*, edited by Robert Brooke et al., NCTE, 1994, pp. 7–30.

were the thoughts expressed so that I fully understood them. I think I realized that I had to explain things to myself before I could explain them to someone else.

—EXCERPT FROM A STUDENT'S FINAL LEARNING LETTER

I think the source of the most personal gain through this class was in the small group discussion of works in progress. Through the group I was able to refine my own writing through feedback, but they did more than just that. The group experience helped me develop a critical eye and combine that with a constructive attitude in voicing my criticism. I also learned a great deal about being prepared not only with materials, but with discussion of materials. It is up to the writer to keep things moving along. That can often mean that you, as writer, must articulate your concerns about the piece and keep the discussion moving toward that goal.

—EXCERPT FROM A STUDENT'S FINAL LEARNING LETTER

In the field of composition, what we want to happen when students take writing courses is a topic of significant debate. The answer everyone seems to agree on is that we want our students to become better writers; the debate emerges when we try to define what the phrase "better writers" means. As I view the profession at present, this phrase takes on several overlapping definitions. To cite just four: David Bartholomae (Bartholomae and Petrosky 1986; 1990) and his colleagues at Pittsburgh argue that "better writers" means writers who have become members of academic communities, who are able to write professionally in college and for college audiences. Linda Flower (1982) and John Hayes and their colleagues at Carnegie Mellon argue that "better writers" means writers who are more conscious of their writing processes and who are more able to manipulate the elements of that process to meet any given rhetorical situation. Richard Haswell (1991) of Washington State University argues that "better writers" means writers who are maturing developmentally toward the organizational and stylistic features of competent writers' prose. And researchers as diverse as Kenneth Bruffee (1984), Ann Berthoff (1982), and Peter Elbow (1981) argue that "better writers" means writers who are able to use writing to understand their lives and their learning, and who are able to use writing as a means of participating in ongoing discussion with other writers.

All of the definitions of "better writers" have consequences for the design of writing classrooms. The sequence of activities, the kinds of writing students do, and the evaluation procedures used will all differ depending on which definition a teacher employs. The choice to use small groups as part of writing pedagogy is one of the items that depends on a teacher's definition of "better writers." Given their definitions, for example, both Bartholomae and Haswell have proposed programs which argue against the use of small groups in writing classes. The argument from Pittsburgh is that peer response from people who do not understand the conventions and purposes of academic discourse can't help students grasp these matters. Haswell's argument is that developing writers need individualized sequences that respond to organizational and syntactic problems and that a knowledgeable teacher is the best person to diagnose an individual's needs and design these sequences. The choice to use small groups in a writing class, therefore, isn't just a methodological choice between equal means of getting across the same information—it's a choice that derives from the way a teacher defines the "better writers" she wants her students to become, from the goals of her teaching. Writing groups function well when they are an integral support to one's teaching goals, but they are bound to be frustrating when they are peripheral or even opposed to those goals.

Ruth [Mirtz], Rick [Evans], and I have talked a good deal about the goals of our teaching and about the ways small groups provide essential support for those goals. What's emerged from these discussions is a tentative consensus on the way we define the "better writers" we hope our students will become. I articulate our consensus this way: we want our students to understand writing as a lifelong practice, especially as a means of reflecting on their experience and their learning, on the one hand, and as a means of participating more fully in the communities they are a part of, on the other. To be "better writers" means, for us, to understand the ways in which writing can be useful in many areas of one's life, as well as to have experiences which adapt writing to any of those uses.

Such goals, I think, bring the three of us closer to the Flower and Hayes or Berthoff and Elbow goals of our profession than to the Bartholomae and Haswell goals. I know this is true in my case. I am attracted to Flower and Hayes's emphasis on knowing how to manage the problems and processes of writing across rhetorical contexts, to Berthoff's emphasis on writing as a means of discovering how one's mind makes sense of one's world, and to Elbow's emphasis on writing for multiple purposes throughout life. I frequently cite the following passage from Elbow's recent "Reflections on Academic Discourse" (1991a) when I find myself in discussion with university colleagues and am asked to explain my pedagogy:

> [T]he best test of a writing course is whether it makes students more likely to use writing in their lives: perhaps to write notes and letters to friends or loved ones; perhaps to write in a diary or to make sense of what's happening in their lives; perhaps to write in a learning journal to figure out a difficult subject they are studying; perhaps to write stories or poems for themselves or for informal circulation or even for serious publication; perhaps to write in the public realm such as letters to the newspaper or broadsides on dormitory walls. I don't rule out the writing of academic discourse by choice, but if we teach only academic discourse we will surely fail at this most important goal of helping students use writing by choice in their lives. (136)

I want my students to see the usefulness of writing throughout their lives and to be self-aware enough to make appropriate use of writing when the situation calls for it.

These goals for our teaching arise, no doubt, out of our own and our students' past experiences. Our personal stories of growth into writing groups will show the ways we've used writing as reflection on life's events and as participation in communities important to us. In many ways, our pedagogical goals arise directly from these aspects of our own lives. Our students, we've found, share many of these aspects. . . . [M]any students also experience a need for writing as a means of bridging the "private" sphere of deeply held opinions and the "public" sphere of open discussion, as well as a need for exploring the diversity that daily surrounds us all. In our talks at national conferences, we've heard these same student needs identified by teachers across the country, from large urban centers in the North and East, from private and public colleges, and from both coasts and the Midwest. In developing a pedagogy that meets our own needs as writers, we've thus found that we address many of our students' needs as well.

At the same time, our pedagogical goals have also developed from working with many different students at the University of Nebraska and the Florida State University, listening to the various ways these students feel alienated from writing, especially in academic settings. The majority of traditional-aged Nebraska students, for example, come to us having had three years of high school English courses and are able to write tidy, mostly correct Standard Written English (supported no doubt by home and community backgrounds where English is the dominant language and a good deal of practical writing and reading goes on [Roebke 1977]). They come to us expecting to study hard in college (but often without having had to study hard before) and understanding much of what is involved in taking lecture classes with multiple-choice final exams. Yet, perhaps because of these relative strengths in scholastic preparation, many of our students come to us alienated from their learning, unsure of what to make of the large and often impersonal college campus and of what place academic study will take in their lives. Other students, who come to us in their mid-twenties or thirties or forties from the urban centers of Omaha, Lincoln, Sioux Falls, and Kansas City, find that they are trying to commit energy and attention to schoolwork now, after spending several years in the work force, and feeling the same restlessness they used to feel in school while also feeling frustrated because the jobs and lives they've been able to find without a college diploma are not as rewarding as the ones they imagine for themselves. Still others come to the University of Nebraska–Lincoln from the Lakota or Sioux reservations within the state, or the Hispanic communities around Scottsbluff, or the ethnically diverse areas of North Omaha, or on sports scholarships from large cities on either coast. These students find themselves often baffled at the provincialism and ethnocentrism of the Nebraska campus, and often struggling, as a result, to build bridges between their own experience and the lives of their professors and classmates.

The alienation students can feel from university life is perhaps best indicated by university attrition statistics. According to statistics for the University of Nebraska–Lincoln, over 20 percent of our entering students drop out of college before their sophomore year; only 40 percent graduate within the traditional four years (with a rise merely to 50 percent in a fifth year); and an ever-growing number of undergraduate students (29 percent) now fit into the "nontraditional" category of older students who are trying college for a first or second time after part of a life spent following different drummers.[1]

Given these students and these demographics, our emphasis on writing as lifelong practice has emerged almost necessarily from the interactions in our classes. Our students are many and varied, but one consistent need is the need to connect the life of thinking, reading, and writing (the so-called "life of the mind") with the other lives they lead (lives of work, of farming or small city communities, of relationships with friends, loved ones, relatives).

The metaphor I have consequently developed for thinking about our courses is the metaphor of invitations to a writer's life. In our courses, we invite our students to try out a writer's life for a semester, to see what it offers and what its potentials are, so that they will leave having some experience from which to decide whether writing can enhance the lives they already live.

Obviously, in the metaphor of a writer's life, I'm not talking about the life of a publishing creative or freelance writer supporting herself financially by writing. I'm talking instead about a person, holding any job, who uses writing as a means of enhancing her life through reflection and participation. I mean the whole range of uses of writing Elbow lists in the passage quoted above: writing as reflection in diaries and learning logs and responses to reading; writing as participation in letters, editorials, creative and polemical pieces; and, when appropriate, professional or scholarly writing.

Small groups are an essential support for these goals for our students. In their interactions in small groups, students are able to explore their own possibilities for a writer's life through participation in a small community of writers; repeated attention to the effect of their words and topics on other people; reflection on their topics, writing processes, and the responses of their group; and observing the ways in which their group members choose to use writing within the contexts of their diverse lives. While class time consists of a range of activities besides small groups, we see small groups as an integral, necessary part of the invitation we offer to a writer's life.

In the rest of this chapter, I will characterize what I see as the essential elements of a writer's life, in order to suggest these elements as organizing principles for writing courses which emphasize small groups. But the point . . . is wider than an introduction to a single set of principles for teaching writing. The point is that the best teaching of writing emerges out of a sympathetic awareness of the lives of teachers and students. We teachers teach best when we understand our own past and present lives, when we understand something of our students' pasts and imagined futures, and when we've reflected enough on the differences between our lives and theirs to understand in what ways writing might support each of us in those lives.

CHARACTERISTICS OF A WRITER'S LIFE

If writing courses are to be invitations to a writer's life—to a life in which writing serves as a constant aid to reflection and participation—then they need to be structured around the essential elements of such a life. I have identified four such elements:

Time: Writers set aside time for writing regularly, perhaps by journaling three or four times a week after the family has gone to bed, or by spending the first two morning hours of the average workday writing down important (rather than urgent) ideas, or just by filling a spiral notebook each month. In order to benefit from the reflective and participatory rewards of writing, people need to develop writing rhythms that work for them, that make writing a habitual instead of occasional activity.

Ownership: Writers maintain ownership over their uses of writing. By and large, they choose the topics they will write about during their writing time. They decide when a piece is worth continuing, or when to crumple it and throw it out, or when it needs to sit in a drawer and gestate for five years. They decide what the purposes of their writing will be, from the self-help purposes of private journals to the political purposes of letters to their elected officials. And they decide how to fit in the writing their job requires of them among the other writing they do.

Response: Writers rarely write in a vacuum. Writers need response, need a community of other people with whom they can discuss their words. Responders can take many forms, from journal/reading groups who meet because all the members share an interest, to individual dialogues in letters or with journal partners, to political action groups, creative writing groups, even the editors and readers of published work. All such responders make writing more than a solitary act; they make writing a means of ongoing participation with others who are important to the writer.

Exposure: Writers give themselves regular exposure both to other people's writing and to other writers. They read often in material directly relevant to their work and their own writing, as well as material which introduces them to other kinds of writing. They talk with other writers about the processes of writing, sharing their own experiences and learning from the experiences of others.

These four essentials all function in one way or another for people who have made a writer's life part of the overall life they lead, from the computer programmer who writes science fiction in her spare time to the secretary who journals with his "Parents Without Partners" group. Because these elements are so prevalent in the lives of practicing writers, they need to become structuring elements in writing courses which seek to introduce students to such a life. For students for whom school writing often seems divorced from other uses of writing—for whom the private sphere of opinion and intimate conversation often seems separated from the public sphere of school and job interaction— these elements can provide a means of identifying and exploring the possible connections between these artificially separated areas of their lives.

I didn't come up with these four elements on my own, though they are certainly supported by my experiences as a writer and teacher. I've borrowed most of them directly from writing teachers and researchers who have studied what children need as they first develop into writers. In the studies Donald Graves and his colleagues conducted at Atkinson Academy on young children learning to write (Graves 1984; Calkins 1983), time, ownership, and response were identified as elements essential for such learning to occur. Calkins's narrative of children's growth in that project documents the significant gains first-through sixth-grade children make in writing when they are provided these elements. Since her study focuses on children very early in the process of learning to write, her book is a wonderful antidote to any colleague who assumes such a classroom would be "advanced" and that entering college students need to have "the basics" first.

Since the publications of Graves's and Calkins's reports in the early 1980's, the notion of time, ownership, and response as structuring elements for a writer's growth has taken on a wider life of its own. In her Shaughnessy Prize–winning *In the Middle*, Nancie Atwell (1987) uses these three elements to describe the developing structure of her writing workshop for middle school students, and she returns to these elements in order to refine them in her recent *Side by Side* (1991), aimed at kindergarten through twelfth-grade teachers. These elements also inform, in general, the classes designed by Linda Rief (1992) for junior high school students; by Tom Romano (1987) for senior high school students; and, to a degree, by Donald Murray (1985; 1990) for college students. There is a sense, then, in which the notion of time, ownership, and response as structuring elements of writing classrooms has been slowly moving through the entire curriculum over the past decade from elementary to college classes. (I've added "exposure" to the list to make explicit yet another essential that is sometimes obscured but is tremendously important for my students.)

Since these elements appear to be essential at so many grade levels, I can't help but wonder if they might not turn out to be connected to the ways in which human beings naturally become writers. Atwell (1991) writes:

> [T]he processes I wrote about are not unique to eighth graders. Although I observed writing, reading, and learning among junior high kids, writing, reading, and learning are human activities that cut across age, ability level, and ethnic background. In terms of their language learning, middle school kids are not a separate species. All of us, ages four to ninety-four, want our reading and writing to be meaningful, to make sense, and to be good for something. And teachers of all ages and subjects want to sponsor authentic contexts for learning and respond to their students as individuals. (137)

When students need to be exposed to a writer's life—to be introduced to the rich possibilities that writing has for enhancing any kind of life—it may be that they then need the essential elements of time, ownership, response, and exposure, no matter what their academic or age level. Although these elements consistently need to be adapted to the particular students, teachers, and contexts in which they appear, they may prove to be ideas that can organize the curriculum, kindergarten through college.

The profession of English studies is recognized by many scholars as now being in the midst of a profound paradigm shift, as throughout the field more and more competing specialties arise with more and more competing ideas about what is essential to English classes. I am heartened, therefore, whenever ideas appear that seem to make sense to teachers across the English curriculum. Such ideas are worth a careful look. And points of consensus do, occasionally, seem to arise. In the most recent national attempt to carefully reexamine the whole of the English curriculum—the 1987 English Coalition Conference sponsored by the Modern Language Association, the National Council of the Teachers of English, and several other organizations—many of the kindergarten through college-level teachers gathered there arrived at a kind of consensus about the essential goals of English instruction.[2] Writing with surprise at the general consensus he found emerging from such a diverse assemblage of teachers, Peter Elbow reported that

> [t]he way of talking that probably best sums up this idea for all participants is this: learning involves *the making of meaning and the reflecting back on this process of making meaning*—not the ingestion of a list or a body of information. At all levels we stressed how this central idea is deeply social. . . . In short, the main conclusion of the conference may be that we see the same constructive and social activity as the central process at all levels of the profession of English. (1991b, 18)

Of course, the particular ways teachers at different levels spoke of this consensual idea reflected their different contexts:

> There was a constant refrain from elementary and secondary teachers on the need to get students to be habitual writers and readers; only then can we be effective at getting them to be reflectors and examiners of language.
>   Virtually everyone acknowledged repeatedly that the main practical finding of the last ten or fifteen years' renaissance in composition has been that students (and teachers!) should engage in more writing—even in class. This movement has taught us that we can't teach writing by just looking at models of others' writing or even by just talking about our own writing process: we have to emphasize production—the practice of writing—and devote plenty of time to this oddly neglected practice.
>   Similarly, college people stressed repeatedly that we should focus not on asking students to study theory as a content but on using theory as a lens through which to look at our actual reading and writing. Implicit here is the need to get people to engage with a text. (19–20)

I cite the documents of this conference at this length for two reasons: first, because the tentative consensus arrived at does hint at the possibility that English teachers across grade levels can be validly working with aspects of the same ideas; and second, because this particular conference's consensus emphasized regular engagement in and reflection on writing and reading—an emphasis that comes close to supporting the elements of time, ownership, response, and exposure which I've identified above. Elbow's call for students to become "habitual" writers and readers and for classes to "emphasize production" seems to me a recognition of *time* as a need. Similarly, for students to become "engaged" with texts, for them to reflect back on their production of writing and their interpretation of reading as a primary means of learning, also seems an acknowledgment of the need for *ownership* over the purposes of writing, reading, and learning, and for *response* that helps individuals reflect and engage more forcefully. And the emphasis on habitual reading and on the conscious uses of theory in reading and of process in writing seems a substantiation of the need for *exposure* to many different types of writing and writers. I am heartened to see evidence in the reports of this national conference of ideas that seem translatable into the elements of time, ownership, response, and exposure which I believe are so crucial to my students' development as writers.

The elements of time, ownership, response, and exposure, moreover, almost inevitably imply the use of small groups in writing classes. Small groups provide writers with all four of these elements, either directly or indirectly. Obviously, groups provide writers with direct response—that's what groups are set up to do: individuals meet, read their texts to each other, and talk about their reactions. But groups also provide direct exposure to other kinds of writing and to other writers: when individuals see the various kinds of writing other people attempt, when they see the uses to which other people put writing, and when they can talk with others about the rewards, problems, and blocks that emerge in the process of writing such pieces, they receive wide exposure to aspects of writing outside their own experience.

Where small groups provide response and exposure directly, they support time and ownership indirectly. People don't usually spend time writing their own pieces while in groups—they have to find time for writing elsewhere during the week. But, for people who may be unaccustomed to writing as a habitual activity, the existence of regularly scheduled small-group meetings creates an artificial stimulus for making time to write. In my classes, the need to have a substantial piece of writing to read aloud to a group every Thursday creates a demand for writing time during the week; this demand is an indirect support for making the time necessary to write part of one's life. Groups likewise supply indirect support for the ownership element of a writer's life. From seeing the range of choices that others make in what they write, from needing to make personal decisions about the often conflicting and complex responses groups provide to writing, and from discussion of the many uses and processes of writing engaged in by group members, any individual's range of writing widens, providing more options, more choices, and hence more ownership over the writing he or she does.

Small groups, then, are not just an arbitrary method for classes that serve as invitations to a writer's life. They are an essential method, an integral support to the elements of time, ownership, response, and exposure. In the rest of this chapter, I'd like to focus a bit more on these elements and the role they play in my writing classroom.

Time

Of the four essentials of a writer's life, *time* is the one element teachers can't provide students within the college curriculum. In classes that meet twice or thrice a week for about an hour, it's become nearly impossible to provide sufficient, regular chunks of time for student writing. Even when teachers devote an entire class period to individual writing, they end up providing only about an hour per week. When I think of time as an essential for writers, I find myself envying elementary teachers who meet with students five days a week for several hours a day—in their situation, I could follow their lead and block out regular, daily in-class time for writing.

As it is, in the limited setting of the college class schedule, time is the single essential students need to provide on their own. In my classes, I make explicit the need for time and then confer with students individually to help them identify ways in which they can make regular time for writing in their busy lives. Small groups become indirect aids for establishing regular time, because each student needs to bring a substantially new piece of writing to the group each week and because in groups, students often talk about time-management issues. But each student still needs to make time for writing outside of class. For some students, this means tackling head-on the serious problem of scheduling their lives so that they can protect the same six hours each week for writing; for others, this means carrying small notebooks with them, so that they can write for fifteen minutes here and there when it's slow at work or when there's a break between classes; for still others, who by personality resist any attempts at scheduling hours during the week, this means setting other goals for themselves that imply time spent writing (for instance; setting a goal of writing ten new pages each week, some of which they will be ready to share in their group).

In each of these attempts to make time for writing, students are repeating the same strategies I see over and over again in the testimonials of professional writers, for whom the need for time often gets discussed in terms of the rhythms they create for writing in their lives. Donald Murray, who has collected many testimonials supporting the essential need for time in writing as an aid to discovery (see Murray 1978), writes of his own need for almost rigidly scheduled writing times: he spends the first morning hours of each day doing his own writing, hours he consciously protects (see Murray 1985). Joan Didion (1968) writes of the notebooks she keeps with her, writing down ideas or images as they strike her, claiming that this practice is useful both for clarifying her own experiences as well as for the indirect support it gives her professional work. And Natalie Goldberg (1986) describes her practice of contracting with herself to fill a notebook with writing each month, not worrying too much about when or where it gets filled—sometimes, she confesses, this means that she gets to the 25th of the month with most of a notebook yet to fill and that subsequently she spends a whole weekend writing. But most of the time, she finds that this method leads to daily writing without the stress of fixed writing hours. These are the same strategies my students endlessly come up with: their ways of managing the rhythms of their writing lives end up being the same as those of our culture's professional writers.

What's equally interesting is that students discover things about the regular practice of writing that professional writers have often articulated. Roger, a junior-level student in one of my classes last year, wrote at midterm:

> I believe the most important progress I am making is with the time aspect of my writing. Although I am not fully locked into a writing time of my own, I am past the last minute production that I entered the course with. This is to me the most important concept I have encountered in the course. Without spending regular time with pen and paper, the writing

process can never get out of the blocks. Peer groups can offer little help if there is no time spent on writing.

At the end of the semester, he continued in much the same vein:

> When I left a specific time slot open for my own writing time, my writing did improve. I was able to explore many different approaches to the pieces I was working on. This allowed me to dance around a subject until I actually got to the meat of what I had deep inside.

In these passages, Roger identifies regular writing time as a "most important concept" because without it, the writing process can't operate. He goes on to write that, for him, the writing process requires a slow circling around his subject through a number of different approaches until the essential ideas—the "meat"—emerge. Roger here sounds remarkably like Kurt Vonnegut:

> [Novelists] have, on the average, about the same IQs as the cosmetic consultants at Bloomingdale's department store. Our power is patience. We have discovered that writing allows even a stupid person to seem halfway intelligent, if only that person will write the same thought over and over again, improving it just a little bit each time. It is a lot like inflating a blimp with a bicycle pump. Anybody can do it. All it takes is time. (Qtd. in Atwell, 1987, 56)

Both Roger and Vonnegut present images of writing as a slow, time-intensive process, a process in which their ideas are refined. Time, for both student and professional, is the key to this process.

Peg, a student who spent her semester splitting her time between private journals and public pieces for her group, wrote of a different outcome of regular writing time:

> I have come to understand what my reason for writing is, or who I write for: ME!! Past experiences caused me to feel the need to write well, or on certain things, for a grade, or for my peers, or as entertainment to the class. Now I understand and know that if those things happen, that's fine, but if they don't, that's okay, as long as I have learned and grown and benefitted from what I've written.

Peg's emphasis on the personal benefit of regular writing sounds here remarkably like the emphasis of Natalie Goldberg, who writes, in *Writing Down the Bones* (1986), that

> [o]ne of the main aims in writing practice is to learn to trust your own mind and body. . . . One poem or story doesn't matter one way or the other. It's the process of writing and life that matters. Too many writers have written great books and gone insane or alcoholic or killed themselves. This process teaches about sanity. We are trying to become sane along with our poems and stories. (12)

For both Peg and Goldberg, it's the personal rewards of greater self-understanding and greater sanity that most result from regular writing. Good products ("A" papers; published poems) are an important by-product of regular writing practice but not the energizing reason for writing. In short, as these comparisons between Roger and Vonnegut, Peg and Goldberg, show, in exploring time as an essential element of a writer's life, students arrive at the same sorts of insights about themselves and their writing that professional writers have long described. They explain how time spent on regular writing improves both the writer's product and the writer's life.

Ownership

The second essential element of a writer's life is *ownership*, a term which refers to the choices writers have over their material, their processes, as well as how they understand and feel about their material and processes. People who write regularly usually write for a number of different purposes, from their own private notebooks, to their writing on the job, to letters to friends and business associates. In managing their writing, they exercise ownership when they choose what kind of writing to do at what times, when they reflect on their writing to identify blocks they are having and to devise strategies for overcoming them, and when they develop ways to keep themselves engaged in writing tasks which have become stale but which they still want to complete. In all of these areas, writers have control over many choices, and it's that feature of choice which is highlighted by the essential element of ownership. Ownership, obviously, is complex because it doesn't reflect the spoiled adolescent's attitude of "I'll do only what I want to do when I want to do it," but more the reflective adult's control over multiple choices for how to use writing in a world where some kinds of writing are required by job, family, friends, politics, while other kinds of writing are more individually motivated.

Roger, the student who wrote so much about time in his learning letters, identified the complexity of ownership at another point in his writing:

> I have realized the importance of ownership in the writing process. Yes, a teacher could have directed my writing when I became frustrated at trying to find a subject and a style that I felt suited me. I think it is more important that I had a chance to explore and discover what concerned me. It inevitably helped me to look at my writing, no matter how frustrated I was. I think it is likely that an assigned subject would not have focused my writing. I attempted to do so myself by dictating to myself that I would write poetry NOW and choose a subject. That decision went by the wayside after a few lines and I realized that I was not in the mood to try writing poetry at that time. So, I moved on to other things.

Roger puts his finger on the major complexity of ownership: the problem of frustration. Writers feel frustrated because of both too much and too little ownership. Roger became frustrated with himself both when he was "trying to find a subject that suited me," as well as when he assigned himself a poem on a particular subject and soon found that choice too restrictive. Like Roger, writers can become frustrated when the available choices over what they might do with writing seem so vast as to be overwhelming—they feel too much owner-ship over these choices and lack strategies for choosing between them. Like Roger, writers can also become frustrated when they feel the range of choice has been so narrowed that they don't feel any ownership over the writ-ing—they feel too little ownership and lack strategies for making the writing personally engaging. These twin feelings of too much and too little ownership lead to frustration, a frustration which highlights that ownership isn't essen-tially a matter of choice over the topic: ownership, instead, involves an aware-ness of how to manage the many processes of writing that a writer engages in; an ability to devise strategies to overcome frustrations that appear whether a given writing seems to have too much or too little definition; and a recognition of the opportunities for choice that the writer has in each of these situations (for it's at those points of choice that the writer can make the writing her own). As Roger points out, having his teacher take ownership away from him by assigning him a topic wasn't the answer, because it was "more important that I had a chance to explore and discover what concerned me." Roger was aware that what he needed were strategies for developing personal engagement with his writing, and that such strategies would prove, in time, more important than any artificial narrowing of the choices he was making about his writing.

Ownership, in short, is a complex idea for writers, extending far beyond the usual meaning of ownership as the possession of property with which you can do what you like. That meaning doesn't really work for writing. In writing, it isn't enough to say "choose any topic you want and do with that topic what-ever you want." In writing, ownership also involves the attitudes you take toward the writing you do, both "assigned" and "unassigned," and the strate-gies you employ for making whatever writing you do personally engaging.

In *Side by Side*, Nancie Atwell writes that she has reconsidered the term "ownership" for this essential element, wondering if the connotations of the word don't lead to unrealistic implications. If she were to rewrite *In the Middle* now, she says:

> I would never have used the word *ownership*. Students' *responsibility* for their writing and reading is what I sought, not control for its own sake. I worry that I helped readers infer that in order for students to take owner-ship of their learning, the teacher has to abdicate ownership of his or her teaching, lower expectations, and let students' choices rule the work-shop. . . . My expectations of my students were enormous, and some-times my nudges were, in fact, assignments to individual students: "Here, now try this." . . . The problem with ownership is the implication that any direction or assignment from the teacher is an infringement on students' rights. . . . When Tom Newkirk wrote to me about *In the Middle*, he said that for him the key term is *engagement* rather than ownership. (1991, 149–50)

Atwell, from the vantage point of five years' distance from her earlier work, suggests two alternative terms for the essential element she had called *owner-ship*: *responsibility* and *engagement*. These two terms certainly express aspects of what students like Roger are going through. Roger does feel responsible for his writing. He feels responsible for the choices of genre and topic he is making; he feels even more responsible for the way he is managing his writing time; and he describes significant learning about the practice and uses of writing at the same time as he describes some frustration with the products he produced. Similarly, Roger does express engagement with his writing—he is deeply engaged in the search for the kinds of writing "which suit him," even when he finds himself frustrated with particular pieces of writing. And, in his repeated attempts to write poetry and his repeated "dancing around" the same subject from different approaches, he shows definite engagement in particular genres and particular topics, even when he feels that he hasn't yet finished a product that does justice to his engagement. Responsibility and engagement are certainly key aspects of Roger's experience, necessary additions to his concerns with topic choice and genre.

The essential element of a writer's life that I've identified as *ownership*, thus, derives from writers' needs to be engaged with their work, to be able to identify the choices they have and devise strategies to help make those choices, to be responsible for the practice and product of their writing. Ownership in this sense is *owning the process* of your writing as much, if not more, than owning the more narrow choices of topic and genre. Writers own their products, if at all, in very odd ways, but owning the practice of writing, in all its complexities, is something essential to the workings of a writer's life.

Response

The third essential element of a writer's life is *response*. People who use writing in their lives usually surround themselves with responders to their writing. Such responders can take many forms: from the official editors and reviewers for published work, to the various writing groups where writing is shared (see Gere 1987, also p. 20 in this volume), to support groups which recommend journal writing or political action groups which jointly produce newsletters and pamphlets, to letter writers. All of these kinds of responders engage writers in discussion about the ideas they present. Some, but not all, of these responders also talk directly about the form and effectiveness of the writing itself.

Writers need response to their writing for three reasons. First, getting response to writing brings the writer into a kind of community where writing is valued. Discussion of the ideas a writer is wrestling with, no matter how little they seem connected to the text itself, creates a context where the writer's ideas have social value. Second, through listening to the responses of others to their writing, writers learn about the reactions of other people, about the various ways different minds make sense of the same passages and deal with the same writing problems. Such learning helps them become better able to predict their readers' reactions while they write and improves their writing processes, as well. Third, response to particular drafts can often help writers see new possibilities and problems in their pieces, often leading to revisions that significantly improve the writing. Response provides new ideas for managing the problems a writer faces and models alternative ways for thinking about the text. In short, response to writing does more than just "fix" the writing by catching errors the writer has made in content, organization, or editing. Instead, response helps writers develop the feelings of social approval necessary to continue writing, an understanding of audience reactions and their own writing processes, and the ability to revise particular pieces effectively.

The experiences of my students Peg and Roger highlight these multiple purposes for response. Peg found the social-value purpose of group response to be the single most important precursor to her writing. For her to really begin to work as a writer, she needed to feel that the writing she was attempting had value for those she worked with: "It really surprised me how much the people made a difference to me," she wrote in her final learning letter. "Because my second small group felt or behaved a lot like I do, and because we all had writings that were pretty emotional, it was loads easier for me to break the separation I had with the personal/public writing." Writing became something she wanted to do once she found herself in a group with others who were using writing for the same purposes as she — once she found, in short, social approval for what she was attempting. Roger, by contrast, most valued the way the group experience helped him learn new strategies for dealing with writing in the future: "Through the groups, I was able to refine my own writing through the feedback, but they did more than just that. The group experience helped me develop a critical eye and combine that with a constructive attitude in voicing my criticism." While Roger noticed that the group feedback did improve his drafts, he stated in his final learning letter that he wasn't, in the end, pleased with his writings that semester. He found that problems still remained and that the groups hadn't helped him overcome all of them. Yet, he wasn't displeased with his group experience. Instead, he felt that the groups had helped him achieve a more important purpose in improving his ability, in general, to critique his own writing and to comment on the writing of others. The groups had improved his critique strategies perhaps more than they had improved any given piece he'd written. For both Peg and Roger, then, the short-term task of "fixing" individual drafts proved less important than more long-term concerns: finding that there was social value to certain kinds of writing because other people also used writing in the same ways; finding that one's abilities to critique writing generally improved through repeated group discussion.

Once we teachers recognize that response to writing serves all three purposes, both short and long term, it then becomes obvious that we need to provide many different kinds of response in our classrooms. To meet the short-term goal of helping to improve the specific texts our students write during the semester, we do need to provide response that highlights the strongest parts of drafts, points out potential problems in them, and makes suggestions for what the writer can try next. But this isn't the only purpose for response; if it were, then there would have been no need for the field of composition as a whole to critique the current-traditional practice of correcting student essays with marginal "awks" and "comma splices" as the only form of response in writing classes. Rather, since response also helps develop the writer's own strategies for writing and the writer's sense of the social value of her work, our classes need other response opportunities, as well.

I suggest that writing classes need to provide, at minimum, the following kinds of response regularly during the semester:

1. To meet the short-term goal of improving individual texts, writing classes need to provide response from other writers, response that provides direct suggestions for how and why the students might develop their texts further. Such response should come from several different writers, including the writer of the piece herself (as writer most engaged with the text), the teacher (as a more experienced writer sharing some strategies that might work), and other writers in the class (as peers facing the same issues).

2. To meet the long-term goal of helping the writer develop more strategies for writing and a better sense of how readers respond to texts, classes need to provide:

   a. frequent opportunities for readers to describe how they read a text, presenting the "movie of their minds" (Elbow, 1981), so that writers can hear the differences in how minds read (and so that both writers and readers can practice becoming conscious of how their own minds read); and

   b. frequent opportunities for writers to reflect on the response they have received, to identify the kinds of advice and reactions they are getting, to speculate about what this means for their writing, and to formulate their own plans for what to do next. Together, these two kinds of response provide writers with the data and the opportunities with which to identify and practice new strategies and ideas they might want to incorporate into their own writing processes.

3. To meet the long-term goal of helping writers see the social value in the kinds of writing they are doing, classes need to provide frequent opportunities to discuss the ideas and purposes underlying the writing. Writers need opportunities to talk about the ideas they are writing about, to share stories about these ideas with other people, to hear how other writers are also exploring these ideas. Writers also need opportunities to talk about why they are interested in writing certain kinds of pieces, to share stories about these purposes with other people, and to hear how other writers are also exploring these purposes. Such discussion, while not directly about individual texts, does much to support the social value of writing because it shows developing writers that other people are also involved in similar uses of writing.

Together, these kinds of response all encourage writers to develop an ongoing writer's life. Together, they create an ongoing social context for writing, a habitual practice of reflecting on one's own work and others' reactions, and an ability to use feedback to improve specific drafts.

Exposure

Exposure, the fourth and final essential element of a writer's life, is in part an extension of the social-value purpose for response. In the same way that open discussion of a writer's ideas and purposes gives social value to the writing and makes that kind of writing more appealing to the writer, so, too, positive exposure to the other people's ideas, purposes, and uses of writing can make new kinds of writing appealing. Writers need exposure to other writers and their writing in order to see what's possible, in order to widen the range of what they themselves might try.

A long-standing maxim in composition instruction puts it that writers learn to write by reading, that good writers develop by reading lots of different kinds of writing and after a while come to incorporate (and extend) aspects of what they've read in what they write. The idea behind this maxim is that writers learn much about writing by submerging themselves in the world of writing; we learn much about writing through a love of reading. To my mind, this time-worn maxim points toward the importance of exposure in a writer's life: writers develop best in an environment that is rich in literacy, where they are exposed to reading material of many kinds and, even more importantly, to other people who write and read frequently themselves. Such exposure helps us imagine ourselves as writers, helps us see the social value of literate activities.

In *In The Middle*, Nancie Atwell dramatizes the importance of exposure by using the metaphor of the dining-room table:

> [D]uring dinner one night Toby discovered that one of our guests actually read and, better yet, appreciated his favorite author. Long after the table had been cleared, the dishes washed and dried, and everyone else had taken a long walk down to the beach and back, Nancy Martin and Toby sat at our dining room table gossiping by candlelight about Anthony Powell's *Dance to the Music of Time*. This didn't help me appreciate Anthony Powell, but it did open my eyes to the wonders of our dining room table.
>
> It was a literate environment. Around it, people talk in all the ways literate people discourse. . . . And our talk isn't sterile or grudging or perfunctory. It's filled with jokes, arguments, exchanges of bits of information, descriptions of what we loved and hated and why. The way Toby and Nancy chatted, the way Toby and I chat most evenings at that table, were ways my kids and I could chat, entering literature together. Somehow, I had to get that table into my classroom and invite my eighth graders to pull up their chairs. (1987, 19–20)

In the same way that children whose families are engaged in writing and reading come to appreciate literate activities just by taking part in dinner-table conversation, so, too, growing writers need to be surrounded with literate talk. By hearing and taking part in such talk, growing writers come to recognize that other people are, in fact, excited by reading and writing, finding value in certain books and projects, and may come to realize their own interest in such activities, too. Since, given the current demographics on the average American family, we teachers can rarely expect the majority of our students to have grown up around a dining-room table as literature-rich as Atwell's, part of our course's invitation to a writer's life needs to be a semester-long exposure to "all the ways literate people discourse."

I see three main ways to bring this exposure into our classrooms. First we need to set aside some time for individuals to share writing and reading with the whole class and with small groups. Student writers need to hear from each other what sorts of things they do read and appreciate and what sorts of things they write. In our classes, this first kind of exposure occurs most often through public reading days, in which each person in class reads a section of his or her best writing aloud to the class. These days provide direct exposure to the writing other class members do and are well received. (Frequently, students tell me that though reading their own piece aloud is frightening, they really enjoy hearing what other people have written and hope we will do this often.) Ruth, Rick, and I have also experimented individually, in a variety of ways, with bringing outside reading into the classroom, from individual book talks on a writing the students admire, to open letters to the class about a group-selected reading, to full-class discussion of the same essay, story, or poem. All of these methods are ways to set aside time for individuals to share writing and reading with the class, functionally exposing class members to writing they wouldn't otherwise consider. Roger, for example, found himself attempting poetry in the second half of the semester, largely because of what he'd heard others try. As he put it, "Looking back on my own goals for this half of the term, I recall I hoped to make an attempt at writing poetry. I did do this. Hearing the poetry that others in class were able to produce, I hoped to be able to duplicate that feeling." It became possible for Roger to try his hand at poetry because other classmates read poetry aloud at full-class readings and for book talks, and he liked what he heard.

Second, small-group discussion of writing is an ongoing forum for exposure. Each time a group meets to share drafts or ideas, the members of the group are functionally exposed to three or four other people's interests in writing and reading, and they are likely to hear why the person wants to write the kind of piece she's writing and what sort of pieces this writing reminds her of. Group meetings consequently provide ongoing exposure to the literate activities that the group members value and participate in. In Roger's group, for example, this kind of exposure led Bill, a nontraditional student who'd come to school after a term of enlistment in the Navy, to a kind of writing he had never imagined before. While Bill's first pieces were attempts at traditional essays on the death penalty and motorcycle laws, Carl, one of his group members, brought in drafts toward a historical drama about the Civil War. Carl, it turned out, was involved in Civil War battle recreations at Fort Kearney in the summer, knew something about military writing, and shared his knowledge of military authors with his group as background to his writing. Within a month, Bill had embarked on his own military writing: a dramatic account of life aboard a Navy cruiser in the South Pacific.

Third, our own writing and reading as teachers provides direct exposure to the literate activities we value, and this exposure is often useful for growing writers who haven't spent much time with any adult who openly admits to a love of reading and writing. I regularly share my writing with my students, doing my own writing on the board on days when we write individually in class, sharing my writing with small groups on small-group days, and taking my turn on public reading days. Similarly, I share my reading with them as well, mentioning in groups the pieces I've read that their work makes me think of, and loaning these pieces to individuals when I have them in my private library (under the threat, if necessary, of a "No Report" if I don't get them back by the end of the semester). Our own behavior as teachers often provides a kind of model of literate activities that students can try out. Over the past two years, for example, while I've worked in class on a personal collage essay about a hiking trip I took with my father when I was ten years old, several students in each class have started writings that explore their own relationships with their fathers. With these students, I've then shared personal essays about father-son relationships from journals like *Georgia Review* and *Prairie Schooner*, only to find these essays—and some of the techniques they demonstrate—spreading as if by magic to comments in students' letters to me, to small-group discussions, and to the kinds of pieces other students attempt.

T. S. Eliot wrote that beginning writers borrow, but mature writers steal—an adage pointing humorously to the importance of exposure in literate life. Exposure to writers and writing is the final essential element of a writer's life that we try to emphasize in our classrooms, so that developing writers will have some taste of the rich world of reading and writing from which they can borrow or steal in the creation of their own purposes and uses for writing within the contexts of their own lives.

CONCLUSION

Time, Ownership, Response, and *Exposure* are elements of a writer's life which I consider crucial for our students. Taken together, these four elements surround developing writers, at least for a semester, with some of the tempos, issues, and discourses that make up writers' lives throughout our culture.

Small groups, as I've suggested, can be an integral means of providing these four elements to writing students. Small groups provide response and exposure, directly, and support time and ownership, indirectly. Since Ruth, Rick, and I have all decided that we want our teaching to help our students explore writing as a life practice, we've all found small groups to be important to our teaching because of their direct and indirect support of these essential elements of a writer's life.

As I've tried to present them here, time, ownership, response, and exposure are guiding principles that can be used in many contexts by teachers who want to teach writing as an invitation to a writer's life. I've tried in this chapter to present these principles as principles, out of the particular context of any single writing class, largely because Ruth, Rick, and I believe that there are many ways of making these principles operative in classrooms and that each teacher needs to design her own classroom in response to the needs of her students and her own past experience. Consequently, we believe that any single classroom must be uniquely structured, even if it is also based on principles similar to these four. Although we do share a guiding philosophy, the three of us don't teach in the same way. Every teacher, we believe, needs to be creative in designing writing courses that fit the philosophy, the students, and the individual who teaches the course—and hence we expect that every classroom will be necessarily unique.

NOTES

1. These statistics are excerpted from a Chancellor's memorandum to the faculty of the University of Nebraska–Lincoln, September 1992.

2. The results of this conference are recorded officially in *The English Coalition Conference*, edited by Richard Lloyd-Jones and Andrea Lunsford (1989), and impressionistically by Peter Elbow in *What Is English?* (1991b), the book which the MLA asked him to write about the conference.

WORKS CITED

Atwell, Nancie. 1987. *In the Middle: Writing, Reading, and Learning with Adolescents*. Portsmouth, NH: Boynton/Cook-Heinemann.

———. 1991. *Side By Side: Essays on Teaching to Learn*. Portsmouth, NH: Heinemann Educational Books.

Bartholomae, David, and Anthony Petrosky. 1986. *Facts, Counterfacts, Artifacts: Theory and Method for a Reading and Writing Course*. Upper Montclair, NJ: Boynton/Cook.

———, eds. 1990. *Ways of Reading: An Anthology for Writers*. 2nd Ed. Boston: Bedford Books.

Berthoff, Ann E. 1981. *The Making of Meaning: Metaphors, Models, and Maxims for Writing Teachers*. Upper Montclair, NJ: Boynton/Cook.

———. 1982. *Forming/Thinking/Writing: The Composing Imagination*. Upper Montclair, NJ: Boynton/Cook.

Bruffee, Kenneth. 1984. "Collaborative Writing and the Conversation of Mankind." *College English* 46: 635–52.

Calkins, Lucy McCormick. 1983. *Lessons from a Child: On the Teaching and Learning of Writing*. Exeter, NH: Heinemann Educational Books.

Didion, Joan. 1968. "On Keeping a Notebook." In *Slouching Toward Bethlehem*, 131–41. New York: Farrar, Strauss & Giroux.

Elbow, Peter. 1981. *Writing with Power: Techniques for Mastering the Writing Process*. New York: Oxford University Press.

———. 1991. *What Is English?* New York: Modern Language Association of America.

Flower, Linda. 1982. *Problem-Solving Strategies for Writing*. New York: Harcourt Brace Jovanovich.

Gere, Anne Ruggles. 1987. *Writing Groups: History, Theory, Implications*. Carbondale: Southern Illinois University Press.

Goldberg, Natalie. 1986. *Writing Down the Bones: Freeing the Writer Within*. Boston: Shambala.

Graves, Donald H. 1984. *A Researcher Learns to Write: Selected Articles and Monographs*. Portsmouth, NH: Heinemann.

Lloyd-Jones, Richard, and Andrea A. Lunsford, eds. 1989. *The English Coalition Conference: Democracy through Language*. Urbana: National Council of Teachers of English/Modern Language Association of America.

Murray, Donald M. 1978. "Internal Revision." In *Research on Composing: Points of Departure*, edited by Charles R. Cooper and Lee Odell, 85–104. Urbana: National Council of Teachers of English.

———. 1985. *A Writer Teaches Writing*. 2nd Ed. Boston: Houghton Mifflin.

———. 1990. *Write to Learn*. 3rd Ed. Fort Worth: Holt, Rinehart and Winston.

Rief, Linda. 1992. *Seeking Diversity: Language Arts with Adolescents*. Portsmouth, NH: Boynton/Cook-Heinemann.

Roebke, Jenny. 1977. "English in the Context of Community." *Nebraska English Counselor* (Fall): n.p.

Romano, Tom. 1987. *Clearing The Way: Working with Teenage Writers*. Portsmouth, NH: Heinemann.

Vonnegut, Kurt. 1981. *Palm Sunday*. New York: Dell.

11 *Using Group Conferences to Respond to Essays in Progress*

SUSAN K. MILLER

When I began teaching first-year composition as a teaching assistant, one of my biggest challenges was encouraging students to respond to each other's writing in helpful, constructive ways that would facilitate revision. I also found that once they had written responses to each other, they were often reluctant to revise according to what other students suggested, although they would listen to what I said about their essays. I wanted to combine the benefits of peer response (Brooke, Mirtz, and Evans 3) and teacher response (Harris 5), so I began conducting group conferences on work in progress, a strategy originally introduced to me by Greg Glau.

Responding to work in progress not only helps authors see their writing through another's eyes, but it also helps readers see their own writing in a new way. Erika Lindemann claims that a class where students discuss their work in progress "enables students to see themselves as real writers and readers, engaged with others in using language to shape communities" (34). I wanted my students to see themselves as part of a writing community, negotiating meaning (Gere 73–74). I also wanted to create an environment in which all students would be encouraged to participate, in which they would still feel ownership over their own writing, and in which they would be exposed to the writing of others. I find that carefully constructed group conferences meet these goals.

I conduct group conferences by having students bring in first drafts of their essays and then distributing copies of that first draft to the other members of their writing group (usually two to three other people). If the class meets in a computer-mediated classroom, I usually have them send their essays by e-mail or post them to an asynchronous discussion forum. They read each other's essays as a homework assignment and write responses based on questions I have given them in class. Finally, we meet at a scheduled conference time to discuss the drafts together, looking at each student's essay in turn. Everyone

---

From *Strategies for Teaching First-Year Composition*, edited by Duane H. Roen et al., NCTE, 2002, pp. 307–18.

(including the teacher) must say one thing he or she thinks each author did well and one thing each author could work on in a revision. The author is always given a chance to clarify or ask questions, and then we go around the circle and say what we will revise before the next class. Students give their written responses to the authors to help in their revisions, and they are all expected to bring revised second drafts to the next class period.

As we go around the circle and share our comments, we often find that we have similar ideas. The confidence level in the classroom rises as students realize that many of their suggestions are the same as the teacher's. They begin to acknowledge that their peers have helpful, constructive comments to offer. At the end of the semester, several students always comment that group conferences were the most useful part of the class; they realized that we could all help each other in the process of writing.

Group conferences have helped me with the challenges mentioned earlier. They give students a framework for offering their comments, so that they have a model for writing helpful suggestions that will facilitate revision. In addition, they hear the comments of other students and the teacher about the same essays, clarifying for them what was expected in the assignment while providing additional examples of the kinds of comments they could make. Although most students are still reluctant to offer their suggestions in front of the whole group at first, their comments are usually confirmed by the others in the group, either by students saying things like, "Yeah, I noticed that, too," or by other students making similar comments during their turns. Authors are always given the choice of using the comments they find the most helpful—nobody is required to change everything suggested to them.

The day students bring their first drafts to class, I give them the following instructions:

Group Conference Instructions

1. *Read the essay thoroughly and critically.* As you read, consider whether the author has fulfilled the essay assignment.

2. *Read through the questions we discussed and practiced answering in class* (usually questions I have given them in class or questions from a text). Write *at least* one page in response to these questions for the author.

3. *Be certain to pay equal attention to things the author did well and places in which the author could improve the essay.* Try to phrase your response so that it gives specific help, so the author has an idea of what to revise. Try to write a response that you would like to receive—one that gives praise and also suggests places to begin rewriting.

4. *Finally, remember that this is the most exciting step in the writing process.* This is when we get to see our writing through the eyes of our audience, a luxury we often don't have when we hand in writing for an assignment or send it out to be published. Come to conferences with an open mind; be prepared to listen to your peers' comments, and be ready to share constructive comments of your own.

I always give them questions to respond to in step 2 that we have already discussed in class (and often they have written the questions themselves). Ideally, we would have spent a class period prior to this one answering the questions together for an essay we have all read. This process helps students feel comfortable as they answer the questions for each other, because they have seen an example of what I expect them to do.

The following draft of an essay by one of my students, Lynn, along with group conference comments from her classmate Nancy and from me, provide an example of how this process works. Lynn wrote an essay about an event that was significant in her life, a rock-climbing trip that she took shortly after arriving at college. Her first draft follows:

A Remembered Event 1

"I can't believe I survived after the three days" that was the first thing I said on Thursday morning, the day we were doing back from the trip. I went to a rock climbing with my teacher and friends last spring. I hadn't done rock climbing before and I was not good in any of the sports. I was really scared and I thought the trip was going to be long for me, but instead, it was a wonderful experience. Kayo is one of my good friends. We decided to go on that trip together. Both of us were beginners. We were all scared and couldn't believe we just sign up for a rock climbing trip. A week before the trip, we when to the library and borrowed a lot of rock climbing magazines. We were looking at the pictures and day dreaming. We were dreaming about being one of them, even we knew it's impossible. We were climbing up and down the bathroom door, tables. . . .

We left the school in the Monday morning. There were seven other girls went with us. On the way to the rock climbing jam, we didn't really talk to each other. As soon as we got to the Jam, we started to help each other out, we started to talk. The jam was really big that had six climbing well in the middle. There were made for different levels of people. It took me a long time to find the right size shoes for me and to put them on. The shoes were tight on me, they weren't comfortable to wear.

When I was walking, I couldn't walk too fast because the sticky thing in the bottom of the shoes. On the wall, there were things stick out from the wall that we could use to climb. I started with the easiest one on the walls. It wasn't hard. I tried the harder one, then another one. When I was climbing, my friends would watch me and tell me what's to do. The second day, we went out to a real climbing place a lot of big rocks. The teacher taught us the right way to climb. We were learning fast. People were helping each other again, then, we got closer to each other. The third was the best day in the whole trip. We took a long hike in to a mountain. We were walking with our equipment, lunch, water. . . . It wasn't an easy hike with all those things.

Finally, we got there. We put sunscreen on because the sun was really strong at that time. Susan the teacher and other two girls went to set the climbing equipment up. There were two of them. One was a easy one the other was harder. We took turns went up the easy one. I made it the first time. It was easy so not a big deal. The fun part is the harder one. It was a tall one with a slid patter and smooth surface. Some of the people went up there easily because they had been climbing before. It was my turn. It wasn't hard at the beginning but on the half way, I could started feel the wind blowing, I couldn't find any thing for my right hand to hang on, then I couldn't find any space for my foot. I almost cried. My friends were telling me where to put my hands and feet, but I just couldn't find any way to do it. Suddenly I herded Susan said "Lynn, you are doing great, just keep going, you are safe up there." I felt much better.

But still, my legs were shaking. I decide to try one more time see if I could go any further. Then I did. I made it all the way up there. I stood there for one minute just look at the view. The fifteen minutes I was climbing I felt like one year. The view was really beautiful.

I didn't think the trip could be so fun for me. I went all way up there when most of them didn't make it. Other then that, I met a lot of friends. After I came back from the trip, I felt stronger. That was a good thing for me to do.

Lynn's first draft gives us the chronology of what happened, but she doesn't provide the reader with specific details. Several of the students in her conference group asked her questions about the details of her story, demonstrating to Lynn that she had to consider her audience as she wrote her story.

Nancy, a fellow student in Lynn's conference group, made the following comments to Lynn about her first draft:

> To Lynn,
>
> I think it's a well-told story. I think the climax of this story is when you were trying to climb up the harder wall on the third day. It was described minutely, so I could imagine you climbing up the wall easily. I, however, can't understand some basic things and the significance. I want to know more abut the rock climbing and the trip. What is rock climbing? (What kind of equipment does it need? Where can you do it?) Why did you and your friend decide to go on the trip? Was it a tour of many clubs? How did you know that? Did you practice something before leaving for the trip? Where, when and to whom did you say, "I can't believe I survived after the three days."?
>
> I think most of the story is described vividly, but you need to describe how you felt on each day. If you add them, the story will be more vivid and more autobiographical. What did you feel after you experienced the rock climbing for the first time? What was the sticky thing in the bottom of your shoes? Did it affect your climbing? What did you think when you saw the real climbing place? Did you feel excited at night of the second day or before you tried the harder wall? "After I came [back] from the trip, I felt stronger." I think this sentence means how important the trip was for you, so it will be better if you add more information about the feeling or the life. After the trip, did this experience affect your life? If so, how? The organization of your story is so nice, I think. The beginning arouses my curiosity and lets me want to read it. You should describe the second day more minutely. And add your feeling or opinion to the ending.

Nancy helped Lynn start the revision process by asking specific questions about details in the story. She asked about details of the trip, how Lynn felt at different times, and she asked for more description of parts that she didn't understand or that she thought were underdeveloped. All students don't naturally ask questions about the essay in their written comments, so I model this technique in class when we practice responding before the first group conference. To encourage them to use questions in their responses, I demonstrate how much easier it is to start revising when we have specific questions to answer. Nancy did not comment on the mechanics or overall organization of Lynn's essay because I emphasize that we are looking at the content of the essay in the first draft. We conduct a workshop on editing toward the end of the writing process, and at that time we look at mechanics, organization, and overall clarity.

When I commented on Lynn's first draft, I asked about several details that Nancy mentioned. We both asked for more information about the car trip on the way home, Lynn's introduction to the story. In addition, we wanted to know more about the events on the third day—the main focus of the trip. We both asked specific questions about how she felt and what she saw on that day, and Nancy asked for more information about the other days, too. My comments also focus on specific things that I like in Lynn's essay:

Lynn,

I'm impressed with the fact that you went rock climbing! It's a very challenging and dangerous sport, and you should be very proud of your accomplishment! I love to go hiking, and I can relate to your excitement at finally reaching the top. I am a little scared of rock climbing, however, so I admire your courage.

I really liked how you started the essay in the car on the way home. It's almost as if you started at the end and then went back . . . a "flashback." Can you tell us more at the very beginning about how you felt on the way home? Were your muscles sore? Were you tired? Were you happy that you went, even though you didn't think you could do it? Did you feel like you would ever go again? You don't have to give us a lot of detail there, but I just wanted to know more about how you felt . . . what your emotions were.

In the middle part of your essay, you give some details about each of the three days of the trip. I was wondering if you could focus on Day 3. It seemed like that was the most exciting and challenging day. Can you give us more details about that day? How did you feel as you climbed? Where did you put your feet and your hands? Who was in front of you and who was behind you? Were you roped to your instructor? Were you scared? Did you ever look down? These kinds of details will help us to imagine the climb as if we were there.

Finally, I wondered if you could go back to the car scene that you have in the introduction at the end of the story. This would provide a frame for your essay that would help to conclude it. Just an idea . . . perhaps you can think of an even better way to end it.

Good job, Lynn! I look forward to reading your revision.

Lynn used Nancy's and my responses, along with the comments from the other students in her group, to revise her draft. Everyone asked for more description of the third day, so Lynn focused on that part of the essay in her revision. The varied sets of comments she received from her group members helped her to look at her draft through several sets of eyes, and then she chose the suggestions she found most important to start her revision. In the draft that follows, Lynn has included more details about her trip, including large-scale revisions such as a more complete description of her climb on the third day and smaller explanations such as describing the purpose of the sticky substance on the bottom of her shoes:

Rock Climbing

"I can't believe I survived after the three days." That was the first thing I said on Thursday morning, the day we were coming back from the trip. I went rock climbing with my teacher and friends that week. I hadn't done rock climbing before and I was not good in any sports. I was really scared, and I thought the trip was going to be long for me, but instead, it was a wonderful experience.

Kayo is one of my good friends. We decided to go on that trip together. Both of us were beginners. We were all scared and couldn't believe we just signed up for a rock-climbing trip. A week before the trip, we went to the library and borrowed a lot of rock climbing magazines. We were looking at the pictures and day dreaming. We were dreaming about being one of the rock climbers, even though we knew it was impossible. We were climbing up and down the bathroom door and tables.

We left the school on Monday morning. There were seven other girls who went with us. On the way to the rock climbing jam, we didn't really talk to each other. As soon as we got to the jam, we started to talk and help each other out. The jam was really big, and had six climbing walls in the middle. They were made for different levels of people. It took me a long time to find the right size shoes for me and to put them on. When I was walking, I couldn't walk too fast because the bottom of the shoes were sticky to help me climb. On the wall, there were things sticking out from the wall that we could use to climb. I started with the easiest wall. It wasn't hard. I tried the harder one, then another one. When I was climbing, my friends would watch me and tell me what to do.

The second day, we went out to a real climbing place, which had a lot of big rocks. The teacher taught us the right way to climb. We were learning fast. People were helping each other again, and, we got closer to each other.

The third day was the last and best day in the whole trip. We walked for almost one hour. Finally, we got to the bottom of the wash. It was such a beautiful place. There were two big walls on our left and right side. The rocks were red just like the sun on top of us. We almost forgot to put sunscreen on because of the beautiful scenery. We all sat on a big rock for lunch. The lunch was only some cold sandwiches I made that morning, but, I thought that was the best thing I had ever eaten because I was so hungry by the time. After the lunch, our teacher Susan who was also a very good climber went another way to set up the ropes. After that, we started to take turns climbing.

Brook had been rock climbing for several years, so she went up first. All of us were watching her. She was so good that she didn't even need to think. We weren't surprised when she made it. She came back down and told us how beautiful the view was on the top. After her, I watched several people climb. The beginning part was easy, but it got harder at one point. Most of the people gave up right at that point.

It was mine turn to go up. I put the harness on and took several steps forward. When I was climbing, I felt it was different from what I saw. It was much harder to do by myself. I put my hand on, then feet. Very fast, I was in the middle of the wall. I got to the hard part where almost everyone stops at. I looked down; I couldn't see people's faces because I was so high. The wind started blowing and my legs started shaking. I couldn't move either of my legs. I started yelling for help: "God, I am so scared what should I do! Somebody help me!"

People down there just tried to calm me down. I could hear people saying:

"Lynn, you are doing good, just put your right hand in that crack and put your foot into that hold."

I took a big deep breath and decided to move on again. I put my right hand in a crack so I could push my self up. But when I put my right hand in the little space, I felt something just pinch my hand. That hurt, but I couldn't let my hand go. Until I pulled myself up, I realized my hand was on a cactus. The next step was even harder. I got to put my balance on my left leg. It wasn't an easy thing for a beginner to do. I tried to put my weight on my left leg, but I felt like I wasn't going to stay on any more. My arms started shaking not only that, my throat was so dries that I couldn't even say anything. I was stuck. I didn't know what to do.

"Maybe I should just give up right here."

These words kept coming up to my head. When I was just going to give up, I heard Susan say, "Lynn, you are doing good. Try to go further if you can. You are doing just fine."

After I heard that, I felt much better. I took another deep breath, I found another crack that I could hang on to. Then, I tried the best I could. I was up. I just did the hardest part and the rest was easy. I just kept going, try to find place to put my hands and feet. Suddenly, I heard people clapping. Then I realized I was on the top of the wall. I made it! My legs and arms were still shaking though. I looked around. The wind was blowing, but I felt good. I was on the top for a minute to just enjoy the view and the happiness. I could see the top of the mountains and the world.

On the way back, all of us were in the van singing because every inch of our bodies was so sore that couldn't we move anything except our mouths. We were singing and talking as loud as we could because we were so happy. All of us were glad we went on this wonderful trip together. Not only learned how to rock climb, I also got some great friends and a good memory.

Although Lynn revised her essay further after her second draft, she was pleased with the description of her climb in her revision, and she began to realize the importance of having a real audience read her writing. The group conference helped Lynn by providing her with a forum for discussing those comments openly before revising. In addition, the conference helped Nancy by providing her with a model for writing comments to the author and giving her the opportunity to listen to other comments about the same draft.

WORKS CITED

Brooke, Robert, Ruth Mirtz, and Rick Evans. *Small Groups in Writing Workshops: Invitations to a Writer's Life*. Urbana, IL: NCTE, 1994.
Gere, Anne Ruggles. *Writing Groups: History, Theory, and Implications*. Carbondale: Southern Illinois UP, 1987.
Harris, Muriel. *Teaching One-to-One: The Writing Conference*. Urbana, IL: NCTE, 1986.
Lindemann, Erika. *A Rhetoric for Writing Teachers*. 3rd ed. New York: Oxford UP, 1995.

12   *Reflection on Peer-Review Practices*

LISA CAHILL

MY TEACHING BACKGROUND

At this writing, I have been teaching composition for three years, but when I
began teaching composition I was not necessarily a proponent for *or* an oppo-
nent of peer review. Initially, work in the classroom was primarily informed by
my understanding of the critical reading process. I tried to incorporate peer
review, rather unsuccessfully, in the first course that I taught, because I did
not really understand how to facilitate a productive review session. My first
composition teaching experience metamorphosed into a writing-across-the-
curriculum (WAC) partnership at Northern Arizona University between the
English department and the School of Forestry. This experience helped me
see ways that the peer-review process could function differently and more productively. During this time, I recognized a need to know more about the social,
academic, and personal exigencies for writing.

My WAC experiences taught me a great deal about the value and logistics
of peer review and collaborative writing experiences. The students with whom
I consulted were regularly engaging in discussions of their work with their
classmates; they trusted one another as credible readers and as responsible,
careful, and knowledgeable reviewers. Sharing a discipline enabled them to
bypass some of the obstacles that often confront students in first-year composition courses. The students in forestry were part of an established discourse
community that provided them with certain advantages over students in first-
year comp. Forestry students shared a language, a methodology, and an understanding of acceptable discursive forms. Students in my composition class had
different disciplinary affiliations and experiences, and different reasons for participating in peer review.

Students in first-year composition courses bring a variety of writing
experiences to the table. Some are familiar with peer review, while some have
had fewer opportunities to carefully critique others' work, provide specific

From *Strategies for Teaching First-Year Composition*, edited by Duane Roen et al., NCTE,
2002, pp. 301–07.

suggestions, and illustrate their concerns with examples from their peers' texts. Another very human factor tends to compound this difference of experience—a protocol of politeness that tends to impede an honest exchange of ideas. Understandably, some students are somewhat leery about pointing out "weaknesses" in their peers' work, while others may feel overwhelmed at not merely having to discover specific ways to strengthen the paper but also having to pose questions that will encourage a productive peer-review meeting. While peer review may seem like a simple exercise in building a sense of classroom community and in applying critical reading skills, it really is a more complex endeavor for students.

Likewise, peer review can be a complex endeavor for instructors who want to successfully implement it in their classrooms. In the fall of my first semester at Arizona State University, I taught English 101. My approach to peer review was predicated on one major goal—helping students learn how to recognize and respond in detail to the "right" questions during peer-review meetings. What was not fully clear to me at the time was the fact that there are not necessarily "right" or "wrong" questions. Questions for peer review are really only guided by one principle—the fact that writers' texts, as well as their rhetorical goals, vary from text to text and from situation to situation. Therefore, peer-review questions are contingent on the context of the writing assignment; different writing tasks call for new sets of questions. Instead of challenging students to write their own questions for peer review *and* to negotiate their concerns and responses with one another, I took responsibility for creating the questions to be used at different stages of the peer-review process. For each paper, I also prepared long peer-review response sheets derived from the criteria appearing in our text, *The St. Martin's Guide to Writing*.

THE THEORY BEHIND MY NEW PRACTICES

In 1985, Faigley argued for the social perspective in studying nonacademic writing; however, applying this perspective in the composition classroom is just as important. With the rise of social constructivism that followed soon after, compositionists began to realize the necessity of looking beyond the visible signs offered by a text to deeper issues of ideology and discourse communities' conventions—writers' reasons for making certain choices about content, organization, and style. Faigley's social perspective acknowledges the textual and individual perspectives that focus on genre-specific conventions, writers' perceptions of tasks, and writers' applications of strategies. The social perspective takes off in an important direction, however, a direction that is important when peer review is present in the composition classroom. Faigley's advocacy for researchers to "study how individual acts of communication define, organize, and maintain social groups" (235) is a task just as crucial for both teachers and students. James Berlin supported the notion of teachers as researchers, and it is time also to encourage our students to be researchers—to reflect on their practices and goals as well as the real and potential impact of their communications.

I am now working to make the peer-review process more than a series of questions that function in the textual vein—analysis of the way that stylistic and rhetorical figures are used. I want my students to "view written texts not as detached objects possessing meaning on their own, but as links in communicative chains, with their meaning emerging from their relationships to previous texts and the present context" (Faigley 235). To expand their notions of audience, purpose, context, and argumentation, students need to reflect on the traditions out of which their papers may come. In my English 102 class, for example, my students write the following series of essays: justifying an evaluation, taking a position, speculating about causes, and proposing solutions. I encourage them to think beyond their classmates and me as their only interested readers. I ask them to identify communities that are or have been realistically affected by the issues they write about and to investigate the histories of controversies and solutions surrounding that issue.

In doing so, the peer-review stages have to be altered. During group brainstorming sessions, I encourage students to invent a general list of questions related to the genre in which they are writing. Then students work in pairs and trios to work through different stages of the writing process. I ask them to set their own agendas, and I also encourage them to use peer review for more than the reading of a draft or polished document. Students will discuss the range of topics and positions under consideration, the communities related to these topics, possible counterarguments they may encounter, potential organizational structures, implications of their arguments, and previous progress made on these issues. All of this constitutes my response to Lester Faigley's 1985 call.

Rather than having my students begin peer review one week before the final draft is due, I integrate the process at the beginning of each unit. I want students to talk about their reasons for choosing to include particular subjects, positions, and evidence in their texts. In Lee Odell's ethnographic study of supervisors and administrative analysts who evaluated proposed legislation, he suggests that students "could benefit from discussion throughout the composing process" (277). Furthermore, Odell warns that teaching students fixed sets of analytic procedures designed to elicit ideas and reader responses may not necessarily be the best approach. His concern is that "in trying to reduce cognitive complexity we unwittingly increase it" (276). The sets of questions I posed to students for the four genres in English 101 were, for the most part, productive. They were only productive, however, in that moment and may not have translated beyond the scope of each assignment. Furthermore, these predetermined questions may have limited students to a certain degree. Odell is justified in asserting that "the writer must also be able to translate those terms [from heuristics or analytic procedures] into specific strategies or questions that will enable him or her to investigate a particular subject matter" (276).

Peer-review practices need to make students self-sufficient and capable of reading and writing in a variety of contexts and able to respond to a variety of rhetorical situations—be they civic, personal, professional, or academic. I have come to understand the composition classroom as a testing ground for students' professional, civic, personal, and academic endeavors. The classroom is a site for practicing heuristics, taking communicative risks, and participating in social efforts to create and interpret meaning. Peer review is one way to provide students with the chance to "practice the interpersonal skills that will enable them to function effectively in a dialogue or group discussion" (Odell 278). Allowing them to generate questions, direct their own meetings, and negotiate tensions are important precursors for their roles outside of the classroom.

Reflecting on Past Practices

My original intentions were good ones; I wanted students to assist their peers in writing cogent papers of which they could be proud. But the means I used to achieve my goals were not necessarily the best. Throughout the semester, I provided students with lengthy worksheets that asked them to answer open-ended questions that required more than a yes or no response. Rather than gradually weaning students away from canned or prepackaged questions and making them responsible for devising the questions as a class and as partners, I continued to use the worksheets. I discovered that, as readers, students were spending more time in quiet, individual contact with the paper than in discussion. They could not look up long enough to really *talk* to the writer; they felt compelled to answer all the questions and then return their responses to the writer. In turn, as writers, the students had to individually confer with the written responses instead of talking to their readers.

Because my approach to peer review in the composition classroom was to supply students with the "right" kinds of questions—questions that I took sole responsibility for creating and distributing—my students had a difficult time taking responsibility for directing the reading of their papers. I put students in pairs and gave them a twenty- to thirty-minute time slot during which to work. I provided them with very general directions: talk to one another, share concerns, help direct your partner's reading, and be prepared to discuss strengths as well as possible revisions. Although I left it up to my students to negotiate the ethics and logistics of peer review, I exempted them from a crucial part of the process—the development of a set of reading heuristics.

While I do not consider my original approach to peer review a total failure, I do recognize the flaws inherent in it. I also realize how important it is for me as a teacher to take a moment to examine my own assumptions and goals for peer review *before* creating classroom activities. That kind of examination, however, cannot stop there. It is vital to engage my students in a discussion about their concerns, goals, anxieties, and ideas related to peer review. In this way, we can co-construct an approach that is more fluid and flexible—one capable of responding to their ever-changing rhetorical goals. In this way, we can get closer to a community, to a communal ethic of trusting one another like that of the forestry students.

WORKS CITED

Berlin, James A. *Rhetoric and Reality: Writing Instruction in American Colleges, 1900–1985.* Carbondale: Southern Illinois UP, 1987.

Faigley, Lester. "Nonacademic Writing: The Social Perspective." *Writing in Nonacademic Settings.* Ed. Lee Odell and Dixie Goswami. New York: Guilford, 1985. 231–48.

Odell, Lee. "Beyond the Text: Relations between Writing and Social Context." *Writing in Nonacademic Settings.* Ed. Lee Odell and Dixie Goswami. New York: Guilford, 1985. 249–80.

PART FOUR

Recognizing Linguistic and Cultural Diversity

Introduction to Part Four

Group dynamics are at the center of peer response activities—an important factor to recognize as writing classrooms grow increasingly diverse. The essays collected in this section explore the many complex concerns that come with understanding linguistic and cultural differences in relation to peer response activities. We've chosen readings that reflect on the abilities and needs of multilingual and multicultural students, seeking to include authors who challenge and complicate comfortable notions of a one-size-fits-all peer review and response pedagogy.

Opening this section is Gail Stygall's "Women and Language in the Collaborative Writing Classroom" (1998), which employs feminist-critical discourse analysis (framed via Foucauldian theories of discursive formations and relations) to argue for a reconsideration of the importance of teacher involvement in peer response groups. Stygall's linguistic analyses of peer response transcripts, originally published by Kenneth Bruffee, Martin Nystrand, and Lester Faigley, reveal discursive evidence that works against utopian notions of democratic or equitable participation. Repeatedly, in the transcripts, Stygall finds evidence of gender inequalities as they are performed by group participants—inequities exacerbated by the (seeming) absence of instructor direction and control. Overall, Stygall argues that teachers need to pay close attention to what goes on in peer response groups. Instructors should consider the importance of playing a more active role in student group activities, especially watching out for and confronting inequalities in peer groups and being willing to coach students toward alternatives.

Our second selection, Laurie Grobman's "Building Bridges to Academic Discourse" (1999), starts with the premise that basic writers should be treated as intellectuals and that peer response groups should be geared toward fostering the critical capacities of these students. Paralleling works included in previous sections of this sourcebook, Grobman offers a case study of a peer response group leader in action. Illustrating the advantages of having an experienced peer tutor facilitating basic writing response groups, Grobman argues that having peer group leaders model response strategies to students who are unfamiliar with these critical moves improves the writing abilities of all participants. Grobman's case study offers strategies for nudging students toward focus, comfort, and confidence in working with peers in response groups.

Our next selection, Sonja Launspach's "The Role of Talk in Small Writing Groups" (2008), synthesizes a number of central ideas about the role of peer response group leaders and the negotiation of identity and diversity issues in peer groups. Launspach's study focuses on one student, a freshman African American female named Ricki. Launspach studies several teaching-assistant-led response group interactions, analyzing how these interactions progressively affected Ricki's composing performances as she moved through drafts of her papers. Launspach illustrates how Ricki, with the help of her peer group leader and members, increased her strength and awareness of both declarative and procedural knowledge as she moved between the group conversations and revised her assignments. The author further claims that due to the gradual, exploratory nature of the peer group interaction, Ricki was able to draw on her "home discourses" to help scaffold the new academic discursive knowledges she was attempting to acquire and perform.

Todd Ruecker, in our fourth selection, "Analyzing and Addressing the Effects of Native Speakerism on Linguistically Diverse Peer Review," offers a 2014 case study of seventeen international nonnative English-speaking (NNES) students in peer response groups. Framed by Lev Vygotsky's theory of the zone of proximal development (ZPD) and theories of native speakerism, Ruecker's study provides evidence for ways that NNES students often offer each other successful reciprocal help in response groups. When provided the proper structural guidance, students in Ruecker's study proved capable—often surprisingly more than their native English-speaking classmates—of providing higher-order (over sentence-level) feedback on each other's work. The author offers several suggestions for how to work toward successful peer response experiences for NNES students, including having them work with peer group-mates both face-to-face and online, and making sure instructors take an active role in the design, scaffolding, and coaching of students (including instructor-led peer-group conferences).

And in our final selection, "Learning Disability and Response-Ability" (2015), Steven J. Corbett offers a case study of a tutor-led peer response group in a basic writing class, highlighting the partnership between a tutor and a student who both have learning disabilities. Via contextually rich, personal backstories, Corbett demonstrates the confidence and comfort achieved by tutor and student as they struggle to realize their place in the challenging world of academia and work successfully with their peers over several years. These intimate glimpses into student experience offer important implications for research on and work with peer response groups in writing classes, reminding instructors that patience, thoughtfulness, and trust building are central to the effectiveness of peer-centered learning environments.

Part Four's readings highlight ways that we can do more to think about how peer response groups reflect broader social opportunities and inequalities. In all, these readings suggest that instructors and researchers interested in peer response and review activities must be mindful of the ways these groups enact and entrench social conditions. Peer response groups cannot be extracted from the powerful social determinants that order other human interactions—but with reflection on these dynamics, instructors may be able to adjust the traditional imbalances, influencing—if only in small part—group patterns of response or making these interactions part of course learning. Researchers should also be careful to account for social dynamics in their work on peer response activities in writing classes.

13 Women and Language in the Collaborative Writing Classroom

GAIL STYGALL

Many of the problems they experience in the classroom could be alleviated, some of the women said, if talk were more collaborative. Discussing a classroom situation she had enjoyed, one woman said: "It was just wonderful. There were integrated, reciprocal, coexisting dialogues happening most of the time. There were people interrupting people and there were all kinds of things happening. The dialogues, the interaction, was in sync so I was very comfortable."

–CHERIS KRAMARAE AND PAULA A. TREICHLER

What is happening during a collaborative task is a dialogue between men's and women's language. Although we would expect that male language would dominate, the new social structure of the peer learning group, the lack of a patriarchal presence "teaching," and the presence of strong and vocal women in the group can combine to give women's language the power to surface and to replace men's language.

–CAROL STANGER

"Discipline" . . . is a type of power, a modality for its exercise, comprising a whole set of instruments, techniques, procedures, levels of application, targets; it is a "physics" or an "anatomy" of power, a technology. . . . [O]ne can speak of the formation of a disciplinary society . . . [n]ot because the disciplinary modality of power has replaced all the others; but because it has infiltrated all the others, sometimes undermining them, but serving as an intermediary between them, linking them together, extending them and above all making it possible to bring the effects of power to the most minute and distant elements.

–MICHEL FOUCAULT

As an educational technology, collaboration has received very little scrutiny at the same time that it has become widely used in both composition and feminist classrooms. Cheris Kramarae and Paula A. Treichler find female students attracted to classrooms in which the process of discussing

From *Feminism and Composition Studies: In Other Words*, edited by Susan C. Jarratt and Lynn Worsham, Modern Language Association, 1998, pp. 252–75.

knowledge is more highly valued than the production of knowledge. Carol Stanger posits a new gender equality in the talk of the collaborative group. Both uses of collaboration, in composition studies and in feminist teaching, were born of the liberal hope in the expansion of educational franchise of the early 1970s, and both set equality of opportunity as the goal of pedagogy. Liberal ideology in both cases assumes that the classroom is a free, open forum, because the instructor can mediate inequalities by articulating, modeling, and enforcing the rules of respectful, relevant exchange and development of positions. But in both the composition and feminist versions of collaboration, when the instructor withdraws, hierarchy and inequality may reappear.

Michel Foucault teaches us that all technologies of talk are part of discursive formations and relations, disciplining at the "most minute" levels (*Discipline* 216), and the collaboration under discussion here is not exempt from the forces of discipline. What scrutiny collaboration has received in the past fifteen years has been primarily from a left-progressive perspective; none at all has come from a feminist position. This essay elaborates, from the perspective of a feminist-critical linguist, the reasons that unstructured collaboration in the writing classroom jeopardizes participatory learning for women students. Given what feminist-critical linguists have known about how women fare generally in conversations outside the classroom, it should come as no surprise that women fail to thrive in classroom working groups, whether the field is composition or women's studies. Does collaboration produce the non-patriarchal classroom of feminist hope? In the absence of a feminist-critical authority in the writing classroom, the answer must be no.

To examine how collaborative talk works in the writing classroom, I employ a feminist-critical linguistic approach. While I am not suggesting that feminist-critical linguistics yields empirical truth, I do claim that it provides another position, a platform from which the workings of collaborative talk can be viewed. In this essay I review the perspectives provided by feminist-critical linguistics, then reanalyze three published conversations that are offered as examples of good collaboration. The first conversation, an invented one, is provided by Kenneth Bruffee. In it, we see a female acting as the helpmate for a male struggling to find a topic for his essay. She does all the work; he gains all the benefits. Although the conversation is made-up, it inscribes deeply held attitudes about conversation in our culture. The second conversation, a recorded and transcribed student working group, is drawn from Martin Nystrand. It demonstrates that students do serious work on their writing in peer groups and also gives evidence of gender roles in talk—and of the discipline that works at the "most minute" level—when one of the female group members, the student-author of the piece under discussion, is nearly silenced while another takes on the voice of the institution for the group. In the third conversation, a transcript drawn from Lester Faigley, we see the forces of gender and language at work in the computer-mediated classroom. Although this transcript demonstrates a radical reallotment of speaking roles, I argue that gender roles are reinscribed here by other means.

Technologies of talk—such as collaboration—are part of discursive relations in educational institutions. In the writing classroom, where collaboration acts to displace teacher authority, we can expect that the intertwined discursive practices of education and patriarchy will reproduce themselves in the absence of authoritative comment from a feminist teacher. From the findings of Elizabeth Sommers and Sandra Lawrence, from bell hooks's discussions of teaching, and from Susan Jarratt's theorizing about feminism and argument, I conclude that women fare better in collaborative talk when the feminist teacher explicitly teaches and models new forms of talk.

FEMINIST-CRITICAL LINGUISTICS, CONVERSATION, AND EDUCATION

Feminist linguistics has taken many forms over the past twenty years, from the theoretical projects of the radical feminist linguists such as Dale Spender to the empirical sociolinguistic and discourse-analytic studies by researchers such as Deborah Tannen to the theoretical discussions of the French feminists to the Hallidayan analyses by scholars such as Cate Poynton. I focus here on the empirical analysis of gender and conversation, because much of the work on collaboration in the writing classroom presumes some sort of conversation as its basis. But we must move beyond naive empiricism and also think about the discursive formations of education working in conjunction with those of gender.

As Foucault describes in *Discipline and Punish*, it is not only prisons that act to discipline; it is also schools in which students are made into individual files, ranked, sorted, collected, all under the surveillance of the institution. It is a commonplace that the teacher at the head of the classroom embodies the panopticon. But discipline does not necessarily disappear when the teacher moves away from the head of the classroom. We should expect discipline to continue to operate, if in different forms. With collaboration, we have simply deputized our students to act, in the absence of instruction to the contrary, as those who discipline, that is, using the social roles they bring to the classroom. There are two discourse consequences: first, some student will take up the role and voice of teacher, directing students to the task of collaboration; second, whatever gender roles students bring to class will necessarily be part of the talk of the group. In both cases, institutional discipline is still operating—despite the liberal hope that the need for the teacher, like the state, will eventually wither away.

Unlike feminism or even contemporary composition studies, linguistics has been resistant to poststructural accounts of language, because linguistics is predicated on the assumption of structure in language. All linguists, whether the theoretical descendants of Noam Chomsky's MIT linguistics, of the sociolinguistics of William Labov or Peter Trudgill, or of the combinations of language and the social made by M. A. K. Halliday, believe that language may be analyzed in levels—the divisions into phonetics, phonology, morphology, syntax, semantics, and discourse. Although there is considerable dispute about the relative importance of the different levels and their relation to the social, linguists generally assume that, at least for purposes of analysis, these levels exist. All linguistic analysis begins with the assumption of structure. Analysis of language and gender identifies the structures sensitive to change when gender is a variable.

Both sociolinguists and discourse analysts assign different weight to the reality of their findings. Some report their findings as if they discovered a natural wonder on a colonial expedition: the structure of language emerging from their analysis. Others, such as Deborah Cameron ("Demythologizing"), have attacked the nonpolitical stances of some sociolinguists. Teun van Dijk and other followers of critical linguistics argue that the basic task of that linguistics is to center analysis "on the role of discourse in the (re)production and challenge of dominance. . . . More specifically, critical discourse analysts want to know what structures, strategies or other properties of text, talk, verbal interaction or communicative events play a role in these modes of reproduction" (249–50). Because work in critical linguistics invokes social theorists such as Foucault, Pierre Bourdieu, and Louis Althusser to examine how language, ideology, power, knowledge, and cultural capital interact, I believe Dijk's recent work avoids some of the criticisms developed in Faigley's *Fragments of Rationality*. Faigley's primary criticism of the critical linguistics movement is that it posits a simple one-to-one correspondence between ideology and language. It is a valid criticism of the early forms of critical linguistics but doesn't do justice to the later work of Robert Hodge and Gunther Kress in *Social Semiotics* or Dijk's articulation of a complex critical discourse analysis. Critical discourse analysis informed by social theory is my frame for this essay. As a feminist-critical linguist I expect that, apart from gender, institutional education is generating, maintaining, and situating discursive formations—metarules about speaking rights genres, erasures.[1]

Issues of language and gender in linguistics have been relatively muted in the United States by the dominant linguistic approach, which posits an autonomous linguistic mental faculty and a universal grammar and has no interest in the social, where gender factors are often most visible. As Cameron observes, "It's hard to imagine a feminist account of Gaelic vowel mutation or a women's phonetic alphabet" (3). That is to say, linguists disagree not about what the forms are but about what the study of those forms means. Thus the feminist linguist doesn't argue that a sound or sentence exists, but that the existence varies with gender. To study forms and not their social uses is to exclude gender (and other hierarchies) from linguistic study. Cameron suggests the possibility of a feminist critique of linguistics. Indeed, in sociolinguistics and in discourse analysis, both subfields of linguistics that are less influenced by the dominant autonomous paradigm, gender has emerged as a relevant category of analysis. While any structuralism-based subfield of linguistics is open to poststructuralist criticism, the observations these two subfields have made about the effect of gender on the language of middle-class, white American adults remain an important means of triangulating accounts of gender and language. Some of these observations are listed in figure 1.

Figure 1   Sample empirical observations of gender in conversational interaction.

Sociolinguistic or Discourse Finding	Researcher(s)
Women use more tag questions in cross-sex conversation.	Lakoff
Women use more addressee-oriented, affective tag questions; men use more speaker-oriented, modal tag questions.	Holmes; Cameron, McAlinden, and O'Leary
Women use more hedges.	Lakoff
Men in cross-sex conversations tend to interrupt women more than women interrupt men.	Zimmerman and West
Men and women both interrupt, but they interrupt in different contexts.	James and Clarke
Women in conversation with women overlap cooperatively.	Tannen, *You* and "Relativity"; Coates, "Gossip"
Women frame conversation as a process of rapport building; men frame conversation as independence maintaining.	Tannen, *You* and *Gender*
Men talk more than women in cross-sex conversation.	James and Drakich
Men's turns on the floor are longer.	Edelsky
In cross-sex relationships, women do more of the conversational caretaking.	Fishman; DeFrancisco

The studies reported in figure 1 are not comprehensive, because they do not integrate the intersections of gender with race, class, and ethnicity, but they do outline some of the most discussed observations in empirical studies of conversational interaction and gender. Robin Lakoff's 1975 work, *Language and Woman's Place*, opens the debate by making observations about stereotypes of language and gender, drawing solely on her own reflections (a typical practice of linguistic theorists in the U.S.) and on the experiences of her close associates. Sociolinguists and later discourse analysts took issue with many of her declarations, but some felt that she had described a powerless form of language—a phenomenon whose existence was confirmed in several later studies.[2] Although all these observations are now quite complicated by context, it would appear that insofar as women are less powerful than men in middle-class American culture, so is their language less powerful, more oriented to relational issues. Many studies of childhood and classroom interaction suggest differentiation along lines of gender. Daniel Maltz and Ruth Borker's discussion of gender and language, for example, suggests that because in the

United States boys and girls are socialized into language quite differently, they have grown up in what amount to separate sociolinguistic subcultures. The rules for conversation, Maltz and Borker argue, are learned from ages five to fifteen, when single-sex relationships dominate, and carry over into late adolescence and early adulthood. Thus it would be highly surprising if male and female students came to the collaborative writing group with the same conversational socialization and strategies in hand.

The feminist-critical linguist would want to examine transcripts of classroom conversations in which collaboration was used and ask questions about those conversations before concluding that collaborative peer groups are beneficial to women students. If male students talk more and get their topics onto the conversational floor more readily than female students do, if they ask fewer questions of female students than of male students and interrupt female students more often than they do male students, we might want to give serious thought to the kinds of authority that should operate in the collaborative group in the writing classroom. And if a student takes on the role of the teacher, we would want to interrogate that interpretation of authority and discipline as well.

Bruffee: It Could Be "Any Undergraduate"

Taking a closer look at some published conversations from the perspective of the feminist-critical linguist, I begin with Bruffee's *Collaborative Learning*. While Bruffee's earlier work does not provide transcripts, even invented ones, his 1993 book does. Though Bruffee includes responses to criticisms made in the composition community, especially those made by John Trimbur, the audience for *Collaborative Learning* seems to be college administrators more than other scholars in composition. Bruffee shows a familiarity with postmodern, poststructural thought about knowledge communities; but in the end the book is a curriculum proposal, one that advocates a nonfoundationalist program in which the knowledge students bring to college is affirmed, the social justification of knowledge is examined, the situatedness of knowledge is explored. The "conversation" in figure 2 is invented, and if Bruffee were not so earnest in his presentation of the benefits of collaboration, I might have thought he was parodying a male-female conversation. Bert's assignment is that Bert must "explain to his classmates something he has learned in another course." Conveniently, he runs into Ernestine, who "sees the worried look on his face, and puts two and two together" (58–59). Apparently, Ernestine is supposed to help Bert find a topic for his paper, and she works at this task accordingly. At first glance, the conversation may not seem problematic. Each speaker—one male, one female—has the same number of turns. Though there is some difference in the number of utterances, Bert having 57% of the total, Ernestine 43%, the difference doesn't seem excessive. It is striking, however, when we examine the kinds of utterances. Ernestine asks fifteen questions, whereas Bert asks five, and those five only after she has convinced him that he has a topic. The role Ernestine assumes is very close to the role Pamela Fishman describes in her analysis of transcripts of three couples' ordinary, daily

FIGURE 2   Bruffee's invented transcript.

Ernestine:	Hey, Bert, what're you going to write your comp essay about?
Bert:	Gee, Ernestine, I don't know.
Ernestine:	What courses are you taking besides comp?
Bert:	Music. Phys Ed. Psych. Physics.
Ernestine:	Which one do you like best?
Bert:	Physics. I'm doing great. I think I'm going to ace it.
Ernestine:	Why not write about that?
Bert:	No.
Ernestine:	Why not?
Bert:	No, Ernestine. No. Absolutely not. It's too hard. Nobody'd understand what I'm saying. Anyway, nobody cares about physics. They think it's boring. Everybody'd be bored.
Ernestine:	I wouldn't be. I liked physics in high school. I'm taking it next term. What're you doing in physics right now?
Bert:	Well, we just finished atomic structure and radiation.
Ernestine:	What about them?
Bert:	Well, uh . . . oh, Ernestine, no. I tell you I can't write about physics and that's that.
Ernestine:	Aw, come on, Bert. What's radiation?
Bert:	It's energy. Different kinds of matter give off different kinds of energy.
Ernestine:	What kinds?
Bert:	Light. Light is radiation. There are different kinds.
Ernestine:	Bert, come on. What other kinds?
Bert:	Oh, X-rays, cosmic rays, particle radiation, that sort of thing.
Ernestine:	So, there you are. Write about them.
Bert:	Mm, . . . no. Too complicated. But you know what? I could write about what radiation does to you if you get too much of it.
Ernestine:	Do you have enough to say about that for a paper?
Bert:	Sure. The teacher lectured about it. Showed pictures too. Ugh. And you know, I remember seeing a TV show about it last spring. There's a section in the textbook about it, too. That may help.
Ernestine:	What could you say about it? What kind of position would you take?
Bert:	Well, maybe something like, Radiation changes cell structure. How about that?
Ernestine:	What does changing cell structure do to you?

FIGURE 2   *continued*

Bert:	Mainly it gives you cancer and gives your children birth defects.
Ernestine:	There you are, Bert. You've got a position—radiation changes cell structure—and two paragraphs to support it, one on radiation-induced cancer and one on radiation-induced birth defects. You're home free.
Bert:	Gee, Ernestine, do you think so? Do you think people would be interested? Radiation sickness is really awful, Ernestine. Why, do you know what happens first if you get too much radiation? Your . . .
Ernestine:	Wait. Wait. Stop, Bert. Don't tell me any more about it. Make the comp teacher sick, not me. Serve him right. But you know what?
Bert:	What?
Ernestine:	I'm not bored.
Bert:	Gee, Ernestine, thanks.

Source: Bruffee, *Learning* 58–59.

conversation. Fishman finds that women work to keep conversation going, by asking questions, by having their topics deferred in favor of those offered by their male partners, and by engaging in a subordinate role that is supportive and encouraging. Women, she says, are the "'shitworkers' of routine interaction" (405).

Bruffee remarks at the close of his invented conversation that Ernestine has done a considerable amount of work in this conversation but that, of course, "any undergraduate" could have fulfilled the same role (60). But it wasn't any undergraduate, it was a female undergraduate, and she was acting in accordance with her allotted conversational role: to maintain the conversational floor for the benefit of the male speaker.

NYSTRAND: TALKING ABOUT WRITING

Much of the research done on peer writing groups has been descriptive, focused on what the group members say to one another. Even with a social constructivist model of language and learning, it has been difficult to theorize about collaborative writing groups. There should be a good match between a theory that says that we learn language socially and a practice that says that writing is best taught in collaborative groups. Yet although a gesture has been made toward studying how collaboration suppresses dissent (see Trimbur, "Consensus") and enforces class lines (see Myers), we have looked very little at how gendered social roles operate in collaborative writing groups. Specifically, we have not considered how collaboration produces and instills discipline at the microlevel.

Foucault contends that seriation and hierarchization produce discipline in schools:

> From the seventeenth century to the introduction, at the beginning of the nineteenth, of the Lancaster method, the complex clockwork of the mutual improvement school was built up cog by cog: first the oldest pupils were entrusted with tasks involving simple supervision, then of checking work, then of teaching; in the end, all the time of all the pupils was occupied either with teaching or with being taught. The school became a machine for learning, in which each pupil, each level and each moment, if correctly combined, were permanently utilized in the process of teaching. (165)

Though collaboration rarely works as efficiently as Foucault describes it (nor did the Lancaster method work that well), thinking about collaboration as discipline is useful. Because the teacher is not in direct control, some student must move into that vacated supervisory position. It should be no surprise that in Martin Nystrand's transcript of a collaborative session in a writing classroom the student is a woman. Most of the teachers college students have had in language arts and English courses in their precollege education were women. Sociolinguistic research indicates, also, that women are more likely to act as language conservators than as language innovators. Though this finding has been disputed by feminist linguists, it remains a widely held view of the relation between women and language.[3] Whom do we imagine correcting our grammar? The image is almost always female.

Nystrand provides striking examples of how social roles affect a peer group's discussion. We see a woman writer remain silent while three others discuss her text; we see a woman function as the group's voice of discipline. In neither case does the woman student materially benefit from being a part of the collaborative group. Both the silent author and the voice of discipline only reproduce the available gendered roles.

Figure 3 is taken from Nystrand's extensive transcript of a writing group's discussion of a paper. Before this segment begins, a female group member's paper has been read to the group. Only three of the four members speak; the writer of the paper is silent. She is not required to remain silent, as some forms of peer writing groups prescribe. The assignment was to write a critical essay and her topic was how the media slant representations of events. Defining features of the genre of critical essay was, in Nystrand's view, a significant part of the discussion. And, indeed, a reading of the transcript shows that the students are talking about genre in relation to personal experience and about the writer's relation to experience and evidence.

Tom opens the discussion in turn 1 by stating that he enjoyed the paper, but his statement is marked by several false starts and hesitations. Perhaps his training in group work—"Always start with something positive"—is in conflict with his difficulty with the language of feeling, a difficulty typical of young adult males. With an initial false start and a switch in focus from the paper ("That was really") to his feeling ("I—I enjoyed the first paragraph"), combined with three place-holding *ums*, Tom conveys that he is afraid that he

FIGURE 3   Nystrand peer writing group transcript, first segment.

Turn	Speaker	Text of Turn
1	Tom:	That was really—I—I enjoyed the first paragraph really good. I thought—um—"slant"—"slant" was a good word—"slant their stories"—um—stuff like that—um—
2	Jean:	Um—this one right here on the second page it says "one day on the way to school"—I think that's too related to you—It's—you gotta detach it more.
3	Tom:	Yeah—Make it—make it general.
4	Jean:	Should I do that on my paper too?
5	Rick:	You can't do that on your paper.
6	Jean:	Maybe my whole paper just stinks.
7	Rick:	No, just 'cause you have personal experiences in it doesn't mean it stinks. I don'—*your* paper was about band. When you document—you know—you can't use documented proof on something like that.
8	Jean:	So I have to use my own—right.
9	Rick:	Well, unless you know of something—
10	Jean:	'Cause when she was reading that through I noticed it on hers and then I thought it's the same on—as mi—mine—like—
11	Rick:	But hers—hers is a paper where she could get—you know?—examples and stories that didn't *have* to deal with her.
12	Tom:	Yeah, I think that would end up—you have to—

Source: Nystrand 191.

can't hold the conversational floor. Because this group is working well into the semester, Tom's fear may be based on an expectation of losing the floor to Jean or to Rick. Indeed, at Tom's second hesitation, Jean echoes his *um* and initiates her first bid for the floor. Without waiting for the writer to ask for specific commentary, Jean selects herself as the next speaker. She changes the direction of the discussion by her topicalization "this one right here" and in effect tells the author not to use "I" or be too personal in a critical essay. Tom confirms Jean's criticism in turn 3 by interpreting not being personal as being general.

Jean introduces a new topic with her question in turn 4 about her own paper, and this second topic remains on the floor until she connects it back to the writer's paper in turn 10. Rick enters the conversation at turn 5 and assists Jean in maintaining her topic. Jean's declaration in turn 6 is an indicator of her intention to continue control of the conversation. The type of statement in turn 6 is sometimes called response-controlling, because normal conversa-

tional politeness demands that any respondent deny the truth of the statement. Predictably, Rick says no at the beginning of his turn, releasing Jean
from the obligation of providing evidence in her paper because of its grounding in personal experience. Jean confirms Rick's response in turn 8, with a
topic-closing "right." Rick actually offers to continue Jean's second topic in
turn 9, with a slight shift in orientation indicated by his "well." Jean's topics
and interests hold throughout this twelve-turn segment, with the writer completely outside the conversation.

Figure 4 is a continuation of the discussion in figure 3. Though the writer
does speak in this and subsequent segments, it is always in response to

FIGURE 4   Nystrand peer writing group transcript, second segment.

Turn	Speaker	Text of Turn
1	Rick:	That's why I think that you—it—it—
2	Jean:	You just have to change the phrasing a little bit.
3	Author:	How about if I just started out "I heard a conversation that gave a perfect example of the media slanting a story"?
4	Jean:	That's still—I think it's still too close.
5	Tom:	Yeah.
6	Rick:	But if she doesn't do that she's gonna have to like say where—where she's got this information from—That's what I—I kinda want to know about this.
7	Jean:	What is the bus? What does the bus have to do with it maybe? Take the bus out too—
8	Rick:	That's where—where she heard it.
9	Author:	Yeah.
10	Jean:	Right. But that doesn't have anything to do with the story.
11	Tom:	No. It doesn't.
12	Author:	Okay.
13	Jean:	And that's kind of—
14	Author:	How could I—how could I introduce the story into the paper so that it didn't sound like something—that—something that I'm just making up?
15	Jean:	Okay.
16	Tom:	Does anybody have that one paper on—um—
17	Jean:	How 'bout for—for instance—um—
18	Rick:	Mention the conversation a little bit.

Source: Nystrand 192–93

Jean's queries and directives. The author is like students in student-teacher conferences who cannot direct attention to their concerns. We are never really sure that she wished to discuss the issue of her personal knowledge of her essay topic. Because Jean blocks her access to the floor by speaking in the disciplinary voice, the author never initiates discussion. Even more important, Jean's control of the floor is in the service of filling the teacher's vacated role. Jean focuses on nuance of phrase (turns 2 and 4), narrowness of topic (turns 7 and 10), unity of story line (turn 10). And she makes suggestions. We could imagine a teacher in a student-teacher conference making these same points. And it fits educational and patriarchal discursive practices that Jean is a woman. With discipline's requirement that some students take on the teaching role so intertwined with the patriarchal educational system that distributes the pre-college and first-year college composition slots to women and the serious scholarly roles to men, it may be easy to miss that the disciplinary discourse is itself gendered. Neither Jean nor the writer can advance an independent agenda. While Nystrand appropriately characterizes his students' conversation about the text at hand as a discussion of genre, he avoids the issue of the relations among discipline, education, and gender.

FAIGLEY: GENDER ITERATIONS IN THE COMPUTER-MEDIATED CLASSROOM

Although Lester Faigley was initially entranced by the multiplicity of voices and displacement of the teacher in the computer-networked classroom, his subsequent experience made him less sanguine. The final transcript he offers shows a devolution into gender warfare and name-calling that would dismay any teacher, a kind of behavior made possible probably only by the use of pseudonyms and the iterations and echoes of computer-mediated communication.

It is to the original, more hopeful first transcript that I turn here. In a class in which the female-to-male ratio is 17:4, Faigley presents and discusses 87 messages of a 191-message session from a computer-mediated writing course titled Writing and Thinking. He initiates the discussion by offering two paragraphs from an assigned reading from James Spradley and Brenda Mann's *The Cocktail Waitress*, an ethnography of the working life of bar waitresses. The paragraphs deal with the gender-role confusion of a waitress named Holly.[4] Holly's confusion is generated by a job in which her sexuality plays so prominently; she works in a male world, serving primarily male customers, so her livelihood is dependent on her ability to stay in a traditional woman's role. Faigley's asking the class who wrote the passage, Spradley or Mann, prompts a discussion of gender, authorship, and text. Faigley tells of the exceptionally high student participation rate and the occurrence of "hot messages"—messages to which there are many responses (180). On gender issues arising from the transcript, he says, "Even if patriarchal social structures do not vanish when students use *Interchange* (note that several of the women chose male pseudonyms), some of the socially defined limits are mitigated" (181).

I challenge this observation. If some socially defined limits based on gender are mitigated, others arise to take their place, leaving us with little in the way of net improvement for women students conversing by computer in the writing classroom. The ideologies of gender, instead of being identified in the usual back-and-forth classroom exchange among a handful of high-participation students, are more thoroughly, more completely dispersed throughout the classroom, powerful iterations on the theme of gender determinism. And although computer-mediated discussion does allow an opening for everyone's response, the number and rapidity of message exchanges are too great for the instructor to monitor them all.

In the ordinary classroom, talk is controlled by the teacher. The teacher decides who talks and when, decides when a student must stop talking, decides which topics are appropriate, what connections from one's reading or personal experience may be publicly linked to the topic, and what digressions are acceptable. Although the degree of control over classroom talk in fact varies, classrooms in which teachers talk and students listen or students talk one at a time are the most common. Discourse analysts working in classrooms have observed what has been called the IRE (initiation, response, evaluation) pattern, in which the teacher opens with an inquiry, the student makes a response, and then the teacher evaluates that response.[5] As Courtney Cazden observes, the teacher is thereby guaranteed two-thirds of the classroom floor time (160). It has also been observed in United States classrooms at all age levels that a small group of high-participation students usually controls the classroom floor, the rest of the class remaining silent listeners. Thus the broad participation that Faigley describes in his study is unusual. Figure 5 shows a radical redistribution of classroom speaking roles.

Twenty out of twenty-one students attending that day participated. A graduate student teacher, JoAnn Campbell, also participated (the class she was teaching used the same reading materials as Writing and Thinking but did not meet in the computer-mediated classroom). She wrote more than Faigley did; her words, in eight turns, accounted for about 10% of the transcript. In six turns, President Reagen (the student's spelling) accounted for 8.4%, and Faigley accounted for 7.7%. Thus the two teacher figures accounted for 18.4% of the messages. The next ten students in the table produced remarkably similar passages of the transcript.

The issue of pseudonyms does not straightforwardly mitigate social limits, as it might first appear. Two of the males are identified by Faigley—President Reagen and Greg Harvey. Faigley indicates that there are four males in the class altogether. But only six names are female—jane doe, Karen, angel, Rae, Megan, and Dolly Wolly—though of course we have no reason to assume that the students behind these names are all female. There are three ambiguous names (t.c., Mickey, and LSP) and nine male names (Art, A. Hitler, jimmy, Kenny g, xerxes, Gordon Sumner, fred, George Strait, and Mickey Mouse). Clearly, the anonymity of typically male names is preferred by many, perhaps even by a majority, of the female students. Rhetorical cross-dressing contributes to our understanding of gender displayed in the classroom discussion. As I have argued in

FIGURE 5   Distribution of talk in Faigley transcript.

Name	Words	Turns	Percent of Floor	Words per Turn
JoAnn	374	8	10.7	47
President Reagen*	294	6	8.4	49
Lester Faigley	270	9	7.7	29
LSP	259	5	7.4	52
Kenny g	229	5	6.6	46
Mickey	218	5	6.2	44
Art	212	5	6.1	42
t.c.	190	5	5.5	38
Karen	176	6	5.1	29
Rae	162	2	4.5	81
xerxes	148	4	4.3	37
jimmy	132	3	3.8	44
Gordon Sumner	128	5	3.8	26
jane doe	120	3	3.4	40
angel	102	3	2.9	34
Mickey Mouse	98	2	2.8	49
A. Hitler	96	4	2.8	24
fred	77	2	2.2	38
Megan	59	1	1.7	59
Dolly Wolly	58	1	1.7	58
Greg Harvey*	43	1	1.2	43
George Strait	40	1	1.1	40
Total	3,485	87	100.0	40

*Asterisk indicates a known male student.
Source: Faigley

"Gendered Textuality: Assigning Gender to Portfolios," one result of rhetorical cross-dressing may be that students take on gender roles that create opportunities for repetition of restrictive understandings of sex and gender (see Stygall et al.). Students who choose a gender role different from their sexed body are likely to select the most stereotypical version of that role—the hard-edged, argumentative male; the soft, self-disclosing female—rather than an androgynous or less conventional mixture of traits.

The overall redistribution of speaking roles in this computer-mediated classroom led Faigley to conclude that he had "become a student in his own class" (181). Yet the discursive formations of education are powerful, and looking at the data in another way yields a different impression. The two teachers perform their roles through the use of interrogatives. Faigley asks six questions in his nine turns; Campbell asks twelve questions in her eight turns. No student uses his or her turn to pose questions to the entire group. Also, although the attention paid to the teachers does indeed diminish by the end of this eighty-seven-message transcript, participants' responding to them accounts for half the messages. Control of the talk, then, is still very much in the hands of the teacher figures.

But it is in the discussion about the gender of the writer of the paragraphs that the ideological functions of gender in this culture become apparent. Most of the initial messages are in response to the two teacher messages posed at the beginning of the session, first Faigley's asking which coauthor of *Cocktail Waitress* wrote the paragraphs, then Campbell's query about the possibilities of women working together for change. Messages 4 through 21, and several more after Campbell's hot message (22), respond directly to Faigley's question. Twelve respondents think Brenda Mann wrote the passage, six think James Spradley did, and three feel either could have been the writer. But then the participants begin to respond to message 22, in which Campbell asks why waitresses accepted such behavior from their male coworkers and customers.

Two positions that emerge in the transcript could be expected to appear in a regular classroom when women's issues are raised: the feminist position and the "men have rights too" position. In figure 6, xerxes exemplifies the first and LSP the second. In message 14, xerxes tentatively moves into the discussion by agreeing with Karen. Karen said she thought Spradley wrote the paragraph, because it ended with "Mark or another bartender would give you a loving pat—and tell you how much you were appreciated. It was a good feeling to be needed" (qtd. in Faigley 169). Karen commented that she couldn't see a woman discussing the feeling of being needed in that way. Xerxes, taking a step further, connects feeling needed with feeling used. After the discussion turns to Campbell's question, xerxes sketches a scenario in which waitresses are powerless to change how they dress and how they are treated. By message 61, xerxes is agreeing enthusiastically with what xerxes perceives Campbell's position to be, that contemporary popular culture offers women few good roles and that radical change must ensue. Finally, in message 74, xerxes undercuts the validity of the argument that discrimination happens to men as well; in one of the few interrogatives from a student in this transcript, xerxes points to the "small instances" where such discrimination occurs.

If xerxes marks out some textual, feminist space, LSP seems to mark space for the more traditional male, in ways quite different from the conservative economic arguments advanced by President Reagen. In LSP's first turn, LSP

FIGURE 6   Messages of xerxes and LSP.

Turn	Text of Turn
	xerxes
14	I agree Karen. The statement about "feeling needed" bothered me, too. I mean feeling needed is one thing, but feeling used is quite another.
46	I think the waitresses dress the way they do because the person in charge gives them certain dress codes. Also, if they complain too much to the men they serve they are in danger of losing their tips and possibly their jobs.
61	JoAnn, yes! The role of women in this society is laid out on t.v. in magazines—everywhere and the role that is prescribed is not a good one. But, if enough women realize that to look like a fashion model and to please men is not where it's at eventually some radical changes will happen.
74	LSP, there will always be small instances where reverse discrimination occurs, but really can we justify everything by saying it happens to a few men as well?
	LSP
16	I think Brenda Mann wrote it, or at least said it in an interview.
31	Maybe these women like the way the men treat them. There are people out there who have to find other ways of being needed. It does sound as if women are putting themselves in demeaning positions, but maybe it's true. I don't know.
45	I agree with Old Pres. I think the waitresses probably make themselves to look good to get better tips. That's different from dressing up to impress your boyfriend or girlfriend.
66	I think that if the women don't want to put up with the men they should find another line of work or wait tables in a different setting. I know a lot of women don't like the way men treat them, but what about the men who get tormented by a bunch of drunk women and strip joints. They could be dancing and taking their clothes off too, yet you never hear much about them complaining about the harassment because they are getting tips put into their G-strings.
80	There are more than a few places. Pres. Reagan said that he gets remarks from women who have had a few drinks and he's a waiter that works banquets and stuff like that. I'm not saying that male discrimination is more prevalent than female discrimination, but it does exist and you don't hear about it as much. What about the things male nurses go through, or male secretaries. It's out there.

Source: Faigley

seems to suggest that Mann is just another waitress for Spradley to interview and not the coauthor of *The Cocktail Waitress*. In LSP's next turn, LSP suggests that perhaps waitresses like being treated as they are, even though what they live with on the job might be "demeaning." In turn 45, LSP agrees with President Reagen that waitresses try to look better to get better tips, a hint at prostitution, when that behavior is contrasted with making oneself look better for a romantic partner. By turn 66, LSP expresses sympathy for "the men who get tormented by a bunch of drunk women and strip joints" and says strippers shouldn't complain about sexual harassment because they're getting good money. In turn 80, LSP retreats somewhat, replying to xerxes by acknowledging that the occurrences are higher for women and that although discrimination against men isn't as widely discussed as discrimination against women, it does exist. LSP accounts for 7.4% of the talk, behind only the two teachers and President Reagen.

The other responses that emerge in the transcript we might not expect in a regular classroom: the ongoing iterations of gender ideology. In figure 7, three repeating messages are grouped:

1. Traditional sexual orientation is binary.
2. Women must observe restricted sexual roles.
3. The world is naturally controlled by financial Darwinism.

FIGURE 7   Gender iterations.

Turn	Speaker	Text of Turn
Sexual Orientation as Binary		
5	A. Hitler	Brenda Mann must have said this, unless James Spradley likes getting called sweetie and honey by men.
21	George Strait	I think Brenda wrote the paragraph because it describes what men do to waitresses in bars. I doubt these men were doing this to other men.
Women's Sex Roles and Sexual Aggression		
41	fred	I think the waitress is partially to blame in her situation. She could protest this environment if the waitresses banded together. It seems that the waitresses acted this way to define their femininity, just as the men wanted to show their masculinity. The women work at the bar because they cannot express their femininity in their situations such as school and other jobs.

FIGURE 7   *continued*

| 83 | Art | The point being that when men make comments about women, and grab at them, it is almost accepted by most people as normal, but when a woman makes comments to a man she is considered loose. |
| 84 | A. Hitler | Correct, Lester. It is socially accepted for a man to grab a woman's butt or make a remark towards her, but if the roles are reversed people think the woman is drunk or crazy or a whore. |

Financial Darwinism

40	A. Hitler	I think the women, divided for some reason, were afraid to protest their conditions individually for fear of being fired.
52	Gordon Sumner	You have to remember that it is a job requirement to dress in a certain fashion, and an occupational hazard to be bothered by drunken men. They can always quit if they don't want to put up with it.
54	Kenny g	Xerxes has a good point. IF the waitress says anything to her customer or her boss she/he runs the risk of losing money. The reason most people are in this line of work is for the money.
57	Mickey Mouse	Waitresses are not the only ones who have to put up with being called things such as "sweetie" and "honey." I work in an office where the women secretaries are called these sorts of names by the older (and higher status) men. They have to put up with it also, because if they don't they will get on these people's bad side real fast.
69	Mickey	Basically, I think it is just whoever is at the bottom end of the totem pole has to put up with everyone else. It just so happens that the waitresses are below the customers and the waitresses are female while the customers are male. Can anyone give me an example of where women are above men on the totem pole?

Source: Faigley

Although the first message is repeated only once, it sets an important and early frame in the discussion for the other repeating messages. No one in this classroom suggests that sexual orientation is anything but traditional and heterosexual, yet of course there are other options. After the discussion centers on gender roles as stereotypically binary, the message posters who want to articulate a feminist position have difficulty. Both turns 5 and 21 imply that to step outside traditional gender roles is to risk homosexuality. Thus, in this classroom, if you are a feminist—that is, if you do not act in a traditionally feminine way—you risk being called deviant, even if you are decidedly heterosexual. Feminism is a position outside the binary gender roles available. This attitude is expressed throughout the discussion but is perhaps most focused in fred's midpoint comment about women wanting to work in a job like waitressing so that they can "express their femininity." Toward the close of the transcript, Art and A. Hitler speak about the sexual double standard, once again affirming that only a binary choice is available.

Even more pervasive than the double standard in this discussion is the ideology of financial Darwinism and the role gender plays in economic realities. A. Hitler, Gordon Sumner, Kenny g, and Mickey Mouse all recognize the problem of being a female employee in a patriarchal economy. The lack of agency in the waitress's working conditions is apparent in all four messages. A. Hitler mentions the fear of protesting working conditions but does not say to whom such a protest might be addressed. Gordon Sumner speaks of job requirements and occupational hazards—unpleasant, to be sure, but the result of natural forces at work. In Kenny g's message, the waitress is responsible for the situation, the male customer is not: if she "says anything," she will not make money. Mickey Mouse says that in white-collar offices as well the female workers must get along, go along. Mickey broadens the scope by offering the observation that waitresses are below customers in the world's hierarchy, which problem is not based on gender inequality but "just so happens."

Faigley tells us that all eighty-seven messages were written in a twenty-minute period. Though there were two teachers responding, the rapidity and wide dispersion of student response served to undercut the feminist-critical authority Faigley and Campbell represented in the classroom, the most collaborative classroom discussed in this essay. Faigley reports that some researchers, Cynthia Selfe and Jerome Bump among them, have praised the computer-mediated writing classroom for increasing women's participation in classroom discussion. But women's increased participation only produces textual echoes of the gender ideologies that progressive teachers hope to overcome.

Missing in these three conversations is a feminist-critical authority who can act as a counterweight to the disciplining of students by gender and education. Elizabeth Sommers and Sandra Lawrence have examined classroom conversation in peer writing groups under two different frameworks. The first, originally the position of Sommers, was that for women students peer groups would work best with little or no teacher intervention. She reports, "Believing that schools give too little control to students, she wanted students to retain ownership of their drafts, their groups and their talk, and to understand that meaning is not handed from teachers to students but developed in collaboration." Lawrence, her collaborator in this project, provided the second framework; she "felt that students had little experience responding to one another's written texts or working in groups, [so] she gave them specific guidelines and procedures for conducting peer group sessions" (9). Lawrence's rules included a fairly prescribed speaking protocol, in which each student was required to speak in turn while the others listened. Sommers and Lawrence selected eight peer-group sessions out of approximately a hundred (for both teachers in an academic term) and analyzed the tapes of those sessions for women's participation compared with men's. They found that in the teacher-directed peer groups, women's participation rates matched men's but that in the student-directed groups, women's participation was markedly lower. Sommers and Lawrence conclude, "Female participants in student-directed groups learned yet another lesson about gender and power, providing female students with one more 'chilling' school experience" (29).

Bruffee, Nystrand, and Faigley certainly didn't abandon their classrooms to student chaos, a fear of many newcomers to collaborative pedagogy, but all three advocated the teacher's withdrawal from the activities of the collaborative group. Bruffee advocates a particular activity for collaborative groups in the form of descriptive outlining but clearly recommends that teachers "remain uninvolved in any direct way" (45). For Nystrand, the teacher's withdrawal from the peer group serves a Vygotskyan rearticulation of the social aspects of learning to write. He says:

> We may regard intensive peer review as a formative social arrangement in which writers become consciously aware of the functional significance of composing behaviors, discourse strategies, and elements of text by managing them all in anticipation of continuous reader feedback . . . [and what] writers take from their groups largely emerge in ways that are often evident first in the social interaction of peer review. (211)

If that social interaction turns out to reinscribe gender inequalities, and this feminist-critical linguistic analysis shows it does, then teacher withdrawal from the group and teacher trust in the social interaction are unwarranted. For Faigley, even though gender ideologies were not scrutinized as in a feminist-critical linguistic analysis, the agonistic quality of the classroom discourse becomes apparent, as does the need to theorize postmodern discourse more deeply.

Advocating a general, academic knowledge community, as Bruffee does, and a feminist, cooperative, collaborative utopia, as Stanger does, oversimplifies and flattens the complexities and conflicts of students struggling to position themselves in relation to the academy and in complex social forces. Susan Jarratt makes a case for the feminist teacher who, like bell hooks, creates the classroom in which rigorous, critical argument takes place and for the teacher who helps students confront truths "in the heat of argument" ("Feminism" 121). The feminist teacher of composition who uses collaboration must also be willing to use her authority in the classroom to model a different kind of discourse for women students. The model proposed by Sommers and Lawrence is a beginning but remains insufficient in the face of more complex intersections of the forces of discipline in education and gender, such as those found in the Nystrand conversation. Moreover, if we know now that unstructured collaboration holds hazards for women students, we can assume that the same is true for students of color. A constant analysis of the technologies of talk used in writing classrooms can address the problem. Chandra Mohanty argues:

> Resistance that is random and isolated is clearly not as effective as that which is mobilized through systemic politicized practices of teaching and learning. Uncovering and reclaiming subjugated knowledge is one way to lay claim to alternative histories. But these knowledges need to be understood and defined pedagogically as questions of strategy and practice as well as of scholarship in order to transform educational institutions radically. (qtd. in hooks, *Teaching* 22)

Using feminist-critical linguistics to foreground the discourse features and interactions sensitive to gender differentiation and inequality, we can be more active in collaborative writing classrooms, in confronting, analyzing, and teaching alternatives in the feminist writing classroom.

NOTES

1. For a discussion about the relation between critical discourse analysis and Foucauldian social theory, see Stygall, *Trial Language*, chapter 1.
2. See especially O'Barr for a discussion of powerless language in the courtroom.
3. See Spender's *Man Made Language* for a discussion of the paradox of women being both language conservators and language innovators.
4. The two paragraphs read:

> At times, some of the girls sensed it vaguely. But for Holly, the mixture of feelings was always there, sometimes clear and intense, other times beneath the surface. Working at Brady's made her feel more like a woman and less like a woman than anything she had ever experienced. And these conflicting emotions were often simultaneous, causing her to both question and accept the identity of "Brady Girl."
>
> Brady's Bar was a man's world and being part of it brought an excitement all its own. You dressed for the men, served drinks to the men, laughed at jokes told by the men, got tips and compliments from men, ran errands for men. Men called you sweetie and honey and sexy. Men asked you out and men made passes. . . . And as you left after work, Mark or another bartender would give you a loving pat—and tell you how much you were appreciated. It was a good feeling to be needed. (qtd. in Faigley 169)

5. For a more complete discussion of classroom discourse patterns, see Barnes; Stubbs; Cazden.

WORKS CITED

Barnes, Douglas. *From Communication to Curriculum.* London: Penguin, 1976.
Bruffee, Kenneth A. *Collaborative Learning: Higher Education, Interdependence, and the Authority of Knowledge.* Baltimore: Johns Hopkins UP, 1993.
Cameron, Deborah. "Demythologizing Sociolinguistics: Why Language Does Not Reflect Society." *Ideologies of Language.* Ed. John E. Joseph and Talbot J. Taylor. London: Routledge, 1990. 79–93.
———. *Feminism and Linguistics Theory.* 2nd ed. New York: St. Martin's, 1990.
Cameron, Deborah, Fiona McAlinden, and Kathy O'Leary. "Lakoff in Context: The Social and Linguistic Functions of Tag Questions." Coates and Cameron 74–93.
Cazden, Courtney B. *Classroom Discourse: The Language of Teaching and Learning.* Portsmouth: Heinemann, 1988.
Coates, Jennifer. "Gossip Revisited: Language in All-Female Groups." Coates and Cameron 94–122.
———. *Women, Men, and Language: A Sociolinguistic Account of Sex Differences in Language.* New York: Longman, 1986.
Coates, Jennifer, and Deborah Cameron, eds. *Women in Their Speech Communities.* New York, Longman, 1988.
DeFrancisco, Victoria Leto. "The Sounds of Silence: How Men Silence Women in Marital Relations." *Discourse and Society* 2 (1991): 413–23.
Dijk, Teun A. van. "Principles of Critical Discourse Analysis." *Discourse and Society* 4 (1993): 249–83.

Edelsky, Carole. "Who's Got the Floor?" Tannen, *Gender* 189–227.

Faigley, Lester. *Fragments of Rationality: Postmodernity and the Subject of Composition.* Pittsburgh: U of Pittsburgh P, 1992.

Fishman, Pamela. "Interaction: The Work Women Do." *Social Problems* 25 (1977): 397–406.

Foucault, Michel. *Discipline and Punish: The Birth of the Prison.* Trans. Alan Sheridan. New York: Pantheon, 1977.

Hodge, Robert, and Gunther Kress. *Social Semiotics.* Ithaca: Cornell UP, 1988.

Holmes, Janet. "Women's Language: A Functional Approach." *General Linguistics* 24 (1984): 149–78.

hooks, bell. *Teaching to Transgress: Education as the Practice of Freedom.* New York: Routledge, 1994.

James, Deborah, and Sandra Clarke. "Women, Men, and Interruptions: A Critical Review." Tannen, *Gender* 231–80.

Jaems, Deborah, and Janice Drakich. "Understanding Gender Differences in Amount of Talk: A Critical Review of the Research." Tannen, *Gender* 281–312.

Jarratt, Susan C., "Performing Feminisms, Histories, Rhetorics." *Rhetoric Society Quarterly* 22 (1992): 1–6.

———. *Rereading the Sophists: Classical Rhetoric Refigured.* Carbondale: Southern Illinois UP, 1991.

Kramarae, Cheris, and H. Jeanie Taylor. "Women and Men on Electronic Networks: A Conversation or a Monologue?" Taylor, Kramarae, and Ebben 52–61.

Lakoff, Robin. *Language and Woman's Place.* New York: Harper, 1975.

Maltz, Daniel M., and Ruth A Borker. "A Cultural Approach to Male-Female Miscommunication." *Language and Society Identity.* Ed. John J. Gumperz. Cambridge: Cambridge UP, 1982. 192–216.

Mohanty, Chandra Talpade. "On Race and Vice: Challenges for Liberal Education in the 1990s." Giroux and McLaren 145–66.

Nystrand, Martin. *The Structure of Written Communication: Studies in Reciprocity between Writers and Readers.* Orlando: Academic, 1986.

O'Barr, William F. *Linguistic Evidence.* Chicago: U of Chicago P, 1983.

Poynton, Cate. *Language and Gender: Making the Difference.* Oxford: Oxford UP, 1989.

Sommers, Elizabeth, and Sandra Lawrence. "Women's Ways of Talking in Teacher-Directed and Student-Directed Peer Response Groups." *Linguistics and Education* 4 (1992): 1–36.

Spender, Dale. *Man Made Language.* 2nd ed. London: Pandora, 1990.

Spradley, James, and Brenda Mann. *The Cocktail Waitress.* New York: Wiley, 1975.

Stanger, Carol. "The Sexual Politics of the One-to-One Tutorial Approach and Collaborative Learning." Caywood and Overing, *Teaching* 31–44.

Stubbs, Michael. *Discourse Analysis: The Sociolinguistic Analysis of Natural Language.* Chicago: U of Chicago P. 1983.

Stygall, Gail. *Trial Language: Differential Discourse Processing and Discursive Formation.* Amsterdam: Benjamins, 1994.

Stygall, Gail, et al. "Gendered Textuality: Assigning Gender to Portfolios." *New Directions in Portfolio Assessment: Reflective Practice, Critical Theory, and Large-Scale Scoring.* Ed. Laurel Black et al. Portsmouth: Boynton-Heinemann, 1994. 248–62.

Tannen, Deborah, ed. *Gender and Conversational Interaction.* New York: Oxford UP, 1993.

———. "The Relativity of Linguistic Strategies: Rethinking Power and Solidarity in Gender and Dominance." Tannen, *Gender* 165–88.

———. *You Just Don't Understand: Women and Men in Conversation.* New York: Ballantine, 1990.

Trimbur, John. "Consesus and Difference in Collaborative Learning." *College English* 51 (1989): 601–16.

West, Robin. *Narrative, Authority, and Law.* Ann Arbor: U of Michigan P, 1993.

Zimmerman, Don H., and Candace West. "Sex Roles, Interruptions, and Silences in Conversation." *Language and Sex: Difference and Dominance.* Ed. Barrie Thorne and Nancy Henley. Rowley: Newbury, 1975. 105–29.

14

Building Bridges to Academic Discourse: The Peer Group Leader in Basic Writing Peer Response Groups

LAURIE GROBMAN

David Bartholomae's landmark essays "Inventing the University" and "Writing on the Margins: The Concept of Literacy in Higher Education" locate the basic writer outside academic discourse, lacking the authority academic writers possess. This exclusion is manifested, among other ways, in peer response groups, where basic writers often shy away from critiquing substantive issues of content or organization in each other's work. Their hesitancy is understandable, given that the university has told them (by virtue of their placement in a "remedial" writing course) that they do not know how to write. In this article, I will describe a study of writing groups in which I attempted to build the bridges between basic writers and academic writers by incorporating a *peer group leader*—a sophomore student who guides basic writers during peer response sessions—in an electronic classroom with online peer response sessions.[1] I hypothesized that efficacy of peer response would increase, expecting that the peer group leader would be able to provide a bridge between basic writers' and academic communities, enabling basic writers to model academic discourse as they authorize themselves as participants.

The theoretical support for peer response groups in composition is by now well known: social theories of language and learning suggest that students should construct meaning not in isolation but within the context of social interaction. Although the use of peer response groups is common practice in writing classrooms, research on peer response groups offers mixed reviews, largely because students typically lack the skills and knowledge for peer response (see Zhu). Indeed, much of the research on writing groups focuses on ways to promote more effective, substantive response in students (see Zhu) and on the causes and characteristics of successful and unsuccessful peer response groups (see Bishop). Furthermore, a great deal of this research focuses on composition rather than basic writing students.

Nevertheless, Bartholomae's work with basic writers has led many researchers and instructors, including myself, to use peer response groups as a way to

From *Journal of Basic Writing*, vol. 18, no. 2, 1999, pp. 47–68.

empower basic writers (Weaver 31). Basic writing pedagogy emerging from social constructivist views of writing encourages students to see their written texts as part of academic discourse, a larger conversation taking place in writing. This approach presupposes, as do I, that developmental writers can produce intelligent writing if instructors challenge them with serious content and enable them to enter academic conversations. Peer response groups are one means through which students can potentially enter these conversations.

However, Wei Zhu notes that the opportunities for peer interaction offered by peer response groups often go unfulfilled (517). Though many factors influence peer response group efficacy and inefficacy, group members' lack of confidence in peers' expertise and members' fear in offering criticism are among the most salient characteristics of peer response group failure (Bishop 121). Clearly, these problems are more pronounced for basic writers, whose reluctance and/or inability to offer substantive critique hinders meaningful learning from knowledgeable peers. Basic writers' precarious position as outsiders in the academic community and subsequent lack of confidence in their own writing abilities lead these students to shy away from assuming any measure of authority in offering meaningful response. Basic writers tend to resist honest and authoritative critique, even in electronic classrooms which otherwise contribute to community-building (see Gay; Varone).

Zhu points out that while a significant amount of research on peer response centers on its benefits to students, less research examines the factors that influence peer interaction (518). My project incorporating a peer group leader in basic writing peer response groups sought to examine such conditions. I attempted to make writing groups more effective in basic writing classrooms based on what I knew of the research in this area as well as my experiences with writing groups and basic writers. Rather than give in to what Sandra Lawrence and Elizabeth Sommers conclude about instructors' doubts about the value of peer response groups for inexperienced writers, I sought to find ways to make this experience meaningful and valuable. Moreover, I sought to promote writing groups in which basic writers, like their composition counterparts, reconceptualize substantive issues in their writing, countering Joan Wauters' claim that for basic writers, "there is an excellent rationale for offering only positive reinforcement, if the goal is to encourage confidence on the part of reluctant writers" (157). Basic writers should be treated as intellectuals learning a new discourse, and peer response sessions should reflect such academic work. By making academic discourse visible through the use of a peer group leader, I could help students in their understanding and appropriation of academic discourse.[2]

This article describes and analyzes how I used a peer group leader to provide a bridge between basic writers and academic discourse. I strongly believe in the *potential* of peer group leaders in basic writing classrooms. In this article, I hope to convey that potential by identifying the strengths and weaknesses of what happened in my classroom in the context of peer collaboration research and theory. While my study can not cover the range and variety of basic writing classroom situations and dynamics, it does raise significant issues that beg further research and practice. In the remainder of the article, I discuss the theoretical basis for the use of peer group leaders, turn next to the experiences in my classroom, and end with my conclusions about the present and future of peer group leaders in basic writing.

BUILDING BRIDGES IN PEER COLLABORATION RESEARCH: PEER GROUP LEADERS IN BASIC WRITING

Using limited funds from an internal grant, I selected one student as the peer group leader for my basic writing class.[3] I theorized that peer group leaders, who have only recently become academic writers themselves, could constitute a bridge between basic writers' and academic communities. David Bartholomae and Anthony Petrosky suggest we "engage students in a process whereby they discover academic discourse from the inside" (36). Peer group leaders make academic discourse's inside visible, so basic writing students do not have to invent it blindly. At once insiders and outsiders, peer group leaders provide a vital link between writer and audience, writer and academic discourse. As James Gee argues, discourses are mastered by "enculturation into social practices through scaffolded and supported interaction with people who have already mastered the Discourse" (qtd. in Zhu 518). Straddling the fence somewhere between academic and basic writers' communities, this young woman could, I hoped, provide the scaffolding and supported interaction upon and through which basic writers would enter academic discourse. In so doing, peer group leaders provide what Kenneth Bruffee would call a "conversation" to model or what subscribers to the competing model of academic authority would see as a means to challenge it. In both cases, peer group leaders could aid basic writers' appropriation of academic discourse.

I chose a student I had known from my basic writing class a year earlier. She was among the strongest writers in my class (and I knew she had been successful in English Composition), but more importantly, I felt she had characteristics that would suit the peer group leader role: leadership, integrity, maturity, and sensitivity. Tyisha, the peer group leader, attended my class during peer response sessions, joining one or two groups and guiding them through and participating in response.[4] I instructed her to be descriptive and to pay attention to global issues of meaning, content, and organization rather than mechanical issues in students' writing. I expected Tyisha to model these responses for students as well as guide them to suitable modes of critique. Additionally, I informed students that they could seek the peer group leader's help outside of class as well, through email or phone calls.

The peer group leader thus straddled the roles of the two primary types of peer collaboration in basic writing: peer response in basic writing classrooms and peer tutorials in Writing Centers. I envisioned the peer group leader as a mediary between peers in a peer response group and tutors in Writing Center tutorials, and I believed that by bringing the peer tutor *into* not only the classroom, but the peer response group, I would be able to draw at once from the advantages of both peer response groups and peer tutorials. Of course, there is a flip side as well, for peer group leaders have the potential to degrade the collaboration of peers in peer response groups.

Muriel Harris' widely known and respected work on the similarities and differences between peer tutorials and peer response, though now seven years old, remains a significant contribution to the study and practice of these important collaborative methods in basic writing classrooms. Harris asserts that both writing center tutorials and peer response groups are "collaborative learning about writing" ("Collaboration" 369) in which "one writer claims ownership and makes all final decisions" (370); moreover, the goal of the tutor and peer group members is the same: "all are working toward more effective writing abilities and heightened awareness of general writing concerns" (373). Bringing peer group leaders into peer response sessions leaves these important general similarities unchanged.

It is the distinctions Harris makes, however, which interest me more in the context of peer group leaders, particularly in terms of how the peer group leader can take advantage of these distinctions and become a force in basic writers' peer response sessions and meaningful learning in collaboration with knowledgeable peers. Among the most significant of these differences is the widely accepted view that peer tutors in writing tutorials become "neither a teacher nor a peer" as they assist writers with writing issues beyond "fixing" a particular paper under consideration while peer response readers focus on and critique a specific draft (371). Peer tutors explain issues and problems and give instructional assistance. As Stephen North notes, the tutor's job "is to produce better writers, not just better writing" (qtd. in Harris 372). In tutorials, tutors individualize and personalize the concerns, while in peer response groups, readers offer mutual assistance in a back-and-forth interaction that deals with general skills (373).

Peer group leaders take on both roles, neither teachers, peer tutors, nor peers, straddling multiple communities as they join the peer response group. In their unique role, peer group leaders can bring individualization to peer response groups since they do not have writing to be critiqued and do not seek mutual assistance. This difference from other members of the peer response group allows for an additional layer of instruction in peer response groups, beyond a focus on the writing under scrutiny to more general writing concerns, including instructional assistance on *how to respond to peers' writing*, which the tutorial lacks. Learning the nuances of critique can in and of itself lead to improved writing abilities. Thus, Harris' assertion that peer tutors' methods and concerns for uncovering writers' problems are not appropriate for peer response groups no longer holds when we introduce peer group leaders into peer response groups. Peer group leaders can individualize response, and, more importantly, can lead students away from purely directive response.

Harris' distinction in terms of collaboration is important in this context. She argues that peer response groups are closer to collaborative writing (i.e., joint authorship) than writing tutorials, for peer response group work emphasizes informing, while writing tutorials emphasize the student's own discovery ("Collaboration" 377). On first glance, it may seem that using a peer group leader might move the peer response group away from collaborative writing, since peer group leaders do emphasize students' own discovery. However, peer group leaders can simultaneously increase the level and quality of informative modes. Peer group leaders raise peer response beyond simple informing on specific issues, a goal of many instructors who use peer response groups, despite Harris' claim that these groups tend to be prescriptive (see Benesch; Zhu; Bishop). Peer group leaders guide group members into larger, substantive issues and thus students' own discovery of the writing process. Moreover, unlike tutorials, peer response groups with peer group leaders also facilitate students' discovery of group processes; that is, peer group leaders guide and model peer group response and critique, so students discover not only their own writing issues, but how to benefit from and contribute to peer response. In peer response work with peer group leaders, basic writing students not only attempt to critique their peers' draft but themselves learn about the possibilities for revision in the process. Therefore, despite the potential to undermine collaboration among peers, peer group leaders can enhance it by raising the efficacy of peer group members' informing *and* multiple layers of discovery.

In their multiple roles, peer group leaders thus provide a bridge between what Thomas Newkirk calls peers' and instructors' distinct "evaluative communities" (p. 47 in this volume). His study suggests that peer response groups may reinforce students' abilities to write for their peers but not the academic community, and, subsequently, that "students need practice applying the criteria that they are now learning" and should be viewed as "apprentices, attempting to learn and apply criteria appropriate to an academic audience" (p. 55). Newkirk argues for teachers' active role in peer response; however, I believe peer group leaders can more effectively "mak[e] the norms of that community clear and plausible—even appealing" (p. 56). Ideally, peer response enables students to enter academic discourse through working with knowledgeable peers, breaking free from one evaluative community to enter another, and it empowers students who do not see themselves as academic writers. However, in practice, students' crossover is more problematic. Peer group leaders can expose students to the conventions—appealing and not-so-appealing—of academic discourse. Peer group leaders, though, do not impose on students what Benesch calls the "teacher's code," but instead allow them to respond to writing issues in "their own language" (90), since peer group leaders have, in Harris' words, "a foot in each discourse community" (380). With the use of peer group leaders, therefore, basic writers develop this language more independently of the teacher and in collaboration with peers.

Using peer group leaders in peer response groups also bridges what Tim Hacker describes as the two main approaches to peer response: the broad categories of "teacher-directed" and "modeling." The former category includes teacher intervention in the form of worksheets (a set of heuristics for approaching an essay) and/or instructions on how to proceed, while "modeling" consists of teacher intervention prior to actual student-directed peer response sessions through teaching students how to evaluate and critique their peers' essays before peer response sessions. Using peer group leaders, however, reduces the need for teacher intervention in either model.[5] That is, with peer group leaders, students can "model" effective response, but they do so in-process, and they do not need a set of heuristics provided by the instructor. Moreover, with peer group leaders, more authentic collaboration occurs because peer response groups remain decentered. Students cannot blindly invent the language of academic discourse, but peer group leaders make its inside visible. With peer group leaders as facilitators, basic writers take on a more active role in the invention of academic discourse. Like peer tutors, peer group leaders can empower student writers who "want to have power over their environment, to be in control of what happens to them, . . . and manipulate language the way their teachers do before they will be able to play the academic game the way the insiders do" (Hawkins 64).

Harris makes the further point that students in peer tutorials typically trust peer tutors and have confidence in their skills and knowledge. Students' perception of the peer group leader is also an important component of the peer group leader's usefulness in peer response groups. For peer response to work, peer group members must have confidence in their peers' knowledge. However, for basic writers especially, trust in peers' knowledge is suspect, mainly because they have been designated as underprepared for college writing. Peer group leaders can play a significant role in leading basic writers to see themselves and their peers as knowledgeable, skilled writers. Moreover, because peer group leaders can pass their knowledge to basic writing students, they more evenly distribute knowledge in the classroom. As a result, the classroom becomes a more authentic decentered, collaborative learning environment, in practice as well as in theory.

While peer group leaders can bring the advantages of both peer response groups and peer tutorials to their roles in peer response sessions, they may also degrade peer response. Harris points out that because peer tutors are more acquainted with academic discourse than the tutees, "the further they are from being peers in a collaborative relationship" ("Collaboration" 379). Students come to them seeking prescriptives, thereby making it difficult for tutors to remain collaborators rather than co-authors and frustrating both student and tutor (379). Certainly the potential exists as well when we bring peer group leaders to peer response groups. Peer group leaders, straddling both the basic writers' and academic communities, are not completely "equal" to other peer group members. Without writing of their own "out there" and under scrutiny, peer group leaders have less at stake than the other peer group members. Harris makes the point that the peer tutor's unique position as interpreter of academic jargon is in peril if the tutor, "enamored of the jargon of the field, moves too far into the teacher's world" (380). Clearly, this risk of co-authoring and co-opting student writing exists with peer group leaders in peer response groups, but can be minimized with effective training and guidance.

Relatedly, peer group leaders may interfere with what Harris identifies as peer response groups' give-and-take process of negotiation that leads to consensus about how the group will undertake peer response (374). With the peer group leader's participation in peer response, the negotiation between students will likely be less democratic, for part of the peer group leader's role is to help guide students to specific kinds of response. Moreover, as in tutorials, the tutor's and students' goals may often conflict, since students want particular papers fixed while the tutor attempts to address larger issues (374–75). Clearly, if students have the goal of fixing a particular piece of writing in their peer response group, they may find themselves in conflict with the peer group leader who will be guiding them to more global issues as well. On the other hand, since peer response groups with peer group leaders can effectively address both specific and general writing concerns, the conflicts between students and peer group leader are likely to be reduced.

Harris' identification of the tutor's "unique advantage of being both a nonjudgmental, non-evaluative helper—a collaborator in whom the writer can confide" (376)—cannot be ignored when we bring the peer group leader into peer response. Arguably, the peer group leader may face difficult hurdles in getting group members to perceive him/her as non-evaluative and non-judgmental, given the peer group leader's connection to the instructor. Instructors can make it clear to students that the peer group leader is there to offer assistance, not to evaluate or judge them. Instructors can also inform students that even though they will consult with the peer group leader throughout the semester (much like peer tutors in Writing Centers confer with instructors), the peer group leader will not be involved in grading the students in any way. In my class, students' participation in peer response did influence their grades to some degree, but it was my assessment of the logged transcripts of the sessions, not anything the peer group leader told me, that affected my evaluation of students' participation in this process. Although I do not think I was able to completely overcome my students' association of the peer group leader with myself, I believe they did come to see her as non-evaluative, enabling her to evoke honest and authoritative response.

BUILDING BRIDGES TO ACADEMIC DISCOURSE: THE PEER GROUP LEADER IN BASIC WRITING

How well did using a peer group leader work in my class? What advantages and/or disadvantages did this young woman bring to basic writers' peer response groups? In the following pages, I offer my analyses of the peer group sessions. Since most of our response sessions occurred online, I was able to use these transcripts to monitor and assess the peer group leader's effectiveness in leading students to substantive response.[6] I hope to suggest, finally, that this study has significant implications for further research and practice using peer group leaders as a bridge to academic discourse for basic writers.

In the basic writing class under study, I challenged students with difficult work, connecting content with methodology as we studied varied aspects and definitions of literacy, each assignment building off the others so that the writing assignments, as Berthoff suggests, "encourage conscientization, the discovery of the mind in action" so students "learn . . . how meanings make future meanings possible, how form finds further form" (755). Moreover, class content, focused on academic literacy itself, wedded content with methodology and put discourse at the center of analysis. Thus, course content and methodology began the process through which basic writers could enter academic discourse. The peer group leader helped these students make this difficult leap, as the following examples demonstrate. At the same time, however, her work illuminates some of the potential perils of peer group leaders in basic writers' peer response.

One strength of the peer group leader was her ability to both inform and model. In the following example, Tyisha, the peer group leader, guides students away from mechanical issues, without specifically instructing them not to consider such surface features.

STAN: yo Paul i guess you read my review

PAUL: yup

PAUL: it was good

STAN: good content

PAUL: yes

STAN: i found it very interesting

PAUL: but I found a lot of little mistakes

PAUL: did you catch any?

TYISHA: I liked your paper also Stan, it was really good, Paul is there anything in his paper that you thought he could work on, besides a few spelling mistakes.

Tyisha's language effectively downplays "a few spelling mistakes" and re-focuses students' attention to more substantive issues, without specifying what these should be. This exchange demonstrates Tyisha's ability to simultaneously focus on the essay under consideration while leading students to discovery.

In the next example, Tyisha successfully keeps the group focused and elicits effective critique.

TYISHA: what can he do about that 5th paragraph

STAN: break it up

TYISHA: It is too big- break it up how?

STAN: hold on i have to read it again to get that answer

PAUL: I think I could break it up at the word people

LARRY: LEHIGH IS BETTER THAN BERK

PAUL: yea yea

TYISHA: Larry we're having a discussion

PAUL: Larry is the man

STAN: ok i just want to get to main sooooooooooo i don't really care

STAN: but berks has more that one building and we have a guy

PAUL: that really doesn't bother me

TYISHA: Anyways, what can we do with this para. lets get back on track

TYISHA: just 5 more minutes

PAUL: I could break it up at the word "people"

TYISHA: Good and from there what could he do Stan

STAN: that is what i was just about to say

STAN: back up the ideas in greater detail

TYISHA: should he change the intro. sentence to that paragraph or keep it the same.

STAN: just make sure you have good transition between the two paragraphs

PAUL: ok

STAN: yep . . . . change the intro

When Larry interrupts Paul's and Stan's academic conversation, Tyisha takes a leadership role, trying to get them back on track. Though Stan momentarily gives in to Larry's disruptions, he does re-focus his attention on the task. This is an important example of the peer group leader's potential role, for all too often, basic writers get off track—and stay there. Although Tim Hacker claims that students in writing groups tend to take on the role of teacher, I rarely see this occur with basic writers. It is difficult for these students to get back on track on their own, perhaps afraid to take on such a leadership role, questioning their own authority as writers.

Furthermore, the above exchange also illuminates the ways in which the peer group leader can simultaneously focus on a particular piece of writing and more global writing instruction. Even though Tyisha and the peer group members are discussing Paul's essay, Tyisha's comments are directed at Stan, the responder. Paul's comment that "I could break it up at the word 'people'" and Stan's comment that "that is what I was just about to say" indicate their understanding of both how to "fix" this particular paragraph and its applicability to issues of paragraphing generally.

Similarly, the following exchange also illuminates the peer group leader's ability to straddle the roles of tutor and peer, focusing on specific and general concerns.

SARA: In some of the papers I write, I start out with a question

TYISHA: so how does this help Joes paper

TYISHA: what idea do you have for Joe that he could use with a question in his paper

SARA: He could have started out with "What is Technical Literacy?"

TYISHA: and then what could he have done in his intro to support this?

JOE: why would I want to start with a question that I don't know the answer to?

. . .

SARA: Explain how many definitions it had and use each definition to start a new paragraph

TYISHA: good point how would you answer that, you went right to the point in your starting paragraph.

. . .

SARA: Joe what do you say?

JOE: The point that I am attempting to say is that I do not know the exact definitions.

SARA: Did you try looking them up?

JOE: no, because we are suppose to find our own.

Sara begins this exchange over Joe's introductory paragraph by pointing to her own strategy for introductions. Tyisha then pushes her to apply it to Joe's essay. Despite Joe's disagreement, Tyisha effectively guides these students to consider not only Joe's essay but a particular rhetorical strategy more generally. Sara and Joe debate the issue in academic terms, Joe responding that "looking it up" is not what academic discourse is about. Instead, Joe realizes the role he must play as a knowledge-maker.

The following example demonstrates an impressive interchange of substantive ideas between Tyisha, Jennifer, and Stan that occurred fairly late in the semester. Jennifer begins by asking both her peer and the peer group leader for response:

JENNIFER: Tyisha, do you think I stay on track or do I drift off my topic?

JENNIFER: Also, do you think my thesis is okay, or more like what do you think my thesis is?

JENNIFER: Stan, give me some input. What do I need to change? Remember I did this late last night.

STAN: well you talk about culture and beliefs and than you jump to standard english. It just needs something to blend the idea that even though a person likes to keep their beliefs that they still need standard english.

TYISHA: Your paper is very good however, Stan can you identify Jennifers thesis, and does it go along with her paper.

Tyisha directs Jennifer and Stan to consider a particular problem in Jennifer's essay, the lack of a clear thesis/focus, specifically responding to Jennifer's request for help but in the process guiding Stan to respond. The discussion continues:

STAN: well I think it can be improved upon. I really did not understand what the article was going to be about when I read it.

JENNIFER: I think I am still talking about Standard English. I throw in culture and beliefs because that is why people stray from Standard English, it is so they can keep close to their culture.

TYISHA: Okay, so then how does all this information tie in to Rachel Jones facing disadvantages-what do you think Stan.

JENNIFER: I don't understand. Didn't I introduce my thesis in the opening? I thought I made it clear what I was talking about, but I could be wrong.

TYISHA: Your thesis should be in the introductory paragraph last sentence before you get into your supporting paragraphs.

JENNIFER: I used Rachel Jones because I like how she expresses that people are faced with disadvantages without speaking Standard English.

Tyisha presses Stan to help Jennifer with this problem of purpose and simultaneously propels Jennifer into thoughtful consideration of her rhetorical choices. Even though Jennifer notes, as a writer questioning her own authority, that "I could be wrong," she continues to explain the reasoning behind her own understanding of her thesis and its placement in the essay. Tyisha's presence has helped this basic writer gain confidence in her own and her peer's knowledge and writing. The conversation concludes this way:

STAN: try adding something like this; Standard english pulls from cultural independence. Some people feel that without there cultural distinction they will be lost. For a person to truly accelerate in our society they must have a little of both. Cultural diversity is not acceptable in todays world and for a person to not understand or use standard english they will be lost.

JENNIFER: so, she was my spark for this paper. I am responding and giving my idea of her views.

. . .

TYISHA: It's good you used Jones however, what is your thesis, is it that last sentence, because if so then you could talk about the things SHE FACED, I think it could be the 2nd and 3rd sentences combined, how do you feel Stan.

STAN: well I wrote what I think it should be

JENNIFER: thanks Stan, I like that response you gave me previously. I wrote it down because I like it a lot.

Tyisha's membership in the academic community is evidenced by her stronger, more nuanced reading of Rachel Jones' essay, "What's Wrong with Black English?" and her clearer sense of how to respond to an outside reading in one's essay. She prods Jennifer into a deeper reading in a way that both models and guides Jennifer and Stan in the conventions of academic discourse. Benesch argues that peer response is often disconnected—that is, utterances are left suspended, other comments are raised, and an emerging conversation rarely materializes (93). With the aid of Tyisha, we see a substantive conversation emerge (temporarily interrupted by the lag time inherent in online synchronous conversations) because Tyisha enables them to "enter *imperfectly* into peer group conversations" (Benesch 93, emphasis mine), as Stan's misstatement that "Cultural diversity is not acceptable" indicates. Indeed, Stan's rewriting of Jennifer's introductory paragraph (which shows his own sense of authority as a knowledgeable peer) illuminates the perils of peer response generally. I would like to believe that peer group leaders could lessen the impact of such difficulties, though admittedly, Tyisha did not "catch" it this time.

The above examples and analysis point to the strengths of peer group leaders in basic writers' peer response, but there were some pitfalls as well. Mainly, these occurred when the peer group leader became overly prescriptive, as the following two examples demonstrate:

> **STAN:** overall the paper was good. Some things that need to be worked on is unity. Also what is that delta 9 stuff about.
>
> **STAN:** is that the code for the tetrahydrocannabinal
>
> **PAUL:** yea
>
> **TYISHA:** define cannabis in your paper so your reader knows what it is.
>
> **PAUL:** ok
>
> **TYISHA:** what can Joe do to make his first sentence sound interesting?
>
> **TOM:** Joe could tell the reader what his point of view is
>
> **TYISHA:** yes or he could also do what
>
> **TYISHA:** where are you Joe
>
> **TOM:** he could state what the controversy is
>
> **JOE:** I don't want to include my opinion in the beginning because I was writing from a non-bias point of viewpoint
>
> **TYISHA:** Tom, do you think you would pick up an article like Joe's why or why not?
>
> . . .
>
> **TOM:** I would because in reading the first sentence I want to know what the controversy is
>
> . . .
>
> **TYISHA:** Joe your paper is good, just work on making the introductory sentence sound appealing to the reader, by having a sentence like, As I looked into the subject of cultural diversity, I noticed how it was such a controversial topic.

There are probably a number of reasons why instances such as these occurred, beginning with Harris' identification of peer tutors' tendency to become "enamored of" their more authoritative role (380). There were times when I observed Tyisha reveling in her role as more knowledgeable, and why not? She was a former basic writer, and her work as a peer group leader by its very nature indicated how far she had come. At the same time, like peer tutors, Tyisha was still very much a part of her peers' community, only one year ahead of them in school, as her comments from various peer response sessions reveal: "what can Paul do to make his paper more personal to his audience"; "Maybe in your intro you could mention that there are bad effects of weed"; "Let's flip to Paul's [essay]"; and "you're a nut Paul." In the first comment, Tyisha uses academic terminology ("audience"), though somewhat awkwardly. In the second sentence, her use of the word "weed," rather than the more formal "marijuana" (as I would call it), discloses her ties to basic writers' community. The final two comments also reveal her connection-as-peer with the basic writers in my class.

I also believe that Tyisha was genuinely concerned about the writers in my class, and she wanted to help them improve their essays and get good grades, perhaps losing sight of her alternate roles. Her impulse to jump in with ways to "fix" their essays may have been a result of this concern. Moreover, there were times when she probably became frustrated with students in her group, as she prodded and pushed them to areas they did not want to go.

Relatedly, Harris' identification of the conflict over objectives of tutor and tutee may also explain some of the difficulties I experienced with the peer group leader. In the impressive exchange between Tyisha, Stan, and Jennifer previously discussed (I reproduce it below), there are also some signs of discontent.

> STAN: try adding something like this; Standard english pulls from cultural independence. Some people feel that without there cultural distinction they will be lost. For a person to truly accelerate in our society they must have a little of both. Cultural diversity is not acceptable in todays world and for a person to not understand or use standard english they will be lost
>
> JENNIFER: Also, she was my spark for this paper. I am responding and giving my idea of her views.
>
> . . .
>
> TYISHA: It's good you used Jones however, what is your thesis, is it that last sentence, because if so then you could talk about the things SHE FACED, I think it could be the 2nd and 3rd sentences combined, how do you feel Stan
>
> STAN: well I write what I think it should be
>
> JENNIFER: thanks Stan, I like that response you gave me previously. I wrote it down because I like it a lot.

The transcript itself shows less of the conflict than did Tyisha's comments to me after class. Tyisha felt that Jennifer was defensive, rejecting Tyisha's input and guidance, though I wonder whether some of this was not a misperception on her part. Nevertheless, I do believe the dialogue highlights two of Harris' points. First, it is possible that Jennifer saw Tyisha as judgmental, since Jennifer clearly felt strongly about her essay. The fact that the peer group leader does not have writing to be mutually critiqued alters the dynamic of peer collaboration and may have led Jennifer to feel defensive about her writing. Secondly, I think it is conceivable that Jennifer wanted what Stan gave her: a more direct answer to her questions about the thesis. Indeed, Stan rewrites the paragraph for her. Tyisha, on the other hand, prods Jennifer into making the discovery for herself, which may have been frustrating for Jennifer. Moreover, Tyisha's use of capital letters when she wrote '"It's good you used Jones however, what is your thesis, is it that last sentence, because if so then you could talk about the things SHE FACED," may have been offensive to Jennifer, although I think Tyisha only meant to emphasize the point she was trying to get across. Jennifer's "thank you" to Stan at the end of the discussion, absent one to Tyisha, may be further evidence of the conflict Tyisha sensed.

THE FUTURE OF PEER GROUP LEADERS IN BASIC WRITING

This study of the peer group leader in basic writing has significant implications for further research and practice. Above all else, it points to how peer group leaders can aid basic writers' appropriation of academic discourse. The benefits of peer response groups for writers include cognitive, global issues like "better sense of audience" and "motivation to revise," specific task-oriented activities like increased effectiveness in proofreading and editing, and emotional benefits such as offering emotional support and developing a sense of community (Harris, "Collaboration" 372). I have shown how Tyisha contributed to each of these areas in her work with my basic writers.

This study also identifies areas of concern in using peer group leaders, but I do not think the concerns are unsolvable. Rather, I think there are ways to lessen their impact, and I will suggest some of them here. Indeed, I am using peer group leaders again in my current basic writing classes, and I have made many of these changes in my own classes. First, I believe peer group leaders need more training and integration into the basic writing class than the project under study allowed. Tyisha had only one day of training at the beginning of the semester (due to limited funds as well as my inexperience). Moreover, although she and I discussed issues as they arose for her throughout the semester, our conversations were informal and spontaneous. I suggest incorporating more training time, including structured, formal supervision and guidance throughout the semester. I also believe the research on selection and training of peer tutors in Writing Centers can inform this work (see Cobb and Elledge).

Currently, I am using three peer group leaders in my basic writing classes, and I have spent more time with ongoing assessment and adjustment of their work with students as well as with their initial training. It is very difficult for peer group leaders to walk that fine line between offering help and solving the problem for the basic writers with whom they work, an issue tutors in writing centers also face. Indeed, these students' recent roles as peer responders in peer response groups (in English Composition last semester) make the multiplicity of their new roles even more challenging. Thus, their ongoing training centers on these issues.

My current peer group leaders began the semester by reading Richard Straub's "Responding—Really Responding—to Other Students' Writing" and excerpts from Muriel Harris' *Teaching One-to-One: The Writing Conference*. They participated in a mock peer group session, and they attended class on the date I introduced peer response groups to my basic writing students. Additionally, we continue to discuss and assess their work with students, and two of the three peer group leaders are co-presenting their experiences as peer group leaders at this year's National Conference on Peer Tutoring in Writing. They will also attend other panels at the conference to learn more about writing center tutorials and the distinctiveness of their roles as peer group leaders.

Furthermore, I suggest that peer group leaders be more integrated into the class than my initial study allowed. Due to limited funding, Tyisha attended class only on peer response days, which lessened the opportunity for students and tutor to bond. Subsequently, the trust that is so important between tutor and student may have been curtailed.[7] At the same time, I believe Tyisha's sense of investment in the class could have been stronger (I am a bit suspect about whether she read all the assignments), although I do think she cared about the students with whom she worked. Attending more classes would have also helped her to feel like part of the class rather than an intruder on peer response days.

Again, I have begun to address some of these problems in my current work with peer group leaders. These students (all were in my English Composition classes last fall, and one was also a former basic writer in the class under study) are attending the basic writing classes an average of two out of three class meetings per week, including the dates when we discuss the readings.[8] Moreover, the peer group leaders attend class and work with students during workshop classes when students are working on prewriting, drafting, and/or revision. I am attempting to find additional ways to expand their role as peer leaders in the class, though again I am somewhat limited by financial constraints.

I also think it would have been helpful for Tyisha to attend class when we discussed the readings in order to obtain a more sophisticated understanding of them. Though more advanced with academic discourse than the basic writers, she still was, after all, a sophomore, and I do not think all her difficulties with the readings were because she did not read them. Relatedly, Tyisha's performance also raises the issue of peer group leaders' age and maturity. I foresee many benefits of using older students as peer group leaders, such as more serious investment in academic work, greater reliability, and higher skill levels in reading difficult texts.[9] However, these benefits might be offset by older students' distance from first-year basic writers and the potential for degradation of peer collaboration.

Additionally, I think it is important to use more peer group leaders in a basic writing classroom. Ideally, each writing group should have a peer group leader. Tyisha's potential to help the students was undermined by the fact that there was only one of her to go around. Subsequently, she had less opportunity to get to really know the students with whom she worked and individualize instruction based on specific needs. Additionally, I felt somewhat uncomfortable about the fairness of having her work with some students rather than others. In designing the project, I had expected that Tyisha could work with all the students over the course of the semester by working with two or three groups during each peer response class. However, during the first class I learned that she could not go from one group to another because doing so disrupted conversations-in-progress.

Currently, I am using two peer group leaders in one class and one in the other, still less-than-ideal situations.[10] Clearly, funding is a potentially serious obstacle to maximizing the benefits of using peer group leaders in basic writing. As a result, I have begun to think about other ways to support peer group leaders. For example, I am beginning discussions with the Honors Coordinator at my college about finding ways to integrate using peer group leaders with our Honors program. Other possibilities include for-credit internships, community service, and/or senior capstone experiences. Currently, I am involved in designing a major in Writing and Rhetoric for our college, and this major might offer opportunities to integrate the peer group leader experience with students' course of study.

Finally, my study also raises issues related to computer-mediated-communication (CMC) and online peer response sessions. I chose to conduct my peer response sessions online for a number of reasons, but primarily because I have experienced the ways in which "technology can help build a sense of community and change basic writing dynamics" (Varone 213). Because electronic forums challenge teacher-centered pedagogies and provide students with the means to question academic (and other) authority, online peer groups potentially foster basic writers' meaningful participation in the review process. Research on online forums and collaborative writing suggests that students respond well to this less-threatening atmosphere, especially for students who perceive differences in status or knowledge, and engage more collaboratively and intensely with writing (see Schriner and Rice).

In this study, I chose not to focus on CMC issues largely because I was mainly concerned with the use of the peer group leader. I also believe that the implications of peer group leaders hold for both traditional and electronic classrooms, though I expect that there are advantages and disadvantages to each. As I continue to use peer group leaders in my basic writing classes, I will look more closely at the convergences and divergences of electronic and traditional classrooms, including CMC-specific issues such as lag time, space, and anonymity. Indeed, in my current basic writing classes using peer group leaders, I have chosen to conduct peer response sessions face-to-face, even though I hold class in a computer classroom two out of three days per week. Clearly, the specific dynamics of peer group leaders and online peer response is an area ripe for research.

Bishop asserts that teachers who use peer writing groups must be researchers in the sense that they monitor and evaluate the process. They must be "willing to experiment, to redefine group failures as steps in a larger process that leads to success, and to have realistic expectations for this holistic teaching method. Before long, those expectations will be met and hopefully surpassed" (124). I am one of these teachers, eager to continue working with peer group leaders to help basic writers cross the bridge to the academic community. When they cross that bridge and appropriate academic discourse, they will have the opportunity to make their mark on the world.

NOTES

1. I thank my collegue Candace Spigelman for the term, "peer group leader."

2. Margaret Weaver rightfully acknowledges the debate over authority and peer response groups in basic writing research. That is, some theorists advocate consensus, that peer response enables students to join our conversations, while others advocate dissent, that peer response groups enable basic writers to resist academic discourse (though she perhaps creates a false dichotomy). Nevertheless, because I believe the use of peer group leaders can facilitate both dissensus and consensus, debating the issue itself is beyond the scope of this essay.

3. I received this grant in conjunction with a colleague, Claudine Keenan. Claudine used a peer group leader in her basic writing class at the Lehigh Valley Campus of Penn State University, Berks-Lehigh Valley College, but I am writing only about my class at the Berks Campus.

4. Throughout this article, I am using pseudonyms for both the peer group leader and the basic writers.

5. I am not encouraging teachers to disappear completely, however. Indeed, I introduced a writing rubric to my students, one that closely resembled my own set of writing assessment criteria with greater emphasis on content and meaning than mechanics, and throughout the semester, we circled back to these issues in numerous ways. However, my attention to rhetorical issues had more to do with my general approach to teaching academic discourse, rather than specifically focused on modeling for peer response groups.

6. I have edited the transcripts to make them legible (students writing online tend to rush and transcripts can be difficult to read), but I have been very careful not to appropriate their words or language.

7. Students will offer more critical and high-quality response in an atmosphere of support and sharing. That is, group members need to gain some sense of group identity, have a sense of shared goals, and feel invested in their peers' work. Robert Brooke, Ruth Mirtz, and Rick Evans' study of student writing groups stress that for groups that worked well together, "a significant number of students describe their small groups as friendly and family-like in their unconditional acceptance" (34). Similarly, groups fail when students do not feel comfortable with their group members and do not get along.

8. Thus far, the peer group leaders have only listened to, rather than participated in, class discussions of the readings. I am currently weighing the advantages and disadvantages of allowing them to be more involved in this aspect of the class, especially when students work in groups to analyze and interpret the difficult reading selections. Clearly, the peer group leaders' participation in this aspect of the class raises issues both similar to and different from their participation in writing groups.

9. Penn State University, Berks-Lehigh Valley College, was only in its second full year as a four-year college when I undertook this project. Therefore, I had few juniors and seniors from which to choose. I expect a greater pool of potential peer group leaders as our college grows.

10. I received funding for two peer group leaders per class, but unfortunately I received the funding so close to the start of the semester that I was unable to find a fourth student whose schedule met my needs.

WORKS CITED

Bartholomae, David. "Inventing the University." *Journal of Basic Writing* 3.1 (1986): 4–23.
———. "Writing on the Margins: The Concept of Literacy in Higher Education." *A Sourcebook for Basic Writing Teachers.* Ed. Theresa Enos. New York: Random House, 1987. 66–83.
Bartholomae, David, and Anthony R. Petrosky. *Facts, Artifacts, and Counterfacts: Theory and Method for a Reading and Writing Course.* Upper Montclair, NJ: Boynton/Cook, 1986.
Benesch, Sarah. "Improving Peer Response: Collaboration Between Teachers and Students." *Journal of Teaching Writing* 4.1 (1985): 87–94.
Berthoff, Ann E. "Is Teaching Still Possible?" *College English* 46.6 (1984): 743–55.
Bishop, Wendy. "Helping Peer Writing Groups Succeed." *Teaching English in the Two-Year College* 15.2 (1988): 120–25.
Brooke, Robert, Ruth Mirtz, and Rick Evans. *Small Groups in Writing Workshops: Invitations to a Writer's Life.* Urbana: NCTE, 1994.
Bruffee, Kenneth. "Collaborative Learning and 'The Conversation of Mankind.' " *College English* 46.7 (1984): 635–52.
Cobb, Loretta, and Elaine K. Elledge. "Peer Tutors as a Source of Power for Basic Writers." *Teaching English in the Two-Year College* 9.2 (1983): 135–39.
Gay, Pamela. "Questions and Issues in Basic Writing and Computing." *Computers and Composition* 8.3 (1991): 63–81.
Hacker, Tim. "The Effect of Teacher Conferences on Peer Response Discourse." *Teaching English in the Two-Year College* 23.2 (1996): 112–26.
Harris, Muriel. "Collaboration Is Not Collaboration Is Not Collaboration: Writing Center Tutorials vs. Peer-Response Groups." *College Composition and Communication* 43.3 (1992): 369–83.
———. *Teaching One-to-One: The Writing Conference.* Urbana: NCTE, 1989.
Hawkins, Thom. "Intimacy and Audience: The Relationship Between Revision and the Social Dimension of Peer Tutoring." *College English* 42.1 (1980): 64–68.
Jones, Rachel L. "What's Wrong with Black English?" *Encountering Cultures: Reading and Writing in a Changing World.* Ed. Richard Holeton. Englewood Cliffs: Blair, 1992. 17–19.

Lawrence, Sandra M., and Elizabeth Sommers. "From the Park Bench to the (Writing) Workshop Table: Encouraging Collaboration among Inexperienced Writers." *Teaching English in the Two-Year College* 23.2 (1996): 101–11.

Schriner, Delores K., and William C. Rice. "Computer Conferencing and Collaborative Learning: A Discourse Community at Work." *CCC* 40.4 (1989): 472–78.

Straub, Richard. "Responding—Really Responding—to Other Students' Writing." *The Subject Is Writing: Essays by Teachers and Students.* Ed. Wendy Bishop. 2nd ed. Portsmouth: Boynton/Cook, 1999. 136–46.

Varone, Sandy. "Voices from the Computer Classroom: Novice Writers and Peer Response to Writing." *Teaching English in the Two-Year College* 23.3 (1996): 213–18.

Wauters, Joan K. "Non-Confrontational Critiquing Pairs: An Alternative to Verbal Peer Response Groups." *Writing Instructor* 7.3–4 (1988): 156–66.

Weaver, Margaret E. "Using Peer Response in the Classroom: Students' Perspectives." *Research and Teaching in Developmental Education* 12.1 (1995): 31–37.

Zhu, Wei. "Effects of Training for Peer Response on Students' Comments and Interaction." *Written Communication* 12.4 (1995): 492–528.

15 The Role of Talk in Small Writing Groups: Building Declarative and Procedural Knowledge for Basic Writers

SONJA LAUNSPACH

Like many composition teachers, I have struggled with finding ways to help my students, especially underprepared students, acquire the language of the academy. Since talk is key to the acquisition of academic discourse and the pragmatic strategies necessary for academic writing, modeling the discourse within appropriate situational contexts becomes a primary means by which to assist students' learning. Discourse, like language, is complex, especially for learners new to a particular discourse. Is it possible to observe their learning process as a first step toward unraveling the complexity of the discourse for them? The systematic analysis of the talk of our students using conversation or discourse analysis as a linguistic framework is one method by which to help instructors gain a better understanding of how discourse acquisition takes place and facilitate the process for basic writing students in multiple contexts.

This study examines the talk of writing students in peer groups led by a teaching assistant in order to explore how conversational interaction facilitates the acquisition of discourse. Since learning is socially negotiated, proficiency in a new discourse community, Lave and Wenger claim, may be acquired through limited peripheral participation which they define as a way to gain access—to learn gradually through ever-growing involvement (37). Situated learning, or "learning-in-practice," takes place by interacting with experienced members of the community through talk, observation, and practice (Lave and Wenger 101). As talk is a central socio-cultural practice, learning to talk about writing in mediated social interactions allows composition students to negotiate the meanings of the new discourse such that conversation becomes the "matrix" for their acquisition process (Levinson 284).

The work presented in this article is part of a larger research project on interactional strategies and the acquisition of academic discourse. For that project, I videotaped freshman composition students in small writing groups

From *Journal of Basic Writing*, vol. 27, no. 2, 2008, pp. 56–80.

that were a component of the Freshman Composition Program at a large southeastern university, a program implemented to replace the university's remedial composition courses and set up to work in tandem with the freshman composition course, English 101. The students in each group are all enrolled in English 101 and attend a writing group session led by a teaching assistant once a week in addition to their regular composition class.

Through the use of a case study, I trace the progress of one paper from the student's first attempts at understanding the assignment to the writing of her first through final drafts. I argue that the small writing group functions as a means of socialization into a new community of practice used to build both procedural and declarative knowledge about writing. Specifically, I show how the students use talk to develop declarative knowledge and try out different strategies, building procedural knowledge, to bridge the gaps between knowing *what* to do and *how* to do it. In addition, I consider the role of the teaching assistant as an experienced community member in creating a social setting wherein students practice new proficiencies in academic writing.

FRAMEWORKS OF DISCOURSE ACQUISITION

As a composition instructor, I have often observed a significant gap or mismatch between the knowledge and abilities that my students bring to the classroom. This gap can be seen when students are clearly able to speak about the changes they need to make in revising their draft, yet the essay that gets turned in does not match the students' plans. In other words, they are not yet able to carry over that verbal understanding of the process into their actual writing. What causes this gap between knowledge and ability—between the ability to define a rhetorical term, like pathos, and the inability to write a rhetorical analysis? For successful essays, composition students need to control different levels of language competence. Like all language users, they function linguistically on two basic levels: competence and performance. A speaker has many different underlying, or subconscious, competences including grammatical, communicative, pragmatic, and discursive. The second level, that of performance or "the actual use of language in concrete situations" (Chomsky 4), is often an imperfect reflection of underlying language competences. This is especially true when speakers learn new languages or enter new discourse communities, as do our freshman writers.

Frameworks for looking at levels of competence and performance from the field of second language acquisition provide composition instructors with alternative insights for understanding the learning processes of beginning college writers. One valuable perspective, first proposed in 1986 by Faerch and Kasper, claims that students employ two types of knowledge: declarative and procedural. Drawing on the research of cognitive science, they define declarative knowledge as an understanding of the "what" or knowing "that" of something, and procedural knowledge as "knowing how." In this framework, declarative knowledge consists of linguistic, pragmatic, discourse, and socio-interactional knowledge (8), knowledge which the speaker or learner internalizes. Both levels of language, structural and social, interact with each other to create an individual's language competences. In order to become competent speakers of the discourse, newcomers must learn the pragmatic and discourse rules of each community of practice they enter. Therefore in order to be successful writers, composition students must first develop this internal knowledge of the socio-linguistic rules of academic discourse.

Simultaneously, students must also build their procedural knowledge. A parallel concept to performance, procedural knowledge is the use of one's declarative knowledge and consists of a speaker's strategies for accomplishing various language tasks. Drawing on the socio-interactional resources of their declarative knowledge, speakers within a discourse community develop their procedural knowledge, which in turn allows them to regulate the discourse, use language forms in socially appropriate ways, and create coherent texts. According to Faerch and Kasper, part of successfully developing procedural knowledge requires knowing how to use language appropriately in particular situations in order to accomplish different language tasks. Assessing the context means knowing the appropriate things to say as well as the appropriate ways to accomplish tasks. This aspect of acquisition involves developing successful communication strategies, or "strategic competence" (Canale and Swain as qtd. in Faerch and Kasper 11). For it is through the organization of their talk that speakers display the many types of competences necessary to be considered a proficient member of a particular discourse community. Within this framework, composition students need to develop competences in more than one level of language. However, like all language learners, they acquire these types of knowledge at different rates, often engendering a gap between their declarative and procedural knowledge, or between their ability to talk about writing and their ability to write an academic paper.

Thus instructors must help students build strategic competences as a way for them to bridge the gap between their declarative and procedural knowledge. As beginners in the discourse, composition students will move through different stages of development and test hypotheses about the rules of the discourse they are learning. This process of hypothesis formation and testing is shaped by way of several factors: their access to the discourse; selection of input; and modeling of the discourse by experienced community members. First, access to the discourse is critical. In order to acquire declarative knowledge, students must have structured access to academic discourse, which will enable them to revise their internalized language model(s). According to Klein, access consists of two components: the amount of input, or language exposure, a learner receives, and opportunities for communication (44). Furthermore, the process of structured access combines these two components so that the learner's acquisition process is guided by more experienced community members who provide parallel information about both the content and function of discourse features.

Exposure to fluent speakers who can model and clarify the language/ discourse is especially vital for the new learner. According to Beaugrande, each student comes to the discourse learning process with "a model of the language, with the limitations and approximations peculiar to that speaker's experiences and abilities. In this sense, learning a language means revising one's model . . . through a succession of stages" (126). Since more than just comprehension of the discourse is necessary to be successful in a new community of practice, new schemas or language models need to be developed for all the language tasks associated with academic writing. Guiding students toward a new or more viable language model is one of the tasks that instructors, as experienced community members, must undertake since "what gets performed or learned on any one occasion always depends on the learner's current model" (Beaugrande 126). In order to help learners revise their language models, Long and Crookes argue that instructors should design "pedagogic tasks which provide a vehicle for the presentation of appropriate language samples to learners" (qtd. in Cook 151). Thus through the guided exploration of different genres of writing and speaking, students learn to negotiate both their own writing process and the meaning of writing within the larger academic community. As with second language learners, students enter more fully into academic communities of practice as they "begin to understand the distinct communities that are held together or separated by not only genres and vocabulary, but also practices and values" (Guleff 214).

The Writing Groups (WG)

To help instructors determine which students would benefit from the WG, all students in freshman English 101 courses are given a diagnostic essay the first week of class. These essays are evaluated together with writing samples from high school writing portfolios that all in-coming freshman students are requested to bring with them to class. Students are then recommended to the WG based on the quality of their writing, and/or their attitude toward writing. Some of the writing qualities which suggest that a student could benefit from the WG are a lack of content or development, evidence of dialect differences, and an abundance of mechanical and/or grammatical issues. Emotional responses such as fear or dislike of writing or a negative writing experience are more reasons to recommend a student. Also any student who wishes to volunteer for the WG may do so.

A writing group normally consists of four or five students from several different English 101 classes and a group leader, who is either an experienced teaching assistant (TA) or an English faculty member. All the TAs who work in a WG have taught composition as well as tutored in the writing center. During the semester, they participate in a weekly meeting with the WG director where they can talk through any problems in their groups as well as draw on the expertise of their peers in devising writing strategies for their students.

In a typical session, students meet in the WG room, where they sign in. There is usually some initial social talk, and then the group begins to discuss the essays each student has brought to share. Each student reads her/his essay aloud, and then the other students and group leader comment. If possible, the group leader tries to build discussion on peer comments. This practice validates the students' comments and encourages greater involvement among participants. However, it is not uncommon for students to bring an assignment without a draft because they don't understand what the assignment requires. In these cases, the group will talk the students through it.

DATA ANALYSIS

The data for this article is drawn from videotapes of a writing group that were recorded and transcribed according to conventions established by linguist Gail Jefferson.[1] The excerpts presented are taken from three group sessions over a period of four weeks during a single semester. This particular group includes three students and the group leader. The analytical framework is Conversation Analysis (CA), often used in research pertaining to both ordinary and institutional talk or discourse. Within the CA theoretical framework, it is the job of the researcher to discern the categories—the systematic and orderly properties of the discourse—that are meaningful to the participants and not impose a set of predetermined categories on the data. When examining the talk of composition students, it is therefore important to identify the structural and other elements in the talk that are meaningful to the students themselves, as these also offer clues to pragmatic competence.

The student in the case study is Ricki (all names used are pseudonyms), an African American freshman in her first semester. Like many students who are speakers of vernacular or non-standard language varieties, Ricki starts the process of acquiring academic discourse at a greater distance from the target discourse than students whose middle-class dialect and discourse practices more closely resemble institutionalized school practices (Heath). Thus, for Ricki, like other students in the WG, the differences in her home/primary discourse require that she engage in bridge building—in creating new language models—that negotiate between primary and secondary ("academic") discourses (Gee 156–57). My analysis focuses on Ricki's attempt to understand her instructor's challenging rhetorical assignment as she is supported by her peers and a group leader working in collaboration. Although most of the excerpts presented focus on Ricki's interactions with the group leader, the entire group was present at each session.

Every semester, the instructor of Ricki's English 101 class, a composition and rhetoric graduate student, gives her students a rhetorical analysis assignment, for which the students select an essay from the class reader and analyze its use of either ethos, pathos, or logos. A list of questions is designed to show them how their author is using the rhetorical strategy they have chosen, and the instructor expects students to use examples from their selected essays to demonstrate the effectiveness of specific rhetorical devices they must identify. The essay that Ricki chose for her paper is "Sexploitation" by Tipper Gore. However, the assignment proved difficult for her, since it required a level of textual analysis generally beyond the experience of writers such as Ricki, as it involved at least two separate analytical tasks. The first task is analysis of pathos, showing how Gore generates an emotional reaction from her audience as determined by textual structure apart from content. The second task is the creation of Ricki's essay. Through the group, she recognizes that she must discuss word choice and textual examples rather than summarizing or criticizing the reading's content—an approach typical of students at this level (Launspach 217).

So while not typical for freshman composition, the assignment functions as a good example of the cognitive gap between declarative and procedural knowledge for beginning college writers as it highlights an assignment which, if done successfully, effectively would situate students within an academic language-oriented community of practice. Yet the entire premise of the assignment is quite challenging to the experience and expectations of Ricki as a beginning college writer. She has no mental representation of pathos as a rhetorical device and must therefore build declarative knowledge before she can devise procedural strategies to write her essay. The data will show how talking through stages of the assignment in the writing group helps Ricki to develop an understanding of the rhetorical terms as well as a sense of the writing process.

The First Session

The first time the assignment is discussed, Ricki is just starting to work on her paper. At this point, she does not have a clear idea of what the assignment is asking her to do. One strategy the group leader, Jean, a teaching assistant, employs is to get Ricki to restate the assignment in her own words. In Excerpt 1, Ricki describes the assignment as she currently understands it.

Excerpt 1

RICKI: Okay, we had like uhm. (2.9) a list of words like, logos ethos and pathos. (4.3) I chose pathos. and I can't think of the meaning right now.

JEAN: Uh it would have to do with emotion.

RICKI: Yeah. how da-how da-da feel, yeah how she felt (.) about what she was writing, or what not.

Ricki is vague about the assignment as she is also uncertain about the meaning of the rhetorical terms her instructor has used. In her first turn, she is unsure of what pathos means. In her second turn, having been given a definition, she states how she envisions pathos would be used in an essay. She associates it with the attitude or feelings of writers toward their content rather than as a means to engage the emotions of a reader. It is clear that she does not understand the conventional definition or rhetorical use of pathos. Like most instructors, Ricki's instructor had explained the assignment in class and defined each term. Despite this preparation, there exists a mismatch between the conventional definition and Ricki's understanding of the term.

In Excerpt 2, Jean is aware that Ricki is lost on several levels. She tries to get her to think about how she will approach her paper, pressing for Ricki to connect the terminology and the drafting process.

Excerpt 2

JEAN: Now, what an-when-when you do your essay? what are you supposed to do with the pathos?

RICKI: Well? that's something I don't kno(h)w. uh I guess I supposed to write like. (2.5) jus' analyzing (.) how she felt about the sex entertainment. (2.1) without stating my opinion on how I think she was feeling. but jus' write what she really was meaning. I guess.

Ricki recognizes that her paper must analyze how Gore feels about her topic, sex entertainment, but at this point she doesn't understand that she will need to do more than discuss the general topic or Gore's feelings about it. Ricki will need to discuss how Gore touches the emotions of her readers. Initially, Ricki enters into the assignment by focusing on Gore's *what*, not on her *how*. Like other students I have studied, she does not yet realize that it is possible to analyze the essay's structure separate from its content. One of the group's tasks then is to help Ricki devise successful strategies to write just such an analysis. Jean approaches this in several ways. First she works with Ricki to construct a definition for the rhetorical term, pathos. Second, she stresses that Ricki's paper should be analysis, not summary. She states the point directly: "You know not to just summarize the article/ but to analyze which means to pull out/ just pull out specific pieces and look at them." Later she rephrases the point, "You want to analyze it/and that means that you'll pull out certain/relevant pieces to look at in more detail/does that make sense?" In the same turn, she reminds Ricki not to get involved in the issue, i.e., the content, but to look at how Gore writes about it. Third, Jean solicits peer input from Seth, another student, in order to help Ricki devise some practical writing strategies.

Excerpt 3

SETH: 'Cause we did something. sort of like that, we did a critical analysis my 12th grade year. of a writer. we had to analyze his writing, and how it reflected his background. and I was kinda like tryin' to (.) reflect it towards that.

JEAN: Yeah so you were thinkin. (0.9) wh-hearing the analysis. how did you see that analysis being the same, from what you did? and-and what uh Ricki's doing?

SETH: 'Cause we had to like. we had uhm-I had. T.S Eliot. Eliot I believe. and uh (2.4) what did I write. I think I wrote about his ah. I wrote about the poem uh. Love Song of J Alfred Prufrock. and uhm I just pulled out of there, like different lines that showed you, like a lonely man. and stuff like that. that reflected on his background, and that's what he wrote about, and all that other kind of stuff. it's like (.) pulling certain verses, or something like that.

JEAN: So it means that you don't tell the whole thing over.

SETH: Yeah.

At the beginning of this excerpt, Seth compares Ricki's assignment to one he did in high school. He has picked up on its analytical aspect. His class was asked to analyze how a writer's background affected his writing. The group leader then encourages Seth to elaborate on his comparisons in her next turn. Seth talks about his essay and emphasizes picking out parts of the text that will support the thesis. He stresses that his analysis used lines that showed the loneliness of the writer, and compares this process to Ricki's of using examples to show how word choice affects the reader's emotions.

Next Jean and Seth collaborate to give Ricki suggestions for getting started, reemphasizing the main points touched on in earlier parts of the interaction: study the assignment sheet, reread Gore's essay, and look for examples. Seth also suggests that Ricki practice on something easy, to get the hang of it before writing her actual essay.

Thus, the first group session lays important groundwork for Ricki in terms of building both her declarative and procedural knowledge. Ricki has been led to construct an understanding of rhetorical terms and build her declarative knowledge. At the same time, the collaboration between Jean and Seth has modeled for her both the concept of analysis and a strategy for writing her essay. In the discussion of writing strategies, Ricki also progresses toward academic discourse: analysis, and the use of examples to support ideas.

THE SECOND SESSION

One week later, Ricki's assignment is discussed again. This time she brings the first draft of her paper. Today the group will continue to help her understand the assignment and offer suggestions for revision based on her teacher's comments. Twice Ricki is asked to explain her assignment, once at the beginning and later when the group actually discusses her draft. Excerpt 4 shows her initial restatement.

Excerpt 4

JEAN: After we hear what Ricki's doing. Ricki tell us what you're doing.

RICKI: Well. we had to write on our rhetorical analysis. well the subject I chose, was curbing sexploitation industry by Tipper Gore? and I write like about pathos. how she stir-red the audience (.) emotions. (1.3) to uhm limit (.) the sex entertainment. for uh children. (10.0) *{Jean writing notes}*

JEAN: Uh how are you going to? how is pathos uh. work in what you are doing. how-how do you see that as important in your assignment?

RICKI: Uhm. (2.7) I see how she's showin' (.) the feeling of a woman. and a parent. how children they imitate stuff they see on TV, like they imitate violence, so she-she believe that once a child sees the sex. the stuff on TV. or what they hear through lyrics, that they might imitate it, and then it's also how it degrade women. degrading to women. (2.4) so she stro-she trying to strike up feelings. in the female. as well as both parents. as how this affects their child.

Here Ricki is able to give a concise explanation of the assignment. She identifies the important elements of the assignment, that is, to analyze an essay and describe the author's use of pathos. Her new way of thinking is reflected in her switch from pathos as it relates to Gore's feelings or attitudes toward her content to pathos as a means Gore has to touch the emotions of her audience.

Similar to her approach in the first group meeting, Jean works with Ricki on two levels: building her understanding of the rhetorical terms, and relating these terms to writing. We can see this strategy in her turn, where she asks Ricki to apply her new understanding of pathos to the construction of her own text. However, Ricki is still unable to analyze pathos separately from the content of Gore's essay, and so the first part of her turn involves a recounting of some of Gore's content. In the end of her turn, she finally articulates that it is the examples that will "strike up feelings" in the audience.

In Excerpt 5, Jean points out to Ricki her improved understanding of the assignment compared to last week.

Excerpt 5

JEAN: Yeah okay. so you made some progress on that haven't you?

RICKI: Not really.

JEAN: hahhuh I think you made some progress on thi:nking. on the thinking about it. 'cause you have a sense of, what-of how you're supposed to do the analysis. you have a better sense of it, than you did before. that you're supposed to look at how Tipper G<u>o</u>re. (0.7) uh. (2.1) how pathos acts in what she (.) is writing. it that-does that seem how you are thinking of it?

RICKI: I'm thinkin of it. but I jus' ain't, writing like that. it's kinda hard . 'cause I keep- I don't want to keep quoting her and I cain't <u>s</u>ummarize it. and I ain't never did no paper like this before. so it's kinda hard for me to try an' do this.

The group leader notes the progress in Ricki's 'thinking' about the assignment at the same time she recognizes that such meta-awareness is an important aspect of writing. However, Ricki initially denies this progress. Instead she focuses on some of the main difficulties of the assignment: she doesn't want to quote the author; she knows she may not summarize; and more importantly, she has no previous experience with this type of writing. Her ability to articulate these problems further indicates her growing meta-awareness of her own writing process.

These two excerpts from the second session evince the gaps between the student's declarative and emergent procedural knowledge. The group leader focuses on and praises Ricki's growth in her meta-awareness—her ability to articulate her knowledge of the terms of the assignment, while Ricki in contrast focuses on her struggles with drafting—with the translation of her declarative knowledge of the terms to the writing itself. She is not really conscious yet that the meta-awareness she is building will eventually help her to create a successful essay. Neither will Jean ignore Ricki's concerns as the group proceeds to discuss her first draft.

INTRODUCING THE FIRST DRAFT

Ricki passes out copies of her paper, and Jean asks her to again explain her assignment. Ricki reads aloud from the assignment sheet to remind the group of the requirements; she then reads aloud her essay.

One strategy employed by group leaders in these small writing groups is to set up the other students as leaders of the discussion. This strategy encourages students to become active participants in the discussion of each other's papers. Through this type of limited peripheral participation, the students in the WG gradually increase their participation in the different practices of academic writing. These interactional strategies provide a way of gaining access through a growing involvement in a type of "social practice that entails learning as integral constituent" (Lave and Wenger 35). Jean gets the other students to "take over" by asking Ricki to explain the assignment to Seth. Through his questions and comments, he provides the direction of the discussion for the next eight turns. Notably, he asks Ricki, "Is it persuasive writing?" That is, is her essay supposed to persuade her readers that Gore is right in her claim?

Excerpt 6

SETH: or you trying to convince them to go one way or the other? or are you just tryin to get them to think? (.) yeah she's right.

RICKI: Well see, okay for what I'm doing, is-I'm-I'm describing how she striking the feelings up. within another person. like how she feels. toward that uhm that topic. she's also using like different examples. and that's like one way of. like the one example she uses uhm. (2.6) she's talking about she watching a game show one morning. and then they had a preview of a soap opera, with a rape scene in there. so I have to show how's that uhm. how would that-how would that feel towards the audience, you know your child looking at a morning show, and then a rape scene comes up. and your child might try to imitate that, that's what's she's trying to.

In Excerpt 6, Ricki shows that she is now oriented toward the idea of demonstrating pathos and showing how an audience would react to Gore's examples. But she is still not quite certain about her intentions for the paper. She knows that her essay should describe how Gore "strikes up feelings" through the use of different examples, and that she must explain to her own readers the intended effect of Gore's examples on the audience, which Ricki has identified as parents with children. Of course Gore's essay is intended to be persuasive. However, Ricki does not give Seth a definite answer as to whether her own essay should be persuasive, which was probably the intent of his question. Rather she interprets it as relating to Gore's text. In subsequent turns, Jean responds to Ricki's confusion as she tries to reinforce the difference between the two papers: Gore's paper is persuasive, while Ricki's should be analytical.

THE FIRST DRAFT

Like many beginning or inexperienced writers, Ricki writes like she talks. According to Beaugrande, the differences in the conditions of talk vs. writing produce "manifestations of interference when experienced talkers must act as inexperienced writers" (129). However, the transfer of dialect features is not a

simple one-to-one proposition and many students, like Ricki, exhibit an intralect in their writing which contains features not found in either their vernacular dialect or standard written English.[2] As we will soon judge by way of her
final draft, the more Ricki is engaged in using talk as a means to acquiring the
language of the academy, the greater the impact will be on such intralectical
features of her writing as can be identified here.

Ricki's First Draft

Curbing the Sexploitation Industry Tipper Gore

Tipper Gore purpose towards the parents is to convince them on limiting sexual

messages that children acquire through television, radio and other entertainment. Also

open eyes to the degrading of women. Throughout the essay there is great concern of the

welfare of the children. Children mimics what they see on T.V. as for example a five-year

old boy from Boston got up from watching a teen-slasher film and stabbed a two-year girl

with a butcher knife. The same as a child might mimic a preview of a rape scene of a soap

opera that interrupts during a morning show. Gore states that "we cannot control what

our children watch, but we can let the industry know we're angry." She also is stating that

children is going to watch whatever they like, but we can cut down on most of the

advertisement of different sexual acts. She continues her pathos view by portraying another

"teen-slasher" film which depicts the killing, torture and sexual mutilation of women in

sickening detail. This is an example of degrading women in such that it is intolerable and

despicable towards the nature of a woman. She is opening eyes to our environment as a

woman and a woman with children it is time to limit this sex entertainment. Gore is also

describing how the industry is poisoning our children mind with pornography.

  The group's discussion of Ricki's draft centers around several main
points. One aspect they discuss is Ricki's concern about not using too many
quotes, something she has stated earlier (Excerpt 5). Another is the group's
attempts to get Ricki to focus on Gore's use of language as the means to affect
the emotions of her audience. The group tries to work this idea out with Ricki
by suggesting the use of concrete examples—either from the essay or by way
of comparisons drawn from experience. Through the process of discussing
her essay, Ricki realizes that what she has done is mainly summary.
  The group advises her to look at the words that Gore uses to affect parents. Jean asks her, "Can you find some quotes in there/that you would use/

have you picked out some uhm quotes/some words/images/passages where you would say she's using pathos." Seth points out several words that seem strong to him as possible examples she might use, "mutilation and all that kinda stuff/it-it's not like the usual words that float through/it jus sorta like pops out at you/it's like you don't every day read the newspaper." In addition, they also recommend that she try to imagine herself as Gore when she was writing her essay—to try to figure out why Gore made the choices she did. Seth says, "A good way to put it/you got to think/what Tipper Gore was thinking/when she wrote the paper." Both Seth and Jean stress to Ricki that her paper should be an analysis of Gore's. Jean says, "So it's like/it's a-it's a double thing isn't it/it's layered/Tipper Gore has written about sexploitation/and you're not to write about that/but you're to write about how Tipper Gore writes about it." Later Seth states, "So you're not writing about the sexploitation/she's writing about what Tipper Gore wrote about."

While Ricki has made progress in building her declarative knowledge of the rhetorical terms from one group meeting to the next, her paper tells a different story. At this second group meeting, Ricki has demonstrated from her discussions that she understands that pathos relates to the emotions of the reader and that she needs to talk about the effect of pathos on Gore's readers. She can make that distinction when *talking* about her paper—however, the text itself does not yet reflect her new meta-knowledge about the definition of pathos and its role in an essay.

For instance, Ricki states in her check-in for this session that she needs to demonstrate how Gore shows the feeling of a woman (Excerpt 4). While she focuses on the content, that children will imitate what they see and how such content is degrading to women, she fails to show the feelings that Gore wants to produce from the use of these examples in her own essay, even though she is very clear that Gore is trying to strike up feelings in parents, especially women. Later in Excerpt 6, she again is able to articulate that she needs to describe how Gore strikes up feelings and later show how an audience would feel or react to Gore's example. However, when she writes about the rape scene used to advertise a soap opera, she does not make the leap in her own text to demonstrating how Gore uses this example to provoke a reaction from her audience.

In her writing, we see a difference between Ricki's new declarative knowledge and her performance abilities, or her procedural knowledge—the set of skills that will allow her to "perform" a rhetorical analysis. From the WG discussions, Ricki has absorbed the importance of using examples; she mentions several, but does not articulate how they function to create certain types of feelings in the reader. Her primary focus in this draft is still on Gore's content—on the information that Gore is giving readers rather than the techniques, or "the pathos view," that Gore uses to persuade her readers. But while this draft contains a lot of summary, restating the examples that Gore uses, it is not entirely summary. Ricki writes about two purposes that she believes Gore has—opening the reader's eyes to this problem and limiting the sexual messages that children are exposed to. She implies that Gore's target audience is women, especially ones with children. In this way, her draft shows some limited evidence of analysis. In addition, Ricki's draft gives evidence that she is able to perceive genres. She understands that Gore's essay is a persuasive essay, when she states Gore's "purpose towards the parents is to convince them."

Despite the flaws in the draft, Ricki is making progress in her apprenticeship process. Through the guided talk in the WG, she has made important steps in the development of her understanding of several key rhetorical concepts: pathos, analysis, summary. Within the safety of the group, she has been able to negotiate through her participation, the academic meaning of pathos and make initial strides toward a workable textual structure. Still she has moved only so far toward participation in her new community of practice.

THE NEXT DRAFT

At the third and last session in which this paper is discussed, Ricki is asked again to restate the assignment as a preface to reading her new draft aloud. The following excerpt presents her restatement.

Excerpt 7

JEAN: tell us-tell us what you were supposed to do in this paper

RICKI: okay what I supposed to have done was uh tell how and why that she reaches out to her audience evokes feelings which is uhm pathos and I jus' use some of the words and how it might affect a parent which was her audience it suppose like limit the sexploitation in the industry like get some of that uhm sex entertainment off the TVs or like rock groups or what not that's what I was supposed to done

JEAN: okay okay let's see if she did it

In her turn, Ricki is now better able to summarize the main points of the assignment. One further improvement that Ricki has made in her understanding of the assignment is the connection between Gore's word choices and evoking pathos. This realization marks an important step in her verbal understanding—she is moving from what the term means, a definition of pathos, to being able to perceive what resources an author might use to create pathos.

The draft that Ricki has brought is one that has been returned to her with the teacher's comments. Like her earlier draft, it also contains African American English features, intralect features, and standard written English usage. The draft is now two pages typed (half a page longer than previously), and organized in only two paragraphs: introduction and a single body paragraph. In the introduction, she states her main points; in the body, she uses quotes and examples from Gore's essay.

Excerpt 1 from Ricki's Final Draft

"Sentiment of Gore towards Sexploitation"

Tipper Gore uses pathos in her essay, "Curbing the Sexploitation Industry" to reach out to the women and parents with children under the age of fifteen. She is letting her audience know of the deep need to limit the children to sex entertainment. As to back her

argument she shows examples how easily influence the children are by what they watch

before they hit adolescence.

Gore has a great concern for the welfare of the children and women reputation. She

evokes a suddenness of protection and at the same time anger combine together at these

entertainers The crucial words as sadomasochism, brutality, mutilation and titillate gives

harsh images of what a child might be seeing done to the women.

Overall this paper is more organized and contains less summary than the first version. Ricki has selected four different words that she feels Gores uses to evoke a response in the reader. For each of the words she has chosen, Ricki uses examples from Gore's essay that illustrate their use. The following excerpt is one example of this strategy. Here she starts with *mutilation* and connects it through the example to the next word—*titillate*.

Excerpt 2 from Ricki's Final Draft

Which lets me go to the next crucial word she uses mutilation. The example used by Gore is: "teen slasher' film, and it typically depicts the killing, torture and sexual mutilation of women ins sickening detail." That is despicable showing how one can remove a necessary part of a woman and then show it to the children. Which only increase their curiosity (Titillate) of what would happen next.

The excerpt that follows is from later in the essay: here she has chosen the word *brutality*, but unlike in the earlier excerpt, she doesn't present her reader with any of Gore's examples to demonstrate brutality. Instead she comments on the emotional impact she feels the word would have on Gore's readers.

Excerpt 3 from Ricki's Final Draft

The word brutality hits close to the heart of majority of women. This is another one of crucial words that she uses to throw pain in her audience heart, because of the fact that they been in the situation once or twice.

Evincing analysis, these excerpts make it possible to observe Ricki implementing the advice she has been given in the WG; she is trying to connect the emotions of the reader to the words used by Gore. We can see the beginning of her new procedural knowledge.

Despite this progress, the conclusion of the paper returns to what Ricki feels is Gore's main message rather than focusing on the emotional impact of Gore's essay.

Excerpt 4 from Ricki's Final Draft

Gore concluding statement, "The fate of the family, the dignity of women, the mental health of children—These concerns belong to everyone.", make you think that everybody suppose to come together and put an end to this sexploitation. Lets her audience come into an agreement that the family should stick together on the issue of anybodies child state of being.

While the teacher's comments on the draft emphasize a need to work on the organization, she praises Ricki's progress with the assignment, and gives the impression that overall she is pleased with Ricki's draft. Ricki, on the other hand, lets the group know that while happy with her grade, she is not pleased with what she views as her mistakes. Firstly, she doesn't think that she did the best job she could have since she got hung up on the idea of the paper being hard. She states that she needed to get beyond the idea of it being hard and just convince herself that she could do it. Secondly, she is aware of the mechanical errors in the paper: spelling errors, skipped information, and problems with sentence structure. She feels it falls short of the requirements of the assignment as she has now come to understand them.

DISCUSSION

As this study shows, for basic or inexperienced writers, access to talk in peer groups enables students to construct meaning in social interaction through collaborative learning, facilitating their participation in the larger academic conversation. As evidence of socially situated learning, the data in this study is useful to composition instructors as we trace Ricki's process of development over the course of four weeks, watching her grapple with acquiring new declarative knowledge and struggle with translating that new knowledge into actual writing strategies. Excerpts of conversation with a supportive peer group show that she is able to move from having no understanding of pathos as a rhetorical term, to associating pathos with the writers' feeling toward their content, to understanding pathos as a means to touch the reader's emotions. Thus, the talk in the Writing Group serves as an "institutionalized" guide for Ricki, providing essential discourse input for her and highlighting important aspects of academic discourse and practices.

Writing is a multiple step process. We have to know "what" to do as well as "how" to do it, and beginning academic writers, like Ricki, often struggle with more than one type of knowledge gap when confronted with writing in the academy. Their acquisition process needs to take place on both cognitive and pragmatic levels, affecting declarative and procedural knowledge. The small writing group provides Ricki with a "safe" forum to negotiate the meaning of new rhetorical terms as well as an apprenticeship-like setting, a place for guided participation in the academic writing process.

In addition, the Writing Group provides what Faerch and Kasper refer to as accessibility (14). They explain, "To become a full member of a community of practice requires access to a wide range of ongoing activity, old-timers, and other members of the community; and to information, resources, and opportunities for participation" (Lave and Wenger 100–101). Conversational interactions in the Writing Group make available to basic writers, like Ricki, important linguistic and discourse resources, that are not usually overtly articulated for students during a composition course. It is a place where, for example, rhetorical terms are not only defined, but modeled by the group leader as well as by peers.

Moreover, like other speakers of vernacular dialects, Ricki also experiences a difference between her home and academic discourses. She must find a way to bridge that gap, to negotiate the differences, without losing her voice. Rather than forcing such students to abandon all of their discourse norms, one way to enhance their acquisition of academic discourse is to build on their expertise in their home discourses. Smitherman advocates using the oral language resources that African American students possess to help them promote learning through social interaction. Thus instructors might use what students already know to "move them to what they need to know" (219). Like Smitherman, Perez holds that use of linguistic knowledge from students' home discourse can ease the transition and provide scaffolding for learning new discourse norms. Thus, instructors can draw on the linguistic resources that students bring with them as a way of providing students structured access to academic discourse in order to facilitate their acquisition process.

As a writer, Ricki is still working out the appropriate relationships between herself and her audience (her peers and instructor), and the assigned topic (a rhetorical analysis). What is the best way for her to negotiate these different elements? As the number of options for instruction of basic writers has widened in the field, the use of small groups may fit a variety of basic writing contexts: basic writing courses, groups run out of a writing center, or pull-out workshops such as the one described in this study. Writing groups could be implemented in writing programs, either by individual instructors within a classroom setting using a teaching assistant, or by a program as a whole. Both the methods and results of this study advocate for such small group or studio arrangements as productive places of discourse development for basic writers.

Through the discussions in the Writing Group, Ricki is able to increase her declarative knowledge, allowing her to shift from writing a summary of Gore's essay to the beginnings of an analysis of Gore's use of pathos. The Writing Group's discussions assist her in coming up with strategies for writing her paper such as selecting, connecting, and analyzing words she feels that Gore used to invoke responses in her reader. It is a sound strategy. However, we can see in her draft that Ricki's inexperience as a writer, her lack of procedural knowledge, does not allow her to translate this new approach into a well-organized paper. While she has gained through the Writing Group interactions a strategy to approach a rhetorical analysis of a text, she is struggling with other aspects of expository writing. She is still working on building the strategic competences that will improve her actual writing skills. At this point in her acquisition process, Ricki's declarative knowledge has outstripped her performance ability.

A primary advantage that Ricki has is access to an experienced community member, the teaching assistant, Jean, who models the discourse and provides links between the discourse and creating texts for Ricki and her peers. The TA uses a series of interactional strategies: restating the assignment, using focus questions,[3] giving advice, and soliciting focused input from Ricki's peers. This last strategy provides Ricki with advice and suggestions that are framed in language that she can relate to and at the same time builds the linguistic competence of her peers. Further, the group leader's language use models for students suitable responses, allowing them to reframe their talk in ways that come to match more and more accepted discourse practices. This type of structured access to the discourse is especially beneficial to basic writers like Ricki, who start farther from the target discourse than other students who may have had some exposure to it in other contexts. All language learners need sufficient exposure to the target discourse: the more meaningful the language input they receive, the faster their acquisition process will become.

Other studies also show that there are additional benefits for composition students when an experienced language user, such as a peer group leader, an instructor, or a teaching assistant is present in a writing group. For example, Grobman, in her research, found that peer group leaders can function to "build bridges between basic writers and academic writers" by making academic discourses "visible" (45). Similarly, Brooke, O'Conner, and Mirtz also found that students, in peer groups with an experienced leader who modeled discussion about writing as well as genres of writing, made more relevant connections between talk about writing and the act of writing itself than did students in peer groups without a group leader. Those students had a harder time connecting their talk and their writing process (83). Thus, students in writing groups with an experienced group leader have more structured access to the discourse and can negotiate meanings related to the composition process more productively than those in peer groups alone.

Like our students, we can also benefit from collaboration and talk about writing. This study demonstrates that we, as teachers and researchers, can gain important insights into our students' acquisition of writing when we examine the talk that goes into the creation of a draft—as well as examining the draft itself. Despite some of the problems with adapting research methods from other fields, Mortensen acknowledges that examining the talk of writing students can make more visible the process by which texts are constructed. In his critique of analyzing talk about writing, he states that "theoretically, then, analyzing talk about writing gives us a way of studying how texts are socially constructed. As a method, it offers a frame in which to arrange and interpret observations about the writing experience" (Mortensen, 120–21). He further observes that talk about writing is situated at the boundaries of text and individual perception. This intersection of text and consciousness leaves "traces" that can be recorded and utilized to further our understanding of a particular student's writing process. One way these traces can be seen is when we examine how talk about a text shapes the text itself. The intersection between talk and text is a meeting place of oral and written, between Ricki's talk about her draft, her draft, and prior drafts like it.

So what do the data imply about the relationship between Ricki's talk about her paper and her paper? Are there specific features/characteristics we can point to and use in other situations and with other writers? One aspect of the talk we can observe is the effect of repetition. Over the course of a month, Ricki is asked to restate her assignment at the beginning of the group session and right before her paper is discussed later in the same session. Guided by the TA and her peers, she is able to construct an understanding of the assignment through this process of stating and restating. How else can we view the shaping effect of talk on Ricki's essay? Organizationally, the emphasis of analysis over summary and advice to use examples given to Ricki from the first session onward support her effort to move from summary to analysis to incorporating examples in both her drafts. In the first draft, she uses examples taken from Gore's content, and in the second draft, she uses examples of words that express pathos. Phrases such as "degrading to women," "feelings of a parent," "pathos view," "children imitating TV" appear in the talk and reappear in the text. As a basic writer, she is relying heavily on others to provide her with the phrasal building blocks for her text.

These types of psychological, social, and discourse perspectives on writing gained from the analysis of talk are valuable to researchers and instructors. A systematic look at how students' talk is structured and what topics they focus on offers important insights into basic writers: the gaps in their knowledge, their learning process, and their view of the writing process. As a result, a deeper understanding of the discourse acquisition process and the way talk shapes texts could lead to changes in teaching methods and the way talk is framed in peer groups. In addition, as Smitherman, Heath, and others have claimed, the greater the awareness and understanding that instructors have of the distances that many students—minority, working class, first generation, and basic writers—have between their home discourses and the target discourse, the better they will be able to design curriculum that places those discourse modes more at the center of the students' learning experience.

Furthermore, our students benefit when we can take what they show us in their talk and transform it into ways they can improve their writing processes and acquire academic discourse more effectively. When we can go beyond analysis and integrate the insights gained from talk back into peer groups and the classroom, we help our students enter a new community of practice. As Mortensen tells us, "Studying talk about writing allows for the discovery of unexpected openings situated among people, ideas and discourse. And it allows us to see how these openings permit both the consensus and conflict that rhetorically, make and break the bonds of community" (124). It can create change by allowing new voices into the academic discourse community.

NOTES

1. Conversation is not organized the same way as written texts, and it can appear fragmented in comparison with writing, since speakers/hearers have different resources at their disposal. For example, intonations patterns, stress on words or individual vowels, pauses, repetition, discourse markers, and use of continuers such as "uhm" all serve to signal and create coherence and meaning within a conversation. In a transcription of a conversation, different symbols are used to indicate vocal cues. Punctuation is used to signal intonation, underlines indicate places of greater stress. Pauses are timed in seconds (the numbers placed in parenthesis), while a slight pause is

indicated by just a period inside a parenthesis. Some of the transcription conventions that appear in the excerpts of speech cited in this article: a colon : indicates a lengthened sound, usually a vowel; a period . indicates a stopping fall in tone; a single dash - indicates an abrupt cut off; an underline, e.g., a, indicates emphasis; numbers in parentheses, e.g., (0.1), indicate intervals between utterances, timed in tenths of a second; empty parentheses ( ) indicate that part of the utterance could not be deciphered (see Sacks, Schegloff, and Jefferson).

2. One stage that learners go through in learning a second language is called interlanguage. Interlanguage features are often different from either the learner's first language or the target/ second language. Scott Cobb makes a parallel claim for non-standard dialect learners of academic writing. They also go through an intermediate stage she calls intralect.

3. The larger research project focused on the types of interactional strategies that the beginning student writers developed over the course of the semester. As part of the analysis, the types and functions of the questions used in the discourse were categorized. (See Launspach. "Interactional Strategies and the Role of Questions in the Acquisition of Academic Discourse." Diss. U of South Carolina, 1998).

WORKS CITED

Beaugrande, Robert. "Linguistic and Cognitive Processes in Developmental Writing." *International Review of Applied Linguistics* 21.3 (1983): 125–44.

Brooke, Robert, Tom O'Conner, and Ruth Mirtz. "Leadership Negotiation in College Writing Groups." *Writing on the Edge* 1.1 (1989): 66–85.

Chomsky, Noam. *Aspects of the Theory of Syntax*. Cambridge, MA: MIT P, 1965.

Cook, Vivian. *Second Language Learning and Language Teaching*. 3rd ed. London: Arnold Publishing, 2001.

Faerch, Claus, and Kasper, Gabriele. "Procedural Knowledge as a Component of Foreign Language Learners' Communicative Competence." *AILA Review* 3 (1986): 7–23.

Gee, James. *Social Linguistics and Literacies: Ideology in Discourses*. 3rd ed. London: Routledge, 2008.

Gore,Tipper. "Curbing the Sexploitation Industry." *Little Brown Reader*. Ed. Marcia Stubbs and Sylvan Barnet. Short 5th edition. Glenview, IL: Scott, Foresman, 1989. 478–80.

Grobman, Laurie. "Building Bridges to Academic Discourse: The Peer Group Leader in Basic Writing Peer Response Groups." *On Location Theory and Practice in Classroom-Based Writing Tutoring*. Ed. Candace Spigelman and Laurie Grobman. Logan, UT: Utah State UP, 2005. 44–59.

Guleff, Virginia. "Approaching Genre: Pre-writing as Apprenticeship to Communities of Practice." *Genre in the Classroom: Multiple Perspectives*. Ed. Ann M. Johns. Mahwah, NJ: Erlbaum, 2002. 211–23.

Heath, Shirley Brice. *Ways with Words*. 2nd ed. Cambridge, UK: Cambridge UP, 1999.

Klein, Wolfgang. *Second Language Acquisition*. Cambridge, UK: Cambridge UP, 1997.

Launspach, Sonja. "Interactional Strategies and the Role of Questions in the Acquisition of Academic Discourse." Diss. U of South Carolina, 1998.

Lave, Jean, and Etienne Wenger. *Situated Learning: Legitimate Peripheral Participation*. Cambridge, UK: Cambridge UP, 1991.

Levinson, Stephen. *Pragmatics*. Cambridge, UK: Cambridge UP, 1983.

Mortensen, Peter. "Analyzing Talk about Writing." *Methods and Methodology in Composition Research*. Ed. G. Kirsh and P. Sullivan. Carbondale, IL: Southern Illinois UP, 1992. 105–29.

Perez, Bertha, ed. *The Sociocultural Contexts of Language and Literacy*. Mahwah, NJ: Erlbaum, 2004.

Richardson, Elaine. *African American Literacies*. London: Routledge, 2003.

Sacks, Harvey, Emanuel A. Schegloff, and Gail Jefferson. "A Simplest Systematics for the Organization of Turn-Taking for Conversation." *Language* 50.4 part 1 (1974): 696–735.

Scott Cobb, Jerrie. "Accommodating Nonmainstream Language in the Composition Classroom." *Language Variation in North American English*. Ed. A. Wayne Glowka and Donald Lance. New York: Modern Language Association, 1993. 331–45.

Smitherman, Geneva. *Talkin and Testifyin*. New York: Harper & Row, 1977.

16 Analyzing and Addressing the Effects of Native Speakerism on Linguistically Diverse Peer Review

TODD RUECKER

Since its introduction to mainstream writing classrooms in the late 1960s by scholars such as Donald Murray and Peter Elbow, peer review has become a commonly used process pedagogy in both second language (L2) and mainstream writing classrooms. Despite its frequent use, dissatisfaction with the peer review process from both teachers and students has been consistently reported throughout its history. In response, researchers have extensively explored different aspects of peer review, including student satisfaction with the process, the effects of training students beforehand, and the role of cultural backgrounds on the success of peer review. While this research has provided many useful insights, it has been limited in a major way: it has focused on either mainstream or L2 environments, failing to recognize that linguistic diversity is increasingly becoming a major part of mainstream writing environments in US colleges. This chapter is an attempt to address that gap, drawing on data from a study at a 6,000-student university in the Midwest, Lev Vygotsky's theory of the zone of proximal development (ZPD), and the theory of native speakerism to examine the power imbalances in linguistically diverse peer review groups. After discussing these imbalances, I will offer a few different ways writing teachers can combat the negative effects of native speakerism on peer review.

LINGUISTICALLY DIVERSE PEER REVIEW

As mentioned above, there has been very little research focused on peer review between native English speaking (NES) and non-native English speaking (NNES) writers,[1] but extensive work dealing with these learners in separate environments. In researching L2 classrooms, Kate Mangelsdorf and Ann Schlumberger reported that the more desirable collaborative feedback was the least common. Joan Carson and Gayle Nelson made the argument that because constructive

From *Peer Pressure, Peer Power: Theory and Practice in Peer Review and Response for the Writing Classroom*, edited by Steven J. Corbett et al., Fountainhead Press, 2014.

criticism did not exist in Middle Eastern and Asian cultures, any form of criticism could be destructive for these students in peer review. Arguments such as this emerged from theories of cultural difference and contrastive rhetoric, the latter of which has been heavily critiqued by scholars such as Ryuko Kubota for being essentialist and deterministic. Studies by both L1 and L2 scholars such as Jane Stanley, Wei Zhu, Cathrine Berg, and Hui-Tzu Min found that extensive training greatly increases the success of peer review.

To learn more about linguistically diverse peer review, it is necessary to turn to a few other studies, even though they did not explicitly focus on peer review. In "ESL Students in First-Year Writing Courses: ESL Versus Mainstream Classes," George Braine briefly mentions NNES students' experiences with peer review: "During peer review of papers in groups, [NNES] students felt that the [NES] students were impatient with them, and one student said that he overheard a [NES] student complain to the teacher about her inability to correct the numerous grammatical errors in his paper" (98). This statement is situated in a discussion on why NNES students in the study chose to withdraw from mainstream composition classes. Negative experiences, such as the ones associated with peer review, contributed to a NNES student first-year composition withdraw rate of 24.4% over four semesters in Braine's study, compared to an 7.7% withdraw rate of NES students over the same period (97).

In a 1999 study, Paul Kei Matsuda and Tony Silva explored the value of "mediated integration" of NNES and NES students in what they called a "cross-cultural composition course." Matsuda and Silva reported that the course goal of mediated integration helped students learn about each other and promote international understanding. The comments of one student in the study, Park, reveal that the NNES students valued feedback given by NES US students in peer review sessions and learned about US culture and thinking through reading US student papers.

Wei Zhu's study "Interaction and Feedback in Mixed Peer Response Groups" was the first and only major study focusing on peer review groups involving NNES and NES students. In this study, Zhu focused on 11 students in 3 peer response groups and examined their turn-taking procedures, language functions,[2] and similarities and differences between their comments. Zhu found that the NNES students used fewer types of functions than the NES students, as they were less likely to use a more direct and authoritative function like "advising" (200). In regard to turn-taking, Zhu discovered that the NNES students were more likely to be interrupted and less likely to regain their turn after being interrupted. While the NES students produced much more evaluative and local feedback than the NNES students, the NNES students were able to match the NES students on global comments, comments that tended to be content-based. Overall, Zhu felt that NNES students were valuable contributors in mixed peer review groups and that more should be done to increase their level of participation. This lower level of participation seen by NNES students can be better understood by examining the power dynamics in linguistically diverse peer review groups through two theoretical lenses: Vygotsky's theory of the zone of proximal development (ZPD) and the theory of native speakerism.

NATIVE SPEAKERISM AND THE ZPD

Adrian Holliday has written extensively on recognizing English as an international language, not one that belongs to a small group of countries like the US and the UK. In the context of teaching English, Holliday has defined native speakerism as "an established belief that 'native-speaker' teachers represent a 'Western culture' from which spring the ideals both of the English language and of English language teaching methodology" (6). As a respondent in his book said, native speakerism involves recognizing difference and using this difference to "deliberately put 'native speakers' in an advantageous position . . ." (Holliday 28). While Holliday was focused specifically on English teachers in foreign countries, where linguistic and even racial prejudice is very open and visible and well-qualified NNES teachers have trouble finding work teaching English, native speakerism also has an impact on NNES students who have been shown to internalize the belief that they are inferior to NES speakers.

For instance, Ivor Timmis surveyed over 600 students and teachers about native speaker preference, finding that students had a stronger desire to sound like a native speaker than teachers did. Yuko Goto Butler's study revealed how sixth grade Korean students expressed a preference for US English accents even though they were able to comprehend a Korean accent as well as a US accent in a listening test. An NNES college professor, Jacinta Thomas, explains that all the gratification she received from positive student evaluations one semester was erased upon reading the following comment: "We need native speaker teacher. It will be better" (10). While the comments and research referenced here point to students preferring NES teachers, it may be assumed that students will similarly view themselves as inferior because they are not NESs. This negative self-perception can become a problem in trying to activate the ZPD.

Vygotsky's theory of the ZPD has provided an important framework for the implementation and study of peer review. The theory was first appropriated from cognitive psychology by educators in the 1960s, an era in which teachers emphasized the value of socially constructed knowledge and peer interaction (Marsh and Ketterer). The ZPD involves "the distance between the actual developmental level . . . and the level of potential development" which is bridged "under adult guidance or in collaboration with more capable peers" (Vygotsky 86). At its most successful, all students in peer review produce and receive feedback that helps them progress to new stages of writing development.

Student attitudes play an important role in activating the ZPD because student willingness to accept peer feedback is an important determinant of students using feedback from peer review sessions in improving their writing (Litowitz). Unfortunately, because of native speakerist discourses, NNES writers may not be confident in giving feedback and NES writers are often likely to question the feedback provided by a NNES student. This distrust was evident in Kate Mangelsdorf's study in which she found that 77% of the NNES students in L2 classrooms who did not like peer review did not trust their peers' advice. In another study, Andrea Murau found that NNES writers expressed more negative attitudes towards peer review than positive, with these comments centering on their anxiety or lack of confidence in providing feedback in English. Due to lack of confidence from NNES writers and lack of trust as expressed by NES writers in Braine's study, the ZPD may not be activated successfully in linguistically diverse peer review. My presentation of data in the next few sections will provide a more detailed look into the effects of native speakerist ideologies on the success of linguistically diverse peer review.

THE STUDY

The study discussed here was conducted to better understand the dynamics of linguistically diverse peer review and focuses on examining student attitudes towards giving and receiving feedback to students of different linguistic backgrounds. For this study, I interviewed 17 NES students and surveyed 14 NNES students regarding their peer review experiences in mainstream first-year composition (FYC) classrooms at Adams State University, a 6,000-student university in the Midwest.[3] All students who participated in this study either had taken or were currently enrolled in ENG 190: Writing as Critical Thinking, a FYC course required for all students. ENG 190 was a semester long course taught by a mixture of professors and TAs. The classes generally included four original essays and one revision and expansion of a previous essay. Before submitting each essay, the classes held a writing workshop in which they collectively read and gave feedback on anonymous student essays under the instructor's guidance. While students were not trained to the extent that students were in the Stanley, Zhu, and Berg studies, the writing workshop helped prepare students for peer review sessions by showing them how to develop and give helpful feedback. After the workshops, students brought essays to class the day of peer review, read them, and discussed their feedback. Peer review sessions involved both small-group and paired work.

The seventeen L2 students who participated in this study were chosen for three reasons: (a) They had participated in peer review in similarly designed FYC classes at Adams, (b) they represented a wide variety of countries and cultural groups, and (c) they came from countries where English was not the primary language.[4] See Table 1 for names and country of origin of the NNES students. None of them had participated in formal peer review sessions in their own countries. Before taking ENG 190, some of the NNES students in this study had participated in ENG 309: Academic Writing for Non-native Speakers, a preparatory course that did not fulfill the ENG 190 requirement. However, because only one section of ENG 309 was offered per semester, most students were mainstreamed without taking this course.

Data were collected from the NNES students via interview and from the NES students via survey. After collecting data from each group, I transcribed

TABLE 1   Country of Origin of the NNES Students

Name	Country
Adelina	Albania
Miranda	Albania
Jana	Albania
Dafina	Bulgaria
Lorina	Bulgaria
Daniel	Bulgaria
Kim	Vietnam
Lily	China
Naomi	Japan
Sho	Japan
Takai	Japan
Monica	Nepal
Nana	Nepal
Petr	Tajikistan
Andrew	Ghana
Michael	Ghana
James	Ghana

the NNES interviews and read through them recursively to find patterns or themes. In searching for these patterns, I used inductive data analysis, letting "research findings emerge from the frequent, dominant, or significant themes within the raw data" (Mackey and Gass 179).

GIVING FEEDBACK

Over one third of the NNES students interviewed expressed that they had strong anxiety when they first began peer review because they were unfamiliar with the process. Sho from Japan revealed that this anxiety also may have stemmed from native speakerist beliefs, saying, "one of my friend took the class before and she said, like peer editing, and it's kind of hard for you, because you are not American." Before even trying peer review, Sho was told he would be an inferior member of a peer review group because he was not an "American." This demonstrates the common assumption that Americans are "native speakers," illustrating the strong pull of standard language ideologies.

While participants reported becoming more comfortable with peer review after engaging in the process, giving feedback was consistently the least favorite part of peer review for the NNES students. For both Petr from Tajikistan and Lily from China, time pressure became an issue. Petr said, "I was kind of nervous, because I'm not too sure, I tried to be responsible. And when I'm too slow, I'm a slow reader, like they go too fast and I tried to make, like as clear notes, to give a feedback on them as they do." Lily was nervous for similar reasons:

> Because, when I do peer teaching, because since I'm not a native English speaker, I'm afraid that I cannot give really helpful comments and also, I cannot finish the paper using the same time as others and, while I feel sorry if I, delay somebody's time, so I'll try to just scan the paper really really quick, and find out what's the general ideas and comment on it.

Lily and Petr's comments reveal a few different issues that may arise during peer review interactions in linguistically diverse groups. First, peer review is a complex process that involves reading, formulating feedback, and communicating that feedback. Naturally, someone who is doing this complex process in a language other than their first may need more time than someone doing it in their first and/or only language. Second, as these comments reveal, any problems caused by simple time constraints are exacerbated by the ever-present belief commonly held by NNES students that they are inferior and "cannot give really helpful comments." In a later statement, Petr expanded on the above comment, saying, "Because probably I was not more open to give them instruction or something as a non-native speaker. I didn't have that sense that I know more than them." Similarly, Naomi from Japan said, "I think I'm not supposed to say anything like bad . . . because English is not my first language and they know much more better than I do."

While most students in the study did not express feelings of rejection and hurt by a NES student openly rejecting their feedback, Lorina from Bulgaria appeared to be the victim of NES condescension, which was also reported in Braine's study. She said, "They don't appreciate nothing of your opinion as a critic. Here they think that because we are international students, we are not aware of the grammar, the punctuation, the way the Americans write maybe."

RECEIVING FEEDBACK

While the NNES participants generally did not like having to give feedback, receiving feedback from peers was one of their favorite parts of the peer review process. For instance, Lily expressed enthusiasm towards receiving comments: "I cannot wait to turn to the back and see how people think of my paper." While this enthusiasm is understandable, Takai from Japan revealed the continued inequality in this part of the peer review process: "My favorite part is to get the knowledge, the English knowledge by the American student. Especially, I don't have a, the much idioms, or American sayings, American proverb." Here, Takai is depicting himself as a passive receiver, receiving knowledge from the knowing NES student he is interacting with. This inferior positioning has problematic effects when NNES students are asked to give feedback, as detailed in the previous section.

All students were not as enthusiastic as Lily and Takai about receiving feedback. For instance, Naomi from Japan said one feedback form "was so harsh . . . this author [of the comments] was basically rambling, ranting . . . and not like really nice comments" and she was "really disappointed, discouraged." According to Naomi, no one would be so negative in Japan.

Michael from Ghana, referring to a peer review session, shared a similar experience when expressing his thoughts towards some fellow reviewers: "After I had written something nice about you, why should you give me such a mean . . . marks on my paper, that's why I feel very bad about myself." Michael and the other two Ghanaian students interviewed seemed more resistant to critical feedback from the NES US students than others. This is likely because they were educated in English throughout their life and claimed the NES label for themselves. However, as Immaculée Harushimana has written, Africanized forms of English may be treated as error-ridden and inferior because they are different from those found in places like the US and the UK. It appears that the Ghanaian students interviewed here were facing similar difficulties because they had confidence in their academic English but were told by peers that their English was not good.

NNES Advantage

While the previous discussion centered on the problems relating to NNES students giving feedback, NNES students have the potential to be more helpful peer reviewers than their NES counterparts. For example, Zhu discovered that NNES reviewers were just as likely to provide written global feedback as their NES peers ("Mixed Peer" 268). In the present study, a few NES students recognized NNES students' ability to provide content-based feedback. One student wrote, "I actually found the native speaker to be more helpful with grammar while the non-native speakers were better able to connect to the piece and be a true 'reader' not just 'editor.'" Under this student's assessment, the NNES students are doing exactly what we as teachers want them to do, responding to essays as readers and providing content-based feedback. Another student seconded this view by writing that the NNES reviewer was "helpful in development of ideas, but not so much with grammar." These comments show the great value that well-trained NNES speakers can bring to the peer review sessions.

Only a couple of NNES students explicitly discussed giving grammar-based feedback; the rest gave either content-based feedback or mostly positive feedback. Dafina from Albania viewed giving feedback as giving advice, not criticism: "More kind of like advice or something. Just how they can improve their paper, just adding new stuff and taking out some of the old one." Daniel from Bulgaria similarly focused on content-based feedback: "I'm just trying to focus on the things that they can just add or something, or how can they support their argument, their point. Just their argument, I'm just trying to focus on, like introduction, and stuff." For some, this focus stemmed from an awareness of the language inequality. Kim from Vietnam explained, "I worry that my grammar is not good so I don't want to give grammar recommendations . . . I'm going to just give on content," while Lorina from Bulgaria said straightforwardly, "I'm not supposed to give the American students here grammar."

DISCUSSION

As evident by the data presented in the previous section, many NNES students enter peer review with NES students with trepidation. This is certainly due in part to the expectation, supported by discourses of native speakerism, that NES peers are considered possessors of English and therefore the ultimate authorities concerning its use. This anxiety and unequal power hierarchy often serve to silence NNES voices in peer review groups by creating the belief that they are incapable of giving feedback to NES peers. As a result, the likelihood of ZPD activation in linguistically diverse peer review groups may be limited because of students' perception that one group is superior to the other. On one hand, and this was revealed in the above-referenced comments, NNES students may reach higher levels of development because they feel they are working with "more capable peers." On the other hand, revealed by comments in both this study and Braine's study, NES students may perceive their NNES peers as inferior and fail to develop as a result. In order to better promote ZPD activation and the subsequent success of linguistically diverse peer review groups, I have developed strategies that build on the strengths of NNES students and limit the negative influences of native speakerism.

The first strategy aims to prepare students to give and receive feedback more collaboratively. It is generally agreed upon that collaborative feedback, in which reader and writer work together to produce meaning, leads to the most effective peer review comments and the best revisions (Brammer and Rees; Lockhart and Ng; Mangelsdorf and Schlumberger; Nelson and Murphy). However, as revealed in previous research and by the student comments in the project discussed here, it is also the least common type of feedback. For instance, the writers in Wei Zhu's study on linguistically diverse peer review elicited feedback minimally, and in the case of an NES writer in Zhu's study, generally. The only two eliciting comments that this student provided were "Okay, go ahead, tear my paper apart" and "What did you guys think?" (266). In a similar vein, comments from students in my study along with the findings of Rysdam and Johnson-Shull reveal that the readers often think of themselves as editors, feeling the need to focus on telling the writer what was wrong with her paper. This becomes especially problematic in the case of linguistically diverse peer review groups because an NNES student may feel uncomfortable giving feedback to an NES, who is viewed as superior when it comes to English knowledge. If students work collaboratively, there will be less discomfort resulting from this hierarchy because one student is not expected to tell another student what is wrong; rather, they are expected to work together to formulate suggestions for revision.

In order to increase collaboration in peer review, it is important to train students to play active, collaborative roles. Stanley reported that trained students provided more comments overall and collaborative and questioning responses increased from .7% of comment totals to 8% and 6% respectively. In training my students to enter more collaborative roles, I share the four peer review roles in Charles Lockhart and Peggy Ng's study while workshopping a paper as a class, and have students model the different types of comments (see Table 2 for these roles). Then, for the first peer review, I meet with groups individually like Zhu, Ching, Corbett, and Corbett, Serenita, Gruessner, Brown, and Gordon have done, training them on how to work collaboratively to formulate feedback ("Training"). These group meetings focus on getting the writer to play a more active role in the peer review process because my experience confirms the findings of Zhu's study in that writers tend to elicit feedback minimally and superficially (i.e., "tear my paper apart") ("Mixed Peer" 266). For instance, when a peer makes a comment that is generic or needs more clarification, I push the writer to ask for more specific feedback. If necessary, I formulate a statement for the writer to use to elicit more feedback and have them repeat it after me. It can be an awkward process, but the students often need such specific guidance. During the training process, I also emphasize the importance of content-based feedback, explaining that all students are equally capable of providing this type of feedback and that it is the most valued feedback in peer review sessions.

While training students to work more collaboratively helps address discomfort felt by NNES students in giving NES students feedback, hybridizing

TABLE 2   Lockhart and Ng's Peer Review Stances

Stance	Description
Authoritative	The reader dominates and directs the discussion while viewing the session's purpose as the "transmission of knowledge" (617).
Interpretative	The reader gives her personal reaction of both the good and bad aspects of the piece; however, although to a lesser extent than the authoritative reader, the interpretative reader still controls the discussion (620–24).
Probing	The reader asks questions to discover the writer's purpose and meaning. The discourse is more give and take as neither side truly controls it (626–28).
Collaborative	According to Lockhart and Ng, "Collaborative readers negotiate with the writer to discover the writer's intention and build meanings" (628). As with probing, the communication here is dual sided and open (632).

the peer review process by adding an online component helps further ease discomfort by addressing two problems: difficulty in providing critical feedback to another student's face and the time constraints placed on slower readers to read and respond quickly. As revealed by the student comments in this study, NNES students may take longer to read and develop feedback than their NES counterparts. In traditional peer review, this is a problem because a student may feel rushed to complete if her peer finishes reading significantly more quickly. Similarly, researchers like Ruiling Lu and Linda Bol have found that some students may be less comfortable than others in giving critical feedback to one's face. Both of these problems can contribute to a decline in the quality of feedback that emerges from peer review interactions.

In response to these issues, I have found it useful to have students read each other's work and provide initial feedback by first exchanging their essays in an online space, such as a course management system like Blackboard or on a course Wiki. When using a course management system like Blackboard, I create discussion threads for each peer review group, with the header message including specific instructions on how to post and how to respond to other students. In order to ensure participation by all students, it is important that the online component counts significantly towards students' grades (such as 5–10% of their essay grade). While participation in the first round may not be perfect as students get used to the process, I have found that this changes with subsequent peer reviews. . . .

Adding an online component gives students the time they need to read through papers and develop feedback for the writer. Similarly, while this hybridization does not completely anonymize the process, creating a certain distance between reader and writer can make the writer more comfortable in providing critical feedback. While Lu and Bol found that students conducting peer review anonymously online provided the most feedback and helped their peers improve their writing more than non-anonymous groups, I prefer non-anonymous peer review so that there is still a face-to-face component. Having students meet face-to-face after providing online commentary gives them the opportunity to further develop the online feedback collaboratively as both readers and writers are able to ask each other questions and clarify their feedback.

CONCLUSION

Research has shown that hierarchies constructed by native speakerist ideologies can have negative effects on the success of linguistically diverse peer review. In order to fully activate the ZPD, students need to be confident in their own and their peers' abilities to provide useful suggestions for revision, which means giving students enough time to develop feedback and helping minimize discomfort caused by providing critical feedback. Moreover, students need to play an active role in formulating feedback regarding their own writing so that they can value the feedback produced in peer review sessions because it is truly a collaborative project. By training students to work collaboratively and by hybridizing peer review, teachers can take important steps to make linguistically diverse peer review more successful, helping students lead each other to higher levels of development as promised by the theory of the ZPD.

NOTES

1. While I find the labels NES and NNES problematic in that they are associated with a hierarchy that situates L2 learners as inferior, I will use them in this chapter since I am directly addressing and challenging the inequality constructed by these labels.

2. These functions were divided into reader and writer roles. The writer language functions included pointing, advising, announcing, reacting, eliciting, questioning, elaborating, hedging, confirming, and justifying. The writer language functions included responding, eliciting, and clarifying (Zhu, "Interaction" 192–3).

3. This study was approved by and conducted in accordance with the requirements of the University's IRB board. All students signed consent forms before participating. All names are pseudonyms to protect the identity of the University and the study participants.

4. The Ghanian students were an exception because they named English as their first language. However, they possessed an English that was different enough from US English to classify them as non-native speakers of US English for the purposes of this study.

WORKS CITED

Berg, Cathrine Essy. "The Effects of Trained Peer Response on ESL Students' Revision Types and Writing Quality." *Journal of Second Language Writing* 8.3 (1999): 215–41. Print.

Braine, George. "ESL Students in First-Year Writing Courses: ESL Versus Mainstream Classes." *Journal of Second Language Writing* 5.2 (1996): 91–107. Print.

Brammer, Charlotte, and Mary Rees. "Peer Review from the Students' Perspective: Invaluable or Invalid?" *Composition Studies* 35.2 (2007): 71–85. Print.

Butler, Yuko Goto. "How Are Non-native-English-Speaking Teachers Perceived by Young Learners?" *TESOL Quarterly* 41.4 (2007): 731–55. Print.

Carson, Joan, and Gayle Nelson. "Writing Groups: Cross-Cultural Issues. *Journal of Second Language Writing* 3 (1994): 17–30. Print.

Elbow, Peter. "A Method for Teaching Writing." *College English* 30.2 (1968): 115–25. Print.

Harushimana, Immaculée. "Colonial Language Writing Identities in Postcolonial Africa." *Reinventing Identities in Second Language Writing*. Ed. Michelle Cox, Jay Jordan, Christina Ortmeier-Hooper, and Gwen Grey Schwartz. Urbana, IL: NCTE, 2010. 207–31. Print.

Holliday, Adrian. *The Struggle to Teach English as an International Language*. Oxford: Oxford UP, 2005. Print.

Kubota, Ryuko. "Discursive Construction of the Images of U.S. Classrooms." *TESOL Quarterly* 35.1 (2001): 9–38. Print.

Litowitz, Bonnie E. "Deconstruction in the Zone of Proximal Development: A Revolutionary Experience." *Contexts for Learning: Sociocultural Dynamics in Children's Development*. Ed. E. Forman, N. Minick, and C.A. Stone. Oxford: Oxford UP, 1993. 184–96. Print.

Lu, Ruiling, and Linda Bol. "A Comparison of Anonymous Versus Identifiable e-Peer Review on College Student Writing Performance and the Extent of Critical Feedback." *Journal of Interactive Online Learning* 6.2 (2007): 100–15. Print.

Lockhart, Charles, and Peggy Ng. "Analyzing Talk in Peer Response Groups: Stances, Functions, and Content." *Language Learning* 45 (1995): 605–55. Print.

Mackey, Alison, and Susan M. Gass. *Second Language Research: Methodology and Design*. Mahwah, NJ: Lawrence Erlbaum Associates, 2005. Print.

Mangelsdorf, Kate. "Peer Reviews in the ESL Composition Classroom: What Do the Students Think?" *ELT Journal* 46 (1992): 274–84. Print.

Mangelsdorf, Kate, and Ann Schlumberger. "ESL Student Response Stances in a Peer Review Task." *Journal of Second Language Writing* 1.3 (1992): 235–54. Print.

Marsh, George E., and John J. Ketterer. "Situating the Zone of Proximal Development." *Online Journal of Distance Learning Administration* 8.2 (2005): n. pag. Web. 21 Dec. 2012.

Matsuda, Paul Kei, and Tony Silva. "Cross-Cultural Composition: Mediated Integration of US and International Students." *Composition Studies* 27.1 (1999): 15–30. Print.

Min, Hui-Tzu. "The Effects of Trained Peer Review on EFL Students' Revision Types and Writing Quality." *Journal of Second Language Writing* 15 (2006): 118–41. Print.

Murau, Andrea. "Shared Writing: Students' Perceptions and Attitudes of Peer Review." *Working Papers in Educational Linguistics* 9.2 (1993): 71–79. Print.

Murray, Donald. "Finding Your Own Voice: Teaching Composition in an Age of Dissent." *College Composition and Communication* 20.2 (1969): 118–23. Print.

Nelson, Gayle L. and John M. Murphy. "An L2 Writing Group: Task and Social Dimensions." *Journal of Second Language Writing* 1.3 (1992): 171–93. Print.

Stanley, Jane. "Coaching Student Writers to be Effective Peer Evaluators." *Journal of Second Language Writing* 1 (1992): 217–33. Print.

Thomas, Jacinta. "Voices From the Periphery: Non-native Teachers and Issues of Credibility." *Non-Native Educators in English Language Teaching*. Ed. George Braine. Mahwah, NJ: Lawrence Erlbaum Associates, 1999. 5–13. Print.

Timmis, Ivor. "Native-Speaker Norms and International English: A Classroom View." *ELT Journal* 56.3 (2002): 240–49. Print.

Vygotsky, Lev S. *Mind in Society: The Development of Higher Psychological Processes*. Cambridge, MA: Harvard UP, 1978. Print.

Zhu, Wei. "Effects of Training for Peer Response on Students' Comments and Interaction." *Written Communication* 12.4 (1995): 492–528. Print.

———. "Interaction and Feedback in Mixed Peer Response Groups." *Journal of Second Language Writing* 10.4 (2001): 251–76. Print.

17 Learning Disability and Response-Ability: Reciprocal Caring in Developmental Peer Response Writing Groups and Beyond

STEVEN J. CORBETT

W hat does it mean to be responsible, to work hard and smart, to struggle, to persevere? If these terms, often called "intangibles," sound like words used more frequently in sports than in writing and composition studies, then let's quickly take a look at the *Framework for Success in Postsecondary Writing* (2011) developed by representatives from the Council of Writing Program Administrators, the National Council of Teachers of English, and the National Writing Project. The eight umbrella "habits of mind essential for success in college writing" are meant to be cross-disciplinary, perhaps even transdisciplinary, learning principles: curiosity, openness, engagement, creativity, persistence, responsibility, flexibility, and metacognition. And while readers can probably map these terms onto the people and events I report on throughout this article, that is not my main purpose here. Nor is it to grapple too broadly with a literature review of learning disability (LD) and the teaching of writing scholarship. Others have done a much better job of that than I could (see, e.g., Dunn [1995] 2011; Lewiecki-Wilson and Brueggemann 2008; Snyder et al. 2002). My overarching purpose in this article is to attempt to render the compelling stories of the participants in as vivid and trustworthy (Bishop 1999) a manner as possible. All references to the "habits of mind" and to the literature on connections between LD students and the teaching of writing follow from this storytelling attempt.

During ongoing research in course-based peer tutoring (see, e.g., Corbett 2002, 2005, 2011; Corbett et al. 2010) at my former institution, Southern Connecticut State University, I left my researcher's curiosity open just long enough to get to know an amazing group of colleagues, two of whom identify as LD. My study involved recruiting exemplary students from a first-year composition stretch course to be course-based peer tutors in subsequent sections of the

From *Pedagogy: Critical Approaches to Teaching Literature, Language, Composition, and Culture*, vol. 15, no. 3, Special Issue, Fall 2015.

course. In the past, such topics as race (Corbett et al. 2010) and instructional method—especially the nuances of directive/interventionist and nondirective/noninterventionist instructional strategies (Corbett 2005, 2011)—have emerged, causing me to focus subsequent inquiry on such issues. While I originally intended to further my study of directive/nondirective tutoring strategies, I also went in eyes wide open. And I am happy I did. In this qualitative study I treaded previous research ground in designing and writing institutional review board applications and supporting materials, in imagining possible ethical issues, and so forth. But I was still not fully prepared for the challenging questions surrounding ethos, logos, and pathos all qualitative field researchers in writing studies must face (Mortensen and Kirsch 1996).[1] As I began to observe and interview the participants in this case study, I quickly became engaged in not only the fascination stirred up by their unique stories but also the problematics involved in the ethics of representation.

This article is thus intended to provide readers with a pertinent study that frames and enhances the focus on participant stories. The first part engages arguments involving connections between LD and typical basic writing students. I offer peer review and response groups as a locus for those connections. In the second part, I narrate the sorts of ethical choices that emerged as I began to focus on the participants in this study, the instructor Mya, tutor Sara, and student Max. I describe the interactions of all three participants as they worked together, and with other students, in two peer review and response sessions. As Andrea Greenbaum claims, "There is still a scholarship-gap in addressing, in realistic and practical terms, how we include these [LD] students into our classrooms" (2010: 41). The third part provides a more intimate gaze into the backgrounds and experiences of all three participants. There I hope to offer readers a sense of just how compelling and unexpected the participant stories proved to be, behind the scenes and beyond the classroom.

And it is all of the major players' voices in this study/story that I would like for readers to hear as loudly and clearly as possible. Patricia Dunn advocates the study/story approach explicitly in relation to the value of LD students telling their own life stories when she writes,

> It should go without saying that the personal experience of our students matters, that what they say about themselves is credible, that their stories are true, that what they know about the way they learn, what they must do as they read, write and study, is informed by years of life experience. . . . Young people's versions of their experiences should be just as valid as the version given by the most credentialed among us. ([1995] 2011: 97)

It is in the synergistic reporting of our actions, thoughts, certainties, and uncertainties that, we hope, readers will gain the most intimate sense of the importance of including LD (and all "othered") students in the same experience of dynamic teaching, learning, and critical refection—the potential for reciprocal caring—that exists in the truly peer-centered writing classroom.

MORE IS MORE IN THE DEVELOPMENTAL WRITING CLASSROOM

Should LD students receive more institutionally sanctioned time, attention, and pedagogical care than mainstream students, especially if they are also in basic writing courses? In "Learning Disabilities and the Writing Center" (1994), Julie Neff claims that students with various LDs require more and longer appointments—or more time and attention. Kimber Barber-Fendley and Chris Hamel (2004) agree and, echoing an argument made by Jonathan Kozol (2005: 59) involving minority students and students from lower socioeconomic classes, assert that "LD scholars should boldly, assertively declare students with LD will receive alternate assistance, special treatment, unique opportunities, singular advantages that mainstream students will not receive" (Barber-Fendley and Hamel 2004: 532). However, the authors further argue that it is impossible to establish a neutral or equal playing field for LD students in the writing classroom. Instead, they propose alternate assistance programs that provide supplemental instructional resources *outside* of class. They argue that supplemental instruction conducted outside of the classroom can better support LD students' privacy and dignity.

In "Discourses of Disability and Basic Writing" (2008) Amy Vidali questions Barber-Fendley and Hamel's claim that LD students should be separated from the writing classroom, especially the basic writing classroom, for additional support. Vidali argues, rather, that similarities abound between LD and basic writing students: they are both talked about in terms of difficulty and overcoming deficits, they often share identities and classrooms, and both are "defined according to a dominant (white, male, abled) other" (53). Vidali urges us to do what we can to unify basic writing and LD pedagogy. She believes that LD students would then benefit from the structural support systems afforded basic writers in all their various diversities. This integrative belief also echoes the argument made by Mark Mossman (2002) that, for LD students, classroom environments need to be places where they can claim power and equality through what he posits as a process of "authentification." This process occurs, Mossman explains, "when disability is understood as 'normal,' and in our classrooms this process of normalization happens only when we allow our students, all of them, to speak, to fully participate in the discussion, when we give them, all of them, a normalized status" (656).[2] So what might possibly be one of the strongest instructional authentifcation support systems available for the individual student writer at just about any sociocognitive level or ability?

The argument for more focused tutorial attention for students who may be categorized as "nonmainstream," "developmental," or "basic" offers a place to begin thinking about the sorts of connections called for by Vidali and Mossman. For example, scholars argue that, when it comes to such cognitively and socially complex reciprocal teaching-learning (caring) situations as peer review and response, we need a better understanding of how various groups of students perform (Corbett et al. 2014; Harris 1992; Spigelman and Grobman 2005). Attempting to understand the nuances of peer review and response with LD and basic writing students is well worth the effort. According to Shari Harrison (2011), the same collaborative learning theories that undergird the use of peer response groups in all writing courses can be especially beneficial to LD students. She claims, "Such social learning experiences promote group construction of knowledge, and allow students to observe each other's models of successful learning and encourage emulation" (176; also see Dunn [1995] 2011: 104, 128–29, 174; Johnston and Doyle 2011: 58). A collaborative learning environment where students see examples of various degrees of ability (inter)-enacted day-to-day can lead to increased learning performance gains. Further, each of the three LD students interviewed in Dunn's study explained that they were (often much) better at orally demonstrating their understanding of material than reading or writing about it. There appears to be a valuable pedagogical connection here between the oral/conversational acts involved with collaborative group work, including peer review and response, and facility with course material and communicative performances. Dunn argues: "For most students, it is especially important that small-group discussions and *peer response* be incorporated into the writing class" (174, emphasis added).

Course-based peer tutoring—where guided peer review and response often takes center stage—may provide a means for instructional unification between LD and basic writing pedagogies. Granted, writing centers have long existed to support the sundry needs of the individual learner. But other tutorial support systems, such as course-based tutoring and supplemental instruction (see Spigelman and Grobman 2005; Stone and Jacobs 2006), ideally take the best of collaborative learning theory—from the classroom and the center—and bring them on location where students, teachers, and tutors work elbow-to-elbow, day in and day out, on improving their writing performances and products, while practicing and developing other important communicative social skills as well.

THE ETHICS OF PRACTICING AND REPORTING ON-LOCATION VISIBILITY

In the fall of 2009, during one of my visits to a classroom to observe and record the interactions between the tutor Sara, instructor Mya, and students during a peer review and response session, I witnessed an amazing moment that immediately piqued my interest.

I noticed one student in particular, Max, having a visibly tough time understanding what he was supposed to be doing, while his two peer group partners seemed to be experiencing no trouble at all. The peer tutor, Sara, who was circulating around the room, saw that Max was having trouble. "I noticed Max looking nervous over in his seat so I went over to see what I could help him with. His partners, Kim and Adrianne, already had their computers set up and were starting the assignment. Max wasn't as far along. He hadn't even logged into the computer," she later said. Sara spent much of the remaining class session helping him get on track with the multiple organizational and communicative tasks students needed to negotiate during this peer review and response session: working with online files, following the response guidelines and instructions, and reading and offering feedback to his group members.

As Mya circulated the room, she went over to Max's group. Max groggily said "I'm tired today, the weather." Sara continued to good-naturedly and patiently help him navigate the review process. She turned to his two group members at one point for help. Kim came over to help out, succeeded, and then moved back to her computer. At one point, Max deeply sighed and Kim chipped in a tip on commenting. Max said "yeah, yeah, yeah" in relief. A few minutes later, Max said to Sara that he is "falling apart" and "can't concentrate." She continued trying to coach him on how to handle things.

After class, Max came up to me, we said hi, and then he just stood there for a second. I asked how he is doing. He told me that he is not feeling all that well and that he is having a hard time with this peer review. We chatted a little more before he left for his next class.

During this entire visit, I noticed how patient and caring Sara was with Max. And I started to think that there was something very important taking place here. But, as I have in previous research with "other(ed)" student populations (see Corbett et al. 2010), I also began to wonder about the ethics of research with LD students. I especially worried about the implications of reporting my observations of LD students in action. The tension between wanting to provide LD students with the best possible individualized instruction and not wanting to single them out too much—and this same idea in relation to the ethics of reporting research with LD students—has warranted some important discussion among LD scholars. Georgina Kleege (2002) illustrates her ambivalence regarding this tension with a story of an undergraduate student in one of her fiction-writing classes who came out about his LD. Kleege and the student argued issues of identity politics and the question of non-LD people writing about LD people: "'I hate the way they always want us to be inspirational,' he said. I wanted to caution him against divisive generalizations and thought of asking, 'Can we really say *always*?' But in this instance I found myself on his side of the divide, so I said, 'I hate it, too'" (313).

This question of how we represent nonmainstream students in our research reporting struck me right from the moment I started noticing Max's discomfort during my visit. Because I did not know Max very well yet, because I had traveled down the potentially slick path of the ethics of representation before, and because I knew not to jump to conclusions this early in the research, I decided not to make too much out of this one observation. But it really got the study/storytelling wheels spinning in my mind. I started to wonder about the idea of Max being visibly singled out in class. In "Constructing a Third Space" (2002), James C. Wilson and Cynthia Lewiecki-Wilson address similar situations, observing that LD students just want to be treated like everyone else. The authors' argument on this point, importantly, applies to both the issue of LD student visibility in the classroom and to the problem of ethics in reporting on LD student research: "While there is no single answer to this dilemma, teachers need to reflect on ways they might acknowledge and creatively accommodate differences without turning a disabled student into an object, a token representative, or a victim. Such acknowledgment requires flexibility on the part of instructors, who need to learn to understand that disabled students themselves hold a range of views and levels of comfort in identifying as disabled" (300). As my research progressed into a later classroom observation, and later still as I began to interview and follow up with the participants in depth, I came to hear interpretations and points of view that made me reconsider my initial concerns about Max being singled out.

Dunn ([1995] 2011) further illustrates the desire to understand what LD students themselves think about the tension between their explicit acknowledgment of disability in the classroom and just blending in or "bootstrapping" their way through. She reports on an extensive interview with Nick, an undergraduate LD student who in high school had resisted going to the resource room that he tellingly called the "reject room," choosing instead to remain in a regular classroom until his junior year in high school. When Dunn asked Nick if he had any specific dos and don'ts for writing instructors regarding LD students, he replied that "probably the number one don't would be to look at them differently—because a student usually is uncomfortable with their disability anyway, and any time a teacher almost looks down upon them and says, 'You don't have to do this quality of work because you have a disability,' that, in my mind, says that they don't think that we can do the work, so therefore they're not making us do the work" (105). In some ways, then, Max's anxiety during my initial observation—and, importantly, the way Mya, Sara, and his group partners reacted to his difficulties—could be viewed as natural reactions to any student having trouble with any given classroom activity. Since Mya and Sara were both available to any student showing signs of needing extra help, the fact that Max needed some extra attention on that particular day, with that particular activity, was perhaps not out of the ordinary. The idea that this was just one instance of a student needing help and not necessarily being singled out was verified later during my second observational visit.

During a visit one month later, I noticed both Max and his peer response partners taking on much more interactive collaborative roles. Max, today, seemed in much better shape—no visible worries, and so on. I noticed that, rather than frequently asking Sara for help, he seemed to be much more involved with his two partners. In contrast to what I witnessed during my earlier visit, Max seemed to have a good grasp of what he was supposed to be doing. He asked his partners a question, and they helped him; they asked him questions, and he helped them.

Sara gives her impressions of her involvement with Max and his group members in this second peer review session: "Like always, Max was right on track with what he was supposed to do. He was just double-checking that he was up to speed. I looked at Max's work and realized he was very ahead of the game."

Again, my observations confirm Sara's impressions that, while Max certainly takes advantage of Sara's uniquely beneficial presence, he does not demand any more energy from her than any other student in the class. Vidali's claim that basic writing LD and non-LD students should be interacting and learning in the same milieus was gaining serious traction in my mind. Later, I would find out, however, that Sara did actually feel a special connection with Max and did feel a certain impetus to help him as best she could.

DEEPER QUESTIONS, DEEPER STORIES: PARTICIPANTS' POINTS OF VIEW

Student Max

When I later began interviewing Max and Sara, the emerging stories proved more compelling than I had first imagined. Rather than talking solely about his learning struggles, Max also divulged his social struggles with trying to make friends. Max is an accounting major. He told me that he really appreciated the attention he received from Sara, his group members, and Mya. He said he especially appreciated Kim's help. He told me that his mom is a teacher's aide and frequently helps him with his homework assignments. As Max began to compare his experiences in high school with college, I began to hear a moving, throat-lumping testimonial regarding his experiences as an autistic student in high school.

He told me that his disability involved trouble with speech and language and that he did not speak until he was five years old.[3] He felt like he had a tough time connecting with his peers in high school and that he never had attention from and bonding with his peers, while he feels his college professors treat him more like an adult. He also said that there are many more group projects in college than in high school and that he likes that much more. He told me about the time he "overcame" one of his biggest struggles by forcing himself to read in the summer after eighth grade in preparation for his freshman year of high school. He spoke of special education classes where other students were "unstable," causing him to have trouble learning. He said he had a tough time concentrating and that he was sensitive to loud noises, afraid of telephones, and so forth.

Max also talked about specific teachers, such as a sixth grade teacher in the resource room who was arrogant and would yell at him (recall Nick naming it the "reject room" above). Max said "she was crazy." He went on to talk about a history teacher in his sophomore year of high school who was "ignorant of him and not a very nice person" and made fun of him outside of class to the teacher's other classes. Max said this teacher "said very resentful things to the class as a whole."

Max described how he has trouble with writing prompts and does not do well with standardized tests like the SAT. He said that he does not think it is fair that students with LDs have to take and pass those tests. He feels, rather, that they are far too time-consuming and that a better indication of any student's intelligence is how hard they work. Regarding the SAT and ACT, he said, "It's hurting a lot of people, especially those with learning disabilities."[4] He feels that in college he is better able to advocate for himself; he has become more independent and relies on the campus Disability Resource Center only for paperwork to give to his instructors asking for extended times for test taking. He said he was given the option by Mya to move from English 110 to English 112, but he chose to go to the intermediary English 111 instead because he wants to eventually "kick butt in English 112!" He said that while he feels he is getting much stronger in so many things with his writing, he believes all the constant practice with planning and revising is making him so much better.

At this point I told him that I had no more questions and that we could stop. He gently interrupted, saying that he wanted to reemphasize something:

> In grammar school I didn't have a lot of friends. I knew a lot of people and my classmates seemed to like me, but I only had one close friend in grammar school. I had some trouble fitting in with my peers in middle school and high school. . . . I had an easier time socializing with adults than with kids because I've got nothing to say if they are going to say something immature. I always felt very quiet in the cafeteria where I didn't have a lot in common with their conversations.

My time with Max reinforced my belief in the importance of the sort of "habits of mind" Max's education forced him to develop. He had to sustain his engagement by staying persistent, even in the midst of social circumstances that seemed to work against him. Max had to learn to take responsibility for whom he could trust. When I first saw Max interacting with Sara and his group members, I think he was still developing that trust. By the time I saw him in action during my second visit, he seemed to have realized that trust. He stayed open enough to let trustworthy people in. And he had the meta-cognitive wherewithal to share his story with us.

Tutor Sara

Things proved even more interesting when I interviewed Sara. At the time of our interview she was a nursing major who intended to transfer to the University of Connecticut in Storrs. She felt her involvement as a course-based tutor for the class went "different, but better than I thought it would." She thought it was wonderful that students had the option of asking either her or Mya questions during classroom activities. She also felt she was able to engage with students on a personal as well as academic level. She said that if she could give other course-based tutors any advice, it would be not to be too worried or hesitant to approach and interact with students. She felt that in the first few weeks she did not want to bother or interfere too much, but then she started to realize that students really appreciated her attention. Sara said she felt her experiences as a student in English 110 the term just prior to this one prepared her well for her role as a course-based tutor because Mya worked with students just as much on general skills for succeeding in college as on their writing skills. She admitted that, while peer review helped prepare her for her tutoring role, she tried harder when helping students with peer review for this course than she did as a "student" in the previous course. On working with Max, she understood that he might need a little more help and attention. She said that he was very hard on himself but that he was willing to call on her for help. As the course went on, she was pleased to see how he "loosened up and started to talk to everyone and ask peers for help."

I was actually surprised and intrigued to find out that Sara also has an LD (dyslexia), though a much less noticeable one than Max's, that she "works very hard to overcome." She said:

> Throughout my grade school years I was kept separate from all my other classmates because of my disability. When I reached seventh grade I was allowed to go into normal math, history, and science classes. I found it very difficult at first learning with many other students in the room. I also found it very hard to interact with the other students. Over time I got comfortable with the new environment. When [the professor] asked me to participate I was very nervous, but I knew this was a once in a life-time opportunity so I had to take it.

She intimated that when she talked to her mom about becoming a peer tutor, her mom actually laughed in disbelief. And Sara said that, even though English has always been hard and a struggle for her, "I've never been ashamed of my disability."

But I was really struck to find out that Sara had to deal with another "dis" in her social and personal life: a rather dysfunctional home life with a pair of alcoholic parents, two older sisters, and a younger brother. She told me the story of her life spent balancing taking care of her parents, looking after her little brother and herself, and trying to do well in her studies:

> Overall both my parents are alcoholics. My mother has been a nonfunc-tioning alcoholic for over twelve years. My dad has been a functioning alcoholic for about ten years but in the past year he has also turned to a nonfunctioning alcoholic. I have three siblings and we are very close. We help each other get through our parents' issues. . . . I have overcome my parents' problem and have focused on making a good, happy life for myself.

Sara also wrote a more impressionistic version of her family's experiences in her "This I Believe" paper for her subsequent English course. While there is not room here to reiterate her essay in its entirety, I could not help but be struck especially by her final paragraph:

> As the years went on and I entered adulthood my family is very different. Unfortunately there are no longer six people at our family dinner. The par-ents who taught their children family comes first have forgotten this lesson even though their children still remember. My three siblings and I still gather around the table for family dinner when we can. Put any plans we have aside until our family time is over. The moral our parents taught us has stayed with us even though they have forgotten it for now.

When I asked Sara if she'd be willing to be a course-based peer tutor again, she said "absolutely." She feels this experience has made her a **better** writer and an all-around more confident student, expanding her comfort level with English and with helping others in general. She said she especially loved working with Mya. Sara told me about the final day of class. Her words illustrate the sense of community and camaraderie that had developed through fifteen weeks of intensely close collaboration:

> Today we had a party for our last day of class. If the students wanted to, they were asked to bring a food that meant something to them. This tied back to their first paper when they wrote about a food that meant something to them. Many of the students participated. Max brought Thai tapioca pudding, and he brought a copy of the recipe for all the students to take home. . . . It was amazing to see Max interacting with all the students. They were including him in the conversation and you could hear the joy in his voice.

Like Max, Sara embraces her role in her story of an overall successful experience. The interpersonal connections she made with Max and Mya, the way this entire experience made her reflect on her own disability and her deeply personal experiences coming to terms with her LD, and the way she used her sense of what it means to listen, care, persist—and to openly and confidently share her story with us—offer teachers a deeper view into what it means to listen, care, and persist in our best efforts toward inclusive teaching and learning.

Instructor Mya

Mya is an award-winning teacher with about ten years of teaching college English, two years of teaching high school, and fifteen years as a home educator prior to this case study. She particularly enjoys teaching English 110 because she believes that she "can see more progress from students in 110." She already had a "bond" with her tutor Sara, since they were together in English 110, and this familiarity allowed Sara to take a very active and highly informed role in assistant teaching for the course. She said Sara started off a little slowly at first, but very soon she felt that students started to warm up to Sara and really lean on her for questions and support. She would often help jump-start class discussions if students were initially silent. She felt that Sara was like a "life preserver" that she could throw out at any time in the classroom for *any* particular student who needed it. Although she did feel this class was stronger than usual in terms of their engagement, she very much appreciated having Sara to help circulate throughout the room and give more individual attention to others. She said that even though Sara did not say a lot in class all the time, she was very upbeat and always had wonderfully positive energy.

EMBRACING INSPIRATION: CONCLUSIONS

In the end, I believe the collaborative learning environment established by the close instructional partnership between Mya and Sara enabled *all* students in this basic writing course to experience learning to write and writing to learn at an optimal level. Max was not singled out in the course for his LD any more than any other student in the course (as a basic writer) was singled out, adding credence to Vidali's (2008) important argument. Max ended up being the only student in the course to earn an A. But he did not earn it because of or in spite of his LD. He earned it (as I imagine he might say) because he worked his butt off and—unlike many non-LD students we have all encountered— had the pride and work ethic to give it his best efforts. Further, Sara was not singled out to be a tutor because she had an LD. Rather, she was recruited by Mya for the same sorts of intangibles found in Max—many of the same intangibles we as a field (à la the *Framework*) want all of our students to develop and hone: curiosity, openness, engagement, creativity, persistence, responsibility, flexibility, and metacognition.

This poignant experience with two LD students is teaching me the true value of what it means to struggle, to persevere, and to make the most of what "others" of all backgrounds and abilities have to offer. Max continued to work hard through the remainder of his required English and writing courses and maintained an A average overall. He also reported to me that, for the first time, he earned an A in every one of his courses in the fall 2011 term. Sara went on to transfer to the University of Connecticut and is doing quite well there in her studies. Like Max, she maintained an A average in her English courses, at both universities, and she is currently applying to graduate schools at both.

In the spring of 2011, I asked Mya, Max, and Sara if they would join me in a campus presentation to talk a bit about their experiences with this project, and they all agreed. Mya reiterated much of what she shared above and also let us know how proud she is of both Max and Sara. Max summed up his struggles as an LD student who had always "hated English dearly" (to the chuckles of the Anglophile audience). He said that Sara would "help me understand what I was trying to write about. I would have felt more anxious without her there to help me." He also said, "I felt comfortable joining in on classroom conversations because I knew that no one there would ridicule me."

Yet despite the confidence and security that Max has experienced, we should consider one more ethical question: Max seems to be doing quite well in college, but will he be able to sustain these sociocognitive gains after he graduates? In the broadcast "For Adults with Autism, Few Support Options Past Age 21" (2011) Robert MacNeil reports on the fact that after the age of twenty-one federally subsidized educational support for LD students ends. Further, for the hundreds of thousands of autistic people, after age twenty-one few support programs are available. Hundreds of thousands of families must face the stark reality that full responsibility for the care and support of one of their precious members is now on them. Hopefully Max's (as well as Sara's) newfound and hard-won confidence and sense of responsibility will enable enough self-regulation to realize a safe, happy, and prosperous life. If Max continues to listen and to stay engaged, open, curious, self-critical, and reflective, perhaps he will continue to travel the admittedly difficult path of lifelong learning—a path both Sara and Max have set themselves up to travel as successfully as possible.[5]

It was the brief yet poignant words of Sara that really shook the crowd—maybe suggesting the path of self-regulation and lifelong learning Sara and Max are traveling—and with which I would like to end this article. Since that presentation, I have thought a lot about what it means to struggle and persevere to such a degree that you can eventually tell or hear your story comfortably and confidently and maybe, just maybe, become comfortable with the knowledge that that story has inspired someone and could potentially inspire more to pay attention and to care:

> At the beginning of this project I was extremely nervous. It was out of my comfort zone. I always struggled with English. As [the professor] said, I have a learning disability that pertains mainly to English. I was told all of pretty much growing up in elementary and high school that I was different and that English wasn't my strength and I needed to find something that had nothing to do with English. . . . So I went in very hesitant and nervous, and I didn't know how it was going to work out. But it ended up being the most wonderful educational experience I've ever encountered. It helped boost my self-esteem with English. It helped me be able to sit down with someone to give helpful advice, if I thought they could do something better with their writing. . . . I would have never thought that before I did this because I never thought I could do something with teaching another. It was something I was always told I would never be able to do. And now I have the confidence to do it.

NOTES

1. Several essays in Mortensen and Kirsch 1996 argue various positions on the ethics of reporting qualitative research, especially the idea of participant collaboration. Thomas Newkirk (1996: 14) asserts that researchers should take forthright and co-inquisitive steps during all phases of the research process, including being up-front with participants about the possibility that "bad" news might get reported and that participants should at least be given the opportunity to respond to problematic interpretations (see also Brueggemann 1996; Dale 1996; Williams 1996).

2. Also see Dunn [1995] 2011: 110, 163–64; compare with Lerita M. Coleman Brown's notion of the "destigmatization process" (2010) and Lennard J. Davis's "dismodernism" argument (2010). The concept of normalization in disability studies is a complicated one. Mossman's idea draws on Brown's claim that "stigmas will disappear when we no longer need to legitimize social exclusion and segregation" (2010: 189–90). For counterresponses to this conception of normalization, see especially Bell 2010 on race and disability and Davis 2010 on disability identity politics.

3. For a comprehensive and user-friendly source on the latest research and reporting on autism, see *PBS NewsHour's* Autism Now website (www.pbs.org/newshour/news/autism/); see also Gerstle and Walsh 2011 and Strauss 2010.

4. Of course, Max is not alone in his thoughts on standardized tests; see especially Colin Barnes and Geof Mercer (2011: 106), UK disability studies scholars who have argued against standardized testing in relation to disabled students.

5. When I asked Max what he thought about the manuscript for this article and if he had anything he wanted to add or if he wanted me to change anything, he wrote back (and I excerpt from his longer response): "Dear Dr. Corbett, I just wanted to let you know that I read your report and I really liked it! I was very emotionally touched by your written report. You give such a detailed description of the people that you wrote about, including me. I feel honored and respected to be a participant of your research. My time with [Mya], Sara, and Kim was one of the best learning experiences I have ever had. I was fortunate to start my college education with them to support me. I am glad that you care about the students at Southern, and you are an inspiration to me. I look at you as a hero that convinces people to never give up on their dreams to a brighter future."

WORKS CITED

Barber-Fendley, Kimber, and Chris Hamel. 2004. "A New Visibility: An Argument for Alternative Assistance Programs for Students with Learning Disabilities." *College Composition and Communication* 55.3: 504–35.

Barnes, Colin, and Geof Mercer. 2011. *Exploring Disability: A Sociological Introduction*, 2nd ed. Cambridge: Polity Press.

Bell, Chris. 2010. "Is Disability Studies Actually White Disability Studies?" In *The Disability Studies Reader*, 3rd ed., ed. Lennard J. Davis, 374–82. New York: Routledge.

Bishop, Wendy. 1999. *Ethnographic Writing Research: Writing It Down, Writing It Up, and Reading It.* Portsmouth, NH: Boynton/Cook.

Brown, Lerita M. Coleman. 2010. "Stigma: An Enigma Demystifed." In *The Disability Studies Reader*, 3rd ed., ed. Lennard J. Davis, 179–92. New York: Routledge.

Brueggemann, Brenda Jo. 1996. "Still-Life: Representations and Silences in the Participant-Observer Role." In Mortensen and Kirsch, *Ethics and Representation in Qualitative Studies of Literacy*, 17–39.

Corbett, Steven J. 2002. "The Role of the Emissary: Helping to Bridge the Communication Canyon between Instructors and Students." *Writing Lab Newsletter* 27.2: 10–11.

———. 2005. "Bringing the Noise: Peer Power and Authority, On Location." In Spigelman and Grobman, *On Location*, 101–11.

———. 2011. "Using Case Study Multi-methods to Investigate Close(r) Collaboration: Course-Based Tutoring and the Directive/Nondirective Instructional Continuum." *Writing Center Journal* 31.1: 55–81.

Corbett, Steven J., Michelle LaFrance, and Teagan Decker, eds. 2014. *Peer Pressure, Peer Power: Theory and Practice in Peer Review and Response for the Writing Classroom.* Southlake, TX: Fountainhead Press.

Corbett, Steven J., Sydney F. Lewis, and Madeleine M. Cliford. 2010. "Diversity Matters in Individualized Instruction: The Pros and Cons of Team Teaching and Talkin' That Talk." In *Diversity in the Composition Classroom*, ed. Gwendolyn Hale, Mike Mutschelknaus, and Thomas Alan Holmes, 85–96. Southlake, TX: Fountainhead Press.

Dale, Helen. 1996. "Dilemmas of Fidelity: Qualitative Research in the Classroom." In Mortensen and Kirsch, *Ethics and Representation in Qualitative Studies of Literacy*, 77–94.

Davis, Lennard J. 2010. "The End of Identity Politics: On Disability as an Unstable Category." In *The Disability Studies Reader*, 3rd ed., ed. Lennard J. Davis, 301–15. New York: Routledge.

Dunn, Patricia A. [1995] 2011. *Learning Re-abled: The Learning Disability Controversy and Composition Studies.* Portsmouth, NH: Heinemann-Boynton/Cook, http://wac.colostate.edu/books/dunn/.

Framework for Success in Postsecondary Writing. 2011. Council of Writing Program Administrators, National Council of Teachers of English, and National Writing Project, http://wpacouncil.org/framework.

Gerstle, Val, and Lynda Walsh, eds. 2011. *Autism Spectrum Disorders in the College Composition Classroom: Making Writing Instruction More Accessible for All Students.* Milwaukee, WI: Marquette University Press.

Greenbaum, Andrea. 2010. "Nurturing Difference: The Autistic Student in Professional Writing Programs." *Journal of the Assembly for Expanded Perspectives on Learning* 16: 40–47.

Harris, Muriel. 1992. "Collaboration Is Not Collaboration Is Not Collaboration: Writing Center vs. Peer Response Groups." *College Composition and Communication* 43: 369–83.

Harrison, Shari. 2011. "Creating a Successful Learning Environment for Postsecondary Students with Learning Disabilities: Policies and Practice." In *Teaching Study Strategies in Developmental Education: Readings on Theory, Research, and Best Practices*, ed. Russ Hodges, Michele L. Simpson, and Norman A. Stahl, 166–79. New York/Boston: Bedford/St. Martin's.

Johnston, Nancy, and Tina Doyle. 2011. "Inclusive Teaching: Perspectives of Students with Disabilities." *Open Words: Access and English Studies* 5.1: 53–60. www.pearsoncomppro.com/open_words_journal/index.php.

Kleege, Georgina. 2002. "Disabled Students Come Out: Questions without Answers." In Snyder et al., *Disability Studies*, 308–16.

Kozol, Jonathan. 2005. *The Shame of the Nation: The Restoration of Apartheid Schooling in America.* New York: Crown.

Lewiecki-Wilson, Cynthia, and Brenda Jo Brueggemann, eds. 2008. *Disability and the Teaching of Writing: A Critical Sourcebook.* New York/Boston: Bedford/St. Martin's.

MacNeil, Robert. 2011. "For Adults with Autism, Few Support Options Past Age 21," *Autism Now, PBS NewsHour*, 22 April, www.pbs.org/newshour/bb/health/jan-june11/autism5adults _04-22.html.

Mortensen, Peter, and Gesa E. Kirsch, eds. 1996. *Ethics and Representation in Qualitative Studies of Literacy*. Urbana, IL: National Council of Teachers of English.

Mossman, Mark. 2002. "Visible Disability in the College Classroom." *College English* 64.6: 645–59.

Neff, Julie. 1994. "Learning Disabilities and the Writing Center." In *Intersections: Theory-Practice in the Writing Center*, ed. Joan A. Mullin and Ray Wallace, 81–95. Urbana, IL: National Council of Teachers of English.

Newkirk, Thomas. 1996. "Seduction and Betrayal in Qualitative Research." In Mortensen and Kirsch, *Ethics and Representation in Qualitative Studies of Literacy*, 3–16.

Snyder, Sharon L., Brenda Jo Brueggemann, and Rosemarie Garland-Thomson, eds. 2002. *Disability Studies: Enabling the Humanities*. New York: Modern Language Association.

Spigelman, Candace, and Laurie Grobman. 2005. *On Location: Theory and Practice in Classroom-Based Writing Tutoring*. Logan: Utah State University Press.

Stone, Marion E., and Glen Jacobs. 2006. *Supplemental Instruction: New Visions for Empowering Student Learning*. San Francisco, CA: Jossey-Bass.

Strauss, Joseph N. 2010. "Autism as Culture." In *The Disability Studies Reader*, 3rd ed., ed. Lennard J. Davis, 535–59. New York: Routledge.

Vidali, Amy. 2008. "Discourses of Disability and Basic Writing." In Lewiecki-Wilson and Brueggemann, *Disability and the Teaching of Writing*, 40–55.

Williams, Cheri L. 1996. "Dealing with Data: Ethical Issues in Case Study Research." In Mortensen and Kirsch, *Ethics and Representation in Qualitative Studies of Literacy*, 40–57.

Wilson, James C., and Cynthia Lewiecki-Wilson. 2002. "Constructing a Third Space: Disability Studies, the Teaching of English, and Institutional Transformation." In Snyder et al., *Disability Studies*, 296–307.

PART FIVE

Writing Across the Curriculum and Writing in the Disciplines

Introduction to Part Five

The essays included in Part Five treat the close connections between becoming a stronger writer in disciplinary contexts and the opportunities afforded by peer response activities. Authors in this section discuss the benefits of using peer response feedback activities in courses that prepare students to write as scientists, engineers, and other disciplinary professionals, and the challenge presented by positioning students as respondents and reviewers when they are novices in their disciplines, unfamiliar with the content, rhetorical, and disciplinary conventions central to written work in their fields. Authors also foreground the importance of effective peer review design, noting that peer response activities need to be closely integrated with course goals and that students in disciplinary contexts particularly benefit from the coaching and facilitation of disciplinary faculty.

In our first selection, "A Model for Facilitating Peer Review in the STEM Disciplines" (2014), Katharine Brieger and Pam Bromley discuss the benefits of student-led workshops for graduate students in the fields of science, technology, engineering, and math. While writing is a prevalent component of courses in the sciences, peer review is less frequently encouraged, but Brieger and Bromley point out that students are positively affected by peer review experiences, and they "revise more fully, write stronger manuscripts, feel more empowered to interpret information, better understand complex processes, and better comprehend the scientific writing process and the importance of peer review in science" (p. 304 in this volume). Brieger and Bromley provide models for facilitating peer review sessions and discuss their observations over the evolution of these workshops.

The second selection, "Developing Authority in Student Writing through Written Peer Critique in the Disciplines" (2007), authored by Barbara Schneider and Jo-Anne Andre, explores the close relationships between student writing development and disciplinary expertise/authority. Focusing on the experiences of students in a second-year communications studies course, the authors note that asking students to compose written feedback is an important, but often missed, learning opportunity. Written peer response helps students value their experience as readers and develop a sense of "authorial presence" as they compose their feedback. While Schneider and Andre found that student comments often mimic the tone of instructors when giving feedback—a factor perhaps not surprising, according to the authors, as instructor feedback is such a familiar form of "commentary" for most students—students tend to include more personal voice in their comments, a means of developing voice, authority, and critical abilities.

The final selection in this section, "Adopting and Adapting: Three Examples of Peer Review/Response Activity Design from Disciplinary Writing Courses" (2014), presents a study of three faculty members adapting peer review activities to the contexts of their psychology, history, and literature courses, respectively. In this essay, Michelle LaFrance details the design of peer review activities each faculty member employs in courses for undergraduate majors. The study finds that these three instructors view forms of disciplinary expertise and awareness of written form as interconnected knowledge domains, or as one participant notes, "learning how to think like a psychologist cannot be separated from learning to write as a psychologist" (p. 329). The study highlights the importance of faculty taking on the role of disciplinary guide for student writers learning to compose within the contexts of their disciplines. The instructors profiled reveal how they go about making themselves a guiding presence in the peer review processes they implement.

In all, readers interested in peer response and the contexts of disciplinary writing instruction will note several themes that emerge from these readings. The first is that instructors in the disciplines often acknowledge the connections between writing and learning long espoused by the WAC/WID movements, but they also frequently treat their existing workload—particularly in large lecture or content area courses—as a deterrent for including peer response activities (or any writing assignments) in their courses. The second is that faculty in the disciplines do not always have a developed vocabulary for discussing writing, detailing writing conventions, or explaining their own expectations for student writers—a factor that may complicate their desire to use peer response in contexts that allow it. These concerns are ripe for further research-based exploration and increased understanding.

18 A Model for Facilitating Peer Review in the STEM Disciplines: A Case Study of Peer Review Workshops Supporting Student Writing in Introductory Biology Courses

KATHARINE BRIEGER AND PAM BROMLEY

Writing and peer review are essential features in all scholarly disciplines; these practices should be developed and encouraged, especially in undergraduate courses where students are just beginning to think critically in a new discipline. Writing and peer review feed into one another to promote essential elements of critical thinking, including conscious conceptualization, categorization, application, evaluation, and synthesis (Halpern, 2013). However, while writing is an essential feature of many undergraduate STEM courses, peer review is less frequent.

Writing is a powerful way to learn science (e.g., Reynolds, Thaiss, Katkin, & Thompson, 2012; Stout, 2011). Writing not only enables students and instructors to better discover when concepts are mastered (Campbell, Kaunda, Allie, Buffler, & Lubben, 2000) but also pushes students to synthesize material from lecture, reading, and lab (Beiersdorfer & Haynes, 1991). In fact, undergraduates report being more comfortable with scientific writing, proposing a research question, and designing an experiment after writing a research proposal (Stanford & Duwel, 2013). True synthesis of complex material often comes only as students write about it, such as when discussing experiment results (Lerner, 2007). Thus, writing is an important way to promote various aspects of critical thinking, including conceptualization, application, and synthesis.

However, many undergraduates focus on the technical aspects, or "rules," of scientific writing, such as section requirements and table formatting, rather than on writing as communication of scientific information or as a means of scientific discovery (e.g., Gladstein, 2008; Stout, 2011). Students' focus on the more technical aspects of writing may stem from the fact that many science writing guides focus on the rules of the discipline (e.g., Matthews & Matthews, 2007; Zeiger, 1999) or on writing as a way to communicate scientific information without adequate interpretation (e.g., Paradis & Zimmerman, 2002; Pechenik, 2010), instead of on writing as a "thinking and learning tool," a means to understand, evaluate, synthesize, and apply concepts (Stout, 2011,

From *Double Helix* 2 (2014), www.qudoublehelixjournal.org. Accessed July 1, 2015.

p. 2). Students need to be taught that writing in STEM is not simply conforming to technical standards but also a method of critical thinking.

While writing is a regular feature of many undergraduate STEM courses, peer review is less common, though increasing (Nicol, Thompson, & Breslin, 2014; Trautmann, 2009). Peer review involves students giving, receiving, or, most commonly, both giving and receiving critique about a shared assignment; peer review can be conducted in person, in writing, and/or online. Studies show that students who give and receive peer review revise more fully, write stronger manuscripts, feel more empowered to interpret information, better understand complex processes, and better comprehend the scientific writing process and the importance of peer review in science (Guilford, 2001; Rangachari, 2010; Trautmann, 2009). In fact, a study on co-authorship teams found that novice scientists discovered that the writing and revising process influenced the quality of the science produced (Florence & Yore, 2004). Because peer review asks students to repeatedly evaluate and judge their own work and that of their peers, a recent study argued that peer review is a "fundamental . . . skill" that should be taught explicitly (Nicol et al., 2014, p. 102). Thus, like writing, peer review helps students think critically, especially through improved conceptualization, synthesis, evaluation, and application of new information.

When used together, writing and peer review enable students to think more critically and understand scientific material more fully than they otherwise would (e.g., Quitadamo & Kurtz, 2007; Reynolds & Thompson, 2011; Stout, 2011). Students learn more when concepts are taught through a combination of writing and peer review than when taught with lecture alone (Pelaez, 2002). Writing and peer review also underscore the collaborative, iterative nature of the professional scientific community, as experiments and research articles are worked on by teams and go through many rounds of feedback and revision (FitzPatrick, 2004).

However, bringing more writing and peer review into STEM courses — particularly large, introductory courses — can be challenging, given that faculty generally have heavy workloads and large classes. Faculty often must rework their courses to make room for students to participate in writing and/or peer review, and/or take more time responding to student work (e.g., Guilford, 2001; Reynolds, Smith, Moskovitz, & Sayle, 2009; Reynolds & Thompson, 2011; Stout, 2011). Web-based peer review is one strategy for incorporating more writing and peer review into courses without taking up substantial course or instructor time (Pelaez, 2002; Nicol et al., 2014), but the virtual environment can be challenging because reviews can be impersonal, without back-and-forth oral communication and idea exchange (Breuch, 2004). Writing programs provide another way to bring more writing and peer review into STEM courses, but this, too, has a cost, as it often requires, in order to be successful, a significant investment from the writing program. For instance, directors of one program asked students about their concerns and developed and delivered workshops to help students communicate their findings (Bayer, Curto, & Kriley, 2005). Others rely on lecturers from the writing program to directly assess student writing or to create rubrics to help faculty assess student writing (Lerner, 2009; Reynolds et al., 2009). Still other writing programs use trained peer writing tutors to conduct one-on-one or small group writing consultations (Franklin, DeGrave, Crawford, & Zegar, 2002; Gladstein, 2008).

In this report, we present a model for facilitating peer review of student writing assignments that requires comparatively less investment from the STEM department and from the writing program. These workshops provide a relatively easy way to incorporate writing and peer review into STEM courses—and thus perhaps also to promote critical thinking, which has been demonstrated to occur when students undertake writing and/or peer review. At our institution, Pomona College, peer review workshops tailored to specific introductory biology lab reports were led by peer writing fellows with STEM backgrounds, already trained by the writing program (all writing tutors are called writing fellows at Pomona). Thus, additional training for the workshop leaders was minimal. Biology faculty integrated the workshops into their syllabi and provided each assignment's grading rubric to facilitate peer review. The workshops were optional and took place outside of regular instruction time. This approach enabled faculty to cover the same amount of course material while underscoring the importance of writing and peer review. Student and faculty feedback show that these peer review workshops emphasized the importance of writing in biology and may have helped to improve the overall quality of introductory students' lab reports. In addition, as the workshops evolved from a more formal approach focused on science writing in general to a less formal, more student-centered approach, student satisfaction and attendance increased. This writing-in-the-disciplines program stressed the importance of writing and peer review, giving students a focused introduction to collaborative writing in a particular STEM discipline (biology).We recognize that for an institution that does not yet have trained writing fellows with experience in STEM, such a program would be a nontrivial investment. However, the organized, section-by-section nature of lab reports lends itself to standardized, widely applicable fellow training focused on underscoring the importance of argument and organization as students move from section to section (Gladstein, 2008).

BACKGROUND AND METHODS

Pomona College is a small, private, selective liberal arts college with 1500 students. At this institution, writing in biology begins in the introductory courses (cellular biology, genetics, and ecology and evolutionary biology) and continues throughout the major. Most, but not all, students in the introductory courses are first-years and sophomores, and most are considering some kind of science major. (Students declare a major at the end of their sophomore year.) Pomona has always required students in introductory biology courses to take a concurrent lab section and to write extended laboratory reports (Genetics faculty).[1] However, the level of formality, length, and complexity of the reports has changed over time. In general, biology curricula are becoming more process-based (e.g., Treacy et al., 2011), and our biology major has followed suit. For instance, our cellular biology course used to have five shorter experiments but now has two longer ones (Cell biology faculty). Likewise, starting in 2008, the genetics faculty began to assign the reports in sections, progressing to more complete lab reports at the end of the semester, recognizing the need to introduce scientific writing in stages (Genetics faculty).

As lab reports in the introductory courses became more extensive, faculty recognized the need for more writing assistance (Genetics faculty). Students spent copious amounts of time asking how to write a lab report. Some professors started conducting a writing advising session, but that took up a large amount of class time. Moreover, the instructions provided in the laboratory manual were not sufficient, even with carefully explained details and expectations, because students needed an experienced writer to address unanticipated questions (Cell biology professor). Biology faculty members decided to have a renewed emphasis on the components of good writing, and one of the professors approached the writing program director for her ideas. At first, neither the biology professors nor the writing program director knew exactly how to best support students. Though one-on-one and small group consultations between trained peer tutors and science students have proven effective at other institutions (Franklin et al., 2002; Gladstein, 2008), the small number of trained science writing fellows and large number of introductory biology students made such strategies impractical at our institution. It was thus determined that the program would have to rely on a few science writing fellows to lead large student workshops. The science writing fellows, though, were prepared, as the previous semester they had interviewed faculty and prepared a student handout about successful science writing (Writing program director; Pomona College Writing Program, 2007).

Together, the biology department and the writing program created writing and peer review workshops to support students in the two largest introductory biology courses: cellular biology and genetics. The first workshop was held in Fall 2007 to assist students with lab reports in cellular biology and expanded to genetics in Spring 2008. Workshops have continued for both courses.

Because genetics is a prerequisite for the other introductory biology courses, it also serves as students' introduction to writing in the discipline. Students submit three written reports for genetics; for the first, they submit a title, results section, and responses to a few discussion questions; for the second, they add an introduction and a literature cited section; for the third, they write a full lab report with all the component sections. For genetics students, we offered three 90-minute workshops (each repeated over several evenings), focused on each of the three different assignments. For students in cell biology, we offered one 90-minute workshop (again, repeated over several evenings) tailored to their assignment to write a complete lab report. Because genetics is a prerequisite for cell biology, students are therefore at least somewhat familiar with writing in biology when they enter the second course.

To investigate the origin and evolution of the writing workshops, in Spring 2011 Brieger conducted interviews with the biology faculty, the writing fellows who created the workshops, and the writing fellows who ran the workshops through 2011. She also asked the biology faculty to evaluate the workshops through an online survey. Student feedback was collected through a short exit survey; workshop evaluations, like most teaching evaluations, were completed right after a session; while there was likely an overly positive response from immediate survey completion, teaching evaluations have been found to be "reliable and stable . . . , relatively valid against a variety of indicators of effective teaching, [and] relatively unaffected by a variety of variables hypothesized as potential biases" (Marsh, 2007, p. 319). Student evaluations were collected in the last semester of the more formal workshop method (Fall 2009) and for the first three semesters of the less formal workshop style (Spring 2010, Fall 2010, and Spring 2011). This enabled us to compare student satisfaction with the workshops in two different formats.[2]

While there have been changes since the workshops began in 2007, much has remained the same. First, a common lab manual and a common grading rubric are used by all sections of each course, regardless of faculty member. Second, because of large enrollments, faculty are not able to provide feedback on student drafts. Third, workshops are always included in the syllabi and held in the evenings in the week before the lab reports are due, though due dates are sometimes staggered by lab section; faculty encourage students to attend earlier workshops. Fourth, since 2009, students have worked with a lab partner to conduct the experiments and write the reports. The pairs do not necessarily attend the workshop together, and each student is encouraged to take full responsibility for the collaborative report. Finally, while the workshops are integrated into the course, attendance is not mandatory and students do not receive extra points for attending, though we note that, at other institutions, such workshops could become mandatory, part of class participation, or associated with extra credit if desired.

WORKSHOP EVOLUTION

In consultation with biology and writing program faculty, the science writing fellows began by creating a classroom-style writing workshop. Designing the workshops from scratch was extremely challenging, as fellows had to determine the workshops' key goals and how best to accomplish them. Biology faculty wanted to be certain that the fellows would not provide students help with the science and that the workshops would help students take advantage of writing resources already available in the lab manual. Students were asked to arrive at the workshop with their draft. Fellows spent the first part of the workshop walking students through the different sections of a lab report, using the chalkboard and handouts to illustrate important points. With the lab manual as a guide, fellows explained what material should be in each section of the lab report; they also presented good and bad samples of each section, drawn from lab reports faculty had received in the past as well as published scientific papers. In the latter part of the workshop, fellows asked students to pair up and trade drafts. Students would note what their peers could improve on, based on the lab manual and the earlier workshop discussion, while writing fellows circulated around the room answering writing-related questions (Writing fellows). Thus, the first iteration of the workshops was classroom-based, where the fellows assumed more of a teacher-like role. There was a "how to" presentation about science writing focused on each section, and opportunities for questions, followed by peer review.

After the first series of workshops, the writing fellows, with input from students and biology and writing program faculty, evaluated and revised the workshops. Over time, the fellows moved from a workshop model that began with more lecture, chalk talk, and discussion of good and bad examples to one that focused more on peer review.

Though changes took place gradually since the inception of the workshops, beginning in Spring 2010, we made three important changes. First, we re-structured the workshops to make them less instructional, with more opportunities for questions and discussion, enabling students to engage in peer review earlier in the session. Fellows did not begin with a formal discussion of what goes in each section. Instead, they started by introducing common errors to be wary of. Fellows did not show any examples of reports, good or bad, either, but instead encouraged students to use each other's drafts as models; toward the end of the workshop, fellows encouraged students to identify and share with the larger group particularly strong examples. Second, the workshops were more clearly tied to the courses. As in the earlier workshop format, students paired up and exchanged drafts, while fellows circulated around the room and answered writing-related questions. However, instead of using the lab manual as a guide for peer review, students used that lab's grading rubric as a way to assess each other's reports. Third, the group of fellows who led the workshops broadened. While the fellows leading the workshops all had a scientific background, they were no longer only biology or science majors with experience in biology. Though students with coursework in biology continued to be the lead fellows, other fellows with a non-biology STEM background, with a few hours of additional training, helped facilitate the workshops, which made staffing the workshops much easier. In the revised workshop format, science writing fellows talked with students informally about what made for an effective lab report; students then engaged in peer review, pairing up to trade reports, evaluating each other's papers, and noting possible areas for revision.

It is worth noting that the fellows themselves benefit immensely from leading the workshops. Particularly for those who hope to go on to teach in the STEM disciplines, guiding students through the writing and peer review process—and, necessarily, critical thinking—of laboratory reports was a valuable experience. Several fellows who have gone on to pursue doctoral degrees in the sciences reported that their communication and writing skills are highly valued by their research groups (Writing fellows); improved writing and communication skills are two of the major long-term benefits of working as a peer tutor, as noted in a cross-institutional study of former peer tutors (Hughes, Gillespie, & Kail, 2010).

In Fall 2013, the biology department took over running the workshops. Science writing fellows now train the department's student mentors to conduct the workshops; the advantage to this is that the mentors can help students who have questions about both writing and science. Because student mentors meet with the course coordinator on a regular basis, training the mentors to conduct the writing workshops has been included in one of these meetings. This change has meant that there has not been much more additional investment from the biology department and much less investment from the writing program. While the department now conducts the workshops, the overall mission for the workshops remains deeply rooted in writing pedagogy: by reading and revising drafts, students focus on, and hopefully improve, their own critical thinking and writing.

RESULTS AND DISCUSSION

We gauged the overall success of the workshops through two methods: faculty feedback about the quality of student lab reports they received, and student feedback about, attendance at, and satisfaction with the workshops. We hope that, over time, these workshops will increase awareness of how writing and peer review function, both in biology and in STEM disciplines more generally.

Student Feedback

Direct student feedback provided one way to evaluate the success of the workshops. In evaluations of the Fall 2009 workshops, students commented that the workshops were "extremely useful" and even that "peer review = great." In addition, students found the progressive assignment arc helped them feel more comfortable with science writing, given that the requirements of each section are so specific (Writing fellow). Fellows noted that students found the workshops helpful from the outset, and that students were very grateful to have a resource available outside class to help them with their lab reports (Writing fellows). However, students had complaints. Although workshops were "good on the specifics of format/structure/language," many students felt they were "too structured." Students felt that too much time was spent on the lecture-style portion where the fellows explained what was necessary for each section and went through examples of good and bad lab sections. Common challenges of peer review included students' difficulty taking it seriously and being critical of each other's work (Writing fellow); similar concerns have been noted in the divided literature in this area (Nicol et al., 2014). Since the change in format from a more formal, classroom-oriented workshop focused on lab report sections to a less formal workshop focused on guided peer review based on the lab's grading rubric, students have seemed to feel more comfortable. Allowing students to refer directly to the grading rubric helped emphasize what to look for in their peers' work; psychologically and socially, too, the rubric empowered students

TABLE 1   Student Workshop Evaluations, 2009–2011

Semester	Course	Enrolled Students	Average Workshop Attendance	% of Enrolled Students Attending	% of Students Satisfied
Fall 2009	Cell Biology	101	40	39.6%	65.4%
Spring 2010	Genetics	111	69	62.5%	90.2%
Fall 2010	Cell Biology	114	70	61.4%	90.9%
Spring 2011	Genetics	151	103	68.4%	91.0%

Note. Fall 2009 was the last semester of the old workshop format. Spring 2010 was the first semester of the new workshop format. Average attendance is the average attendance at all the workshops in a given semester. Percentage of students satisfied with the workshops is the percentage of students each semester who responded "yes" when asked the question, "Did you get out of the workshop what you were hoping for?"

to constructively comment on peers' work with less risk of appearing hypercritical (Writing fellow).

Two specific indicators point to the workshops' growing success: increased attendance and increased student satisfaction, shown in Table 1.

After the change to the workshop format, a larger percentage of enrolled students were attending the workshops and a larger percentage of students attending the workshops reported they were satisfied with their experience. The attendance and satisfaction data directly demonstrates that students increasingly sought the workshops out and found them helpful. Increased attendance is particularly meaningful because students received nothing extra for coming to the workshops.

Faculty Feedback

Members of the biology faculty believe that the workshops have been successful in helping students improve their writing in biology. Many faculty interviewed in Spring 2011 noted that the overall quality of the lab reports they see has improved. As one of the fellows who helped originate the workshops explained, "the faculty I worked with noted immediate improvement in the writing quality following the workshops" (Writing fellow). In interviews, some professors noted that they can tell who has been to the workshops based on the quality of the reports. Several faculty members noted that, since the introduction of the workshops, there have been few truly terrible lab reports and fewer egregious errors, perhaps an indication that students are engaging in drafting and revision, rather than last-minute writing (Genetics and cell biology faculty). Faculty also reported that the overall quality of student writing has improved since the introduction of the workshops, though some feel this may not be the direct result of the workshops (Genetics and cell biology faculty). Faculty thus felt that the workshops have had a direct impact on the quality of the lab reports. There is strong departmental acceptance of the importance of the workshop model, with the biology department and the writing program collaborating each year to make sure the workshops still address student and faculty needs.

In the Spring 2011 survey, faculty rated their introductory students' writing on a scale of 1 to 5: Poor (1)—Fair (2)—Good (3)—Very Good (4)—Excellent (5). Faculty gave ratings of good or very good in all five categories: (a) proper style, formatting, tables, figures, etc.; (b) student responsiveness to professor instruction/feedback; (c) clarity of writing; (d) demonstration of mastery of scientific concepts; and (e) logical flow of ideas. In particular, we believe that the last three categories provide insight into students' critical thinking abilities; if, as the biology faculty agreed here, students have performed well in these categories, this is a testament to students' ability to conceptualize and categorize information and apply, evaluate, and synthesize concepts. Given the complaints that faculty had about the quality of student writing before the institution of the workshops, it is reasonable to see the Spring 2011 faculty ratings as an indication of students' writing improvement.

LIMITATIONS AND CONCLUSIONS

Faculty noted they were frustrated that more students do not take advantage of the workshops, as the students who attend generally have better reports. However, we recognize it is possible that students who attend are simply overachievers to begin with; they may have written better lab reports in any case, and may well already be more invested in the idea that writing is important to science. The improvement in student writing is likely due to a combination of factors, but faculty believe it is related both to the peer review workshops (including students who attended the workshops potentially helping others who did not attend) and to the faculty doing a better job of emphasizing what constitutes good writing in the discipline (Cell biology faculty). It is also important to note that other factors play into the success of the workshops since they began in 2007. The workshops are not the only component of the courses focused on writing. As noted above, since 2009, students have written their reports with their lab partners; such collaboration builds in the possibility of revision and peer review. Progressing slowly through the lab report sections may help students feel more comfortable with science writing; in their first assignment, students begin by writing the title, results, and responses to a few discussion questions, adding the introduction and literature cited, submitting a complete lab report only at the end of the semester. In addition, students are now given detailed grading rubrics with instructions about writing, tables, figures, etc. Finally, the quality of students admitted to the college is gradually improving and more students have had previous research experience (Cell biology faculty).

Generalizability of these findings is limited by the fact that it was conducted on two introductory courses at a single institution. However, we believe that this model—using trained peer writing tutors to facilitate peer review workshops about writing assignments in large introductory science courses—might prove useful in other contexts. Our approach brings into large undergraduate courses two strategies—writing and peer review—that have been demonstrated to promote student learning and critical thinking in STEM disciplines, and it does so in a way that enables students to learn about writing in a specific discipline. Moreover, this model uses relatively minimal resources, essential in this time of shrinking budgets and cost-cutting, as it does not increase faculty workload, add additional material to the syllabus, or demand much additional investment from the STEM department or the writing program.

NOTES

1. This and all subsequent references to interviews are from in-person interviews undertaken, and email responses collected, by Brieger in January and February 2011. All interviewees participated in some capacity in the creation, implementation, and/or reformulation of the workshops. We thank André Calvalcanti, Kris Cheney, and Len Seligman (Genetics faculty); Karl Johnson, Karen Parfitt, and Bruce Telzer (Cell biology faculty); Carolyn Bacon, Hannah Doll (née Salim), and Erik Lykken (Writing fellows); and Dara Rossman Regaignon (Writing program director).

2. Complete information about our data collection procedures is available at http://research .pomona.edu/pam-bromley/research/science/methods-supplement/

REFERENCES

Bayer, T., Curto, K., & Kriley, C. (2005, June 26). Acquiring expertise in discipline-specific discourse: An interdisciplinary exercise in learning to speak biology. *Across the Disciplines*, 2. Retrieved from http://wac.colostate.edu/atd/articles/bayer_curto_kriley2005.cfm

Beiersdorfer, R. E., & Haynes, J. (1991). An integrated approach to geologic writing for non-science majors based on study of a California river. *Journal of Geological Education*, 39(3), 196–198.

Breuch, L. A. K. (2004). *Virtual peer review: Teaching and learning about writing in online environments*. Albany: State University of New York Press.

Campbell, B., Kaunda, L., Allie, S., Buffler, A., & Lubben, F. (2000). The communication of laboratory investigations by university entrants. *Journal of Research in Science Teaching*, 37(8), 839–853.

FitzPatrick, K. A. (2004). An investigative laboratory course in human physiology using computer technology and collaborative writing. *Advances in Physiology Education*, 28(3), 112–119.

Florence, M. K., & Yore, L. D. (2004). Learning to write like a scientist: Coauthoring as an enculturation task. *Journal of Research in Science Teaching*, 41(6), 637–668.

Franklin, J. T. I., DeGrave, K., Crawford, M., & Zegar, I. (2002). The science experiment: Improving scientific writing through collaboration. *Writing Lab Newsletter*, 26(10), 1–4.

Gladstein, J. (2008, March 29). Conducting research in the gray space: How writing associates negotiate between WAC and WID in an introductory biology course [Special issue on Writing Fellows]. *Across the Disciplines*, 5. Retrieved from http://wac.colostate.edu/atd/fellows /gladstein.cfm

Guilford, W. H. (2001). Teaching peer review and the process of scientific writing. *Advances in Physiology Education*, 25(3), 167–175.

Halpern, D. F. (2013). *Thought and knowledge: An introduction to critical thinking* (5th ed.). New York: Psychology Press.

Hughes, B., Gillespie, P., & Kail, H. (2010). What they take with them: Findings from the peer writing tutor alumni research project. *Writing Center Journal*, 30(2), 12–46.

Lerner, N. (2007). Laboratory lessons for writing and science. *Written Communication*, 24(3), 191–222.

Lerner, N. (2009). *The idea of a writing laboratory*. Carbondale: Southern Illinois University Press.

Marsh, H. W. (2007). Students' evaluations of university teaching: Dimensionality, reliability, validity, potential biases, and usefulness. In R. P. Perry & J. C. Smart (Eds.), *The scholarship of teaching and learning in higher education: An evidence-based perspective* (pp. 319–383). Dordrecht (Netherlands): Springer.

Matthews, J. R., & Matthews, R. W. (2007). *Successful scientific writing: A step-by-step guide for the biological and medical sciences* (3rd ed.). Cambridge (UK): Cambridge University Press.

Nicol, D., Thomson, A., & Breslin, C. (2014). Rethinking feedback practices in higher education. *Assessment & Evaluation in Higher Education, 37*(6), 719–731.

Paradis, J. G., & Zimmerman, M. L. (2002). *The MIT guide to science and engineering communication* (2nd ed.). Cambridge (MA): MIT Press.

Pechenik, J. A. (2010). *A short guide to writing about biology* (7th ed.). New York: Pearson Longman.

Pelaez, N. J. (2002). Problem-based writing with peer review improves academic performance in physiology. *Advances in Physiology Education, 26*(3), 174–184.

Pomona College Writing Program. (2007). Writing in the sciences. Retrieved from http://www.pomona.edu/academics/resources/writingcenter/files/sciencewritingoverview.pdf

Quitadamo, I. J., & Kurtz, M. J. (2007). Learning to improve: Using writing to increase critical thinking performance in general education biology. *CBE-Life Sciences Education, 6*(2), 140–154.

Rangachari, P. K. (2010). Teaching undergraduates the process of peer review: Learning by doing. *Advances in Physiology Education, 34*(3), 137–144.

Reynolds, J. A., Smith, R., Moskovitz, C., & Sayle, A. (2009). BioTAP: A systematic approach to teaching scientific writing and evaluating undergraduate theses. *BioScience, 59*(10), 896–903.

Reynolds, J. A., Thaiss, C., Katkin, W., & Thompson, R. J. (2012). Writing-to-learn in undergraduate science education: A community-based, conceptually driven approach. *CBE-Life Sciences Education, 11*(1), 17–25.

Reynolds, J. A., & Thompson, R. J. (2011). Want to improve undergraduate thesis writing? Engage students and their faculty readers in scientific peer review. *CBE-Life Sciences Education, 10*(2), 209–215.

Stanford, J. S., & Duwel, L. E. (2013). Engaging biology undergraduates in the scientific process through writing a theoretical research proposal. *Bioscene, 39*(2), 17–23.

Stout, R. P. (2011, June 27). "It's a shame to put such wonderful thoughts in such poor language": A chemist's perspective on writing in the discipline. *Across the Disciplines, 8*(1). Retrieved from http://wac.colostate.edu/atd/articles/stout2011/index.cfm

Trautmann, N. M. (2009). Interactive learning through web-mediated peer review of student science reports. *Educational Technology Research and Development, 57*(5), 685–704.

Treacy, D. J., Sankaran, S. M., Gordon-Messer, S., Saly, D., Miller, R., Isaac, S. R., & Kosinskia-Collins, M. S. (2011). Implementation of a project-based molecular biology laboratory emphasizing protein structure-function relationships in a large introductory biology course. *CBE-Life Sciences Education 10*(1), 18–24.

Zeiger, M. (1999). *Essentials of writing biomedical research papers* (2nd ed.). New York: McGraw-Hill.

19 Developing Authority in Student Writing through Written Peer Critique in the Disciplines

BARBARA SCHNEIDER AND JO-ANNE ANDRE

Students come to university as "strangers" to the academic conversation (Maimon, 1979); however, there is no one-style-fits-all discourse that students can learn and use successfully in all their classes. Each discipline has its own set of conventions in which particular ways of constructing and communicating knowledge are embedded. In learning a particular academic discourse, students must come to understand what research questions are appropriate, what counts as acceptable evidence, and the ways in which sources may be used in building arguments. They must also begin to master the specialized terminology and the myriad nuances of expression that mark a discipline, including subtle conventions regulating the use of personal pronouns, references to the literature, and the inclusion or exclusion of certain kinds of information in a paper (Giltrow & Valiquette, 1991). As instructors, one of our challenges is teaching students to become participants in our disciplinary conversations, to understand the discourse conventions in our disciplines, and to write with confidence and authority. In this article, we propose the use of written peer critique—the practice of having students read and comment on the work of their classmates—as a means for instructors to help students learn to engage in academic discourse with authority.

Over the past several decades, peer critique has become a popular pedagogical strategy aimed at helping students improve their papers based on comments from their peers. The literature suggests that peer response encourages students to revise more substantively (Gere & Abbott, 1985; Herrington & Cadman, 1991), to become more sensitive to their audience, to improve their critical reading and evaluation skills, and to expand their understanding of the range of acceptable approaches in writing (Gere & Abbott, 1985).

Although peer critique is often done in groups in which students respond orally to the work of other students in the group (e.g., Gere & Abbott, 1985; Her-

From *The Writing Instructor*, Sept. 2007, www.writinginstructor.org. Accessed 14 Jan. 2014.

rington & Cadman, 1991), many researchers advocate written peer response (e.g., George, 1984; Halden-Sullivan, 1996; Holt, 1992; Wauters, 1988). However, with the notable exception of Herrington and Cadman (1991), the literature addresses the use of peer critique in writing classes and does not examine its use in developing disciplinary knowledge or discourse skills in content-area courses. Moreover, the literature focuses primarily on the benefits to the writers of the texts being critiqued rather than to the student responders. In this article, we focus on how written peer critique can help student responders to develop a confident and authoritative voice and identity as they begin to enter our disciplinary conversations. We argue that two factors are key in the success of peer critiques as a vehicle for developing authority: positioning students to write their critiques from a strong knowledge base and having them respond in writing to their peers' work.

THEORETICAL FRAMEWORK

When instructors assign academic writing in content-area courses, they seek to have students take up particular academic identities by using conventions associated with their disciplines, for example, asking relevant research questions, employing terminology from the discipline, using certain kinds of sources, and documenting sources scrupulously. But even when students begin to shape their papers according to these conventions, they do not always manage to write with authority.

As Clark and Ivanic (1997) point out, authority can be seen in the degree to which writers take up the identities inscribed in a particular set of conventions and position themselves as members of a particular group. They identify three representations of self that appear in written texts: the autobiographical self, the discoursal self, and the authorial self. The autobiographical self refers to a writer's life history, experiences, values, and beliefs. It is a constellation of factors that shapes a writer's sense of competence and authority as a writer in various contexts. The discoursal self is the writer's representation of self through writing practices, discourses invoked, and discursive features in a text. Through their generic, rhetorical, and stylistic choices, writers take on the identities made available by particular discourse conventions. As Clark and Ivanic's work implies, writers' handling of discourse conventions may also mark them as experts or novices. For example, students may convey their lack of identification with academic discourse through their misuse of citation conventions or specialized terminology or through their failed attempts at employing complex sentence structures in order to sound more academic. Finally, the authorial self refers to the writer's representation of self as someone who has something to say. Clark and Ivanic identify a number of textual features associated with establishing authorial presence in a text. These include the ways in which writers position themselves in relation to authorities and other writers, the extent to which they comment on and evaluate the work of others, their use of modalizations and qualifications, the types of reporting verbs they use with sources, their use of first-person pronouns, and the extent to which they claim authority for their personal experiences. The authorial self, according to Clark and Ivanic, encompasses the textual "evidence of writers' feeling of authoritativeness and sense of themselves as authors" (p. 152).

The work of Walvoord and McCarthy (1990) can also illuminate the concept of authority in student writing. Based on their study of student writing in four disciplines, they identified three roles that students adopt in academic writing: the layperson role, the text-processor role, and the professional-in-training role. Students taking the layperson role address the issues and problems described in an assignment but neglect the knowledge and methodology being taught in the course. Walvoord and McCarthy give an example of a student in a business course who approaches a decision-making assignment about a baseball stadium from the perspective of a baseball fan rather than a business manager. Students taking a text-processor role fail to address the issues or the problems in the assignment and focus instead on some aspect of text-processing, such as summarizing, synthesizing, or reviewing. Here, Walvoord and McCarthy cite an example of a student who summarizes the textbook section on decision-making for the stadium assignment rather than using the requisite methodology to defend his decision. Students adopting a text-processor role may also string together material from various sources without constructing an argument about the assigned problem or topic. Ideally, we want to move our students toward the third role that Walvoord and McCarthy describe, which is that of the professional-in-training. In the professional-in-training role, students use the knowledge and methods from the course as well as knowledge from outside the course to address assigned issues and problems.

These models describing representations of writers in texts suggest that our goal as instructors should be to give students opportunities to develop a sense of themselves as "professionals-in-training" (Walvoord & McCarthy, 1990) by developing an "authorial self" (Clark & Ivanic, 1997) in their texts. We propose written peer critique as a way to do this.

POSITIONING STUDENTS FOR EFFECTIVE WRITTEN PEER CRITIQUE

If we want to hear an authorial voice in student writing, we must ensure that students write their critiques from a strong knowledge base. This knowledge base will be different in different courses, but it should generally include knowledge of disciplinary content and genre conventions. Students have no hope of writing an effective critique in an authoritative voice if they do not understand the material that forms the subject matter for their peers' writing. When enrolled in a course in a particular discipline, students cannot know all the course material, but they can know aspects of it very well before they undertake critique tasks.

In order to critique others' work effectively, students must also have an understanding of the relevant genre conventions. Although a number of theorists (e.g., Diaz, Freedman, Medway, & Paré, 1999; Freedman, 1994) have expressed considerable pessimism about the usefulness of explicit teaching of genre conventions, we believe that lack of explicit teaching of academic genres is one of the factors explaining why students experience confusion in trying to write well for courses in different disciplines. While we agree with Freedman and Diaz et al. (1999) when they argue that learning rules for constructing genres does not ensure that students will use them appropriately, we take the position that expecting students to learn academic genres tacitly through trial and error may slow their progress toward mastering academic genres. As Coe (1994) puts it, "the social processes of tacit genre acquisition [may] serve to limit genre knowledge" (p. 188).

Of course, even when students have sufficient content-area knowledge and a good understanding of the relevant genre conventions, they may still not write with authority. Factors such as class, ethnicity, sexuality, gender, age, and educational attainment may play a role in inhibiting their development of an authoritative voice (Clark & Ivanic, 1997; Penrose & Geisler, 1994). A deeper barrier, however, may lie in students' epistemological assumptions. As Penrose and Geisler argue, students will be reluctant to take a critical attitude toward sources and to write with authority if they "see all texts (except their own) as containing 'the truth,' rather than as authored and subject to interpretation and criticism" (p. 516). Indeed, for such students, peer critique may be the stepping stone to acknowledging the constructed nature of texts and to assuming authority in their own writing.

More immediate problems for students faced with the task of critiquing a peer's paper are determining what constitutes effective commentary for a writer who may use the feedback in revising, and finding an appropriate tone in which to frame critical comments. In any particular course, both students and instructors can generate a list of the features of an effective critique. If instructors do not provide guidance in what is expected in a peer critique, students may simply focus on grammar, spelling, and punctuation errors in their peers' writing (Flynn, 1984). While such surface errors may distract readers, they should not become the main focus in peer critiques. And while instructor and students may collaboratively develop a list of considerations to guide peer responders, students will have no chance to develop an authoritative voice if the assigned peer critique takes the form of a series of ticks on a checklist of criteria (Halden-Sullivan, 1996). Of course, what counts as an effective peer critique will depend on the academic context; at a minimum, however, a critique should address content, comment on strengths in the critiqued writing, and suggest areas for improvement. It should also offer a genuine reader response to the text.

Peer Critique in Barbara's Communications Studies Course

In Barbara's second-year course *Cultural Studies in Communication,* for communications studies students, one of the early readings in the course was a difficult essay by Raymond Williams, "Culture Is Ordinary" (1958/1997). Students were assigned to write a one-page summary capturing the main points of the essay and to develop three questions for class discussion based on it.

The audience specified for the summary was a hypothetical classmate who had missed the class on the reading and needed help to understand it. To help prepare students for writing (and later critiquing) their summaries, Barbara spent class time having students generate a list of the features of an effective summary given the context specified. Students were asked to bring copies of their summaries to class the following week.

The next week, the class began with a discussion of Williams' essay. Barbara divided the class into groups, assigned each group a section of the essay, and asked each group to discuss that section, develop a joint understanding of it, and present their thoughts to the rest of the class. The whole class discussion also considered questions suggested by the students. After the discussion, Barbara collected the summaries and redistributed them randomly for peer critique. Before having students begin the critique task, she asked the class to generate a list of features of an effective critique, which she recorded on the board. She then asked the students to write a memo critiquing the summary they received. Both the summaries and the peer critiques were identified only by student number.

The peer critiques written in Barbara's class embodied a strong authorial presence revealed in three main areas. First, the authorial self was distinct in students' evaluative comments related to disciplinary content, in particular in their comments on how accurately and completely their peers' summaries had captured the key ideas in Williams' essay. Second, authorial presence was evident in students' evaluative comments on their peers' handling of the summary genre. Finally, authorial presence was established as students drew on personal authority derived from their experience as readers.

Authorial Presence in Students' Comments on the Content of Their Peers' Summaries

In the following excerpts from students' critiques of their peers' summaries of the Raymond Williams article, we see students adopting an authoritative stance as they comment on how well the summaries captured the main points in Williams' essay:

> The analysis of Williams is very well done. The only comment that I would present is that Williams does not think that industrialization is bad, instead he felt the industrialization is positive.
>
> Great job of nailing the purpose of this article right on the head. Williams is refuting the theory of mass culture, and defining what his view of culture is.
>
> You should have mentioned mass society and mass culture theories (not the theories themselves but noted that the article is about them) and that he [Williams] was debunking them.
>
> You provided a very clear and concise summary of what the article was about, especially at the beginning. . . . [However] I must admit that I

wish you had expanded a little more on the views of Marx and Leavis that Williams had been exposed to.

Even when students did not address their peers directly, as in the following critique excerpt, the sense of authority—the authorial self—is clearly present:

> My peer states [that Williams] "dismisses the definition of culture as the behavior and manners of upper classes." This is an underlying perception in the article; however, Williams' reason for this definition was more distinct and direct than the examples given in the summary.

A final excerpt combines the sense of authorial confidence with a personal note:

> "You have exposed a psycho-political agenda in the article that I didn't notice!"

In the excerpts above, the confident academic voice and the sense of disciplinary understanding conveyed through the students' comments are unmistakable.

All these excerpts indicate the value of positioning student writers to critique from a strong knowledge base. In this case, the students in Barbara's class gained a good understanding of Williams' essay not only through their own attempt to summarize the article but also through the class discussion that preceded the writing of the critiques. This preparation enabled them to comment confidently on whether their peer's summary had captured Williams' main points. This confidence is evident in students' comments on the value of what was included in the summary and in their request for clarification or more detail on points that had been misunderstood or left out. The critique assignment encouraged students to think critically about the summaries they were reading and gave them an opportunity to check their own understanding of Williams' essay against someone else's, forcing them to reevaluate and thereby deepen their own understanding of Williams' arguments.

AUTHORIAL PRESENCE IN STUDENTS' COMMENTS ON THEIR PEERS' HANDLING OF THE SUMMARY GENRE

In their critiques, Barbara's students also commented with authority on the effectiveness of their peers' handling of the summary genre and of their peers' writing styles. In some cases, the comments offered praise:

> Your paraphrasing skills are excellent.

> Nice transition paragraph between the drinking hole/teashop mentalities and the main cultural influences (Marxism & Leavis) in [Williams'] life.

In other cases, the students confidently pointed to problems or offered suggestions for improvement, as in the following excerpts:

> A very brief and clear introduction telling me as the reader what Williams' article is about. . . . Your summary was quite clear and to the point.

> But, a recommendation is in your next summary, do have a concluding paragraph.
>
> This summary seems to be half critique and half summary.
>
> I don't think the sentence "People need . . . " came from William's [sic] article. It's ok to have it there but make sure the reader knows if it's your editorializing . . . or if it's what Williams actually said.

One student even commented on the lack of authority in her peer's writing:

> Your style of writing when you summarized the Marxist and Leavis['] criticisms is clear and confident. Before this however, I found your writing to appear appollogetic [sic] and tentitive [sic]. . . . Can I suggest avoiding such statements as . . . "from what I understand."

When students write their critiques from a sound base of knowledge of the relevant genre conventions, they do not have to guess whether their peers' grasp of the genre is appropriate. Explicit teaching of conventions positions students to comment with an authoritative voice on others' use of the discourse conventions; it also strengthens their own understanding of the conventions, thereby developing their discoursal selves (Clark & Ivanic, 1997).

AUTHORIAL PRESENCE IN STUDENTS' COMMENTS DRAWING ON THEIR EXPERIENCE AS READERS

Peer critique allows students to draw on the authority of their own experience as readers. In Barbara's class, the authority of this position was reinforced by the assignment's specification of a peer audience for the summary assignment. In the following comments, we can see the students' confident authorial presence as they offer personal reactions to their peers' summaries:

> Wow! I really appreciated the way you broke down the theories being argued against and the arguments of the author. This format is straightforward and easy to understand.
>
> I like the way you boiled everything down to a few sentences. This is actually very useful in learning simply the main points of the article.
>
> I really like your summary of the Marxist side and Williams['] counter argument. It is way clearer to me after reading your summary.
>
> While reading your summary I felt relaxed & at ease—contrary to what I felt while reading the article. . . . I must admit that I wish you had expanded a little more on the views of Marx and Leavis that Williams had been exposed to. For me that was the most complex part of the composition so a little clarification would have been appreciated.

In the following critique excerpts, the authority of the reading experience provided grounds for critical comments as students noted how problems or lapses in the text led to problems for them as readers:

> I found that the ideas [in the summary] did not flow together the way they should. This caused some confusion on my part.

> Your summary didn't give me many details of William's [*sic*] argument ... which would have helped me to evaluate the strengths of his argument; I guess I like a certain amount of precision in academic pieces.

In these excerpts, we see how the students' autobiographical selves—through their reading experiences—inform a strong authorial presence in their critiques.

As Clark and Ivanic's (1997) model points out, students arrive in our classes with a history of reading and writing experiences that they call on and integrate to develop an authorial self. As students begin to immerse themselves in the literate practices of their disciplines, they must seek ways to integrate their autobiographical selves with the subject positions offered by academic discourse. That integration is not always an easy task (Harvey, 1994), particularly as the academy tends to suppress the personal element in academic writing (Clark & Ivanic, 1997; Penrose & Geisler, 1994). Peer critique, however, opens a space in which students' personal knowledge and responses as readers are valued. The opportunity afforded by peer critique to develop a sense of authorial presence in responding to texts may turn out to be centrally important in developing authority in students' academic writing. As Penrose and Geisler (1994) argue, even when students possess sufficient domain knowledge to write with authority, they will remain reluctant to do so if they believe that knowledge resides within texts and that their own knowledge, experience, and voice has no legitimacy within the academic sphere.

TEMPERING THE AUTHORIAL VOICE

Before we go on to consider the epistemological underpinnings and pedagogical implications of authority in student writing, let's look at the ways in which students temper the authorial voice in their peer critiques. In many of the excerpts quoted in this article, students' comments on the completeness and accuracy of their peers' summaries could easily be mistaken for instructors' comments. However, the students' critiques sometimes included a personal voice often lacking in teacher commentary. A more striking feature of the students' critiques can be seen in the ways in which students tempered their authorial voice through the use of politeness hedges. These included framing remarks and qualifications, as evident in the following examples:

> Please forgive me if I have made any unfair judgment. Thank you.

> I found it difficult to understand your second paragraph about the definition of culture. Maybe I am more unclear on the definition than you are, and that is the cause of my confusion.

Students often framed their responses as invitations to the writer to "consider" their "suggestions," and they frequently used modal constructions to qualify their comments: "Maybe you could ..."; "You might want to ..."; "It might be better to ..."; "One suggestion may improve your ..."; and "I would like to suggest ... ," to take just a few examples.

While these strategies temper the voice of authority embodied in the critiques, they can be seen as a natural outcome of the rhetorical situation in which students are writing to each other as equals rather than as authorities in a position of power over each other. At first glance, this feature of the students' critiques seems slightly disconcerting but perhaps only because instructor commentary—the voice of critique with which we are most familiar—almost never shows this kind of sensitivity to its student audience. We can barely imagine an instructor ending her comments with a disclaimer like "If you don't agree with any of my comments, feel free to disregard it," as one student wrote in her critique. In fact, although student responders may appear to relinquish authority through hedging remarks, qualifications, and polite constructions, their writing displays an awareness of what it means for their colleagues, and themselves, to develop an authoritative voice and a critical perspective in their writing. As Clark and Ivanic (1997) note, "being considerate to the reader involves making space for the readers' own intentions and interpretations" (p. 168). At some level, these strategies may also reflect a healthy resistance to the kind of comments that students often receive from teachers—comments that speak in the voice of authority to provide ultimate assessments on student texts while closing off avenues for dialogue or competing interpretations.

EPISTEMOLOGICAL UNDERPINNINGS AND PEDAGOGICAL IMPLICATIONS

The perspective we have taken in this article rests on a set of assumptions that have come to be called the social approach to writing (Faigley, 1985). In this view, writing is not just a means of transmitting existing knowledge but a social activity that "accomplishes meaningful social functions" (Walvoord & McCarthy, 1991, p. 21), including sharing communal ways of thinking and knowing. In teaching newcomers to write appropriately for our disciplinary and professional communities, we socialize them into the ways of thinking and knowing that characterize our disciplines and professions. We bring them into our conversations and help them on their way to becoming literate members of our communities. We also help them to understand that what we are doing in our disciplines and professions is carrying on a conversation—that those impenetrable essays in the journals of our fields are not just isolated pieces of writing; they are contributions to an ongoing exchange of ideas. This social and constructivist understanding of academic work is central if students are to move from an "information-transfer model" of education (Penrose & Geisler, 1994) to a view that sees all texts as contingent and open to response and criticism.

As we have seen, written peer critique can be a valuable tool not only for the writers but also for the student responders as well. Through written critique that is grounded in a strong base of content-area knowledge and a sound understanding of genre conventions, students can begin to develop an authoritative presence and a confident voice in their academic writing. Written peer critique uniquely positions students to write to a real audience of their peers. In the process, students strengthen their disciplinary knowledge base, develop critical reading skills, begin to master genre and academic discourse conventions, and acquire a confident and authoritative voice in their writing. In first- and second-year courses, written peer critique can help initiate students into the basic discursive genres that constitute our disciplinary conversations and afford them a space in which to develop their own authoritative voices as they comment on their peers' texts. In upper-level courses, written peer critique can provide a forum for a more advanced textual dialogue through which students can expand their range of discursive strategies and sharpen the precision of their expression, the effectiveness of their arguments, and their understanding of complex concepts and relationships in their disciplines. At the simplest level, written peer critique activities promote a real textual conversation among students in our classrooms. But more than that, such activities ask them to write first as members of a community as they compose their original texts and then to engage in a meta-conversation about the ways in which their peers' work is an appropriate contribution to the academic discourse of the classroom or to the larger disciplinary or professional conversation.

Of course, it might be possible to have this meta-conversation orally rather than in writing. But a tenet of the social approach to writing is that people discover and refine their thoughts through the act of writing. Asking students to respond to each other in writing gives them the opportunity to discover that they have something to say in the meta-conversation of their classrooms or in their disciplines or professions, and it allows them the time they need to construct a considered response. Peer critique activities also engage students as participants in a written conversation in which their contribution performs a meaningful social function, that of helping their peers to revise their writing and to deepen their understanding of concepts from their disciplines and of the consequences of their discursive strategies and stylistic choices.

By positioning students to engage in this meta-conversation, written peer critique gives students a uniquely effective opportunity to bring together their autobiographical experiences as readers and their growing understanding of academic or professional discourse conventions to develop their authorial selves and to comment with authority on the work of others. Students who fail to develop a sense of authority in their academic writing may remain trapped in text-processor or layperson roles, subservient to others' knowledge claims and reluctant to adopt the identity of legitimate—albeit novice—members of their disciplines and professions. Written peer critique moves students beyond these limited subject positions by situating them as professionals-in-training (Walvoord & McCarthy, 1990) called upon to apply what they have learned to respond with authority to the writing of their peers. As they take up this challenge, they begin their journey toward becoming full members of their disciplines and professions.

REFERENCES

Clark, R., & Ivanic, R. (1997). *The politics of writing*. New York: Routledge.
Coe, R. (1994). "An arousing and fulfillment of desires": The rhetoric of genre in the process era. In A. Freedman & P. Medway (Eds.), *Genre and the new rhetoric* (pp. 181–190). London: Taylor and Francis.

Diaz, P., Freedman, A., Medway, P., & Paré, A. (1999). *Worlds apart: Acting and writing in academic and workplace contexts*. Mahwah, NJ: Lawrence Erlbaum.

Faigley, L. (1985). Nonacademic writing: The social perspective. In L. Odell & D. Goswami (Eds.), *Writing in nonacademic settings* (pp. 231–248). New York: Guilford Press.

Flynn, E. (1984). Students as readers of their classmates' writing. *The Writing Instructor, 3,* 120–129.

Freedman, A. (1994). "Do as I say": The relationship between teaching and learning new genres. In A. Freedman & P. Medway (Eds.), *Genre and the new rhetoric* (pp. 191–210). London: Taylor and Francis.

George, D. (1984). Working with peer groups in the composition classroom. *College Composition and Communication, 35,* 320–326.

Gere, A., & Abbott, R. (1985). Talking about language: The language of writing groups. *Research in the Teaching of English, 19,* 362–385.

Giltrow, J., & Valiquette, M. (1991). The outsider is called in: Audience in the disciplines. *Inkshed—Newsletter of the Canadian Association for the Study of Writing and Reading, 10*(2), 5–11.

Halden-Sullivan, J. (1996). Reconsidering assessment: From checklist to dialectic. *Assessing Writing, 3*(2): 173–195.

Harvey, G. (1994). Presence in the essay. *College English, 56*(6), 642–654.

Herrington, A., & Cadman, D. (1991). Peer review and revising in an anthropology course: Lessons for learning. *College Composition and Communication, 42,* 184–199.

Higgins, R., Hartley, P., & Skelton, A. (2002). The conscientious consumer: Reconsidering the role of assessment feedback in student learning. *Studies in Higher Education, 27*(1), 53–64.

Holt, M. (1992). The value of written peer criticism. *College Composition and Communication, 43,* 384–392.

Maimon, E. P. (1979). Talking to strangers. *College Composition and Communication, 30,* 364–369.

Penrose, A. M., & Geisler, C. (1994). Reading and writing without authority. *College Composition and Communication, 45,* 505–520.

Walvoord, B. E., & McCarthy, L. P. (1990). *Thinking and writing in college: A naturalistic study of students in four disciplines*. Urbana, IL: NCTE.

Wauters, J. K. (1988). Non-confrontational critiquing in pairs: An alternative to verbal peer response groups. *The Writing Instructor, 8,* 156–166.

Williams, R. (1989). Culture is ordinary. In A. Gray & J. McGuigan (Eds.), *Studying culture: An introductory reader* (2nd ed.) (pp. 5–14). London: Arnold.

20   *Adopting and Adapting: Three Examples of Peer Review/ Response Activity Design from Disciplinary Writing Courses*

MICHELLE LaFRANCE

The struggle of the student writer is not the struggle to bring out that which is within; it is the struggle to carry out those ritual activities that grant our entrance into a closed society.

        —David Bartholomae, "Writing Assignments, Where Writing Begins"

This project began with a question about how far the ideals and practices central to peer review/response activities in composition programs may have made their way into classrooms that focus on disciplinary writing. In the course of my conversations with instructors using peer review/response in their disciplinary writing courses, however, I came to realize that a more interesting question waited to be explored. The three instructors discussed here had not only adopted peer review/response activities in their classrooms, but had substantially adapted the practice to more deeply reflect the highly specialized nature of writing in their disciplines. As such, I began to wonder how their designs of peer review/response activities modeled ways to think more purposefully about the design and implementation of peer review/response for those teaching more general writing courses, such as first-year composition.

While there is a well-established corpus of work on peer review and response activities in composition courses, as the introduction to this collection and the chapters included here attest, treatments of peer review in the disciplinary-writing or writing-intensive course are more difficult to find. Those pieces that do nod to the role of peer review/response within content-area, writing-intensive, or disciplinary-writing courses often only treat the mechanics of conducting peer review/response or set out to reinforce the important pedagogical gains of peer review activities for student writers in general. In *Sharing Writing: Peer Response Groups in English Classes,* for instance, Karen Spear notes the potential of the writing across the curriculum movement to

From *Peer Pressure, Peer Power: Theory and Practice in Peer Review and Response for the Writing Classroom,* edited by Steven J. Corbett et al., Fountainhead Press, 2014.

"clarify the nature of writing as a central component of learning in all disciplines" (10), but then situates the remainder of her discussion about peer review/response squarely within the context of composition courses. Other examples of the disciplinary course as backdrop for a discussion of the general benefits of peer review/response activities, such as the essay "Peer Review and Revising in an Anthropology Course: Lessons for Learning" by Herrington and Cadman, ignore the disciplinary contexts that surround this practice almost entirely, suggesting that the peer review activities and student responses they explore could have taken place in any class, let alone any writing class. Indeed, even in more recent pieces, such as Barst, Brooks, Cempellin, and Klejan's essay from 2011, "Peer Review Across the Disciplines: Improving Student Performance in the Honors Humanities Classroom," the authors each describe the organization of peer review/response activities and the tasks they asked students to carry out in courses across the curriculum. Yet, despite the nod to disciplinarity in the title of their article, the authors of this piece do not explicitly address writing as a disciplinary-learning goal for their students or how their learning activities assist students to more effectively write within the contexts of a disciplinary tradition.

These conversations of peer review/response seem to miss out on the long emergent thinking in composition that has drawn from extensive work in writing across the curriculum and writing in the disciplines, especially that audience expectations and the conventions of argument are often shaped by participation in discipline-specific ways of knowing. As such, I wondered how instructors of writing-in-the-disciplines courses might challenge these generalized notions of peer review. In what ways might these instructors collapse content and conventions? And, how might instructors in disciplinary-writing courses devise rubrics, worksheets, or workshops to assist students in understanding that language practices are always reflective of a disciplinary tradition? What might be revealed in the ways instructors negotiated the ideals of original expression, necessary mastery of content, and familiar disciplinary forms? What could we learn from them?

David Russell has famously used the metaphor of ball handling in sports activities to demonstrate the ways, subtle and not so subtle, that writing calls on different skill sets and ways of problem solving from situation to situation. "To try to teach students to improve their writing by taking a GWSI [General Writing Skills Instruction] course," Russell writes, "is something like trying to teach people to improve their ping-pong, jacks, volleyball, basketball, field hockey, and so on by attending a course in general ball using" (58). Downs and Wardle argue likewise that general composition courses often reify features of writing (e.g., syntax, mechanics, and process) in ways that are ultimately not instructive for students who must step into multiple, flexible, and adaptive writing situations. They write, "It is often assumed that 'skills' or moves such as taking a position, building arguments, developing paragraphs, and writing clear and forceful sentences are 'general writing skills' that transfer across all situations" (579). Wardle has argued that these oversimplifications of thinking about writing instruction result in "Mutt Genres" and Downs and Wardle argue that even if some elements of writing are shared across disciplines—for instance "taking a position . . . the ways of doing so vary radically across disciplines, and therefore can only meaningfully be taught within a discipline" (579).

The difficulty for composition instructors becomes—especially as their courses and composition programs may float above or refuse the very disciplinary affiliations that compel the intricate imbrications of content and convention—how to pose writing and activities like peer review/response as a specific and situational response that mirrors the values, goals, and ways of knowing central to disciplinary work. Exploring the ways that instructors of disciplinary-writing courses adopt and adapt peer review/response activities stands to offer models for thinking about peer review/response with this sort of specificity. Understanding the contexts of writing and writing instruction that students will face following the general composition course offers some perspective for instructors who seek to more actively prepare students for the disciplinary and professional writing to come in later courses.

Here, I present three brief case studies of instructors using peer review/response in a course about writing for psychology, a two-semester senior capstone in history, and a gateway course that introduces English majors to written literary criticism in English studies. As their interview responses and peer review/response designs reveal, the instructors of these courses design their peer review/response activities in ways that redefine notions of "better writing" as a product of general writing knowledge. Rather, these instructors actively design their peer review/response exercises in ways that enable their students to become more skilled in the thinking processes central and specific to their disciplines' ways of writing.

Three trends in thinking emerge from the following stories about peer review/response in disciplinary writing courses shared here: (1) the instructors contend that students develop disciplinary-writing muscle when worksheets and activities reinforce the intricate relationship between effective written response within a discipline and the thinking practices and ways of doing central to the discipline; (2) against notions (such as Spear's; Herrington and Cadman's) that peer review/response can be a decentering activity in writing classes, . . . each of the instructors held that they must be *highly* involved in the process of review/response—prompting, directing redirecting, and affirming students' reactions and responses as burgeoning readers/writers within a discipline—what Corbett has called . . . "iterative coaching" (Ching 26); (3) peer review/response is a very time-intensive process for these three instructors, but each claims that with supported practice student writers do become more aware and thoughtful readers and writers over the course of a term. These students also become more familiar and practiced with the particular expectations for writing within the disciplinary communities they are entering.

METHODS AND DATA COLLECTION

When discussing this project with a colleague who teaches upper-level writing courses, she asked me quite skeptically if I had actually identified instructors outside of composition who used peer review/response activities in their writing courses. In fact, it was not difficult to find instructors outside of composition courses who were using peer review/response activities in their classes. The notion that students may learn something from working with peers on written drafts in progress has filtered with some frequency across disciplinary lines into the classrooms of those who teach writing in disciplinary contexts. Making inquiries through colleagues at different institutions, I was quickly able to locate several instructors who use peer review/response as a staple in a variety of differently structured and purposed writing courses—biology, linguistics, art history, political science, Spanish, anthropology, business, even engineering.

Finding three of these instructors who were also willing to discuss their pedagogical approach to peer-based work proved a bit more difficult. The three I discuss here all agreed to participate in my study about their use of peer review/response. However, each asked that I not divulge their identities or home institutions. As such, the instructors' names have been changed and a few details of the locations they teach in have been divulged to honor their gracious participation in my study.

As a precursor to more in-depth discussion via e-mail and in-person, I administered a brief survey to each instructor asking a number of questions. I was interested in understanding their general educational philosophies and pedagogical approaches to writing instruction, including the use of peer review/response activities more specifically. Questions on this survey asked them to share where and how they may have first learned about peer review/response, how effective and/or important they rated typical elements of peer review/response design, and to comment more generally on factors that seemed to most interfere with or enable productive peer review/response sessions in their courses. I collected peer review/response worksheets from two of the instructors and conducted follow-up interviews via e-mail and in-person. One instructor additionally shared with me a lengthy report on her course design that she had written as part of her involvement in a faculty development initiative on her campus.

PSYCH-WRITING: Peer Review/Response in a Disciplinary Writing for Psychology Class

---

Writing in the Discipline of Psychology (Sophomore/Junior Level)

An introduction to critiquing the literature and methods of psychology and to scientific writing in the style of the American Psychological Association.

Prerequisite: PSYC+3. Corequisite or Prerequisite: MATH+3. Fulfills: WM

Jackie is a popular instructor in one of the most popular undergraduate majors at her small liberal arts college in the Northeast. On the vanguard of disciplinary writing instruction on her campus, Jackie created and began to teach the psychology-writing course well before the WAC program on her campus was jump-started. She credits these experiential philosophies as predisposing her to design the writing-for-psychology class to include peer review/response activities. Jackie believes that learning how to think like a psychologist cannot be separated from learning to write as a psychologist. The specific moves endemic to psychology writing are simply outside the experience and awareness of most of her students as they enter the major, Jackie notes.

Jackie uses peer review/response exercises in her classes for a number of reasons. She finds that students do rely slightly less on her instructor comments when they have the opportunity to hear what their peers think of their work. She has seen that students can help one another work through their written arguments and identify issues of genre, organization, and cohesion. She believes that peer review/response can prompt students toward more effective revisions than work on their own.

She's less convinced that students are able to help one another recognize the conventions of writing in the discipline, and that's where her methods of class design and instruction begin to come in. Jackie holds off on peer review/response activities for the first paper because of this. Early in the semester she devotes ample class time to discussing many of the conventions and activities central to written research in psychology with her students. Activities of critical reading are central to this portion of the semester, as students begin to build their vocabulary, their understanding of research questions and protocols, and their familiarity with the accepted genre-forms of written psychology research. Once the first paper and a number of readings and discussions are under the students' belts, Jackie asks students to peer review/respond to one another's second and third papers.

In class, she keeps her peer review/response groups small (two or three students) and devotes an entire class period (an hour and 15 minutes) to the session. During peer review/response days, she walks around, "supervising" the work of groups. "I check in with each group at least a couple of times, looking at their comments and the original papers. I provide feedback to the peer reviewer," she reports. "Student reviewers are often much kinder *and less accurate* than I am," she continues. "They seem to have difficulty either identifying aspects of papers that are poorly written and need improvement, and/or feel uncomfortable giving negative feedback. This is less true of the stronger writers in the course, but very true of the weaker students." Jackie tailors her in-person feedback to each peer review group member, encouraging them to take a more critical stance as they read.

Jackie's "Evaluation Rubric for Peer Review" form supports students in identifying a range of possible issues in the papers of their classmates. She asks peer reviewers to consider the introduction, evidence, language, research question, and citation style of their classmates. For each question, Jackie describes what an effective, a less effective, and a struggling paper may look like. What's notable about her form is its specificity. The form reminds students of class discussions about the conventions of research writing and about the specifics of the assignment prompt. It asks students to make a clear choice; for instance, if the studies included in the paper are "reviewed at an appropriate level of specificity," "are not reviewed in enough detail," or if they are reviewed with "unnecessary details." The form ends with a space to solicit further questions or comments from peer reviewers/responders.

Coupled with her ongoing, semester-long conversation about what it means to conduct research and write in the discipline of psychology, Jackie's "Evaluation Rubric" and peer review/response activities foster the notion that writers' choices are highly demonstrative of how authors within a particular community assert their credibility as researchers who share their findings with other researchers. The questions on Jackie's form and her in-class involvement with peer review/response groups build upon and deepen student understandings of in-class discussion about the rigorous practices of psychologists and the norms of writing for psychology. These not only reinforce the thinking processes of Jackie's students as burgeoning researchers themselves, but also help them understand how their choices relate to the *ethos* necessary to effectively present original research and methods of critical problem solving central to effective research in psychology.

HIST-WRITING: Writing Workshops in a Medieval History Senior Capstone

> **Introduction to History (300-Level)**
> Introduction to the discipline of history for new or prospective majors. Emphasizes the basic skills of reading, analysis, and communication (both verbal and written) that are central to the historian's craft. Each seminar discusses a different subject or problem.
>
> **Colloquium in History (400-Level)**
> Each seminar examines a different subject or problem. A quarterly list of the seminars and their instructors is available in the Department of History undergraduate advising office.

Rowan, a full professor at a large research university, and her colleagues in history were frustrated; students who took the junior seminar (Introduction to History) did not always come prepared or able to transfer their learning in the capstone senior seminar they took the following year (Colloquium in History). Students seemed particularly underprepared when it came to writing effectively in the course; the capstone project required an independent research project, and few students were writing in the ways that faculty expected of the senior history major. As Rowan relates:

> Students routinely come into the 498 with little or no background either in the general subject matter of the course, or in the research and analytical techniques common in the field in which they are being asked to work.

> Indeed, many of them [had] often never been taught in any focused man-
> ner how to write historical prose: they must glean what they can from
> instructors' comments on papers written from previous history classes.

One issue that complicated preparing students to write effectively in the senior
capstone was the wide disparity in course offerings on both the junior and
senior levels—the courses offered diverged wildly from quarter to quarter,
offering little opportunity for students to sustain or build on the work they had
completed in previous quarters.

Rowan redesigned the two courses, originally taken in different years of
study, to occur back to back in the senior year. She signed on to teach both quarters. She designed the first quarter's study to introduce students to a range of
primary sources on a very specifically chosen topic ("heresy"). Her focus was
on the content necessary for students to understand how historians went about
reading, evaluating, citing, debating, and situating primary texts. Class discussions in the first quarter focused on the methodologies that historians might use
when thinking through and writing about primary sources. Discussions and exercises that Rowan designed—a debate and a mock heresy trial, for example—
required students to practice the foundational skills of effective history-writing.
As she describes these, students were asked to "summarize complex narratives,
muster evidence in support of an argument, and present that argument in a
logical and sequential fashion." Students also produced four "micro-essays"
(1 to 2 pages long) with the knowledge that each of their papers would be work-
shopped in class in collaboration with their peers. Students then revised those
drafts following the comments they gathered from others in the class.

The students' work on heresy continued into the next quarter, where students were asked to develop a much longer research paper of 15 to 20 pages.
Rowan's teaching strategy picked up where the previous quarter had left off,
scaffolding the assignments so that "the readings in the senior seminar followed naturally on from the readings done the previous quarter." This time,
however, the critical reading focus was on secondary sources—as Rowan
explains, "what historians have made of those [primary] sources."

Rowan's ultimate goal was to integrate writing instruction into both
courses so that her students would be more prepared to tackle their major
research paper in the second quarter. However, she found the amount of writing students were asked to do in the class a bit daunting in terms of the
commitment she had laid out for herself to comment, grade, and encourage
revision. She describes the design strategy she enacted to overcome this:

> I asked for two brief written progress reports on the seminar paper, and
> inquired every week as to whether students were facing problems in the
> writing or conceptualization of their papers that they wished to bring up
> for general class discussion. (Only once did it actually happen that a stu-
> dent brought up frustrations she was facing with her paper and ask for
> her classmates' advice.) I also had them write a response to their reading
> before beginning discussion one week, although I did not collect what
> they did.

Rowan devoted the last three weeks of the class to workshopping rough drafts of these research papers.

Rowan admits that the in-class workshopping took a bit of time to gel. At first, her students were a bit hesitant. Their comments defaulted to the surface mechanics of drafts. However, "as they got more and more comfortable with the idea of criticizing each other's work," she writes, "the discussions became more and more animated — and hugely longer." Rowan reports that the workshops were surprisingly popular among her students. Students who self-reported to her that they were terrified at first, became eager and active learners; they were pleased that their peers had things to say about their writing and that they had things to say about the works-in-progress of their peers. "[S]tudents soon began asking questions about writing conventions that they had clearly been wondering about for a long time."

Students began thinking more about the rhetorical conventions and functions of history-writing, to Rowan's delight, moving away from thinking of writing for history in terms of right or wrong, or "good" as merely grammatically and syntactically correct. Instead, they became interested in the "impact" of writing upon readers and how the rhetorical features of texts asked for particular responses and/or positions. Rowan describes this:

> This proved to be a very profitable way of getting at some otherwise extremely intangible aspects of writing: what is the impact of a rhetorical question? Does it affect the reader differently when it occurs as the first or last sentence in a paper? Is humor ever acceptable? Does intentional dramatic scene-setting add to or distract from the seriousness of an academic paper? And so on.

Her students began to notice, respond to, and evaluate the authorial moves their peers enacted in their papers. Moreover, Rowan reports that students learned how to be more effective writers from listening to their peers comments and reading/editing their peers' papers. They "transferred the lessons learned from other people's prose to their own," according to Rowan.

Rowan now recommends an extensive process of "modeling" for instructors interested in helping their students understand the complex ways that rhetoric and content knowledge work together in effective written texts. Her goal is to get students "to reflect on the choices other authors have made (stylistic, structural, rhetorical, etc.) and the impact those choices have had on them." While this method of instruction was far more time intensive than Rowan would have liked, she reports that the papers she received were more sophisticated and more engaged than she had seen in previous quarters.

CRITICAL METHODS: Introductory Theory-Writing for English Majors

> ### Critical Methods, Theory and Practice
>
> A foundation course for English majors in the literature concentration. Introduces students to literary criticism, as well as critical thinking and writing in English Studies. Emphasis is on the application of principles and methods of literary study to selected texts, which prepares students to examine and respond to texts from a variety of critical perspectives
>
> Prerequisites: Required completion of ENL 101 and ENL 102

For Ben, an assistant professor at a small, Eastern state university known for its commitment to non-traditional students and teaching excellence, peer review/response activities are far from one size fits all. Close integration of peer review/response activities with course goals is central to his course design. "I'm constantly reworking my questions in relation to my goals for students. I'm continually rethinking what I really truly want my students to get out of my class and how I design peer review is a large part of that." He believes that the activities and processes that students conduct when engaged in peer review/response activities must reinforce and entrench the larger skill sets he's seeking to help his students develop: critical and close reading practices, an eye for the language and function of literacy criticism, and an ability to pose and explore the questions that emerge from fiction.

Ben first encountered peer review/response activities as an undergraduate, though he admits with a wry smile that he was not necessarily a fan of such activities. He recalls himself thinking, "What is in it for me?" As a teacher — first of high school and later of college-level fiction and writing — he came to see the advantages of using peer review/response over time and through a great deal of "stubborn" experimentation. Ben notes that he is never one to take a pedagogical tool at face value; for something like peer review/response to be a part of his classes, he must think it through substantially, exploring what different approaches do for student learners. He now uses peer review/response in many of his classes on all levels of instruction.

While a strong advocate for the benefits of peer review/response activities in his classroom, Ben is also more skeptical of the benefits of peer review/response than the other instructors interviewed herein. Like Jackie and Rowan, he does not buy into the belief that peer review/response activities encourage students to rely less on an instructor's comments or to make effective plans for revision. In his experience, students struggle to give each other effective feedback, even when asked about elements of writing that many other instructors would consider foundational, such as the organization of or cohesion in a draft. He finds that students are particularly limited in their ability to give feedback around the conventions of written literary criticism. Students simply lack the necessary experience with the form.

Even when it comes to proofreading and editing, Ben says, some students may even give each other bad advice. "Students are able to identify problems in one another's drafts," Ben notes, "but what to do about those problems most often has to come from me." This is only natural, he believes. The ways of thinking and working with texts central to the disciplinary forms of writing he's teaching are generally unfamiliar to even his strongest students. As such, Ben's primary goal for his students is to consider the ways that other students have approached writing assignments and to reflect upon how a peer's response lends insights into their own work with texts. In Ben's experience, students profit more from giving feedback as readers than from getting it. His interest is in helping students to develop the burgeoning awareness that readers *respond* to texts in particular ways; the criticisms and insights students offer to others, he hopes, help them to increase their awareness of how their own writing may or may not act upon readers as well.

For these reasons, Ben feels that he must be an active presence in the process of peer review/response in order for students to truly gain the benefits of the process, prompting and encouraging, reinforcing stronger comments and redirecting as necessary as peer review/response groups meet and comment on one another's drafts. "It's not a day off. If anything I work harder during peer review than I do on other days," Ben tells me. During peer review/response, Ben tends to circulate while his students are reviewing one another's papers, interacting with groups in process, reinforcing the directions and methods central to the writing assignment. In this way he is able to redirect his students' attentions when necessary and support what they may be doing effectively. While he is energetic, he does note that "it is impossible to give all the attention that's necessary to every student." He tends to follow up days dedicated to peer review/response activities in class with one-on-one personal conferences where he can prompt his students to reflect upon the ways an assignment requires them to work with a text.

Ben's peer review/response sheet is highly tailored to the primary goal that he has for students in his class—that they become more effective in making "interpretive interventions" into the fiction they are reading for his class. He asks his students to look for the ways the "interpretive intervention" has been supported by their peers, to consider how word choice or other elements might play into the development of their argumentative points, and if there are any clear weaknesses in the ways a peer has provided textual support in a draft. In this way, Ben's peer review/response activity reflects the central activities in his class—reading effectively, interpreting fiction with some sophistication, and writing up what students' see in ways that are convincing and effective within the contexts of literary criticism. "What I want them to get out of peer review is this," Ben says. "How do you find your way into a text? I want to see students engaging in particular ways with the text." Ben's entire design and execution of peer review/response activities reiterates this process and its attendant skills for students. By the end of the semester he begins to see gains in their ability to read, analyze, and write about texts.

DISCUSSION

Writing is an attempt to exercise the will, to identify the self within the constraints of some discourse community. We are constrained insofar as we must borrow the traces, codes, and signs which we inherit and which our discourse community imposes. We are free insofar as we do what we can to encounter and learn new codes, to intertwine codes in new ways, and to expand our semiotic potential—with our goal being to effect change and establish our identities within the discourse communities we chose to enter.

        —JAMES PORTER, "INTERTEXTUALITY AND THE DISCOURSE COMMUNITY"

Adoption. Adaptation. The process of coming to own an instructional practice for any instructor often results in changes, large and small, to the centers, shapes, and inflections of that practice. Each of the above case studies high-lights the ways instructors in the disciplines have remade practices central to general writing instruction into activities that support students towards the very specific forms of writing in their fields. These instructors have done so in slightly different ways. Jackie's focus in the peer review/response activities for her Writing for Psychology class familiarizes students with ways that psy-chology research presents itself as credible, thorough, and grounded in an ongoing research conversation central to the field. Rowan's two-quarter senior capstone in history created an invested community of interlocutors who discussed the effects of particular rhetorical choices made by peer-authors writing their way into greater knowledge of historical events and the secondary sources that treat them. Ben's course in literary theory and writing integrated the problematic of interpretive reading into the process by which students would think through the appropriateness and complexity of one another's texts.

Notably, each instructor is very clear that, while peers are the primary audience and first line of reader response in these activities, their involvement as disciplinary professionals is also crucial; each instructor keeps an active presence in the process, acting as a disciplinary guide, directing the tenor, extent, focus, and type of responses to the best of their abilities. To build upon Corbett's call . . . for peer review to help students think about higher-order skills, these instructors ask students to move beyond commenting on lower-order concerns and to grapple with what makes for effective writing within a particular, disciplinary context (236). Each instructor also notes that peer review/response requires a good deal of their time and energy, but that the payoff is that students do strengthen their disciplinary reading and writing abilities in the course of the term. There are connections to be made here, as well, to discussions of teacher authority and of peer review/response as men-toring or modeling; while the instructors I observed and interviewed obviously do not shirk their authority or run a completely decentered peer review process, they do shift the typical frameworks of writing instruction when they take on the crucial role of disciplinary guide and ask students to think about how the heuristics of a field shape the expectations of readers. Finally, each instructor also approaches peer review/response as a process of informing students about their roles as readers and writers within a disciplinary community with very specific notions of writing. . . . [T]his exercise helps students to understand the rhetorical nature of writing and the responsive flexibility of genre-forms, particularly in relation to the disciplinary nature of problem solving.

These ways of adapting peer review/response activities in disciplinary writing classes bring to mind the claims of WAC/WID scholars, such as Bartholomae, Porter, and Williams, that writing effectively in disciplinary communities is as much a process of socialization as it is a way of putting words on the page. Knowing how to take up an appropriate ethos, to write for and respond to others within a community, and work through the problematics that matter are central to effective writing in any field. We often speak of these things as if they are generalities; but in practice, as these instructors show, the face of written knowledge is shaped by the specific contexts of disciplinary problem-solving processes. Composition instructors may benefit their students in peer review/response activities by foregrounding a similar awareness of the differences between writing tasks in different settings, especially the ways written responses change in relation to varied purposes, audiences, and genres.

A final note returns us to consider the benefits of peer review and response activities in disciplinary writing classes. Among the results of a long-term study on student learning transfer undertaken by Linda Bergmann and Janet Zapemick is the finding that undergraduates would prefer to learn writing from experts in their fields. As Bergmann and Zapernick write, "the students in our study were much more open to learning to write like historians, chemists, or electrical engineers in the context of studying chemistry, history, or electrical engineering than they were to learning to write like students in the context of a writing class" (141). Bergmann and Zapernick go on to note that few faculty members in the disciplines are entirely comfortable taking up the role of writing instructor, however. These examples of the adoption and adaptation of peer review/response, then, may offer further insights for instructors in composition *and* instructors in the disciplines interested in, but still hesitant to work explicitly toward preparing their students for writing in their fields. The case studies highlighted in this essay show the importance of continuing to seek and build upon such examples so that we may use what we learn to work inside and outside of writing classes, general and disciplinary, toward more specific ends.

WORKS CITED

Beaufort, Anne. *College Writing and Beyond: A New Framework for University Writing Instruction.* Logan: Utah State UP, 2007. Print.

Bergmann, Linda S., and Zapernick, Janet. "Disciplinarity and Transfer: Students' Perceptions of Learning to Write." *WPA: Writing Program Administration* 31.1-2 (Fall/Winter 2007): 124–49. Print.

Barst, Julie M., April Brooks, Leda Cempellin, and Barb Kelinjan. "Peer Review Across Disciplines: Improving Student Performance in the Honors Humanities Classroom." *Honors in Practice—Online Archive. Paper 128.* (2011): n. pag. Web. August 11, 2012.

Bartholomae, David. "Writing Assignments: Where Writing Begins." *Forum.* Ed. Patricia L. Stock. Upper Montclair, NJ: Boynton/Cook, 1983. Print.

Bazerman, Charles. *Shaping Written Knowledge: The Genre and Activity of the Experimental Article in Science.* Madison: U of Wisconsin P, 1988. Print.

———. "The Life of Genre, the Life in the Classroom." Ed. Wendy Bishop and Hans Ostrom. *Genre and Writing: Issues, Arguments, Alternatives.* Portsmouth, NH: Boynton/Cook, 1997. 19–26. Print.

Bazerman, Charles, and James Paradis, eds. *Textual Dynamics of the Professions: Historical and Contemporary Studies of Writing in Professional Communities.* Madison: U of Wisconsin P, 1991. Print.

Berkenkotter, Carol, Thomas Huckin, and John Ackerman. "Conventions, Conversations, and the Writer: Case Study of a Student in a Rhetoric Ph.D. Program." *Research in the Teaching of English* 22 (1988): 9–44. Print.

Ching, Kory Lawson. "The Instructor-Led Peer Conference: Teachers as Participants in Peer Response." *Peer Pressure, Peer Power: Collaborative Peer Review and Response in the Writing Classroom,* edited by Steven J. Corbett, Michelle LaFrance, and Teagan Decker, Fountainhead Press, 2014, pp. 15–28.

Corbett, Steven J. "Tips toward More Productive CPRR." *Peer Pressure, Peer Power: Theory and Practice in Peer Review Response for the Writing Classroom,* edited by Steven J. Corbett, Michelle LaFrance, and Teagan E. Decker, Fountainhead Press, 2014, pp. 235–43.

Downs, Douglas, and Elizabeth Wardle. "Teaching about Writing, Righting Misconceptions: (Re)Envisioning 'First-year Composition' as 'Introduction to Writing Studies'." *College Composition and Communication* 58.4 (2007): 552–87. Print.

Herrington, Anne, and Deborah Cadman. "Peer Review and Revising in an Anthropology Course: Lessons for Learning." *College Composition and Communication* 42.2 (1991): 184–99. Print.

Herrington, Anne, and Charles Moran. *Writing, Teaching, and Learning in the Disciplines.* New York: Modern Language Assn., 1992. 86–98. Print.

Hyland, Ken. *Disciplinary Discourses: Social Interactions in Academic Writing.* Michigan classics ed. Ann Arbor: U of Michigan P, 2004. Print.

Kaufer, David S., and Richard Young. "Writing in the Content Areas: Some Theoretical Complexities." *Theory and Practice in the Teaching of Writing: Rethinking the Discipline.* Ed. Lee Odell. Carbondale: Southern Illinois UP, 1993. 71–104. Print.

Petraglia, Joseph, ed. *Reconceiving Writing, Rethinking Writing Instruction.* Mahwah, NJ: Lawrence Erlbaum, 1995. Print.

Porter, James. "Intertextuality and the Discourse Community." *Rhetoric Review* 5.1 (1986): 34–57. Print.

Russell, David R. *Writing in the Academic Disciplines: A Curricular History.* 2nd ed. Carbondale: Southern Illinois UP, 2002. Print.

Spear, Karen. *Sharing Writing: Peer Response Groups in English Classes.* Portsmouth, NH: Boynton/Cook Publishers, 1988. Print.

Walvoord, Barbara, and Lucille McCarthy. *Thinking and Writing in College: A Naturalistic Study of Students in Four Disciplines.* Urbana, IL: NCTE, 1990. Print.

Wardle, Elizabeth. "'Mutt Genres' and the Goal of FYC: Can We Help Students Write the Genres of the University?" *College Composition and Communication* 60.4 (2009): 765–90. Print.

PART SIX

Digital Environments

Introduction to Part Six

Our final section offers readings on the development of peer review in computer-enhanced and digital environments. We've selected readings to present basic technological considerations that may complicate and enrich how we teach and theorize peer review and response in the context of the increasingly digital landscape of writing courses. We've also included here readings that make clear the connections between pedagogical goals and the design of peer review and response activities—as a number of notable scholars of computers and writing have argued, it is a mistake to think of digital environments, software platforms, and other technologies for writing and writing group interactions as simple and/or neutral tools. These environments mediate human behavior, shaping what writers do and how they understand what they do. Researchers interested in how these environments and tools may mediate writing as artifact and activity have only just begun to understand the many processes that undergird these digital mediations of peer review in writing classes.

The first selection, Arlene A. Russell's "The Evolution of Calibrated Peer Review" (2013), provides an overview of the creation, development, and multiple uses of Calibrated Peer Review (CPR). The tool has been shown to increase the content knowledge, exam scores, and writing clarity of students as it provides a process of calibration and review via web-based peer interactions. In this essay, Russell argues that CPR has the potential to help faculty understand that quality in student writing is closely related to the quality of the prompts students are given; when students are explicitly guided to pay attention to the elements of writing most valued by their instructors (and effectively compensated for this attention to form or rhetorical awareness), students will both attend to these details and potentially improve in digital environments with scaffolded instructional support.

Guided by the principles of activity theory and Vygotsky's social theories of learning, Li Jin and Wei Zhu consider student motives and their engagement in particular activity systems, especially around their use of instant messaging as a tool for giving and gathering peer response feedback. In "Dynamic Motives in ESL Computer-Mediated Peer Response" (2010), the authors argue that interactive online tools may trigger, support, and alter student motivations toward participation in peer response activity systems, while the lack of "knowledge and experience" with a particular tool may mediate the formation of new and/or abolishment of old motives for some students. We include this essay here because, as the authors claim, this study indicates that for some students the integration of technology may increase the difficulties and/or complexities of engagement in peer review activities.

The final essay of this section, Joanna Wolfe and Jo Ann Griffin's "Comparing Technologies for Online Writing Conferences: Effects of Medium on Conversation" (2012), is a comparative study of face-to-face writing center conferencing with two forms of digitally mediated peer response activities. We include it here for its contribution to a discussion of how digital environments and tools shape and enable interactions in peer response groups. The findings of this study include that some forms of technology-enabled conferencing allow writing center tutors to exert more control in sessions — the authors suggest that this is a product of the software's focus on the document at the center of the tutorial over places to take personal notes or other forms of interaction. Wolfe and Griffin call for further research on the impact of audio, visual, and desktop sharing digital environments as they impact peer-feedback interactions.

In all, the readings included in Part Six highlight the opportunities and constraints that accompany developing peer response and review activities within digital environments. The readings clearly suggest that the selection of a digital tool or environment cannot be separated from other reflexive processes of pedagogical investment and understanding. While technological innovations in the last two decades do allow for more flexible and interactive design options, these environments and tools may mediate student engagement in peer response activities in ways that the field might yet better understand. It is our hope that these readings will offer a strong starting point for the next generation of researchers interested in how peer response activities take shape and continue to evolve in our increasingly digital era.

21 *The Evolution of Calibrated Peer Review*™

ARLENE A. RUSSELL

"Calibrated Peer Review™ *(CPR) is a web-based, instructional tool that enables frequent writing assignments in any discipline, with any class size, even in large classes with limited instructional resources."*

Thus, begins the website introduction (http://cpr.molsci.ucla.edu) to an instructional tool conceived in the early 1990's before Wikipedia (2001), and when MS Office, ChemDraw, and Spartan were being delivered on discs and installed on each computer. Proposing web-based instruction as a goal of the Molecular Science Project in 1995 (*1*) was daring and high risk. Fortunately, the Chemistry Division of the Division of Undergraduate Education under the leadership of Susan Hixson, was willing to take the risk; the ensuing years have validated that choice, as many of the then ambitious goals have become expected teaching practices fifteen years later.

INCEPTION

The learning goals of the Molecular Science Project were to prepare students (1) who would have a deep understanding of chemistry concepts and principles, (2) who had learned collaboration skills through doing chemistry, (3) who could use the modern technology tools of the chemist, and (4) who could write about chemistry. The radical component of the vision, however, was that the project would meet these goals through the integration of technology and telecommunications into the instructional process, and shift the instruction from lecture to active student learning. Faculty from six institutions

From *Trajectories of Chemistry Education Innovation and Reform*, edited by Thomas Holme et al., American Chemical Society, 2013, pp. 129–43.

(Crossroads School—Joe Wise, East Los Angeles College—Carcy Chan, Pasadena City College—Victoria Bragin, Mt. San Antonio College—Eileen Di Mauro and Iraj Nejad, California State University, Fullerton—Patrick Wegner, and the University of California, Los Angeles—Orville Chapman and Arlene Russell) formed the scientific core of the project. This cross-section represented the common and shared responsibility that still exists for teaching the first two years of chemistry and the diversity of students in the nation. Even by the second year of the project others had come under the Molecular Science umbrella: community college faculty from Albuquerque—Marie Villarba, San Francisco—Tim Su, Houston—John Magner, Seattle—Joann Romascan, and Las Vegas—Carolyn Collins were active participants, through an "Adopt and Adapt" FLASH grant in 1999 (2), which formalized the collaboration; Mike Mosher at the University of Nebraska, Kearney soon began to contribute to the project also through the "Adopt and Adapt" program at NSF (3). While the community college faculty saw the CSU-Fullerton on-line Mastering Chemistry homework and active learning products as the primary boons for their students, Mosher seized the centerpiece project developed at UCLA, Calibrated Peer Review™, to teach students scientific report writing. He utilized the Calibrated Peer Review program to manage the instruction and writing in an innovative, intensive-writing laboratory curriculum. For each experiment, students focused on a different component of a lab report, thus providing manageable, scaffolded instruction throughout the term leading to the proficiency expected in upper division courses. The dilemma Mosher was facing then on how to teach technical writing to large classes, and to give students practice writing and targeted feedback, is still shared by many faculty. Scientific report writing forms the core of writing in lower division chemistry courses, yet these are the courses that carry the highest enrollments. Mosher's foresight, to use CPR to teach report writing skills, has been replicated in other institutions and disciplines in the ensuing years. A review of the assignments created in the original CPR program shows dozens of assignments connected to laboratory experiments and to the communication of scientific data. A few of the CPR users have published the results of their work (4, 5).

CPR, however, is not restricted to implementation in existing writing arenas. The topics of assignments are far ranging, and the use of CPR is limited only by the creativity of the faculty who have envisioned writing as a way of learning (6, 7). Not only have more than 300,000 students used the program in over 1,500 institutions around the world, many instructors have used CPR as a research tool to investigate and improve student learning.

Calibrated Peer Review, which is based on the scientific practice of expert peer review, is the most enduring of the products of the Molecular Science project. Earlier articles have elaborated on the details of the CPR process (8–12). We provide here a brief synopsis of the process to give context to the evolution of the program and the research in learning that the tool has facilitated. Although the program has evolved in response to users' needs and changing technology, the embedded pedagogical structure has proved sound.

THE CALIBRATED PEER REVIEW PROCESS

Writing-across-the-curriculum and adjunct-writing courses continue to have strong and widespread advocacy in higher education (*13, 14*). These courses are, however, resource intensive and writing in the STEM disciplines has often been relegated to the upper division or the graduate level, particularly in large institutions. Through web-based management of the text submission and review process, CPR was the first program to enable writing in any size class without additional teaching resources. The success of a CPR assignment relies on precise and clear articulation of the topic of the assignment. The aphorism "clear writing demonstrates clear thinking" captures the pedagogy of CPR, that writing provides a window on student understanding of the topic and an alternative means to assess learning. To do this, the CPR program is grounded on the precept that peer review is first and foremost a fundamental instructional strategy for engaging students through critical thinking *and* secondarily a mechanism for evaluation of their peer's writing. Effective peer review, however, depends on "qualified judges" (*15*). Training students to become those qualified judges or capable reviewers, that is "CALIBRATING" them to understand the nuances of the content of the assignment and to recognize errors and misconceptions, *when they have just learned about the topic*, constitutes the signature component for each and every writing assignment. It is fundamental to the pedagogy. Monitoring that training, providing feedback on the training, and tracking the training so that poorly trained reviewers carry little weight on the reviews they give their peers give confidence to the reviewers and reliability to the reviews.

As an instructional tool, Calibrated Peer Review serves to teach higher-order thinking skills through scaffolding the writing and evaluation tasks. An assignment consists of four components that are interwoven to encourage learning at each stage (Figure 1). Students are first presented with a writing task, which is supported by resources, references, and guidance for preparing for the actual text writing. This guidance enables students to address the topic of the assignment, yet gives them freedom to articulate their ideas in their own words. Even students recognize the power of writing-to-learn (*12*), which undergirds the strong and widespread advocacy for writing in higher education (*16, 17*), and serves as the initial motivation for many faculty to try using CPR.

The second stage of the CPR process, the calibration training, begins only after students have wrestled with the writing and submitted their work for review. The program presents the students with three pre-written texts, which span the range of responses expected from their peers. Studying and evaluating these texts not only prepares them for peer reviewing, it also provides a directed opportunity for students to continue to learn the topic. Generally one text will be an exemplar, and the other two will contain the common errors and misconceptions that frequently occur. Students evaluate and rate these texts using a rubric that addresses the critical issues and concepts of the topic. Prior guidance on how to rate texts helps to provide the common understanding

FIGURE 1   Tutorial flow-chart of the process and stages of an assignment as seen
by a student.

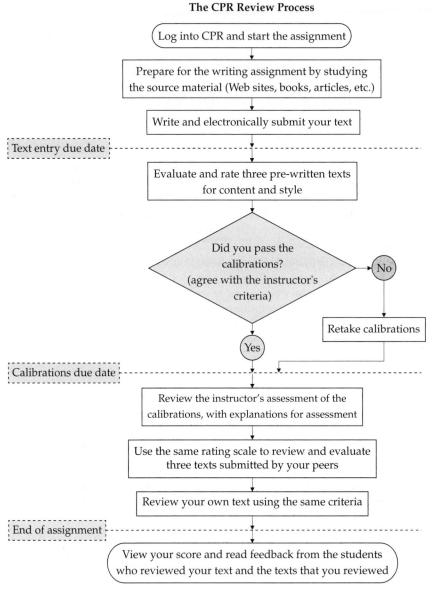

The CPR Review Process

From "The Evolution of Calibrated Peer Review" by Arlene A. Russell (2013 American Chemical Society).

that experts use to value student work. The consistent goal of the training is to bring all students to an "expert" level of understanding. Realizing that the rate of deep learning is not necessarily correlated to mastery, the CPR program does not penalize students who require a second attempt at mastering the training component of the program. Even with a second attempt, not all students will make "expert status." Thus, behind the scenes, the program tracks student calibration performance and assigns a "reviewer competency index" (RCI) to each student. The RCI subsequently is used as a weighting factor in the scoring algorithm to determine what impact the reviewer will have on the peer's text rating.

The third stage of the CPR process involves the double-blind review of three peer texts. The program randomly selects from the full set of texts only after all texts have been submitted. Laggards in text submission are just as likely to be assigned a text from an early bird as from a text submitted any time before the due date. Students then use the peer assessment rubric, which they learned during calibration training. In this stage, however, students are required to give written feedback to their peers on the reasons for their assessments and ratings. As in the academic world, the most useful reviewer's comments can serve to support improvement. With CPR, good feedback from a peer's voice can be a powerful learning object. For example, a student in an organic chemistry class wrote:

> **Rating: 4; Explanation:** You have the general concepts of base peak and molecular ion peak down, but your explanations [*sic*] of how you obtain these peaks is incorrect. First, when you determine the molecular ion peak, you add the weights of the ions that were given with the problem (i.e., C=12, not 12.01, H=l, not 1.01, etc.). Hence, your molecular ion's weight will be 84, not 84.93. Although your concept is correct, your calculation is wrong. Also, your explaination of the 86 m/z and 88 m/z readings is very difficult to follow. You never directly tie the 86 m/z reading to CH2C135C137+. Your explaination of the differing levels of 86 m/z and 88 m/z is good in that you correctly state that it has to do with the ratios that the isotopes occur in nature. The details of your explaination, however, are incorrect. The fact that there are two C137 atoms, which have a 25% chance of occurring in nature, present in the molecule LOWERS the chance of that molecule being present, since there are two "one in four" chances that have to be overcome instead of just one in the case of only one C137 atom being present. You do not add the 25% chances together and get a 50% chance. Also, you have a few spelling errors and you neglect to put the plus radical (+.) after each ion. You also don't have a summary sentence. Additionally, you lack an explaination of why low pressure upheld in the machine (it is done to reduce the amount of intermolecular processes). Overall, your general understanding is good, but you need to work on the details.

By utilizing the role of feedback to guide revision of written work, some faculty have developed assignments for lab reports where the CPR process constitutes the "pre-write" and drafting stage of the report. Only the final report, with responses to the peer feedback, are submitted to the instructor for grading (*18*). The next version of CPR, which is in development, will include a revision feature as one of the options, which faculty can select, for an assignment.

The final stage of the CPR process brings closure to the assignment for the student. After training and reviewing peers' texts, each student has the opportunity to critically evaluate their original work in light of their new understanding. The articulation of conceptual change by recognizing problems in their original ideas solidifies the progress towards a greater understanding.

CPR4 AND CPR5: AUGMENTING AND ENHANCING CALIBRATED PEER REVIEW

In 2004, a major restructuring of the delivery mechanism for CPR began. It had become apparent that many institutions were interpreting federal regulations (FERPA) (*19*) as a restriction on student work and grades from existing outside of the campus technology firewalls. Because all CPR data at that time were stored at UCLA on a master server, faculty were prevented from using the program. In particular, the faculty at Texas A&M, which had endorsed CPR as a mechanism to meet their new academic senate requirement for writing in every discipline, required a new approach. As a short-term solution the University of California and Texas A&M entered into an agreement, which allowed the latter to house and use a copy of the program on their College Station campus. With one problem solved, another arose. The Texas A&M faculty were now able to use the program, but were isolated from the shared community of users who were developing and modifying discipline-based assignments. Likewise, others could not benefit from their intellectual creativity in developing assignments as part of a science and math initiative (*20*).

The concept of a two-server distributed version (CPR Central and CPR Local) of the program emerged. Once again NSF responded and supported the vision of a shared community of users (*21*). CPR Central, located at UCLA, was developed to provide a place for authoring, storing, and sharing assignments. This central assignment library includes all assignments that were part of the old CPR server library as well as a place to continually grow assignments that are created by the community of CPR authors. Figure 2 contrasts the assignment resources now available through the Central Library with the number of assignments that have been shared in the original CPR program over 15 years.

CPR Local became the entity of the program that was designed to be installed on a server at the user's institution. Students' records and work are now stored entirely on the host campus, safely behind its firewalls. The institution copy of CPR Local communicates with CPR Central only when an instructor is setting up an assignment for subsequent class use. After an assignment is copied to the CPR Local server, the institution is no longer dependent on a server at UCLA and students no longer have to share the UCLA server's processing power and resources with other institutions.

The revision and rewrite of the CPR program furnished an opportune moment to add many new features for students, for instructors, and for assignment authors. Perhaps the most important new feature for students in CPR4

FIGURE 2   Comparison of the growth and number of assignments available to the community of CPR users in the original CPR program (solid line) hosted at UCLA and in the shared Central CPR Library (dashed line) used with the distributed CPR4 and CPR5 versions of the program.

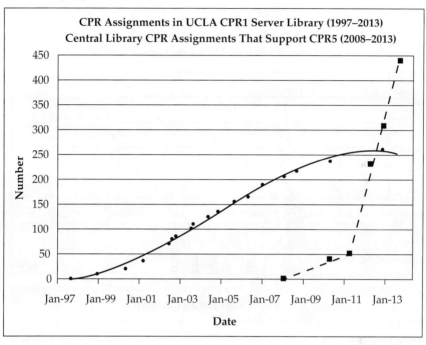

CPR Assignments in UCLA CPR1 Server Library (1997–2013)
Central Library CPR Assignments That Support CPR5 (2008–2013)

From "The Evolution of Calibrated Peer Review" by Arlene A. Russell (2013 American Chemical Society).

has been a new function at the end of an assignment for students to see how others reviewed the texts that they had pondered over and evaluated. Evaluation is new and often intimidating to students. The hope that students would gain confidence in their own evaluation skills when they saw that others detected the same strengths and weaknesses in their peers' work as they did has been borne out. In a 2008 pilot test of the tool, 65% of the students agreed or strongly agreed that their "confidence increased by comparing others' reviews." They value this new feature for a variety of reasons (Figure 3). Students are relieved to find that their peers provide reviews consistent with their own.

The most innovative feature of the new distributed CPR4, however, was a new tool that addressed a faculty need. The Texas A&M collaboration had shown that faculty scholarship was an integral part of CPR assignment development (22). Assignment authors bring to the process a deep knowledge of content and a recognition of student learning. Because of the need to know how students struggle with the topic, well-crafted assignments rely on the wisdom of experienced instructors. As the faculty brought to bear their creativity as authors they wanted a way to document this new scholarship of teaching (23).

FIGURE 3   Student explanations of the reasons on the Likert scale ratings of the statement, "Comparing my peers' ratings of the texts I reviewed improved my confidence in my understanding" [of the topic of the assignment]. (gray—gained confidence in my reviewing ability; checkered—helped in understanding content; white—liked comparing understanding with peers; black—not useful for me but would be for others; diagonal—not useful; horizontal—no explanation).

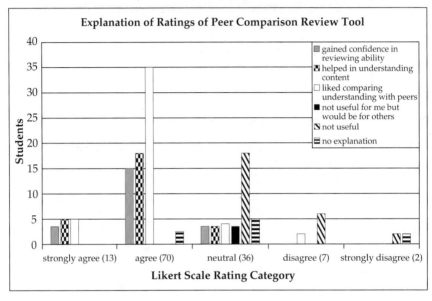

From "The Evolution of Calibrated Peer Review" by Arlene A. Russell (2013 American Chemical Society).

They also asked how to give credit to the authors whose assignments they were adapting or adopting. Plagiarism of others' intellectual ideas is not acceptable.

Because the hours, effort, and teaching experience necessary to create a successful assignment, as well as the need for fair attribution of scholarly work requires recognition, a citation index function was built into the new CPR Central Library. New and old users can now search the database of hundreds of assignments and ethically use, copy, or modify an existing assignment. The program automatically maintains a record of the usage of each assignment by the original author, and the derivative works that have emanated from the original creation. As more schools require accountability for teaching in tenure and promotion portfolios CPR can be used to document the impact of an assignment beyond an author's campus.

Development of Calibrated Peer Review, Version 5 followed logically and quickly after CPR4. The rapid growth in networking technology, in both software and hardware, had finally enabled the feasibility of creating a tool to support an endemic component of scientific writing—visual representations of graphs, tables, pictures, spectra, or other images. However, the new tool that allows students to upload a file with their text submission or in lieu of text opened the door for other uses for CPR. The program is no longer limited to writing and writing assessment. Driven by the need for Engineering departments to assess multiple forms of communication, CPR5 became a vehicle to handle such a process (*24*). In CPR5 file uploads can have any format; what students upload to their campus CPR server is limited only by the requirements of an assignment and local policies. The program is robust. Files with more than 11 different extensions were successfully used by students during the first pilot test of this new feature. Thus, the evolution of CPR in response to STEM needs, has broadened its applicability to peer evaluation of posters, PowerPoint slide decks, videos, oral presentations, and music. New and creative uses continue to appear. The future promises tools that more fully adopt the revision processes of scientific publications.

RESEARCH ON LEARNING USING CPR

Creation of new CPR tools and materials has not occurred in a vacuum. Since the inception of the program, faculty have been concerned with the effectiveness of a web-managed, peer-review process. As well as instructors, institutions are increasingly being held accountable for assessment of student learning. They see CPR as a way to show they are meeting their learning objectives. Again Engineering is on the forefront. For example, CPR documentation is being used in ABET accreditation reviews at UCLA and in at least one other Engineering department (*25*).

Much of the research on the impact on learning using CPR has focused on test scores on the topics of the CPR assignments (*26–28*). The studies repeatedly show exam score increases of the order of 10%. Pelaez instituted a "time series design" for a single class of 42 students. She alternated topics taught using didactic lectures and CPR assignments with lectures, group work, and multiple choice quizzes to provide the assessment feedback intrinsic in CPR. Pelaez found that students performed better on exams on the topics of the course that included CPR assignments than on the questions on topics where the lectures were augmented with group discussion and quizzes. She saw similar gains across all levels of student ability on the multiple choice questions on exams, but the top performing students (on exams) had larger gains on the essay questions than the weaker performing students (*26*). Chapman's early work in Economics gave the first insight into the additive learning effected by the evaluation components of CPR. His "intact class comparison" involved three large classes (>100) taught by the same instructor using the same ten case studies in all classes. One of the classes was assigned the CPR writing component only; the other two classes completed full CPR assignments with peer evaluations and self-assessment. Chapman repeated the experiment the following semester. He observed that on common exams, across every quintile, the grades for his students were higher in those sections that had completed the full CPR assignments rather than just writing about the topic before the class discussion (Figure 4). Rudd et al. carried out a similar study in an introductory Geology course for non-science majors with two sections taught by the same instructor. Like Pelaez and Chapman, they found that scores on essay

FIGURE 4   Comparison of midterm performance by students who only performed the writing component of CPR assignments and those who
completed the reviewing stages also. Graphing the scores by quintile shows that the gains occur at all levels. Economics 200, Fall 1999.
K. S. Chapman, COBAE Faculty Report (1999–2000).

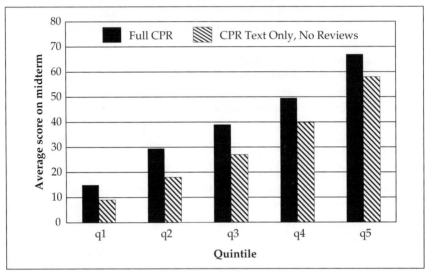

From "The Evolution of Calibrated Peer Review" by Arlene A. Russell (2013 American Chemical Society).

questions on exams were significantly higher for the group who had completed
full CPR assignments than the group who had only written about the topic.
Performance on multiple choice questions was also higher for the CPR group,
but the difference was not statistically significant (27).

Others have also documented the impact of the peer review process on
learning. When students' opinions on their learning gains from using CPR are
collected, the importance of peer review always surfaces:

"Truthfully, I enjoyed CPR. Writing the essay was a great way to review
the specifics of cyclohexane strain, but when I reviewed the peer essays I
think I learned most. I was able to see what strong points my essay had,
and more importantly where I was lacking." (29)

"When I read other people's essays, I see 'Oh, this is what tied into
that idea' like the streamlined body makes [penguins, et al.] move faster.
If I didn't mention that [point] in my essay or didn't realize that, then
reading someone else's essay is what showed me that that's how I was
supposed to answer the question." (30)

More recently Enders et al. (31) carried out a detailed analysis of learning
throughout an assignment. They found that the top students in their graduate
statistics class learned the content of the assignment (linear regression) during

FIGURE 5   Location in a CPR assignment (white—text entry, light gray—
calibration stage, dark gray—post review) where students demonstrate
understanding of graphing skills. Twenty-four of the 31 students
showed understanding at the end of the calibration training stage
although not all (only 19) recognized the error in their own work.
Three additional students learned the principles when reviewing their
peers' work and correctly identified the errors in their own work.

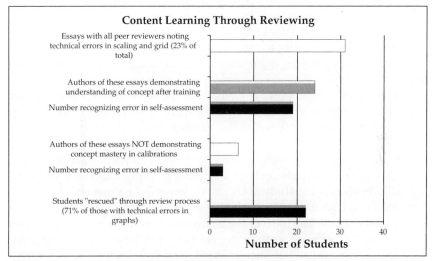

From "The Evolution of Calibrated Peer Review" by Arlene A. Russell (2013 American Chemical Society).

the calibration training stage, while the median and low-performing students
did not master the concepts until the self-assessment phase of the assignment. Their work parallels the findings of this author in a 2010 study in which
students assessed the quality of Beer's Law graphs prepared by their peers
(Figure 5).

Seventy-one percent of the students whose original graphs did not meet
expected standards, learned through the calibration and reviewing stages of
the assignment and subsequently identified the weaknesses and problems in
their own work (*33*).

Writing-to-learn and learning-to-write are not synonymous. While "clear
writing demonstrates clear thinking," clear writing can also demonstrate erro-
neous thinking and poor writing can obfuscate correctly understood concepts.
Improving students' science writing skills has been a driving force for adoption
of the CPR process for many instructors. Most reported studies have found that
writing clarity does improve when courses have used CPR (*4–6, 33*). However,
the results of studies that have teased out writing-to-learn from learning-to-
write are mixed. Hartburg et al. (*5*) found significant writing gains for students
whose biochemistry reports were evaluated by peers and losses for those whose
reports were graded by teaching assistants. Walvoord et al. (*34*) found no gains.

Reynolds and Moskovitz's analysis of the emphasis or attention placed on writing skills in a random sample of the STEM assignments posted on the CPR website sheds light on these contrasting results (35). They found that 90% of the assignments lacked clear expectations for writing in the prompt students were given. Rather, the writing prompts and evaluation focused on content. Although no guidance was provided in the prompt, some assignments had implicit writing expectations. However, even those assignments that did address writing quality in the rubric tended to concentrate on the lower-order skills of mechanical and grammatical errors. They found that few assignments addressed the higher-order writing skills of effective argumentation, the use of evidence-based analyses, organization, or appropriate use of sources. Attention to audience also seldom occurred.

That students' higher-order writing skills do not improve when they are not explicitly addressed should not be surprising (36). Instructors of large lower division classes know well that students generally do only what they are asked to do. Therefore, explicitly articulating to students the writing expectations and providing them with feedback on their writing performance is just as important if an instructor's goals for a CPR assignment include scientific writing skills. In an ongoing study at UCLA, higher-order writing skills are being imbedded into both the guidance and the rubric of CPR assignments. This first step has established that 100% of the students believe their own essays "have logical flow." Their peers often disagree! However, when the writing guidance specifies an explicit trait that leads to logical flow, such as the use of transitions, the idea of logical flow becomes tangible and students are able to recognize this quality or lack of it in their own writing. Student use of transitions and other elements that improved organization increased and their self-assessment showed no significant differences with the assessments from their peers' evaluation of their "logical flow." Students will attend to writing if asked to do so and can improve their writing skills if the practices inherent in scientific writing are properly scaffolded into the instruction.

TABLE 1   Comparison of the change in confidence in one's ability to recognize the quality of one's own writing and in one's knowledge of the skills necessary to assess one's writing by students who received instructor feedback on their four writing assignments (non-CPR) and those who reviewed peers' texts and provided feedback to their peers. L. Likkel *J. Coll. Sci Teaching*, 41, no. 3 (2012)

*Perceived ability to tell if own essay good**			*Perceived skill in assessing own writing**		
	CPR (54)	Non-CPR (21)		CPR (88)	Non-CPR (30)
more positive	65%	29%	more positive	43%	23%
no change	20%	38%	no change	51%	77%
more negative	15%	33%	more negative	6%	0

* Excludes students who indicated they were 'very confident' at both start and end of term.

particularl
peer feedb
lus' study
writing by
compositic
feedback v
age of revi:
that has e>
through e>
approach
writer role
1992; Lock
focusing o
complexity
assume dif
terns of int
The ac
sibilities fo
Over the p
Warschaue
classroom
group wor
on compu
computer-r
English as
peer respor
other's wri
writing cla
2001; Liu &
on student
studies inv
focused on
(2004) four
from peers,
in generatii
that studen
Existin
valuable in
of peer fee
gated conce
tion in peer
tasks, syncl
become the
generation
municative
language ir

Finally as the knowledge in the STEM fields expands exponentially, teaching students to have confidence in their ability to be independent life-long learners becomes more critical. Likkel recently reported on the impact of using CPR on students' confidence in their abilities (37). Like Chapman, her study involved three intact classes. Two used CPR for their writing assignments, for which she provided the feedback. Her other two astronomy classes used CPR to manage and assess the four essays in the course. Table 1 shows her students' changes in their confidence in knowing whether they had written a "good" essay and in their perceived skill in evaluating their own work. On both criteria, those who had the opportunity to engage in active evaluation and peer review were more positive about their ability to assess their own work when they left the course.

References to other studies using the Calibrated Peer Review program as a research tool may be found on the program website (http://cpr.molsci.ucla.edu).

CONCLUSIONS

During the past 15 years, student writing and peer review using the CPR program has been employed by more than 300,000 students in over 1,500 institutions and 3,500 courses. What began as a convenience for economies of scale has serendipitously evolved for many instructors as a more powerful method to teaching critical thinking within their disciplines. It has been used as a research tool for assessing learning, for improving instruction, for documenting adoption of innovation, and most recently for validating new digital lexical analysis tools. The program has found application beyond the STEM disciplines (Table 2) and is expanding into other areas of communication. CPR Version 6, which will allow for revisions after review portends to bring this instructional resource even closer to the authentic practice of science. Lichter asserted that "the goal of peer review is improved products" (15). The goal of CPR remains steadfast: to increase students' learning and their understanding of the importance and validity of peer review in the improvement of scientific knowledge.

TABLE 2   Discipline distribution of the 500 assignments in the CPR Central Library, March 2013

Astronomy	5	Computer Science	1	General Science	20
Biochemistry	4	Earth and Space Sciences	7	Non-STEM	
Bioengineering	2	Engineering	60	Social Sciences	58
Biology	91	Environmental Science	7	Humanities	47
Physiology	7	Mathematics and Statistics	31	Medicine, Dentistry, Public Health	44
Chemistry	115	Physics	13	Other	9

2̲2̲

the development of speaking and writing skills. It would be intriguing to closely examine student participation in peer response in the instant-message-mediated environment. Such investigation would shed considerable light on how the use of technological tools influences students in CMPR tasks and how students may develop through their participation in CMPR tasks.

This paper reports a case study investigating how the use of a synchronous tool, an instant messenger program, influenced the participation of two ESL students in three CMPR tasks in an ESL academic writing class in the summer semester of 2006. More specifically, through the lens of activity theory (Engeström, 1987, 1999; Leont'ev, 1981), which posits that development originates from social interaction that is constantly mediated by a variety of physical and psychological tools (Vygotsky, 1978) or artifacts (Wertsch, 1991; Wertsch, 1998) and that all human social interaction is a mediated learning and developmental process that can only be understood through the analysis of participants' motives, the reported study examined how the use of instant messaging mediated the motives of two ESL students who participated in three CMPR tasks.

2. THEORETICAL FRAMEWORK

This study was theoretically guided by activity theory, which was extended from Lev Vygotsky's (1978) sociocultural theory, further developed by Vygotsky's best friend and pupil Alexei Leont'ev (1981) in the 1930s, and later expanded by Engeström (1987, 1999) and other scholars. Activity theory is a social psychological approach to understanding human mental functioning, social contexts, and processes surrounding mental behaviors. It provides a cultural historical view of human behaviors that result from socially and historically constructed forms of mediation through mediational artifacts in all human activities (Engeström, 1987; Lantolf, 2000). The mediational artifacts in a human activity are comprised of both physical tools, such as computer tools and books, and symbolic/psychological tools, such as languages, signs, and concepts (Luria, 1973, cited in Lantolf, 2000). In a sociocultural view of human learning and development (Vygotsky, 1978; Wertsch, 1991, 1998), using tools makes it possible for humans to act in a more functional and powerful way and enhances and alters human development. Activity theory, however, does not represent a monolithic theoretical approach. Victor Kaptelinin (2005) argues that activity theory "can be described as a variety of approaches sharing basic principles but differing in how these principles are implemented" (p. 8). Kaptelinin considers work by Leont'ev and Engeström as representing two key approaches to activity theory, and Kaptelinin maintains that these approaches are "complementary" rather than competing.

Leont'ev (1981) argues that human practices can be analyzed at three levels: activity/motive, action/goal, and operation/conditions. Meaning "doing in order to transform something" (Kuutti, 1996, p.25), the *activity* is the unifying element and the unit of analysis in activity theory. An activity is driven and defined by its motive and is realized as goal-directed actions, the chains of which are related to an underlying motive. In order to thoroughly under-

For th
stude
writii
(Grab
Hedg
cess a
ing a
intera
classr
cussic
and e
sourc
build
tion a
Tang
(Man
menta
of exp
sary f
berge
have

N
in fac
on stu
Paulu
Resea
opme

From

stand why humans conduct certain practices, it is essential to decipher the motives that drive individuals' activities. That is, human practices can only be understood if their motives are considered. Leont'ev (1981) proposes that "there is no unmotivated human activity. . . . the object of an activity is its true motive. It is understood that the motive may be either material or ideal, either present in perception or existing only in the imagination of thought" (p. 62). According to Kaptelinin (2005), the "object" of activity in Leont'ev's approach is related to human's need and motivation (p. 11). In addition to emphasizing the role of motive in directing human activity, Leont'ev also proposes that an activity can have multiple motives when it responds to multiple needs. In other words, one activity can be driven by multiple motives. Further, these motives can be ranked hierarchically according to their directional functions in the activity system. However, it is not clear exactly how to rank the motives methodologically.

Embracing activity theory in the analysis of computer-human interaction, computer scientists (e.g., Kaptelinin, 1996; Kaptelinin & Nardi, 2006; Kuutti, 1996) advocate an examination of computer technologies' transformational mediation in human behaviors from a theoretical view of activity. Kari Kuutti (1996) proposes that information technology can support and penetrate human activities at all levels. The mediation of technology at the activity level can be reflected in the technology's existence, which makes an activity possible and feasible. Some computer-human interaction researchers (Kuutti, 1996; Nardi, 1996) admit that the relationships between information technology and human activities may be more complex than we expect. Activity theory provides an inspiring and useful framework to understand human-human interactions in a computer-mediated environment. In particular, it allows for the examination of the effect of technology on the formation of new motives and the consequent reconfiguration of the activities—in other words, the reshaping of existing activities.

Other important concepts provided by activity theory that are relevant to the present study include conflicts and contradictions, which are considered to be the trigger of development (Thorne, 2004). According to the third generation of activity theory expanded by Engeström (1987), Engeström (1999),[1] each subject engaged in an activity system also functions as an individual agent who has an individual history and may react to the context in various ways. This indicates that subjects may be driven by different motives although they are involved in the same task. Activity theory sees contradictions as sources of development; activities are virtually always "in the process of working through contradictions" (Kuutti, 1996, p. 34). The learner's development occurs when confronting these contradictions and undertaking a series of actions to change and solve the contradictions. These changes in turn may produce new contradictions. Thus, learning and development occur in an ongoing contradiction-change cycle. This contradiction solving and new object/activity creating process is perceived as development from the activity theory perspective.

The introduction of computer technologies in language learning has triggered more questions about students' participation in technology-enhanced learning tasks. In the case of L2 peer response, how technology influences students' participation in CMPR tasks needs to be examined. In the sections below, we report a study that was designed to address this issue. Inspired by Leont'ev's proposition of human motive/object as well as Kuutti's (1996) view of computer mediation at the activity/motive level, we examined the role of technology in two ESL students' participation in three CMPR tasks with a focus on (1) the students' motives when participating in CMPR and (2) the mediation of technology (i.e., instant messaging) in the formation and shift of the students' motives. Drawing from other perspectives and constructs of activity theory, such as contradiction and development, we also discuss development which occurred due to motive shift during students' participation in the CMPR tasks.

3. METHODOLOGY

3.1. Study Context

The study was conducted in the English Language Institute (ELI) at a metropolitan research-oriented public university in the Southeast U.S. in summer 2006. More specifically, it took place in a low-advanced-level (Level 4) academic writing class whose purpose was to improve ESL students' written communication skills in the U.S. higher-education academic discourse. A total of 11 students from Belgium, Belize, Mexico, Saudi Arabia, Taiwan, Turkey, and Venezuela were enrolled in the class. This writing class took place from 10:00 to 11:00 am every weekday, and one of the researchers was the class instructor. In addition to taking the writing class, all enrolled students also took required courses in listening, speaking, and reading in the morning as well as other elective courses such as the Test of English as a Foreign Language (TOEFL) and Graduate Record Examination (GRE) preparation in the afternoon. The purpose of the study was explained to the students at the beginning of the course to obtain consent from them for participation in the study.

Students in the writing class were required to write a two- to three-page academic essay in each of five writing modes: compare and contrast, exposition, summary-analysis, argumentation, and problem-solution. A writing process approach with peer response as an integral component was adopted in this class. Before conducting the first computer-mediated peer response (CMPR) task, the instructor explained the rationale for peer response and the steps to be taken during each task. She emphasized the purpose of improving writing skills through peer response in terms of exchanging peer feedback on the content, organization, structure, and usage, as well as the format of peer writing and thoughtfully using the feedback for revision to achieve increased effectiveness in writing. The instructor made it clear that feedback would consist of comments on various aspects of peer writing as well as suggestions for revision, and she explained how to provide helpful feedback. A reader's worksheet was also provided to the students to guide them on what feedback to provide.[2] Students also practiced giving feedback on each other's written paragraphs in a face-to-face peer response exercise. In preparation for the CMPR tasks, students who were not familiar with instant messaging were asked to set up an instant messenger account.

For each CMPR task conducted after the students finished the first essay draft in each rhetorical mode, each student was instructed to swap his/her draft with a partner who could be either pre-assigned by the instructor or self-selected by the student. The students would then read through each other's essay and write comments and suggestions on the reader's worksheet, which was a writing evaluation guide developed by the instructor and distributed upon the essay exchange. During the peer response tasks, conducted every two to three weeks via instant messenger, students exchanged and discussed feedback on their partner's essay. A writer's worksheet, which contained similar questions to those in the reader's worksheet, was also provided to help each student writer actively and selectively seek comments and suggestions from their partner. Students were instructed to revise their first draft after each CMPR task and to submit a second draft to the teacher. A total of five peer response tasks were conducted throughout the semester. The first task was conducted face to face in the regular classroom, and the last four, namely CMPR tasks, were conducted in the institute's computer lab.

The study reported below was part of a larger study designed to examine the impact of technology on student participation in peer response. Data provided in this paper were collected from two student participants: Anton, a 23-year-old Belgian woman, and Iron, a 45-year-old Turkish man (pseudonyms are used here). Anton and Iron were selected for the present study because of their differing levels of knowledge of, and experience with, computer tools and IM. This knowledge level difference was revealed by the participants' responses to an ethnographic survey. Both Anton and Iron volunteered to participate in the study. Since the study's focus was on the mediation of computer technologies in peer response, and since the two participants in this study only took part in the first three CMPR tasks, data were collected from them only during the first three CMPR sessions.

3.2. Participants

According to the ethnographic survey to be described below, Anton was a 23-year-old Belgian student whose native language was French. She graduated with a bachelor's degree in Economics from a college in Belgium one year before the study began. In order to work in the international trade company owned by her sister-in-law, she came to the U.S. to improve her English. She had no intention to enroll in any other higher-educational institution in the U.S. or in any other English-speaking country. Anton had taken English courses for three years in a high school in Belgium, and most of the instruction she received in Belgium focused on grammar and translation. She was not trained to speak English or to compose academic papers in English. She had never heard of peer response until she was enrolled in an intermediate (Level 3) academic writing course at the ELI in spring 2006, which was also her first semester at the ELI. When Anton joined the ELI in January, 2006, she could not speak English fluently. However, she made dramatic progress in the spring semester. When she started the low-advanced-level academic writing class, she was one of the most proficient students in English speaking and writing. She had no obvious communication problems within or beyond the classroom. Anton had her own computer and reported that she had been using it for more than three years and that she was an enthusiastic CMC user. She used email, public chat rooms, instant messenger, and voice-over-Internet-protocol (VOIP) programs to communicate with her friends and family. The IM tool she usually used most was MSN messenger, which she used daily but only for less than one hour per day. She had never used IM to discuss academic issues with classmates.

The other participant, Iron, was 43 years old when he joined the ELI. He was a financial manager in an international finance auditing company located in Istanbul, Turkey. His native language was Turkish, and he obtained his master's degree from a university in Turkey. He had taken English classes in Turkey for roughly three years. However, he had rich experience with English speakers because of his trips to London for business meetings. Thus, although the summer semester was Iron's first semester at the ELI, he was placed at the low-advanced level. Iron could comprehend, read, and write in English with no significant difficulties, but his speaking ability needed improvement. He reported that his sole purpose at the ELI was to improve his English proficiency. He expected to learn how to express himself in both spoken and written forms in English at the ELI. Iron was a frequent computer user before the course although he only used email to communicate with his colleagues in Turkey and occasionally with colleagues in London. Iron could not type on the computer very quickly, especially in English, because his staff usually typed for him when he was in Turkey. He had neither heard of instant messenger nor participated in any peer response sessions prior to his attendance at the ELI.

3.3. Data collection and analysis

A case study approach was adopted in the study with a focus on Anton and Iron's participation in the three CMPR tasks. Anton and Iron were partners during the first two CMPR tasks, and they were paired with new partners in the third CMPR task. Data were collected with qualitative data collection techniques including 1) an ethnographic survey administered at the beginning of the semester to gather information about the participants' age, cultural background, and prior experience with English academic writing instruction, peer response tasks, as well as computer use. This background information, according to activity theory, could help the researchers understand historical factors that might have shaped Anton and Iron's motives in the CMPR tasks; 2) on-screen behavior observations during each CMPR session; 3) beyond-screen behaviors captured by two digital video cameras and through observation by one of the researchers; 4) three rounds of interviews each conducted after a CMPR session as well as informal interviews conducted during class breaks and through online chat, all concerning students' motives and perceptions of CMPR; 5) reflective journals kept by one of the researchers; and 6) Anton and Iron's first and second drafts of papers. The on-screen behavior data included chat transcripts as well as all mouse-clicking and typing on the computer during the three CMPR sessions, which was captured by the free screen-motion-capturing software Wink 2.0 (DebugMode Inc., 2005). The interview data included the participants' responses to questions eliciting their reflections on what they did during the task; their purposes for conducting peer response and for certain behaviors during CMPR; and how they interacted with their partner during the peer response task.

As mentioned earlier, knowing motives is instrumental to understanding human activity. However, identifying human motives is by no means a simple matter. To date, no particular method has been proposed as the prototypical method for analyzing human motives when people participate in an activity. Researchers and scholars, however (e.g., Nardi, 2005; Miettinen, 2005), have mentioned interviews and observations as data sources for this purpose. Following Leont'ev's (1978) definition of motive and using data sources identified as helpful in understanding human motives in activities (Nardi, 2005; Miettinen, 2005), we identified the participants' motives by analyzing information directly from the participants' interviews (i.e., what they thought motivated their behaviors in the CMPR tasks) and by inferring motives from online and offline observations (i.e., what they really did during the tasks), and, if necessary, from other relevant materials such as the students' first and second drafts. It was hoped that the triangulation of direct and indirect information could help us better understand the students' motives in each CMPR task, which in turn would assist us to understand how technology influenced student participation in CMPR. In our analysis, we considered the entire writing class to be driven by an overarching purpose: to develop English academic writing skills.

To examine the role of technology in student participation in CMPR tasks, we first identified the participants' motives, then probed the mediation of technology in the participants' motive formation and shift. A three-step analysis was conducted for each participant to understand the participant's motives. The analysis began with data collected from Anton. In the first step of analysis, transcripts from Anton's interviews following each CMPR task were analyzed to identify her tentative scheme of motives during participation in each CMPR task. The constant comparison method (Lincoln & Guba, 1985) was used to identify and categorize the motives that were expressed explicitly in the interviews. Sentences with key phrases such as "I wanted to . . ." were identified and categorized to analyze what prompted Anton to participate in the task.

In the second step of analysis, Anton's on-screen and off-screen observation data were analyzed to infer the underlying motives that drove her behaviors. To analyze Anton's on-screen behaviors, we segmented Anton's chat transcripts from the three CMPR tasks into e-turns, then numbered the e-turns Anton took during each task, and finally categorized them either as on task (when the turns were devoted to discussing the CMPR task) or off task (when the turns were devoted to topics unrelated to the CMPR task). Following Thorne (2000), we defined an e-turn as "a bounded individual submission to a CACD (computer-assisted classroom discussion) dialogue that takes its final form and placement on the screen." After the e-turns were identified, the number of on- and off-task e-turns Anton contributed during each CMPR task was calculated. On-task e-turns were subsequently coded in terms of their language functions, for example *give opinion, ask for suggestion,* and *ask for clarification.* One on-task e-turn might be segmented and coded into multiple language functions. The number of on- and off-task e-turns as well as the functions of the e-turns helped us infer whether Anton was participating in peer response for the purpose of learning or if she was performing the peer response task for other reasons. For example, if Anton's on-task e-turns substantially outnumbered her off-task e-turns and the functions of her on-task e-turns focused on meaningful discussion with Iron, we considered Anton's motive to be improving her writing skill through peer response. We also noted the mouse-clicking activities and analyzed Anton's off-screen behaviors to better understand what she was doing during the CMPR task. A tentative scheme of motives was established based on Anton's on-screen and off-screen behaviors. As part of the data analysis, a revision analysis was conducted, and, when needed, the results of the revision analysis were used to inform and corroborate our analyses based on the interview and observation data.[3]

In the third step of analysis, the motives identified through interview data and observation data were triangulated. If there was inconsistency between Anton's self-reported motive and her motive as constructed based on the observation data, both the interview data related to the self-reported motive and the observation data were constantly compared and contrasted to see whether Anton shifted her motive during the task or if she did not report a motive in the interview. In a few cases, we noted more motives from the observation data than reported by Anton in the interviews. This is not surprising given that humans may not always be conscious of their motives (Lantolf & Thorne, 2006) and that Anton might not want to report a motive to the interviewer, who was also her instructor. Motives identified based on the observation data were included in the results section if they could be triangulated within the multiple sources of observation data (i.e., beyond-screen and on-screen observations).

After the analysis was completed with data from Anton, all three steps as described above were applied to data collected from Iron. As indicated in the description of the three steps above, the process of identifying the participants' motives was not linear, simple, nor straightforward. Rather, it was a recursive, complex, and interpretative process.

After the participants' motives were identified, the motives were reviewed along with the raw data to probe whether and how the use of IM played a role in Anton and Iron's motive formation and shift. The identified motives were reviewed to see whether any new motive emerged because of the availability of IM. Drawing from data already analyzed, we also explored how Anton and Iron's use of IM impacted their interaction, which, in turn, affected their motive shift within and across tasks.

4. FINDINGS

4.1. Anton and Iron's Motives in Three CMPR Tasks

According to activity theory, activities are driven by motives, which in turn are realized in goal-directed actions. Students who participate in a learning task may be driven by different motives and, as a result, may obtain different levels of development (Lantolf & Thorne, 2006). Further, students' motives are not static and may be influenced and reshaped in different physical environments. By analyzing data from multiple sources, we identified Anton and Iron's motives, namely, the activity systems they respectively were engaged in when participating in each CMPR task. This section first presents the identified motives for each participant and then a discussion on how the use of instant messenger influenced Anton and Iron's motive formation and shift.

4.1.1. Anton's Motives in CMPR Tasks.   The first CMPR task was conducted in week six. During this task, Anton collaborated with Iron. Regarding her motive, Anton revealed in the interview that "I never took academic writing class before. Yes, I want to know how to write expository essays" (interview with Anton, 6/25/06). Anton's motive to learn was reflected in her comments on what she did with Iron's feedback: "Iron told me I had problems in my introduction paragraph. So I rewrote my thesis statement and added new information. I also changed some phrases and words because I feel these new words are clearer and better" (interview with Anton, 6/25/06). Anton's comments indicate that Anton took the CMPR task and Iron's comments seriously and was interested in improving her writing through collaborating with Iron. The revision analysis revealed that Anton incorporated Iron's feedback in her revision and made the changes that she reported during the interview.

The data of Anton's beyond-screen behaviors (Appendix A) showed that she concentrated on the online interaction throughout the task. This was reflected in several ways: 1) she did not have any verbal interaction with other students and the instructor during the task, and the only verbal interaction that she had with Iron was during her return of Iron's essay at the end of the session; 2) she was intensely typing and reading messages on the screen and occasionally paused to check Iron's essay, which, as she explained in the follow-up interview, was undertaken to look for more aspects to comment on and to ensure the appropriateness of her comments; and 3) she occasionally glanced over at Iron to check whether he was on task.

Her on-screen behavior recordings (Appendix B) also showed that Anton did not chat on any off-task topic throughout this task. Anton produced a total of 26 e-turns during the first CMPR task, and all of the e-turns were on task. During the chat, Anton made comments in the areas of content, organization, format, and references in Iron's essay. She also asked Iron to provide feedback on her essay. When Iron pointed out some weaknesses in the essay's organization, Anton actively sought suggestions from him.

As shown in the chat transcript (see Excerpt 1 for an example), during her message exchange with Iron, Anton used various language functions to fulfill her roles as a writer and a reader such as *give opinion/suggestion, ask for opinion/ suggestion, structure,* and *ask for clarification.* In the following excerpt, Anton provided feedback and asked for Iron's comments on her essay. . . .

> *Excerpt 1:*
>
> Anton says: So, Iron. . . . Your writing is well-organized and very interesting . . . I have nothing very important to tell you actually. . . . But, this is a peer review . . . so I will try to help you to do better than you do!
>
> Anton says: First, concerning the format of the paragraph . . . You have to know that in an academic writing, you have to follow certain rules.
>
> Anton says: Do not use Bold
>
> Anton says: No space between paragraph (only indent)
>
> Anton says: Also, the line spacing is double and not single
>
> Iron says: I am reading your essay about learning style now.
>
> . . .
>
> Anton says: Can you tell me what you think of my essay?

In all, the interview transcript as well as Anton's beyond- and on-screen behaviors indicate that in the first CMPR task Anton was driven by a motive of improving her writing skills in an expository essay through peer feedback. This motive was maintained throughout her participation in the task.

For the second CMPR task conducted in week eight, Anton's behaviors deviated dramatically from her behaviors in the first task. During the interview conducted after the second CMPR task, she confessed the difficulties that she experienced with Iron during the task, mentioning in particular Iron's lack of experience with instant messaging: "Iron didn't know how to use instant messenger. He is so slow. His English is not bad. But he doesn't know how to help me . . ." (interview with Anton, 7/17/06). In an informal IM chat with the course instructor after the task, Anton also revealed that "I don't like talking to Iron on messenger because it is boring to talk to him. He doesn't know how to use the smiley faces on messenger" (informal interview with Anton, 7/18/06). This indicates that from Anton's perspective, Iron's lack of skills in IM communication affected their interaction.[4] When asked whether she wanted to collaborate with Iron again in the following CMPR task, Anton expressed explicitly, "I don't want to. But if you want me to, I can. But I don't think that will help anyone" (IM chat with Anton, 7/18/06). This shows that Anton lost interest in collaborating with Iron, and she would conduct the next CMPR task with Iron only because she wanted to please the instructor, which hinted at her motive shift in the second CMPR task.

The observation data indicated two emergent motives during the task. The beyond-screen behavior recordings (Appendix A) showed that although Anton performed the peer response task by completing the reader's worksheet, checking Iron's essay, and chatting with Iron, she did not concentrate on her online interaction. She was constantly checking whether the instructor was looking at her before putting on her earphone set, and she immediately took off the earphone set when she noticed the instructor was approaching her area. Anton also chatted briefly with her neighbor for information about online music, and she stuck her tongue out and made faces toward the camera several times when she noticed nobody was looking at her. All these behaviors indicate that she was not genuinely participating in the online interaction with Iron.

The on-screen behavior recordings (Appendix B) further verified that during the second CMPR task, Anton was not participating in the learning activity system as the instructor expected. While chatting with Iron on her essay, Anton opened three more IM chat windows and browsed several music web sites throughout the lab time. In other words, she was simultaneously chatting with four persons: with Iron on the peer response task, with an online friend on topics irrelevant to the course, and with two classmates, Diane and Jillil, respectively, on off-task topics relevant to the course. While Anton might have been reluctant to reveal to the researcher who conducted the interview her motives for participating in this task, she shared them with one of her online friends during the CMPR task: "I am here just to be a good student . . . Let's just have some fun here." When she chatted online with Diane, she complained about how boring and unhelpful her partner Iron was and said that she did not want to work on the task with him. Then, she started to play an online poker game with Diane. When she chatted with Jillil, he suggested that Anton visit an online music website. Anton immediately started browsing the website sent by Jillil and only put on her earphones when she noticed that the instructor was not looking in her direction.

In her chat with Iron, Anton only produced nine e-turns, among which seven were on task and two were off task. In the seven on-task e-turns, she rejected all the opinions and suggestions that Iron gave about her essay and explicitly expressed her resentment toward his comments, as shown in Excerpt 2 from the chat transcript. Although Iron's comments were relevant and might have prompted other writers to seek further clarifications and suggestions for revision, Anton refused to consider them. In addition, Anton did not provide any comments or suggestions on Iron's essay. Anton's messages to Iron later during this exchange suggest that she resented the manner in which Iron provided feedback via the instant messenger. This point will be discussed further in the section on Iron's motives.

Excerpt 2:

Iron says: Firstly, You have chosen very intresting subject, but I don't agree with your analysis approch and your idea.

Anton says: Iron . . . You shoudn't make any judgement concerning my ideas

Anton says: The work consists in helping in wrting better

Anton says: Therefore, I will ask you not to say things like that

Anton says: they don't inprove my writing

The observations and analyses indicate that Anton was not truly participating in the activity system oriented toward using peer response to gain knowledge and skills relevant to writing a summary-analysis essay. Although Anton did not truly participate, she sat in the lab and appeared to be conducting the CMPR task by chatting with her partner and checking the essay. Data analysis indicated that Anton was driven by two alternative motives in this task. The first was to maintain her good-student image, which was revealed in her messages to her online friend and reflected in her behaviors to comply with the CMPR procedures (i.e., checking the essay and completing the reader's worksheet). Her second motive was to have fun with her friends online. Neither of her two motives was congruent with the expectation conveyed by the instructor. Between these two motives, the first one seemed to be the primary motive that drove Anton to come to class to participate in the CMPR task. During the CMPR task, she realized that she could simultaneously chat with her friends to kill some time in class, which stimulated her second motive.

In the third CMPR task, Anton was paired with Diane. In the interview, Anton explicitly expressed that "Diane is my good friend. I know she needs help. I want to help her. I think her English is good too. We can help each other" (interview with Anton, 7/23/06). Her interview comments indicate that Anton was motivated to help Diane and improve her own writing through collaboration in the third CMPR task. The beyond-screen behavior recordings (Appendix A) showed that Anton had no interaction with the instructor and only had two brief (less than two minutes) verbal interactions with her classmates during the task. The first brief verbal interaction was initiated by a classmate who asked how things were going with her when he passed by Anton's computer desk. The other brief talk occurred between Anton and her partner Diane in the middle of their IM chat when Diane stepped over to ask if Anton had a hard copy of her essay.[5] After the exchange, Anton started reading Diane's essay carefully to identify and mark grammatical errors on the paper.

The on-screen behavior recordings (Appendix B) revealed that Anton was not only participating in the CMPR task with Diane, but also actively involved in another IM chat. In her interaction with Diane, Anton was very engaged, which was demonstrated by both the number of e-turns produced and the range of language functions used. She produced a total of 46 e-turns, 34 of which were on task and 12 were off task. Among the 34 on-task e-turns, Anton used language functions such as *structure, give opinion/suggestion, ask for suggestion, indicate intention, clarify,* and *ask for clarification* while playing her roles as a critical reader and a self-reflective writer. She also structured the conversation proactively by suggesting what Diane and she could do to optimize the efficiency of peer response at both the beginning and the end of the task.

The interview and observation data indicate that in the third CMPR task, Anton was driven by the motive of improving both her and her partner's writing skills in an argumentative essay through peer response. However, Anton's observation data also indicate that she was simultaneously driven by an additional motive: having fun in IM chat. The on-screen behavior recordings showed that as soon as Anton logged onto the messenger and started chatting with Diane, she opened another IM chat window and initiated a conversation with an online friend. The beyond-screen behavior recordings showed that Anton was smiling all the time while chatting with both Diane and this online friend. In addition, Anton constantly checked the screen to see whether her online friend sent her new messages even when she was editing the grammar mistakes in Diane's essay.

The analyses presented above indicate that Anton held heterogeneous motives within and across CMPR tasks. Anton's motive shift throughout the three CMPR tasks is illustrated below:

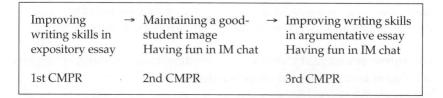

Improving writing skills in expository essay	→	Maintaining a good-student image Having fun in IM chat	→	Improving writing skills in argumentative essay Having fun in IM chat
1st CMPR		2nd CMPR		3rd CMPR

4.1.2. Iron's Motives in the CMPR Tasks. Iron was a very dedicated student for the entire semester. However, his motives of participating in the CMPR tasks were not always congruent with his partners' motives, and his motives shifted chronologically as well. The first CMPR task was Iron's very first time conducting online chat, and he was not skilled at typing on the keyboard. Before the CMPR session, the instructor helped him register a new MSN instant messenger account and showed Iron how to find his partner on his MSN buddy list and to chat with her.

In the interview, Iron said, "I don't know anything about academic writing. In Turkey, I only learn grammar. I don't know many things we learn here. That is why I am here" (interview with Iron, 6/21/06). This clearly stated Iron's motive to improve his academic writing when he joined the class. His comment on the first CMPR task was, "I don't know about expository essay. I want to improve my writing," which indicated his motive to improve his writing through the first CMPR task.

Iron's beyond-screen behavior recordings (Appendix A) showed that throughout the entire CMPR session, he did not have any other behaviors beside reading messages on the screen, typing on the keyboard, and occasionally checking his partner's essay and the CMPR worksheet given by the instructor. Iron's on-screen behavior recordings (Appendix B) confirmed his devotion to this task. All his contributions in the online chat were task-related although he only contributed a total of 14 turns due to his lack of typing skills. During the CMPR chat, the language functions that Iron employed included *greetings, express intention, give opinion, give suggestion, agree, phatic*, and *inform action*. Further, Iron did not chat with anyone else. Although he was very slow at typing, Iron managed to offer some feedback on Anton's essay. Using the CMPR reader's worksheet, he pinpointed some weaknesses in Anton's essay: her thesis statement was too broad and her conclusion paragraph was weak. During the chat, Iron's partner Anton suggested that he follow the academic writing format such as space between lines and paragraphs, provide reference information for the data he cited, and balance the information discussed in the introduction and conclusion paragraphs. Iron incorporated most of the suggestions in his second draft, which revealed the value he placed on peer feedback for the purpose of improving his writing. Thus, all the data suggest that Iron was genuinely participating in the activity system of learning knowledge and skills of writing an expository essay through computer-mediated peer response.

IM was a completely new tool for Iron. In spite of his efforts, Iron's lack of computer skills created a problem: he and his partner Anton were not able to finish their task. As indicated in the excerpt below, they ran out of time and had to continue the task the following day. Anton was not very happy about this.

Excerpt 3:

Anton says: there are only three minutes left. . . .

Anton says: we are in a hurry!:-p

Anton says: ok . . . so I think we have to leave now. . . .

Anton says: we will continue this conversation tomorrow morning!

In the second CMPR task, Iron was paired with Anton again. However, he seemed to be driven by two divergent motives in this task. When asked what he wanted to achieve in this task, Iron confessed, "I didn't do so well last time because I typed so slowly. I wanted to do better this time. So we could talk more and help each other. Anton has good English" (interview with Iron, 7/13/06). These comments indicate that he was hoping to improve his performance as a CMPR partner. Also, since he obtained some useful feedback from Anton in the first CMPR task and realized that Anton had high English proficiency, he retained faith in the usefulness of this task and was eager to participate in it. However, Iron's desire to improve his writing through CMPR only ended with his disappointment. During the interview conducted after the second CMPR task, Iron complained to the instructor that "Anton didn't give me any comments on my essay. So I didn't get any help from her" (interview with Iron, 7/13/06). His complaint reflected his hope to receive feedback from Anton.

The beyond-screen behavior recordings (Appendix A) showed that Iron again completely concentrated on his chat. When he was waiting for responses from Anton, he constantly compared his comments on Anton's essay with the CMPR worksheet. The on-screen behavior recordings (Appendix B) showed that he initiated the conversation and contributed comments on Anton's essay despite her negative attitude as reflected in the IM chat transcript (see Excerpt 2). Eight out of nine of Iron's e-turns were on task, and the language functions he performed included *give opinion, give suggestion, indicate intention,* and *agree.* These behaviors and the interview data indicate that Iron was motivated to develop his writing skills by collaborating with his partner in the CMPR task.

On the other hand, the observation data also confirmed Iron's secondary motive: remedying his image as an incompetent CMPR partner due to his lack of computer skills. In the first CMPR task, the chat was constantly led by Anton, who contributed the majority of the e-turns, directed the conversation, and urged Iron to type faster. Iron was not able to finish the chat within class time, which caused the pair to have an additional CMPR session the following day. Worse yet, Anton formed an impression of Iron as an unhelpful partner. Iron seemed to have sensed this and intended to change this impression during the second CMPR chat. His efforts were reflected in three aspects. First, after the first CMPR task, he stayed in the lab to practice typing after class, which enabled him to type faster. Second, he tried to play a more active role in the CMPR task. With his faster typing speed, he initiated the conversation and led most of the topics during the second task, which contrasted with his behaviors during the first task. Last but not least, as shown in Excerpt 4, he defended his image as a competent partner when Anton rejected his comments on her essay. He defended himself by indicating that he was a boss in a big company in Turkey and he could not type fast because his staff did all the typing for him. He brought up this point again in the interview with the instructor. These behaviors indicate that Iron was very self-conscious about his image as a competent partner and did not want to be looked down upon by his partner due to his limited computer skills.

Excerpt 4:

Anton says: What you say is unreadable . . . and I'm wondering why bcs your essay is sooooooooo clear! there is a contradiction between the way you express yourself on the Internet and the way you write. . . .

Iron says: That is right, I couldn't use internet and competer much quickly. my staff does these things why I don't have free time for chat etc. But I try.

Anton's comments about the contradiction between how Iron expressed himself in instant messaging and how he communicated ideas in his essays suggest a gap between Iron's communicative effectiveness as an IM user and an essay writer. They also suggest that what caused difficulties in Anton and Iron's interaction was not just Iron's lack of typing skills, but also his inability to effectively use IM tools to communicate ideas during CMPR.

It seemed that Iron's motive to develop writing skills through peer collaboration was demolished by Anton's objections during the second CMPR task, which caused his hesitation to wholeheartedly participate in the third CMPR task. Despite his unsuccessful and unhappy experience in the second CMPR task, Iron participated in the third CMPR task without any complaint. He was paired with Nicky, who was his friend. They occasionally chatted during class breaks since they sat close to each other, so Iron knew Nicky's English proficiency. When asked to reflect on his motive for participating in the third CMPR task, Iron revealed that "Nicky needs a lot of help. I can help her. I don't need any help. I am good" (interview with Iron, 7/21/06). The interview data showed that Iron was not particularly excited about getting feedback from Nicky to improve his writing, but he was willing to provide help for Nicky.

According to the beyond-screen behavior recordings (Appendix A), Iron encountered some technical problems when he tried to log onto the MSN messenger at the beginning of the lab time. In contrast to the eagerness he demonstrated in the first two CMPR tasks to participate in peer interaction, Iron seemed indifferent to conducting the third CMPR task. He did not report his logon problem immediately to the instructor; instead, he began reviewing Nicky's essay and writing down comments on the CMPR worksheet. Until the instructor and Nicky discovered the problem and helped him log in, Iron did not show enthusiasm in conducting the online task. However, while waiting for responses from Nicky after he sent out each message during the chat, Iron was attentive to the task by constantly comparing Nicky's essay and his comments with the CMPR reader's worksheet to "make sure my comments are correct" (interview with Iron, 7/21/06). These behaviors indicate that Iron did not wholeheartedly participate in the CMPR task but tried to comply with the task procedures.

Iron's on-screen behavior recordings (Appendix B) revealed that Iron did not finish reviewing Nicky's essay before the class, and he tried to finish the review before he started to chat. This further verified that he was not eager or ready to participate in the CMPR task. Due to the technical problem he encountered at the beginning of the task, Iron had only 20 minutes to conduct the task. During his chat, Iron contributed eight e-turns and all of them were on task. The language functions that he employed included *ask for suggestion, clarify, give opinion, give suggestion, express intention, inform action,* and *ask for permission.* Although at the beginning of the chat Iron asked Nicky to give suggestions on his essay, he was not genuinely motivated to obtain help from Nicky, which was indicated in his interview comments presented earlier. He seemed more concerned about finishing the CMPR task within the allotted time and complying with task procedures, which indicates his motive of maintaining a good-student image.

However, this motive started to change toward the end of the task. After hearing some very positive comments from Nicky and her statement that she did not have any further suggestions for him, Iron started providing more detailed comments on her essay. After they ran out of time, Iron suggested they continue the CMPR task during the lunch break. During his interview with the instructor, Iron revealed that he gave his partner more comments in their follow-up peer response. Although he did not obtain any helpful suggestions from his partner, he enjoyed the process very much "because she is willing to learn. Also I am willing (to share)" and because he liked portraying the image of a competent writer who could help Nicky, as indicated in this comment: "I give some suggestions, she will change all of them" (interview with Iron, 7/21/06). Thus, the data indicate that Iron was motivated in the second half of this task to maintain an image of a competent writer by providing help to his partner.

The data analyzed above indicate that Iron was driven by two motives that not only differed qualitatively, but also shifted chronologically. Although he did not explicitly express it, the observation data indicate that at the beginning of the third CMPR task, Iron was interested in maintaining a good-student image by finishing up reviewing Nicky's essay before the chat; sharing his comments and suggestions with Nicky; and politely asking for Nicky's suggestions about his essay—behaviors that were all required by the instructor. After hearing the compliments and appreciative words from his partner, Iron realized that Nicky, unlike Anton, respected his comments; this realization motivated him to provide more detailed suggestions to Nicky and even suggest they have a follow-up discussion during the lunch break. Iron enjoyed the interaction with Nicky even though he did not obtain any constructive feedback from her on his essay, and he enjoyed his image as a competent writer in front of Nicky. Thus, his actions in the second half of the task were driven by the motive of maintaining an image of a competent writer.

Iron's motive shift across the three CMPR tasks is illustrated below:

Improving writing skills in expository essay	→ Improving writing skills in the summary-analysis essay	→ Maintaining a good-student image
	Reshaping his image as an incompetent IM user and partner	Maintaining an image of a competent writer
1st CMPR	2nd CMPR	3rd CMPR

4.2. Mediation of IM in Anton and Iron's Motive Formation and Shift

The analyses presented above and the results from the survey, particularly results about Anton and Iron's respective prior experience with instant messaging, indicate that the use of instant messenger had significant influences on Anton and Iron's participation in the CMPR tasks at the activity level. The influences were reflected in the mediation of the instant messenger in Anton and Iron's motive formation and shift.

In a traditional peer response task, students collaborate with each other by verbally exchanging comments on each other's essays. However, when the collaboration is moved to the Internet, the change of the interaction environment may trigger and nurture new motives as well as abolish existing ones. For example, during the second CMPR task, Anton discovered that she could chat with her friends online simultaneously when she was working on the CMPR task with her partner Iron. Anton started participating simultaneously in two activity systems, and her participation in the activity driven by the motive of "having fun in IM chat" would not have been possible without the use of IM. In the third CMPR task, Anton was immediately engaged in two activity systems: improving writing skills in the argumentative essay and having fun in IM chat. It seems that the use of IM not only stimulated the emergence of an additional activity system, but also afforded its maintenance. Further, the use of IM played an additional role in mediating motive formation and shift through its capacity to influence participants' experience and interaction. In particular, Iron's lack of knowledge and experience with IM affected his interaction with Anton, which in turn mediated the formation of new motives and abolishment of old motives for both participants. More specifically, Iron's image of being a competent collaborator, which he firmly believed in at the beginning of the first CMPR task, was smeared due to his clumsy online performance caused by his lack of IM chatting experience and poor typing skills. A new motive thus emerged when he participated in the second CMPR task: changing his image of being a dysfunctional CMPR partner.

On the other hand, the use of IM also distracted students from existing activity systems. For example, in the first CMPR task, Anton was driven by the motive of learning writing through collaborating with her partner but realized that her partner could not type quickly and could not provide feedback efficiently online. Anton also realized that she could participate in an alternative activity system. As a result, Anton withdrew from the activity system of improving writing through CMPR when she participated in her second CMPR task.

In addition to allowing participants to join in new IM-afforded activity systems and to withdraw from previous activity systems across different learning tasks, the use of IM also enabled participants to shift between activity systems within one learning task. For example, during the third CMPR task, Anton participated in the activity of improving writing through peer collaboration at one moment but switched to the activity of having fun in IM chat the next moment. All these could happen smoothly without disturbing other community members in each activity system because of the online interaction afforded by IM.

In sum, in the present study, the use of IM not only triggered the formation of new motives within and across learning tasks but also afforded flexible motive shift among the activity systems within and across tasks. To some extent, this augmented participants' agency by affording a variety of interaction venues (Vygotsky, 1978) in learning processes. In other words, the students had more freedom to decide which activity system they wanted to participate in at a given moment.

5. DISCUSSION

The study reported in this article investigated the influence of technology on two ESL students' participation in three CMPR tasks using the lens of activity theory. A particular contribution of the reported study lies in the insight it provides on student motive formation and shift within and across CMPR tasks as well as on the mediating role of technology in this process. Analyzing Anton and Iron's participation from an activity theoretical perspective (Leont'ev,

1978, 1981), we discovered that Anton and Iron were often driven by multiple heterogeneous motives that were triggered and maintained by the use of technology and their previous experience with the technological tool. As shown in our analyses, the IM tool played an important role in mediating Anton and Iron's motive formation and shift.

The integration of computer technologies into peer response tasks has significantly changed the physical conditions of the CMPR task. As pointed out by some activity theory researchers and computer-human interaction researchers inspired by activity theory (e.g., Kuutti, 1996), changes at the operation level, meaning the physical environment, cause changes at the activity level. In this study, conducting peer response in the IM-mediated environment stimulated discrete motives that may otherwise not exist in a face-to-face peer response task. Additionally, the power of different motives in different learning tasks may shift due to both the opportunities afforded and challenges presented by the use of IM. For example, in the first CMPR task, Anton was motivated to improve her writing skills. This changed in the second CMPR task, during which Anton was driven by the motive to have fun in IM chat because the use of IM allowed her to escape from collaborating with Iron. Also, instant messenger use stimulated motive formation and shift because the demands associated with the use of IM presented challenges that had to be addressed. The emergence of Iron's motive to remedy his image as an incompetent CMPR partner in the second task reflected this type of mediation.

The IM mediation of Anton and Iron's motive formation and shift is also attributed to their divergent prior experience with the use of IM. In other words, the mediation of tools is not only situated in the current social cultural context, but also closely intertwined with each participant's history with it. Anton had used IM frequently prior to her participation in the CMPR tasks. Therefore, she could not tolerate Iron's slowness and lack of IM chat skills while conducting online interaction, which caused her to withdraw from the expected learning activity system as well as to become involved in an alternative activity system supported by the use of IM. In contrast, Iron had never used IM before. His anxiety and eagerness to become skillful at IM chat amplified the challenges caused by the use of IM as a communication tool in peer response. Due to his lack of experience with IM and his negative experience with Anton, Iron formed a new motive to change his image as an incompetent IM user and CMPR partner in the second CMPR task.

As shown in our analyses, the use of IM in the peer response tasks caused conflicts and tensions in Anton and Iron's partnership as well as between the different motives that Anton and Iron respectively held in the CMPR tasks. According to activity theory (Engeström, 1987, 1999; Thorne, 2004), each person engaged in an activity system is constantly communicating with other components such as other members in the same system and the tools used to help achieve the object. Contradictions and conflicts often occur during those interactions, but they also trigger development. In other words, development results from the learners being actively engaged in seeking appropriate solutions to the conflicts and contradictions. There was some evidence of this development process in Iron's participation in the second CMPR task. Due to Iron's lack of IM chat and typing skills, online interaction-related conflicts emerged between Anton and Iron, and these conflicts were amplified during the second CMPR task. Anton did not actively seek solutions to reduce the conflicts. On the contrary, she resented further collaboration with Iron online by sending unfriendly and even humiliating messages to him during the second CMPR task. Thus, Anton did not successfully resolve the conflicts between her and Iron. In contrast, Iron realized his lack of computer skills and the problem it caused in the first CMPR task. In response, Iron made efforts to resolve those conflicts before and during the second CMPR task. He spent a great amount of time in the lab practicing typing on the keyboard with help from the instructor and classmates. During the second CMPR session, he tried very hard to initiate the majority of the topics despite Anton's negative attitude toward his suggestions. Although Iron did not obtain help from Anton as he expected, he did improve his typing skills and his participation in the second CMPR task as a result of his efforts to seek solutions to the conflicts.

There was one more contradiction between the participants' individual motives, such as having fun in IM chat, and the task's purpose of improving writing skills in a certain writing style through CMPR. However, due to the disguise afforded by online interaction, the instructor was not able to identify the students' off-task activity systems in a timely manner. This contradiction was resolved by neither the students nor the instructor, which may have aggravated the collaboration failure between Anton and Iron in the second CMPR task.

Our study indicates that the integration of technology into peer response tasks can add to the complexity of such tasks. Face-to-face peer response is already a complex task influenced by a wide array of factors such as the participants' language proficiency, interpersonal skills, and ability to comment on peer writing. CMPR introduces yet another variable that may affect student performance of the task: participants' computer-related skills. In our study, Anton and Iron's interaction was evidently influenced by Iron's lack of experience with the technological tool used. Anton used computer skills as one criterion for assessing Iron's competence as a CMPR partner, and the result of her assessment influenced her participation in the second CMPR task. By rendering the participants' technological skills a necessary condition for the successful performance of peer response tasks, computer-mediated peer response introduces new challenges that must be addressed in order for students to fully benefit from peer response.

Our study suggests interesting connections between students' motives and findings reported in peer response research concerning student revision (e.g., Paulus, 1999) as well as interaction during peer response (e.g., Lockhart & Ng, 1995). Our analyses show that when the learners' motives for participating in a peer response task are consistent with each other and with the purpose of the task, learners are more likely to consider peer feedback for revision and to enjoy the instructional benefits of the task. For example, during the first CMPR task, Anton and Iron's motives were not only compatible with each other but were also consistent with the purpose of the task. They exchanged feedback and, similar to the participants in studies that revealed the positive impact of peer response on student revision (e, g., Paulus, 1999), incorporated peer feedback in their revisions. On the other hand, when participants' motives are not compatible with each other nor with the purpose of the peer response task, writing improvement through discussion and revision of drafts may not occur, as shown in Anton and Iron's experience during the second CMPR task. Further, our study indicates that student interaction during peer response may influence and be influenced by students' motives for participating in a peer response task. Anton and Iron's experience during the first two CMPR tasks indicates a bi-directional relationship between student motive and interaction. An understanding of this dynamic relationship, we hope, may inform future research on CMPR processes.

In all, findings of this study show that the use of IM in peer response tasks influenced students' motive formation and shift. In addition, the mediation of instant messenger is historically dynamic (Engeström, 1987). In our study, because each student bore differing prior experience with the instant messenger, each student was usually driven by multiple and heterogeneous motives triggered by the adoption of the instant messenger. In particular, depending on an ESL student's prior experience with the instant messenger, the student may make decisions about how to use the instant messenger in various learning tasks. In addition, students' prior and current experiences with IM use during each CMPR task may also cause conflicts among different motives held by different members in the same task. Only the students who actively seek solutions to the conflicts can experience development.

6. CONCLUSION AND IMPLICATIONS

In this study, we adopted Leont'ev's (1978, 1981) concepts of motive/object and acknowledged the notion of poly-motivated activities to understand what motives two ESL students had while participating in computer-mediated peer response tasks. We also used important constructs from the third generation of activity theory (Engeström, 1987, 1999) such as conflict and contradiction to shed light on student development as a result of participation in computer-mediated peer response activities. At a time when computer-mediated communication is becoming an influential social interaction practice in society and is increasingly integrated into learning tasks such as peer response in the writing classroom, understanding students' motives when performing computer-mediated learning tasks becomes essential for teachers to understand student task engagement and to support student development. However, identifying an individual's motives is not a simple task. We hope that the method used in this study sheds some light on analyzing students' motives in a learning task, particularly in a computer-mediated learning task. It is also hoped that researchers will continue to explore the research methodology that may allow for a better understanding of learner motives in computer-mediated writing tasks.

A few modern activity theory researchers (e.g., Kaptelinin, 2005; Nardi, 2005) find it ambiguous and potentially problematic when object and motive are conflated in analyzing poly-motivated activities because it cannot explain how multiple motives in one activity system work together to direct the activity. To address this issue, Kaptelinin (2005) proposes distinguishing objects from motives. According to Kaptelinin, one activity can be motivated by multiple motives yet only be structured and directed by one object, which may be constructed and redefined due to the changes in the tools used and people involved in the activity. The notion of motive versus object is very attractive for a deeper understanding of what directs learners in a learning task. We hope that future studies will be conducted to examine how the object directs learner behaviors in CMPR and other computer-mediated writing tasks.

This study unveiled that tools, specifically computer tools, could cast a significant influence on students' motives and behaviors. It also disclosed the historically dynamic relationship between the use of instant messenger and ESL students' motives. Computer-mediated peer response may still be a new learning task for many ESL students. While it may have great potential as a learning task aimed at supporting student writing improvement, it may cause difficulties for students who have no prior experience with peer response and computer technologies.

Because only two cases were examined in the present study, the findings are by no means intended to address all issues experienced by all students in online ESL peer response. However, it is hoped that the study sheds some light on the pedagogical concerns of writing teachers of second-language learners, particularly in terms of developing and planning online peer response and other collaborative tasks. When new technologies are introduced into learning tasks, students' proficiency in employing the technology should be taken into serious consideration. Research examining face-to-face peer response (e.g., Berg, 1999; Stanley, 1992) has revealed that training students for peer response tasks through explaining the purpose of peer response and helping students develop feedback strategies is essential for the success of face-to-face peer response tasks. The findings of this study indicate that in CMPR tasks, teachers also need to make sure that the students have adequate technological skills so that CMPR tasks are successfully performed. Effective training in the technology area, however, should go beyond simply helping students acquire general technological skills to focusing on helping students develop skills and strategies for using technology specifically for the purpose of exchanging and negotiating peer feedback.

Results of the present study indicate that during a CMPR task, students may not participate in the learning activity system in which the teacher expects them to participate. The study further indicates that integration of technology in peer response tasks may create tensions and contradictions between participants in the same learning task when student participants do not possess the relevant skills. Therefore, it is paramount for teachers to be aware of the activities that the students participate in as well as the tensions and contradictions that emerge within and between activity systems. To make CMPR tasks conducive to learning and development, teachers need to play an important role in guiding students in their efforts to resolve the tensions and contradictions that occur due to computer technologies and the presence of divergent learner motives. More specifically, teachers need to help students understand that their peers may have differing levels of proficiency with technology and caution students against judging their peers' competence as writers and peer response partners based solely on their computer skills. Teachers also need to help students develop effective online communication strategies as well as strategies for resolving contradictions. According to activity theory, all human practices contain tensions and contradictions, which are triggered by the constant interactions between the human subjects, the tools used, and the community members involved in an activity. Only through participants' actively seeking solutions to the tensions and contradictions can development occur. Thus, a teacher who is ready to provide helpful guidance on resolving technology-triggered human tensions and contradictions within and across activity systems is instrumental for a successful computer-mediated peer response task.

As more and more computer-mediated communication tools such as blogs, Wikis, and Facebook are becoming the social communication norm in modern society, it can be expected that they will be integrated into the first- and second-language writing classroom. However, taking advantage of these emerging and popular tools to achieve academic objectives requires a deeper understanding of students' needs, motives, and learning behaviors. We hope that more research examining how technology influences writing will be conducted to allow a better understanding of the complex and dynamic writing process students go through when performing computer-mediated writing tasks.

Appendix A

Beyond-Screen Behavior Matrix

Beyond-Screen Behaviors Matrix: 1st CMPR Task

Participant	Interaction with the instructor	Verbal interaction with peers	Body movement	Facial expression
Anton	Informed the instructor of her situation at the end of task	Returned Iron's paper at the end of task	1. Concentrated on typing; 2. checked Iron's essay; 3. paused to wait for response; 4. checked Iron's behaviors	Smiled once

Iron	None	1. Chatted with Anton shortly at the beginning; 2. chatted with Anton at the end of task	1. Concentrated on typing with one hand; 2. checked Anton's essay, CMPR worksheets and teaching materials; 3. typed with one hand; 4. wrote down words on the worksheet	Smiled while reading a message

Beyond-Screen Behaviors Matrix: 2nd CMPR Task

Participant	Interaction with the instructor	Verbal interaction with peers	Body movement	Facial expression
Anton	Came late and obtained instruction about the task	1. Checked whether Iron was online; 2. chatted briefly with neighbors at the beginning of the task; 3. confirmed a web link with a neighbor	1. Checked Iron's status; 2. looked at her essay to check the appropriateness of Iron's comments; 3. filled up the reader's worksheet; 4. marked down mistakes in Iron's essay; 5. checked the location of the instructor; 6. put on earphones to listen to music	1. Smiled constantly and laughed a couple of times; 2. made faces toward other students
Iron	None	None	1. Typed intensively with both hands; 2. compared the essay with the worksheet while waiting for responses; 3. paused to read the essay and wrote down notes on the worksheet	Serious looking, frowned occasionally

Beyond-Screen Behaviors Matrix: 3rd CMPR Task

Participant	Interaction with the instructor	Verbal interaction with peers	Body movement	Facial expression
Anton	None	1. Briefly chatted with classmates passing by; 2. talked to Diane about the essay and exchanged her essay	1. Smiled at other students in the lab and listened to their talk; 2. read Diane's essay and constantly checked the messenger while waiting for response; 3. read messages on the screen for a long time.	Smiled for the majority of time
Iron	Spent ample time logging into IM with the help from the instructor	Informed Nicky of what problem he had and what he was doing when Nicky checked	1. Read Nicky's essay while the instructor was helping him solve the problem; 2. constantly checked the CMPR worksheet; 3. typed intensively when the IM was on; 4. constantly checked Nicky's essay, the worksheet, and the instant messages.	Constantly smiled in chat

Appendix B

On-Screen Behavior Matrix

On-Screen Behavior Matrix: 1st CMPR Task

Participant	On-task/ off-task e-turns	Language function	Emoticon use	Online resource checking	Multiple chat windows	Notes
Anton	26/0	Greeting: 2 Compliment: 2 Give suggestion: 8 Indicate intention: 1 Phatic: 5 Structure: 5 Ask suggestion: 2 Express appreciation: Ask clarification: 1	4	None	None	Anton initiated most topics
Iron	14/0	Greeting: 2 Indicate intention: 3 Give suggestion: 3 Give opinion: 3 Phatic: 1 Agree: 1 Inform action: 1	None	None	None	

On-Screen Behavior Matrix: 2nd CMPR Task

Participant	On-task/ off-task e-turns	Language functions	Emoticon use	Online resource checking	Multiple chat windows	Notes
Anton	7/2	Disagree: 5 Phatic: 1 Clarification request: 1	None	1. Check email; 2. check online music video; 3. online poker	3 other windows	Initiated 2 chat windows
Iron	8/1	Give opinion: 4 Give suggestion: 2 Indicate intention: 2 Clarify: 2 Agree: 1	None	None	None	Initiated chat with Anton

On-Screen Behavior Matrix: 3rd CMPR Task

Participant	On-task/ off-task e-turns	Language function	Emoticon use	Online resource checking	Multiple chat windows	Notes
Anton	34/12	Structure: 3 Express intention: 1 Indicate difficulty: 2 Compliment: 6 Give opinion: 1 Disagree: 1 Agree: 2 Give suggestion: 4 Ask for suggestion: 1 Clarify: 5 Clarify request: 1 Encourage: 2 Self-correct lapse: 1 Self-identify problem: 1 Express gratitude: 1 Phatic: 7	7 (happy, unhappy, "you got it," wink) Phatic	None	2 windows: one with online friend, the other with a classmate	Initiated one off-task window; initiated chat with Diane
Iron	8/0	Greeting: 1 Inform action: 1 Ask suggestion: 1 Express intention: 1 Give opinion: 1 Give suggestion: 2 Clarify: 1 Ask for permission to give suggestion: 1	None	None	None	Spent long time logging into MSN IM, then changed to Yahoo!

NOTES

1. Engeström (2001) concludes there are three theoretical generations in the evolution of activity theory: Vygotsky's model of mediated actions, Leont'ev's three-level model of activity, and Engeström and Cole's work on interacting activity systems.

2. The reader's worksheet provided 16 specific questions for students to consider during peer response. The questions were grouped into 4 different categories: content (5); organization and style (7); punctuation, capitalization, and spelling (2); and references (2). For each question, space was provided for students to indicate 1) whether they found any problems and 2) what they would suggest for revision.

3. A descriptive revision analysis was performed by comparing each student's first draft with the second draft produced after each CMPR task. The purpose of the descriptive revision analysis was to identify what revisions each participant made in the second draft and the stimulus for each revision. The revision analysis was used as one additional data source to assess the participants' attitude toward peer feedback and to infer their motives for participation in CMPR. A revision rubric, adapted from Chris Hall (1990), was used to facilitate the analysis.

4. Anton did not complain about the quality of Iron's feedback during the interview after the second CMPR task.

5. The IM chat transcript revealed that neither Anton nor Diane printed out a hard copy of each other's essay. Instead, they exchanged drafts via email the day before the CMPR task. Both Anton and Diane found it difficult to discuss grammar issues via IM chat, so they decided to print out hard copies and mark the grammar mistakes directly on the paper. Diane printed out her own essay and walked over to exchange her essay with Anton's.

REFERENCES

Berg, Catherine. (1999). The effects of trained peer responses on ESL students' revision types and writing quality. *Journal of Second Language Writing, 8*, 215–241.

Braine, George. (2001). A study of English as a foreign language (EFL) writers on a local area network (LAN) and in traditional classes. *Computers and Composition, 18*, 275–292.

DebugMode, Inc. (2005). WINK 2.0.

Engeström, Yrjö. (1987). *Learning by expanding: An activity-theoretical approach to developmental research.* Helsinki: Orienta-Konsultit Oy.

Engeström, Yrjö. (1999). Activity theory and individual and social transformation. In Yrjö Engeström, Reijo Miettinen, & Raija-Leena Punamaki (Eds.), *Perspectives on activity theory* (pp. 345–374). New York: Cambridge University Press.

Engeström, Yrjö. (2001). Expansive learning at work: Toward an activity theoretical reconceptualization. *Journal of Education and Work, 14*(1), 133–156.

Ferris, Dana, & Hedgcock, John. (2005). *Teaching ESL composition: Purpose, process and practice* (2nd ed.). Mahwah, NJ: Lawrence Erlbaum Associates, Publishers.

Grabe, William, & Kaplan, Robert. (1996). *Theory and practice of writing: An applied linguistic perspective.* London: Longman.

Guerrero, Maria C. M. de, & Villamil, Olga S. (2000). Activating the ZPD: Mutual scaffolding in L2 peer revision. *Modern Language Journal, 84*(1), 51–68.

Hall, Chris. (1990). Managing the complexity of revising across languages. *TESOL Quarterly, 24*(1), 43–60.

Hedgcock, John, & Lefkowitz, Natalie. (1992). Collaborative oral/aural revision in foreign language writing instruction. *Journal of Second Language Writing, 1*(3), 255–276.

Jin, Li. (2008). Instant messenger-mediated intercultural learning. In S. Magnan (Ed.), *Mediating discourse online* (pp. 275–304). Philadelphia, PA: John Benjamins Publishing Company.

Kaptelinin, Victor. (1996). Activity theory: Implications for human-computer interaction. In A. Nardi Bonnie (Ed.), *Context and consciousness: Activity theory and human-computer interaction* (pp. 53–59). Cambridge, MA: MIT Press.

Kaptelinin, Victor. (2005). The object of activity: Making sense of the sense-making. *Mind, Culture, and Activity, 12*(1), 4–18.

Kaptelinin, Victor, & Nardi, Bonnie. (2006). *Acting with technology: Activity theory and interaction design.* Cambridge, MA: MIT Press.

Kuutti, Kari. (1996). Activity theory as a potential framework for human-computer interaction research. In A. Nardi Bonnie (Ed.), *Context and consciousness: Activity theory and human-computer interaction* (pp. 17–44). Cambridge, MA: MIT Press.

Lantolf, Jim. (2000). *Sociocultural theory and second language learning.* Oxford: Oxford University Press.

Lantolf, Jim, & Thorne, Steve. (2006). *Sociocultural theory and the genesis of second language development.* Oxford: Oxford University Press.

Leki, ILona. (1990). Potential problems with peer responding in ESL writing classes. *CATESOL Journal, 3*, 5–17.

Leont'ev, Alexei. (1978). *Activity, consciousness and personality.* NJ: Prentice-Hall.

Leont'ev, Alexei. (1981). The problem of activity in psychology. In James Wertsch (Ed.), *The concept of activity in Soviet psychology* (pp. 37–71). Armonk, NY: M. E. Sharpe.

Lincoln, Yvonna, & Guba, Egon. (1985). *Naturalistic inquiry.* Newbury Park, CA: SAGE.

Liu, Jun, & Hansen, Jette. (2002). *Peer response in second language writing classrooms.* Ann Arbor, MI: The University of Michigan Press.

Liu, Jun, & Sadler, Randall. (2003). The effect and affect of peer review in electronic versus traditional modes on L2 writing. *Journal of English for Academic Purposes, 2*(3), 193–227.

Lockhart, Charles, & Ng, Peggy. (1995). Analyzing talk in ESL peer response groups: Stances, functions, and content. *Language Learning, 45*(4), 605–655.

Mangelsdorf, Kate. (1989). Parallels between speaking and writing in second language acquisition. In Donna M. Johnson & Duane H. Roen (Eds.), *Richness in writing: Empowering ESL students* (pp. 134–145). New York: Longman.

Mangelsdorf, Kate. (1992). Peer reviews in the ESL composition classroom: What do the students think? *ELT Journal, 46*, 274–284.

Mangelsdorf, Kate, & Schlumberger, Ann. (1992). ESL student response stances in a peer-review task. *Journal of Second Language Writing, 1*(3), 235–254.

Mendonca, Cassia O., & Johnson, Karen E. (1994). Peer review negotiations: Revision activities in ESL writing instruction. *TESOL Quarterly, 28*(4), 745–769.

Miettinen, Reijo. (2005). Object of activity and individual motivation. *Mind, Culture, and Activity, 12*(1), 52–69.

Mittan, Robert. (1989). The peer response process: Harnessing students' communicative power. In Donna M. Johnson & Duane H. Roen (Eds.), *Richness in writing: Empowering ESL students* (pp. 207–219). New York: Longman.

Nardi, Bonnie (Ed.). (1996). *Context and consciousness activity theory and human-computer interaction.* Cambridge, MA: MIT Press.

Nardi, Bonnie. (2005). Objects of desire: Power and passion in collaborative activity. *Mind, Culture, and Activity, 12*(1), 37–51.

Paulus, Trena M. (1999). The effect of peer and teacher feedback on student writing. *Journal of Second Language Writing, 8*, 265–289.

Stanley, Janet. (1992). Coaching student writers to be effective peer evaluators. *Journal of Second Language Writing, 1*, 217–233.

Storch, Neomy. (2002). Patterns of interaction in ESL pair talk. *Language Learning, 52*(1), 119–158.

Tang, Gloria M., & Tithecott, Joan. (1999). Peer response in ESL writing. *TESL Canada Journal, 16*(2), 21–38.

Thorne, Steven. (2000). Beyond bounded activity systems: Heterogeneous cultures in instructional uses of persistent conversation. In S. Herring & T. Erickson (Eds.), The proceedings of the thirty-third Hawaii International Conference on Systems Science. New York: IEEE Press. Retrieved from http://language.la.psu.edu/~thorne/cmchicss33.html.

Thorne, Steven. (2004). Cultural historical activity theory and the object of innovation. In O. St. John, K. van Esch, & E. Schalkwijk (Eds.), *New insights into foreign language learning and teaching* (pp. 51–70). Frankfurt, Germany: Peter Lang Verlag.

Tuzi, Frank. (2004). The impact of e-feedback on the revisions of L2 writers in an academic writing course. *Computers and Composition, 21*, 217–235.

Villamil, Olga S., & Guerrero, Maria C. M. de. (1998). Assessing the impact of peer revision on L2 writing. *Applied Linguistics, 19*(4), 491–514.

Vygotsky, Lev. (1978). *Mind in society: The development of higher psychological processes.* In Michael Cole, Vera John-Steiner, Sylvia Scribner, & Ellen Souberman (Eds.). Cambridge, MA: Harvard University Press.

Warschauer, Mark. (1996). Comparing face-to-face and electronic discussion in the second language classroom. *CALICO Journal, 13*(2), 7–26.

Warschauer, Mark, & Kern, Richard (Eds.). (2000). *Network-based language teaching: Concepts and practice.* New York: Cambridge University Press.

Wertsch, James. (1991). *Voices of the mind: A sociocultural approach to mediated action.* Cambridge, MA: Harvard University Press.

Wertsch, James. (1998). *Mind as action.* Oxford: Oxford University Press.

Zamel, Vivian. (1982). Writing: The process of discovering meaning. *TESOL Quarterly, 16*(2), 195–209.

Zhu, Wei. (2001). Interaction and feedback in mixed peer response groups. *Journal of Second Language Writing, 10*(4), 251–276.

23

Comparing Technologies for Online Writing Conferences: Effects of Medium on Conversation

JOANNA WOLFE AND JO ANN GRIFFIN

In its 2011 report, the CCCC Committee on Best Practice in Online Writing Instruction (OWI) states that it "takes no position on the oft-asked question of whether OWI *should be* used and practiced in postsecondary settings because it accepts the reality that currently OWI *is* used and practiced in such settings" (Hewett et al. 2). The committee claims that teachers and administrators, including those in writing centers, "typically are simply migrating traditional face-to-face writing pedagogies to the online setting—both fully online and hybrid. Theory and practice specific to OWI has yet to be fully developed" (7). Hewett's recent book on OWI echoes these concerns, and she claims that without a theory of OWI, it is "disturbingly easy" to assume that face-to-face pedagogy is better than computer-mediated instruction (*Online* 32).

Certainly, writing center scholars have traditionally assumed that OWI is inferior to face-to-face instruction. Breuch describes online writing conferences as "less than impressive" (29) and suggests "some may argue that online tutoring goes much against the idea of a writing center—the idea of Burkean Parlors, of ongoing conversation" (31). A respondent to Neaderhiser and Wolfe's survey expressed similar reservations by quipping that "an online writing center isn't really a writing center is it?" (72). Even while asserting the need for writing centers to invest in technology, Harris ("Making") sees the lack of real-time interaction and phatic cues in online conferences as a deficiency, a concern echoed by Hobson and Castner. More specifically, scholars have worried that the limited opportunities for give-and-take interaction promote a fix-it mentality (Castner; Harris, "Using") and that the absence of face-to-face cues can cause consultants to fall back on working with the text rather than the writer (Enders).

Part of this dissatisfaction with online conferencing may be that the majority of these conferences rely exclusively on text-based technologies that

From *Writing Center Journal*, vol. 32, no. 2, 2012, pp. 60–92.

lack media richness. Neaderhiser and Wolfe report that over 90% of online writing center conferences take place through email with another 9.6% occurring through synchronous text-based chat. Fewer than 0.2% of online conferences reported by the 266 institutions responding to their survey took place using media-rich synchronous technologies, such as real-time audio or real-time screen sharing—technologies that Neaderhiser and Wolfe argue are much better poised than exclusively text-based tools to support the dialogic, collaborative interactions writing centers aspire to achieve (61, 69).

Despite the overwhelming use of email in OWI, some innovative methods for conducting writing conferences have recently been studied. Hewett ("Synchronous") has examined the use of whiteboards combined with text-based chat in writing centers, finding that the interactions resulted in improvements to student writing quality, but only one or two substantive changes were discussed per session. Jones, Georghiades, and Gunson similarly found that students responded very positively to the use of screen capture digital video (which combines audio and screen capture videos) as a form of asynchronous instructor feedback on their work. Yergeau, Wozniak, and Vandenberg experimented with synchronous audio-visual technology that allowed student and tutor to use web cameras to see streaming video of one another.

These studies, however, have rarely attempted to compare OWI directly with face-to-face interactions to see what is gained or lost in the virtual environment. Such comparisons are needed both to persuade skeptics of OWI to reconsider the medium's potential advantages and to begin developing theories and practices of OWI. By directly comparing face-to-face and OWI, we better position ourselves to see what practices we can directly migrate to new settings, which practices need to be modified or transformed, and what new practices we need to add to our collective pedagogical repertoire. Moreover, we believe that it is also important to compare different versions of OWI in order to develop clearer theories of how changes in the conferencing environment can affect the consultant-writer dynamics that occur there.

Our current study therefore directly compares face-to-face writing center consultations with two closely related variations of OWI. Although this study takes place in a busy, dynamic writing center, we try to make our comparisons as systematic as possible so we can better foreground some of the benefits and disadvantages of various conferencing environments. Our study uses qualitative, naturalistic data (transcripts of sessions, surveys) but analyzes them using quasi-experimental methods (expert ratings, patterns of responses) in order to highlight trends across the copious data we collected (over 500 transcript pages). Although we realize that some in the writing center community are skeptical of such methods, many others have been calling for systematic, empirical inquiry into writing center concerns (Bergmann qtd. in Jaschik; Jones; Hewett, "Synchronous"). Such inquiry both produces insights that may not be readily visible using other methods and can persuade administrators and others across the university of the need to invest more resources and support rigorous research into writing center pedagogy.

CONFERENCING TECHNOLOGIES: CHOOSING AMONG OPTIONS

Our first question was which OWI environments to study. We concluded we were most interested in conferencing environments that allow for rich, interactive conversations that approximate the give-and-take of face-to-face writing conferences. Although Hewett (*Online*) has made a case for the effectiveness of asynchronous OWI, we wanted to explore how easily available media-rich conferencing environments would compare to the face-to-face setting most writing center practitioners seem to privilege.

Research suggests that audio-based conferencing has many advantages over text-based commenting. Neuwirth et al. found reviewers recording audio comments were more likely to mitigate their comments and were perceived as more likeable than the same reviewers writing text comments. Ice, Curtis, Phillips, and Wells similarly found that asynchronous audio feedback was more effective than text-based feedback in conveying nuance and was associated with increased student involvement, content retention, and student satisfaction. Perhaps more striking, audio feedback was associated with the perception that the instructor cared about the student. Further support for these conclusions can be found in Oomen-Early and colleagues' research which concluded that using asynchronous audio communication in online classes enhances instructor presence, student engagement, student mastery of content, and student satisfaction. Likewise, in a pilot study of synchronous writing conferences, Brown, Cazan, and Griffin found users preferred audio-based conferencing over text chat and were able to accomplish more within the real-time audio environment. Finally, Bos et al. found groups using audio conferencing produced better solutions to complex problems than those using text chat—with audio groups performing nearly as well as those collaborating face-to-face.

In addition to audio communication, we felt that a shared workspace was essential to supporting synchronous OWI. Harris ("Using") notes that online writing conferences suffer when consultant and writer lack a shared space in which they can interact with and manipulate the writer's text. Researchers in human-computer interaction similarly believe a shared workspace significantly improves the efficiency of speech communication (Whittaker), particularly among co-authors (Cohen et al.).

Since we were interested in providing support for nonverbal communication, one might wonder why we did not use video-based conferencing, such as Harris ("Using") recommends. However, research in intense collaborations suggests video has no benefits over audio and, in some cases, may even have a detrimental effect on intense collaborations (Bradner and Mark; Heath and Luff). Video collaboration has proven disappointing partly because video captures many distracting movements and background information without communicating the entire environment in which these movements take place. As Whittaker summarizes, visual information about work objects (such as a shared desktop provides) is far more important than visual information about participants. Finally, Yergeau, Wozniak, and Vandenberg have noted that video may give unnecessary or distracting class and status information about participants by allowing each other to see their homes or workspaces. For these reasons, we chose not to pursue video-based conferencing in the current study, although such environments may be useful in future research.

We assessed two different variations of our online space. In the first version, which we call WordShare, the student writer and consultant used the Adobe ConnectPro conferencing environment to communicate through an audio channel and share a common desktop, allowing them to access the same word processor, web browser, and other applications.[1] With the shared desktop, both participants can manipulate the cursor and scrollbar and have access to all of the features normally available in Word, so both can modify the text, use the highlighter, or change text formatting. The shared desktop allowed participants to easily redirect conversation to different parts of the document by scrolling and using the cursor to point to the relevant sections. Similarly, when participants wanted to change parts of the document, the shared desktop allowed them to simply implement the changes in the shared word processor. Such support prevents participants from having to negotiate a shared perspective with lengthy phrases such as "on page 3, paragraph 2."

Our second variation is the Tablet PC condition, which used the same setup except that the consultant was given a Tablet PC instead of a regular desktop computer. A Tablet PC allows participants to use special ink annotation features in Microsoft Word or other software programs to write on digital documents directly with a pen, much as a reviewer or instructor might mark on a standard sheet of paper. Such tools for marking and editing a document can support distinct authoring roles for writer and consultant—something that prior research suggests improves communication and coordination of the document-creation process (Lowry and Nunamaker). In particular, we hypothesized that giving the consultant a digital pen and the writer a keyboard might encourage the consultant to make teacherly digital ink markings that lay over the main document while investing the writer with primary authority to make direct changes to the primary text. In addition, the Tablet PC's digital ink annotations have the potential to recoup some of the gestures that prior research has shown coauthors and reviewers use to help direct attention and construct a shared sense of the document (Cohen et al.; Thompson; Wolfe). Since Tablet PC users often take advantage of digital ink to create markings that are roughly analogous to physical gestures (Anderson et al.), we hypothesized that Tablet PCs might help writers discussing a shared text to recoup some of the nonverbal communication lost in digital environments.

The study described below examined two variations on an audio and desktop-sharing conference environment: a setup with normal workstation computers (WordShare) and a setup in which consultants worked from Tablet PCs. We had four basic research questions:

- How does a best-case virtual conferencing environment (with synchronous audio and desktop sharing support) compare to face-to-face? Does the conferencing environment appear to affect the pedagogical quality of the conferences or the nature of consultant-writer interactions?

- How does the Tablet PC compare to the WordShare environment?
- What recommendations might this study yield for tutor training or technology set up that could improve conferencing in virtual environments?
- How might this study lead to recommendations for a theory of online writing instruction, such as called for by the CCCC Committee on Best Practice in Online Writing Instruction?

METHODS

Eight writing center consultants were observed working with student writers in each of three conditions—face-to-face, standard WordShare conferencing environment, and Tablet PC environment—for a total of twenty-four sessions observed. Both consultants and students were inexperienced with discussing writing in a synchronous audio and desktop sharing environment. We analyzed transcripts of these sessions on a number of different scales in order to assess qualitative differences such as consultant control of the sessions or overall pedagogical quality of the sessions. In addition, surveys were collected to analyze the attitudes of writers and consultants towards each of the three conditions.

Study Site and Participants

This research took place at a Midwestern state-supported metropolitan research university that generally enrolls 20,000 students, 15,000 of whom are full- or part-time undergraduates. This university's writing center hires approximately twelve graduate students as consultants and holds over 2,200 student consultations annually. There is a 50-minute limit on consultations.

Consultants.   The eight writing center consultants (five female, three male) who participated were the first to respond to an open invitation to join the study. Seven of the eight consultants were native English speakers, and the one non-native participant functioned at an extremely high level of proficiency. All consultants were graduate students in English with at least two semesters of experience working in the writing center. Four had experience consulting via email and synchronous text-based chat but had not had opportunity to experience audio consultations. Consultants received $100 compensation after participating in all three sessions.

Student Writers.   Sixteen student writers (ten female, six male) participated in the study. Of the sixteen student writers, eight completed WordShare conferences while the other eight completed both Tablet PC and face-to-face sessions. We asked these eight participants to complete two sessions each because our original intent was to focus on fine-grained differences between the Tablet PC and face-to-face environments (a focus that our results caused us to put aside in favor of other differences that arose). Student writers were recruited by first soliciting regular writing center clients and inviting them to participate in the study and then by inviting students who showed up at the door with papers. Ten of the student writers reported prior experience with face-to-face writing center consultations, and all were experienced with the World Wide Web, email, and word processing. Students received $20 compensation after their session for participating in the study.

Procedures and Surveys

When student writers showed up at the writing center with electronic copies of their essays, they were invited to participate in the study. In order to keep the sessions as consistent as possible, we invited only students who had already completed drafts to participate. Those accepting the invitation then completed a pre-consultation survey consisting of thirteen questions about their prior writing center and online communication experiences (see Appendix A). Students were next paired up with a consultant and assigned to one of the three conditions: face-to-face, WordShare, or Tablet PC. We tried as much as possible to vary the order in which consultants were introduced to the two online environments; however, because of conditions beyond our control, five of the eight consultants (rather than the four of eight that would have been ideal) were exposed to the Tablet PC condition before the WordShare condition.

If the consultant/student pair was assigned to the face-to-face condition, they were instructed to proceed as they would ordinarily with the exception that their session was videotaped. For technology sessions, the consultant and writer were ushered into different rooms with computers hooked up to the university's high-speed Internet connection and loaded with the Adobe Acrobat ConnectPro software that we used as a conferencing environment. A researcher then opened the shared meeting space, introduced the writer's text into the meeting, and gave the participants a rudimentary demonstration of how to manipulate the tools available in either the WordShare or tablet condition. The researcher also stayed nearby to help the participants if any technology problems arose during the session. All participants were videotaped, and Adobe Acrobat ConnectPro's meeting software recorded the screen and audio activity of participants in the online sessions. At the end of the online sessions, writers were emailed copies of the text the participants worked from, with all comments and revisions included.

Following each session, both consultants and student writers completed a post-consultation survey (see Appendix B) querying their perceptions of the consultation using a combination of thirteen Likert-scale and four open-ended questions.

Transcript Creation

The twenty-four consultations were transcribed using *Transana 2.0* software. In order to keep our raters blind to the experimental condition and our analysis focused on the pedagogical work conducted during the session, we opted to eliminate turns concerned with manipulating the technology. Thus, turns dedicated to equipment setup (adjusting volume or document view), manipulation of the technology (how to scroll, edit, etc.), or self-conscious discussion of participation in the study were eliminated.

Data Analysis

Conversational Control.   Transcripts were first divided into turns and the number of consultant and writer turns was tallied. The researchers then coded each turn to identify which participant was "in control" of the exchange. We focused on control because writing center professionals strongly believe that students should maintain ownership over their writing (Black; Kreiser; Walker and Elias). Moreover, some have worried that online conferences, in particular, will encourage consultants to control and dominate the session (Castner; Harris "Using"), although Hewett ("Synchronous") believes that online instructors try hard not to co-opt student writing or to provide inappropriately directive advice (20). We were therefore curious as to whether we would see any evidence of the online environments affecting the dynamics of conversational control.

"Control" was determined by identifying which participant directed the flow of the conversation in each turn. In identifying the controlling partner, the pertinent question is, Who is pushing the exchange forward? When a participant introduces a new topic into the conversation or asks a direct question that the other participant must answer, that participant is usually controlling the direction of the conversation. However, when a participant's turn consists solely of affirming his/her partner's utterances (e.g., saying "Yes, that's a good point" or simply "OK") or responding to a direct question, that person is usually following his/her partner's lead and thus is not in control of the conversation. Only successful attempts to shift control of the conversation were counted; attempts to redirect that were interrupted and/or ignored by the other participant were not counted as a shift in control. To assess the reliability of the coding, the two researchers independently coded 15% of the turns, obtaining an inter-rater reliability of $k = .73$ using Cohen's simple kappa, a level that represents good agreement above chance (Fleiss).[2]

Document Marking.   As Hewett ("Online") has observed, in OWI, much of the learning takes place through textual interactions. Therefore, we were particularly interested in how the conferencing environment might affect who wrote on texts and what types of comments and markings they made. The markings made on documents provide clues about the type of learning that is occurring, and looking at who made these markings can suggest who is taking the initiative for this learning. To this end, we noted whenever document marking occurred, who did the marking, and the type of marking. Table 1 notes the four main marking types identified:

TABLE 1   Types of markings made on the shared documents

Function	Description	Examples
Editing	Turns spent editing or revising existing text. This includes fixing punctuation, figuring out how to spell a word, and dealing with formatting issues such as indenting, spacing, and font size.	Writer: uh [reading text] "with students" sounds funny. We'll take this out. [deleting text]
Generating	Turns spent generating substantive new text. For a turn to count as generating text, the writer must be working on a new sentence that did not exist in the original document brought to the session.	Consultant: Think about reparations too because you're going to go into a discussion about reparations. Writer: Mmm hmm [typing: "repay African-Americans of African descent for the injustices that we. . . ."]
Focus	Turns spent marking sections of text for the purpose of drawing the other participant's attention to that particular section. Includes underlining, highlighting, and drawing arrows or lines to get the other participant to focus on the same section of text.	Consultant: Okay, let's stop there [makes squiggle mark at the end of the relevant paragraph].
Notes	General text that the writer will use to implement future changes. Includes writing reminders to add content, outlining the structure of the paper, and highlighting or otherwise marking a sentence to remind the writer to come back and edit it later.	Consultant: OK, I'm bracketing everything that you need to move up to the previous paragraph [brackets 5 lines].

We also recorded places where a participant marked on a private (usually paper) copy of the text that could not be seen by the other participant. Such private markings can lead to disjointed views of the text the participants are collaborating on, a condition Whittaker argues can contribute to communication difficulties. Private markings occurred in the OWI sessions when writers, instead of engaging with the shared electronic version of the text, made notations or revisions on paper without announcing their actions. The two researchers independently coded 10% of the turns for the use of document markings, obtaining an inter-rater reliability of $k = .72$ using Cohen's simple kappa.

Holistic ratings.   To assess the overall pedagogical effectiveness of the conferences, three writing center professionals from different institutions were recruited to read and evaluate the transcripts. Two of these raters were PhD students with a strong interest in writing center research. The third rater had recently completed her PhD in Rhetoric and Composition and had previously served as an assistant director at a writing center. The three raters first read each transcript and labeled turns they would characterize as either "good" (productive for the writer) or "bad" (evidence of miscommunication or not communicating effectively). This activity both helped the researchers hone in on interesting sections of the sessions and ensured that raters read the entire transcripts with due attention. Next, the three raters each evaluated the quality of the conference using 5-point Likert scales to respond to criteria considered important to successful writing conferences, including

- Overall success of consultation
- Writer engagement in session
- Writer taking responsibility for his/her own learning
- Consultant guided by writer's agenda
- Degree of comfort writer and consultant demonstrated with each other.

In situations where multiple judges are used, a common measure for reporting inter-rater reliability is Cronbach's alpha coefficient. In this study, Cronbach's alpha coefficients were above .75 for "Writer engagement in session" and "Writer taking responsibility for his/her own learning." This represents substantial agreement above chance. Cronbach's alpha coefficients were between .41–.58 for the other three measures, which represent moderate agreement above chance (Fleiss). In addition, raters used a four-point scale to assess the frequency of various activities during the session, including "Fixing the writer's paper," "Attending to mechanics," "Providing elaboration or explanation," "Building rapport," and "Providing praise or affirmation." Cronbach's alpha coefficients were between .62–.76 for these five measures.[3]

Surveys.   Post-consultation surveys were analyzed for both writer and consultant attitudes towards the content of the sessions and to the conferencing environments.

RESULTS

Quantity and Control

Table 2 shows face-to-face sessions averaged over 50% more turns per session than computer-mediated sessions, a marginally significant difference, $F(1,23) = 4.25$, $p < .06$. (Although we realize many in the writing center com-

TABLE 2   Participant control by turns

Condition	Average turns (and standard deviation) per session	Consultant-controlled turns	Writer-controlled turns
Face-to-face	531 (305) †	66%	34%
WordShare	320 (147)	66%	34%
Tablet PC	368 (150)	73%*	27%

*$p < .0001$; † $p < .06$

munity will not recognize the specific statistical tests we have performed, we include this information because it has meaning outside this community. Novices to statistical analyses need only focus on the p value, the last number reported in the tests. The p value indicates the likelihood that a distribution is due to chance. Thus, the lower the p value, the more reliable the reported trends are believed to be. A p value of .01 indicates a 1% likelihood that results are due to random chance; a p value of .05 indicates a 5% likelihood of chance; a value of .10 indicates a 10% likelihood of chance. Values of less than .05 are considered statistically significant; those from .05–.10 are marginally significant. It is worth noting that a statistically significant finding does not automatically mean the researcher has interpreted the data correctly.)

Some of the difference between face-to-face and computer-mediated sessions in the number of turns is due to our decision to delete from the transcripts turns that dealt specifically with negotiating the conferencing environment (such as turns focused on figuring out how to work the controls). If the turns focused on wrangling with the technology are reinserted, the average turns per WordShare session rises to 327 and average turns per Tablet PC session rises to 393 turns. Since all sessions were capped at 50 minutes, these findings may suggest that some writing-focused instruction is lost in the computer-mediated sessions, particularly as participants struggle to adjust to unfamiliar technologies.

Table 2 also provides support for the concern that online conferencing environments may become consultant focused. Although the face-to-face and WordShare conditions exhibited equivalent rates of consultant control, the percentage of consultant controlled turns increased in the Tablet PC condition, $\chi^2(2) = 38.01$, $p < .0001$. Thus, the consultants initiated and controlled significantly more of the discourse in Tablet PC sessions than they did in either face-to-face or WordShare sessions.

Document Marking on Shared Text

The conferencing environment also seemed to influence both who wrote on documents and the types of markings made. Figure 1 indicates that the total amount of writing on the shared document increased from 10.5% of all turns in the face-to-face environment to 12.1% and 14.2% of all turns in the WordShare

FIGURE 1   Percentage of turns in which participants marked on text

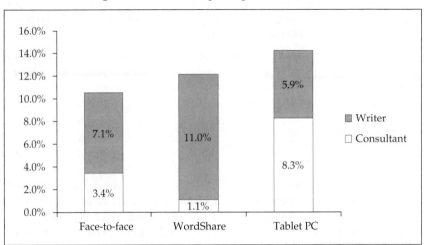

From "Comparing Technologies for Online Writing Conferences: Effects of Medium on Conversation" by Joanna Wolfe and Jo Ann Griffin.

and Tablet PC environments, respectively, $\chi2(2) = 17.5$, p < .001. More strikingly, Figure 1 also shows writers marked on the text significantly more often in the WordShare condition than the other two conditions, while consultants marked on the text significantly more often in the Tablet PC condition, $\chi2(2) = 172.2$, p < .0001.

Table 3 provides additional insight into these trends. We can see from the third row of Table 3 that the increase in consultant markings in the Tablet PC condition can be attributed to consultants using the digital ink tools to estab-

TABLE 3   Types of document markings made by consultants and writers in the three consultation conditions (expressed as percentage of all document markings per condition)

Condition	Editing text	Taking notes	Generating text	Establishing attention
Consultants				
Face-to-face (n = 140)	56%	38%	1%	1%
WordShare (n = 27)	76%	10%	0%	7%
Tablet PC (n = 242)	49%	22%	0%	29%
Writers				
Face-to-face (n = 301)	87%	12%	0%	0%
WordShare (n = 281)	70%	8%	20%	3%
Tablet PC (n = 172)	95%	1%	2%	2%

lish joint attention in the Tablet PC setting. These markings replace the act of pointing in face-to-face conversations and help the remote participants establish a common frame of reference. Table 3 also shows us that note-taking decreased in both of the online conditions with writers taking almost no notes in the Tablet PC condition. Finally, Table 3 shows us that a striking amount of writer activity was spent generating new text in the WordShare condition. While new text was rarely generated in the face-to-face environment (mostly occurring when a consultant transcribed a writer's thoughts), text generation accounted for nearly 20% of the writing activity in the WordShare sessions.

Transcript 1 provides an example of a writer generating new text in a WordShare session while the consultant looks on and provides advice and encouragement. Such real-time text generation seems to be facilitated by the shared computer screen, both because the screen (as opposed to handwritten notes) helps consultants see exactly what is being written and because writers know that whatever additions they make can be saved. Even though it should be noted that the majority of new text generation in this study occurred in a single WordShare session, such extensive generation of new text seems to be a unique feature of OWI.

Transcript 1: A writer generating text in a WordShare session

CONSULTANT: [suggesting wording] "His idea makes sense, but I personally think that it would only work in a perfect society which does not and will not exist." Then you get all these facts that show an example of how the society is not perfect.

WRITER: OK. Um [typing "a perfect society"]

CONSULTANT: Like the mere fact that you can have a Declaration of Independence that says all men are endowed and created equal but yet you have slavery.

WRITER: Mmm Let me see. So "in relation to"

CONSULTANT: So how, how could you make that

WRITER: "has" um [typing "has strengthened the fact that"]

CONSULTANT: Mmm hmm

WRITER: [typing "there will never be"] Um

CONSULTANT: Mmm hmm Yeah. you're on the right track. That's good.

WRITER: Let me think for a second here.

CONSULTANT: Mmm hmmm

WRITER: [typing "a way to"]

CONSULTANT: Yeah. You're on the right track. You're making a connection. Think about reparations too because you're going to go into a discussion about reparations. How can you fit reparations in there?

WRITER: Mmm hmm [typing "repay African-Americans of African descent for the injustices that we. . . ."] [intake of breath]

CONSULTANT: Yeah. That's good. Keep going.

At the same time that OWI allowed for more extensive text generation during sessions, the environment seemed to discourage note-taking and writers almost completely stopped taking notes on the common document in the Tablet PC condition. Transcript 2 suggests that one reason for this decrease in writer activity may be confusion over how to use the electronic tools—particularly when the consultant had a different set of tools than the writer, as was the case in Tablet PC sessions:

Transcript 2: Writer asking consultant to write for him in Tablet PC session

WRITER: Right. Right. So can I get control of [the Word document] back, or what?

CONSULTANT: Um

WRITER: Just to type that real quick? Or can you, can you write for me?

CONSULTANT: I'm gonna go ahead. I'm trying to get this thing working um. Let's see. Black. I don't want to do red cause it's—yeah—Sorry about that. uh ok. . . . I'm gonna write down here at the bottom.

Finally, it is worth noting that in the electronic sessions the spell- and grammar-checker often became a distraction. Fixing spelling errors accounted for 5% of document markings in the Tablet PC condition and 3% in the Word-Share condition, but only 1% of document markings in the face-to-face sessions. Many times the OWI conferences seemed to be temporarily derailed because of errors identified by Microsoft Word, a phenomenon Buck also reports. The writers and consultants spent time discussing and correcting these low-level and easily fixable errors when time might have been better spent on more substantive concerns.

Document Marking on Private Copies of Texts

The conferencing environment not only influenced the type and quantity of document markings made on the shared text but also influenced the extent to which participants (usually writers) marked individual, private copies of the text. Table 4 shows that writers in the Tablet PC setting made over twice as many markings on a private paper copy of their text as in the WordShare set-

TABLE 4   Number of turns writers spent marking on a private copy of the text

Condition	Number of turns spent marking a private copy of the text
Face-to-face	4
WordShare	14
Tablet PC	28

ting and seven times as many as in face-to-face. These private markings are an area of concern both because they might reflect writers' reluctance to engage with the computer controls and because having multiple versions of a text increases the opportunities for miscommunication (Whittaker; Heath and Luff).

We see this potential for miscommunication in Transcript 3 when the writer justifies a long silence by explaining that he is taking notes. Had the participants been face-to-face, or had the writer been making notes with the computer, the consultant would have been able to see this activity and no explanation would have been needed. Thus, writers' apparent reluctance to engage with the computer in the Tablet PC condition may result in less efficient communication.

Transcript 3: Writer marking a private paper copy of the text in a Tablet PC session

CONSULTANT: And it wouldn't have to be too much more, just like a sentence. But just, I, I would, as a reader, I would be curious to see who directs this correctional officer, [follows "correctional officer" with cursor] and he is obviously carrying some kind of order out.

WRITER: Yes sir. [making notes to self in paper copy of text]

CONSULTANT: Well, how is he carrying that order out?

WRITER: And how is he carrying it out. [pause] I'm long-handing your notes. Okay.

CONSULTANT: Do you? Okay.

Holistic Ratings

Holistically, there was little difference in how writing center professionals evaluated the quality of conferences across the three environments. Although Table 5 shows face-to-face sessions were generally ranked highest and Tablet PC sessions lowest on all measures, these differences were far from significant. In particular, evaluators perceived just as much writer engagement and agency in WordShare as face-to-face sessions.

While overall conference quality appeared consistent across all three environments, the consulting environment did appear to influence the types of

TABLE 5   Average evaluations (and standard deviations) raters gave the sessions based on a 5-point scale (1 = strongly disagree; 5 = strongly agree)

Evaluation criteria	Face-to-face	WordShare	Tablet PC
Successful consultation	3.9 (.80)	3.7 (.50)	3.5 (.82)
Comfortable with one another	4.2 (.50)	4.0 (.79)	3.9 (.66)
Writer engaged	4.2 (.71)	4.2 (.67)	3.8 (.99)
Writer responsible for own learning	4.2 (.69)	4.0 (.84)	3.7 (1.00)
Consultant guided by writer's agenda	4.0 (.49)	4.0 (.67)	3.9 (.89)

TABLE 6   Average frequencies (and standard deviations) of strategies observed in consultations (0 = never; 1 = occasionally; 2 = often; 3 = very often)

Strategies observed in consultation	Face-to-face	WordShare	Tablet PC
Fixing the writer's paper	0.5 (.50)	0.6 (.42)	1.1 (.90)†
Attention to mechanics, syntax, grammar	1.6 (.60)	1.8 (.67)	2.1 (.50)
Providing elaboration or explanation	1.8 (.64)	1.5 (.40)	1.6 (.70)
Building rapport	1.8 (.62)*	1.3 (.47)	1.2 (.78)
Providing praise or affirmation	2.0 (.71)	1.9 (.53)	1.6 (.73)

*$p < .05$; † $p < .07$

pedagogical strategies consultants used. Table 6 shows consultants were perceived as doing marginally more fixing of writers' papers in the Tablet PC condition than in the other two media, $F(1,23) = 3.91$, $p < .07$. This finding is consistent with the increase in consultant control in Table 2.

Transcript 4 illustrates consultants' tendencies to correct on writers' behalf rather than allow them to implement changes themselves. The consultant in Transcript[4] corrects punctuation directly on the shared document with relatively little explanation. Meanwhile, the writer seems to have been turned into a passive observer of the consultant's actions, a situation perhaps most tellingly encapsulated in the consultant's query, "Are you keeping up with me?"

Transcript 4: Consultant fixing a writer's text in a Tablet PC session

CONSULTANT: OK, [reads] "five point star" [adds "nt" to end of word] "is," uh, the [adds "the"] "struggle of the emancipation against," um, maybe the, maybe the emancipation from [replaces "against" with "from"] "colonialism." The, it would be "the struggle against colonialism," or "emancipation from" it. "Struggle.". . . So maybe, um, maybe "the struggle toward emancipation from colonialism?" [replaces "of the" with "toward"]. Does that work for you?

WRITER: Um, yeah, yes.

CONSULTANT: OK, so [reads] "The flag of Ghana." . . . Let's just go, let's go back to this sentence up here. Are you keeping up with me, or am I going too fast?

By contrast, participants in WordShare sessions were more likely to hand off control back and forth to one another, as in Transcript 5.

Transcript 5: Consultant and writer sharing control in a WordShare session

CONSULTANT: Right. What I would do—this is just a suggestion—I would start off with your discussion here [indicates location in text with cursor] where you're talking about exactly what [the speaker] was talking about. Then, I would put this stuff in where you're adding your extra commentary and your extra research [indicates location in text with cursor]. Flip it around. . . .

WRITER: So this part right here would go up where "[The speaker] also discussed" [indicates location in text with cursor]

CONSULTANT: Mmm hmmm. . . . Put it here [indicates location in text with cursor].

WRITER: OK.

CONSULTANT: I'll let you put that in there. You can just copy and paste.

Table 6 also indicates less rapport-building was observed in the two technology conditions than in face-to-face sessions, $F(1,23) = 4.37, p < .05$, although this finding may be due to the decision to eliminate turns explicitly focused on technology. In other words, there may be rapport-building not reflected in the transcripts as consultants and writers collaborated to manage the logistics of conducting the electronic sessions. No significant differences were found in the amount of elaboration or praise that raters perceived in the three conditions.

Surveys: Session Satisfaction

Table 7 suggests both consultants and writers were equivalently satisfied with consultations in the face-to-face and technology mediated environments. All but one of the student writers agreed or strongly agreed that they were satisfied with the consultation. The one student writer (in a WordShare session) who responded "neither agree nor disagree" to the satisfaction question commented that at least some of her dissatisfaction was due to her perception that the consultant did not have a strong handle on "technical grammar rules." Consultants similarly were equally satisfied with the overall quality of technology and face-to-face consultations. The high levels of self-reported satisfaction immediately following the conference are typical for this writing center.

In their responses to other survey items, student writers were slightly more likely to agree that it was easier to communicate their concerns in the face-to-face environment (average agreement 5.0 on a 5-point Likert scale) than in WordShare (3.9) or Tablet PC (4.9) environments. The student writers also tended to agree that the Tablet PC (average agreement 4.3 on a 5-point Likert scale) and WordShare (3.8) environments were more impersonal than the face-to-face (3.1) environment. However, none of these differences is significant.

TABLE 7   Average agreement (and standard deviations) on a 5-point Likert scale with the statement "I was satisfied with this consultation" (5 = strongly agree; 1 = strongly disagree)

Satisfaction with consultation	Face-to-face	WordShare	Tablet PC
Consultant satisfaction	4.00 (.93)	4.13 (.35)	4.00 (.00)
Student writer satisfaction	5.00 (.00)	4.50 (.76)	4.86 (.50)

Surveys: Environment Preference

Student writers were far more enthusiastic about the online consultations than consultants. Table 8 shows that, while 75% of the consultants preferred face-to-face to online consultations, only 13% of student writers agreed. Instead, 87% of student writers who participated in an online session either preferred the online environment or had no environment preference.

When students provided reasons for their preferences, they focused on the convenience of the online environment, commenting on the ease and travel time saved by working at home, factors that the CCCC Committee for Best Practice in Online Writing Instruction similarly found students prized. However, students also mentioned pedagogical benefits such as "the ability to make changes on the spot." Several participants explicitly contrasted the real-time application-sharing and audio support used in this study with text-based chat, saying "I really liked that we could both look at the screen at the same time. It was very helpful to be literally on the same page. I'm glad there was a mic instead of text messaging. That made it more personal." Seven of the sixteen students in online sessions emphasized the importance of having a shared screen as contributing to their positive evaluations of the sessions.

Most of the student criticisms of the online environment focused on technological problems such as "echoing" in the headset, "lag time," and "mushy controls." One student also mentioned feeling he and the consultant had gotten into a "tug of war over the cursor." In addition, nearly one third of the students complained of a decrease in either the quantity or quality of communication in this environment. For instance, one student wrote, "I seemed to get more accomplished in an hour of face-to-face tutoring than in the online," and "it was hard for me to express myself without confusion without being face-to-face."

In contrast to the students' overall enthusiasm for online consultations, consultants were much more negative about the online environments. Half of

TABLE 8   Consultant and student writer preference for online vs. face-to-face consultations. Only writers who participated in an online session are included.

Participant groups	Preferred online	No preference	Preferred face-to-face
Consultants after participating in an online session (n = 8)	13% (n = 1)	13% (n = 1)	75% (n = 6)
Student writers participating in an online consultation (n = 16)	56% (n = 9)	31% (n = 5)	13% (n = 2)

the consultants complained about inefficiency in the online sessions—a perception consistent with the finding that online sessions had fewer turns than face-to-face sessions. Consultants also found the absence of body language and facial cues made online communication more difficult. One consultant, for instance, wrote that "it is easier in a face-to-face tutorial to use body language as an instructional tool. For example I can use gestures, etc. to convey an idea." Another consultant noted that online sessions seem to have a text-driven focus that make it difficult to "talk about more global concerns; it's so easy to fall into an editing mode," echoing concerns voiced by Enders, Castner, and Harris ("Using").

DISCUSSION

Because our research was conducted in a busy writing center, the operations of which we wanted to disrupt as little as possible, many variables in this small study were beyond our control. Nonetheless, we do believe this study offers provisional evidence that media-rich online conferences can be nearly as pedagogically effective as face-to-face sessions. We found no significant differences in our expert raters' perceptions of the instructional quality of the sessions; moreover, participants were equally satisfied with the consultations regardless of environment. We did, however, note that environment seemed to affect how instruction was implemented. In particular, online environments saw a decrease in the number of notes participants took about planned changes to the text and an increase in the quantity of new text generated during the session. This shift from note-taking to actual text production has mixed benefits, and we suggest below some steps instructors may want to take to ensure that text production does not lead the sessions off track.

Our most surprising finding was that the Tablet PC variation of our conferencing environment exhibited some negative effects when compared with the other session types. The Tablet PC seemed to encourage consultants to assert more control over the sessions: consultants were more likely to dominate turn exchanges, were more likely to write *for* students, and were perceived as more likely to "fix" student papers rather than encourage students to implement changes themselves. So why did the Tablet PC seem to encourage consultants to exert greater control over the sessions? While we obviously do not have access to participants' mental states, we hypothesize that the unequal distribution of tools available to participants changed the dynamics of the sessions. Whereas in the WordShare sessions both participants manipulated the text and screen through the familiar mechanism of a computer keyboard, in the Tablet sessions consultants were given a relatively novel tool that was unavailable to writers. This inequality may have reinforced a perception that the consultant was in charge of the session—or at least in charge of the computer—and subsequently writers were more hesitant to engage with the technology. One consequence of this hesitance is that writers in the Tablet PC sessions turned instead to making notes on separate paper copies of their essays. Such personal note taking was not visible to consultants and contributed to a lack of shared awareness of participants' activities during the session.

Support for our hypothesis that unequal tools contributed to consultant dominance of the Tablet PC sessions comes from one of the most highly rated conferences in our sample. This Tablet PC conference received a score of 4.7 (out of 5) for overall success, tying it with two other face-to-face consultations as most successful. Tellingly, both participants in this session mistakenly believed that the writer also had access to digital ink tools. At one point, the writer even picked up a ballpoint pen left near the computer and tried to use it on the desktop computer screen only to give up, saying "my marker sucks." Thus, this consultation may have been successful partly because the participants were under the impression that they both had access to the same novel technology. Future research is needed to determine if providing both student writers and consultants with Tablet PC tools would improve this condition.

One final result worth mentioning is the decided difference in student and consultant preferences for OWI. While over half of our student participants stated that they preferred OWI, only one consultant expressed a similar preference. Most consultants raised concerns about the pedagogical effectiveness of OWI—concerns our data suggests are mostly unwarranted. Although fewer turns may have been covered in OWI, our raters found these sessions pedagogically equivalent to face-to-face sessions. With a small amount of training, consultants could learn to overcome many of the obstacles we report (such as negotiating cursor control or becoming distracted by the spell- or grammar-checker). Hewett believes that instructors have too much "misguided" faith in the efficacy emerging from the comparative intimacy of face-to-face interactions (Online, 13). Our findings lend some support to this assertion.

Several shortcomings in our study design may have affected results. The participants received minimal training in the technology and most were inexperienced with the virtual environments. Thus, we might expect to see some changes in both the quality and quantity of the online sessions as participants became more familiar with the possibilities and limitations of the online tools. It should also be emphasized that, while the participants (particularly the student writers) were very positive about the online conferences, they were experiencing these environments in ideal conditions: the technology was set up for them on computers with very high connection speeds and a researcher was nearby to help them troubleshoot problems. More frustrations are to be expected if participants conduct conferences from their home computers. Our results are also affected by the fact that students in the Tablet PC sessions were more likely to have been regular writing center visitors than those in the WordShare sessions.

Finally, we must mention that this study was conducted in a naturalistic environment (a very busy university writing center), and we therefore were unable to control for the types of papers and the skill levels of the writers included in the study. Thus, we cannot dismiss the possibility that the differences between the Tablet PC and WordShare environments are due to differences in the participants. It is also the case that students were compensated for their participation in the study, which may have affected their satisfaction with the OWI and their tolerance for technological problems.

Recommendations for OWI and Directions for Future Research

Despite any problems with our study design, our experiences conducting this research do allow us to propose the following recommendations for setting up writing conferences in virtual environments:

- Real-time audio and desktop-sharing are highly desirable. Many participants particularly singled out these features as contributing to the success of the online conferences; we believe these features allowed the online conferences to approach the pedagogical quality of face-to-face sessions.

- Online conferences may warrant longer session times, particularly when participants are new to the technology. We found that online conferences averaged 30% fewer turns (once turns focused on technology were factored out) than face-to-face, and, not surprisingly, participants claimed that these sessions felt less efficient than face-to-face. Thus, longer session times may be needed to overcome some of the difficulties of negotiating unfamiliar technology. Future research should examine how more experienced participants perform in online settings.

- Spell-check and grammar-check functions should be turned off to avoid the temptation to focus on these relatively low-level and straightforward errors during the conference time. Fixing spelling errors accounted for approximately 4% of the document markings in the online sessions but only 1% in the face-to-face sessions. Writers and consultants spent time discussing errors highlighted by the word processor, time that might have been better spent addressing other concerns.

- If the goal of the session is for writers to exert control and ownership over their own writing, then both participants may need to have equivalent tools. We hypothesize that one reason consultants dominated Tablet PC sessions is that they controlled tools unavailable to writers. More research is needed to test the hypothesis that unequal tools lead to unequal dynamics in other aspects of collaborative writing environments.

- Consultants and writers should receive training and advice on how to use tools to support distinct authoring roles. In Tablet PC settings, this could involve having the consultant use digital ink tools to draw attention to specific areas of the text and write notes in the margins while the writer uses the keyboard to change the text. In the WordShare condition, consultants might be coached to use the commenting feature and highlighting tools to comment on the text while the writer executes changes. More research is needed to examine how such training influences the quality of the conferences.

Writing center professionals are recognizing the importance of separating evidence-based research from lore. Although some lore suggests face time is the ideal form of communication, the findings from this small study give us reason to hope that, with training, experience, and the right selection of tools, OWI may offer pedagogical benefits rivaling—or even exceeding—those of face-to-face conferencing.

Appendix A: Pre-consultation Survey

1. Have you ever used the University Writing Center?   Yes   No

2. If yes, circle all that apply:

   a. I met a consultant in the Writing Center

   b. I submitted a paper for an email response

   c. I met with a consultant through Blackboard

3. Your academic status:

   Freshman   Sophomore   Junior   Senior   Graduate

4. Age: 17–25   26–30   Older than 30

5. Gender: Male   Female

6. I use email as a communication tool:

   Never   An hour per week   An hour per day   3–5 hours per day
   More than 5 hours/day

7. I am connected to the World Wide Web (on the Internet):

   Never   An hour per week   An hour per day   3–5 hours per day
   More than 5 hours/day

8. I use an Instant Messaging Program:

   Never   An hour per week   An hour per day   3–5 hours per day
   More than 5 hours/day

9. What Instant Message applications are on your computer? (circle all that apply)

   a. None/I have no clue

   b. AOL Instant Messenger

   c. MSN Messenger

   d. Yahoo Messenger

   e. ICQ

   f. Other

10. I use Instant Messaging to (circle all that apply):

    a. I never use Instant Messaging programs

    b. Chat with friends

    c. Work with someone on homework

    d. Send a picture/file

    e. Waste time

11. How would you rate your overall computing experience compared to the average student?

    a. Very below average

    b. Somewhat below average

    c. Average

    d. Somewhat better than average

    e. Much better than average

12. My previous face-to-face consultation(s) helped me improve my paper.

    Strongly agree   Agree   Neutral   Disagree   Strongly disagree

13. I found all my concerns addressed in previous face-to-face consultations.

    Strongly agree   Agree   Neutral   Disagree   Strongly disagree

APPENDIX B: POST-CONSULTATION SURVEY

1. I am a (circle one): Freshman Sophomore Junior Senior Graduate

2. I am a (circle one): Male Female

3. What is your major? _____

4. How many times have you visited the Writing Center in the past?

    _____

5. For what class is the assignment you discussed today?

    _____

6. How close are you to being finished with this assignment?

    _____

7. It was easy to convey my concerns about writing to the consultant:

    Strongly agree   Agree   Neutral   Disagree   Strongly disagree

8. I know what I need to do in order to revise my paper:

    Strongly agree   Agree   Neutral   Disagree   Strongly disagree

9. I found the consultant impersonal:

    Strongly agree   Agree   Neutral   Disagree   Strongly disagree

10. My consultant addressed all my concerns about my paper:

    Strongly agree   Agree   Neutral   Disagree   Strongly disagree

11. Based on my experience today I would choose an online tutorial over a face-to-face tutorial in the future:

    Strongly agree   Agree   Neutral   Disagree   Strongly disagree

12. Why would you make this choice?

13. I am satisfied with this consultation:

    Strongly agree   Agree   Neutral   Disagree   Strongly disagree

14. What was the best or worst feature about today's consultation?

15. What would you like to be able to do in a consultation that you could not do?

16. Additional comments?

NOTES

1. We used Adobe ConnectPro as our conferencing environment due to its ability to record conferences in addition to allowing participants to share a desktop and communicate via audio. Many other conferencing environments exist, including WebEx and Yuuguu (a free application).

2. Inter-rater reliability is a key concept in conducting ethical empirical research. It indicates that two or more individuals observe the same phenomenon independently from one another. Cohen's kappa and Cronbach's alpha are statistics that determine these observations are not due to random chance. The higher the statistics are, the more similar the raters' observations. A statistic of .75 or greater typically indicates excellent agreement; statistics greater than .40 represent fair agreement (Fleiss).

3. Four other criteria have been dropped from the evaluations because of low inter-rater reliability. These low levels of agreement are not surprising: it has long been recognized that the more complex and fluid the subject area being assessed, the more difficult it is to achieve high levels of inter-rater agreement (Coffman; Diederich). Writing center transcripts are certainly a fluid subject matter and there is a great deal of debate in writing center communities about the relative merits of particular strategies.

WORKS CITED

Anderson, Richard J., Crystal Hoyer, Steven A. Wolfman, and Ruth Anderson. "A Study of Digital Ink in Lecture Presentation." *CHI 2004*. New York: ACM, 2004. 567–74. Print.

Black, Laurel. *Between Talk and Teaching: Reconsidering the Writing Conference*. Logan, UT: Utah State UP, 1998. Print.

Bos, Nathan, Judy Olson, Darren Gergle, Gary Olson, and Zach Wright. "Effects of Four Computer-Mediated Communications Channels on Trust Development." *Proceedings of the SIGCHI Conference on Human Factors in Computing Systems: Changing Our World, Changing Ourselves*. New York: ACM, 2002. Print.

Bradner, Erin, and Gloria Mark. "Social Presence with Video and Application Sharing." *Group '01*. New York: ACM, 2001. Print.

Breuch, Lee-Ann K. "The Idea(s) of an Online Writing Center: In Search of a Conceptual Model." *Writing Center Journal* 25 (2005): 21–37. Print.

Brown, Kate, Roxana Cazan, and Jo Ann Griffin. "Chatting in the Center: An Investigation of the Current Uses and Potential of Synchronous Chat in the Writing Center." Conf. on Coll. Composition and Communication. Chicago. Mar. 2006. Presentation.

Buck, Amber M. "The Invisible Interface: MS Word in the Writing Center." *Computers and Composition* 25.4 (2008): 396–415. Print.

Castner, Joanna. "The Asynchronous, Online Writing Session: A Two-Way Stab in the Dark?" *Taking Flight with OWLs: Examining Electronic Writing Center Work*. Ed. James A. Inman and Donna N. Sewell. Mahwah, NJ: Erlbaum, 2000. 193–202. Print.

Coffman, William E. "On the Reliability of Ratings of Essay Examinations in English." *Research in the Teaching of English* 5 (1971): 24–36. Print.

Cohen, Andrew L., Debra Cash, Michael J. Muller, and Curtis Culberson. "Writing Apart and Designing Together." *CHI 99*. New York: ACM, 1999. 198–99. Print.

Diederich, Paul B. *Measuring Growth in English*. Urbana, IL: NCTE, 1974. Print.

Enders, Doug. "Virtual Success: Using Microsoft NetMeeting in Synchronous, Online Tutorials." *Writing Lab Newsletter* 24 (2000): 12–16. Print.

Fleiss, Joseph L. *Statistical Methods for Rates and Proportions*. New York: Wiley, 1981. Print.

Frank, Alex, and Mary Beth Lakin. *Distance Education: Challenged to Move Ahead yet Leave No Students Behind*. 2007. Web. 22 Apr. 2008.

Harris, Muriel. "Using Computers to Expand the Role of Writing Centers." *Electronic Communication Across the Curriculum*. Ed. Donna Reiss, Dickie Selfe, and Art Young. Urbana, IL: NCTE, 1998. 3–16. Print.

———. "Making Up Tomorrow's Agenda and Shopping Lists Today: Preparing for Future Technologies in Writing Centers." *Taking Flight with OWLs: Examining Electronic Writing Center Work*. Ed. James A. Inman and Donna N. Sewell. Mahwah, NJ: Erlbaum, 2000. 193–202. Print.

Heath, Christian, and Paul Luff. "Disembodied Conduct: Interactional Asymmetries in Video-Mediated Communication." *Technology in Working Order: Studies of Work, Interaction, and Technology.* Ed. Graham Button. London: Routledge, 1993. 35–54. Print.

Hewett, Beth L. *The Online Writing Conference: A Guide for Teachers and Tutors.* Portsmouth, NH: Boynton/Cook, 2010. Print.

———. "Synchronous Online Conference-Based Instruction: A Study of Whiteboard Interactions and Student Writing." *Computers and Composition* 23.1 (2006): 4–31. Print.

Hewett, Beth, Deborah Minter, Keith Gibson, Lisa Meloncon, Sushil Oswal, Leslie Olsen, Scott Warnock, Christa Ehmann Powers, W. Webster Newbold, Julie Drew, and Kevin Eric De Pew. "Initial Report of the CCCC Committee for Best Practice in Online Writing Instruction (OWI)." 12 Apr. 2011. Web. 30 Nov. 2012.

Hobson, Eric. "Introduction: Straddling the Virtual Fence." *Wiring the Writing Center.* Ed. Hobson. Logan, UT: Utah State U P, 1998. ix–xxvi. Print.

Ice, Philip, Reagan Curtis, Perry Phillips, and John Wells. "Using Asynchronous Audio Feedback to Enhance Teaching Presence and Student Sense of Community." *Journal of Asynchronous Learning Networks* 11.2 (2007): 3–25. Print.

Jaschik, Scott. "How to Tell Whether Writing Instruction Works." *Inside Higher Ed* 28 Dec. 2007. Web. 21 Jun. 2012.

Jones, Casey. "The Relationship Between Writing Centers and Improvement in Writing Ability: An Assessment of the Literature." *Education* 122.1 (2001): 3–20.

Jones, Nigel, Panicos Georghiades, and John Gunson. "Student Feedback Via Screen Capture Digital Video: Stimulating Student's Modified Action." *Higher Education* 64 (2012): 593–607. Print.

Kreiser, Chris. "Silence in the Writing Center: Comparing Student to Consultant Word Ratios." Conf. on Coll. Composition and Communication. Chicago. Mar. 2002. Presentation.

Lowry, Paul Benjamin, and Jay F. Nunamaker, Jr. "Using Internet-Based, Distributed Collaborative Writing Tools to Improve Coordination and Group Awareness in Writing Teams." *IEEE Transactions on Professional Communication* 46.4 (2003): 277–97. Print.

Neaderhiser, Stephen, and Joanna Wolfe. "Between Technological Endorsement and Resistance: The State of Online Writing Centers." *Writing Center Journal* 29.1 (2009): 52–81. Print.

Neuwirth, Christine M., Ravinder Chandhok, Davida Charney, Patricia Wojahn, and Loel Kim. "Distributed Collaborative Writing: A Comparison of Spoken and Written Modalities for Reviewing and Revising Documents." *Human Factors in Computing Systems.* New York: ACM, 1994. 51–57. Print.

Oomen-Early, Jody, Mary Bold, Kristin L. Wiginton, Tara L. Gallien, and Nancy Anderson. "Using Asynchronous Audio Communication (AAC) in the Online Classroom: A Comparative Study." *MERLOT: Journal of Online Teaching and Learning* 4.3 (2008): 267–76. Print.

Thompson, Isabelle. "Scaffolding in the Writing Center: A Microanalysis of an Experienced Tutor's Verbal and Nonverbal Tutoring Strategies." *Written Communication* 26.4 (2009): 417–53. Print.

Walker, Carolyn P., and David Elias. "Writing Conference Talk: Factors Associated with High- and Low-rated Writing Conferences." *Research in the Teaching of English* 21 (1987): 266–85. Print.

Whittaker, Steve. "Things to Talk About When Talking About Things." *Human-Computer Interaction* 18.1 (2003): 149–70. Print.

Wolfe, Joanna. "Gesture and Collaborative Planning: A Case Study of a Student Writing Group." *Written Communication* 22.3 (2005): 298–332. Print.

Yergeau, Melanie, Kathryn Wozniak, and Peter Vandenberg. "Expanding the Space of f2f: Writing Centers and Audio-Visual-Textual Conferencing." *Kairos: A Journal of Rhetoric, Technology, and Pedagogy* 13.1 (2008). Web. 12 Aug. 2010.

OTHER SELECTED READINGS AND RESOURCES FOR FURTHER STUDY

This section (though not exhaustive) identifies additional works and online resources.

ADDITIONAL READINGS BY PART

Part One — Practical and Theoretical Foundations

Bruffee, Kenneth A. "Collaborative Learning and the 'Conversation of Mankind.'" *College English*, vol. 46, no. 7, 1984, pp. 635–54.

Macrorie, Ken. *Writing to Be Read*. Hayden Book, 1968.

Moffett, James. *Teaching the Universe of Discourse*. Houghton Mifflin, 1968.

Murphy, James J. "The Key Role of Habit in Roman Writing Instruction." *A Short History of Writing Instruction: From Ancient Greece to Modern America*, edited by James J. Murphy, 2nd ed., Hermagoras, 2001, pp. 35–78.

Murray, Donald M. "The Listening Eye: Reflections on the Writing Conference." *College English*, vol. 41, 1979, pp. 13–18.

———. "Teach Writing as a Process Not Product." *The Leaflet*, Nov. 1972, pp. 11–14, reprinted in *Cross-Talk in Comp Theory*, edited by Victor Villanueva, 3rd ed., NCTE, 2011, pp. 3–6.

Part Two — Shaking the Foundations: Questioning and Revaluing Assumptions

Bishop, Wendy. "Completing the Circuit: Why (Student) Writers Should Share Products." *Public Works: Student Writing as Public Text*, edited by Emily Isaacs and Phoebe Jackson, Boynton/Cook, 2001.

Berkenkotter, Carol. "Student Writers and Their Sense of Authority over Texts." *College Composition and Communication*, vol. 35, no. 3, 1984, pp. 312–19.

Ching, Kory Lawson. "Peer Response in the Composition Classroom: An Alternative Genealogy." *Rhetoric Review*, vol. 26, no. 3, June 2007, pp. 303–19.

———. "Apprenticeship in the Instructor-Led Peer Conference." *Composition Studies*, vol. 39, no. 2, 2011, pp. 101–19.

Covill, Amy E. "Comparing Peer Review and Self-Review as Ways to Improve College Students' Writing." *Journal of Literacy Research*, vol. 42, no. 1, 2010, pp. 199–226.

Falchikov, Nancy, and Judy Goldfinch. "Student Peer Assessment in Higher Education: A Meta-Analysis Comparing Peer and Teacher Marks." *Review of Educational Research*, vol. 70, 2000, pp. 287–322.

Flynn, Elizabeth A. "Re-Viewing Peer Review." *The Writing Instructor*, Dec. 2011. Web. 14 Jan. 2014.

George, Diana. "Working with Peer Groups in the Composition Classroom." *College Composition and Communication*, vol. 35, no. 3, 1984, pp. 320–26.

Gere, Anne Ruggles, and Ralph Stevens. "The Language of Writing Groups: How Oral Response Shapes Revision." *The Acquisition of Written Language: Response and Revision*, edited by Sarah Warshauer Freedman, Ablex, 1985, pp. 85–105.

Gere, Anne Ruggles, and Robert D. Abbott. "Talking about Writing: The Language of Writing Groups." *Research in the Teaching of English*, vol. 19, 1985, pp. 362–86.

Grego, Rhonda C., and Nancy S. Thompson. *Teaching/Writing in Thirdspaces: The Studio Approach*, Southern Illinois UP, 2008.

Harris, Muriel. "Collaboration Is Not Collaboration Is Not Collaboration: Writing Center vs. Peer-Response Groups." *College Composition and Communication*, vol. 43, no. 3, 1992, pp. 369–83.

Healy, Dave. "A Defense of Dualism: The Writing Center and the Classroom." *The Writing Center Journal*, vol. 14, no. 1, 1993, pp. 16–29.

Holt, Mara. "The Value of Written Peer Criticism." *College Composition and Communication*, vol. 43, no. 3, 1992, pp. 348–92.

Nystrand, Martin. "Dialogic Discourse Analysis of Revision in Response Groups." *Discourse Studies in Composition*, edited by Ellen Barton and Gail Stygall, Hampton Press, 2002, pp. 377–92.

Paulson, Eric J., Jonathan Alexander, and Sonya Armstrong. "Peer Review Re-Reviewed: Investigating the Juxtaposition of Composition Students' Eye Movements and Peer-Review Processes." *Research in the Teaching of English*, vol. 41, no. 3, Feb. 2007, pp. 304–35.

Slembrouch, Jane Van. "Watch and Learn: Peer Evaluation and Tutoring Pedagogy." *Praxis: A Writing Center Journal*, vol. 8, no. 1, Fall 2010, www.praxisuwc.com/journal-page-81/.

Soliday, Mary. "Shifting Roles in Classroom Tutoring: Cultivating the Art of Boundary Crossing." *The Writing Center Journal*, vol. 16, no. 1, 1995, pp. 59–73.

Spigelman, Candace, and Laurie Grobman, editors. *On Location: Theory and Practice in Classroom-Based Writing Tutoring*, Utah State UP, 2005.

Stallings, Lynne, and Dawn M. Formo. " 'Where's the Writer?' Examining the Writer's Role as Solicitor of Feedback in Composition Textbooks." *Teaching English in the Two-Year College*, vol. 41, no. 3, Mar. 2014, pp. 259–77.

Stewart, Donald C. "Collaborative Learning: Boon or Bane? *Rhetoric Review*, vol. 7, 1988, pp. 58–83.

Thomas, Dene, and Gordon Thomas. "The Use of Rogerian Reflection in Small-Group Writing Conferences." *Writing and Response: Theory, Practice, and Research*, edited by Chris M. Anson, NCTE, 1989, pp. 114–26.

Trimbur, John. "Consensus and Difference in Collaborative Learning." *College English*, vol. 51, 1989, pp. 602–616.

———. "Peer Tutoring: A Contradiction in Terms?" *The Writing Center Journal*, vol. 7, no. 2, 1987, pp. 21–28.

Part Three — Theory into Practice

Armstrong, Sonya, and Eric Paulson. "Whither Peer Review? Terminology Matters for the Writing Classroom." *Teaching English at the Two-Year College*, vol. 35, no. 4, 2008, pp. 398–407.

Bean, John. "A Method of Peer-Evaluation of Student Writing." *College Composition and Communication*, vol. 30, 1979, pp. 301–02.

Bishop, Wendy. "Helping Peer Writing Groups Succeed." *Teaching English in the Two-Year College*, vol. 15, 1988, pp. 120–25.

Brooke, Robert E. *Writing and Sense of Self: Identity Negotiation in Writing Workshops*. NCTE, 1991.

Bruffee, Kenneth A. *A Short Course in Writing: Composition, Collaborative Learning, and Constructive Reading*. 4th ed. Pearson, 2007, especially pp. 169–87.

Byland, Heather. "Educating Students about Peer Response." *Young Scholars in Writing: Undergraduate Research in Writing and Rhetoric*, vol. 2, Fall 2004, pp. 56–67.

Corbett, Steven J. "A Better Way to Grade." *Inside Higher Ed*, 7 June 2010, www.insidehighered.com/views/2010/06/07/better-way-grade.

Danis, Francine M. "Catching the Drift: Keeping Peer Response Groups on Track." *College Composition and Communication*, vol. 39, no. 3, Oct. 1988, pp. 356–58.

Grimm, Nancy. "Improving Students' Responses to Their Peers' Essays." *College Composition and Communication*, vol. 37, no. 1, 1986, pp. 91–94.

Harris, Joseph, et al., editors. *Teaching with Student Texts: Essays toward an Informed Practice.* Utah State UP, 2010.

Lunsford, Andrea. "Teacher to Teacher: Tips for New Teachers #7: Effective Peer Groups." *Bedford Bits: Ideas for Teaching Writing,* 16 June 2011. Web. 14 Jan. 2014.

Perkins, Joan, et al. "Requiring Revision, Juggling the Work Load." *The WAC Casebook: Scenes for Faculty Reflection and Program Development,* edited by Chris Anson, Oxford UP, pp. 126–29.

Roen, Duane. "A Possible Sequence of Peer-Group Responses to a Student's Emerging Text—Autobiographical Essay." *Strategies for Teaching First-Year Composition,* edited by Duane Roen et al., NCTE, 2002, pp. 318–24.

Schaffer, Jane. "Peer Response That Works." *The Journal of Teaching Writing,* vol. 15, no. 1, 1996, pp. 81–90.

Trim, Michelle. *What Every Student Should Know about Practicing Peer Review.* Pearson/Longman, 2007.

Vatalaro, Paul. "Putting Students in Charge of Peer Review." *The Journal of Teaching Writing,* vol. 9, no. 1, 1990, pp. 21–29.

White, Edward M., and Cassie A. Wright. *Assigning, Responding, Evaluating: A Writing Teacher's Guide.* 5th ed., Bedford/St. Martin's, 2016, especially pp. 49–69.

Woods, Peggy M. "Moving beyond 'This Is Good' in Peer Response." *Practice in Context: Situating the Work of the Writing Teachers,* edited by Cindy Moore and Peggy O'Neill, NCTE, 2002, pp. 187–95.

Part Four—Recognizing Linguistic and Cultural Diversity

Berg, E. Cathrine. "The Effects of Trained Peer Response on ESL Students' Revision Types and Writing Quality." *Journal of Second Language Writing,* vol. 8, no. 3, 1999, pp. 215–41.

Carson, Joan, and Gayle Nelson. "Writing Groups: Cross-Cultural Issues." *Journal of Second Language Writing,* vol. 3, 1994, pp. 17–30.

Denny, Harry. "Queering the Writing Center." *The Writing Center Journal,* vol. 25, no. 2, 2005, pp. 39–62.

Liu, Junn, and Jette G. Hansen. *Peer Response in Second Language Writing Classrooms,* U of Michigan P, 2002.

Lockhart, Charles, and Peggy Ng. "Analyzing Talk in Peer Response Groups: Stances, Functions, and Content." *Language Learning,* vol. 4, no. 5, 1995, pp. 605–55.

Lundstrom, Kristi, and Wendy Baker. "To Give Is Better Than to Receive: The Benefits of Peer Review to the Reviewer's Own Writing." *Journal of Second Language Writing,* vol. 18, 2009, pp. 30–43.

Lutes, Jean Marie. "Why Feminists Make Better Tutors: Gender and Disciplinary Expertise in a Curriculum-Based Tutoring Program." *Writing Center Research: Extending the Conversation*, edited by Paula Gillespie et al., Lawrence Erlbaum Associates, 2002, pp. 235–57.

Mangelsdorf, Kate. "Peer Reviews in the ESL Composition Classroom: What Do the Students Think?" *ELT Journal*, vol. 46, 1992, pp. 274–84.

Mangelsdorf, Kate, and Ann Schlumberger. "ESL Student Response Stances in a Peer-Review Task." *Journal of Second Language Writing*, vol. 1, no. 3, pp. 235–54.

Min, Hui-Tzu. "The Effects of Trained Peer Review on EFL Students' Revision Types and Writing Quality." *Journal of Second Language Writing*, vol. 15, 2006, pp. 118–41.

Nelson, Gayle L., and John M. Murphy. "An L2 Writing Group: Task and Social Dimensions." *Journal of Second Language Writing*, vol. 1, no. 3, 1992, pp. 171–93.

Nelson, Marie Wilson. "Interdependence in the Writing Group — 'We Get By with a Little Help from Our Friends.'" *At the Point of Need: Teaching Basic and ESL Writers*, Boynton/Cook, 1991, pp. 49–98.

Okawa, Gail Y. "Redefining Authority: Multicultural Students and Tutors at the Educational Opportunity Program Writing Center at the University of Washington." *Writing Centers in Context: Twelve Case Studies*, edited by Joyce A. Kinkead and Jeanette G. Harris, NCTE, 1993, pp. 166–90.

Stanley, Jane. "Coaching Student Writers to Be Effective Peer Evaluators." *Journal of Second Language Writing*, vol. 1, 1992, pp. 217–33.

Villanueva, Victor. "Blind: Talking about the New Racism." *The Writing Center Journal*, vol. 26, no. 1, 2006, pp. 3–19.

Zhu, Wei. "Effects of Training for Peer Response on Students' Comments and Interaction." *Written Communication*, vol. 12, no. 4, 1995, pp. 492–528.

———. "Interaction and Feedback in Mixed Peer Response Groups." *Journal of Second Language Writing*, vol. 10, no. 4, 2001, pp. 251–76.

Part Five — Writing Across the Curriculum and Writing in the Disciplines

Brieger, Katharine, and Pam Bromley. "A Model for Facilitating Peer Review in the STEM Disciplines: A Case Study of Peer Review Workshops Supporting Student Writing in Introductory Biology Courses." *Double Helix*, vol. 2, 2014, qudoublehelixjournal.org/index.php/dh/article/view/26/115.

Carlson, Patricia A., and Frederick C. Berry. "Using Computer-Mediated Peer Review in an Engineering Design Course." *IEEE Transactions of the Professional Communication Society*, vol. 51, no. 3, 2008, pp. 264–79.

Cho, Kwangsu, and Christian D. Schunn. "Scaffolded Writing and Rewriting in the Discipline: A Web-Based Reciprocal Peer Review System." *Computers & Education*, vol. 48, no. 3, 2007, pp. 409–26.

Cho, Kwangsu, et al. "Validity and Reliability of Scaffolded Peer Assessment of Writing from Instructor and Student Perspectives." *Journal of Educational Psychology*, vol. 98, no. 4, 2006, pp. 891–901.

Cho, Kwangsu, Christian D. Schunn, and Davida Charney. "Commenting on Writing: Typology and Perceived Helpfulness of Comments from Novice Peer Reviewers and Subject Matter Experts." *Written Communication*, vol. 23, no. 3, 2006, pp. 260–94.

Eliason, John, and Thomas Schrand. "Exploring Response Cultures in the World of WAC." *The WAC Journal*, vol. 21, 2010, pp. 21–36.

Fernsten, Linda. "Peer Response: Helpful Pedagogy or Hellish Event?" *The WAC Journal*, vol. 17, 2006, pp. 33–41.

Florence, Marilyn, and Larry D. Yore. "Learning to Write Like a Scientist: Coauthoring as an Enculturation Task." *Journal of Research in Science Teaching*, vol. 41, no. 6, 2004, pp. 637–68.

Ford, Michael. "Disciplinary Authority and Accountability in Scientific Practice and Learning." *Science Education*, vol. 92, no. 3, 2008, pp. 404–23.

Gopen, George. "Why So Many Bright Students and So Many Dull Papers? Peer-Responded Journals as a Partial Solution to the Problem of the Fake Audience." *The WAC Journal*, vol. 16, 2005, pp. 22–48.

Hafner, John, and Patti Hafner. "Quantitative Analysis of the Rubric as an Assessment Tool: An Empirical Study of Student Peer-Group Rating." *International Journal of Science Education*, vol. 25, no. 12, 2003, pp. 1509–28.

Ortoleva, Giulia, and Mireille Bétrancourt. "Collaborative Writing and Discussion in Vocational Education: Effects on Learning and Self-Efficacy Beliefs." *Journal of Writing Research*, vol. 7, no. 1, June 2015, pp. 95–122.

Patchan, Melissa M., et al. "Writing in Natural Sciences: Understanding the Effects of Different Types of Reviewers on the Writing Process." *Journal of Writing Research*, vol. 2, no. 3, Feb. 2011, pp. 365–93.

Patchan, Melissa M., et al. "A Validation Study of Students' End Comments: Comparing Comments by Students, a Writing Instructor, and a Content Instructor." *Journal of Writing Research*, vol. 1, no. 2, March 2009, pp. 124–52.

Pelaez, Nancy J. "Problem-Based Writing with Peer Review Improves Academic Performance in Physiology." *Advances in Physiology Education*, vol. 26, no. 3, 2002, pp. 174–84.

Reed, Irene, et al. "Peer Assessment of Writing and Critical Thinking in STEM: Insights into Student and Faculty Perceptions and Practices." *Double Helix*, vol. 2, 2014, qudoublehelixjournal.org/index.php/dh/article/view/40.

Reynolds, Julie, and Vicki Russell. "Can You Hear Us Now? A Comparison of Peer Review Quality When Students Give Audio versus Written Feedback." *The WAC Journal*, vol. 19, 2008, pp. 29–44.

Scorcinelli, Mary Deane, and Peter Elbow, editors. *Writing to Learn: Strategies for Assigning and Responding to Writing Across the Disciplines.* Jossey-Bass, 1997, especially pp. 1–52.

Seuba, Mariona Corcelles, and Castelló Montserrat. "Learning Philosophical Thinking through Collaborative Writing in Secondary Education." *Journal of Writing Research*, vol. 7, no. 1, June 2015, pp. 157–200.

Sherrard, William R., et al. "An Empirical Study of Peer Bias in Evaluations: Students Rating Students." *Journal of Education for Business*, vol. 70, no. 1, 1994, pp. 43–47.

Walvoord, Mark E., Mariëlle H. Hoefnagels, Douglas D. Gaffin, Matthew M. Chumchal, and David A. Long. "An Analysis of Calibrated Peer Review (CPR) in a Science Lecture Classroom." *Journal of College Science Teaching*, vol. 37, no. 4, 2008, pp. 66–73.

Yucela, Robyn, et al. "The Road to Self-Assessment: Exemplar Marking before Peer Review Develops First-Year Students' Capacity to Judge the Quality of a Scientific Report." *Assessment and Evaluation in Higher Education*, vol. 39, no. 8, 2014, pp. 971–86.

Part Six—Digital Environments

Alexander, Kara Poe. "More about Reading, Responding, and Revising: The Three Rs of Peer Review and Revision." *Multimodal Composition: Resources for Teachers*, edited by Cynthia L. Selfe, Hampton Press, 2007, pp. 113–31.

Anderson, Daniel. "Web-based Peer Review: An Opportunity for Conversation." *Teaching Writing in the Late Age of Print*, edited by Jeffrey Galin et al., Hampton Press, 2003.

Breuch, Lee-Ann Kastman. "Virtual Peer Review and Technological Flexibility." *Virtual Peer Review: Teaching and Learning about Writing in Online Environments.* SUNY P, 2004.

Carlson, Patricia, Arleen A. Russell, et al. "Improving Engineering Education with Enhanced Calibrated Peer Review: Assessment of a Collaborative Research Project." *Proceedings of the 2012 Annual Conference of the American Society of Engineering Education*, 2012, peer.asee.org/21501.

Formo, Dawn M., and Kimberley Robinson Neary. "Constructing Community: Online Response Groups in Literature and Writing Classrooms." *Teaching Literature and Language Online*, edited by Ian Lancashire, MLA, 2009, pp. 147–64.

Fosmire, Michael. "Calibrated Peer Review: A New Tool for Integrating Information Literacy Skills in Writing-Intensive Large Classroom Settings." *Libraries and the Academy*, vol. 10, no. 2, April 2010, pp. 147–63.

Goldin, Ilya M. *A Focus on Content: The Use of Rubrics in Peer Review to Guide Students and Instructors.* Unpublished dissertation, U of Pittsburgh, 2011.

Hart-Davidson, William, et al. "A Method for Measuring Helpfulness in Online Peer Review." *Proceedings of the 28th ACM International Conference on Design of Communication,* Association for Computing Machinery, 2010, pp. 115–21.

Hartberg, Yasha, Adalet Baris Gunersel, Nancy J. Simspon, and Valerie Balester. "Development of Student Writing in Biochemistry Using Calibrated Peer Review." *Journal for the Scholarship of Teaching and Learning,* vol. 8, no. 1, 2008, pp. 29–44.

Hewett, Beth. "Characteristics of Interactive Computer-Mediated Peer Group Talk and Its Influence on Revision." *Computers and Composition,* vol. 17, 2000, pp. 265–88.

Honeycutt, Lee. "Comparing E-Mail and Synchronous Conferencing in Online Peer Response." *Written Communication,* vol. 8, no. 1, 2001, pp. 26–60.

Keeney-Kennicutt, Wendy, et al. "Overcoming Student Resistance to a Teaching Innovation." *International Journal for the Scholarship of Teaching and Learning,* vol. 2, no. 1, 2008, pp. 1–26.

Lu, Ruiling, and Linda Bol. "A Comparison of Anonymous versus Identifiable e-Peer Review on College Student Writing Performance and the Extent of Critical Feedback." *Journal of Interactive Online Learning,* vol. 6, no. 2, 2007, pp. 100–15.

McLeod, Michael, et al. "Theorizing & Building Online Writing Environments: User-Centered Design Beyond the Interface." *Designing Web-Based Applications for 21st Century Writing Classrooms,* edited by George Pullman and Baotong Gu, Baywood, 2013.

Reynolds, Nedra. "Peer Review in Practice in the Paperless Writing Class." *Bedford Bits: Ideas for Teaching Writing,* 24 May 2013. Web. 14 Jan. 2014.

Sayed, Osama H. "Developing Business Management Students' Persuasive Writing through Blog-Based Peer-Feedback." *English Language Teaching,* vol. 3, no. 3, Sept. 2010, pp. 54–66.

Schunn, Christian D., et al., guest editors. "Redesigning Educational Peer Review Interactions Using Computer Tools." Special Issue of *Journal of Writing Research,* vol. 4, no. 2, Nov. 2012.

Strasma, Kip. "'Spotlighting': Peer-Response in Digitally Supported First-Year Writing Courses." *Teaching English in the Two-Year College,* vol. 37, no. 2, 2009, pp. 153–60.

Volz, Tracy, and Ann Saterbak. "Students' Strengths and Weaknesses in Evaluating Technical Arguments as Revealed through Implementing Calibrated Peer Review in a Bioengineering Laboratory." Special Issue of *Across the Disciplines,* vol. 6, 2009, wac.colostate.edu/atd/technologies/volz_saterbak.cfm.

ONLINE RESOURCES

Calibrated Peer Review: Web-Based Writing and Peer Review
cpr.molsci.ucla.edu/Home.aspx

Eli Review
elireview.com/

My Reviewers
myreviewers.com/

Peerceptiv (formally SWoRD Peer Assessment)
www.peerceptiv.com/

WriterKEY
www.writerkey.com/

Corbett, Steven J. "Great Debating: Combining Ancient and Contemporary Methods of Peer Critique." *Kairos: A Journal of Rhetoric, Technology, and Pedagogy*, vol. 19, no. 2, Spring 2015, praxis.technorhetoric.net/tiki-index.php?page=PraxisWiki%3A_%3AGreat+Debating.

Fitzpatrick, Kathleen. "Peer-to-Peer Review and Its Aporias." *Planned Obsolescence: Falling Indelibly into the Past*, www.plannedobsolescence.net/blog/peer-to-peerreview-and-its-aporias/.

MIT TechTV. *No One Writes Alone: Peer Review in the Classroom*. Videos on peer review—one for students and one for instructors—that place student practices of peer review in professional context:

"A Guide for Students," techtv.mit.edu/genres/25-humanities-arts-and-social sciences/videos/14629-no-one-writes-alone-peer-review-in-the-classroom-a -guide-for-students.

"A Guide for Instructors," techtv.mit.edu/genres/25-humanities-arts-and-social sciences/videos/14628-no-one-writes-alone-peer-review-in-the-classroom-a -guide-for-instructors.

ABOUT THE EDITORS

Steven J. Corbett is director of the University Writing Center, and assistant professor of English in the Department of Language and Literature at Texas A&M University-Kingsville. He is the author of *Beyond Dichotomy: Synergizing Writing Center and Classroom Pedagogies*, and coeditor (with Michelle LaFrance and Teagan E. Decker) of the collection *Peer Pressure, Peer Power: Theory and Practice in Peer Review and Response for the Writing Classroom* (Fountainhead Press, 2014). His work in writing studies research and pedagogy has appeared in a variety of academic journals and collections.

Michelle LaFrance is assistant professor of English and directs the Writing Across the Curriculum program at George Mason University. Michelle teaches graduate and undergraduate courses in qualitative research methods, ethnography, the discourses of writing studies, and activist rhetorics. She has published on peer review, preparing students to write across the curriculum, e-portfolios, e-research, the connections between writing centers and WAC-pedagogy, labor concerns, and institutional ethnography. With Steven J. Corbett and Teagan E. Decker, she is the coeditor of *Peer Pressure, Peer Power: Theory and Practice in Peer Review and Response for the Writing Classroom* (Fountainhead Press, 2014).

Acknowledgments

We would like to thank Bedford/St. Martin's for agreeing to make this resource available to fellow teachers of writing. We are especially indebted to Karita dos Santos, Program Manager, who helped us develop this project from start to finish with grace and patience. Stephanie Cohen, Assistant Editor, provided fine-tuned feedback on several drafts of our book.

We owe a debt of gratitude to our reviewers—especially, Michele Eodice, Doug Downs, and Teagan E. Decker—for their thoughtful and detailed critical feedback on early drafts. Caitlin Dungan and Tyler Caldwell helped with the preproduction process. We also deeply thank the authors, publishers, and editors of the works republished in this anthology.

Finally we thank our friends and family for their never-ending love and support: Margaret and John Steele, Victoria Steele, Fred and Elaine LaFrance, Marci and David West, and Anicca Cox.

Bedore, Pamela and O'Sullivan, Brian. "Addressing Instructor Ambivalence about Peer Review and Self-Assessment," *WPA: Writing Program Administration* 34.2 (Spring 2011): Pp. 11–26. Copyright © 2011 by Council on Writing Program Administrators. Used with permission.

Belcher, Lynne. "Peer Review and Response: A Failure of the Process Paradigms as Viewed From the Trenches" from *Reforming College Composition*, edited by Ray Wallace, Alan Jackson, and Susan Lewis Wallace. Copyright © 2000 by Ray Wallace, Alan Jackson, and Susan Lewis Wallace. Reproduced with permission of Greenwood Publishing Group via Copyright Clearance Center.

"Peer Review from the Students' Perspective: Invaluable or Invalid?" By Charlotte Brammer and Mary Rees. From *Composition Studies;* Fall 2007; 35, 2; ProQuest Education Journals, pp. 71–85. Used with permission from the author.

Brieger, Katharine and Pam Bromley. "A Model for Facilitating Peer Review in the STEM Disciplines: A Case Study of Peer Review Workshops Supporting Student Writing in Introductory Biology Courses," *Double Helix* 2 (2014). Used with permission.

"Invitations to a Writer's Life: Guidelines for Designing Small-Group Writing Classes" by Robert Brooke from *Invitations to a Writer's Life*. Pages 7–30. Copyright 1984 by the National Council of Teachers of English. Reprinted with permission.

"Reflection on Peer-Review Practices" by Lisa Cahill. From *Strategies for Teaching First-Year Composition*. Published by the National Council of Teachers of English (NCTE). Pp. 301–307. Copyright 1984 by the National Council of Teachers of English. Reprinted with permission.

Corbett, Steven J., "Learning Disability and Response-Ability: Reciprocal Caring in Developmental Peer Response Writing Groups and Beyond," in *Pedagogy*, Volume 15, no. 3, pp. 459–475. Copyright, 2015, Duke University Press. All rights reserved. Republished by permission of the copyright holder, Duke University Press. www.dukeupress.edu

"Peer Response Groups in the Writing Classroom: Theoretic Foundations and New Directions" by Anne DiPardo and Sarah Warshauer Freedman. *Review of Educational Research*, Vol. 58, No. 2 (Summer, 1988), pp. 119–149. Published by American Educational Research Association. Copyright © Sage Publications. Reproduced with permission of Sage Publications, Inc. via Copyright Clearance Center.

Peter Elbow and Pat Belanoff, "Cover Letter" and "Procedures for Giving and Receiving Responses" From *Sharing and Responding*, Pages 3–5, 7–16. Copyright © 1999 by McGraw-Hill Education. Used with permission.

From *Writing Groups: History, Theory, and Implications* by Anne Ruggles Gere. Southern Illinois University Press. Pages 99–123. Copyright © 1987 by the Conference on College Composition and Communication of the National Council of Teachers of English. Reprinted with permission.

Grobman, Laurie. "Building Bridges to Academic Discourse: The Peer Group Leader in Basic Writing Peer Response Groups," *Journal of Basic Writing*, Vol. 18, No. 2, 1999, pp 47–68. Copyright © 1999 by Journal of Basic Writing. Used with permission.

"Dynamic Motives in ESL Computer-Mediated Peer Response" by Li Jin and Wei Zhu. Available online at www.sciencedirect.com. Pages 284–303. Copyright © 2010 Elsevier. Reprinted with permission from Elsevier.

LaFrance, Michelle. "Adopting and Adapting: Three Examples of Peer Review/Response Activity Design from Disciplinary Writing Courses." From *Peer Pressure, Peer Power: Theory and Practice in Peer Review and Response for the Writing Classroom*, edited by Steven J. Corbett, Michelle LaFrance, and Teagan E. Decker. Copyright © 2014 by Fountainhead Press. Used with permission.

Launspach, Sonja. "The Role of Talk in Small Writing Groups: Building Declarative and Procedural Knowledge for Basic Writers," *Journal of Basic Writing*, Vol. 27, No. 2, 2008, pp. 56–80. Copyright © 2008 by Journal of Basic Writing. Used with permission.

"Using Group Conferences to Respond to Essays in Progress" by Susan K. Miller. From *Strategies for Teaching First-Year Composition*. Published by the National Council of Teachers of English (NCTE). Pp. 307–318. Copyright 1984 by the National Council of Teachers of English. Reprinted with permission.

Donald M. Murray. "Writing as Process: How Writing Finds Its Own Meaning" from *Learning by Teaching: Selected Articles on Writing and Teaching*. Copyright © 1982 by Donald M. Murray. Reprinted by permission of The Rosenberg Group on behalf of the author's estate.

From "Direction and Misdirection in Peer Response" by Thomas Newkirk. *College Composition and Communication*, Vol. 35, No. 3 (Oct., 1984), pp. 301–311. Copyright 1984 by the National Council of Teachers of English. Reprinted with permission.

Ruecker, Todd. "Analyzing and Addressing the Effects of Native Speakerism on Linguistically Diverse Peer Review." From *Peer Pressure, Peer Power: Theory and Practice in Peer Review and Response for the Writing Classroom,* edited by Steven J. Corbett, Michelle LaFrance, and Teagan E. Decker. Copyright © 2014 by Fountainhead Press. Used with permission.

"The Evolution of Calibrated Peer Review" by Arlene A. Russell. From *Trajectories of Chemistry Education Innovation and Reform* by Thomas Holme, Melanie M. Cooper, and Pratibha Varma-Nelson. Published by the American Chemical Society (ACS), by Oxford University Press. Pages 129–143. By permission of Oxford University Press, USA.

Schneider, Barbara and Andre, Jo-Anne. "Developing Authority In Student Writing Through Written Peer Critique in the Disciplines," *The Writing Instructor,* September 2007. Copyright © 2007 by Parlor Press. Used with permission.

"Habits of Mind: Historical Configurations of Textual Ownership in Peer Writing Groups" by Candace Spigelman. *College Composition and Communication*, Vol. 49, No. 2 (May, 1998), pp. 234–255. Copyright 1984 by the National Council of Teachers of English. Reprinted with permission.

"Women and Language in the Collaborative Writing Classroom" by Gail Stygall. From *Feminism and Composition Studies — In Other Words,* edited by Susan C. Jarratt and Lynn Worsham. Published by The Modern Language Association of America, 1998. Pp. 252–275. Reprinted by permission of the copyright owner, the Modern Language Association of America.

Joanna Wolfe and Jo Ann Griffin, "Comparing Technologies for Online Writing Conferences: Effects of Medium on Conversation," *The Writing Center Journal,* Vol. 32, No. 1 (2012). Copyright © 2012 by Writing Center Journal. Used with permission.

INDEX